PROVENCE

the collected traveler

Also in the series by Barrie Kerper

CENTRAL ITALY
The Collected Traveler

PARIS
The Collected Traveler

PROVENCE

the collected traveler

PRIORITAIRE
PRIORITY

INCLUDING MONACO AND THE CÔTE D'AZUR

AN INSPIRED
ANTHOLOGY & TRAVEL
RESOURCE

Collected by Barrie Kerper

Three Rivers Press / NEW YORK

See page 579 for credits to the part title pages' quotations.

Anthology copyright © 2001 by Barrie Kerper

Published by Three Rivers Press, New York, New York.
Member of the Crown Publishing Group.
Random House, Inc. New York, Toronto, London, Sydney, Auckland
www.randomhouse.com

THREE RIVERS PRESS is a registered trademark and the Three Rivers Press logo is a trademark of Random House, Inc.

Printed in the United States of America

DESIGN BY LYNNE AMFT

Library of Congress Cataloging-in-Publication Data
Provence: the collected traveler: an inspired anthology & travel resource /
collected by Barrie Kerper. Includes bibliographical references.
1. Provence (France)—Guidebooks.   2. Travelers, writings.   3. Provence
(France)—Description and travel—Sources.   I. Kerper, Barrie.
DC611.P958 P725 2001
914.4'90484—dc21   00-068300

ISBN 0-609-80678-5

10 9 8 7 6 5 4 3 2 1

First Edition

Once again, for my mother, Phyllis,
who always believed my boxes of files
held something of value.

acknowledgments

As I've noted before, publishing a book requires a staggering amount of work by a team of dedicated people. An anthology, however, requires the participation of an even greater number of people, ensuring the project will be that much more complex. Though this volume has been a little easier to pull together than the first two editions in this series, it remains essential to extend my heartfelt thanks and deep gratitude once again to the following colleagues, family, and friends: Al Adams, Alison Gross, Amy Boorstein, Amy Myer, Andrea Rosen, Anne Messitte, Becky Cabaza, Bradley Clough, Brian Belfiglio, Bruce Deegan, Dan and Leslie Cummins, Derek McNally, Florence Porrino, Gordon and Jennifer Kerper, Holly Clarfield, Joan DeMayo, Karine Lefrere, Kathy Burke, Lauren Shakely, Linda Loewenthal, Maha Khalil, Marcia Purcell, Murray Berman, Patty Flynn, Philip Patrick, Rebecca Strong, Rich Romano, Roberto Diaz, Stacy Laufer, Steve Ross, Teresa Nicholas, Vivian Fong, Wayne and Lydie Marshall, and the staff at the Maison de la France tourist office in New York. Special thanks are due to each of the individual writers, agents, and permissions representatives for various publishers and periodicals—especially Leigh Montville of The Condé Nast Publications and Rose Cervino of *The New York Times*—without whose generosity and understanding there would be nothing to publish; Shaye Areheart, my extraordinarily talented editor and friend, with whom I am honored to work; Whitney Cookman, who grasped the essence of my idea quicker than anyone and once again designed a cover that is truly *magnifique*; Mark McCauslin and Lynne Amft of Crown's production-editorial and art departments, who again proved that a complicated manuscript with missing text and insufficient artwork was not too challenging for them; Chip Gibson, my boss, for opportunities and kindnesses large and small; and Lorraine and Luc Paillard, who never fail to send an enormous number of postcards, reviews, tips, and invaluable observations in support of my project. Lastly, sincere thanks to everyone not mentioned here—you know who you are—for continually inquiring about my progress, and to my husband, Jeffrey, and daughter, Alyssa. Jeff once again came to the rescue and assumed babysitting duty a few more times than he would have preferred; certainly without his help I would have had to scrap the entire project. Alyssa, age two, is too young to realize it now, but I hope our home and, by extension, this series, will inspire in her a love of reading and travel, ensuring she will grow up to be a true *citoyenne du monde*.

contents

PROVENCE

the collected traveler

Fondation Maeght

06570 Saint-Paul

téléphone 04 93 32 81 63   télécopie 04 93 32 53 22

2 7 MAI 2000

1 x 50

Ouvert tous les jours sans exception
du 1.10. au 30.6., 10h–12h30, 14h30–18h;
du 1.7. au 30.9. 10h–19h (sans interruption)

Introduction

"A traveller without knowledge is a bird without wings."
—Sa'di, *Gulistan* (1258)

Some years ago, my husband and I fulfilled a dream we'd had since we first met: we put all our belongings in storage and traveled around the countries bordering the Mediterranean Sea for a year. In preparation for this journey, I did what I always do in advance of a trip: I consulted my home archives, a library of books and periodicals. I have been an obsessive clipper since I was very young, and by the time I was preparing for this trip, I had amassed an enormous number of articles from a wide variety of periodicals. After a year of reading and organizing all this material, I then created a package of articles and notes for each destination and mailed them ahead to friends we'd be staying with as well as appropriate American Express offices—although we had no schedule to speak of, we knew we would spend no less than six weeks in each place.

My husband wasted no time informing me that my research efforts were perhaps a bit over the top. He shares my passion for travel (my mother-in-law told me that when he was little he would announce to the family exactly how many months, weeks, days, hours, minutes, and seconds it was before the annual summer vacation) but not necessarily for clipping. He has accused me of being too much like the anal-retentive fisherman from an old *Saturday Night Live* skit, the one where the guy neatly puts his bait, extra line, snacks, hand towels, etc. into individual sandwich bags. In my defense, I'm not *quite* that bad (although I *am* guilty of trying to improve upon pocket organizers, and I do have a wooden rack for drying rinsed plastic bags in my kitchen).

While we were traveling that year, we would occasionally meet other Americans, and I was continually amazed at how ill-prepared some of them were. Information, in so many different forms, is in such abundance today that it was nearly inconceivable to me that people had not taken advantage of the resources available to them. Some people we met didn't even seem to be having a very good time; they appeared to be ignorant of various customs and observances, and were generally unimpressed with their experience because they had missed the significance of what they were seeing and doing. Therefore, I was surprised again when these same people—of varying ages and wallet sizes—were genuinely interested in my little packages of notes and articles. Some people even offered to *pay* me for them, and I began to think that my collected research would perhaps appeal to other travelers. I also realized that even the most well-intentioned people were often overwhelmed by trip planning or didn't have the time to put it all together. Later, friends and colleagues told me they really appreciated the packages I prepared for them, and somewhere along the line I was being referred to as a "modern-day hunter-gatherer," a sort of "one-stop information source." Each book in *The Collected Traveler* series provides resources and information to travelers—people I define as inquisitive, individualistic, and indefatigable in their eagerness to explore—or informs them of where they may look further to find it.

While there is much to be said for a freewheeling approach to travel—I am not an advocate of sticking to rigid schedules—I do believe that, as with most things in life, what you get out of a trip is equal only to what you put into it. James Pope-Hennessy, in his wonderful book *Aspects of Provence,* notes that "if one is to get best value out of places visited, some skeletal knowledge of their history is necessary, and this seems particularly true of Roman places, for classical history, last read at school, is for most people a subject indistinct and blurred. Whatever aesthetic or romantic pleasure one may experience on gazing at the Pont du Gard or on standing in early morning before the formidable walls of the theatre at Orange, one wishes to know something of the reason for the existence of these giant structures . . . while it is not always possible to name the builder or define the purpose of some specific Roman monument, it is not at all so difficult to ascertain its period, and to keep the dates of the Roman occupation of Provence within one's head. Sight-seeing is by no means the only object of a journey, but it is as unintelligent as it is lazy not to equip ourselves to understand the sights we see." I feel that learning about a place is part of the excitement of travel, and I wouldn't dream of venturing anywhere without first poring over a mountain of maps, books, and periodicals. I include cookbooks in my reading (some cookbooks reveal much historical detail as well as prepare you for the food and drink you will most likely encounter) and I also like to watch movies that have something to do with where I'm going. Additionally, I buy a blank journal and fill it with all sorts of notes, reminders, and entire passages from books I'm not bringing along. In other words, I completely immerse myself in my destination before I leave. It's the most enjoyable homework assignment I could ever give myself.

Every destination, new or familiar, merits some attention. I don't endorse the extreme—spending all your time in a hotel room reading books—but it most definitely pays to know something about your destination before you go—just leave some room for the chance encounter or unpredictable surprise. The reward for your efforts is that you'll acquire a deeper understanding and appreciation of the place and the people who live there, and, not surprisingly, you'll have more fun.

"Every land has its own special rhythm, and unless the traveler takes the time to learn the rhythm, he or she will remain an outsider there always."

—Juliette De Bairacli Levy,
English writer, b. 1937

Occasionally I meet people who are more interested in how many countries I've been to than in those I might know well or particularly like. If "well-traveled" is defined only by how many places I've been to, then I suppose I'm not. However, I feel I *really know* and have *really seen* the places I've visited, which is how *I* define "well-traveled." I travel to see how people live in other parts of the world—not to check countries off a list—and to do that requires sticking around for more than a few days and adapting to the local pace and rhythm. Certainly any place you decide is worthy of your time and effort is worthy of more than a day, but you don't always need an indefinite period of time to immerse yourself in the local culture or establish a routine that allows you to get to know the merchants and residents of your adopted neighborhood. One of the fastest ways to adjust to daily life in France is to abandon whatever schedule you observe at home and eat when the French eat. Mealtimes in France are generally well established, and if you have not bought provisions for a picnic or found a place to eat by one o'clock, restaurants will be full and shops closed. Likewise, dinner is not typically served at six, an hour which is entirely too early for anyone in a Mediterranean country to even contemplate eating a meal. Yvone Lenard, in her delightful book, *The Magic of Provence,* expresses this well in writing that for residents and visitors alike there are inflexible rules to be learned: "Everything will close down at noon sharp, except food stores, which *may* remain open a little longer: shops, post office, gas stations, garages, city hall, banks will shut tight, since their employees shall be going home for *déjeuner.*

And *déjeuner,* as practiced in France, holds nothing in common with what we Americans know as lunch. Some places will re-open around two, or two-thirty, or three, some not until four, and others not at all. So, all errands should be completed before closing time, and if you have plans for the afternoon, or guests over for dinner, get going before it is too late. Besides, nobody wants to miss out on the best part of the morning in town: the hours devoted to food shopping." Adjust your schedule and you'll be on French time, doing things when the French do them, eliminating possible disappointment and frustration. In addition to meal times, I would add that it's rewarding to rise early in Provence. It may be difficult to convince holiday travelers who like to sleep late to get out of bed a few hours earlier, but if you sleep in every day you will most definitely miss much of the local rhythm. By 9:00 A.M. in southern France—and in any Mediterranean country—much has already happened, and besides, you can always look forward to a delicious afternoon nap.

About fifteen years ago, the former Paris bureau chief for *The New York Times,* John Vinocur, wrote a piece for the travel section entitled "Discovering the Hidden Paris." In it, he noted that the French have a word, *dépaysement,* which he translated into English as meaning "the feeling of not being assaulted by the familiarity of things, a change in surroundings where there is no immediate point of reference." He went on to quote a French journalist who once said that "Americans don't travel to be *dépaysés,* but to find a home away from home." This is unfortunate, but too often true. These tourists can travel all around the world if they desire, but their unwillingness to adapt ensures they will never really leave home.

Similar are the people who endorse "adventure travel," words which make me cringe as they seem to imply that unless one partakes in kayaking, mountain climbing, biking, rock climbing, or some other physical endeavor that a travel experience is somehow invalid or unadventurous. *All* travel is an adventure, and unless "adventure travel" allows for plenty of time to adapt to the local rhythm, the so-called adventure is really just a physically strenuous—albeit memorable—outdoor achievement. For example, occasionally I hear descriptions of a biking excursion, where the participants spend the majority of each day making biking the priority instead of incorporating biking into the local cadence of daily life. When I ask if they joined the locals at the café for a morning *café crème* or an evening *apéro* (short for apéritif), shopped at the outdoor *marché,* went to a local *fête,* or people-watched in the *place,* the answer is invariably no. They may have had an amazing bike trip, but they didn't get to know France—one has to get off the bike a bit more often for that sort of knowledge—and if a biking experience alone is what they were seeking, they certainly didn't need to fly to France: there are plenty of challenging and beautiful places to bike in the United States.

I believe that *every* place in the world offers *something* of interest. In her magnificent book, *Black Lamb, Grey Falcon,* Rebecca West recounts how in the 1930s she passed through what was then Skopje, Yugoslavia (Skopje is today the capital of the Federal Yugoslav Republic of Macedonia), by train twice, without stopping, because friends had told her the town wasn't worth visiting. A third time through she did stop, and she met two wonderful people who became lasting friends. She wrote, "Now, when I go through a town of which I know nothing, a town which appears to be a waste land of uniform streets wholly without quality, I look on it in wonder and hope, since it may hold a Mehmed, a Militsa." I, too, have been richly rewarded by pausing in places (Skopje included) which at first appeared quite limiting.

"Travel is fatal to prejudice, bigotry, and narrow-mindedness."
—Mark Twain

"The world is a book, and those who do not travel read only a page."

—St. Augustine

I am assuming if you've read this far that something compelled you to pick up this book, and that you feel travel is an essential part of life. I would add to Mark Twain's quote above one by Benjamin Disraeli (1804–1881): "Travel teaches toleration." People who travel with an open mind and are receptive to the ways of others cannot help but return with more tolerance for people and situations at home, at work, in their cities and communities. James Ferguson, a nineteenth-century Scottish architect, observed this perfectly when he wrote, "Travel is more than a visitor seeing sights; it is the profound changing—the deep and permanent changing—of that visitor's perspective of the world, and of his own place in it." I find that travel also ensures I will not be quite the same person I was before I left. After a trip, I typically have a lot of renewed energy and bring new perspectives to my job. At home, I ask myself how I can incorporate attributes or traits I observed while traveling into my own life and share them with my husband and daughter.

The anthologies in *The Collected Traveler* series offer a record of people's achievements and shortcomings. It may be a lofty goal to expect that they might also offer us an opportunity to measure our own deeds and flaws as Americans, so we can realize that, despite cultural differences between us and our hosts in *any* country, we have much more in common than not. It is a sincere goal, however, and one which I hope readers and travelers will embrace.

About This Series

The Collected Traveler editions are not guidebooks in the traditional sense. However, they *may* be considered guidebooks in that they are books which guide readers to other sources. Each book is really the first book you should turn to when planning a trip. If you think of the individual volumes as a sort of planning package, you've got the right idea. To borrow a phrase from a reviewer who was writing about the *Lonely Planet Travel Survival Kit* series years ago, *The Collected Traveler* is for people who know how to get their luggage off the carousel. If you enjoy acquiring knowledge about where you're going—whether you're planning a trip independently or with a like-minded tour organization—this series is for you. If you're looking for a guide that simply informs you of exact prices, hours, and highlights, you probably won't be interested in the depth this book offers. (That is not meant to offend, merely to say you've got the wrong book.)

A few words about me may also help you determine if this series is for you: I travel somewhat frugally, not out of necessity but more because I choose to. I respect money and its value and I'm not convinced, for example, that if I spend $600 a night for a hotel room that it would be a good value or that I would have a better trip. I've been to some of the world's finest hotels, mostly to visit friends who are staying there or to have a drink in the hotel bar. With a few notable exceptions, it seems to me that the majority of these places are all alike, meant to conform to a code of sameness and predictability. There's nothing about them that is particularly French or Italian or Turkish—you could be *anywhere*. The cheapest of the cheap accommodations don't represent good value, either. I look for places to stay which are usually old, possibly historic, and have lots of charm and character. I do not mind if my room is small; I do not need a television, telephone, or hair dryer; and I most definitely do not care for an American-style buffet breakfast, which is hardly what the locals eat. I also prefer to make my own plans, send my own letters and faxes, place my own telephone calls, and make my own travel arrangements. Not because I think I can do it better than a professional agent (whose expertise I admire), but because I enjoy it and learn a lot in the process. Finally, lest readers think I do not appreciate elegance, allow me to state that I think you'll quickly ascertain that I do indeed enjoy many of life's little luxuries, when I perceive them to be of good value to me.

This series promotes the view of staying longer within a smaller area. Susan Allen Toth refers to this in her book, *England As You Like It,* in which she subscribes to the "thumbprint theory of travel": spending at least a week in one spot no larger than your thumbprint covers on a large-scale map of England. She goes on to explain that excursions are encouraged, as long as they're about an hour's drive away. As I have discovered in my own travels, a week in one place, even a spot no bigger than my thumbprint, is rarely long enough to see and enjoy it all. Each book in *The Collected Traveler* series focuses on one corner of the world, the countries bordering the Mediterranean Sea. I find the Mediterranean endlessly fascinating: the sea itself is the world's largest, the region is one of the world's ancient crossroads, and as it stretches from the Atlantic to Asia it is home to the most diverse humanity. As Paul Theroux has noted in his excellent book, *The Pillars of Hercules,* "The Mediterranean, this simple almost tideless sea, the size of thirty Lake Superiors, had everything: prosperity, poverty, tourism, terrorism, several wars in progress, ethnic strife, fascists, pollution, drift nets, private islands owned by billionaires, Gypsies, seventeen countries, fifty languages, oil drilling platforms, sponge fishermen, religious fanatics, drug smuggling, fine art, and warfare. It had Christians, Muslims, Jews; it had the Druzes, who are a strange farrago of all three religions; it had heathens, Zoroastrians and Copts and Baha'is." Diversity aside, the great explorers in the service of Spain and Portugal departed from Mediterranean ports to discover so much of the rest of the world.

The Collected Traveler also focuses on cities and regions rather than entire countries (there will not be a book on all of France, for example), but France—and especially Provence—is a member of two communities, European and Mediterranean, and an understanding of both is essential to understanding France. This edition covers Provence, the Côte d'Azur, and the Principality of Monaco, three areas which can manageably be seen together. A look at a map of France reveals that the Languedoc-Roussillon, Dordogne, Gascogne, and the Pays Basque regions are close by (in fact, it is often difficult to distinguish much of Languedoc from Provence); but each of these areas deserves to be covered in a separate book, and they are too far outside this particular thumbprint. Readers should note that there are varying definitions and boundaries of what constitutes Provence. To *me,* Provence begins south of Lyon at Valence, goes down to Montélimar, runs due east to Gap and Barcelonnette, continues southeast to Tende, south to Menton on the coast, past the Côte d'Azur to the Camargue, up to Nîmes (even though Nîmes is technically in Languedoc), across the Rhône to Avignon, and north to Orange, Vaison-la-Romaine, and Nyons. Administratively, Provence is divided into five *départements:* Bouches-du-Rhône, Vaucluse, Var, Alpes-de-Haute-Provence, and Alpes-Maritimes, which includes the Côte d'Azur and the Principality of Monaco. But tourist pamphlets will show even more subdivisions: for example, a map I have of northern Provence (the area centered around Valence) is also divided into five sections: Drôme des Collines, Royans-Vercors, Valence-sur-Rhône, Drôme Provençal, and Vallée de la Drôme-Diois. And Provence's native sons, Frédéric Mistral and Jean Giono, barely recognized the existence of the Côte d'Azur, let alone considered it a part of the Provence they knew and treasured.

Each section of this book features a selection of articles from various periodicals and an annotated bibliography relevant to the theme of each section (the *Renseignements Pratiques* section is a bit different, with the books being a part of the A–Z listings). The articles and books were chosen from my own files and home library, which I've maintained for over two decades. The selected writings reflect the culture, politics, history, current social issues, religion, cuisine, and arts of the people you'll be visiting. They also represent the observations and opinions of a wide variety of novelists, travel writers, and journalists. These writers are authorities on the south of France or France in general; they either live there (as permanent or part-time residents) or visit there often for business or pleasure. I'm very discriminating in seeking opinions and recommendations, and I am not interested in the remarks of unobservant wanderers. I am not implying that first-time visitors to France have nothing noteworthy or interesting to share—they very often do, and are often very keen observers; conversely, frequent travelers can be jaded and apt to miss the finer details which make Provence and the coast the exceptional places they are. I am interested in the opinions of people who want to *know* the south of France, not just *see* it.

I've included numerous older articles (even though some of the specific information regarding prices, hours, etc., is no longer accurate) because they were either particularly well written, thought-provoking, or unique in some way, and because the authors' views stand as a valuable record of a certain time in history. Often, even with the passage of many years, you may share the same emotions and opinions of the writer, and equally as often, *plus ça change, plus c'est la même chose*. I have many more articles in my files than I was able to reprint here. Though there are a few pieces whose absence I very much regret, I believe the anthology you're holding is very good.

A word about the dining out section, *À Table!:* I have great respect for restaurant reviewers. Their work may seem glamorous— it sometimes is—but it is also very hard. It's an all-consuming, full-time job, and that is why I urge you to consult three very good books: *The Food Lover's Guide to France,* by Patricia Wells; the red

Michelin France guide; and the *Guide Gantié,* by Jacques Gantié, all detailed in the *À Table! bibliothèque.* My files are bulging with restaurant reviews, and I could have included many more articles about restaurants, cafés, and bistros, but it would be too repetitive and ultimately beside the point. I have selected a few articles that give you a feel for eating out in the south of France, alert you to some things to look for in selecting a truly worthwhile place versus a mediocre one, and highlight some dishes which are not commonplace in America. My files are also bulging with hotel recommendations, but as with dining out, I urge you to consult one or more of the great books listed in *Renseignements Pratiques.*

The annotated bibliography for each section is one of the most important features of this book. Reading about travel in the days before trans-Atlantic flights, I always marvel at the number of steamer trunks and baggage people were accustomed to taking. If it were me traveling then, however, my bags would be filled with books, not clothes. Although I travel light and seldom check bags, I have been known to fill an entire suitcase with books, secure in the knowledge that I could have them all with me for the duration of my trip. Each *bibliothèque* features titles that I feel are the best available, most worth your time. I realize that these lists are subjective, but readers will simply have to trust that I have been extremely thorough in deciding which books to recommend. (I have read and own them all, by the way, with the exception of a few that I borrowed.) If the lists seem long, they are, but the more I read, the more I realize there is to know, and there are an awful lot of really good books out there! I'm not suggesting you read them *all,* but I do hope you will not be content with just one. I have identified some books as *de rigueur,* meaning that I consider them required reading; but I sincerely believe that *all* the books I've mentioned are important, helpful, well written, or all three. There are surely some books I'm unaware of, so if some of your favorites aren't included here, please write and tell me about them.

There are many excellent books that are out of print and I have not hesitated to list them here, because many of these books can be found through individuals who specialize in out-of-print books, booksellers, libraries, and on-line searches. I should also mention that I believe the companion reading you bring along should be related in some way to where you're going. Therefore, the books listed in *Des Belles Choses* are novels and nonfiction titles which feature characters or settings in the south of France, or feature aspects of Provence and the *Provençaux*, such as *The Garden of Eden*, *The Man Who Planted Trees*, *Bella-Vista*, and *Tender Is the Night*. Also, because *Les Personalités* is about people, biographies make up most of the books in this section. The selection isn't meant to be comprehensive—there are many more I could have included—but represents a variety of books about a variety of interesting people, one or more of whom may also interest you. The *Jardins, Musées, et Monuments* section, therefore, doesn't include biographies of artists, as I thought it better to separate art history books and museum catalogs—with their many reproductions of artworks—from memoirs and biographies.

Together, the articles and books lead you on and off the beaten path, and present a "reality check" of sorts. Will you learn of some non-touristy things to see and do? Yes. Will you also learn more about the better-known aspects of Provence? Yes. The Palais des Papes in Avignon and flowers tumbling out of a planter in a narrow street of Roussillon are equally representative of the region. Seeing them *both* is what makes for a memorable visit, and no one, by the way, should make you feel guilty for wanting to see some famous sites. They have become famous for a reason: they are really something to see, the Pope's Palace included. Readers will have no trouble finding a multitude of other travel titles offering plenty of non-controversial viewpoints. This is my attempt at presenting a more balanced picture. Ultimately, this is the compendium of information that I wish I'd had between two covers years ago. I admit it isn't the "perfect" book; for that, I envision a waterproof jacket and pockets inside the front and back covers, pages and pages of accompanying maps, lots of blank pages for notes, a bookmark, photos and beautiful drawings, mileage and size conversion charts . . . in other words, something so encyclopedic in both weight and size that positively no one, my editor assures me, would want to read it. That said, I am exceedingly happy with *The Collected Traveler,* and I believe it will prove helpful in heightening the anticipation of your upcoming journey; in the enjoyment of your trip while it's happening; and in the remembrance of it when you're back home.

It may seem today that the magical phrase "the south of France" is overused, that the region is overrun with visitors and new residents, and overpublished as a subject for books. But no less an authority than Peter Mayle notes in his most recent book, *Encore Provence,* that "Provence is still beautiful. Vast areas of it are still wild and empty. Peace and silence, which have become endangered commodities in the modern world, are still available. The old men still play their endless games of *boules.* The markets are as colorful and abundant as ever. There is room to breathe, and the air is clean." For myself, I have visited Provence in high season and low, and each trip has proved more rewarding than the last. I have hiked in the Esterel and have encountered only a handful of people, have sat in the middle of a lavender field in July—with only my husband and the buzzing bees for company—and wondered where all the tourists were, and have eaten fruit bought at outdoor *marchés* that to this day stand out as the truest and finest specimens of their kind I've ever put in my mouth. There are back roads I've driven on in the high season where the only passing traffic was goats and chickens. No matter how much or little time passes between visits, Provence and its Mediterranean coastline never fail to astonish me. Paradise it's not—corruption, ugly politics, overdevelopment, and the annoying presence of the *Front National* cannot be ignored. Provence is perhaps entirely too popular for its own good, but I am always sad to leave this corner of the world, because I remain grateful that it exists at all. High technology and modern ways have altered life in Provence, but a number of old traditions persist. Many festivals and holidays celebrated with such enthusiasm in the south, which we assume to be Christian, are actually a blend of sacred and secular customs, some of which originate from ancient, pagan observances. As Vladimir Nabokov has noted, "I wander aimlessly from lane to lane, bending a careful ear to ancient times: the same cicadas sang in Caesar's reign, upon the walls the same sun clings and climbs." While writing an article about Provence for *Condé Nast Traveler*, author Mary Blume was reminded of a letter written by Jean Racine in the seventeenth century while he was traveling through the region. In his letter, he wrote, *"Et nous avons des nuits plus belles que vos jours."* (And here we have nights more beautiful than your days.) I hope you will discover both the nights and the days.

Meilleurs vœux pour un bon voyage!

Renseignements Pratiques
(Practical Information)

"The people of Provence are traditionally welcoming but the French rituals of politeness apply in Provence more than any-where. When introduced to someone, it is correct to shake hands. In shops, be prepared to say bonjour *before asking what you want, then* merci *when you receive your change and* au revoir, bonne journée *when you depart."*

—EYEWITNESS TRAVEL GUIDE:
PROVENCE & THE CÔTE D'AZUR

A–Z Renseignements Pratiques

A

Accommodations

Generally speaking, it is not much of a problem to travel around Provence, the Côte d'Azur, or Monaco without reservations, except during the summer months. Summer is defined on the coast as about mid-May to mid-September, the absolute worst time being the month of August when all of Europe is *en vacances*. You may also notice that some places close for the winter or during the month of November, when many *patrons* take their own holiday. However, I maintain that unless you're traveling for an indefinite period of time, it's a good idea to make reservations. Many wonderful inns, hotels, and *chambres d'hôtes* (bed and breakfasts) are quite small with only a few rooms, and they can fill up fast, even in the off-season. It can be very time consuming, not to mention frustrating, to go from place to place and find no vacancy. However, if you do not have a room reserved, the staff at the tourist offices are typically happy to assist you in finding a place. The offices in the larger cities and towns are perhaps better with this kind of assistance, but it has been my experience that the staff at even the smallest office in the smallest village is willing to help. They will not always place telephone calls for you or make the actual reservations, but they will at least tell you what choices there are and give directions. Some offices may charge a fee for booking services. If you have a car and are having trouble finding a room, you may have better luck at one of the French budget motel chains: Formule 1, Première Classe, and Nuit d'Hôtel. (Formule 1 is, in fact, owned by the Accor chain, which also owns Etap, Ibis, Mercure, Novotel, Sofitel, and Motel 6 and Red Roof Inns in the U.S.). Just like Motel 6, these budget lodgings are functional, basic, and clean, and are located on major highways and roads on the outskirts of towns and cities in France. Rooms are small, and bathrooms and showers are often down the hall, but if you haven't reserved in advance this may be your only choice. Be prepared for little to no air-conditioning and a front desk that's staffed only in the morning and early evening; at other times of the day and night guests "check in" by using a computer terminal and a credit card. To research locations or to make reservations, the Accor Web site is www.accor.com; Nuit d'Hôtel's is www.hotelscie.fr/nuit.htm; and the site for Première Classe is www.premiereclasse.fr. The Maison de la France tourist offices here in the U.S. and the Provence/Alpes/Côte d'Azur tourist offices in France have thorough accommodations listings, but these are just listings indicating classification and services, and don't have good descriptive information. I prefer to consult the experts, and feel the same way about books on accommodations as I do about guidebooks: the right one for you is the one whose author shares a certain sensibility or philosophy with you. It's important to select the right book(s) so you can make choices that best suit you and your style. Once you've selected the books you like, trust the author's recommendations. Trying to "validate" your choices by searching the Web, for example, serves no good purpose: remember, *you don't know the people who are writing reviews, and you have no idea if the same things that are important to you are important to them*. The authors of the books you've chosen have shared their standards with you and explained their criteria used in rating accommodations. Stick with them, and move on to the next step in planning your trip. It's been my experience that it is never difficult to learn of places to stay in either the luxury or budget categories; harder is finding the truly beautiful and unique places that fall somewhere in between, which is why the books I consult are my personal favorites. Following are brief descriptions of the various types of accommodations you'll find throughout the south of France, and books I recommend:

Auberges de jeunesses (youth hostels) are the premier choice for those seeking budget accommodations and remain a fun and exciting experience for young and old alike (keep in mind that hostels are not just for the under-30 crowd). Though I do not regret a minute of my summer of vagabonding around Europe, meeting young people from all over the world, and feeling that my life was one big, endless possibility, I now much prefer sharing a room with my husband rather than five twenty-somethings. Younger budget travelers need no convincing that hosteling is the way to go; however, older budget travelers should bear in mind that although some hostels offer individual rooms (mostly for couples), comparing costs reveals that they are often the same price as a room in a real (albeit inexpensive) hotel, where you can reserve a room in advance and comfortably keep your luggage, unlike in a hostel, where you must pack up your luggage every day and you can't make a reservation; additionally, most hostels have an 11:00 P.M. curfew. Petty theft—of the T-shirts-stolen-off-the-clothesline variety—seems to be more prevalent than it once was, and it would be wise to sleep and shower with your money belt close at hand. For a complete list of hostels in the south of France, contact the French tourist offices (here or abroad); the Federation Unie des Auberges de Jeunesse, 27 rue Pajol, 75018, Paris, 01.44.89.87.27; or the national headquarters of Hostelling International here in the U.S. (733 15th Street, N.W., Suite 840, Washington, D.C. 20005, 202-783-6161 / fax: -6171. Hours are 8:00 A.M.–5:00 P.M. eastern standard time, with customer service staff available until 7:00 P.M.). In fact, while there are no age limits or advance bookings, many of the hostels require membership in HI. A membership card is free for anyone up to his or her eighteenth birthday. Annual fees are $25 for anyone over eighteen and $15 for anyone over fifty-five. HI also publishes several guidebooks, one of which is *Europe and the Mediterranean*. The price is either $10.95 or $13.95, depending on whether you purchase it from the main office or one of its council affiliates around the country (HI staff have addresses and phone numbers for affiliates nearest you). I think a better book to get is *Hostels France & Italy: The Only Comprehensive, Unofficial, Opinionated Guide* (Paul Karr and Martha Coombs, The Globe Pequot Press, Old Saybrook, Connecticut). This is one book which lives up to its no-nonsense title. It's a funny yet very practical guide. In "How to Use This Book," the authors state that "what you're holding in your hands is the first-ever attempt of its kind: a fairly complete listing and rating of all the hostels we could find in France and Italy." They invite you to take a quiz (What Is a Hostel?) and they don't hesitate to tell it like it is, using such adjectives as sedate, educational, hoppin', quiet, plain, dirty, chaotic, strict, okay, small. Note that there are also privately run hostels, which do not belong to HI, as well as student dormitory accommodations on some college and university campuses (available during the summer months) and *foyers* and *residences*, all within the realm of budget travel. You'll find some of these are mentioned in various guidebooks, or ask the tourist office staff for help in finding them.

Camping (known simply as *camping* or sometimes *campings municipaux*) is available in nearly every town and village (except Monaco, where camping is not permitted) but visitors should know that the European conception of camping is about as opposite from the American as possible. Europeans do not go camping to seek a wilderness experience, and European campgrounds are designed without much privacy in mind, but they do offer amenities ranging from hot-water showers, facilities for washing clothes and dishes, electrical outlets, croissants and café for breakfast, and flush toilets to tiled bathrooms with heat, swimming pools, cafés, bars, restaurants, telephones, televisions, and general stores. If you find yourself at a European campground during the summer months, you may notice that entire families have literally moved in, having reserved their spaces many months in advance. In fact, many families return every year to spend time with their friends, the way we might return every year to a ski cabin or a house at the beach. It's quite an entertaining and lively spectacle, and camping like this is hardly roughing it. Some campsites along the Côte d'Azur are situated in beautiful spots with great views (I can personally recommend the campsite in Cagnes-sur-Mer), although these tend to cost more than inland campgrounds. It's been my experience that at municipal campgrounds during the off-season, no one ever comes around to collect fees. The campgrounds are still open and there is running water, but the thinking seems to be that it just isn't worth it to collect money from so few campers. (Note that this will not hold true at privately run campgrounds.) Outside of the larger towns and cities you may see signs for *camping à la ferme,* which is camping on a farm. Typically there are no facilities, but the setting is usually beautiful and quiet and often comes with a home-cooked meal or two. Off-site camping is *interdit* (prohibited) in the south because of the very great and real danger of fire. If you plan to camp for even a few nights, I recommend joining Family Campers and RVers. Annual membership (valid for one year from the time you join) is $25. FCRV is a member of the Federation Internationale de Camping et de Caravanning

(FICC), and is the only organization in America authorized to issue the International Camping Carnet for camping in Europe. Only FCRV members are eligible to purchase the carnet—it cannot be purchased separately—and the membership fee is $10. The carnet is like a camping passport, and since many FICC-member campgrounds in Europe are privately owned, the carnet provides entry into these member-only campsites. A carnet offers campers priority status, and occasionally, discounts. An additional benefit is that instead of keeping your passport overnight, which hotels and campgrounds are often required to do, the campground staff will simply keep your carnet, allowing you to hold on to your passport. One FICC membership is good for the entire family: parents and all children under the age of eighteen. To receive an application and information, contact the organization at 4804 Transit Road, Building 2, Depew, New York 14043, 800-245-9755 or 716-668-6242, phone and fax.

Chambres d'Hôtes or *maisons d'hôtes* (bed and breakfast accommodations in private homes) are widespread, and range from basic to almost luxurious. Most *chambres d'hôtes* are members of the *Gîtes de France* network (see below) but their membership is not always obvious as some owners do not always display the *Gîtes* logo. (Some people I know seek out *chambres d'hôtes* that don't advertise their *Gîtes* affiliation, believing them to be a cut above the rest; but I think doing this inevitably results in missing out on some truly wonderful places.) *Chambres d'hôtes* were once viewed as rather quirky accommodations existing solely as a way for farmers and other country people to earn extra money. But in the late 1980s, the bed-and-breakfast tradition was suddenly all the rage (one hopeful writer explained this shift as proof that the French were finally ready to shed their xenophobia), and many French (and a number of foreigners) were eager to buy and renovate properties into rustic-yet-elegant accommodations, especially in Provence. Rates are generally not expensive, usually the equivalent of a one- to three-star hotel, and the pluses are that you often get to spend time with your hosts (and practice your French) and enjoy delicious home-cooked meals. Also, B&B accommodations are great for families—Provençal hosts enjoy fussing over children, and many places offer suites, sometimes complete with a kitchenette. Hosts also like to share their suggestions for local restaurants, cafés, shops, and sites to see, so you'll feel like you're an insider faster than you might if you were staying at a hotel. Books to consult: *French Bed & Breakfast* (Alastair Sawday, edited by Ann Cooke-Yarborough, Alastair Sawday Publishing, Bristol, U.K.; distributed in the U.S. by St. Martin's Press) is my favorite book, and I have used some other titles in Sawday's series (*Special Places to Stay: Paris, Special Places to Stay in Spain and Portugal*, etc.) with happy results. All the listings feature color photos of the property and all the usual practical information. There are pages of maps and a useful vocabulary of French words and expressions. On my last trip to Provence, all the places I stayed in were found in this book, and I could not believe I was sleeping in such old, beautiful *châteaux*, surrounded by vineyards and lavender fields, and not a single one was over $100 a night. One of the main differences between this guide and Karen Brown's below is price—Sawday offers places that are every bit as charming but not always *luxe*, and the prices reflect this. *Karen Brown's France: Charming Bed & Breakfasts* (Clare Brown, distributed by Fodor's Travel Publications). My husband and I have found some of the most wonderful places to stay with the help of Karen Brown's guides. The *chambres d'hôtes* and *gîtes* lodgings in this book are less expensive than those listed in *Karen Brown's France: Inns & Itineraries* (see below under Hotels) but are no less charming or special. Obviously, I very much like bed-and-breakfast accommodations or I wouldn't recommend Alastair Sawday's book above or this one, but the authors of this guide state perhaps the best praise: "We unequivocally feel there is no finer way to travel in France." In addition to thorough descriptions of the lodgings (some of which are in old *châteaux*, farmhouses, and manor houses), *my* favorite features of these guides are ones no one ever mentions: the sample reservation letter (in French and English, so readers can construct a letter or fax of their own) and the tips that appear in the introduction, such as that road signs directing drivers to *chambres d'hôtes* or *Gîtes de France* are often posted with signs indicating *1ère à droite* (first road on the right) and *1ère à gauche* (first road on the left). I find the organization of the guides maddeningly cumbersome—the lodgings are listed alphabetically by individual city, town, or village, but maps are at the back of the book, so you end up constantly flipping back and forth to evaluate all the available choices in any given region of the country. However, this frustration is a small price to pay for the opportunity to stay in memorable lodgings. Provence and the Côte d'Azur are well represented in this guide (and cross-referenced with maps ten and eleven), and as there are so many places to choose from, it's a good guide to consult even if you don't plan on visiting other parts of France. *Rivages Bed and Breakfasts of Character and Charm: France* (formerly published by Fodor's Travel Publications, but 2001 editions are published by Hunter Publishing). The French *Rivages* guides have been popular in Europe for years and a welcome addition to lodgings literature here in the States. All the guides feature color photographs of the properties with one-page descriptions and good road maps. There are plentiful listings for the south; some of the listings will be familiar to readers of other guides but many do not appear in any other books.

   Châteaux accommodations are also an option as both privately owned *châteaux* and *châteaux-hôtels* accept guests in France. Readers might be surprised to learn that some of the most famous *châteaux* in France are privately owned, including Amboise and Chenonceaux in the Loire Valley. At private *châteaux* you are guests in someone's home, and this experience is akin to a bed-and-breakfast establishment (*châteaux-hôtels* are detailed below). Note, too, that some privately owned *châteaux* don't always welcome overnight guests but do offer private tours. Some sources of information include *Châteaux et Hôtels de France* (Michelin-starred chef Alain Ducasse now owns the organization that publishes this annual listing of 480-plus *châteaux, châteaux-hôtels,* and restaurants in France; copies are available at the three French Government Tourist Offices here in the U.S., and reservations can be made through DMI Tours (800-735-2478), directly with the *châteaux,* or on-line at www.chateauxethotels.com); *Relais & Chateaux* (this prestigious organization—see listing below under Hotels for more details—represents a number of properties that are *châteaux;* U.S. reservations number: 800-735-2478; www.relaischateaux.fr); Châteaux & Country Internet Resource (www.chateauxandcountry.com; this Web site, in both French and English, is a complete *châteaux* resource featuring castles available for accommodation, for rent for special events, and for tours. Profiles of each chateau include color photos, its history, location, and practical details. The site also features a "château of the month" and special château-related events). Refer also to the fall 1999 issue of *France Insider's News* for the article "Spend the Night in a Chateau-Hotel."

Gîtes de France accommodations are available as either bed-and-breakfast style or as a weekly or monthly rental. *Gîtes de France* is a network of typically inexpensive accommodations in private homes, and in my experience the families or hosts have been very welcoming and accommodations simple but nice. Breakfast is served either with the whole family around a large table and *café au lait* presented in large bowls (which I hardly ever see in Paris anymore) or completely separate from the household. Towels provided tend to be thin and small, and sometimes there isn't soap, so don't forget to pack your own. There are fifty thousand *gîtes* accommodations throughout France and the Maison des Gîtes de France et du Tourisme Vert has over one hundred guidebooks classified by region, *département,* or theme. These books are available at the main office in France (59 rue St.-Lazare, Paris, 75439; 01.49.70.75.75; fax: 01.42.81.28.53), and at some bookstores in the U.S., or inquire at the French tourist offices here in the U.S. for more information. Guides published are *Chambres d'Hôtes et Gîtes de Charme, Les Nouveaux Gîtes Ruraux,* and *Gîtes d'Étape et de Séjour.* The last guide doesn't apply to hotels, but by way of explanation, *Gîtes d'Étape* are similar to youth hostels in that they are very basic and beds are dormitory-style. They're found in rural areas all over France and are primarily for those who are hiking or biking (*gîtes d'étape* are featured on IGN maps and Topoguides—see Hiking for more details on maps). *Gîtes de Séjour* typically accept guests who plan to stay a minimum of three days as opposed to overnight, but are not considered hotels. Both types of lodging wonderfully accommodate both short- and long-distance walkers. *Gîtes Ruraux* are synonymous with *chambres d'hôtes,* except they typically accept guests for three days or longer. All the *Gîtes* guides have color photos and maps, are in both French and English, and the first guide features a number of listings for families.

Home exchange might be an appealing option: I've read wildly enthusiastic reports from people who've swapped apartments/houses, and it's usually always an economical alternative. Some services to contact include Intervac International Home Exchange (30 Corte San Fernando, Tiburon, California 94920; 800-756-HOME, 415-435-3497; fax: 415-435-7440; www.intervac.com). Intervac is one of the oldest (over fifty years) and largest exchange clubs, and has the largest database of home exchange offers in the world. Intervac clients consistently report "superlative" vacation experiences. Vacation Exchange Club (another leading agency, which publishes multiple directories each year; P.O. Box 650, Key West, Florida 33041; 800-638-3841 phone/fax); Trading Homes International (P.O. Box 787, Hermosa Beach, California 90254; 800-877-8723 / fax: 310-798-3865); Worldwide Home Exchange Club (806 Branford Avenue, Silver Spring, Maryland 20904; 301-680-8950); a general home exchange Web site is www.webhomeexchange.com/. A good but out-of-print book to read is *Trading Places: The Wonderful World of Vacation Home Exchanging* (Bill and Mary Barbour, Rutledge Hill Press, Nashville, Tennessee, 1991).

Hotels: For our purposes here we are referring to hotels as accommodations, but note that the word *hôtel* in French has a number of meanings: it also refers to a private, aristocratic mansion (known as a *hôtel particulier*); city hall (*hôtel de ville;* every French town of any size has one); a hospital *(hôtel-Dieu);* a general post office *(hôtel des postes);* an auction house *(hôtel des ventes);* and a home for wounded *(invalide)* war veterans (the most famous being the Hôtel des Invalides in Paris). As I stated in the introduction, I seek hotels which are distinctive but not over-the-top. Architecture critic Paul Goldberger has written that "A good hotel is a place, a town, a city, a world unto itself, and the aura it exudes has almost nothing to do with its rooms and almost everything to do with everything else—the lobby, the bar, the restaurants, the facade, the signs, even the corridors and the elevators." This applies to hotels large and small, expensive and not. A great range of hotel accommodations are available in the south of France, including the Logis de France chain. This network of over 3,500 modest, good-value hotels in rural areas are good places to spend the night (a few *logis* properties are expensive and rather extravagant, but the majority are simply comfortable and unpretentious). *Logis* properties, which have an average of eighteen rooms, are found near villages, in the countryside, in the mountains, and on the coast, and also have a restaurant offering local cuisine. Each year, a guide is published (in five languages) describing all the *logis,* and it comes with a fold-out map indicating precisely where each hotel is located. The guide costs approximately $15, but I've noticed that every January the French tourist offices here in the States will offer the previous year's guide free—assuming there are copies left over—and I don't find it at all limiting to peruse an older guide. Reservations can be made by calling a hotel directly or by calling the Logis de France central reservations service (1.45.84.83.84). The Federation Nationale des Logis de France offices are at 83 avenue d'Italie, Paris; 1.45.84.70.00;

fax: 1.45.83.59.66; www.logis.de.france.fr. *Relais & Chateaux* is an association of 426 independently owned hotels and restaurants of charm and prestige in forty-three countries around the world. R&C properties offer a perfect balance of exceptional service, food, comfort, and surroundings, with an emphasis on charm rather than luxury. The annual R&C guide features color photos, maps, and all details about each property. The 2000 guide listed thirteen lodgings in Lyon/Rhône Valley, and thirty-three for Provence/French Riviera. Reservations can be made directly with each hotel, through the central reservations department (U.S. number is 800-735-2478), via the Internet (www.relaischateaux.fr), or by a travel agent. *Relais du Silence* is an association of mostly owner-operated hotels in peaceful, pastoral settings. While a noise-free atmosphere is this group's main attribute, the hotels are quite diverse, ranging from grand *châteaux,* small cottages, Alpine chalets, and luxury inns. Relais du Silence started in 1968 and today includes over 300 members, primarily in France but in other European countries as well. Visitors traveling along country roads may see the group's trademark sign, featuring a brown logo of a bird and the outline of a house in the middle of a big tree. As good food is also important to Relais members, some properties display an additional sign: a red tree with a crossed knife and fork in the center. This indicates that the property has a *"table remarquée,"* sometimes with a view to match. An annual directory of Relais properties is available by contacting France, Inc., here in the U.S. (5609 Green Oaks Boulevard, SW, Arlington, Texas, 76017; 800-OK-FRANCE or 817-483-9400 / fax: 817-483-7000; send $5 for handling and priority shipping—which is reimbursed with your first reservation—and make checks out to France, Inc.). Reservations can be made directly with Relais properties or through the central reservations office in Paris (17 rue d'Ouessant, 75015; 1.44.49.79.00 / fax: 1.44.49.79.01). There is also a "frequent stayer" plan *(Cadeau Fidélité):* if you stay at ten properties in a one-year period and your Relais guide is stamped at all ten hotels, you receive a voucher for one free night at any Relais property. Here are some good books to look for when considering hotels: *Charming Small Hotel Guides: Southern France,* edited by Jenny Rees, Duncan Petersen Publishing, Ltd., London. This series features the kind of hotels I really like, and this little edition includes 260 captivating small hotels, *auberges,* and restaurants-with-rooms, any one of which would make a memorable night's stay. "Southern" here includes Bordeaux, the Dordogne, the Auvergne, Massif Central, Languedoc-Roussillon, and the Alps, but there are forty-three listings for Provence and the Côte d'Azur, and seven for the Rhône region. The editor notes that entries with photos have nearly all the qualities she looks for in an ideal place, but don't overlook the half-page entries, which profile sixty-four genuinely charming small hotels; after all, "you can't have stars on every page." Accompanying maps indicate hotel locations for each region. *Hello France! A Hotel Guide to Paris & 25 Other French Cities: $50–99 a Night for Two,* 2nd edition, Margo Classé, Wilson Publishing, Los Angeles, California. The author traveled with her husband to twenty-six of France's most popular cities and discovered this selection of clean, safe, centrally located, inexpensive, and charming hotels (with private bathrooms). There are a number of listings to consider for Aix, Antibes, Arles, Avignon, Cannes, Nice, Nîmes, St.-Rémy, and Tourrettes-sur-Loup. I have stayed at a few of her recommendations. *Karen Brown's France: Charming Inns & Itineraries* (Karen Brown, June Brown, and Clare Brown, distributed by Fodor's Travel Publications). As I mentioned above, I am a longtime fan of the Karen Brown series. This Inns & Itineraries edition highlights unique lodgings, some of which are in magnificent old mills, manor houses, *bastides,* and buildings of historic significance. This guide offers the same features as the B&B book—some noteworthy tips mentioned in the introduction include the warning that some hotels will accept a credit card to hold a reservation but don't allow you to pay the final bill with a credit card, and that *"Faites le plein, s'il vous plaît"* is how you say "Fill it up" at the gas station—but includes sample itineraries. I think these are useful for planning your route in advance and deciding if you want to travel by car, but the descriptions of individual towns and sites is not detailed enough to warrant bringing the book along—this is really a "before you go" book. There are over twenty listings for Provence and the Côte d'Azur (none for Monaco), making this a good guide to consult. *Rivages Hotels and Country Inns of Character and Charm: France* (formerly published by Fodor's Travel Publications, but 2001 editions are published by Hunter Publishing). As mentioned above for the Bed and Breakfasts guide, the French *Rivages* guides have been popular in Europe for years. Each guide (this one is in its fourth edition) features color photographs of the properties with one-page descriptions and good road maps. Just as with the B&B book, there are a great number of appealing listings for Provence and the Côte, and at the back of the book is a section on restaurants. Some listings will be familiar to readers of other guidebooks but many do not appear elsewhere. Character and charm are not exclusively equated with four-star luxury, but there are lots of three- and four-star listings in this guide; however, there are a number of two-, three-, and no-star choices, even though this book will never be of interest to the serious budget traveler. *Hidden Gems of Provence* (compiled by Luc Quisenaerts, English translation by Anne and Owen Davis, D–Publications, Belgium). This is a beautiful book in the new Hotel Gems of the World Series, and these places are to die for, with prices to match; still, I'd rather spend my money on one of these hotels than on an international chain hotel, and off-season rates make many of them affordable. Each hotel is described in four to six pages with photos that make you want to pack your bags *immédiatement* and ten pages of practical information—prices, contact information, a map, etc.—appear at the back of the book. Thirty-one lodgings (plus the Bistrot d'Eygalieres) are featured, including such well-known establishments as La Mirande, Villa Gallici, Auberge de Noves, Oustau de Baumanière, Cloître St.-Louis, and Le Mas de Peint, as well as a number of lesser-known but equally tempting places. *French Hotels & Restaurants* (The Rough Guide/Le Guide du Routard). This is the English translation of the popular *Hôtels et restos de France*, "the book the French take when they travel at home." Though it obviously includes restaurants and family-run bistros, the accommodations listings are so thorough and carefully selected that it's worth perusing just for the hotels. The Routard philosophy is based on good-value, independent establishments, which are assessed annually by a team of locally based writers. A review from *The Sunday Times* of London offers the best recommendation for this great book: "Indispensable to anyone on less than a platinum budget." There are 139 pages of listings for Provence/Alpes/Côte d'Azur and Rhône/Alpes.

Renting an apartment or villa might be a suitable choice depending on how long you'll be in the area and the number of people traveling together. I like the idea of renting because it's a quick way to feel a part of the local routine—you have daily chores to accomplish just like everyone else (except that I would hardly call going to pick up provisions at the local *marché* a chore). Though the tasks are mixed in with lots of little pleasures and trips, you often avoid the too-much-to-do rut. What to eat for dinner suddenly looms as the most important question of the day, the same question that all the local Provençal families are trying to answer. Renting, therefore, forces you to take an active part in the culture, rather than catch a glimpse of it. Organizations which arrange short- and long-term rentals would fill a small book, and it is not my intent here to provide a comprehensive listing. Rather, following are some sources that have either come highly recommended or have provided me with a positive experience: At Home Abroad (405 E. 56th Street, Suite 6H, New York, New York 10022; 212-421-9165; fax: 752-1591); Barclay International Group (3 School Street, Glen Cove, New York 11542; 516-759-5100 / 800-845-6636; fax: 516-609-0000; www.barclayweb.com. A well-established company offering worldwide rentals, Barclay also reserves car rentals, sight-seeing tours, rail passes, theater tickets, cellular phones, and laptop computer rentals; the "Last-Minute Specials" feature of its Web site is a good deal); Citadines "Apparthotels" (B & V Associates, 140 East 56th Street, Suite 4C, New York, New York 10022; 800-755-8266; www.apartment-hotels.com. Apartment hotels may be an especially good choice for business travelers and families, and travelers on modest budgets may welcome them, too. All apartments have faxes, fully equipped kitchens, and a 24-hour reception desk, each is in a great location, and rates include weekly maid service, linens, towels, and hair dryers. I found some apartments in Nice with rates from $60–$150 per night, and one offered access to a private beach for a special discount price. There is a one-night minimum stay, so this is also worth investigating even if you don't plan on staying a week); Frenchvillas.com (Internet Villas, Inc., 8 Knight Street, Suite 205, Norwalk, Connecticut, 06851; 800-700-9549 or 203-855-8161; this Web site—one of the easiest and fastest to use—features "fabulous rentals" in Provence, Côte d'Azur, and Paris, with some fabulous prices to match (although a number are great for families and groups. Internet Villas also offers rentals for Italy and Mexico); Villas and Apartments Abroad Ltd. (420 Madison Avenue, Suite 1003, New York, New York 10017; 800-433-3020; fax: 212-755-8316; www.vaanyc.com; arranges rentals in France, Italy, and the Caribbean; I like that its Web site clearly defines four seasons, low, mid, high, and peak, and gives prices for all four; many of these properties have cooks and housekeepers); Villas and Voyages (David Geen, 2450 Iroquois Avenue, Detroit, Michigan 48214; 800-220-3993; www.savourfrance.com; over fifty villas are available for rent in five areas: the Lubéron, Mt. Ventoux region, St.-Rémy and vicinity, Aix-en-Provence area, and the Côte d'Azur; this company also offers three cooking programs in Provence—see Cooking Schools); Ville et Village (2124 Kittredge Street, Suite 200, Berkeley, California; 510-559-8080; fax: -8217; agency offers rentals in the cities and countryside of France, Italy, Spain, and Portugal); Wimco (P.O. Box 1461, Newport, Rhode Island 02840; 401-849-8012; fax: 847-6290; www.wimcovillas.com; specializes in private vacation villa rentals and select hotels in the south of France, Paris, Italy, Spain, England, Scotland, Ireland, and the Caribbean; there are dozens of deluxe properties available throughout Provence and along the coast, not many under $2,000 per week; well-traveled reservationists have visited nearly every property personally). If you prefer making arrangements yourself, don't forget that *Gîtes de France* properties are also available for rent (see Chambres d'Hôtes above). Also, larger newsstands in the U.S. sell a glossy, full-color publication called *Maisons de Rêve à Louer: Côte d'Azur* (dream houses to rent), which highlights dozens of extremely appealing places. The magazine is in English and French, and its complementary Web site is www.residences-immobilier.com. Additionally, do not overlook the classified ads in magazines and newspapers. By renting directly from the owners, you avoid paying a middle-man fee, and there are plenty of places to rent that are every bit as nice as those represented by agencies.

General accommodation notes to keep in mind: ~Ask for reservation confirmation in writing. Though I may place an initial call to an inn or hotel, I prefer that communication be by fax. This allows for any language errors to be corrected in case my French was faulty, and serves as an official document. While a fax alone does not guarantee something won't go wrong, it certainly helps to produce one at check-in. If you arrive at your lodging and the staff cannot honor your reservation, be polite but firm in asking for a better room elsewhere in the hotel (at the same price) or a comparable room at another lodging (you could also push the envelope here and ask that they pay for your first night). The hotel is obligated to find you comparable, alternate lodgings—not to pay for your first night someplace else, but I figure this is part of a bargaining process in arriving at a solution. You should also ask them to pay for your transportation to the other location, which they should not hesitate to do. ~Some of the larger Provençal cities and towns are noisy, even at night. Even though some streets may be limited or closed to cars, scooters are usually permitted, so select rooms accordingly. ~Breakfast is rarely a good value at a hotel. Save some money—and get the same thing, often better—and join the locals at the corner café. ~When you first arrive at your hotel, ask to see your room first. This is a common practice in Europe, and it is understood that if a room is not to your liking, you may request a different one. This is also your opportunity to ask for a room upgrade; if the hotel is not fully booked (and it rarely will be during low season) you may end up with a significantly nicer room at the same rate, so it never hurts to ask. ~Speaking of fully booked: if you've been told that you can't get a room, call again between 4:00 and 6:00 P.M. and double-check. This is the time of day when many establishments cancel the reservations of guests who haven't shown up. ~If a hotel you choose also has a reservations office in the U.S. (usually an 800 number), call both numbers. It is entirely possible that you will be quoted different rates. Also, some of the more expensive hotels offer a rate which must be prepaid in full, in U.S. dollars, but which is lower than the local rack rate. ~No matter what type of lodging you choose, *always* inquire if there is a lower rate. Reservationists—and even the owners of small inns—always hope the rate they quote will be accepted, and if you don't ask about other possibilities they will not volunteer any. In addition, ask if there are corporate rates; special rates for seniors, students, government and military employees; weekend rates (this usually only applies to city hotels, as business travelers will have checked out by Friday); and even special prices for newlyweds. Hotels and inns large and small all want to fill their rooms, and if you'll be staying four nights or longer, you may also be able to negotiate a better rate. Most important, ask for how long the rate you're quoted is available and how many rooms at that price are left. In smaller places especially, a day can mean the difference between securing a reservation or losing it. ~Useful vocabulary: *oreiller* (pillow); *clef* (key); *draps* (sheets); *couverture* (blanket); *serviette de toilette* (hand or face towel); *serviette de bain* (bath towel); *l'eau chaud* (hot water); *compris* (included, as in, is breakfast included in the price?).

Aigue

The Provençal word for water, as in the Aigues River, *Aigue Brun, Pays d'Aigues, Tour d'Aigues, Aigues-Mortes,* and so on.

Aïoli, Aïoli Monstre, or Grand Aïoli

Aïoli, a delicious, thick, garlic mayonnaise, is a culinary treat every visitor to Provence will surely encounter. Interested cooking enthusiasts will find a recipe for *aïoli* in any Provençal cookbook worthy of its name. The most popular way of serving this mayonnaise is in the form of an *aïoli monstre* or *grand aïoli,* as an accompaniment to a platter of room-temperature vegetables, sliced or flaked cod, and sometimes roasted meat and snails. It is an immensely satisfying warm-weather feast, and I try not to let a summer pass without making some for myself. If you're in Provence during the summer, check the local kiosques in places like the local *poste, café,* or *mairie* for signs announcing the annual *fête*. Why? Because in addition to carousels, parades, and dances, every summer *fête* hosts a *repas populaire,* which is your clue that you've found an open invitation to an *aïoli monstre*. Visitors are most welcome—although be prepared for few English speakers—and "the more the merrier" motto seems to prevail (as more people arrive, more chairs and places at the tables are somehow found). Generally, each village hosts its summer *fête* at the same time every year, and you can contact the local tourist office about the date in advance. A *grand aïoli* is one party you don't want to miss.

Airfares and Airlines

We all know that not everyone pays the same price for seats on an airplane. One of the reasons for this is that seats do not hold the same value at all times of the year, month, or even days of the week. Recently, I was researching some fares to Paris for a long weekend. One of my calls produced a particularly helpful representative who proceeded to detail all available fares for the entire month of September. There were approximately fifteen different prices—based on a seemingly endless number of variables—within that month alone. The best way, therefore, to get the best deal to accommodate your needs is to check a variety of sources and be flexible. Flexibility is, and has always been, the key to low-cost travel, and you should be prepared to slightly alter the dates of your proposed trip to take advantage of those airline seats which hold less value. If you think all the best deals are to be found on the Internet, you're mistaken: airlines, consolidators, and other discounters offer plenty of good fares over the telephone and through advertisements. In order to know with certainty that you've got a good deal, you need to compare fares, which requires checking more than one source. I believe that on any day of the week, the lowest fares can be found equally among Web sites, wholesalers, airlines, charters, tour operators, travel agents, and sky auctions—you don't know until you inquire. With the proliferation of e-fares, more no-frills carriers, and more frequent price wars, there are no longer obvious times to purchase tickets at the best prices. It used to be that advance purchases—whether made months or fourteen days ahead—guaranteed better fares; but nowadays it seems that good fares pop up at random, and only thorough research will reveal them. (Saturday night stayovers, however, remain a relic that the travel industry still rewards with better rates.) I like flying a country's own airline—Air France, for example. And even though Air France fares are usually among the highest available, its off-season fares are among the lowest. Following are some sources I typically consult before I purchase anything (note that I've included corresponding Web sites for some sources, but I typically prefer calling): 1-800-AIRFARE (1-800-247-3273); 1-800-FLY-CHEAP; Cheap Tickets Inc., 800-377-1000; Lowestfare.com, 888-777-2222; 1-800-FLY4-LESS; 800-CHEAP-AIR; Council

Travel (known as "America's Student Travel Leader," this fifty-three-year-old company also offers good fares for adults and a host of useful stuff for students and teachers; 800-2COUNCIL, or counciltravel.com); and the travel section of *The New York Times* (my local daily newspaper), which I scan for ads of all the area agencies offering low prices. Many of these ads typically reveal the same low fares by one or two particular airlines, which are almost always smaller, foreign lines currently trying to expand their business in the U.S. So, for example, a few years ago all the agencies I called were featuring cheap flights to Paris on Pakistan International Air. I bought a round-trip ticket for under $400 on a flight that was destined for Karachi via Paris. (Note that if you do fly on an airline of a Muslim country, there will not usually be alcohol served; Air Saudia, however, employs non-Muslim flight attendants, so alcoholic drinks are available, and Saudia is probably not the only airline to get around the restriction in this way.) Booking travel on the Web works best for people with simple requirements and lots of flexibility. In fact, if you can leave on *really* short notice, some great deals may be in store for you: some Web sites specializing in just such spur-of-the-moment travel are lastminutetravel.com; www.site59.com; and www.travelzoo.com. However, if you have a lot of questions (as I always do), you can't get them answered, and are setting yourself up for potential headaches. And in my experience with sky auctions, I never seem to be able to find a flight scenario that works with my schedule, and I don't like not being able to more finely narrow the criteria when submitting my initial bid—what *time* of day I fly is just as important as the date. The time it takes to continue submitting bids (my initial bid is never accepted) seems wasteful to me, time I could be spending getting concrete information from other sources. Additionally, I have read that the idea of submitting your own price for a ticket is illusory; in fact, the Internet firms buy discounted seats from the airlines, but only sell those seats at fares above an established level. Bids below that level are rejected. Also, travelers seldom have control over which airlines they'll fly or which cities they'll stop in if it's a connecting flight. And most don't allow you to earn mileage points. But if you have no parameters to work around and are just looking for a good fare, here are some Web sites to check: www.skyauction.com; www.previewtravel.com; www.thetrip.com; www.cheaptickets.com; www.priceline.com; www.travelocity.com; www.expedia.com; www.economytravel.com; www.lowestfare.com; www.TRIP.com; www.travelscape.com; www.airfare.com; www.thefarebusters.com; www.itn.com; www.buytravel.com; and Savvio.com, which operates like an auction and also allows you to choose an airline—viewers are shown the length of time discounted prices are valid and as departure day approaches, prices drop, and you can delay purchasing until the rate reaches what you want to pay (note, too, that some of these Web sites also offer opportunities to rent cars and reserve accommodations). And if you're in Provence and want to fly somewhere else within Europe, check with Europe by Air (888-387-2479; www.europebyair.com), which offers $99 fares with over sixteen airlines serving 127 cities in twenty-seven countries. ~Readers who live in the Northeast may want to consider flights from London, a city filled with consolidators (known as "bucket shops"). Since good deals on flights from northeastern cities to London are available most of the year, you just might be able to find a very good fare (and, since you can't fly direct to Provence anyway, the change of planes does not add another leg to the journey). Virgin Express (011.44.322.752.0505) offers inexpensive fares from London to Nice—and other European cities, including Barcelona, Milan, Copenhagen, and Rome—although it is no-frills all the way and you can't earn frequent-flier miles. ~A word about travel agents: though it was perhaps inevitable that a great number of travel agencies would close due to the arrival of the Internet, do not underestimate what a quality agent can do for you. Readers who have one already know this: good travel agents are indispensable and worth their weight in gold. Resourceful travelers will often be able to put a detailed trip together on their own as well as an average agent, but even the most determined travelers will not be able to match the savvy of top-notch agents. I believe that at the end of the day, the Internet is a great resource tool, but it's not a human being watching over every last detail for you. The more specialized or complicated your trip is, the more reason you should employ the services of an experienced agent. To read more about exactly what good agents are capable of, see "Miracles Are Us," by Wendy Perrin (*Condé Nast Traveler,* June 2000). Perrin identified seventy travel consultants described as "better connected than the Internet, faster than a T3 line, able to book the unbookable." Of the seventy, sixty-three of them are members of the Virtuoso network, which specializes in leisure travel for discerning clients. Less than 1 percent of consultants in the Americas are accepted for membership in Virtuoso, which utilizes a worldwide network of four hundred cruise, tour, adventure, property, and ground operator partners in sixty countries. Contact Virtuoso at 800-401-4274 or www.virtuoso.com. ~Don't be afraid of reputable consolidators, but recognize that their lower fares come with more restrictions. If there are flight cancellations or delays, you have no recourse with the airline since it didn't sell you the ticket directly (this holds true with tickets purchased through discount Internet companies as well). If you want to make any changes, you have to pay a penalty. ~Reputable charter flights, too, should not be feared. I've had three good experiences on charter flights and encourage you to investigate them. The limitations are that most charters offer only coach class and tend to be completely full—in fact, a charter operator is legally allowed to cancel a flight up to ten days before departure if it doesn't fill enough seats. I might not, therefore, travel with children or plan a honeymoon on a charter flight. Although I did not experience any problems on my charter flights, I understand that delays are common, and—as with consolidators—passengers don't have any recourse. However, operators who organize charter flights are required to place passengers' flight payments in an escrow account, so if the flight is canceled, or if the operator doesn't abide by its agreement, you receive a refund. A publication called *Jax Fax Travel Marketing Magazine* lists over five thousand scheduled charter flights to over one hundred destinations worldwide. Previously only available to industry folks, the general public can now subscribe. Contact Jax Fax at 48 Wellington Road, Milford, Connecticut 06460; 800-9-JAXFAX or 203-301-0255; fax: -0250; www.jaxfax.com. A single issue can be purchased for about $5 as well as a one- or two-year subscription. ~Flying as a courier may be the best deal of all if you're a light packer (luggage is usually limited to one carry-on bag), although even courier fares are no longer as discounted as they once were. Couriers also can't usually reserve a seat for more than one person, although your traveling companion could purchase a ticket on the same flight. Air couriers are cogs in international commerce; they are completely legal and legitimate, and demand for them in years past has exceeded the supply (because this balance is now shifting, shipping companies no longer need to reduce prices to entice fliers). Couriers are responsible for chaperoning documents through customs and then hand delivering them to a person waiting outside the customs area. They are a necessity simply because companies doing international business send a large number of documents overseas, and those documents can get held up in customs unless accompanied by a person. There are several companies which arrange courier flights in the U.S., but the one I'm most familiar with is Now Voyager (74 Varick Street, New York, New York 10013; 212-431-1616). To review more options, consider joining the International Association of Air Travel Couriers (P.O. Box 1349, Lake Worth, Florida 33460; 561-582-8320). Members receive a regular bulletin with a variety of international routes being offered by air courier companies departing from several U.S. cities. Reservation phone numbers are included so you can make inquiries and schedule your trip yourself. I have seen some *incredible* bargains, and some fares were valid for several months. ~If you're making arrangements directly with an airline, ask if your flight is a "code-share." Code-sharing is complicated, to say the least (Betsy Wade of *The New York Times* says that "the general theory of relativity is not too much more complex" than the code-sharing network). In a very small nutshell, code-sharing is an agreement between airline partners which allows them to share routes, but what it means for the consumer is that each airline sharing a code may offer a different price for the same trip. Find out which other airline(s) is in on the code and compare prices. ~Note that airlines are not required to offer passengers much due to flight delays or cancellations. If you have visions of free meals, hotel rooms, and flights, you may be in for a disappointment. Each airline has its own Conditions of Carriage, which you can request from an airline's ticket office or public relations department, but the legalese is not identical from airline to airline. From what I can tell, the employees who stand at the gates are the ones who have the authority to grant passengers amenities, so if you *don't* ask them for something (a seat on the next flight, a long-distance phone call, a meal, whatever) you *definitely* won't get it. ~Technically, airlines no longer allow passengers to fly standby at a discount, but I've been told that seats are occasionally sold at reduced prices for flights that aren't full. There is, however, an official standby service offered by Whole Earth Travel Airhitch (two U.S. offices: 2641 Broadway, 3rd floor, New York, New York 10025; 800-326-2009 or 212-864-2000; fax: 212-864-5489 and 13470 Washington Boulevard, Suite 205, Marina del Rey, California 90292; 800-834-9192; fax: 310-574-0054; www.4cheapair.com). Very affordable flights are available for worldwide destinations, but you must be flexible, seeing that Airhitch selects the date you travel based on a five-day range, which you provide. Similar to a consolidator, Airhitch offers seats on commercial airlines which are about to be left empty, and the company's philosophy is one akin to *The Collected Traveler:* "The experience of travel is a benefit that should be available to everyone. It is through travel that we each learn to accept the differences in others while realizing the similarity in our common goals. We believe travel is the best road to peace and understanding, and it's a whole lotta fun!" Airhitch also offers an option called Target Flights: you supply the dates of travel and desired destination, plus the best quote you've obtained, and Airhitch will respond in twenty-four hours if it can buy a similar ticket at a cheaper price (when I checked, this feature wasn't available yet on its Web site, but travelers can call the New York office at 800-326-2009 for details). I've also been told that one of the best days of the year to show up at the airport without a ticket is Christmas Day. I can't personally confirm this, and it's doubtful an airline employee can, either. Perhaps this is either a very well kept secret or a myth, but if you're able to be that flexible, it might be worth trying.

Airports

Provence, the Côte d'Azur, and Monaco are served by two airports: the Nice/Côte d'Azur airport and Aeroport Marseille Provence. Additionally, other airports to consider are Satolas Airport in Lyon (only two hours from the Côte d'Azur) and Switzerland's Geneva International Airport (a beautiful, three- to four-hour drive from northern Provence). On occasion, I have looked into Cristoforo Colombo Airport in Genoa and Milano/Malpensa International Airport in Milan, but neither seemed to offer significant savings. A good book to consult is *Salk International's Airport Transit Guide* (Ron Salk, editor-in-chief, Millennium Edition, Salk International Travel Premiums, Inc., Sunset Beach, California), a handy, pocket-size paperback that is indispensable for frequent business and pleasure travelers, and an awfully great resource for everyone else. This millennium edition is the biggest in its nineteen-year history, and includes ground transportation information for 447 airports worldwide. As stated in the introduction, "In the air, others worry about getting you safely from point A to point B. But on the ground you're on your own. And unless you're returning home or being met by a welcoming committee, getting from the airport to point C may require information you don't have. That's what this book is for." The Nice/Côte d'Azur airport entry details taxi fares to the city center, Antibes, Cannes, Grasse, Monte Carlo, and Menton; public bus services; van/shuttle services; and Heli Air Monaco. The Marseille entry details taxi fares to the city, and the airport bus to the Gare St.-Charles, Aix-en-Provence, and Vitrolles. This book is a little hard to find—I used to see it more frequently in bookstores but now I rarely do. I ordered mine from Magellan's mail-order catalog (800-962-4943), but you can also call Salk directly at 714-893-0812 or visit its Web site: www.airporttransitguide.com. The book also features a world time zones map at the back. ~The Nice airport now has a Web site (www.nice.aeroport.fr) with information on flight schedules, airport services, customs, rental cars, business facilities, freight, etc.

Alliance Française

With 1,085 affiliates in 138 nations worldwide (including 142 chapters in 45 states), the aim of Alliance Française—the official cultural arm of France—is to promote awareness, understanding, and appreciation of the French language and culture. French grammar and conversation classes are offered at all levels, and class size is typically small. Plus, members have access to a library of books, videos, compact disks, and periodicals, and special events. I enjoyed my experiences with Alliance very much, and if there is a chapter near you, I encourage you to enroll in a class before you leave—and when you return! Or, consider enrolling at the Alliance in Nice or Marseille, the two affiliates in Provence. To locate U.S. chapters or to enroll in classes in France, contact the Alliance Française at Delegation Generale de l'Alliance Française, 2819 Ordway Street, NW, Washington, D.C. 20008; 202-966-9740 or 888-9-FRENCH; fax: 202-362-1587; www.afusa.org. The Web site features a list of frequently asked questions, as well as the costs for classes and accommodation possibilities. Alliance Française schools are also located in other French cities: Bordeaux, Dijon, Montpellier, Rouen, Lyon, Toulouse, and, of course, Paris.

B

Le Bisou

A kiss, from the verb *baiser*. Actually, *le bisou* is a social kiss, as opposed to *le baiser,* which is a much more passionate kiss between lovers. You may already know that in general the French kiss upon greeting each other, and kiss again when saying farewell. The established practice is to kiss first the left cheek and then the right. But in Provence, you may notice that most people kiss *three* times, always beginning with the left cheek.

Biking

It's not surprising that the country that hosts the Tour de France (now in its 103rd year) welcomes cyclists of all abilities. Provence offers a wealth of biking opportunities for serious enthusiasts and amateurs (so do the Côte d'Azur and Monaco, but to a lesser degree). Bikes can be rented at cycle rental shops in all the larger cities and towns in the region (and in some smaller ones) as well as at some hostels, campsites, train stations, tourist offices, and *gîtes d'étapes*. It is more French to get around by moped or scooter, and these too are easy to find for rent—often, the same places that rent bikes rent mopeds. There is an IGN (Institut Géographique Nationale) biking map available at a scale of 1:10,000 (see Hiking for IGN info). Local tourist offices have information on area biking routes, as well as possible day trips with local guides. Three good books to consult are *Cycling in France* (Carole Saint-Laurent, Ulysses Green Escapes, Ulysses Travel Publications); *France by Bike: 14 Tours Geared for Discovery* (Karen and Terry Whitehill, The Mountaineers, Seattle, Washington, 1993); and *Cycling France: The Best Bike Tours in All of Gaul* (Jerry Simpson Jr., Motorbooks International, 1992). Each book details one or more bike routes in Provence. For some companies (mostly American) that offer organized bike trips, see the listings under Tours. ~Useful vocabulary: *vélo tout terrain* (VTT) is an all-terrain bike.

Boat and Barge Cruises

The southwestern region of France—Bordeaux, the Lot, Gascogne, and Périgord—is better suited for barge travel than Provence. However, one company in particular offers a trip in the Camargue, which begins near Montpellier and ends at Aigues-Mortes. Travel is by *penichette,* now a generic word for any type of canal boat but which is in fact a registered trademark of Locaboat Plaisance (Port au Bois—B.P. 150, 89303 Joigny Cedex, France; 3.86.91.72.72; fax: 3.86.62.06.14; www.locaboat.com). Trips are one week, ten or eleven days, or two weeks, and though not cheap, they are unforgettable.

Bookstores

Like the French (and most Europeans in general), I prefer to buy whatever goods and services I need from specialists. One-stop shopping is a nice idea in theory but has not been very appealing to me, as convenience seems to be its only virtue. Therefore, I buy fish from a fishmonger, flowers from a florist, cheese from a real cheese shop, etc. And when I'm looking for travel books, I shop at travel bookstores or independent bookstores with strong travel sections. The staff in these stores are nearly always well traveled, well read, very helpful, and knowledgeable. An aspect I don't like about nationwide chainstores is that travel guides tend to be shelved separately from travel writing and related history books, implying that guidebooks are all a traveler needs or wants. Stores specializing in travel take a wider view, understanding that travel incorporates many different dimensions. Following is a list of stores in the U.S. that offer exceptional travel book departments (I've also included a few stores specializing in art books and cookbooks, as some of these titles are mentioned throughout the book). Note that all of them accept mail orders, and some publish catalogs and/or newsletters.

CALIFORNIA

Black Oak Books
1491 Shattuck Avenue, Berkeley
510-486-0698

Bon Voyage Travel Books & Maps
2069 W. Bullard, Fresno
800-995-9716
www.bon-voyage-travel.com

Book Passage
51 Tamal Vista Boulevard,
Corte Madera
800-999-7909 or 415-927-0960 locally
www.bookpassage.com

The Cook's Library
8373 W. Third Street, Los Angeles
323-655-3141

Distant Lands
56 South Raymond Avenue, Pasadena
626-449-3220 / 800-310-3220
(California only)
www.distantlands.com

The Literate Traveller
8306 Wilshire Boulevard, Suite 591,
Beverly Hills
800-850-2665 or 310-398-8781 / fax:
310-398-5151
www.literatetraveller.com
~In addition to its regular catalog,

The Literate Traveller publishes
Around the World in 80+ Mysteries.

Pacific Travellers Supply
12 West Anapamu Street,
Santa Barbara
888-PAC-TRAV
pts@maplink.com

Phileas Fogg's Books, Maps & More
87 Stanford Shopping Center,
Palo Alto
800-533-3644
www.foggs.com

Rizzoli (five locations):
2 Rodeo Drive, Beverly Hills
310-278-2247
South Coast Plaza, Costa Mesa
714-957-3331
1 Colorado Boulevard, Pasadena
626-564-1300
117 Post, San Francisco
415-984-0225
332 Santa Monica Boulevard,
Santa Monica
310-393-0101
Rizzoli catalog orders:
800-52-BOOKS

The Travellers Bookcase
8375 West 3rd Street, Los Angeles
323-655-0575
www.travelbooks.com

COLORADO

Tattered Cover
2955 East 1st Avenue, Denver
303-322-7727

WASHINGTON, D.C.

AIA/Rizzoli
1735 New York Avenue, N.W.
202-626-7541
catalog orders: 800-52-BOOKS

Travel Books & Language Center
4437 Wisconsin Avenue, N.W.
202-237-1322 / fax: 237-6022
800-220-2665 (mail orders)
e-mail: travelbks@aol.com

FLORIDA

Andrea's Bookstore, Inc.
308 Highway 19 South, Palatka
904-325-2141 / fax: 325-8352

GEORGIA

The Civilized Traveller (two locations):
Phipps Plaza, Atlanta
404-264-1252
Perimeter Mall, Atlanta
770-673-0111
www.civilizedtraveller.com
~Not exclusively a bookstore, its focus
is more on globes, luggage, and travel
accessories, but the guidebook selection
is thorough. See the sister stores in
New York and Virginia below.

ILLINOIS

The Book Stall at Chestnut Court
811 Elm Street, Winnetka
847-446-8880 / fax: -2894

The Savvy Traveller
310 Michigan Avenue, Chicago
888-666-6200
www.thesavvytraveler.com

Rizzoli
Water Tower Place, Chicago
312-642-3500
Catalog orders: 800-52-BOOKS

LOUISIANA

Beaucoup Books
5414 Magazine Street, New Orleans
504-895-2663 / fax: -9778

MASSACHUSETTS

Globe Corner Bookstore (two locations):
500 Boylston Street, Boston
800-358-6013 / 617-859-8008
28 Church Street, Harvard Square,
Cambridge
617-497-6277

Brattle Book Shop
9 West Street, Boston
617-542-0210 / fax: 617-338-1467
800-447-9595 (mail orders)
~Brattle's specialty is art books, but it
also stocks over 250,000 used, rare,
and out-of-print books.

Rizzoli
Copley Place, Boston
617-437-0700

MINNESOTA

Books For Travel, Etc.
857 Grand Avenue, St. Paul
888-668-8006

NEW HAMPSHIRE

Magellan Travel Books
53 S. Main Street, Suite 211, Hanover
800-303-0011 or 603-643-6100 / fax:
603-643-6014
www.magellantravelbooks.com

NEW YORK

Archivia: The Decorative Arts Book Shop
944 Madison Avenue, New York
212-439-9194
~Beautiful store with a beautiful selection of decorating, garden, style, history, and art titles, some in French.

Argosy Book Store
116 East 59th Street, New York
212-753-4455
~Specializes in old and rare books, some of which are travel-related.

The Civilized Traveller (two locations):
864 Lexington Avenue (at 65th Street), New York
212-288-9190
2003 Broadway (at 68th Street), New York
212-875-8809
www.civilizedtraveller.com

The Complete Traveller
199 Madison Avenue (35th Street), New York
212-685-9007
~In addition to a great selection of current books, a separate room is reserved for rare and out-of-print travel books. Owners Harriet and Arnold Greenberg and their superb staff will do their very best to track down your most obscure request.

Hacker Art Books
45 West 57th Street, New York
212-688-7600 / fax: 754-2554
e-mail: hackerartbooks@
infohouse.com / www.hackerart-books.com
~John Russell, former art critic of *The New York Times,* has written of Hacker that "For an all-round art book-store, this one is something near to ideal."

Kitchen Arts & Letters
1435 Lexington Avenue (between 93rd and 94th), New York
212-876-5550 / fax: -3584

Posman Books
Grand Central Terminal, New York
212-533-2665 / fax: 983-1849
1 University Place, New York
212-533-2665 / fax: 533-2681
e-mail: posmanbook@aol.com

Strand Book Store
828 Broadway (at 12th Street), New York
212-473-1452 / fax: 473-2591
800-366-3664 (mail orders)
e-mail: strand@strandbooks.com

Strand Book Annex
95 Fulton Street, New York
212-732-6070 / fax: 406-1654

Rizzoli (four locations):
Manhattan:
31 W. 57th Street
212-759-2424
3 World Financial Center
212-385-1400
454 West Broadway
212-674-1616
Manhasset:
The Americana
516-365-9393
Rizzoli catalog orders: 800-52-BOOKS

NORTH CAROLINA

Blue Planet Map Company
487 W. King Street, Boone
828-264-5400 / fax: -5400

Omni Resources
10004 South Mebane Street,
Burlington
800-742-2677
www.omnimap.com

OKLAHOMA

Traveler's Pack LTD
9427 North May Avenue,
Oklahoma City
405-755-2924
www.travelerspack.com

OREGON

Book Mark
856 Olive Street, Eugene
541-484-0512 / fax: 686-2957

Powell's City of Books
1005 West Burnside, Portland
800-878-7323 / 503-228-4651 (locally)
www.powells.portland.or.us

Powell's Travel Store
701 SW Sixth Avenue, Portland
800-546-5025
www.powells.com

PENNSYLVANIA

Franklin Maps
333 S. Henderson Road,
King of Prussia
610-265-6277 / fax: 337-1575
~Extraordinary selection of foreign
and domestic maps as well as books.
One journalist wrote, "What travelers
will find at the 15,000-square-feet
Franklin Map store are maps, charts,
and books covering almost every
square inch of earth and universe."

VERMONT

Adventurous Traveler Bookstore
P.O. Box 64769 (for mail orders)
245 South Champlain Street (for visiting), Burlington
800-282-3963 or 802-860-6776 /
fax: 802-860-6667
www.adventuroustraveler.com

VIRGINIA

The Civilized Traveller
Tyson's Galleria, Fairfax
703-917-9535
www.civilizedtraveller.com

Rizzoli
Merchants Square, Williamsburg
757-229-9821

WASHINGTON

Wide World Books & Maps
4411A Wallingford Avenue North,
Seattle
206-634-3453
www.travelbooksandmaps.com

And, because some books I recommend are British publications, I include three excellent stores in London: The Travel Bookshop (13–15 Blenheim Crescent, W11 2EE, 44.171.229.5260; fax: 243.1552; www.thetravelbookshop.co.uk); Books for Cooks (a few doors down from The Travel Bookshop at #4 Blenheim Crescent, 44.171.221.1992; fax: 221.1517); and Stanfords Maps, Charts, Books (12–14 Long Acre, Covent Garden, WCZE 9LP, 020.7730.1354, plus three other locations in and around London. International mail-order service: 44.171.836.1321; fax: 44.171.836.0189).

Additionally, I must mention two favorite mail-order book catalogs: *A Common Reader* and *Bas Bleu*. Both are issued monthly and offer an excellent selection of travel writing, biographies, history, cookbooks, and general fiction and nonfiction books for adults, as well as selected books for children. *ACR*'s selection is more extensive, but this does not make *Bas Bleu*'s offerings any less appealing.

James Mustich Jr. is the man behind the *ACR* venture, and his reviews are of the sort that wander here and there and make you want to read every single book in the catalog (his writing has been an inspiration to me for the annotated bibliographies in *The Collected Traveler*). Not content to simply offer new books, Mustich even arranges to bring out-of-print books back into print by publishing them under his own Common Reader Editions imprint. To add your name to these catalog mailing lists, contact *A Common Reader* (141 Tompkins Avenue, Pleasantville, New York 10570; 800-832-7323; fax: 914-747-0778; www.commonreader.com) and *Bas Bleu* (515 Means Street, NW, Atlanta, Georgia 30318; 404-577-9463; fax: 577-6626; www.basbleu.com). ~If your favorite bookseller can't find an out-of-print title you're looking for, try contacting members of Book Sense, a network of over 1,100 independent booksellers around the country (888-BOOKSENSE or BookSense.com), or search one of the following Web sites: *www.longitudebooks.com* (a wonderful source for travel books—which they define as comprehensively as I do, including travel narratives, art, archaeology, novels, essays, guidebooks, etc.—and maps; when you select a destination, you can view an Essential Reading list plus an accompanying map; when I searched on Provence/Côte d'Azur, I was happy to see many of the same books I recommend—although *Monet's Years at*

Giverny doesn't belong in the mix as Giverny is outside Paris); *www.abe-books.com* (American Book Exchange, which I like because you purchase books directly from independent booksellers); *www.alibris.com* and *www.elephantbooks.com,* which deal in rare and collectible books. For books in French, perhaps the best store in the U.S. is Librairie de France (Rockefeller Center Promenade, 610 Fifth Avenue, New York, New York 10020; 212-581-8810; fax: 265-1094; www.Frencheuropean.com). Books on food, wine, fiction, and travel are all available, as well as dictionaries, Michelin maps, and gifts. The *L'Express "meilleurs ventes"* (bestsellers) are on regular display, and the store sells a great selection of Paris street sign magnets. Mail orders are happily accepted. Also, browse *www.chapitre.com*—*"votre librairie sur internet"*—for the vast selection offered by this Paris store.

ENGLISH-LANGUAGE BOOKSTORES IN PROVENCE, CÔTE D'AZUR, AND MONACO INCLUDE:

The Cat's Whiskers, 30 rue Lamartine, Nice; well-known shop with a good selection, including children's books and secondhand fiction. The owner's cats are shy and stay at home, but if you bring her black labrador a biscuit, you're a friend for life; 04.93.80.02.66.

Centre Franco-Americain de Provence, 10 montee de la Tour, Villeneuve-les-Avignon; 04.90.25.93.23.

Fueri-Lamy, 21 rue Paradis, 1st arrondissement, Marseille. Not an exclusive English-language shop but does have a selection of books in English; 04.91.33.57.91.

Librairie Anglaise, 11 rue Bivouac-Napoleon, Cannes; new and used English-language books; 04.93.99.40.08.

Scruples, 9 rue Princesse-Caroline, Monte Carlo, Monaco; 377.93.50.43.52.

SOME SPECIALTY FRENCH BOOKSTORES INCLUDE:

FNAC, 19 rue de la République, Avignon; Centre Bourse, Marseille; Le Metropole Shopping Center, Monaco; and in the Nice Etoile shopping center, Nice; not a specialty store, but I love FNAC's comprehensive selection.

Librarie des Éditions Parenthese, 72 cours Julien, 6th arrondissement, Marseille; beautiful books on art, architecture, photography, style, and music.

Buses

I can count on one hand the times I've ridden a bus in Provence. Certainly within city and town centers, it is seldom necessary, except perhaps in Nice or Marseille; however, buses often go where the train does not, so I do think they are essential for getting to some smaller villages, if one hasn't rented a car. Service in the south is operated mostly by the SNCF (Société Nationale des Chemins de Fer), France's national train network, because some of the routes replace those once served by rail. A host of private companies (not as many, thankfully, as in Italy) provide service as well, and you can inquire about these at local tourist offices. Visitors should be aware, however, that (as in rural Italy) service outside of the larger towns and along the coast is meant to accommodate local residents, not tourists. Therefore, the schedules coincide with school and market hours, and you may find that in order to visit a particular village, for example, you have to catch an early-morning bus and then only have a few hours to see it (because the return bus departs only once more) or make arrangements to spend the night (because the return bus departs early the next morning). Note that SNCF train passes are also valid on SNCF bus lines, and private lines are typically more expensive. Within the bigger cities of the south, there are several different types of bus tickets available; however, because they are not identical from city to city, I will not detail them here; but visitors may want to know that in addition to single tickets, *carnets* of tickets can be purchased, as well as passes for one day, five days, and one week. Single tickets can be purchased on board the bus, but passes must be purchased at the station or *tabacs* and newsstands. When boarding the bus, insert your ticket into the machine at the front so it can be punched. ~Useful vocabulary: *gare routière* (bus station), which, by the way, is very often located in the same vicinity as the train station, but not always.

C

Cafés

Much more so than in a city the size of Paris, the cafés in the towns and villages of Provence are the center of public life. For residents and visitors alike, cafés are places to relax, drink, sometimes eat, catch up on local gossip, relay messages, buy tobacco, lottery tickets, and stamps, write letters or postcards, meet friends, and play *boules, pétanque,* or *belote.* As visitors from other towns will also stop in at the local café, the *cafetier* (café owner) typically knows everything about everyone, and therefore the café "has naturally become the unofficial information bureau of the town," according to Laurence Wylie, author of *Village in the Vaucluse.* No matter where you're staying in Provence, a quick way to grasp the pulse of a community is to spend some leisure time at the local café.

Les Calanques

This is the name for the beautiful inlets along a twelve-mile stretch of coast between Marseilles and Cap de l'Aigle, just past Cassis. Think of them as miniature Norwegian fjords, many with nice, sandy little beaches. *Les Calanques*—said to derive from the Provençal word *calenco* (steep)—may be among the best-kept secrets of Provence, and they will probably remain so because they're not easily accessible. With few exceptions, you can't drive down to them, and because they are at the bottom of very steep limestone cliffs, many people do not even know they exist. I had certainly never heard of them on my first visit to Provence, but as an energetic nineteen-year-old was easily persuaded to climb down to one with two girlfriends and a handsome young French guy. However, handsome young French guy really did not know what he was doing, and we were not on any sort of footpath; at one point I thought I might die, but somehow we made it to the bottom. The reward was definitely worth the effort, but I was relieved when, after several hours, we were able to get a ride on a boat back to the lovely fishing port of Cassis. By far the easiest way to reach the *calanques* is by boat, either from Cassis or Marseille. There are two types of boat trips, one which simply offers a beautiful round-trip tour, and another which drops you off at some of the beaches, returning later to pick you up. I highly recommend the trip that drops you off because swimming within the coves is a bit like being in paradise, definitely a not-to-be-missed experience. From Cassis, you can walk (about a half hour) or drive to Port-Miou, the closest *calanque*. Calanque d'En-Vau is generally considered to be the prettiest, but it is approximately a two-hour walk from Cassis, depending on your pace and the condition of the path. As these footpaths intersect with the Grande Randonnée 98 route to Marseille, it can be quite confusing to find one's way. It is essential to confer with the Cassis tourist office (there's one right at the port open only during July and August and a bigger one on place Baragnon open year-round) before setting out, and do not attempt to make the hike without proper footwear. Some of the *calanques* closer to Marseille include Mont Rose, Callelongue, Morgiou, and Sugiton. A combination of city buses and walking can get you to most, but those more distant are obviously more easily reached by boat. Note that the surf can be a little rough around the *calanques* in spring and fall, but don't let this be a reason to postpone a trip.

Car Rental

My favorite feature of travel publications is the readers' letters. I have probably learned more from these letters than any other source, and the largest number of complaints seems to be about problems encountered when renting a car. No matter what you read, hear, or assume, the only word that counts is the one from your policy administrator, be it a credit card or insurance company. If you have any

questions about renting a car overseas and what is and isn't covered on your existing policy (including collision damage waiver), contact your provider in advance.
Request documentation in writing, if necessary. It is your responsibility to learn
about your coverage *before* you rent a car. I have never encountered any rental car
problems, but then again I make it a habit to state to the company representative,
"When I return the car to you, I will not pay anything more than this amount"
while pointing to the total on my receipt. I highly recommend renting a car to see
the Provençal countryside. It *is* possible to get around without one as the train and
bus network is extensive, but you can simply see so much *more* with a car. A great
book to get is *France's Best-Loved Driving Tours: 25 Unforgettable Itineraries*
(Paul Duncan, Frommer's). Of particular interest are the four tours for the south:
"East from Marseilles," "The Riviera & Its Hinterland," "Exploring the Côte
d'Azur," and "Through Historic Provence," and peppered throughout the book are
things of interest for children. Some general points to keep in mind: ~You don't
need an International Driver's License in France. Save the $10 fee for driving in less
developed countries, where the absence of the license could open the door for
bribery to cross a border, etc. ~Reserve a car *before* you arrive in France. Anytime
you see ads announcing special rates, those rates apply to those customers who
reserve in advance. Also, rental cars are limited, and you want to avoid a scenario
where there are no cars available, at any price. ~Europe by Car (1 Rockefeller
Plaza, New York, New York 10020; 800-223-1516 or 212-581-3040 / 9000 Sunset
Boulevard, Los Angeles, California 90069; 800-252- or 323-272-0424; www.europe-
bycar.com) offers one of the best values around. In addition to offering good overall rates (with special rates available for students, teachers, and faculty members),
clients can select the tax-free, factory-direct new car vacation plan. This is such a
good deal because technically the program operates more like a short-term lease,
which makes the rental car exempt from European taxes. Cars are from Peugeot,
Citroën, and Renault, and prices include unlimited mileage; insurance with liabil-
ity, fire, collision damage waiver, and theft; and emergency assistance twenty-four
hours a day via a free phone. The only catch is that you have to pay for the car for
a minimum of seventeen days—you don't have to *keep* the car for seventeen days
but the price is the same if you drop it off earlier. All clients receive special discounts at selected hotels and motels (and budget hotels costing about $26 a night),
and free parking. ~Hertz offers a competitive rate with its prepaid car rental
voucher. The conditions are that you prepay in U.S. dollars in advance of your trip,
and vouchers are typically faxed to a U.S. fax number or mailed to a U.S. address.
The prepaid rate does not include such things as drop charges, car seats, collision
damage waiver, or gas, and these must be paid for in local currency at the time you
pick up the car. ~Auto France (P.O. Box 760, 211 Shadyside Road, Ramsey, New
Jersey 07440; 800-572-9655; fax: 201-934-7501; www.auto-france.com) is another
good source to investigate. Similar to the Europe by Car purchase/repurchase pro-

gram, Auto France offers a Peugeot Vacation Plan. You pick up a brand-new Peugeot in one of over thirty cities (participating cities in the south of France are Marseille, Nîmes, Nice, Avignon, and Lyon) and the rate—for trips of seventeen days or more—is VAT- and airport-tax-free (again, you don't have to keep the car for seventeen days, but the price is the same if you drop off the car earlier). The rental price includes unlimited mileage, twenty-four-hour travel assistance, and all-risk auto insurance with full collision. There is free delivery and return of cars in major French cities and airports, and travelers must be permanent residents outside the EEC and visiting France for no more than 175 days within a twelve-month period. The brochure I received featured eight different Peugeots, including wagons and minivans. ~Kemwel Holiday Autos (106 Calvert Street, Harrison, New York 10528; 800-678-0678; fax: 914-835-5449; www.kemwel.com) also offers the Peugeot short-term leasing program (which they refer to as the best-kept "secret" in the business) as well as regular car rentals, chauffeur-driven cars, carpass vouchers, and motorhome rentals, all at competitive rates. The carpass voucher program allows travelers to purchase rental vouchers in three-day segments; you buy as many segments as you think you'll need, and any unused vouchers are fully refundable upon your return. (This is particularly helpful if you're not sure you need to rent a car at all or don't know how long you might need one.) I have used Kemwel on two occasions and have been very pleased. The materials one receives include charts for mileage, miles-to-kilometers, and international road signs; a handy little fold-out guide called "Travel Talk," with basic phrases in English, French, German, Italian, and Spanish; and charts for clothing sizes, kilos-to-pounds, centimeters-to-inches, gallons-to-liters, temperatures, and time differences. ~It's helpful to begin thinking in kilometers instead of miles. I jot down sample distances to use as a ready reference as I'm speeding along the *autoroutes* or motoring along the *routes nationales:* 1 mile = 1.6 kilometers; 12 km = 7½ miles; 16 km = 10 miles; 40 km = 25 miles; 80 km = 50 miles; 160 km = 100 miles; 320 km = 200 miles, etc. ~Road maps and atlases obviously employ route numbers for large and small roads; but the highway and road signs you'll see typically indicate cities or towns quite far away, rather than road numbers. (Initially, this threw me off, and reminded me of a sign I used to see years ago just outside of Philadelphia for a restaurant at the New Jersey shore; the sign advertised that the restaurant was "minutes away" but was in fact two *hours* away.) Begin thinking in terms of *direction* rather than road number and consult your map(s) often—you'll find that it's quite a sensible way of getting around, and it forces the visitor to be better versed in geography. ~Driving in the fast lane on European highways can be a bit harrowing as any car suddenly looming up behind you is closing in at a *much* faster speed than we're accustomed to in the U.S. (the speed limit on the *autoroutes* is 80 mph). These drivers usually have no patience for your slowness and will tailgate you and flash their lights until you get out of the way. So if you're going to pass, step on the gas and go, and return quickly to the right lane. ~Unlike in Italy, there is no nationwide road assistance organization, but there are emergency phones every mile on the *autoroutes* and *routes nationales,* and on other roads you can call Depannage Cote d'Azur (04.93.29.87.87) for twenty-four-hour emergency service. ~I've read conflicting advice on parking tickets, so I would not recommend taking a chance if you're in doubt. Rental agencies do have your credit card number, and it seems to me they can eventually bill you for any tickets you've received, and add a service charge if they're so inclined. ~Gas prices in France are quite high, and tolls in France, as elsewhere in Europe, are extremely expensive. Gas is available twenty-four hours a day, seven days a week, on the *autoroutes,* but on other roads gas stations are typically closed on Sunday and/or Monday. If you'll be driving in mountainous areas, be aware that gas stations are not plentiful, so plan accordingly or bring along a can of gas. ~Attendants at gas stations expect tips for checking the oil, windows, and tires (five francs will do). ~Useful vocabulary: *location de voitures* (car rental agency); *essence* (regular leaded gas); *sans plomb* (unleaded gas); *gasoil* or *gazole* (diesel); *défense d'entrer* (no entry); *horodateurs* (parking meters); *défense de stationner* (no parking); *sortie* (exit); *vous n'avez pas la priorité* (you don't have the right of way—seen mostly at traffic circles, where you give way to traffic already in the circle coming from your left); *passage protégé* (yellow diamond-shaped road signs on main roads indicating that you have priority over traffic on any minor side roads; priority on French roads is always given to vehicles approaching from the right—*priorité à droite*—unless indicated otherwise); *cédez le passage* (give way to traffic); *serrez à droite* (keep to the right); *déviation* (diversion); *péage* (toll); *dépannage* (breakdown); *tout droit* (straight ahead—not to be confused with *à droit,* which means "to the right"; *à gauche,* by the way, is "to the left"); *rappel* (reminder of the speed limit); *près* (near); *loin* (far); *seulement riverains* (private road); *feu tricolore* (traffic light); *hors gabarit* (this is not a common road sign outside of the mountainous areas of Provence, but it bothered me so much when I saw it repeatedly and couldn't decipher what it meant that I thought it might be helpful to mention it here for other readers. My *petit Larousse* wasn't particularly helpful, as it only gave "gauge" as a definition of *gabarit,* so I had to ask my friend Luc for an explanation. While he thought I was rather weird for wanting to include it in this vocabulary, he did offer that the words are a rough translation of "outside the limits"; it is a warning that if you are driving a truck or an RV, it may be too high to fit under the tunnels carved into the mountains).

Children

A few months before my daughter was born, I was feeling anxious that my life as a mother was going to drastically alter my ability to travel. My colleague and friend, Bruce, helped me snap out of this funk by pointing out that my husband and I would have to travel *differently* than we did before but we would indeed still travel, because we love it. As Bruce is both a parent and world traveler, he advised us not to overthink the situation, because then we would find a million reasons *not* to travel. The way I see it, parents can make the decision never to go anywhere and deprive both children and adults of a priceless experience, but I believe that children have as much to teach us as we do them, especially when traveling—their curiosity and imagination make even familiar destinations seem new. Although I have been unable to find a book devoted exclusively to traveling with children in the south of France, some guidebooks—including many of those mentioned below under Guidebooks—offer excellent suggestions for things to see and do with kids. A way to build excitement in advance of a trip is to involve children in the planning, showing them maps and books and talking about the things you'll see and do. Give them a blank book so they can start creating a journal (or, buy a ready-made one such as *How to Draw a Clam: A Wonderful Vacation Planner,* by Joy Sikorski, Clarkson Potter, 2000); and buy them an inexpensive aim-and-shoot camera: they'll show more interest in things if they can take their own pictures, and they can include the photos in their trip journal. Something parents will be sure to notice: in the south of France—as in most other Mediterranean countries—young children stay up late at night, even at restaurants and *cafés.* Do not be surprised if it's 11:00 P.M. and there are lots of kids running around. I've never seen the children looking unhappy or tired, and it seems to make sense in a region with an afternoon siesta tradition. There is not an abundance of books available on traveling with children (although this seems to be a growing area of publishing), but even if there were a lot more I still think the best one would be *Have Kid, Will Travel: 101 Survival Strategies for Vacationing with Babies and Young Children* (Claire Tristram with Lucille Tristram, Andrews McMeel Publishing, Kansas City, Missouri, 1997). It's loaded with good, concrete suggestions and tips, and I wish I'd discovered it before we took our ten-month-old on her first plane flight, from New York to Seattle. Tristram has visited all fifty states and thirty countries, and Lucille, her daughter, has been named "the best baby in the world" by several strangers sitting next to her on long-distance flights (a great recommendation for reading this book!). Among the best words of advice: "Above all, don't let a bad moment become a bad day, and don't let a bad day become a bad week." ~A note about flying: Don't count on getting those roomier bulkhead seats even if you've been promised they would be yours if you check in early. Thanks to an honest employee, I learned recently that these premium seats—and I define them as "premium" for anyone traveling with children—are actually assigned first to passengers in a wheelchair and then to *passengers who paid the most for their tickets.* It's merely a false courtesy when an airline reservationist tells you that by showing up at the airport well in advance of your flight you may be eligible for the bulkhead seats. I think this is abominable, especially since an early arrival at the airport means finding ways to entertain your children for an even longer period of time, and it seems obvious that happy children on a flight means a happier ride for everyone, including the people who paid the most for their seats. I would name the airline of my experience except that this measure is practiced by most if not *all* the airlines, and if I knew a way around it, I'd tell you. I figure if enough of us parents make noise, perhaps the airlines will abandon this practice.

Clothing

It's impossible to talk about clothing without also talking about packing, but I have included a separate packing entry below. I pack light, and unless I have plans to be at fancy places, I pack double-duty items (stuff that can go from daytime to evening) in low-key colors that also mix and match so I can wear garments more than once. I also tend to bring items that aren't my favorites, figuring that if someone does snatch my suitcase or rummage through my hotel room, at least I wouldn't lose the things I love the most. Remember that the French tend to dress up a bit more than Americans (although the south is certainly more casual than Paris), so reserve your jeans and well-worn shorts for casual daytime wear and the most casual of places at night, and leave the color-coordinated jogging suits at home (jogging attire, to the French, is worn *only* when engaging in that activity and is not a fashion statement). The French also dress conservatively when it comes to visiting their religious houses of worship. Visitors will earn respect and goodwill by refraining from wearing sleeveless shirts, short skirts, and shorts, no matter how hot it is. You may find this odd in a country where topless sunbathing is permitted on the beaches, but make no mistake about it: it is still frowned upon, especially in smaller villages, to dress inappropriately around town and in churches. Suits and ties are necessary only at the finest restaurants (even at some Michelin-starred establishments, diners wear *nice* clothes but not finery), and polo shirts and khakis will always serve men well. Although comfortable shoes are of the utmost importance, I never, ever bring sneakers—and I positively forbid my husband to bring them—and you might not either once you realize that they scream "American." (Alice Steinbach, in her book *Without Reservations: The Travels of an Independent Woman,* refers to this truth when she was at a bar in Paris and noticed a woman she thought was quintessentially French: "'I see you're American, too,' she said. I turned toward her, wondering how she had identified me as an American. She seemed to know what I was thinking, and glanced down at my feet. I followed her gaze. She was looking at my black leather Reeboks, which, we both knew, were not the sort of shoes any Frenchwoman over the age of thirty would ever wear.") I prefer Arche, a line of French walking shoes and sandals for men and women, but there are several other lines available (Mephisto, for example, another French line for men and women), which are also stylish *and* comfortable. I recently discovered a unique shoe line just for women: "à propos . . . conversations." I loved the shoes right away when I read they were "influenced by European women whose fashion sense does not include white athletic shoes outside of sports." All the shoes, which are soft and flexible and easily fold down to handbag or briefcase size, are limited editions and sport such names as Liquid Lemons, Peacock Punch, Linen Sands, African Sun, and Khaki Krunch. There are over a dozen styles offered in two collections a year, and many styles are available in two ways: with a solid center elastic band or two cross straps of elastic. "Like a scarf for your feet" is how they're trademarked, and you can view the styles online at www.conversationshoes.com or call 800-746-3724 for a catalog. The following mail-order catalogs offer some practical clothes, shoes, packing accessories, and gadgets for travelers: L. L. Bean Traveler (800-221-4221; llbean.com/traveler); Magellan's (800-962-4943; www.magellans.com); TravelSmith (800-950-1600; www.travelsmith.com); The Territory Ahead (888-233-9954; www.territoryahead.com); and Travel 2000 (800-903-8728; www.travel2k.com).

Club Méditerranée (Club Med)

I have never been an advocate of a Club Med vacation in a foreign country because its all-inclusive package makes it tempting to never leave the compound, ensuring that you will never experience anything of the local culture. However, for parents, Club Med offers one of the few opportunities in the world for a family vacation that allows parents to have time to themselves—at an affordable price. The Club Med package includes airfare, three meals a day, unlimited wine or beer with meals, accommodations for seven nights, and unlimited sports and activities. Although—as my friend Lorraine says—you still have to sleep with your kids and deal with middle-of-the-night and early awakenings, parents can drop their kids off in the morning and pick them up again in the late afternoon. There is a Club Med property in Provence, in Opio (nineteen miles from Nice, between Grasse and Valbonne) that accepts children from age two. Though Club Med rates are not prohibitively expensive at any time of year, there are slower periods for the company, and it is during these times—early April, Thanksgiving, and early to mid December are typically periods when its properties are undersold—that you can often take advantage of even lower rates.

Coins

If you have leftover francs in the form of coins, you can always save them for a future trip; but perhaps a better idea is to give them to a great cause: UNICEF's Change for Good program. A number of airlines pass out the program's envelopes to passengers on flights back to the U.S., but if you've never received one and want to contribute, contact the U.S. Committee for UNICEF (333 East 38th Street, 6th floor, New York, New York 10016; 212-824-6972; fax: 824-6969).

Cooking Schools

The best single source for cooking schools in France—and the entire world—is the *Shaw Guide to Cooking Schools: Cooking Schools, Courses, Vacations, Apprenticeships, and Wine Instruction Throughout the World* (ShawGuides, Inc., New York). Some programs in Provence which may be familiar to cooking enthusiasts, such as the Roger Vergé Cooking School, At Home with Patricia Wells, and À La Bonne Cocotte en Provence, are listed as well as lesser-known programs, and interested food lovers can also view updates to the guide at its Web site: www.shawguides.com. Another good source for classes is The International Kitchen (1209 N. Astor, #11–N, Chicago, Illinois 60610; 800-945-8606, fax: 847-295-0945; www.intl-kitchen.com). Wonderful, hands-on classes for small groups are offered all over France, and some which are in Provence include Cuisine en Provence, Passport to Provence, and Picture Provence. The schools that particularly appeal to me are À La Bonne Cocotte en Provence (led by cookbook author Lydie Marshall—*Chez Nous, Cooking with Lydie Marshall,* and *A Passion for Potatoes*—at her château in Nyons. Not only are students treated to Lydie's warm and lively personality, but accommodations are in the château, classes include a visit to the Thursday market, and this may be the best-value program in all of Provence. Contact Lydie at Château Feodal, 26110 Nyons, France; 0475.26.45.31, fax: 0475.26.09.31; e-mail: ciboulette@juno.com); At Home with Patricia Wells, which is probably the best-known program in the south of France (classes are held in Wells's eighteenth-century farmhouse kitchen just outside Vaison-la-Romaine. The price is a little steep as it doesn't include lodging, but it's difficult to put a price tag on cooking with Wells and being introduced to the food artisans, vendors, and markets on her terrain. Interested students should see the *Fodor's Escapes: Provence* edition, which features Wells's school and includes three pages of color photos. Contact Deborah Orrill, program coordinator, 7830 Ridgemar Drive, Dallas, Texas 75231; fax: 214-343-1227; www.patriciawells.com.); Cooking in Provence (classes are in the Château de Mazenc, once the home of a French president, which has been described as "magnificent." I wouldn't be inclined to recommend this program, especially since it too is in the Nyons area, but much of it is centered around the lovely little villages of Dieulefit—"God made it"—and Le Poët Laval, and includes a trip along the Route des Vins and a visit to a working goat farm, renowned for the local Picodon cheese. For information, contact the school at two addresses: P.O. Box 155, Woodstock, Vermont 05091; 802-457-5169; fax: -1806; La Garenne, 26160 Le Poët Laval, France; 0475.46.49.44; fax: 0475.91.00.56; www.cookinginprovence. com); Cooking with Friends in France (classes are held on the property near Grasse, which was once shared by Julia Child and Simone Beck. Proprietor/instructor Kathie Alex apprenticed at Roger Vergé's Le Moulin de Mougins and studied with Simone Beck. Course includes visits to the Forville market, a butcher, cheese ripener, and Michelin two-star restaurant kitchens, as well as a demonstration by a French chef. Contact Kathie Alex at La Pitchoune, Domaine de Bramafam, Chateauneuf de Grasse, 6740 France; 0493.60.10.56; fax: 0493.60.05.56; U.S. contact: Jackson & Co., 29 Commonwealth Avenue, Boston, Massachusetts 02116; 617-350-3837; fax: 247-6149; www.cookingwithfriends.com); and The Savour of France (the following three programs, which are really more like French food and wine adventures as they offer more than cooking lessons, are offered in the south of France: "The French Riviera," a four-star extravaganza including accommodations at the Carlton and Negresco hotels and dinners at the Michelin-starred Moulins de Mougins and Le Louis XV in Monaco; "Peter Mayle Country," a cooking course for five or seven days at Le Gros Pierre estate; and "The Savour of Provence," which includes visits to the Cavaillon and Avignon markets, cooking instruction in a private home, Côte-du-Rhône wine tastings, and visits to Cassis, Les Baux, Avignon, and the Lubéron. Contact David Geen, 2450 Iroquois Avenue, Detroit, Michigan 48214; 800-220-3993; www.savourfrance.com).

Les Corniches

The three *corniches*—*bas, moyenne,* and *grand*—are three of the most dramatic roads in the world. They wind along the coast between Nice and Monaco, and are, quite simply, breathtakingly beautiful (the Amalfi drive in southern Italy is the only other coastal road I've been on that is comparable). The *bas* (low) road is obviously the busiest, putting you in the thick of local traffic, which, when you're on holiday, is not at all the same thing as being in traffic en route to work (and the Mediterranean is *right there*). The *moyenne* (middle) road puts you midway up the coastal mountain in a bit less traffic than on the *bas* road, with sweeping views out over the sea. The *grand* (high) road will steal your heart. Those scenes of Grace Kelly and Cary Grant driving on the *grand corniche* in *To Catch a Thief* aren't just nostalgic remnants of the fifties: the road still looks the same. It is for this that one should rent a car (except the driver may not have much of a chance to gaze off the cliff). My memories of riding a moped from Nice to Menton and back again, on stretches of all three *corniches,* will never fade. It was the most exhilarating ride I've ever taken in my life.

Course Libre Versus the Mise à Mort

These two terms differentiate two versions of a bullfight, the *course libre* being the French version and the *mise à mort* being the Spanish *corrida* version. Bullfights are held during spring and summer in both Arles and Nîmes, and if you've never seen one, I encourage you to fit one into your itinerary. Lawrence Durrell has referred to the *course libre* as being "close to the heart of Provence." *Course libre* bulls are from the Camargue and are small with lots of particularly sharp horns. These black bulls are familiar with the ways of men (*les gardiens,* cowboys) well before they are brought into the arena. Spanish bulls, on the other hand, have no experience with men until they are face to face with the toreador in the *arène* (arena), and certainly have no familiarity with what men do in or outside of the arena. In the *course libre,* the *razeteurs* (bullfighters) must attempt to remove a knot of ribbons and/or flowers from between the bull's horns with the use of a razor comb. Unlike a *mise à mort,* the bull is not killed. These two distinct styles (there are other differences, which you can read about at length in Lawrence Durrell's *Caesar's Vast Ghost*) coexist in Provence and there is a large audience for both. It pays to find out the dates of the scheduled *ferias* in advance of your trip—you run a great risk of not finding vacancies at any hotels in Arles or Nîmes before, during, or immediately after the bullfights.

Customs

There seems to be a lot of confusion over what items can and positively cannot be brought into the U.S. The rules, apparently, are not as confusing as they might seem, but sometimes neither customs staff nor travelers are up to date on what they are. Some examples of what's legal and what's not include: olive oil, yes, but olives, no (unless they're vacuum-packed); fruit jams and preserves, yes, but fresh fruit, no; hard cheeses, yes, but soft, runny cheeses, no; commercially canned meat, yes (if the inspector can determine that the meat was cooked in the can after it was sealed), but fresh and dried meats and meat products, no; nuts, yes, but chestnuts and acorns, no; coffee, yes, but roasted beans only; dried spices, yes, but not curry leaves; fresh and dried flowers, yes, but not eucalyptus or any variety with roots. If you think all this is unnecessary bother, remember that it was quite likely a tourist who carried in the wormy fruit which brought the Mediterranean fruit fly to California in 1979. Fighting this pest cost more than $100 million. For more details, call the U.S. Department of Agriculture's Animal and Plant Health Inspection Service at 301-734-8645 or view its Web site: www.aphis.usda.gov (click on Travelers' Tips).

E

Eating In and Taking Away

As in other European countries, the price for food and drink is different depending on where you sit in cafés and bars. You'll notice that many Provençaux often stand at the bar, especially in the morning when they stop in at their regular café. If you stand at the bar the price is always cheaper; if you sit at a table, you can expect to pay up to twice as much (although you also have the luxury of remaining in your seat for as long as you like). At larger cafés and restaurants tables are available in the *salle* (dining room) or *à la terrasse* (usually outside on the sidewalk, the prime people-watching spot), and menus for each are priced accordingly. ~Don't let the words *plat du jour, menu dégustation, formule,* or *prix fixe* turn you away from a potentially great meal. Each of these menu choices is almost always a good value, and often includes a carafe or half bottle of wine. ~Some good words of advice from the Cadogan guide to Provence: "If prices aren't listed, you can bet it's not because they're a bargain. If you summon up the appetite to eat the biggest meal of the day at noon, you'll spend a lot less money, as many restaurants offer special lunch menus—an economical way to experience some of the finer gourmet temples." Bread, cheese, sausage, pâté, pâtisseries, and prepared foods are generally of such excellent quality in France that you can create some of the most delicious meals you'll ever eat by picking up provisions at an *alimentation, charcuterie, traiteur,* and *boulangerie.* Except for bread, order the items you want by weight (in kilos), *tranche* (slice), or *morceau* (piece). ~Useful vocabulary: *sur place* is how you say you're going to eat in, and *à emporter* means you'll be taking food away.

Elderly Travel
The two best-known organizations for elderly travelers are Elderhostel (75 Federal Street, 3rd floor, Boston, Massachusetts 02110; 877-426-8056; fax: -2166) and Interhostel (University of New Hampshire, 6 Garrison Avenue, Durham, New Hampshire 03824; 800-733-9753; fax: 603-862-1113; www.learn.unh.edu). I've listed them here instead of under Tours because I wanted them to stand apart from the more general travel companies. For some good articles about these two educational companies and others, see "Senior Classes" and "Catering to Older Travelers," both of which appeared in *The New York Times* travel section, August 25, 1991.

F

Faire le Pont
This French expression is the equivalent of "long weekend" in English. When a holiday falls on a Thursday or a Tuesday, for example, the French like to *pont* ("bridge") the holiday by also taking off on Friday and/or Monday. This is useful to keep in mind if there is a scheduled holiday during your trip, as stores and businesses may be closed for all or part of the time, and the plumber you need to fix a major problem with the pipes at the *gîte* you've rented may be unavailable.

Film
I'm aware the FAA maintains that film less than 1000-speed sent through X-ray scanners won't harm picture developing; but my friend Peggy, a freelance photographer, maintains that multiple trips through the scanner will, indeed, harm the

film. Also, if you pack your film in checked bags, the scanners which inspect them are stronger than those for carry-on bags, and should definitely be avoided. ~I always keep rolls of film—no matter what speed—accessible, and hand them to the security inspectors before I walk through the scanner (remember to retrieve them after you pass, however!). ~If you take a lot of photos you might want to buy some lead-lined pouches from a camera store. They're inexpensive and will even protect film in checked bags. ~Professional film (which is very sensitive and must be kept refrigerated until used and developed a day later) aside, a general guideline for us amateurs is that the higher the film speed, the faster the film—and fast film requires less light. So, think about the situations in which you anticipate taking pictures: if it's off-season and overcast, select 200; if it's spring or summer with bright sunlight, select 400; for indoor gatherings in restaurants, try 800 or higher (unless you want to employ the flash); if you'll be at a bullfight or in Monte Carlo for the Grand Prix, select 400 or higher; for approaching dusk and sunsets, 400. ~I happen to be very fond of black-and-white photos, so I always include a roll or two in my bag.

Fishing

There are numerous opportunities for both sea and freshwater fishing in the south. Freshwater fishing does require a permit, which can quickly be obtained, while deep sea fishing expeditions are available from captains all along the coast. Local tourist offices can provide information about permits and the names of captains.

La France Profonde

Every visitor to France should be familiar with this phrase, which is deeply important to the French. Though the Côte d'Azur and many inland Provençal towns hardly qualify as *profonde,* pockets of Provence do. With the hope you will discover some of these pockets, I share with you one of the best expressions of *la France profonde* I've ever encountered: "When the French start talking about *la France profonde,* stop and listen. They are telling you about one of the secret keys that open the heart of their country. The region they have in mind is somewhat remote, a very long way from Paris, and even farther from any coastline. It leans toward conservatism, prefers the past to the future, the small-town or rural to the urban, and is profoundly unimpressed by fashion. There may be just a whiff of xenophobia there, but this can usually be disguised as an exaggerated love for *la patrie*. Its values are traditional, its architecture small-scale, and the more extreme excesses of the modern world are held at bay—partly by design and partly by economics. It is the world of Balzac and Marcel Pagnol, not Françoise Sagan. It is *boeuf en daube,* not nouvelle cuisine. If it could be bottled it would be concentrated essence of France: *parfum,* not eau de toilette. It is France's center of gravity—and *gravitas*. It is also a region that most foreign travelers never venture into. It's not that it is hard to get there, or that you're not welcome once you arrive; it's just that tourists tend, lemming-like, to prefer the urban delights of Paris, the crowded coast, or the proven cultural uplift of Chartres or the Loire Valley. There are, of course, many *Frances profondes,* scattered all over the country. The idea is supremely elastic, combining—as only the French could—philosophy and geography in one elegant, intellectual package. The trick for the traveler is simple. Abandon any notion of going to a part of France that you have been to before, or, more daringly, that you have *heard* too much about. And then just listen when the French start talking and slowly plan how to steal the key." (Gully Wells, Copyright © 1991 Condé Nast Publications Inc. Reprinted by permission.)

The French Paradox

I always thought the so-called French paradox was a misnomer. There doesn't seem to be much that is paradoxical about a varied diet of fresh, seasonal food (even if it does include some animal fats), and alcohol in moderation, all in combination with regular exercise. Additionally, it is French tradition to sit down to a relaxed, leisurely meal at least once a day (twice a day in more rural parts of France), which I believe is healthful to digestion and spirit, and the French simply eat less than we do. The heaping platters and inches-thick pastrami sandwiches we're accustomed to are viewed as grossly excessive (and uniquely American) to the French. I usually *lose* weight when I'm in France, and you may, too, especially if you make lunch the biggest meal of your day and you walk a lot. But to return to the so-called paradox: Lawrence Durrell, in *Caesar's Vast Ghost,* wrote some of the best passages about how the French view food, which are worthy of repeating here: "It was a heartening surprise to feel that the quality of bread and wine and food were not fads which were kept up for the snobbish and the rich, but the result of a whole people's demand. In this sense my own people remained relatively philistine, it seemed to me. For us *Grande Cuisine* and fine wine were 'upper-class.' Not so here. Food as one of the fine arts, then, is not just the domain of the rich. I recall another small incident which struck me. In the middle of winter at the small hotel near the Fontaine de Vaucluse I arrived somewhat late for dinner. The only other diners were two garage mechanics from Avignon with their wives or sisters—I could not make out which. But the little hotel was an expensive one and known for its rare cuisine. Indeed, when I entered the manageress was busy trying to persuade them to taste the last four portions of venison which remained on her menu. It was such a treat, she pleaded, and such a rare delicacy that they might never come across it again. Why not try it? The enthusiasm of her clients was obvious, but they were not very well off, and hesitatingly they asked the price of the portions. They then turned out their pockets and counted out their money scrupulously before deciding in favour of the adventure—for that was the correct word for it. It was an aesthetic adventure and it also involved a suitable wine. The whole thing was most carefully costed out, and their sober appreciation of the dish was quite professional. Yet they must have been in their early twenties, the four of them, and people of modest station. I could not help mentally setting in their place two English garage mechanics with their wives . . . a contrast of attitudes which would reveal a good deal about national ethos! . . . The secret of the French attitude is simply that cooking is included among the fine arts and accorded the same respect as a gift for painting. But the pleasure and enrichment for an artist living in France is the feeling that the whole population is subtly engaged in the same debate with itself—namely, how to turn living into something more than just existing." (Copyright © 1990 by Lawrence Durrell. Reprinted from *Caesar's Vast Ghost,* published by Arcade Publishing, New York, New York. Canadian rights administered by Faber and Faber Ltd., London.)

Frequent-Flier Miles

From what I've read, it seems the airlines wish they'd never created mileage award programs, and there are now fewer and fewer seats reserved for frequent fliers *and* you need even more miles to earn these seats. Should you happen to have enough miles and want to fly to Nice, Lyon, or Marseille, plan to redeem those miles about six months to a year ahead *or* plan to fly in the off-season (it's also possible that airlines will reduce the miles needed for the off-season flight). Don't immediately give up if your initial request can't be confirmed. Apparently, the airlines fiddle with frequent-flier seats every day as they monitor the demand for paying customers. If the number of paying travelers is low as the departure date approaches, more frequent-flier awards may be honored. Also, check to see if your accrued miles have expired before you try to redeem them. All airlines have expiration dates on frequent-flier miles but they don't all adhere to strict enforcement of those deadlines. Try to reserve your valid mileage for expensive flights, rather than those which you can get for a good price anytime.

G

General Travel

Here are some good books to consult about trip planning in general: The New York Times *Practical Traveler Handbook: An A–Z Guide to Getting There and Back* (Betsy Wade, Times Books, 1994) and *Wendy Perrin's Secrets Every Smart Traveler Should Know: Condé Nast Traveler's Consumer Travel Expert Tells All* (Fodor's Travel Publications, 1997). It might seem like these books cover the same ground but in fact there is very little overlap and I refer to both of them all the time. The *Practical Traveler* really is an A–Z guide, organized alphabetically, and covers such topics as airline code sharing, customs, hotel tipping, and closing up the house. Perrin's book is divided into eight sections plus an appendix, and the anecdotes featured were all previously published in the "Ombudsman" column of the magazine. She covers the fine art of complaining, what to do if your luggage is damaged or pilfered, travel agents and tour operators, car rentals, shopping, and cruises, etc., as well as the ten commandments of trouble-free travel, which I think should be given to every traveler before he or she boards the plane. In a similar but different vein, I highly recommend *Traveler's Tool Kit: How to Travel Absolutely Anywhere!* (Rob Sangster, Menasha Ridge Press, Birmingham, Alabama, 1999). "Tool kit" really is the best description of this travel bible, which addresses *everything* having to do with planning, packing, and departing. Who is this book for? Everyone, really, or at least people who are curious about the rest of the world; people who are thinking about their very first foreign trip; budget travelers; business travelers; people who want to travel more independently; and people who know "that life offers more than a two-week vacation once a year." It's a *great* book, with lots of great ideas, tips, and advice. I've found Sangster's checklists at the back of the book particularly helpful, and his bibliography is the most extensive I've seen aside from my own.

Guidebooks

Choosing which guidebooks to use can be bewildering and overwhelming. I have yet to find the perfect book that offers all the features I need and want, so I consult a variety of books, gleaning tips and advice from each. Then I buy a blank journal and fill it with notes from all these books (leaving some pages blank) and end up with what is, for me, the perfect package: the journal plus two or three guidebooks I determine to be indispensable (I don't carry them around at the same time). In the end, the right guidebook is the one which speaks to you. Go to the France section in the travel department of a bookstore and take some time to read through the various guides. If you feel the author shares a certain sensibility with you, and you think his or her credentials are respectable, then you're probably holding the right book. Recommendations from friends and colleagues are fine only if they travel in the same way you do and seek the same qualities as you in a guidebook. Also, if you discover an older guide which appeals to you, remember, background information doesn't change, so don't immediately dismiss it. Use it in combination with an updated guide to create your own perfect package. Keep in mind, too, that guidebooks within the same series are not always consistent, as they aren't always written by the same authors. Listed below are the guides I consult before heading to the south of France. They appear alphabetically, not in any order of preference. I have, however, noted which features I find particularly helpful in each book, and I've indicated those which I consider to be a "bring-along" (I use some books for very specific reasons, but don't consider them thorough enough to bring along in my suitcase). Note that I do not include books on all of France because the section on Provence in these editions is entirely too condensed.

Blue Guide: Provence & the Côte d'Azur, Paul Stirton, published by A & C Black Publishers, London; distributed in the U.S. by W.W. Norton. Perhaps because it is so authoritative, like Baedeker, I always feel like I *have* to check in with the Blue Guide. In fact, the Blue Guide series has been around since 1918 and the original founders were the editors of Baedeker's English-language editions. Blue Guides are very straightforward and practical with a no-nonsense approach that sets the series apart from so many others. The Blue Guides' strong points are art, architecture, and history, not accommodations and dining out (though these are of course briefly covered). In his preface to this Provence edition, Stirton writes that "in the past, travellers from the north have tended to see the journey to Provence in metaphorical terms. It was a journey of the soul or the mind as much as the crossing of a country and it generally resulted in a change of outlook, a new feeling about their surroundings." Stirton goes on to observe that "Le Style Provençal with its distinctive cuisine and printed cottons is as much an invention of modern advertising as is the Riviera, while beneath its surface the Côte d'Azur has a great deal that is both traditional and historic. To many people seeking an 'authentic' Provence, this can be disappointing but to the open-minded visitor, this is part of the appeal of the region. The interplay between fantasy, history and a vibrant, dynamic culture is what makes the South of France more than simply a holiday resort or museum." With good maps, feature boxes, and some black-and-white illustrations, this is a highly recommended bring-along if used in conjunction with another guide stronger on practical information.

Cadogan: Provence and *Cadogan: Côte d'Azur,* Dana Facaros and Michael Pauls, Cadogan Books plc, London; distributed in the U.S. by Globe Pequot Press, Old Saybrook, Connecticut. Cadogan (rhymes with toboggan) Guides are almost all written by the Facaros-Pauls team (they've written over twenty now), and I consider them to be of the bring-along variety. They're discriminating without being snooty, honest, witty, and interesting. The authors are not very easily impressed, so when they enthuse about something I pay attention. In fact, I occasionally find them too jaded, which can be refreshing in a sea of books which only gush with sentimentality. I'm especially fond of the "History" and "Topics" sections in the front of each book, which reveal how perceptive the authors are and introduce the reader to their style. Some essays in the Provence guide are entitled "Hocus Pocus Popes" and "Up Your Nose," and the authors give advice for visiting the Alpes Maritimes as follows: "*Lacet* means a shoelace, or a hairpin turn. It's a word you'll need to know if you try to drive up here, on the worst mountain roads in Europe, designed for mules and never improved. When you see a sign announcing '20 *lacets* ahead,' prepare for ten minutes in second gear, close encounters with demented lorry drivers, and a bad case of nerves." The Provence edition includes an art and architecture section and "The Best of Provence," a list of the authors' favorites, including castles, follies, gardens, regions of picturesque villages, Roman monuments, and wine touring. The Côte d'Azur edition features a good essay on art and artists and another on "Creating the Côte d'Azur"; plus, there is a list of best beaches, two of which are Villefranche-sur-Mer ("shallow, shingled, good for children") and Cabason ("delicious, simple, and cement-free"). Both books have lodging and dining recommendations for all budgets, good commentary on sights famous and little-known, and the usual maps, menu vocabulary, glossary, and bibliography. Definitely my favorite all-around guidebook. ~Cadogan's *South of France* is also a very good guide, but covers a wider area (including Languedoc, Roussillon, the Pyrenees, etc.) so would be a better companion for those traveling onward toward Spain.

Escape to Provence, photography by Owen Franken, text by Nancy Coons, 2000. This edition is one in the new "Escape to..." series, part of the Fodor's Travel Publications family. As the editors explain, most travel guidebooks are either long on practical information and lacking in evocative photographs or the reverse. They have tried to strike a balance with this new series, feeling that each edition is "rather like the intersection of the most luscious magazine article and a sensible, down-to-earth guidebook." This Provence volume features twenty-one memorable experiences and places that are unique to the region (it focuses only on Provence, not the Côte d'Azur). I think the selection is particularly good and diverse, encompassing the Var, Mont Ventoux, the Camargue, the Luberon, les Alpilles, and Haut Provence, and highlighting such treasures as the Calanques, bullfights, the Avignon Theater Festival, Patricia Wells's cooking classes, the antiques market in L'Île sur-la-Sorgue, and the transhumance, the twice-annual migration of sheep. (In June, the sheep make their way from the Haut-Var to the greener pastures of the Alps, and in October they return to lower elevation. Transhumance still occurs in various areas of the Mediterranean—though the Provençal migration is reportedly the largest—and is discussed at length in Fernand Braudel's *The Identity of France*.) This isn't a bring-along, but it is a good planning volume. With two maps and visitor information details at the back of the book.

Eyewitness Travel Guides: Provence, DK (Dorling Kindersley) Publishing. Like the Knopf Guides (see below), the Eyewitness series features bold graphics, full-color photos, maps, and illustrations. Unlike Knopf Guides, there are lots of bird's-eye views of historic buildings and street-by-street maps, and timelines detailing the history of each place from prehistoric times to the present day. I am crazy for these unique maps and historic timelines, so I am utterly incapable of *not* perusing an Eyewitness Guide. It's no surprise, then, that my favorite feature of Eyewitness Guides—and this Provence edition is no exception—is the introductory section (the one with all those timelines), which includes topics such as "René and the Wars of Religion," "Provence at War," and "Architectural Styles in Provence" (this one is particularly interesting as it features the typical elements of a Provençal *mas* and ironwork bell towers, which are seen all over the region). There are five pages devoted to Monaco in this edition, and the practical-information pages are found at the back of the book. Overall, however, I feel that Eyewitness Guides are more visually appealing than substantive—the descriptive information and historical background aren't thorough enough to satisfy me.

Fodor's Provence and the Côte d'Azur: The Complete Guide to the Hilltop Villages and Mediterranean Coastline (Fodor's Travel Publications). I typically crave more information than Fodor's guides seek to provide; however, I think the entire line of Fodor's guides just keeps getting better and better every year. I *always* read them before I go and *always* discover a handful of useful tips. Once, my husband and I planned on having dinner at a particular restaurant in Antibes, which was recommended in numerous books. Only the Fodor's guide stated that coat-and-tie attire was required for men. This is a small but important piece of information which I consider crucial for business and holiday travelers alike. It would not only be disappointing but embarrassing—and potentially offensive—to appear at a restaurant improperly dressed, all the more so if you had arranged to meet friends or colleagues there. The Rand McNally map at the back of the book; the wider range of choices for lodging and dining; color photos; the boxed "Close-Up" essays and the "Off the Beaten Path" suggestions throughout the book make this gold guide for Provence more valuable than it's ever been. I like consulting the "Fodor's Choice" selections, which list everything from antiquities, beaches, great drives, and gardens to lodging, markets, natural wonders, walks and hikes. ~Definitely worth perusing (but I don't recommend it as a bring-along) is *Fodor's Exploring: Provence,* which is filled with color photographs on every page. I'm fond of the suggested walks and drives (included are routes through the Dentelles, the Alpilles, Sainte-Baume, Grand Canon du Verdon, and Gorges du Loup) and the boxed tips and trivia that appear throughout.

Insight Guides: Côte d'Azur and Monaco and *Provence* (APA Publications, Singapore; distributed by Houghton Mifflin). I have been a fan of the Insight Guides for years. When they first appeared, about twenty years ago, they were the only books to provide outstanding color photographs matched with perceptive text. The guiding philosophy of the series has been to provide genuine insight into the history, culture, institutions, and people of a particular place. The editors search for writers with a firm knowledge of each city or region who are also experts in their fields. I do not think that recent editions are quite as good as they used to be; however, as I mentioned above, some guidebooks in a series are better than others, and I think these two editions are very good. I like the introductory section best of all (it's always been the best section, in my opinion, in *all* the books), a series of magazine-style essays on architecture, food, markets, the people, history, the arts, and politics. Some of the essays in the Côte d'Azur book are "From the Bronze Age to Bikinis," "The British Invasion," "The Blue Train," "The Riviera at War," and "The Sun Cult." Typically for Insight, the selection of hotels is not very helpful unless you have deep pockets, though there is some information on *gîtes,* camping, Club Med, and youth hostels. For advance reading, not a bring-along.

Knopf Guides: Provence (Alfred A. Knopf, originally published in France by Nouveaux-Loisirs, a subsidiary of Gallimard, Paris). I'm fond of the Knopf Guides in general, and the Provence edition is no exception. Just as I'm crazy for the time-lines and bird's-eye maps in the Eyewitness Guides, I'm a bit nuts for the visually enticing layouts and graphics in the Knopf Guides. I like the opening sections of the book on nature (which includes fold-out pages of the Camargue), architecture, historical periods, and Provence as seen by writers and painters. The practical-information pages at the back of the book aren't very thorough but do include a few useful tips, addresses, market and festival schedules, and limited hotel and restaurant suggestions. Surprisingly, for such a *luxe* book, there are listings for bud-get hotels, youth hostels, and campsites. As visually appealing and chunky as Knopf Guides are, they are actually surprisingly short on in-depth information. I wouldn't use this Provence edition exclusively, but it's a great companion to a more sub-stantial guidebook.

Let's Go: France (Bruce F. McKinnon, editor, St. Martin's Press). "The World's Bestselling Budget Travel Series" is the *Let's Go* slogan, which is hardly debatable. This is the only book on France mentioned here because *Let's Go* is still the bible and there is not a separate edition on Provence. If you haven't looked at a copy since your salad days, you might be surprised: each edition now contains color maps, advertisements, and an appendix that features a wealth of great practical information. A team of Harvard student interns still offers the same thorough cov-erage of places to eat and sleep, and things to see and do, and true to *Let's Go* tra-dition, rock-bottom budget travelers can find suggestions for places to sleep under $10 a night (sometimes it's the roof) and travelers with more means can find clean, cozy, and sometimes downright fancy accommodations. The inside back cover of this France guide features important phrases, phone numbers, French symbols, a Celsius/Fahrenheit chart, and a ruler with inches and centimeters, providing a quick reference that's easy to read. I think the presentation of facts and history is quite substantive in *Let's Go*—better, in fact, than in many more so-called sophis-ticated guides—and I would eagerly press a copy into the hands of anyone under a certain age (thirty-five?) bound for France. Definitely a bring-along if you're trav-eling with a backpack and a Eurailpass.

Lonely Planet: Provence & the Côte d'Azur (Nicola Williams). Lonely Planet guides have been among my most favorite for many years. Tony and Maureen Wheeler founded the series in Australia in 1973. Originally, the series focused solely on Asia, but about a dozen years ago they realized that the Lonely Planet approach to travel was not exclusive to any particular geographic area of the world. The series is aimed at independent travelers and each book is organized by chapters such as "Facts for the Visitor" (covering everything from health and gay and lesbian travelers, to pickpockets and legal matters), "Getting Around," "Things to See & Do," "Places to Stay," "Places to Eat," etc. I am fondest of the opening chapters covering history, politics, ecology, religion, economy, and practical facts; the information on sites to see, however, is not nearly detailed enough. I like that hotels and restaurants are presented from least expensive to most expensive, and I like the candid opinions of the contributing authors. This Provence edition features a culinary lexicon (with recipes provided by Patricia Wells, Roger Vergé, and Alain Ducasse), feature boxes covering such topics as "Boules and Bowled Out," "Black Diamonds," and "Pretty in Pink," as well as a good air-travel glossary. There are good black-and-white maps and color photos throughout, and a new feature is the "Highlights" boxes for each town or region of Provence. A percentage of each book's income is donated to various causes such as Greenpeace's efforts to stop French nuclear testing in the Pacific, Amnesty International, and agricultural projects in Central America. Travelers can also check out the Web site: www.lonelyplanet.com. Definitely a bring-along.

Louis Vuitton City Guide—European Cities II: Lyons, Marseilles, Strasbourg, Toulouse (Louis Vuitton Malletier, Paris). When I learned of this series—a boxed set of eight slender paperbacks covering thirty-three cities—my initial reaction was *"non, merci"* as I envisioned page after page of ritz and glitz, with the sort of snooty commentary that makes my skin crawl. So I was pleasantly surprised to find listings for budget hotels in Lyons and Marseille, a selection of affordable and varied restaurants in both cities, and some of my favorite shops (Avec le Temps for antique postcards and Bernachon for chocolate in Lyon, and La Maison Marseillaise in Marseille). Each bright orange guide features a remarkably concise and accurate profile of each city, a page of practical information, and listings for hotels, restaurants, bars, cafés, tearooms, nightlife, shopping (Louis Vuitton stores are, naturally, boxed), galleries, museums, outings and excursions, plus short essays on topics like *savon de Marseille* and contemporary architecture in Lyons. The books—not sold separately—are available at Louis Vuitton stores worldwide, and they are positively addictive. Even though this volume includes Toulouse and Strasbourg (many miles from Provence), it's lightweight enough to be a bring-along.

The Green Guide: Provence and *French Riviera: Côte d'Azur,* Michelin. A Michelin guide might be more trustworthy than your best friend. Its famous star-rating system and "worth a detour" slogan may have become a bit too formulaic, but it's a formula that works. The series was created in 1900 by André Michelin, who compiled a little red book of hotels and restaurants, which today is the *Michelin Red Guide,* famous for the stars it awards to restaurants. The green tourist guides first made their appearance in 1926. Each guide is jam-packed with information and is easy to pack. It will come as no surprise to readers that I prefer even more detail than Michelin offers, but I find it an excellent series, and each guide I've used has proven to be exceptionally helpful. Each Michelin guide is complemented by a Michelin map, of course, and the Provence edition is meant to be used in conjunction with maps 80, 83, 84, 114, 245, and 246; the French Riviera book matches up with maps 84, 115, and 245. I am fond of the touring programs in each book as well as the introductory information, which includes topics such as traditional rural architecture. A new route-planner service, which I happen to think takes much of the joy out of trip planning, is available by visiting www.michelin-travel.com. Viewers type in start and finish points and are provided with a suggested route, travel time, distances, road numbers, and any tolls. A bring-along, especially if you'll be renting a car.

The Rough Guides: Provence & the Côte d'Azur (Kate Baillie, Danny Aeberhard, and Rachel Kaberry, distributed in the U.S. by Penguin Books). When the Rough Guides first appeared, in the early eighties, they had limited distribution in the U.S. Then, the guides were sort-of-but-not-quite the British equivalent of *Let's Go*. I sought them out because I found the British viewpoint refreshing and felt the writers imparted more knowledge about a place than was currently available in U.S. guidebooks. Mark Ellingham was inspired to create the Rough Guides series because he felt at the time that current guidebooks were all lacking in some way: they were, for instance, either strong on ruins and museums but short on bars, clubs, and inexpensive eating places, or so conscious of the need to save money that they lost sight of things of cultural and historical significance. None of the books mentioned anything about contemporary life, politics, culture, or the people and how they lived. Now, since the Rough Guides opened a New York office in the late nineties, the series has evolved into one which is broader-based but still appealing to independent-minded travelers who appreciate the Rough Guides' honest assessments, and historical and political backgrounds (these last are found in the "Contexts" section of each guide and my only complaint is that I think this section should appear at the beginning of each book instead of at the end). After "Contexts," the "Basics" section is my favorite feature of the Provence guide. In this section, readers will find specifics on working and studying in France, gay and lesbian life, accommodations, food and drink, health and insurance, culture and festivals, etc. I also simply enjoy the descriptive writing in "The Guide" portion of the book, and always find useful tips and interesting trivia in the shaded boxes throughout. On-line updates to Rough Guides can be found at www.roughguides.com, for those who feel this is essential. All in all, each edition in the Rough Guides series is dependable and informative. Definitely a bring-along.

Time Out Guide: South of France (Penguin Books). Published by the same hip folks who brought London's *Time Out* magazine to some of our U.S. cities, Time

Out guidebooks are compact, well written, and jammed with information. Truthfully, there is not an enormous difference among Time Out, Rough Guides, and the Lonely Planet series—the style and tone are similar in each; but Time Out guides feature more thorough entertainment listings and are visually more appealing (perhaps because the books are printed on glossier paper), with good design and both color and black-and-white photos. To quote from the book, "While most general guides to the South concentrate on sightseeing, the Time Out South of France Guide has a distinctively cultural slant and includes a full selection of the best places to stay, eat and unwind." My favorite feature of this guide is the "In Context" section. Within this section is an essay entitled "Le Midi Today," which includes one of the best summations I've read on this part of France: ". . . if you've got it, flaunt it. *La frime,* the French call it—showing off. *La Frime* characterises life in France's south-eastern corner, or at least, the tourist part of it. But once you step off the seafront and into the backstreets, a different South emerges, in which corruption, racism, unemployment and the unmistakeable whiff of the Mafia all rear their heads." The French vocabulary section is fairly good, but doesn't include the fuller range of slang and street-wise expressions found in other Time Out guides; still, in addition to the usual useful stuff, you can learn to say *laissez-moi tranquille* (leave me alone), *hors service* or *en panne* (out of order), and that *un billet* is a ticket for a museum and *une place* is a ticket for a concert or theater performance. There are seven color maps at the back of the book, and a plethora of recommendations for music, film, dance, theater, nightlife, sports and fitness, etc. (plus a "Top Ten Choices for Children"). Also, for those who need weekly updated information, Time Out guides can be accessed via the Internet at www.timeout.co.uk. Definitely a bring-along.

Traveler's Companion: Mediterranean France (David Burke, photographed by Nik Wheeler, Kummerly + Frey, AG Switzerland; distributed in the U.S. by Globe Pequot Press, Old Saybrook, Connecticut). This series is a relative newcomer in the U.S., and I like this particular edition but am less fond of those I've seen on entire countries, like Spain, for example. Traveler's Companion is similar to the Insight Guides: the books are approximately the same size, with lots of glossy color photos, but I find the text to be better, and the author of this edition isn't afraid to be candid (under "inexpensive accommodations" in St. Tropez, he writes, "You have come to the wrong place"). Overall, this series offers a wider range of lodging and dining options than Insight. Lodging entries for Cannes, for example, list luxury, expensive, moderate, inexpensive, and camping. The blue pages at the back of the book are an A to Z quick reference guide. Highly recommended.

Ulysses Travel Guide (Howard Rombough, Benoit Ethier, Hans Jorg Mettler, Ulysses Travel Publications, Montreal; distributed in the U.S. by Globe Pequot Press). Ulysses is a relatively new series in the U.S., and though the standard features of the guides, such as maps, practical information, and historic background, are not unique among guidebooks, what makes Ulysses stand apart for me is the overall quality of the writing and its thoroughness. The authors of this Provence edition recommend some good walking and driving tours, as well as restaurants, cafés, bars, hotels, shops, and cultural events. A full range of outdoor activities—including horseback riding, golf, swimming, mountain biking, hiking, fishing, hang-gliding, skiing, canoeing, and kayaking—are mentioned in each chapter, where appropriate. With a few color photographs, this is highly recommended.

H

Health

Staying healthy while in France should not be a challenge, but things do happen. A good general reference book is *Travelers' Health: How to Stay Healthy All Over the World* (Richard Dawood, M.D., former medical editor for *Condé Nast Traveler,* foreword by Paul Theroux, Random House, 1994). This thick, 600+ page book isn't for bringing along—it's for reading before you go. In addition to Dr. Dawood, sixty-seven other medical experts contributed to this volume, which covers everything from insect bites, water filters, and sun effects on the skin to gynecological problems, altitude sickness, children abroad, immunizations, and the diabetic traveler. It also features essays on such topics as "The Economy-Class Syndrome" and "Being an Expatriate." ~Some Web sites to consult include www.cdc.gov/travel, which is the on-line site for the federal Centers for Disease Control in Atlanta. The content on the Web site is from the CDC's *Yellow Book: Health Information for International Travel.* Travel Medicine Inc.'s site is www.travelmed.com, which complements the *International Travel Health Guide* by Dr. Stuart Rose (Chronimed Publishing). ~To find English-speaking doctors, you can contact the International Association for Medical Assistance to Travelers (417 Center Street, Lewiston, New York 14092; 716-754-4883) for a directory of English-speaking doctors around the world. IAMAT is a nonprofit organization and while membership is free, donations are greatly appreciated. In addition to the directory, IAMAT mails members other material on malaria, immunizations, etc., as well as a membership card, which entitles you to member rates should you have to pay for medical help. Travelers can also always contact the closest American Embassy or local U.S. military installation for a list of physicians and their areas of expertise (the only one in France is in Paris; call 202-647-5225, ask for the European division, and a State Department employee will be able to give you the phone number). Additionally, some credit cards offer assistance: American Express's Global Assist program is available to all cardholders at no extra fee. It's a full-service program offering everything from doctor and hospital referrals to emergency cash wires, translation assistance, lost-item search, legal assistance, and daily monitoring of your health condition. When abroad travelers can call card member services at 800-528-4800, international collect at 1-336-393-1111, or the local American Express office. ~For many years, I had been led to believe that one should avoid drinking tap water in Mediterranean countries. I don't have any authoritative evidence on this regarding Mediterranean France, but I admit that I drink bottled water almost exclusively when I'm visiting. I do not go so far as to brush my teeth with it, but I don't drink tap water *(au robinet)* in restaurants either. The southern French themselves consume large quantities of bottled water—both *avec* (with) and *sans* (without) gas—and it may be a good practice for you too if you're worried about any digestive aspects of your health. Plain yogurt (and yogurt pills) are good aids in helping to prevent traveler's diarrhea, and yogurt is widely available at *supermarchés* and smaller food markets in Provence (for yogurt pills, consult your doctor about a prescription or possible over-the-counter brand). Also, before you take a drink from one of Provence's pretty fountains, look first for a posted sign stating *"l'eau non potable"* (nonpotable water).

Hiking

There are some thirty thousand kilometers of long-distance footpaths in France, and countless shorter routes and rambles. Friedrich Nietzsche—for whom the footpath from Eze, where he wrote part of *Thus Spoke Zarathustra,* to the *bas corniche* is named—opined that "Only those thoughts that come by walking have any value." Hiking and walking are not always the same thing, and if you are a dedicated walker who likes to combine modest physical activity with beautiful surroundings and accommodations to match, see Tours for recommended companies that provide such experiences. I believe that whether one hikes or walks, spending some time getting around via your own two feet makes you feel a part of Provence in a special way. Ramblers and serious hikers will be rewarded with the variety of routes in Provence and along the coast. The extensive network of long-distance paths is called the Sentiers de Grandes Randonnées, and the network of shorter paths, which begin and end at the same place, is called the Petite Randonnée. Many routes take walkers across entire sections of the country. Several GR trails meander through Provence and some connect with several local footpaths. Some of these include the GR5 (one of the most famous routes, which begins at the Hook of Holland and ends at Nice), the GR51 ("Balcony of the Côte d'Azur" from Theoule to Castellar), GR52 (Menton to the Vallée des Merveilles), and the GR4 (to the Gorges du Verdon), GR9 (from St.-Tropez to Mont Ventoux), and the GR42 (from the Rhône to Beaucaire). An important point to keep in mind about hiking in France is that what you walk on is a *route*, not a trail. The network wasn't created at random; it connects old paths that have existed for a long, long time. Routes wind through the middle of villages, sometimes across private property where you have to open and close a gate, and are often farm tracks where you'll encounter shepherds and farmers—you may even stumble upon some patches of original Roman cobblestones. Walking a GR is not a wilderness experience, but there are few places in Europe where you can backpack into completely isolated areas and not encounter roads, people, or towns. Conversely, there are few—if any—places in the U.S. where you can backpack and be assured of finding a place to sleep, in a bed, plus a meal with wine or beer at the end of the day. Sleeping accommodations you'll encounter along the route are *gîtes d'étape* and basic mountain huts (huts are found on main GR trails and are typically open in summer only). The location of mountain refuges are close enough to allow you to hike from hut to hut, but it's a good idea to book them in advance. Depending on the route you want to take, contact the appropriate tourist office for hut-to-hut hiking information (for the Alpes-Maritimes: Comité Regional de Tourisme, 55 promenade des Anglais, Nice; 04.93.37.78.78; for the Alpes-de-Haute-Provence: Comité Départemental de Tourisme, 19 rue du Dr.-Honnorat, Digne-les-Baines; 04.92.31.57.29). You'll need a good map to hike the GRs, and there are really only two appropriate choices: *guide topographique* (topoguide) or IGN (Institut Géographique National) *série bleue*. Topoguides contain extraordinary detail, but are available only in French. Fluency is not essential to read them, but a fairly good command of the language is. Topoguides also include locations of accommodations, usually *gîtes d'étapes*. The meticulous IGN *série bleue* maps indicate everything from bodies of water to landmarks and power lines, and are available in English. Both types of maps can be obtained at the national headquarters and information center for the Fédération Française de la Randonnée Pedestre, Comité National des Sentiers de Grande Randonnée (14 rue Riquet, 75019 Paris; 01.44.89.93.93); at the Espace IGN (107 rue la Boetie, 75008 Paris; 01.42.25.87.90); and at bookstores and some newsstands in France. Additionally, Seven Hills Book Distributors in Cincinnati carries the English-language versions of topoguides, published in Great Britain by McCarta. They are called "Footpaths of Europe Guides" in English, and I didn't mention them above because they are not exact translations of the French versions and they're condensed, which means they aren't always as reliable as the originals. However, I do recommend them for shorter-distance walks. Seven Hills offers eight individual guides: *Normandy & the Seine, Paris to Boulogne, Walking the GR5* (in three editions: "Larche to Nice," "Modane to Larche," and "Vosges to Jura"), *Walks in Corsica, Walks in the Cevennes,* and *Walking Through Brittany*. Each edition is five-by-eight inches, 190–250 pages, $19.95, and features sixty to eighty color topo-maps. Contact Seven Hills for a catalog at 1531 Tremont Street, Cincinnati, Ohio 45214; 800-545-2005; fax: 888-777-7799; e-mail: customerservice@sevenhills.com. The catalog also offers some other imported books that may be of interest, such as *The French Directory: The Complete Guide to Learning French in France* and *Trekking in the Pyrenees*. Good hikes are of course available in the Parc National du Mercantour, and there are some great coastal walks, such as the Sentier du Littoral, which follows the coast south from La Faviere (in the Var) and can be accomplished in a day. Note that the Comité Regional pour la Randonnée Pedestre occasionally organizes walks throughout the year in Provence, sometimes with a particular theme. Contact the regional offices (or inquire at the tourist office) for more information: Alpes-de-Haute-Provence (Association de Développement de la Randonnée, 42 boulevard Victor-Hugo, 04000 Digne) and Hautes-Alpes (Direction départementale Jeunesse et Sports, BP 154 passage Montjoie, 05002 Gap Cedex). ~The very best book available on hiking in France is *France on Foot—Village to Village, Hotel to Hotel: How to Walk the French Trail System on Your Own* (Bruce LeFavour, photographs by Faith Echtermeyer, Attis Press, St. Helena, California, 1999). Travelers interested in walking a little or a lot will be well served as LeFavour has thought of everything: trail classification and markers, a typical day en route, maps and trail guides, equipment, lodging and dining, recommended books, costs, packing list—even a handy walker's vocabulary, which you can cut out of the back of the book and carry with you on the trail. He *really* won me over, though, for two reasons: for recommending that readers make their own guidebook in advance (I *always* make a book before I go on a trip, even when there is no hiking on the horizon; my husband wondered if the photo on page 190 of a map, glue stick, scissors, paper, and a glass of wine was taken in our house) and for emphasizing that a walking experience is not the same thing as a backpacking experience (you do carry a pack, but you sleep in hotel beds and eat in restaurants, eliminating the need to carry a tent, cooking utensils, and food). As LeFavour puts it, "Walking in France is a glass of good wine while backpacking is a tumbler of ice water." Walking forces us to slow down, breathe deep, and take notice, the reasons we go on vacation in the first place. Another important point LeFavour emphasizes is that the French make little distinction between sports and leisure, moderation being considered the key to living a good, healthy life. Therefore, exercise goes hand in hand with enjoying wine and food. Overachieving Americans may find it odd to break a sweat at some physical activity and follow it up with pâté, a baguette, and some wine, but it is perfectly normal to the French. (For a hilarious extreme of this, see Adam Gopnik's "The Rules of the Sport," *The New Yorker,* May 27, 1996, in which he tries, unsuccessfully, for four months, to exercise at a health club in Paris.) When you walk from village to village in France, you stop for lunch and have the *plat du jour* and half a carafe of wine. The French way is to embrace a happy medium, which LeFavour endorses. He details several walks in the chapter on Provence and the Côte d'Azur. Even if you're only planning on taking short day hikes, you'll find LeFavour's enthusiasm infectious and his book to be indispensable, inspiring, and absolutely *de rigueur*. ~Another good book to consult for walking in France is *The Independent Walker's Guide to France* (Frank Booth, Interlink Books, Brooklyn, New York, 1996). I took an immediate liking to Booth because he explains that, although he has written a guide about walking in France, his book is also about escaping and avoiding the DROPs (Dreaded Other People). He details thirty-five walks in sixteen regions, with four in Provence and on the coast. Each walk is a day hike between two and nine miles, and a map and trail notes accompany each one. ~For those only planning on hiking in the Parc National du Mercantour, the best companion book I've seen is *Walking the Alpine Parks of France and Northwest Italy* (Marcia Lieberman, The Mountaineers, Seattle, 1994). Even though the book covers parts of Italy you may have no intention of visiting, the author's thoroughness is impressive, and I wouldn't want to be without this book. One hundred ten hikes in all are featured (including the Parc Regional du Queyras, north of Mercantour), with maps, black-and-white photos, and good tips such as "unlike Italian huts, French huts do not provide toilet paper." ~If you're *really* inspired to experience the GR network, you might want to consider a more ambitious trip. A great book about hiking the GR5 is *Walking Europe from Top to Bottom: The Sierra Club Travel Guide to the Grande Randonnée Cinq (GR5) Through Holland, Belgium, Luxembourg, Switzerland and France* (Susanna Margolis and Ginger Harmon, Sierra Club Books, 1986). It's out of print and therefore hard to find, but very much worth tracking down for its wealth of detail and practical tips the authors learned from their 107-day trek. ~Some walking maps and guides published in France, which can all be purchased at local bookstores and some newsstands, include *Balades & Decouvertes*. These individual guides are published by the magazine *Terre Provençale* (see Periodicals for more details), and the Provence edition features twenty-four walks along the sea, in the mountains, in the *garrigue* (limestone hills, notably near Nîmes), and through towns and villages. Though the text is in French, those with a working knowledge of the language should be able to decipher it. Also, *Didier Richard,* which has very good maps on a 1:50,000 scale, with separate editions on Alpes-de-Provence, Haute-Provence, Maures et Haut Pays Varois, Mercantour, and Au Pays d'Azur.

Hours

You'll find that in the larger cities of the south some businesses and shops are open continuously, that is, they don't close for lunch. The behemoth super- and hyper-*marchés* on the outskirts of towns are also open without a lunch break. In smaller towns and villages, however, you can count on most everything closing for lunch at about noon or 12:30, not reopening until 2:00, 3:00, or even 4:00 in the summer months. Additionally, many businesses that are closed Sunday morning are also closed entirely on Monday, although the gigantic *marchés* usually open Monday afternoon. Museums and monuments nearly all close for lunch, too, as well as either all day Monday *or* Tuesday. Houses of worship are often open all day (but be prepared for lunchtime closings), but when they're not, sometimes you'll find a posted sign directing you to someone who has the key.

I

_____

Îles (Islands)

Many visitors overlook the French Mediterranean islands just off the Provençal coast. Linda Dannenberg's article in the section *La Côte d'Azur* reveals the singular pleasures of the Île de Porquerolles (tourist office phone number: 04.94.58.33.76). As lovely as it is to stay there (especially at Le Mas du Langoustier, which was General Patton's headquarters in World War II), visitors should not be discouraged from visiting just for the day (most likely, hotel rates in mainland towns such as Cassis, Giens, and Le Lavandou will be less expensive than on the island itself), and walks—accompanied by some magnificent views—on the island, which is only about nine kilometers long and two wide, can easily be completed within a day: one hike leads walkers to the beautiful Plage de Notre Dame that has markers identifying a variety of flowers and trees; another route, to the lighthouse, reveals a grove of one hundred varieties of olive trees, which flower from early July to the end of August. Neighboring Île de Port-Cros is much more sedate, a true step back in time. There is only one hotel on the island (Hôtel Le Manoir), and there are thirty kilometers of footpaths to explore. It is also home to over one hundred species of birds. The Port-Cros National Park Service is in the old town of Hyères, in the Castel Sainte-Claire (better known as a former home of Edith Wharton). You can call the office (04.94.01.40.70), or better yet visit in person, not only to pick up information but to walk through the gardens, which were reportedly planted by Wharton herself. The Îles de Lérins, a fifteen-minute boat ride from Cannes, are equally tempting, and "appear to have little to do with the modern world" according to the Rough Guide. The two islands which are the Lérins are Île Sainte Marguerite (about three kilometers long and less than one kilometer wide) and Île Saint-Honorat (even smaller). Île Sainte-Marguerite is better known to visitors because of Fort Vauban, where the Man in the Iron Mask was imprisoned by Louis XIV. I am more interested in the Musée de la Mer, also housed in the Fort, which features a collection of amphorae, ceramics, and glass from a Roman shipwreck. Marguerite also has a network of footpaths. Honorat is owned by Cistercian monks (originally from Sénanque), and their Abbaye de Lérins is open to visitors. The monks produce honey; wine, which is of good quality and served at restaurants on the coast; and a liqueur called Lérina, all of which are for sale in the abbey shop. No cars or hotels are to be found on the island, and there is only one restaurant near the ferry dock. Honorat is a perfect respite from the trendy coast: a quiet Mediterranean Eden of vines, lavender, olive trees, wild herbs and flowers, pine trees, and the sea all around. For specifics on getting to the Îles d'Or and the Îles de Lérins, contact the Maison de la France offices here in the States or the tourist offices in Nice, Cannes, or Hyères. Visitors have a choice of ferry service, helicopter, or a water taxi, Le Pélican.

Internet Access

I'm only including this here for business travelers. If you're traveling for pleasure and feel you need to surf the Web, perhaps you should save your money and stay home. I take the view that vacations are for removing yourself from your daily grind, what the French refer to as *vélo, boulot, dodo;* visiting another country is about doing *different* things and putting yourself in unfamiliar situations. Overseas telephone services are generally not as reliable as those in the U.S., ensuring that connecting to the Internet is not so easy or inexpensive. Business travelers who need to check in with the office via e-mail should consider what it will cost for a laptop, power adapter, disk and/or CD-ROM drives, plus any other related accessories, as well as how heavy it will be to carry. You may conclude that cybercafés (or Internet cafés) are more economical (and easier on your back). Cybercafé fees for access to the Internet vary, but when you compare a hotel's charges for the same access— often at slower speeds—cybercafés represent good value. I found cybercafés in Aix, Antibes, Avignon, Fréjus, Lyon, Marseille, Nice, St.-Raphael, and Toulon (some cities had more than one café) by searching www.cybercaptive.com, www.net-cafeguide.com, and www.netcafes.com. Two other sources are *The Internet Café Guide* (Ernst Larsen) and *Cybercafés: A Worldwide Guide for Travelers* (Ten Speed Press), which both feature a comprehensive list of the world's Internet cafés. I personally like the idea of keeping my business tasks away from my hotel room, but for those who can't stand the thought of leaving the hotel premises, you'll be happy to know that hotels are definitely improving their Internet services. Most of the world's major hotel chains are leading the way on this front, and some also have at least one technologically savvy employee who is on hand to assist guests with problems. Additionally, I've noticed recently that many public telephone booths, including those at airports and in hotel lobbies, are now equipped for Internet access.

J

Jet Lag

I have read about a number of methods to reduce jet lag that involve diet and the amount of sunlight one receives during the days leading up to departure (an interesting article to read is "A Cure for Jet Lag?" in *Condé Nast Traveler*, April 2000, which details new research into the use of melatonin). I have never been inclined to try any of these because I've always had success adjusting to local time upon my arrival. No matter how tired I might be, I do not take a nap unless it is after lunch, and then only for no longer than an hour. On the first night, I turn in rather early—by 9:00—to get a very full night's sleep, and I do not sleep late the next morning. If I am fortunate enough to have a bathtub, I do not miss the opportunity to fill it with aromatic *bain moussant* (bubble bath) and get in for a soothing soak. As a result, I have never had a problem with jet lag. I cannot overstate the importance, pleasure, and restorative powers of a daily afternoon nap while in the south of France. Not only do most shops and museums close for a few hours in the middle of the day anyway, but you'll feel refreshed and more alert after a brief rest. As Jane Brody noted in one of her "Personal Health" columns in *The New York Times,* naps "are far better than caffeine as a pick-me-up." Returning to *bain moussant,* I'm loyal to two brands when traveling: Kiehl's (a New York family business since 1851, recently bought by l'Oréal) and l'Occitane (a Provençal company detailed in *Des Belles Choses*). Both offer products for men and women in plastic bottles good for traveling. From Kiehl's (available in many department stores, or call 1-800-KIEHLS-1), I like the Lavender Foaming-Relaxing Bath with Sea Salts and Aloe Vera and the Mineral Muscle Soak Foaming-Relaxing Bath, also with Sea Salts and Aloe Vera. From l'Occitane, I'm particularly fond of the *bain moussant* but also like the *lavande* restorative balm and relaxing essential oils in its aromachologie line.

Jewish History in the South of France

France is home to the fourth-largest Jewish community in the world and the largest Jewish community in Europe. Today Jews represent 1 percent of France's total population, the highest percentage in Western Europe (note, however, that after Catholicism, Islam is the second-largest religion in France). Provence and the coast have a number of things of Jewish interest, including the synagogue in Carpentras, the oldest in France (1741). A good book to consult is *A Travel Guide to Jewish Europe* (Ben Frank, Pelican Publishing Company, Gretna, Louisiana, 2000), which includes profiles of Nîmes, Avignon, Arles, Cavaillon, Carpentras, Monte Carlo, Nice, Cannes, St.-Tropez, Antibes, Marseille, and Aix. Also, Maison de la France (the French Government Tourist Office in the U.S.) publishes two great brochures: "France for the Jewish Traveler," with six pages on Provence and the Côte d'Azur, including synagogues, restaurants—some kosher—and community centers, and "The Road to Jewish Heritage in the South of France," which details the *carrières* (derived from the Provençal word *carreira,* for street) of Jewish communities in Provence and Languedoc.

Journées du Patrimoine

Every September, usually on the third weekend, for the last seventeen years, France has hosted the Journées du Patrimoine (Patrimony Days). Each region of the country puts together an extensive program of events, nearly all of which are free. Many historic buildings, gardens, offices, and embassies that are generally closed to the public are open during the Journées, making this a good time to plan a trip accordingly. I have not been in Provence for the Journées, but I was fortunate to be in Paris once at this time, and the *programme* of events was truly overwhelming. Check with the tourist office in the U.S. or in Provence for the exact dates in 2001.

L

Language

Somewhere, I once read an observation by Lawrence Durrell that if one *really* wanted to know and understand France and the French, one had to learn the language (I cannot for the life of me find this reference again, so if you know of it, please write and tell me). I think he is absolutely right, for the French language really does define so much about the people and the nation. Everyone will tell you, of course, that it is essential to at least try to speak French when in France; this is true—the French warm to anyone who attempts to speak their beautiful language—but it is also true that the natives of *any* country love it when visitors try to speak their language. What people may not tell you is that French is still a nearly universal language. It has been my experience that *someone* always speaks French, even in such seemingly unlikely countries as Egypt, Portugal, Turkey, Greece, and Croatia. Spanish may be the second language in the U.S., but it won't serve you very well outside of Mexico, Central and South America, Spain, and the Philippines. A multitude of French words and phrases have made their way into English, and it would never be a bad investment of your time to either brush up on your high school French or begin learning for the first time. Note that in the south you may see signs in Provençal. Although some people still speak Provençal, it is essentially a written, literary language, and is in fact a dialect of the *langue d'Oc* (see entry below). The French spoken in the south is not like the French spoken in Paris, however. The southern accent is less nasal and more lilting, sounding almost Italian at times (especially in Nice), and the endings of words are pronounced with a marked difference that would surely cause perfectionists to cringe. ~The best language course I've used is Living Language. There are others—Berlitz, Barron's, Language/30, etc.—but Living Language has been around longer (since 1946), the courses are continually updated and revised, and in terms of variety, practicality, and originality, I prefer it. French courses are available for beginner, intermediate, and advanced levels, in either audiocassette or CD editions. The "Fast & Easy" course (referred to as "virtually foolproof" by the New York *Daily News*) is for beginner business or leisure travelers and is a sixty-minute survival program with a cassette and pocket-size pronunciation guide. The "Ultimate Course" is for serious language learners and is the equivalent of two years of college-level study. In a copublishing venture with Fodor's, Living Language also offers the pocket-size *French for Travelers,* which is a handy book/cassette reference designed for business and leisure travelers with words and phrases for dozens of situations, including exchanging money, using ATMs, and finding a hotel room, and also includes a two-way dictionary. To help build excitement for young children coming along, Living Language has the *Learn in the Kitchen* and *Learn Together: For the Car* series. These book/cassette kits are for children ages four to eight, and include a sixty-minute bilingual tape; sixteen songs, games, and activities; a forty-eight-page illustrated activity book with color stickers; and tips for parents on how to vary the activities for repeated use. If you prefer learning by videotapes, a respected course is "French in Action." Call 800-LEARNER for additional information, and see the September 1999 issue of *Paris Notes* for the article "Paris 'In Action,'" by Ellen Williams, about this series. ~Other related language books and tools to consult include *501 French Verbs* (Barron's). In addition to really good descriptions of the various tenses, a full page is allotted to each verb, showing all the tenses fully conjugated, plus the definition, and a useful selection of "Words and Expressions Related to This Verb" at the bottom of each page. As if this weren't enough, there are also chapters on "Verbs Used in Idiomatic Expressions," "Verbs with Prepositions," "Verbs Used in Weather Expressions," "Thirty Practical Situations for Tourists and Popular Phrases," and "Words and Expressions for Tourists." If you're serious about learning or brushing up on French, I really can't see doing it without this essential book. *Fodor's to Go: French for Travelers* (Fodor's Travel Publications, 2000). Not a book but a nifty credit card–size fold-out magnet that you can conveniently keep in your pocket and unobtrusively retrieve when you need to look up a word or phrase. Also, this is great for pretrip quizzing: you can keep it in your kitchen on the refrigerator at eye level and, while holding a glass of wine (Provençal, of course) with one hand, unfold the magnet with the other and test your memory. Note, however, that as this is a magnet, you have to make sure it doesn't touch your credit cards or any other data storage items. *Insiders' French: Beyond the Dictionary* (Eleanor Levieux and Michel Levieux, The University of Chicago Press, 1999) is a smart and infinitely useful book. Much more than a dictionary, it includes terms and phrases that virtually did not exist before 1990. The authors describe the aim of this book as an attempt to present a verbal snapshot of France in the mid to late nineties. They acknowledge (happily) that some classic images and phrases still exist, "But today there are other Frances as well: a France of high unemployment, a France that is hooked on fast food but ambivalent about the country where it originated, a France that is about to experience the European single currency but is not at all certain what being part of Europe is going to entail, a France with a substantial and ever more controversial immigrant population, a France with a much diminished Communist Party and a provocative extreme Right, a France that cannot agree on what nationality and cultural identity mean." So, the entry for *août* is "The missing month in the French calendar because so many people go away on vacation. They become *des aoûtiens* (pronounced 'ah-oo-sien'). Signs on shop doors will inform you, *'Fermeture annuelle du 1er au 28 aout'*; a few factories shut down for the month. *Les parcmètres à Paris son gratuits au mois d'août;* 'You don't have to put money in the parking meters in Paris in August.' Try to find *une boulangerie ouverte, une boucherie ouverte, un marchand de vins ouvert* in August. Try to order wallpaper, take delivery of a new car, or have the *électricien* or the *menusier* come in August: you'll probably have to wait until *la rentrée* (i.e., September). On the last weekend in July or the first one in August, the media will warn about *le chassé-croisé des juilletistes et des aoûtiens,* 'The two-way pattern of very heavy traffic as many people come back from vacation while equally many leave on vacation.'" Brilliant. *Champs-Elysées* (P.O. Box 158067, Nashville, Tennessee 37215; 800-824-0829; www.champs-elysees.com). Not a book but a monthly audiomagazine for intermediate and advanced students of French. Each cassette or CD is a monthly, hour-long program accompanied by a complete transcript with a French-English glossary. The programs include current events, music, cuisine, culture, and business news of France. I have found them interesting, well produced, and good preparation for a trip. Also, they're great to listen to while cleaning up around the house! Subscriptions are available for one year or five months. *Word Routes Anglais—Français: Lexique Thematique de l'Anglais Courant* (Cambridge University Press, 1994). An unusual book unlike any other language book I've ever seen. It's not a dictionary, but the *categories de mots* are presented in alphabetical order. I think learning by categories is a better way to learn more vocabulary. The first category, for instance, is *animaux sauvages* (wild animals), which includes the names of various animals, words used to describe animal characteristics in humans (pig, ass, sheep, fox, etc.), fierce animals, gentle animals, insects, small animals, expressions ("His bark is worse than his bite"), farm animals, pets, animal noises, birds, fish and sea animals, plants, and trees. At the back of the book there is an excellent section on language for communication. Most of this book is in French (including the introduction), so it's not for beginners. *Le Mot Juste: A Dictionary of Classical and Foreign Words and Phrases* (Vintage Books, 1991), which includes French, Italian, German, Spanish, and a smattering of other languages around the world. It's a great reference book which I use all the time. *Les Bons Mots: How to Amaze Tout le Monde with Everyday French* (Eugene Ehrlich, Henry Holt, 1997). Not a dictionary, but rather an alphabetical listing of idiomatic phrases, many of which have found their way into English. If you always wanted to know how to say the equivalent of "don't judge by appearances" *(l'habit ne fait pas le moine),* "seize the moment" *(il faut vivre dans l'instant),* "I couldn't care less *(je m'en fous),* or simply "hangover" *(geule de bois),* you need this book. *Je Ne Sais What?: A Guide to de Rigueur Frenglish for Readers, Writers, and Speakers* (Jon Winokur, Plume, 1996): "Frenglish"—not to be confused with "Franglais"—is grammatically correct *French* that enriches the *English* language. This is a collection of French expressions, maxims, and literary phrases that have found their way into our vocabulary. So one will find *nouvelle cuisine, mauvais gout, enfant terrible,* and *tant pis* and their definitions and related quotations. As Winokur states in the introduction, "Much of our political, military, artistic, and culinary vocabulary originated in France."

Langue d'Oc Versus Langue d'Oil

These terms are referred to often as a way of describing the difference between southern and northern France. Provence's neighbor, Languedoc, takes its name from the *langue d'Oc,* which is derived from *langue d'Occitan*—the language (or tongue) of the Occitan region of France, which long ago was defined as all of the south of France except the parts we know today as Roussillon and Gascogne (the Provençal language should, in fact, be referred to as *Occitan*). As Michael Jacobs has written in his excellent book *A Guide to Provence,* "Provençal is a Romance language having much in common with Italian, Spanish and French, but being particularly close to Catalan, the language spoken both in Catalonia and in the adjoining territory of Roussillon." Both *oc* and *oil* mean "yes" in their respective languages, and both are from the Latin *hoc* and *hoc ille. Langue d'Oc* also refers to the land west of the Rhône to Toulouse, because during the time the popes were in residence in Avignon, the Rhône was the dividing line between land claimed by the popes—known as the Comtat-Venaissin—and that of the French kings. (Lawrence Durrell, in *Caesar's Vast Ghost,* noted that Rhône boatmen actually referred to one bank of the river as "empire" and the other as "kingdom.") Waverley Root, in his classic work *The Food of France,* provides perhaps the best explanation of the *oc* and *oil* terms: "The triumph of the *langue d'oil* over the *langue d'oc* was owing to the fact that the former became a written language, the literary language of its region, and the latter did not. One reason for this was probably the greater uniformity in the spoken language of the north, resulting from greater ease of movement over its more open country. If you looked at a map of the old provinces of France, you might expect the opposite. The southern provinces—Gascogny, Languedoc, Provence—are in general larger than the northern provinces—Île-de-France, Touraine, Anjou—but in the north the cultural units were larger than the political units, while in the south they were smaller. The courts of the north moved freely between Paris and Tours, or even Bordeaux, and spread the language they spoke over the whole area; and the Burgundians, acquiring realms on either side of the French possessions, and dealing constantly with the French, though seldom amicably, came to talk like them as well. Meanwhile in the south each little lorddom maintained its own version of the *langue d'oc,* and as the lords got around less through the difficult and often desolate, largely mountainous (or, in the south, swampy) areas of that part of the country, uniformity of the language was not achieved. But a more important reason for the failure of the *langue d'oc* to become a language of literature is probably the paradoxical one that the south of France had become imbued with the Mediterranean civilization earlier than the north . . . Southern France had made Latin its literary language early. It was firmly rooted and hard to dislodge when the spoken tongues resulting from the collision between Latin and the tongues of Gaul began to crystallize sufficiently to be ready to become new languages. Latin was less firmly rooted as a written language in the north. It gave way more readily to the popular speech. And as this became a written language, and exchanges between the north and the south carried it southward before the *langue d'oc* had been committed to paper, the latter remained a dialect and the former became French." Both phrases also divide north from south gastronomically, designating the north as a cuisine based on dairy products and the south as one based on olive oil. [From *The Food of France* by Waverley Root, Copyright © 1958, 1966 by Waverley Root, reprinted by permission of Alfred A. Knopf, a Division of Random House, Inc.]

Lavande (Lavender)

After I had been to Provence three times, I realized that if I didn't get beyond my aversion to traveling there in the summer months I would never, ever see lavender plants in bloom. I did not know until I witnessed it that seeing swaths of purple lavender fields is a truly unforgettable sight, and, to me, a sight as worthy and memorable as the Grand Canyon, redwood trees, or the Alps. I now have no desire to go to Provence if it's not when lavender is at its peak. And here's a surprising tip: contrary to popular thought, even in July my husband and I encountered no crowds or hordes of visitors in the Drôme and Lubéron parts of the region, and we had glorious lavender fields *all to ourselves* (and the bees). There are three types of lavender grown in Provence: true lavender (this is the kind sought after by perfume makers), spike lavender (looks like true lavender except it has several flower spikes along its stem), and *lavandin* (a hybrid created from pollination of true and spike lavenders). The best book about lavender that I've seen is *Lavender: Fragrance of Provence* (photographs by Hans Silvester, text by Christiane Meunier, Harry N. Abrams, 1996; first published under the title *Provence, terre de lavande* by Les Editions de la Martiniere, Paris, 1995). I was surprised when I read that cultivation of lavender and *lavandin* is a twentieth-century development, and as the author states, "The presence of a permanent and thriving rural population is essential to the continuance and proper usage of the Provençal countryside. The lavender and lavandin fields are now so much a part of the landscape that it is easy to forget that they are in no way 'natural.' They are the result of continuous and exacting labour that has given to an often very unrewarding region all the charm of a garden." The photos in the book present lavender fields during every season of the year—including some with snow blanketing the fields—and Meunier reminds us that each season has its own beauty, "serving as symbols of the sometimes contradictory aspects of the Provençal soul, ever divided between sadness and gaiety, softness and hardness." Travelers who are as nuts for blooming lavender as I am should immediately contact two organizations: Comité Régional de Tourisme Provence-Alpes-Côte d'Azur (Espace Colbert, 14 rue Sainte Barbe, 13231 Marseille, Cedex 01; 04.91.39.38.00; fax: 04.91.56.66.61 for its "Routes de Lavande" color brochure) and the Association "Routes de la Lavande" (BP 36, 2 avenue de Venterol, 26111 Nyons; 04.75.26.65.91 for its package of lavender routes). The lavender package is the most comprehensive information available anywhere—you positively won't find any of this in any book or Web site—and consists of individual, fold-out brochures for eight lavender-growing areas of Provence. Each brochure details itineraries by car, bike, and *à pied* (hikes), and includes maps, lavender-related shops, distilleries, festivals, markets, and gardens, and suggested restaurants and accommodations (including campgrounds, *chambres d'hôtes,* and *Gîtes de France*). I recommend this package so highly that if you learn the tourist office is out of stock, please write to me (c/o Three Rivers Press, 299 Park Avenue, 6th floor, New York, New York 10171) and I will send you a copy!

Luggage

I've read of a syndrome—really—called B.S.A. (Baggage Separation Anxiety), which you may at first be inclined to laugh at; but as reports of lost luggage have escalated in the last few years, I'm not at all surprised (all the more reason, I say, not to check bags, and *definitely* the reason to at least pack some essentials in a carry-on bag). Essentials, by the way, don't add up to much: it's remarkable how little one truly "needs." Recently, one of my bags did not turn up, and the airline representative was honest enough to tell me that when flights are full, sometimes not all the bags are loaded onto the plane—*intentionally* (#&!). Distressing as this is, at least it explains part of the problem, and is one more reason to keep essentials with you. Even if you are the sort of traveler who cannot lighten your load, you will still probably bring a carry-on. As I write this, the standard limit for carry-on luggage is 9″ by 14″ by 22″, otherwise known as 45 linear inches to the airlines. Although not all airlines enforce this policy, it seems foolish not to comply—storage space is limited, and less baggage means more on-time schedules and better passenger safety. Some airlines have even installed sized templates at the security X-ray machines, so if your bag doesn't fit, you can't take it with you. Many luggage manufacturers—including Tumi and Samsonite—have responded by turning out a selection of carry-on bags at varying prices, which are designed to hold enough stuff for about three days of traveling—about the time it takes for a misrouted bag to show up, assuming it isn't lost altogether! The ubiquitous—and always black— suitcase on wheels has taken a beating of late. Some travelers complain that they are too heavy to lift in and out of the overhead bins without hitting someone on the head, and trying to find one at the baggage claim is like Harry the dog trying to find his family's umbrella at the beach in the children's book *Harry by the Sea*. Plus, they've become decidedly un-hip: a writer for *The Wall Street Journal* claimed that "the wheelie has become a fashion faux pas—the suitcase equivalent of a pin-striped suit on a casual Friday." I may be the lone voice in the wilderness, but the wheelie is essential for those of us with back problems. Also, I like the freedom of not having to depend on only one type of ground transportation. With a wheelie, I don't need a porter or a luggage cart, and I can choose from all forms of public (and private) transportation.

Lyon

Now that Delta Airlines flies direct to Lyon, it was tempting to include a section on Lyon in this book. After all, the city's close proximity to northern Provence makes it the gateway to the south of France (Ford Madox Ford felt that entering Provence from the north was the *only* way to enter the region because one could see, feel, and smell the difference). However, once again, my manuscript was already too large to include a separate section on Lyon, but I felt I had to mention it *somewhere* in this edition. Should you decide to begin your trip here, you will find Lyon a perfect introduction to the Midi. Many of the buildings are painted in soft pastel colors, preparing you slowly for the explosion of vibrantly colored buildings in Nice, for example. In December 1998, UNESCO designated Lyon's city center a World Heritage Site (which it justly deserves), and its setting at the point where the Rhône and Saône meet is dramatic. Lyon is, of course, best known as the food capital of France, but there is much, much else of interest. Two good companion books to read are *An Uncertain Hour: The French, the Germans, the Jews, the Klaus Barbie Trial, and the City of Lyon, 1940–1945* (Ted Morgan, William Morrow and Company, 1990) and *"Spotted Dick, S'il Vous Plaît": An English Restaurant in France* (Tom Higgins, Soho Press, 1995; first published in Great Britain by Aurum Press Ltd., in 1994, under the title *Plat du Jour: An English Restaurant in Lyons*). Ted Morgan, a Pulitzer Prize–winning journalist, was a young boy in Paris at the time of the armistice when he and his family left for Spain and then for the U.S. He writes that he regrets they didn't remain in France to live through the occupation, as it was one of those times in history when people were faced with making a moral decision, and since he wasn't there, he's always felt like a deserter. His father, a member of the Lorraine Squadron in the RAF, did not survive a training flight in 1943. Morgan returned to France in 1987 to cover the Barbie trial for *The New York Times Magazine,* and this work is the result of all the memories the trip brought back to him. It is also a record of the years 1940–45 in Lyon; he had access to thousands of pages of secret documents prepared for the Barbie trial, including hundreds of depositions that were never made public. Due to these documents, Morgan was able to provide much more detail about major events—such as the capture and death of Résistance leader Jean Moulin—and the everyday lives of residents under the occupation. A noteworthy point Morgan mentions is that there were more journalists in Lyon for the Barbie trial than at the Nuremberg trials, and that a number of young people, mostly students, stood in line every day for hours hoping to get one of the one hundred seats set aside for the public. The reason for this, he concluded, was "Because the French had to look into this particular mirror, however distorted. Because there was a generation of young people that was still picking up the tab for World War II." (It is appropriate that Lyon is home to the Centre d'Histoire de la Résistance et de la Déportation—one of over forty memorials devoted to the history of the Résistance and the deportation of French residents to concentration camps in France—as it was headquarters for both Klaus Barbie and Jean Moulin.) When Tom Higgins and his wife opened the restaurant Mister Higgins in Lyon, which is known as the gastronomic capital of France, you can imagine the surprise with which the British restaurant was received there. *"Un restaurant anglais? C'est pas possible"* was the usual response. Higgins actually describes Lyon as a "gastrocracy," a word he coined after having a bit of trouble with a Mercedes van, which was stuck in the middle of a busy thoroughfare at evening rush hour and some police officers wanted an explanation as to why the van was overloaded, with defective rear lights, at that particular hour of the day. As soon as he explained that he had a restaurant to return to which was to open in less than an hour, the officers were cooperative and understanding, for the French—and especially the Lyonnais—do not believe, after all, that food is only food, and a restaurant (even an English one at that) must be allowed to carry on without a hitch. It took awhile, but Mister Higgins finally made a name for itself in culinary circles. *"Spotted Dick, S'il Vous Plaît"* is a funny and informative read, as well as an insider's view of the French restaurant world. There are a dozen recipes in the book, including one for, naturally, the famous English pudding, Spotted Dick.

M

Maps
Getting lost is usually a part of everyone's travels, but it isn't always a bonus. Happily, there are maps, and no shortage of good ones. *For individual cities and*

towns: I have found the free maps distributed by local tourist offices perfectly fine for the cities, towns, and villages of Provence. With the exception of Marseille, none of the cities is so big as to warrant a super-duper map. One map series I've seen here in the States which I think is useful is Streetwise (Streetwise Maps, Inc., Sarasota, Florida, www.streetwisemaps.com). Both a Côte d'Azur and Provence map is available, and each is a laminated, fold-out edition. There are individual map panels for bigger towns such as Marseille, Cannes, Monte Carlo, and Nice on one side, and on the other is a bigger map of each region showing relief features (useful for driving). *For driving:* The best choices are the individual Michelin maps for Provence and the Côte d'Azur, numbers 245, 246, 114, and 115. Michelin also publishes a spiral-bound atlas *(Michelin France: Tourist and Motoring Atlas),* which I think is easier than a large fold-out map to employ in a car, but it's for all of France, so it may not be the best buy unless you plan on driving elsewhere in France. ~Note that if you're lost, whether you are walking, biking, or driving, showing the telephone number of your destination to the locals is often helpful. This would never have occurred to me, but on two occasions in Provence the telephone code enabled people to point me in the right direction.

Marchés, Marchés aux Puces, and Brocantes (Food and Flea Markets)
Outdoor markets are one of the unrivaled pleasures of Provence. Even if you have no intention of purchasing anything, visitors should not miss walking around at least one outdoor market, for the daily or weekly *marchés* are an integral part of Provençal life. In "Au Printemps, Au Marché" ("The Sophisticated Traveler" edition of *The New York Times Magazine,* March 13, 1988), Patricia Wells wrote that "France's market structure has changed little since the Middle Ages, when villages throughout the country established weekly marchés for the sale and barter of everything from livestock to clothing." She added that "there are no markets as lively, as appealing, or as abundant as those in the sunny south." Prices for food items are usually clearly displayed and fixed in Provence, and you may find that vendors will ask you when you plan on eating the *fraises des bois* (wild strawberries) or melon that you're about to buy. This is one of the biggest and most obvious differences between how food is grown and distributed in France versus the U.S. A typical Provençal vendor will separate strawberries according to when you should eat them: those ready to eat within a few hours, those for eating tonight after dinner, and those ready for tomorrow afternoon's picnic. This is, of course, the way produce should be purchased. You will not find, therefore, strawberries picked before they are ripe, and no one would dream of selling—or buying—strawberries unless they were going to be eaten no later than one or two days later, at the most. (After you've tasted the *fraises des bois,* peaches, or melons you bought at a *marché,* remember the flavor, and accept nothing less when you return home! Fresh fruits and vegetables are meant to be eaten as soon after harvesting as possible.

Refrigeration does not enhance flavor, and raspberries flown in from Chile are not "fresh," just expensive and flavorless.) Prices at flea markets are sometimes marked, but bargaining is the accepted method of doing business (merchants will tell you if it's not); therefore, a visit to the market should not be an activity you do in a hurry. Take your time, soak up the atmosphere, enjoy your search for that unique *souvenir,* but remember to stop for something to eat or drink so your stomach (or companion) doesn't grumble. Two books you'll definitely want to have are *Markets of Provence: A Culinary Tour of Southern France* (foreword by Patricia Wells, text by Dixon Long, recipes by Ruthanne Long, photographs by David Wakely, CollinsPublishers, San Francisco, 1996; see *Jardins, Musées, et Monuments bibliothèque* for a thorough description) and *Exploring the Flea Markets of France: A Companion Guide for Visitors and Collectors* (Sandy Price, Three Rivers Press, 1999). Price highlights the markets of twelve regions of France, and provides a separate chapter on Provence featuring eight flea market towns: Aix, Arles, Avignon, L'Îsle-sur-la-Sorgue, Jonquieres, Marseille, Nîmes, and Villeneuve-les-Avignon. She also includes practical advice on what to look for at markets, hours, useful vocabulary, how to transport your goods home, a bibliography, and bargaining tips. While most of my own bargaining efforts have been practiced in Turkey and Egypt, here are some tips that have worked well for me in France, too: ~Walk around first and survey the scene. Identify the vendors you want to come back to, and, if prices are not marked, try to estimate what they are for the items you're interested in. If you don't have any idea what the general price range is, you won't have any idea if you're paying a fair price or not. Even better is learning the prices of what items sell for here in the States before you leave home; then you'll also know how much (or how little) savings are being offered. ~If you do spy an item you're interested in, try not to reveal your interest; act as nonchalant as you possibly can; and remember to be ready to start walking away. ~Dealers typically receive a 20 to 25 percent discount off the displayed prices. I was once walking around the *brocante* in L'Îsle-sur-la-Sorgue with a little notepad, innocently writing down the prices of various *pastis* bottles and glasses I wanted to buy. When I returned to one particular vendor, she assumed I was a dealer because I was taking notes, and automatically dropped the price without my having to ask. This was a lucky break, as I'm sure some vendors will ask to see your business card; but it might be worth a try to pretend. At any rate, this is your clue to begin bargaining at a starting point below at least 25 percent of the asking price and go from there. Also, many dealers carry calculators, with good reason: it can be confusing to negotiate and keep all the conversions straight in your head. So, who knows, if you're carrying one you may be mistaken for a dealer, too. ~It's considered rude to begin serious bargaining if you're not interested in making a purchase. This doesn't mean you should refrain from asking the price on an item, but to then begin naming numbers is an indication to the vendor that you're a serious customer and that a sale will likely be made. ~Politeness goes a long way at the *marché*. Vendors appreciate being treated with respect and don't at all mind answering questions from interested browsers. Strike up a conversation while you're looking at the wares; ask about the vendor's family, or a good local restaurant. Establishing a rapport also shows that you are reasonable, and that you are willing to make a purchase at the right (reasonable) price. ~Occasionally, I feign interest in one particular item, though it's a different item I *really* want. The tactic here is to begin the bargaining process and let the vendor think I'm about to make a deal. Then I pretend to get cold feet and indicate that the price is just too much for me. The vendor thinks all is lost, and at that moment I point to the item I've wanted all along, sigh, and say I'll take that one, naming the lowest price from my previous negotiation. Usually, the vendor will immediately agree to it, as it means a done deal. ~Other times, I will plead poverty and say to the vendor that I had *so* wanted to bring back a gift for my mother from "your beautiful country . . . won't you please reconsider?" This, too, usually works. ~If you're traveling with a companion, you can work together: one of you plays the role of the designated "bad guy," scoffing at each price quoted, while the other plays the role of the demure friend or spouse who hopes to make a purchase but really must have the approval of the "bad guy." ~If you discover a flaw in an item, point it out and use it as a bargaining chip. I do this at home as well, and I have never been unsuccessful at convincing the clerk to take some money off the price. A few times I've bought the display sample—the only one remaining in my size, for example—and wasn't charged the sales tax. ~You'll always get the best price if you pay with cash, and in fact, most vendors only accept cash. I prepare an assortment of paper *francs* and coins in advance so I can always pull them out and indicate that it's all I have. It doesn't seem right to bargain hard for something that's 100 francs and pay for it with a 500-franc note. ~Remember that a deal is supposed to end with both parties satisfied. If, after much back-and-forth, you encounter a vendor who won't budge below a certain price, it's likely that it's not posturing but a way of letting you know that anything lower will no longer be profitable to him or her. If you feel you're stuck and have reached an impasse, try asking the vendor once more, "Is this your very best price?" If he or she has spent a considerable amount of time with you, this is the moment when it would be advantageous to compromise, or all that time will have been wasted. ~Pay attention when a merchant wraps up your purchase—dishonest vendors may try to switch the merchandise. Though this has never happened to me, I read a lot of letters from people who didn't know they were had until they got home. ~If you're a real shopaholic and plan to ship your purchases home, remember that rates are based on cubic measurement, not weight. The shipping minimum is one cubic meter, which translates to about $400 on top of fees for packing, insurance, and U.S. customs. Therefore, make sure the savings you receive at the *marché* are truly significant to justify the shipping home. ~If you're interested in buying antiques—

or making large purchases of any kind—it would be worthwhile to get a copy of the "Know Before You Go" brochure from the U.S. Customs Service. You can write for a free copy (1300 Pennsylvania Avenue, N.W., Washington, D.C. 20229) or view it online at www.customs.ustreas.gov/travel/kbygo.htm (first click on Traveler Information, and then select Know Before You Go). Dull as it may sound, I found this document to be incredibly interesting, and concerning shipping purchases I found the following sections to be of special interest: What You Must Declare, Duty-Free Exemption, $200 Exemption, $400 Exemption, Gifts, Household Effects, Paying Duty, Sending Goods to the United States, Freight Shipments, Duty-Free Shops, and Cultural Artifacts and Cultural Property. ~Useful vocabulary: *une tranche* or *deux tranches* (one slice, two slices); *J'en voudrais trois* (I would like three of them); *la moitié de ça* (half that much); *encore un peu* (a little more); *ça c'est parfait* or *suffit* (that's perfect, sufficient/enough); *une bonne poignée* (a good-sized bunch/handful); *trop cher* (too expensive); *c'est pour offrir* or *c'est un cadeau* (it's a gift) . . . *pouvez-vous l'emballer?* (could you wrap it up?).

Frédéric Mistral and *Le Mistral*

It is impossible to travel throughout Provence without being confronted by the legendary Mistral (the man) and the equally legendary *le Mistral* (the wind). Frédéric Mistral was an illustrious poet (he won the Nobel Prize in 1901) and best-known founder of Le Félibrige movement (Joseph Roumanille and Theodore Aubanel were also well-known members of the group), which aimed to preserve the history, culture, and language of Provence, as well as to campaign for the teaching of Provençal in schools. The group of seven poets who officially founded the literary movement on May 21, 1854 were called the Félibres (*félibre* being a vernacular word meaning "writer"). The Félibres were motivated to unite because the French government (based in Paris, of course) had begun to centralize everything it could, including the use of regional dialects, including Provençal. *Le mistral* (the wind) was described by Stendhal in his *Mémoires d'un Touriste* as "the drawback of all the pleasures to be found in Provence . . . When the mistral reigns in Provence you don't know where to take refuge. It is true that the sun is shining brightly, but a cold, unbearable wind penetrates the best closed rooms and grates on the nerves so that the most dauntless person is unwittingly upset." Laurence Wylie, in his excellent book *Village in the Vaucluse,* notes that the wind, which originates in the Alps, blows at a speed of thirty to fifty miles an hour, and occasionally reaches hurricane speed. An old saying goes that Provence suffers from three scourges: the government, the Durance (when it floods), and the mistral. Many believe that the mistral blows in multiples of three days; while this is an old wives' tale, the mighty wind doesn't blow for just a few hours, and it is especially common during December, February, and March. Wylie also notes that "This cold but dry, sunny wind has left its mark on every aspect of life in the whole region. One sees it not just in the cypress hedges that protect fields and houses (that Van Gogh found so picturesque). The olive trees all bend toward the south. The houses seem to bend southward, too, for they are customarily built so as to present a bleak wall and a long sloping roof to the north. Heavy stones are placed along the edge of the roof to keep the tiles from blowing away."

Monaco

The Principality of Monaco, described by Colette as "a country whose frontiers are only flowers," is sometimes forgotten by visitors to Provence and the Côte d'Azur, perhaps because many people do not realize that it is not a part of France, or because it is perceived to be too wealthy to welcome anyone but millionaires. In fact, the Principality became completely independent of France in 1861, and the Monégasques are happy to welcome visitors with pockets both shallow and deep: Monaco is as affordable as it is affluent. Its territory is only three miles long and only a half mile inland up the side of the mountain, so you can spend a very full day there and feel like you saw practically every inch of it. Some general facts: ~French is the official language, but Italian and English are widely spoken. The traditional Monégasque language is mostly spoken only by nationals who've lived there a long time, although the language is enjoying a renaissance in Monaco schools. ~Of the approximately 30,000 residents, over 83 percent are foreigners. Monégasques number only about 5,000. ~French francs are accepted currency although there are also Monégasque coins in circulation that are of the same value as French coins. ~November 19 is the Monaco National Holiday (and Prince Rainier III's birthday). ~The country code for Monaco is 377.

~The Monaco Tourist Office in the U.S. is located at 565 Fifth Avenue, New York, New York 10017; 800-753-9696 or 212-286-3330; fax: 212-286-9890; www.monaco-tourism.com.

The best way to see Monaco and Monte Carlo is simply to walk around. The tourist office has published a great brochure, with colorful watercolors, called "The Enchanted Holiday Planner," which outlines several itineraries: Old Town Day: Rock of Ages Tour; Nature Day: Flora and Fauna Tour; Day of Creation: Design and Architecture Tour; and Retro Day: History and Tradition Tour. As Michael Jacobs noted in *A Guide to Provence*, Charles Garnier—best known as the designer of the Paris Opera—was not only the most influential architect to work on the Riviera, but his casino and opera house project in Monte Carlo is his most important work here. Jacobs points out that some design elements of the opera house—grand staircases, chandeliers, colored marble, and an obvious passion for massive scale—"are to be found in many of the Riviera's turn-of-the-century hotels, which are well worth a visit even if you cannot afford their suitably exorbitant prices." So in Monaco, you can visit the casino and then walk right next door to the Hôtel de Paris, thus affording yourself the opportunity of seeing two of the most beautiful examples of Belle Epoque architecture on the entire French coast-line. (Dress accordingly, however. While finery is not required, men will not be admitted to the casino at night without a jacket and tie; during the day, visitors should wear nice—preferably long—shorts or slacks, or a dress or skirt, and no tank tops or halter tops.)

As Monaco is built into the side of the Alps, there are a number of public ele-vator lifts *(ascenseur public)* which connect some streets and boulevards with var-ious neighborhoods and sites throughout the Principality (readers who've been to Lisbon may recall seeing a few of these in that city, too). These lifts are clearly marked on the "Getting There and Getting About" brochure from the Monaco tourist office; and on the tourist office's *plan* (map) of Monaco, there is a little insert of every driver's dream: a map showing where the public parking lots are located. This is a feature I'm always hoping some clever writer will include in guidebooks, but no one ever does.

Money

The best way to travel is with a combination of local cash, American Express trav-eler's checks (other types are not universally accepted), and credit cards. If you have all three, you will *never* have a problem, but note that you should not rely on wide acceptance of credit cards in the more remote areas of Provence. How you divide these up depends on how long you'll be traveling and on what day of the week you arrive—banks, which of course offer the best exchange rate, aren't generally open on the weekends and most aren't open all day during the week. If you rely solely on your ATM card and encounter a problem, you can't fix it until the banks reopen on Monday (often not until the afternoon). Savvy travelers always arrive with some local currency in their possession (I feel most comfortable with $50 to $100). While the rates of exchange and fees charged obviously vary, it is far more important not to arrive empty-handed—we are, after all, talking about a small sum of money, and it will be money well spent when you get off the plane with the ability to quickly make your way to wherever you're going. After a long flight, who wants to then exchange money, especially while looking after luggage and/or children? And keep in mind that there are very often long lines at the exchange counters and cash machines, and that cash machines are sometimes out of order or out of cash. (Once, I even had the admittedly unusual experience of going directly to a large bank in a capital city only to find a posted sign stating that the bank was closed because it had *run out of money!*). Smart travelers arrive prepared to pay for transportation, tips, snacks, personal items, or unanticipated expenses. Some pointers: ~Overseas ATMs may limit the number of daily transactions you can make, as well as place a ceiling on the total amount you can withdraw. Since you are charged a surcharge each time you use the ATM, keep your transactions to a minimum: make larger, fewer withdrawals. Call your bank and inquire about the exact fees for withdrawals, and ask if there is an additional fee for overseas transactions (there shouldn't be, but ask anyway). Also ask if you can withdraw money from both your checking and savings accounts or from only one, and if you can transfer money between accounts. ~Make sure your ATM password is compatible with French ATMs (if you have too many digits, you'll have to change it), and if, like me, you have memorized your password as a series of letters rather than numbers, write down the numerical equivalent before you leave. Most European cash machines do not display letters, and even if they did, they do not always appear in the same sequence as we know it in the U.S. ~Check the business section of your local daily newspaper for current exchange rates, or check the Web sites www.xe.net and www.oanda.com. ~Though I think this is a bit anal-retentive, even for me, it's possible to view in advance the exact street locations of ATM machines in France online. To see where Plus systems are, check out www.visa.com; for the Cirrus network, go to www.mastercard.com/atm. Once in, select ATM Locator, and you'll be given an opportunity to select a country, city, street address, and postal code (it's not essential to provide the postal code, but for best results, enter cross streets and a city). I found over twenty locations each for Avignon, Nice, Aix, Marseille, and Antibes, just under twenty for Orange, and five for St.-Tropez. ~If you're too busy to get local currency in advance, call International Currency Express and request its Currency Rush mail-order service (888-278-6628; request either UPS second-day or overnight service). With offices in Los Angeles and Washington, D.C., the company offers good rates. Chase Manhattan Bank also offers an on-line service called "Currency to Go" (www.currency-to-go.com), which promises overnight foreign currency delivery, even if you're not a Chase customer. Neither of these services is more economical than getting the currency yourself from a bank, but they come in handy when you're too busy to do otherwise. ~American Express traveler's cheques can also be purchased from AAA. Members may purchase either traditional AmEx traveler's cheques or Cheques for Two in denominations of $20, $50, and $100, and are fee-free (there is usually a 1 percent service fee). The cheques can be purchased at any AAA branch office or by mail (although by mail there is a $500 minimum and a $3,000 maximum; also, allow for first-class mail delivery within fourteen business days). AAA members who also hold a Visa card can purchase traveler's checks by telephone. The checks are delivered to your home and there is no transaction fee or postage, shipping, or handling charges. Additionally, AAA also offers foreign traveler's checks—in French francs, Canadian dollars, Swiss francs, deutsche marks, pounds sterling, and Japanese yen—at competitive exchange rates with no service fee. Call 800-374-1258 for more information and to find out the nearest AAA office to you. ~Refrain from wearing one of those ubiquitous waist bags, or, as my friend Carl says, "Make our country proud and don't wear one of those fanny packs!" A tourist plus fanny pack equals magnet for pickpockets. I know of more people who've had valuables stolen from those ridiculous pouches than I can count. Keep large bills, credit cards, and passport hidden from view in a money belt worn under your clothes, in a pouch that hangs from your neck, or in an interior coat or blazer pocket. And for the person who balks at the suggestion of a money belt in a fine restaurant, it is a simple matter to excuse yourself from the table, head for the WC, and retrieve your money in the privacy of a stall. It is doubtful you'll be robbed walking from the bathroom back to your table. ~If possible, don't keep everything in the same place, and keep a separate piece of paper with telephone numbers of companies to contact in case of emergency. ~Useful vocabulary: *des pièces* (coins); *d'argent* (money); *billets* (bank notes); *chèques de voyages* (traveler's checks).

Movies

Plan a meal from one or more of the cookbooks mentioned in the *Saveurs Provençaux bibliothèque* and invite some friends and family over for dinner and a movie. Some suggestions: *To Catch a Thief, The French Connection II, Lacombe Lucien* by Louis Malle, and the films of Marcel Pagnol: *Manon des Sources, Jean de Florette, La Gloire de Mon Père, Le Chateau de Ma Mère,* and *Fanny*. And while you're cooking, get in the mood by listening to some appropriate music: *Music, Provence & Cézanne* (Art in Concert 113/Philadelphia Museum of Art, 1996; includes the works of Jacques Offenbach, Charles Gounod, Aristide Bruant, Wagner, Debussy, Gabriel Fauré, etc.); *A Table in Provence: Authentic Sounds of the South of France in Twenty-four Vintage Recordings* (EMI); and *A Mediterranean Odyssey* (Putumayo World Music; three of the twelve selections are from France) are all great choices that will have you ready to say *à votre santé!* (to your health/cheers!) when your guests arrive.

P

Packing

Most people, whether they travel for business or pleasure, view packing as a stressful chore. It doesn't have to be, and a great book filled with excellent suggestions and tips is *Fodor's How to Pack: Experts Share Their Secrets* (Laurel Cardone, Fodor's Travel Publications, 1997). You might think it silly to consult a book on how to pack a suitcase, but this is eminently practical and worthwhile. Cardone is a travel journalist who's on the road a lot, and she meets a lot of fellow travelers with plenty of packing wisdom to share. How to buy luggage, how to fill almost any suitcase, how to fold nearly crease-free, the right wardrobe for the right trip, and how to pack for the way back home are all thoroughly covered. Also, some of the best tips from the book are compiled in *Fodor's to Go: How to Pack,* a credit card–size fold-out magnet. Some pointers that work for me include: ~Select clothing that isn't prone to wrinkling, like cotton and wool knits; when I *am* concerned about limiting wrinkles, I lay out a large plastic dry-cleaning bag, place the garment on top of it, place *another* bag on top of that, and fold the item up between the two bags—the key here is that the plastic must be layered in with the clothing, otherwise it doesn't really work. ~If I'm packing items with buttons, I button them up before I fold them—the same with zippers and snaps. ~If I'm carrying a bag with more than one separate compartment, I use one for shoes; otherwise, I put shoes at the bottom (or back) of the bag opposite the handle so they'll remain there while I'm carrying the bag. ~Transfer shampoo and lotions to plastic travel-size bottles, which can be purchased at pharmacies, and then put these inside a sealed plastic bag to prevent against leaks (the plastic bag is then also useful for storing a wet bathing suit). ~Don't skimp on underwear—it's lightweight, takes up next to no room in your bag, and it's never a mistake to have more than you think you need. ~Belts can be either rolled up and stuffed into shoes or fastened together along the inside edge of your suitcase. ~Ties should be rolled, not folded, and also stuffed into shoes or pockets. ~Some handy things to bring along that are often overlooked: a pocket flashlight for looking into ill-lit corners of old buildings, reading in bed at night (the lights are often not bright enough), and for navigating the dark hallways of hotels at night (the light is usually on a timer, and always runs out before you've made it to either end of the hallway); binoculars, for looking up at architectural details; small travel umbrella; penknife/corkscrew; if I'm camping, plastic shoes—referred to in the U.S. as "jellies," which the French have been wearing on some of their rocky *plages* (beaches) for years and years—for campground showers; an empty, lightweight duffel bag, which I fold up and pack and then use as a carry-on bag for gifts and breakable items on the way home; copies of any current prescriptions in case I need to have one refilled; photocopies of my passport and airline tickets (which should also be left with someone at home).

Parler Pointu

A phrase Lawrence Durrell mentions in *Caesar's Vast Ghost,* which translates as "speaking pointed," which is how the natives of Provence show their distaste for the Paris accent.

Passports

For last-minute crises, it *is* possible to obtain a new passport, renew an old one, or get necessary visas (not required for France). Two companies that can meet the challenge: Travisa (2122 P Street, N.W., Washington, D.C., 20037; 800-222-2589) and Express Visa Service, Inc. (353 Lexington Avenue, Suite 1200, New York, New York 10016; 212-679-5650; fax: -4691).

Periodicals

Following are some newsletters and periodicals, many of which are not available at newsstands, that you may want to consider subscribing to in advance of your trip—or upon your return if you decide you want to keep up with goings on in France and/or Provence:

La Belle France: Until I began my subscription, I was rather put off by the subtitle, "The Sophisticated Guide to France." But this monthly, eight-page newsletter (with holes for a three-ring binder) is not stuffy and always includes some useful tips. It's most helpful to those who want critical reviews of hotels and restaurants, which are described and rated. Published by Travel Guide Publications, P.O. Box 3485, Charlottesville, Virginia 22903; 800-225-7825 / 804-977-4885; e-mail: labelle@golftravelguide.com.

FRANCE Magazine: This fine quarterly magazine is possibly the most eagerly awaited item in my mailbox. It's published by La Maison Française at the Embassy of France in Washington, D.C., and is only available by subscription in the U.S. The collection of feature articles in each issue is timely, fascinating, and diverse. Issue No. 46, summer 1998, was a special regional issue on Provence (single copies may still be available). There is no fee to subscribe, but all requests must be made in writing to 4101 Reservoir Road, N.W., Washington, D.C., 20007-2182. For more information: 202-944-6069; fax: -6072.

France on Your Own: A beautifully illustrated—with pen-and-ink drawings—quarterly newsletter for independent travelers to France. Each issue is approximately sixteen pages in length and includes detailed planning advice and practical information as well as reviews of accommodations and feature articles written by residents of or frequent visitors to France. A particular region is also highlighted in each issue; a feature I particularly liked in its recent profile of Languedeoc-Roussillon was a driving route through the Hérault. To subscribe, contact Cold Spring Press, P.O. Box 26098, San Diego, California 92196-0098; www.franceonyourown.com.

France Today: An oversized bimonthly jammed with lots of articles, book and music reviews, trends, travel tips, and stories. One of my favorite columns is "What the French Are Obsessing About," and the classifieds alone are worth reading for the rental listings. Published by France Press, 105 Divisadero, San Francisco, California 94115; 415-921-5100; fax: -0213; www.france-press.com.

France-USA Contacts (FUSAC): More of a directory than a periodical, this is the bible for anglophones who are planning to live, work, or study in France—but it's also incredibly useful for shorter-term visitors. FUSAC contains job and housing listings, classified ads for things to buy and sell, holiday travel information, apartment rentals, to name just a few. Now in its twelfth year, FUSAC is published in France in English and French, and subscribers can choose either first-class ($10) or third-class ($7) postage. Contact *FUSAC* at P.O. Box 115, Cooper Station, New York 10276; 212-929-2929.

Journal Français: For those who read French—or want to improve their French—this is perhaps the best and most pleasant way to feel connected with all that's happening in France. The *Journal* is a monthly covering all the topics of a daily newspaper—politics, business, travel, features, etc. Published by France Press, 1051 Divisadero, San Francisco, California 94115; 415-921-5100; fax: -0213; www.francepress.com.

Maisons Côté Sud: This bimonthly magazine, which is one of my favorite periodicals, is devoted to southern latitudes around the world, but is mainly the leading magazine of Mediterranean culture. The editorial staff is based in Mougins and it doesn't miss a beat on cultural, design, or decorating topics. The text is in French and it's the sort of writing you only dream about, thoroughly transporting readers to the table set under the olive trees or the sleeping couch by the sea. In 1995, an English-language edition entitled *The Very Best of Provence* was published. This issue featured a selection of translated articles from the magazine accompanied by staff recommendations of books and resources. To subscribe, contact Express Mag, 8155 Larrey Anjou, Quebec, H1J 2L5, Canada; 800-363-1310; www.expressmag.com.

Terre Provençale: This monthly magazine is published in French, but even those who do not know the language may find it useful for the photographs and recommendations (it's not difficult, after all, to figure out the names of restaurants, hotels, beaches, and towns). *Terre Provençale* is available at some of the bigger U.S. newsstands or you can subscribe by contacting the magazine directly: Editions Freeway, Abonnements BP 271, 63008, Clermont-Ferrand, cedex 1, France.

Transitions Abroad: The Magazine of International Travel and Life: Though not specific to Provence or France, this bimonthly magazine features the latest information on traveling, learning, living, and working overseas. It's an unbeatable resource for learning about study and work opportunities, volunteering, ecotourism, teaching English, internships, traveling independently or with a group, etc. Ann Waigand, who for many years published *The Educated Traveler* newsletter, now writes a column of the same name for *Transitions Abroad,* focusing on special interest tours and educational programs. *Transitions Abroad* also publishes two useful paperbacks, *Alternative Travel Directory: The Complete Guide to Traveling, Studying & Living Overseas* and *Work Abroad: The Complete Guide to Finding a Job Overseas.* For magazine subscriptions: P.O. Box 3000, Denville, New Jersey, 07834-9768; 800-293-0373. For book inquiries: 413-256-3414. www.TransitionsAbroad.com.

Photography

I would rather have one great photo of a place than a dozen mediocre shots, so I like to flip through photography books for ideas and suggestions on maximizing my picture-taking efforts. Some books I've particularly enjoyed include: *The Traveler's Eye: A Guide to Still and Video Travel Photography* (Lisl Dennis, Clarkson Potter, 1996). Dennis, who began her career in photography at *The Boston Globe*, writes the "Traveler's Eye" column for *Outdoor Photographer*. I like her sensitive approach to travel photography and find her images and suggestions in this book inspiring. After chapters covering such topics as travel photojournalism, shooting special events, and landscape photography, she provides an especially useful chapter on technical considerations, with advice on equipment, film, packing, the ethics of tipping, and outsmarting airport X-ray machines. *Focus on Travel: Photographing Memorable Pictures of Journeys to New Places* (text by Anne Millman and Allen Rokach, photographs by Allen Rokach, Abbeville Press, 1992). More of a tome than *The Traveler's Eye* although this doesn't cover video cameras. The authors offer much more information on lenses, filters, films, and accessories, and there are separate chapters on photographing architecture, shooting subjects in action, and taking pictures in a variety of weather conditions. The appendix covers selecting and preparing your photos after the trip, fill-in flash guidelines, a color correction chart, and a page-by-page reference to all the photos in the book. *Kodak Guide to Shooting Great Travel Pictures: Easy Tips and Foolproof Ideas from the Pros* (Jeff Wignall, Fodor's Travel Publications, 2000). Unlike the books above, which should be consulted before you go, this is a very handy paperback good for bringing along as a reference. Seven chapters present more than 250 color photos, ninety expert tips, and specific photographic challenges—such as city vistas, digital photography, close-ups of faces, mountain scenery, motion, lights at night, silhouettes, and black-and-white images—and each is dealt with on one page with accompanying photos. It's important to note that this guide is meant for experienced *and* point-and-shoot photographers, and many of the images featured in the book are from the Eastman Kodak archives, a great number of which were taken by amateurs. The final chapter is devoted to creating a travel journal.

La Plage (the Beach)

There are more than 270 miles of coast between Marseille and the Italian border, so beach lovers will have no shortage of places to greet the sea. Most Côte d'Azur beaches from Menton to Antibes are made of round, smooth, gray or black rocks and pebbles. Unlikely as it may seem, you really can spread out a towel and, by adjusting the rocks just so, lie or sit in comfort. Sandy beaches are found west of Nice (the largest and most beautiful is Plage de Pampelonne in St.-Tropez), but whether a *plage* is rocky or sandy, most are operated by a *plagiste*, who rents a particular section of beach from the city or town, and who in turn rents you an umbrella and/or chair. Typically, each individual strip of beach operated by a *pla-*

giste has its own name, displayed with bright banners. Some of these are quite luxurious (especially the beaches of the Alpes-Maritimes), complete with changing cabins, swimming pools for kids, and fitness clubs. *Plagistes* also rent out boats, water skis, and windsurfing boards, and operate snack bars and restaurants. By law, a section of each beach must remain free to the public, and if you have situated yourself on a free section, you are welcome to patronize the food concessions, but you can't sit on the pay beach with your snack unless you rent an umbrella. It is still the custom for French women (and many European women in general) to go topless at the beach, and my only advice for American women who choose to do the same is to be vigilant about applying enough sunscreen in the right places. There are a few places where nude sunbathing is permitted, the most famous being the Île du Levant, an island off the coast of Hyères. The beaches of the Var (the western region which includes Hyères) are less developed (with fewer *plagistes*) than those of the Alpes-Maritimes, and sometimes vineyards come right down to the sea. Although the Mediterranean is no longer the healthy and bountiful sea it once was, it is still gorgeous, displaying colors ranging from Caribbean-like turquoise to dark indigo. Water quality is measured weekly (daily in some places) during high season, and is reported in local newspapers and posted at the beaches and the *hôtel de ville* (city hall).

R

Real Estate

If you find Provence and the south *douce* (sweet) and want to stay for the rest of your life, or visit a few times a year, some good sources to consult are *Buying a Home in France* (David Hampshire, Survival Books, London), *Living and Working in France: A Survival Handbook* (also by David Hampshire and published by Survival), *The Grown-Up's Guide to Living in France* (Roseanne Knorr, Ten Speed Press, 2000), and *Living, Studying, and Working in France: Everything You Need to Know to Fulfill Your Dreams of Living Abroad* (Saskia Reilly and Lorin David Kalisky, Owl Books, 1999). Other good sources include periodicals, including *New Riviera Côte D'Azur* (found at larger newsstands in the U.S., this looks like a typical magazine but in fact is composed nearly entirely of ads for houses to buy; 66 route de Grenoble, Nice Leader—Hermes—BP3024, 06201 Nice, Cedex 3, France; e-mail: newriviera@smc-france.com); *France-USA Contacts (FUSAC), Maisons Côté Sud, France Today* (see Periodicals for descriptions on these three); and *Living France: The Monthly Guide to France and French Lifestyle* (a British monthly with a section called "The Property Pages," as well as tons of classified ads; available at larger newsstands or call 011.44.01778.391134 in the U.K.). Take note, however, of an important point that author Bill Bryson emphasized in an excellent piece he wrote for *National Geographic* (September 1995). Bryson explained that the intoxicating landscape of Provence entices a great number of *étrangers* (foreigners) to the region. Many of them, while on vacation, see a house for sale, in brilliant sunshine, and the price seems reasonable compared with where they're from, so they buy it, quit their jobs, and move in. Then winter arrives, and the mistral, and suddenly the cute stone house is cold, drafty, and not at all the adorable abode they thought they were buying. It turns out that almost without exception, *the house faces north*, into the wind, and receives no winter sun. All the locals know that north-facing houses are owned by foreigners who bought them in good weather, so *caveat emptor!*

S

Single Travelers
Those traveling alone (not necessarily looking for romance) might be interested in reading *Traveling Solo: Advice and Ideas for More Than 250 Great Vacations* (Eleanor Berman, Globe Pequot Press, 1997). Berman offers the names of tour operators for different age groups and different types of trips and asks all the right questions in determining if a proposed vacation is right for you. ~Female *and* male solo travelers should beware of revealing too many personal details about your travels. If you admit that you're traveling for an indefinite period of time, for example, the perception is that you are probably carrying a lot of money. I met an Australian man who had the bulk of his money stolen from a youth-hostel safe, and he was certain it was taken by a fellow hosteler he had befriended, but who had disappeared by the time the discovery was made.

Société Nationale des Chemins de Fer—SNCF (Trains)
The French train network—like train networks in most other European countries—is quite extensive, and there are few corners of France one can't reach by train. The SNCF offers a bewildering array of reduced-fare options (in addition to rail passes), so be sure to inquire as it's likely one will apply to you. Some of these discounts include one for seniors (aged sixty and over, known as *troisième age;* the two types of tickets are *carte vermeil quatre temps*—good for four trips—and the *carte vermeil plein temps*—good for unlimited travel); one for children and young adults twelve to twenty-five; one for children under four, and if you're traveling with one child or more, you automatically qualify for a discount; and one for two people traveling together on a round-trip journey (this is known as a *découverte*). A discount is also offered for a certain number of total miles traveled. Days and times of travel are broken down into color-coded price categories: *jour bleu, jour blanc,* and *jour rouge,* which are far too complex to go into here, but they make (somewhat) more sense when you look at the schedule in person. Discounts are, of

course, offered for traveling pets, and travel with a car is possible on some lines. In addition to the popular Eurailpass, rail pass options within France include France Railpass, France Saverpass, France Rail 'n Drive, and France Youthpass. Inquire at Maison de la France offices here in the U.S. about the fares and benefits of these or contact Rail Europe Group (800-4-EURAIL; www.raileurope.com) or Budget Europe Travel Service (BETS; 2557 Meade Court, Ann Arbor, Michigan 48105; 800-441-2387 or 734-668-0529; www.budgeteuropetravel.com). BETS is a wonderful, extremely helpful organization that publishes the annual *European Planning & Rail Guide* (a *great* resource, with lots of tips on rail travel) as well as *Budget Europe Magazine*. Travelers can purchase rail passes directly from BETS, which has been selling European rail passes for over twenty years. Included with your order is a timetable, rail map, and free shipping by certified mail. ~The Train à Grande Vitesse (TGV) now makes the trip from Paris to Avignon in four hours, and there are different fares for first and second class, and round-trip and weekend rates. ~One of the most spectacular train journeys in Provence, if not the world, is the ninety-mile ride from Nice to Digne-les-Bains. The line was completed around 1920 and it runs four times a day in both directions, allowing for travelers to make the trip in one day or spend the night and return to Nice in the morning. The journey is approximately three hours and makes about twenty-one stops, crossing over a dozen viaducts and bridges. Passengers travel through stunning scenery, passing vineyards, olive groves, cliff-top villages, gorges, rivers, valleys, and—if it's August—glorious, purple lavender fields. This trip is a must-do at any time of year, but August is worth waiting for not just for the fields of lavender but for the lavender harvest and festivities. The lavender grown at this elevation is the last in Provence to be harvested, and the celebrations are legendary. During the warmer months of the year, passengers can ride a length of the line called the Train des Pignes, reportedly named because the train crew used to stop along the route and collect pinecones for the pine nuts *(pignes)*. This train runs between Puget-Théniers and Annot and riders sit in cars dating from the turn of the twentieth century. The entire line is operated by the SNCF, and you can inquire at the tourist office for the exact schedule or call the SNCF office at 04.97.03.80.87. ~Remember that any ticket imprinted with the words *à composter* must be validated before you board the train. This is done by inserting the ticket in one of the orange machines at the entrance to the platforms, and your ticket will either be stamped with the date or punched with a hole. If you don't validate, you may be fined once on board. As with train travel elsewhere, if you purchase your ticket on board instead of at the ticket office, you'll pay a surcharge. ~Useful vocabulary: *billet* (ticket); *aller simple* (one-way ticket); *aller et retour* (round-trip); *quai* (platform); *voie* (track; note that *quai* and *voie* are sometimes used interchangeably, as it's possible to have two tracks on either side of a platform); *consigne des bagages* (left-luggage locker); *guichet* (ticket office or window); *horaire* (timetable); *réservation* or *location* (a reservation); *fumant* (smoking); *défense de fumer* (no smoking); *la fenêtre* (window).

Le Soleil

The sun is strong around the Mediterranean, in winter as well as summer. Even if you will not be partaking in hiking, biking, or sunbathing at the beach, bring some protective lotion and use it—liberally. Many people do not realize that for sunscreen to work, you have to apply it copiously, about thirty minutes *before* you go into the sun. Some doctors recommend applying sunscreen even if you're just running errands around town; this would apply to sight-seeing and visiting outdoor markets as well. Women who wear makeup should consider selecting a brand with UV (ultraviolet) protection, and *everyone* should note that by *not* using protective lotion you are exposing your skin to a lot of irreversible damage, even if you don't develop a sunburn. According to recent reports, skin cancer rates are on the rise around the world, not to mention that overexposure to the sun is dangerous to your eyes, with the potential of causing the development of cataracts. Lotions with the ingredient known as Parsol 1789 (avobenzone) have recently been touted as offering the best UV protection on the market. However, my searches have not revealed many sunscreens that have it, and I admit that on the three occasions I used one with Parsol I developed a red, bumpy rash (other people I know did not). It's probably more important to be vigilant with whatever product you use, and mindful of the benefits of wearing a hat and good sunglasses. Kiehl's in New York (1-800-KIEHLS-1) makes ultra-moisturizing eye sticks with SPF 35—one for adults and one for children—that are great for around the eyes, obviously, but also for ears and the tip of your nose. Remember: There is no such thing as a healthy tan.

Stendhal Syndrome

Named for the sick, physical feeling that afflicted French novelist Stendhal after he visited Santa Croce in Florence, this syndrome is synonymous with being completely overwhelmed by your surroundings (my translation: seeing and doing way too much). Visitors to the south of France who arrive with too long a list of mustsees are prime candidates for the syndrome. My advice is to organize your days, factor in how long it takes to get from place to place, and see only what you want. Go forth with confidence, feel good about the way you spend your days, and do not feel guilty about missing a particular site or event. There will be no quiz.

Storage

If you plan on traveling around France (or beyond) for extended periods of time (say, a month or longer) and you want to store some baggage or other belongings, you should first investigate the locker facilities *(consigne automatique)* at SNCF train stations. A locker at one of the stations, if you're traveling by train, may prove to be the ideal storage location. Otherwise, check with the tourist office and ask for recommendations of storage companies. ~Note that in the event there is any terrorist activity in France—even as far away as Paris—locker facilities are immediately declared off-limits.

Studying in Provence

There are dozens of American colleges and universities that sponsor study-abroad programs in the south of France. I am partial to those which have had a presence there for a long time, but no matter which school you decide on, my advice is to select a program that allows you to stay a year, or even longer. And if you have to change your major to go, do it—you won't regret it! Alternatively, investigate attending a French college or university, and remember that studying abroad isn't limited to studying the language—courses are also offered in the fine arts, photography, painting, business, literature, etc.; nor is study abroad limited to full-time students or by one's age—plenty of programs welcome adults, and plenty of adults attend. *The* guide to get is the *Directory of French Schools and Universities,* by Michael Giammarella (EMI International, P.O. Box 640713, Oakland Gardens, New York 11364-0713; 718-631-0096; fax: -0316). This annual guide, $19.95 plus $3 for first-class shipping, details a wide variety of programs—not just language programs—at over sixty schools in France, about thirty of which are in the Provence/Côte d'Azur/Monaco region (additionally, the guide features schools in the broader Francophone world, including Quebec, Switzerland, the Caribbean, etc.). Giammarella handles the bookings for the programs, and also publishes directories for Spain and Italy. ~A good source for both French- and American-sponsored study-abroad programs in France is the annual travel/study guide of *France Today.* This guide usually appears in February or March and is inserted into issues of *France Today* and the *Journal Français,* or can be purchased separately ($5.50 plus postage) by fax (415-921-0213) or e-mail (fpress@francepress.com). ~Other organizations that offer programs and classes in the south include Alpha. B Institut Linguistique (2 rue d'Angleterre, 06000, Nice; U.S. contact: Michael Giammarella—see EMI International above. Courses include continuous, intensive, combination, individual, and express French, plus an A Level Course, which is designed for high school students with four to six years of French. Classes are held in a lovely mansion in the heart of Nice, and in summer, an additional center is located in Cimiez, near the Matisse and Chagall museums); Vacances-Jeunesse (60 East 42nd Street, PMB 1166, New York, New York 10165; 212-370-7981; fax: 986-8731; e-mail: Demontcorp@compuserve.com. In addition to courses in Paris, Nantes, Poitiers, and Toulouse, Vacances-Jeunesse, in its seventeenth year, offers a private language program in Nice for adults over eighteen. Beginner, intermediate, and advanced levels are offered, and accommodations are in residences and hotels); Centre Mediterraneen d'Études Françaises (Chemin des Oliviers, F-06320 Cap d'Ail; U.S. contact: Michael Giammarella—see EMI above. This international summer program for teenagers aged thirteen to seventeen celebrated its fiftieth year in 2000. The center is on a hillside one km from Monte Carlo, and cultural events are held in the amphitheater decorated by Jean Cocteau. The program combines language classes with sporting, cultural, and recreational activities); and IS Aix-en-Provence (9 cours des Arts et Metiers, 13100 Aix-en-Provence; U.S. contact: Michael Giammarella—see EMI above. IS, an international language school specializing in teaching French to foreigners, is registered by the local authorities as a "private establishment of superior learning." IS was established in 1972 and every year welcomes over 1,000 students from twenty-five countries. Four courses are offered: Français General, Français General Intensif, Français General Trimestriel, and Découverte de la Provence, a two-week program combining language with a guided tour of the region and its culture, including a cooking class, wine-tasting, and cultural lectures). ~Remember, too, that the Maison de la France offices here in the States have numerous brochures on language and cultural programs in France.

T

Telephones

Remember that France is six hours ahead of Eastern Standard Time, seven ahead of Central, eight ahead of Mountain, and nine ahead of Pacific. To call France from the U.S., dial 011 + 33 + eight-digit local number (011 = the overseas line, 33 = country code for France, and the local number includes the appropriate provincial and/or city code). The provincial code for Provence is 4. Note that when calling any city or town in France from the U.S. you omit the initial 0 from the local number. When dialing a number from within Provence or France, you must include the 0, and all phone numbers in this book include the 0 because there may be many opportunities when travelers want to place calls after they've arrived in Provence. To call the U.S. from France, dial 00 + 1 + area code + number. Within France, to reach French directory assistance, dial 12. To dial U.S. directory assistance, dial 001 + area code + 555-1212. To reach an English-speaking operator, dial 1933. For tourist information, dial 110. In an emergency (the equivalent of 911 in the U.S.), dial 113. ~Everyone knows that making calls from your hotel room is expensive. Even if some hotels don't exactly gouge you, all of them charge significantly more than it would cost for you to place the call by any other method. AT&T, Sprint, and MCI all offer access numbers which automatically connect you with a U.S. dial tone. (Hotels still usually charge you even for this, but at least they can't charge you for the length of the call.) You enter the number you're calling, followed by your personal i.d. number, and the call is then billed to your home address and appears on your regular phone bill. These access numbers can be obtained by calling the companies directly or viewing their Web sites (AT&T = 800-CALL-ATT; www.att.com; Sprint = 800-877-4646; www.sprint.com; and MCI = 800-444-3333; www.mci.com). Frequent international business travelers (and those with family or friends overseas) may want to investigate other options offered by Sprint, MCI, and other long-distance services; some monthly plans offer low rates that are appealing to those who regularly make overseas calls. ~Remember that almost all public phones in France no longer accept *jetons* (tokens). *La télécarte* (phone card) is now the way of the future and is the most affordable method for making overseas calls (you can also use a *télécarte* to connect with an AT&T operator). There are two types: *télécarte* (typically for making calls in France in either 50 or 120 units) and *télécarte international* (for making calls abroad, in 60 or 120 units). *Télécartes* can be purchased at post offices, train stations, FNAC stores, and some newsstands and *tabacs* (tobacconist shops). The only catch is that you can't get reimbursed for unused units on the card, so try to purchase the *carte* you're sure you'll use. ~If you'd like a *télécarte* before touching French soil, you can order one from Marketing Challenges (10 East 21st Street, New York, New York 10010; 212-529-9069; fax: -4838; www.ticketsto.com). ~You can also place calls at main branches of the post office, where there are individual cabins and you pay after you make the call. Inquire at the tourist office about the least expensive times of day to call, which are usually after 7:00 P.M. during the week, after noon on Saturday, and all day Sunday. ~Useful vocabulary: *annuaire* (telephone directory); *un coup de téléphone* (a telephone call); *ne quittez pas* (hold on, don't hang up); *téléphoner en PCV* (reverse-charge or collect call).

Theft

Whether of the pickpocket variety or something more serious, theft can happen anywhere, in the finest neighborhoods, at the *marché,* in a park, on a street corner. Petty theft is common in the south of France, and travelers may encounter Gypsies who attempt to pick your pockets. They're adept at it, too—no pocket, snap, buckle, or zipper is too difficult for them. (As an aside, read *Bury Me Standing: The Gypsies and Their Journey,* by Isabel Fonseca—Knopf, 1995, hardcover; Vintage, 1996, paperback—for a thoroughly fascinating account of Gypsy life.) It bears repeating not to wear a waist pack, which is nothing but a neon magnet for thieves. I read about a lot of incidences which could so easily have been avoided. In 1998, I read a lengthy piece in the travel section of *The Philadelphia Inquirer* about a husband and wife traveling in France who had a pouch with all their valuables in it stolen. What made this story remarkable was that they were shocked the pouch was stolen. *I* was shocked reading their tale because they seemed to think it was a good idea to *strap their pouch under the driver's seat of their rental car.* This couple had apparently traveled all over Europe and North America every year for twelve years, so they weren't exactly novices. I think it's a miracle, however, that they hadn't been robbed earlier. ~Some pointers: rental cars are easily identified by their license plates and other markings, which may not be so obvious to you and me but signify pay dirt to thieves. Do not leave *anything* in the car, even if you're parking it in a secure garage. My husband and I strictly follow one rule when we rent a car, which is that we never even put items in the trunk unless we're immediately getting in the car and driving away, as anyone watching us will then know there's something of value there. Also, hatchback-type cars are good to rent because you can back in to spots against walls or trees, making it impossible to open the trunk. ~Do not leave your passport, money, credit cards, important documents, or expensive camera equipment in your room (yes, American passports are still very much a hot commodity). The hotel safe? If the letters I read are any indication, hotel safes— whether in your room or in the main office—are only slightly more reliable than leaving your belongings out in plain view. Sometimes I hear about valuable jewelry being taken from a hotel safe, which I find baffling, as there really is only one safe place for valuable jewelry: your home. No occasion, meeting, or celebration, no matter how important or festive, requires bringing valuable jewelry. I happen to also find it offensive to display such wealth. ~Pickpockets employ a number of tactics to prey on unaware travelers. Even if you travel often, live in a big city, and think you're savvy, professional thieves can usually pick you out immediately (and they'll also identify you as American if you're wearing the trademark sneakers and fanny pack). Beware the breast-feeding mother who begs you for money (while her other children surround you looking for a way into your pockets), the arguing couple who make a scene (while their accomplices work the crowd of onlookers), the tap on your shoulder at the baggage security checkpoint (when you turn around, someone's made off with your bags after they've passed through the X-ray machine) . . . anything at all that looks or feels like a set-up. For a look at some common tricks, you might want to see "Traveler Beware!" a video directed by an experienced undercover cop, Kevin Coffey. This is a real eye-opening program exposing all the scams used to target business and holiday travelers. Coffey was founder of the Airport Crimes Detail and investigated literally thousands of crimes against tourists. He's been a guest on *Oprah* and *20/20,* and has been featured in *The Wall Street Journal* and *USA Today.* The seventy-minute video is available from Penton Overseas, Inc. (800-748-5804; e-mail: info@pentonoverseas.com) and is $14.95. ~If, despite your best efforts, your valuables are stolen, go to the local police. You'll have to fill out an official police report, but this helps later when you need to prove you were really robbed, and reporting thefts to the police alerts them that there is a persistent problem. You will also need to call your credit card companies (which is why you have written down these numbers in a separate place), make a trip to the American Express office if you've purchased traveler's checks, and go to the U.S. embassy to replace your passport.

Tipping

Tipping in France is not the mystery some people perceive it to be. At most restaurants, *cafés,* and other types of eateries, the tip—known as *service compris*—is included in the total. You'll see this amount (usually about 15 percent) as a line item on your receipt. It is common to round up the bill, leaving anywhere from one to twenty francs; however, you are not obligated to do so. If you stand at the counter in a café, a tip is not typically included in the bill, so you should leave some change. If you're at a bar and end up in a deep conversation about vintages or fine spirits with the bartender, you might want to leave an extra ten francs. (At fancy hotel bars, however, it's expected to leave a little more, about fifteen to twenty francs.) If you're in a three-star restaurant and the *sommelier* has chosen a special wine for you, it's considered appropriate to give him or her 10 percent of the price of the bottle. If the *maître d'hôtel* has been especially attentive, give him or her about twenty francs. If you receive exceptional service at any establishment, or you want to return and be remembered, you should of course leave a larger tip. Other tipping guidelines: taxis—10 percent; WC attendants—one franc; cloakroom attendants—five francs per coat; tour guides—five francs, or a little more if they've given an exceptional or very long tour; porters—five francs per bag; hotel doormen who call you a cab—ten francs; parking attendants who fetch your car—ten francs; concierges—twenty-five francs per day for overall helpfulness and small tasks requested, or 100–150 francs for special, one-time-only tasks like obtaining reservations or tickets. (Note that if you only use a concierge's services once, it's appropriate to tip on the spot; to thank a concierge for several services during the course of a longer stay, tip on your last day. Should you want to enclose your tip in an envelope marked with the concierge's name, make sure you hand deliver it or it may get shared among *all* the hotel's concierges; a nice gift—such as fine candy—is also appropriate.); chambermaids—five francs per night; room service—as "service" in room service is usually reflected in the bill, tipping isn't expected, but if you're a room service regular, it would be considerate to add an additional five francs for each order; valet—ten francs; barbers and hairdressers—10 percent; theater ushers—two francs; movie ushers—one franc; housekeeping services at a rented villa—5 to 7 percent of the rental price for a cook, 100–150 francs per week for a gardener or driver, and twenty-five francs per day for a maid. ~For the above estimates relating to hotels, double the amounts if you're in a very expensive place. ~Be prepared to tip by putting some small change in your pocket *in advance,* before you arrive at the hotel, for example, or before you go to the theater.

Toilets and Toilet Paper

Never set out each day without stuffing some toilet paper in your pockets or your bag. Public toilets—even those in some of the nicest places—can be abominable, and often do not have toilet paper *(papier hygiénique)*. I have always found good, American-style toilet paper in the bathrooms at American Express offices, which are found in Nice and other cities of the south. You may encounter a few squat toilets (known as Turkish toilets) in the south. These rarely have toilet paper, and you should know that often there will be a bucket in the stall for you to use for the disposal of used tissue. Sometimes a Turkish toilet will flush, but this doesn't always mean you can flush toilet paper—if you see a bucket, you can assume that it's reserved for paper. Finally, note that when some toilets flush they produce quite a wave, with the water coming up over the basin (and onto your feet). Guard against this possibility by not flushing until you're ready to step away, then flush as you simultaneously open the door of the stall.

Tourist (as in, Being One)

Whether you travel often for business or are making a trip for the first time, let's face it: we're all tourists, and there's nothing shameful about that fact. Yes, it's true that one feels a real part of *la vie quotidienne* when you blend in and are mistaken for a native; but since that's not likely to happen unless you live there, it's far better to just get on with it and have a good time.

Tourist Office (Maison de la France)

I cannot stress enough how helpful it is to contact the French Government Tourist Office as soon as you learn you're going to France. Think of it as the ultimate resource: all the information you need is there, or at least the staff will know how to direct you elsewhere. At the New York office, I have never stumped anyone with my questions or requests, and I think readers have come to know that I ask a lot of questions about a lot of little details. A word of advice for dealing with tourist offices in general: it is not very helpful to say you're going to Provence and would like "some information." It will be easier for the staff to assist you if you can provide them with as many details about your visit as possible: Is it your first trip? Do you only need information about hotels? The offices are stocked with mountains of material, but unless you ask for something specific, it will not automatically all be given to you. Sometimes I am amazed at what's available, and for no charge— but you have to ask. Some particularly noteworthy booklets available in the U.S. offices are "France Discovery Guide" (published annually, and includes articles about all parts of France by an impressive roster of journalists, some of whom are featured in *The Collected Traveler* series), "In the Footsteps of the Painters of Light in Provence, 1875–1920," "Domestic Arts of Provence," "The Wine Routes of

Provence," "Gay Friendly France: *Liberté, Égalité, Diversité*" (details a variety of destinations in France with practical information tailored to gay and lesbian travelers), and "The Good Value Guide to France," offering lots of tips to make a visit to all regions of France more affordable. There are four tourist offices in the States: 444 Madison Avenue, New York, New York 10022; 212-838-7800; fax: -7855; 676 North Michigan Avenue, Chicago, Illinois 60611; 312-751-7800; fax: 337-6339; 9454 Wilshire Boulevard, Beverly Hills, California 90212; 310-271-6665; fax: 276-2835; and Consulat Général de France à Miami, 1 Biscayne Tower, Suite 1750, Miami, Florida 33131; 305-373-8177; fax: -5828. Travelers can also access travel information by dialing the France on Call hotline at 410-286-8310 or visiting the Web site: www.franceguide.com.

Office du Tourisme or *Syndicat d'Initiative:* There doesn't seem to be much difference between these two types of offices, but *offices du tourisme* appear solely for tourists while *syndicats d'initiatives* are often more like general chambers of commerce. There are tourist offices in all the large and medium-size cities and towns throughout the south of France. Note that hours of operation during the summer months may not be the same as other seasons of the year, and some branches may in fact only be open during the summer.

Tours

A list of full-service tour companies could fill a separate book, and it is not my intent to promote only one company or one type of trip. Frankly, while I do enthusiastically recommend the organizations listed below, I'm bothered by the fact that too many of them focus on luxury meals and accommodations. I believe there are a great number of people who are seeking the personalized service and knowledgeable guides these companies offer but who do not need or desire five-star elegance every step of the way. The south of France is filled, after all, with a plethora of wonderful, moderately priced lodgings and places to eat, so I often wonder if these companies aren't missing the boat in trying to reach even more clients. That said, it is certainly true that the combination of experience, insider's knowledge, and savvy guides these companies have is most definitely not found by searching the Web, and organizing trips like these requires a substantial amount of research and attention to detail, which some travelers do not always have the time or inclination to do (and for which they are willing to pay a great deal). Also, organized package tours now offer travelers more free time than in years past, as well as more choice in meals and excursions. Following are some companies that have appealed to me and offer an authentic experience:

Alternative Travel Group (69–71 Banbury Road, Oxford, OX2 6PE, England, 011.44.1865.315678; fax: 011.44.1865.315697; info@alternative-travel.co.uk). "The best way to see a country is on foot" is the ATG motto, and I have been very impressed with this group's philosophy and lengthy catalogs. "Painters of

Provence" is one of its popular trips. Additionally, there are the "Footloose" walking and biking trips that offer a variety of less expensive itineraries.

Ambiance France: The French Art of Living (2324 Shorewood Drive, Carmichael, California 95608; 916-484-7730; fax: 483-1826; www.ambiance-france.com). Ambiance was founded by two French women, Danielle and Brigitte, who are passionate about the Midi and want to share their linguistic and cultural knowledge with like-minded travelers. They describe it as a "cultural immersion travel company," and they offer week-long biking and walking trips and general and customized tours of Provence and the Dordogne. Accommodations are in a restored historic château near Aix-en-Provence, and trips include visits to monuments, villages, wineries, and markets and cooking demonstrations.

Art in Provence (P.O. Box 155, Woodstock, Vermont 05091; 802-457-5169; fax: -1806; www.cookinginprovence.com). Host and director, Hans Meijer, introduces participants to truly spectacular painting sites in the northern part of Provence. Accommodations are in the Château de Mazenc, once the summer home of a French president (see description of "Cooking in Provence" under Cooking Schools). Each workshop consists of eight painting days, two free days, and three travel days. Six hours of instruction per day is offered, for painters at all levels, and nonpainting guests are welcome (golf, tennis, swimming, hiking, biking, horseback riding, and canoeing are also available).

Bike Riders Tours (P.O. Box 130254, Boston, Massachusetts 02113; 800-473-7040; www.bikeriderstours.com). Bike Riders limits the size of its tours to sixteen people, and prides itself on the luxurious inns and quality restaurants it selects. Routes typically do not exceed thirty-five miles per day, but optional routes can often be arranged. "Pedaling in Provence" is the seven-day trip it offers in the south, which takes riders from Vaison-la-Romaine in the north to St.-Rémy and Les Baux. The company also offers La Cuisine du Soleil in Provence, one of its "Guest Chef" tours with Alex Lee of Daniel in New York. In between biking tours, guests visit open-air *marchés,* kitchens, a goat cheese producer, and wine *caves,* and gather wild *herbs de Provence* and taste the sea salts of the Camargue.

Breakaway Adventures (3148 Dumbarton Street, N.W., Washington, D.C. 20007; 800-567-6286; 202-944-5006; fax: 202-944-5009; www.breakaway-adventures.com). Breakaway offers cycling, trekking, and walking tours worldwide, and notes that its guests "get a different view of France at a snail's pace." There are several trips to choose from in Provence; one, "Provence—the Alpes du Sud," is a moderate-level walking trip that closely follows the GR4 and includes a full day traversing the best section of the Grand Canyon du Verdon. The company also organizes customized trips for individuals, couples, groups, or families, at any fitness level.

Butterfield & Robinson (70 Bond Street, Toronto, Ontario, Canada M5B 1X3; 800-678-1147 or 416-864-1354; fax: -0541; www.butterfield.com). B&R is the leader in luxury active travel around the world, specializing in biking and walking, and offers about ninety-five trips on six continents. A few lines from its beautiful catalog sum up the B&R philosophy: "We love exploring new places. We think biking and walking are the best way to see a region's people, history and culture. And at the end of each day, we like to treat ourselves well with a great meal and a great hotel. So that's what B&R does." In Provence, there are three biking trips, one walking trip, and two bike-and-walk trips to choose from, and to read a personal account, see *Pedaling Through Provence* (Sarah Leah Chase, Workman, 1995), which is also a cookbook.

Country Walkers (P.O. Box 180, Waterbury, Vermont 05676; 800-464-9255 or 802-244-1387; fax: 802-244-5661; www.countrywalkers.com). This group—whose motto is "explore the world . . . one step at a time"—celebrates its twenty-second anniversary this year, and believes that "to experience a region and its culture, you must see it at your own pace with a small group and a knowledgeable guide." "Perfumed Provence," an aromatic walking tour following in the footsteps of the Romans, and "Lubéron's Luxuries" are the two itineraries offered in the south of France. The Lubéron trip, the more expensive of the two, includes luxury hotel accommodations and dining at a Michelin-starred restaurant.

Cross-Culture: Foreign Travel Programs Designed for Travelers Rather Than Tourists (52 High Point Drive, Amherst, Massachusetts 01002; 413-256-6303; fax: 413-253-2303; e-mail: xculture@javanet.com; www.javanet.com). Its trips to Provence include "Following in the Footsteps of the Painters of Provence" and "Autumn in the South of France: Provence."

Distant Journeys (P.O. Box 1211, Camden, Maine 04843; 888-845-5781 or 207-236-9788; fax: 207-236-0972; www.distantjourneys.com). This hiking and walking tour company offers three trips in Provence: "Provence Inn-to-Inn" (eleven days through classic Provence, from Castellane through the Grand Canyon du Verdon across the Lubéron mountains to Roussillon and Gordes); "Walks in Provence" (seven days in Haute Provence and the Lubéron); and "Grande Traversée des Alps part 2" (fourteen days following the French-Italian border in the Hautes-Alpes and Alpes-Maritimes, ending in Menton on the Mediterranean; lodgings are in mountain huts and hotels). Other trips not far from Provence include "Tour du Mont Blanc" (Europe's premier hut-to-hut route) and "The French Pyrénées Hut-to-Hut." Walks range from easy to strenuous.

Driving Tours of France (2130 NW 95th Street, Seattle, Washington 98117; 800-717-1703; fax: 206-782-3966; www.dtof.com). "Travel anywhere, anytime" is the guiding philosophy of this company, which offers three basic programs of driving itineraries: Silver, Gold, and Platinum. Each program includes a car, Michelin road atlas, all breakfasts, accommodations, and an itinerary-specific travel notebook. But the rest—what you see and do—is up to you (the Platinum Program includes a concierge/escort to assist with making daily plans). The fourteen-day "Southern

France" preplanned itinerary starts in either Bordeaux or Provence, with stops in the Dordogne, Albi, and Carcassonne. I think this is too much to pack into fourteen days; but travelers do have the option of working out a customized itinerary just for Provence. This is a good option for people who want the freedom to plan details of their itinerary within an existing framework.

France in Your Glass (814 35th Avenue, Seattle, Washington 98122; 800-578-0903; fax: -7069; www.inyourglass.com). "For people who enjoy wine, food and France," this company offers exceptional wine and food vacations in the major wine-growing regions of France, including several in Provence and the Côte d'Azur.

France-Vacances: French Travel—Your Style (Candice Lichtenfels, 913 Avenida del Sol NE, Albuquerque, New Mexico 87110; 505-265-6065 or 800-484-9661, x9076; fax: -3110). This is not an organized tour company but a fee-based consulting service that offers custom-designed vacation planning in France and other European countries. Lichtenfels has lived and traveled in France for over thirty years and helps visitors discover *la vraie France* while minimizing the potential stresses of foreign travel. Meticulously designed trip portfolios include such details as driving directions, tickets to performances, hotel and restaurant reservations, car rentals, chauffeurs, recommendations for shopping, language instruction, and tours, and a focus on special interests (such as art, history, wine, children's activities, etc.).

France, Inc. (5609 Green Oaks Boulevard SW, Suite 105, Arlington, Texas 76017; 800-OK-FRANCE or 817-483-9400; fax: -7000; e-mail francehs@gateway.net.) Though primarily a great resource—the company's slogan is "We R France From A to Z"—France, Inc. also offers some tours at competitive prices, as well as private car services, museum passes, Paris opera, ballet, concert, and nightclub performances, etc. The company specializes in offering a wide range of hotels, and readers can request an individual brochure for Provence/Alpes/Côte d'Azur.

The French Experience (370 Lexington Avenue, New York, New York 10017; 212-986-1115; fax: -3808; www.frenchexperience.com). Though it offers some guided tours, The French Experience is not technically a tour operator. However, it's a worthy group to know of as it arranges special packages, self-drive tours, hotels and apartments in Paris and the provinces, car rentals, *gîte* rentals, rail passes, etc.

Les Liaisons Délicieuses (Patricia Ravenscroft, 877-966-1810 or 202-966-1810; fax: 202-966-4091; www.cookfrance.com). "Gastronomic adventures in the French countryside" is what Les Liaisons offers, which may not seem very different from some other tours listed here but in fact it is: participants cook with Michelin-starred chefs in restaurant kitchens and accompany them on visits to markets and special purveyors. The "Savory Splendors of Provence" trip includes four participatory cooking classes with chef Reine Sammut of Auberge la Fenière in Lourmarin (Reine is widely considered to be France's top female chef). Accommodations are at the

Auberge, and the week-long trip includes visits to Île-sur-la-Sorgue, a vineyard, an organic farmer, Apt, a confectioner, and the Château d'Ansouis. (See the September 1997 issue of *Travel & Leisure* for a description and photo of the Auberge and a good word about Sammut's renowned cuisine.)

Randonnée Tours (249 Bell Avenue, Winnipeg, Manitoba, R3L 0J2, Canada; 800-465-6488 or 204-475-6939; fax: 204-474-1888; www.randonneetours.com). Randonnée, founded ten years ago by ecologist Ruth Marr, offers "distinctive self-guided vacations" for travelers interested in walking or cycling (and skiing too). I fell in love immediately with the Randonnée brochure, not just because it's unique and beautiful, but because on page five, Marr refers to La Drôme Provençale as her favorite landscape. It's my favorite part of Provence, too, so I knew her routes would be something special. The "Randonnée Plus" itineraries are the company's pride: these trips are operated personally by the staff, "adding value and flexibility to an individualized experience." What most appeals to me about Randonnée is that, in addition to these itineraries, trips can be customized to accommodate any length or any routes; in fact, you don't have to use a guide at all and you can mix and match accommodations, staying one night in a B&B, another in a two-star hotel. Travelers can start trips on any day of the week, and can combine tours to create exactly the trip they want. Specialized tour options for cycling in the south of France include "Provence," "Provence Sampler," and "Randonnée Remote: Haute Provence." For walking, choose from "Côte d'Azur," "Provence," and "Provence Sampler" (and note that the walks described are not available in English-language guidebooks); Marr has walked every kilometer, so thorough descriptions and interesting insights are provided. Additionally, there are "Short Escapes" trips of two, three, or four nights and two "Drive & Stroll" trips available. The staff's expertise and meticulous research are more thoroughly revealed in its accompanying *Randonnée Road Book,* which combines detailed route instructions with maximum scenery opportunities.

The Wayfarers (172 Bellevue Avenue, Newport, Rhode Island 02840, 401-849-5087 and 800-249-4620; fax: 401-849-5878; www.thewayfarers.com). The Wayfarers have been planning exclusive walking vacations since 1984, and offer two trips in the south: "Cézanne's Provence" and "The Gourmet Provence."

A Week in Provence (Sarah and Michael Brown, Les Martins, 84220 Gordes, France; 04.90.72.26.56; fax: 04.90.72.23.83; e-mail: lesmartins@compuserve.com; U.S. contact: Sheppard Ferguson, 202-537-7202). With the Browns—she holds a Ph.D. in art history and he's a food and wine expert—guests are in the hands of perhaps the most knowledgeable couple in the Lubéron. Sarah has been studying the region since she was twelve years old, and knows the local history like the back of her hand. Michael previously owned a local store, so they both are a real part of the community. Six guests spend an intoxicating week drenched in the history, art, and food of Provence. Accommodations are in the family's own charming home outside Gordes (complete with pool), which they've owned for over forty years. The fee includes lodging, continental breakfast, seven four-course meals with wine, drinks, maid service, six mornings of guided tours, and at least six hands-on cooking demonstrations. And the Browns are flexible: they build the program around the interests of the group. If guests really just want to visit markets and cook, then that's what they'll do (plus, you receive a coveted copy of *Sarah and Michael's Recipes from Les Martins,* a cookbook you'll cherish because Sarah is an outstanding cook). If you just want to soak up history, art, and architecture, you'll get it in heavy doses. Interested in wine? You couldn't be in better hands than Michael's—he's an insider, with more connections than you can count. Antiques? The Browns know all the best places. With room for only six guests a week, Les Martins fills up fast.

~If you do select a tour operator, ask a lot of questions so you get what you expect. For starters, ask if the operator employs its own staff or if it contracts with another company to run its trips. Remember, however, that standards differ around the world, and operators don't have control over every detail. For example, many beautiful old villas and inns do not have screens in the windows, and many first-class hotels don't have air-conditioning. The price you pay for accommodations may not be the same as the posted rates, but you have to accept that you're paying for the convenience of someone else booking your trip. Tour operators also reserve the right to change itineraries, thus changing modes of transportation as well as hotels. If you have special needs, talk about them with the company in advance.

Travel Insurance

I have never purchased travel insurance because I have never determined that I need it, but it's worth considering if you think the risks to you are greater without it. Ask yourself what it would cost if you needed to cancel or interrupt your trip, and how expensive it would be to replace any stolen possessions. If you have a medical condition or if a relative is ill, insurance might be a wise investment. First, check to see if your existing health or homeowner's policies offer some protection. If you decide you need to purchase additional insurance, read all the fine print and make sure you understand it; compare deductibles; ask how your provider defines "preexisting condition" and inquire if there are situations in which it would be waived; and check to see if the ceiling on medical expenses is adequate for your needs.

V

VAT *(Value-Added-Tax)*

The VAT is known as *détaxe* in French. Visitors to France (except from EEC member countries) are entitled to receive a reimbursement of VAT paid. I have an entire file on conflicting information about the VAT, so even if you meet the eligibility requirements, be prepared for a potentially confusing procedure. The best explanation I've read about the VAT is in Maribeth Clemente's great book *The Riches of France* (St. Martin's Press, 1997). She makes a good case for persevering; however, she doesn't mention some of the pitfalls I've read about elsewhere. Frankly, I think the procedure seems to be a lot of bother unless visitors are making a significant purchase, and I think it would be worth asking the retailer to simply not charge any tax; but for those who are determined, you must produce your passport at the time of the purchase, spend at least twelve hundred francs at one store (but retailers are not required to participate in the program nor to match the dollar amount, so ask first), and produce receipts *and* merchandise for inspection at customs. Note that some shops don't have the necessary forms, and that the paperwork must be stamped by customs officials *before* you enter the U.S. Problems seem to arise when the customs desk is closed, although if you'll be in any other country before you return to the States, a customs stamp from that country is also valid (if the officials are willing to validate your forms). Also, it seems customs officials can be rather lax at some borders, and vigilant at others. ~The VAT form is known as a *bordereau de détaxe*. ~For a 20 percent fee, Global Refund will handle your refund through the European Tax-Free Shopping (ETS) network, and many stores in France are now affiliates (contact ETS at 233 South Wacker Drive, Suite 9700, Chicago, Illinois 60606; 312-382-1100). Once your forms are stamped you're able to receive a refund—in the form of cash, check (in francs), or charge-card credit—right away at an ETS counter (or, you can mail the forms from home). ~If you have attempted to have your forms validated in France and were thwarted in your efforts, or if it has been more than three months since you applied for a refund, contact Global Refund (707 Summer Street, Stamford, Connecticut 06901, 800-566-9828; fax: 203-674-8709; www.taxfree.se).

W

Weather

The weather in Provence is not always as gentle as many people think it is. Underneath all that Mediterranean brightness there is, of course, the *mistral* (and 31 other winds!) and violent thunderstorms, even in summer, are not uncommon. Freezing temperatures—ones that destroy olives and vineyards—are also not unheard of, although they're not typical. The region is perhaps most stereotypically beautiful in the summer, when the lavender is at its full-blown peak, but each season of the year has its rewards: by the end of February, almond trees are in bloom (they really do look as explosive as in van Gogh's paintings); March and April bring green leaves on the plane, linden, and chestnut trees, as well as flowering fruit trees; shortly after, everything else bursts into a riot of color and scent; and the fall—a nice time to be many places in the world—is a favorite season for many visitors (it's still warm enough to swim through September and early October); in the winter months, when it's rainy and cold—and it does get cold, especially if the mistral is blowing—you don't have the pleasure of picnicking and hiking outdoors, but prices drop and you'll have little trouble securing reservations at even the smallest hotels and restaurants. Picking the "perfect" time of year is subjective, so go during your favorite season, or when you have the opportunity, and that will be your experience, your Provence. It's true that peak season means higher prices and more people, but if you're determined you want to be in Avignon in July, then the cost and the crowds won't matter. If you're a weather maven, you'll love *Fodor's World Weather Guide* (E. A. Pierce and C. G. Smith, 1998; published in 1998 in Great Britain as *The Hutchinson World Weather Guide, New Edition* by Helicon Publishing Ltd., Oxford). As frequent business or pleasure travelers know, average daily temperatures are only a small part of what you need to know about the weather. It is not helpful to know that the average monthly temperature in Paris in April is 60 degrees without also knowing that the average number of rainy days is thirteen. This guide features weather specifics for over two hundred countries and territories, and also includes a map of the world's climate regions; humidity and wind-chill charts; a centigrade and Fahrenheit conversion table; a rainfall conversion table; and a bibliography pointing interested readers to other sources.

Web Sites

Personally, I don't find a single one of the following Web sites better than the tourist office or the appropriate book, but a few offer some good features:

www.aixenprovencetourism.com—In French and English and complete with music, this is a good site with headings of Events, Heritage, Lodging, Leisure, Conferences, and E-Mail, allowing for clicks on Cézanne, children, crafts, sports, activities, gastronomy, Mt. Sainte-Victoire, restaurants, etc.

www.beyondfr—"Provence—Beyond the Riviera" is this site's raison d'être, and one can click on a number of subjects such as gastronomy (which includes an English-French cuisine dictionary with Provençal equivalents), wine, sports, reference information (which revealed a pottery calendar of events), maps, sites, towns and villages, nature, etc.

www.crt-riviera.fr—at the time I checked, this was the intermediate site for La Comité Regional du Tourisme.

www.enjoyfrance.com—Search here for a selection of accommodations, including hotels, B&Bs, and guest houses. Regional Web sites are also provided, which are useful for contacting smaller tourist offices.

francentral.com—At the time I browsed this site, over half the links I clicked on were empty, but I'm including it because when the site is complete it will have more thorough information—currency exchange, books, cooking schools, specialized tours, French-American Chamber of Commerce, news and trends, etc.—than any other I've seen.

www.info-france-usa.org—The Web site of the French embassy, this has eight divisions: France on the Internet, News and Magazine, Just for Kids, *Tapis Rouge,* France and America, Profile of France, Trade and Technology, and Culture, Language Study, and Travel. Links can be made to French government ministries, regions, cities, media, French consulates, French corporations in the U.S., Alliances Françaises, etc.

www.lagenda.com—In French, but easy to navigate. *"Tous les événements, où, quand, comment"* is what this site offers, and viewers can enter the dates they'll be in Provence (or anywhere else in France) for an exhausting list of festivities and happenings (parents can scroll over to "Agenda" on the far right and click on *enfants* for listings of child-friendly events). Best feature: *vacances scolaires* and *jours fériés* dates.

http://luberon-news.com—In French and English, this is the site for a Lubéron newspaper and includes listings for Lubéron *événements, spectacles,* cinema and theater performances, a calendar of festivities, horoscope, and an indispensable *pages jaunes* for the "Meilleures Adresses du Lubéron."

www.provenceweb.fr—In French and English, this site is a *guide touristique* for villages and towns in Provence. When I clicked on "tchatche room," I could choose boutiques and shopping, *brocantes, châteaux* and monuments, festivals, children's corner, etc.

www.riviera-reporter.com—This site represents *The Rivera Reporter,* an expatriate magazine in Nice (the *Reporter* is distributed free in many places along the Côte d'Azur, including at the area's six English-language bookshops). Lots of useful information can be found at this site, which also lists some other expat periodicals in the Dordogne and other countries around the world.

www.travelwithyourkids.com—Of the family-travel Web sites I've browsed, this is the best. Compiled by a couple named Peter and Mari—who've lived abroad for nearly fifteen years and have two daughters born abroad—I liked it immediately when I read "We like traveling with our children, and wish the same for you. The trade-off from throwing a T-shirt into a backpack before hitchhiking to the airport is the chance to create memories that will for the rest of your life be known by only you and your children." The site is meant to supplement, not replace, guidebooks, and they offer great tips for finding the best airline seats, packing, planning, flying long distances, etc. Not specific to Provence or France, but worthwhile.

www.tourisme.fr/annu/index.htm—This site is in French but is easy to decipher, and is terrifically useful in searching for local tourist offices. Viewers can select a *ville, département,* or region, plus any number of special interests.

Women Travelers

Whether traveling solo or not, lots of great advice is offered in *Travelers' Tales Gutsy Women: Travel Tips and Wisdom for the Road* (Marybeth Bond, Travelers' Tales, Inc., San Francisco, distributed by O'Reilly & Associates, 1996). This packable little book is filled with dozens and dozens of useful tips for women of all ages who want to travel or who already travel a lot. Bond has traveled all over the world, much of it alone, and she shares a multitude of advice from her own journeys as well as that of other female travelers. Chapters address safety and security; health and hygiene; romance and unwelcome advances; money, bargaining, and tipping; traveling solo; mother-daughter travel; travel with children, etc. ~Also, the Women's Travel Club may be of interest. Founded by Phyllis Stoller, this organization plans numerous domestic and international trips a year, and guarantees everyone a roommate. Its great list of travel-safety tips was featured on NBC's *Today* as well as in *Travel & Leisure* (August 1999). Membership is $35 a year, and members receive a newsletter (800-480-4448; e-mail: Womantrip@aol.com/ www.womenstravelclub.com).

Y

Yellow Pages

Sometimes you just need the Yellow Pages, and you can access these electronically by searching on www.pagesjaunes.com.

Travel Light? Yeah, Right!

BY JOANNE KAUFMAN

editor's note

Freelance writer Joanne Kaufman believes the world is made up of two kinds of people: those who pack too much and those who don't pack enough. She is firmly in the pack-too-much category, although I think she probably feels she travels with just enough of what she needs. I include this piece to remind readers to consider your packing requirements sooner rather than later.

JOANNE KAUFMAN writes about an enormous variety of topics for such publications as *The New York Times, New York, The Wall Street Journal,* and *Parenting.*

We all have our favorite oxymorons. "Minor operation" has its proponents. So do "Jerry Lewis comedy" and "family vacation." Personally, I must confess a real weakness for "traveling light."

For me, every trip whether across town or across the Mojave is a journey into the unknown, fraught with potential peril—i.e., the possibility that we are dealing with a region as yet undiscovered by Starbucks—and must be treated as such. I once dated someone who referred to my oversize purse as the bubee bag when he went searching in it for a pen one night and came up with a sewing kit, a toothbrush and toothpaste, Band-Aids, a damp bathing suit, a bottle of Evian, an apple, half a lox-and-cream-cheese bagel and a six-ounce jar of Skippy chunky peanut butter. If he'd kept looking, he swore, he would have found half a roast chicken. Somehow in all the confusion, he missed the white Gap T-shirt and change of underwear I routinely carry during warmer months, when I'm certain to want a change of clothes in the middle of the day.

You can imagine, then, what is involved in my preparations for a trip across multiple state lines. Good sense demands a nod to contingency packing. A given destination may be a bit warmer or colder, dressier or more casual than promised by brochures. But I haven't yet figured out where sensible ends and pointless excess baggage begins.

I don't need a piece of Samsonite to fall on my head to realize I've got a problem. So I eagerly seek out magazine and newspaper articles purporting to take the mystery (to say nothing of the wrinkled clothes) out of packing. Invariably, there are suggestions about the importance of including only those items that can do double duty, for example a nightshirt that can also work as a beach cover-up (I suppose that would also mean using a toothbrush as a lint remover), and hewing to a strict policy of color-coordinated clothing. My friend Ann handily solves this problem by packing only black, while another woman I know used brown as the unifying theme for a recent ten-day trip to France. Indeed, she packed so much taupe knitwear that her husband began to refer to the whole shebang as the squirrel suit.

Those with packing counsel preach the gospel of scarves—the Hamburger Helper of prêt-à-porter—as a way to disguise that you have gone halfway round the world with precisely one change of clothes. But the only two groups I have ever known to do consistently attractive things with scarves are Frenchwomen and magicians.

The how-to articles contain exhortations about sandwiching clothes between layers of plastic, rolling garments into little cylinders and encasing them in tissue paper. But how tightly should they be rolled? Can wax paper substitute for plastic wrap? The complexity of all this is evidenced by the Miss America contestant who spared viewers vocal, instrumental and terpsichorean displays, instead presenting as her God-given talent a demonstration of correct packing.

Renseignements Pratiques *115*

One of my earliest memories is a car trip to northern Michigan, and my parents somehow forgetting to take my suitcase, the valise with my precious shorty pajamas. That incident clearly left its mark. Like Scarlett O'Hara, standing in the war-torn fields of Tara vowing never to be hungry again, I made a similar if less dramatic promise to myself about never being out of clothes out of town again.

Thus, during time that would be most profitably spent trying to hail a cab for the airport, I am last-minute packing my pullover sweater (because I can't remember if I packed the cardigan), beach thongs (I'll need them if I decide to swim), my sneakers (if it's too cold to swim I'll want to jump rope) and my jump rope (which of course can double as a belt or clothesline).

The best face that I can put on my packing is that it suggests an optimism seriously lacking in other areas of my life—the belief that a phalanx of skycaps with open arms and free hands will chaperone my luggage.

It would help if I could just stay practical minded: making sure there is one-to-one correspondence between days away and the pairs of pantyhose snaking around my duffel. But to me, there has always been a fantasy aspect to packing, the belief that going to a different latitude or time zone will unleash a whole new me. Suddenly, I would feel free to wear certain clothes, apply makeup with the kind of heavy hand I would never deploy at home. When I visited New York before moving there from Michigan, I faithfully packed two shades of foundation, three makeup brushes and a Borsalino hat because the city seemed to require a sophistication unknown in the Midwest.

Similarly on trips to Los Angeles, where I perceive there to be a startlingly liberal dress code, I pack, well, light. I've been there a half-dozen times in the last few years and each time I've tucked into my suitcase a black Norma Kamali bathing suit that in Morse code would be translated as two dots and a dash. I bought it when I began dating the man who is now my husband and never quite had the nerve to wear it in public (or come to think of it, in private). But I like about myself that I continue to pack it, that I believe I will someday use it for the purpose so clearly intended: to vamp pool attendants at the Beverly Hills Hotel.

I had not finished working through my own packing issues when I had children (not too critical an issue since it has effectively put my husband and me under house arrest). But there has been the occasional midwestern sojourn to visit my family, and suddenly I was packing for four. I vowed before becoming a mother that I would never be one of those harridans who would force her children, *Sophie's Choice* style, to winnow down their traveling companions.

Thus, on a recent trip to Detroit, the large suitcase with all the outside pockets so dear to me for last-minute additions of shirts and shoes was given over to Barney, Baby Bop, B. J. (my son's sleeping companions) and a flotilla of dolls, among them identical triplets Baby, Karen and Callie (my daughter's bosom buddies). I felt very much like the comedian Alan King, who told of his wife's commandeering an entire set of Gucci luggage for a trip to Europe while his personal effects were consigned to a paper bag dappled with chicken-fat stains.

My husband defines my life as an unceasing attempt to cram six pounds of—well, call it fertilizer—into a four-pound bag. Packing is the literal manifestation of that. I marvel at (and envy slightly) people I see at the airport check-in counter with a bag the size of a legal pad, then I think of Elizabeth Taylor's arriving, years ago, in London with something like 143 pieces of luggage.

Liz and I understand the importance of clean socks.

This piece originally appeared in the travel section of *The New York Times,* January 26, 1997. Reprinted by permission of the author.

isse nationale des **monuments historiques** et des **sites** ◇

AIGUES-MORTES
PLEIN TARIF

22/05/2000

VALABLE LE

VENDU LE 22/05/2000 A 15h27

CAISSE No 01   0002

ticket à conserver en cas de con

RELATIONS
DIPLOMATIQUES
**FRANCE
ISRAËL**

1 9 4 8

1 9 9 9

LA POSTE
RÉPUBLIQUE FRANÇAISE   4.40

BEAU RIVAGE

Le Kiosque—
Points de Vue
(The Kiosque—Points of View)

"Though Provence has been united to France for 400 years or so, there is no part of France which has kept its individuality like the Midi."
—Lawrence Durrell, CAESAR'S VAST GHOST

France's Favorite Country

BY PETER MAYLE

⤳

editor's note

As Peter Mayle so skillfully emphasizes in this piece and in his many books, French ways are often simultaneously admirable and humorous.

PETER MAYLE is the author of more than a dozen books, including *A Year in Provence, Toujours Provence, Encore Provence, Hotel Pastis,* and *Chasing Cézanne,* all published in hardcover by Alfred A. Knopf and in paperback by Vintage.

My most recent experience of the Frenchman's eternal love affair with his country and all things French began with cheese—a five-pound slab of Cheddar, which I had brought back from London for a friend in Provence. It happened to be one of those days at the Marignane-Marseilles airport when the customs officers were feeling either bored or particularly efficient, and they were inspecting the contents of every suitcase.

My case was opened, and the Cheddar removed. The customs inspector looked at it as though it were a compressed corpse. He flicked a finger to suggest that I unwrap it.

"What is this?"

Cheese, I told him.

"Cheese?" His nose wrinkled with disapproval. "You're bringing cheese into France?"

He called across to a colleague. An Englishman was bringing cheese into France. Incroyable. The two of them sniffed it and prodded it and shook their heads in disbelief. Did I not know that the best cheeses in the world—hundreds of them, a different cheese for every day of the year—came from France? There were some unkind remarks comparing it with savon de Marseilles, those blocks of soap that are sold by weight, a few shrugs of incomprehension, and then I was allowed to pack up my cheese and go.

I didn't find their reaction in any way surprising. If you live in France for any length of time, you are treated almost daily to displays of chauvinism—often unconscious, sometimes very funny—that can make the modest Anglo-Saxon feel even more modest. In fact, the French are not only the world champions of chauvinism, they invented it, and pay their respects to its most celebrated supporter, Nicolas Chauvin, by using his name to describe it.

With a couple of ugly exceptions, such as the nastiness preached by some supporters of Jean-Marie Le Pen, leader of the far-right National Front, this conviction that the world is divided into France and less fortunate countries is harmless and quite endearing. French couture, French bread, French joie de vivre—the catalog of French superiority covers every aspect of life.

Most of our French friends take their holidays in France because, as they say, everything is here: the long beaches of the Atlantic coast, the chic bodies side by side like sardines on the Côte d'Azur, the fat hills of Burgundy, the Alps, the lakes, the spectacular countryside of the Lot and the Auvergne (which is never crowded; with approximately the same population as Britain, France is three times the size), the heat of Provence, the coolness of the Haute-Savoie—all this without crossing a frontier or changing languages. And always, wherever you go, on mange bien.

"Who can help loving the land that has taught us 685 ways to dress eggs?" That was Thomas Moore, writing in 1818, and nothing much has changed. The top chefs—Guérard, Blanc, Robuchon, Bocuse and the rest—are deservedly more famous than football players. Three-star restaurants are booked up for Sunday lunch weeks in advance. A French family will happily drive twenty or thirty miles to find the remote little bistro that specializes in truffle omelettes or a bouillabaisse of snails.

It is taken as an indisputable fact—by the French, at least—that food from France is the standard by which all other food is judged, usually unfavorably. The only true lamb is French lamb. If it has the misfortune to come from England, Wales, New Zealand or any other underprivileged country, it is called sheepmeat. The chickens of Bresse are sold with patriotic red, white and blue paper medals on their plump breasts to show that they, like the finest wines, are appellation contrôlée. The olive oil from Provence is not only virgin, but extravirgin. The melons from Cavaillon, the anchovies from Collioure, the foie gras from the Landes, Normandy butter, Brittany oysters—pick anything edible, and you will be told that France produces the most delicate, the most refined, the most delicious examples on earth. There is a small problem when we come to caviar and Scottish smoked salmon, but these are shrugged off as geographical accidents.

Wine prompts a similar mixture of pride in the homegrown vintages and disdain for foreign imitations. I once tried to find Italian and Spanish wines in the shops of two or three local wine merchants, and was politely told that there was no demand for them. We, the French, prefer French wines. This preference is encouraged by the winegrowers with great enthusiasm and some of the most purple prose that ever gushed from a pen. In front of me now is a list from one of the major merchants, a man whose nose for wine is only equaled by his command of the ornamental phrase. Delicate and elegant I can swallow, but when I read that a wine is also coaxing, purring and tender, I'm not sure whether I should drink it or marry it.

The French language, beautiful, supple and romantic though it undoubtedly is, may not quite deserve the reverence that inspires a course of French lessons to be described as a *cours de civilisation*. Nevertheless, it is regarded as a national treasure and a shining example of how everyone should speak. For many years, it was the language of diplomacy, the common language of cultured people of all nationalities and, naturally, the language of love. Alas, times have changed, and we now find all kinds of foreign horrors creeping into everyday French.

It probably started when *le weekend* slipped across the Channel to Paris at about the same time that a nightclub owner in Pigalle christened his establishment Le Sexy. Inevitably, this led to *le weekend sexy*. The invasion of the language has also infiltrated the office. The French executive now has *un job*. If the pressure of work gets too much for him, he becomes *stressé*, perhaps because of the demands of being *un leader* in the business jungle of *le marketing*. It is the worst kind of Franglais, and it goads the elders of the Académie Française into fits of outrage. I can't say I blame them. These clumsy intrusions are *scandaleux;* or, to put it another way, *les pits*. Now there is news that an organization calling itself the Superior Council of the French language wants to change the traditional spelling of five hundred French words. It's enough to make Chauvin writhe in his grave.

Thank Heaven (where they undoubtedly speak correct French) there are still certain vital elements of contemporary life in which France leads the world. Take the simple business of drinking a glass of water, and we are forced to admire the bare-faced audacity that has transformed a dull and tasteless commodity into a semiprecious liquid. Designer water, as it has been called, is a triumph of mystique and packaging, and provides a wonderful example of the obsessive interest the French take in their stomachs and their general state of health.

According to your taste, and bearing in mind your digestive capabilities, you can select from an entire menu of waters: with big bubbles or smaller bubbles, with trace elements of essential minerals, with beneficial properties for the irrigation and purging of the kidneys—fabulous elixirs, all of them, authorized by government decree and more or less guaranteed to put you in top form. One day, we can be sure, the more advanced restaurants will provide a *carte des eaux* which the serious gastronome will study as attentively as the wine list.

Another achievement, and one the French can justifiably take pride in, is the Train à Grande Vitesse, the high-speed rail service connecting Paris with the provinces. After the overpriced squalor of British Rail, the T.G.V. is a revelation. It is clean and fast. I have traveled on the T.G.V. perhaps thirty times in the past few years, and not once has it been late. I never thought the French made enough of their comfortable and efficient trains, given their usual liking for self-promotion. But as it turns out, they were merely biding their time, waiting for the right moment to *épater les Anglais.*

What has been suggested is a direct T.G.V. link between Paris and London when the Channel tunnel is finally opened. This, of course, will need to be given a suitably French and heroic title, and the preferred name is the Napoléon Line. However, someone in the railway bureaucracy, showing a rare sense of humor, has made a further suggestion about where the high-speed Napoléon should finish its journey. Where else but London's Waterloo station?

Another French Revolution: In Marseilles, Europe Confronts Its North African Future

BY JEFFREY TAYLER

༄

editor's note

When the manuscript for this book was in its final stages, I read this article in *Harper's Magazine* and knew it was essential to this collection. France—and in particular Provence—has been especially challenged by its influx of immigrants, both from its former colonies and beyond. As Provence is one of the gateways to France, it comes as no surprise that National Front leader, Jean-Marie Le Pen (whose slogan is "The French First") has scored his biggest victories in the south of France. Not surprising, and yet one cannot escape noticing the great number of small roadside memorials to Résistance heroes in Provence (especially along the Route Nationale 7), still lovingly attended to today, more than fifty years later, with fresh flowers, handwritten notes, and photographs.

The majority of the immigrant population in France, legal or not, is Muslim, and indeed Islam is now the nation's second religion, putting the principle of *Liberté, Egalité, Fraternité* to the test like no other issue in French history since the Dreyfus Affair. It may seem simple to accuse the French of xenophobia, but the reality is much more complex: the French firmly believe that *anyone,* of any race, religion, or nationality, can be French; however, one must not only speak the language but must *really become* French, in ways defined by the French. One of the most publicized examples of applying the law to this principle came in 1993, when two Turkish and two Moroccan girls obeyed their parents and wore head scarves to school, a definite no-no in France's secular public school system. The girls were suspended, a move which was widely interpreted as a signal that the French government would no longer tolerate multiculturalism, that even Islam should become *French* Islam. The French view has always been to treat immigrants as individuals rather than as communities, which can so easily become ghettos. The government has argued that emphasizing cultural and religious differences only further segregates immigrants, leading to intolerance and discrimination.

There is now a sense of urgency in addressing these issues in the new millennium. It was reported in *The New York Times* in early 2000 that Europe may have to raise its immigration quotas and accept a new racial and ethnic makeup. United Nations experts said demographics indicate many European countries have a larger elderly population and fewer babies than ever before. If the Europeans expect to thrive economically and pay for their extensive social services, they will have to look around the world for qualified labor at every level. The U.N. projects that France would have to import approximately two million immigrants to maintain 1995 population levels.

Shortly after the head scarves issue, a French government immigration expert was quoted as saying that "The French are not racists, but they want foreigners to become French, to be discreet about religion, to become integrated at school as individuals." Unlike in America, a melting pot nation where anyone from anywhere can become a naturalized citizen, in France— and other European countries—citizenship is defined by ethnic heritage. Interestingly, the French don't use hyphens to identify immigrant groups the way we do in America—there are no Portuguese-French, Russian-French, or Italian-French, for example. But the French do have a word for the children of Algerian, Moroccan, and Tunisian immigrants who came to France in the '60s and '70s: *beurs,* described as "a generation that is neither Arab nor French" by Mort Rosenblum in his excellent book *Mission to Civilize* (he also explains that *"beur"* is a short form of *Arabe,* spelled backward and jumbled in *verlen,* popular street talk). Despite the current state of affairs presented in this thoughtful piece, in the thirteen years since Rosenblum's book was published the *beurs* have begun identifying themselves as French with Arab roots, and have become nothing less than nationwide cultural trendsetters. The most famous of these is Zinedine Zidane, the star soccer player who scored the two goals that won France the World Cup in 1998; eleven years earlier, the writer Tahar ben Jelloun won France's most prestigious literary award, the *Prix Goncourt;* and *cefran* (which is simply the syllables of *"français"* spoken out of order), the slang language of the *beurs,* has found its way into the daily conversation of French men and women across *l'hexagone.* They aren't only changing the face of Marseille, or France, but much of Europe.

JEFFREY TAYLER is the author of *Facing the Congo* (2000) and *Siberian Dawn: A Journey Across the New Russia* (1999), both published by Ruminator Books, and has contributed frequently to *Harper's Magazine.*

I've hiked up the 500-foot-high hill in the middle of Marseilles on which stands the basilica of Notre-Dame-de-la-Garde, topped by a gilded statue of the Virgin Mary. Above the Mediterranean, clouds obscure the setting sun, but the light is still strong, and the islands beyond the harbor show as scattered clumps of coal in a sea of rippling molten silver. Around me spreads a maze of serpentine lanes and zigzagging avenues, of gabled roofs and stone apartment houses whose ocherous reds and ashen grays harmonize with the pastel hues of the limestone hills defining the northern limits of the city. Such impressionistic allure is what one expects to find in the south of France, whose landscape inspired Cézanne and Van Gogh, Daudet and Pagnol.

I'm not alone beneath the basilica. Families are ambling by, speaking the Arabic dialects of Morocco and Algeria. The men lead, the backs of their loafers squashed flat, the easier to slip them off; women follow in white head scarves and voluminous ankle-to-neck raincoats, pushing baby carriages. Their harsh Semitic gutturals provoke irritated stares from French couples nearby, but for me they call to mind Marrakesh (where I lived as a Peace Corps volunteer a decade ago), a city that, with its sandstorms and withering sun, could hardly be more dissimilar to Marseilles. For a moment the incongruity between my sere memories of Marrakesh and the soft colors of Marseilles overcomes me, and I find myself staring at the newcomers, wondering at their strangeness here in France.

Different though they may be, Marseilles and Marrakesh, or, rather, France and North Africa, are becoming increasingly linked. Since the 1950s North Africans have been moving to Marseilles in great numbers, legally and illegally, and now make up roughly a quarter of the city's population of 803,000. It is estimated that every year at least 100,000 illegal immigrants (of whom possibly half are North African) enter France, where legally registered foreigners already number 3.5 million out of a population of 60 million; the total number of foreigners in the country may be as high as 5 or 6 million. Pan-European statistics reflect a similarly large-scale migratory trend (some 500,000 illegal immigrants slip into the EU each year) that accelerated in the 1990s with wars breaking out or intensifying in Algeria, southeastern Turkey, and the Balkans, and with the opening of borders in countries of the former Soviet bloc. More and more, France and Europe are finding themselves confronted with an issue that parts of the United States (in particular the Southwest and the cities of the Northeast) have been wrestling with for a long time now: how to handle an upsurge in unwanted, mainly economic refugees while preserving constitutionally enshrined individual liberties and human rights.

The influx of people from the Second and Third Worlds has contributed to the recent and rapid growth of right-wing extremist parties in Germany, Austria, Switzerland, Belgium, and Italy, but it was in France in 1972 that the first anti-immigrant political party appeared—the Front National, founded and led by Jean-Marie Le Pen and strongest around Marseilles, if not in it. (Marseilles has traditionally been a bastion of the Left.) Decrying the "silent invasion" of Muslims from across the sea, Le Pen has blamed immigrants for unemployment, crime, drug trafficking, and abuse of the welfare state, among other things, and accused them of threatening the "Christian identity" of France. In 1995, running on a platform of a "French France within a European Europe" and demanding the immediate expulsion of all illegal immigrants, Le Pen won 15 percent of the vote in the presidential election, and the Front captured the administrations of a number of Marseilles's suburbs and neighboring towns. Since then, he has suffered setbacks of his own making, quarreling with his first lieutenant, Bruno Mégret (who left the Front to establish his own party of similar ideological ilk, the Mouvement National Républicain) and losing his seat in the European Parliament after assaulting another politician at a rally.

All this has hurt Le Pen's image, but it will not diminish the anti-immigrant prejudices of his supporters; and he and Mégret together will probably win 15 percent in elections to be held next year.

Although few French who consider themselves moderate or educated will refer to Le Pen and Mégret as anything other than oafs, even if they agree with certain of their views, immigration is no longer an issue raised by the Far Right alone. During the past ten years more and more politicians have been speaking out against immigrants (even President Jacques Chirac has derided their "odors" and "noises"); the formation of a common European policy to stem the tide of illegals has figured prominently on France's agenda since it assumed the presidency of the EU in July; and the public backs the tightening of asylum and naturalization laws.[1] Opinion polls show consistently that a majority of French think there are too many foreigners in the country; colloquially, the word *immigré* has become something close to a slur, evoking larcenous, dark-skinned Muslim freeloaders who demand more and more social benefits from the state as they inundate, pollute, and subvert *La France française.*

Amid the controversy one may discern a fundamental and not unreasonable question: What is France supposed to be? A homogeneous land of Gallic "Christians," as Le Pen would put it, or a *terre d'immigration* welcoming all people who accept the ideals (liberty, equality, fraternity) proclaimed by the French Revolution? If the latter variant is preferable, could it work? Historically, France has been almost exclusively Judeo-Christian (and mainly Catholic)—a fact that has proved critically cohesive in view of the country's many regional rivalries.

[1]Paradoxically, immigration is increasingly vital to the economy, owing to the country's low birth rate and aging citizenry. The United Nations' Population Division recently released a report asserting that France will have to import 1.8 million laborers a year between now and 2050 just to maintain its current ratio of active to retired citizens.

Since my years in Morocco, friends of mine, both French and Arab, have put these questions to me, albeit rhetorically, as a means of expressing disgust with North African immigrants or anger at discrimination, but I've now come to Marseilles to reach my own conclusions, for nowhere else in France has the ingress of outsiders had as visible an impact as it has had here. How Marseilles is handling its new arrivals pertains to the rest of Europe as well. The EU is readying itself for change, with plans to expand to include countries of the former Soviet bloc and possibly even Turkey. Thus, in the next few years, questions of racial, ethnic, and religious diversity will assume greater importance for Europe; they may, in fact, determine the continent's stability, or even its unity. One thing is certain: with 76 million of the planet's 80 million new inhabitants being born each year in Third World countries, and with disparities in wealth increasing between the First and Third Worlds, Europe, and Marseilles in first order, will face more immigrants in the coming decades, not fewer.

The sun drops below the horizon and the wind gusts. From the halls of Notre-Dame-de-la-Garde echo the last hollow chants of the evening mass, then the giant bell above the basilica strikes six, the deafening bronze blows of its gong reverberating over the darkening quarters of the city. Worshippers, mainly working-class French in scuffed shoes and coarse woolen sweaters, file out and shove their way through the Arab strollers, heading for their cars in the lot below.

From the Arc de Triomphe, which rises against the sky amid the broad and airy Place Jules Guesde, I set out for a walk across the center of Marseilles, passing the sleek glass-and-granite headquarters of the regional administration and weaving my way between joggers in spandex tights and fashionably dressed young men and women immersed in cell-phone conversations. I turn down the two-lane Rue d'Aix and enter a shadowy defile of soot-encrusted five-story buildings, and all at once I am in a different world. Arab men in djellabahs crowd the sidewalks. Narrow-faced youths with curly black hair, who might be from any district of Tangier or Algiers, cycle between pedestrians, zinging their bells and shouting, "*Attention!*" At the corner, a turbaned old man whining a beggar's chant in Arabic sits barefoot on a stained sheet of cardboard, his knees drawn up to his shoulders, his palm extended. Tall African women wearing floral scarves and toting bulging plastic bags talk in Wolof and make their way around Berber women with tattooed chins. Side streets weave away into a warren smelling of grilled chicken and harissa—the immigrant neighborhood of Belsunce, which is, from all appearances, as lively and North African as any quarter of the Casbah in Marrakesh.

Rue d'Aix widens into Cours Belsunce, where Senegalese women recline on blankets spread on the pavement, chatting, their babies lolling on their laps. Farther on, clusters of Arab men with lined cheeks gesticulate and argue. Cours Belsunce cuts through La Canabière, the city's largest commercial avenue, which, after a smattering of cheap cafés, narrows and becomes Rue de Rome, where the street fête ends and the Marks and Spencers and Galeries Lafayettes begin—and where most Arabs and Africans, if there are any, are wiping windows or removing garbage.

As one might infer from this walk, the Mediterranean has shaped the history of Marseilles by favoring the migration and mixing of peoples living on or near it. Greeks who set sail from Asia Minor (now Turkey's Aegean coast) founded Marseilles in 600 B.C., and for the next five centuries it was an independent Greek city-state. Julius Caesar began his invasion of Gaul here, and the subsequent blending of Roman and Celtic peoples and cultures produced the Frankish kingdom that was to become the French Republic. Yet for hundreds of years Marseilles remained aloof and recalcitrant, proud of its independent past. It joined the rest of France only in 1481 and in 1792 sided with the revolutionaries; the volunteer force it dispatched to Paris to support the Commune sang a defiant song along the way that became the French national anthem, "La Marseillaise."

Soon after, France began its transformation from European kingdom into colonial empire. The egalitarian values of the French Revolution found paradoxical expression in the *mission civilisatrice* that served as the ideological justification for colonial expansion. The *mission* ordained that the colonized be, in effect, exploited for their own enlightenment; they were to be dragged in irons to civilization, and those who tried to sunder their fetters were savages. The *mission* had little effect on Marseilles, which prospered as the port of empire and maintained its distinct culture, accent, and population—a population that always included Mediterranean immigrants, many of whom were from the colonies. In 1891, Guy de Maupassant wrote that the city "perspires in the sun like a beautiful girl who does not take good care of herself. . . . It smells of the innumerable foods nibbled on by the Negroes, Turks, Greeks, Italians, Maltese, Spaniards, English, Corsicans, and Marseillais, too . . . [who are] recumbent, sitting, rolling, and sprawling on its docks."

Elsewhere in France at that time, however, foreigners were usually of more northern European origin. For a hundred years the country had been relying on Germans, Swiss, Italians, and Belgians to fulfill its expanding economy's need for manpower in heavy industry and mining. After the First World War the labor shortage was especially acute, and the influx of other Europeans increased to meet it: a 1931 census recorded 3 million foreigners in France. The newcomers provoked resentment, but they were mainly Christian and white; most assimilated, and the resentment passed.

It was after the Second World War that the city's present demographic outlines began to take shape. The dissolution of France's empire deprived Marseilles of status and revenue while another war-related shortage of manpower led the French to search for labor abroad, mainly to fill vacancies on construction sites and public works projects and in automobile plants. This time they looked to North Africa. France had just granted citizens of its Algerian territory full civil rights, including the right to live and work anywhere in France. Poverty and overpopulation prompted hundreds of thousands of Algerians to respond to the recruitment drive and take the boat to Marseilles. Other former French colonial subjects from Africa, the Middle East, and Asia would eventually come as well. By the mid-1970s immigrants would swell Marseilles from the 1946 population of 637,000 to 912,000.

The influx of non-Europeans did not cease after 1974, when economic recession motivated the French government to announce a policy of "zero immigration." Legal foreign residents had the right to invite their families, which they did, and then there were the illegals, who kept coming anyway. By the 1980s, for the first time in France's history, primarily Arab or African immigrants were outnumbering European arrivals. It is estimated that about half of the foreigners living in France today are from Africa.

To accommodate the immigrants while quartering them separately from the French, who resented them as much as they needed their labor, Marseilles spilled beyond its traditional boundaries. From Belsunce the city grew north, adding what came to be known as the *quartiers Nord,* or northern districts—immigrant ghettos, really—that spread all the way to the limestone hills visible from

Notre-Dame-de-la-Garde. Beset with crime, street gangs, drug trading, and unemployment as high as 45 percent, the *quartiers Nord* now make up about a third of Marseilles. They are not for casual touring, so I have asked twenty-six-year-old Hafid Benobeidallah, an Algerian who grew up there, to show me around. He has agreed, and offers to introduce me to friends of his in the rap group Fresh.

Hafid drives up to my hotel in a red Renault. He looks hip and relaxed in jeans and floppy salt-and-pepper sweater, a soul patch beneath his lower lip, his hair cropped short and stylishly nappy, Around his chest he carries a cell phone in a leather pouch; on his waist he wears a pager. I ask if we should speak Arabic or French. He tells me that although he understands Arabic, the language his parents still use at home, he is most comfortable in French.

As we follow the grimy Boulevard National out of the city center and into the *quartiers Nord*, heading for his old neighborhood on Rue Félix Pyat, Hafid tells me his story. He was born in a village near Oran. After the Algerian War of Independence (1954–62), his father came to Marseilles to take a minimum-wage job in construction and eventually brought the rest of the family over. The minimum wage sufficed to keep Hafid and his five brothers and sisters fed: families with incomes below a certain level are eligible for welfare and other benefits. Hafid has just finished vocational college, where he earned a degree in automotive engineering, but he can't find work, and he's considering moving to Paris or Quebec if nothing turns up. His car and electronic accoutrements he bought with money he made doing part-time jobs over the summers.

The serried rows of auto-repair shops and dingy cafés on Boulevard National give way to a sparser wilderness of high-rises towering over public housing projects called *HLMs,* an acronym standing for "moderate-income housing" that has become synonymous with tenements and immigrants. In the most decrepit *HLMs,* the windows of abandoned apartments have been cemented over, but in places the concrete has been knocked out and smoke is pouring through the holes. "Squatters," Hafid says. The ground floors of a couple of the high-rises are paneled in glass painted unevenly in blue or green; tiny Arabic signs announce the ramshackle premises behind them as mosques.

We enter the neighborhood of Bassens. Here there are groups of Arab and African youths in baggy jeans and baseball caps standing in the lots between *HLMs,* looking tough and watching the traffic. We come upon two smashed and upturned cars, stripped of every exterior part, even the wheels. "They looted the cars," Hafid says. "For fun they turn them over after they're done. Or they light them on fire. There's nothing else to do here, there's no work." Farther on, a Peugeot chassis lies, burned out and stripped.

We race higher and higher through the *quartiers,* which never deteriorate into the full-blown slums I'm expecting to see (always they look utilitarian and basically inhabitable, if strewn with litter), and finally achieve the summit at Solidarité, a neighborhood of high-rises scattered across rocky land. There's a commotion ahead: a half-dozen helmeted policemen on motorcycles are careening off the main road into an empty lot, heading for a trash container belching smoke and flames. Arab youths are running away into the projects, and the police, circling, are left with no one to apprehend.

The sun breaks free of the clouds, and stark white light washes over the trash and smoke and concrete. We start back down toward Rue Félix Pyat. Hafid calmly explains that the kids *du quartier* ("from the neighborhood") and *d'origine* ("of immigrant background"—most of them are second-generation) quit school early, can't find work, and turn to crime as much to make a living as to kill time, knocking over stores in the city center, mugging pedestrians, or dealing *shit* (marijuana) that they buy off traffickers riding the ferries from North Africa. *Shit* serves both as a source of income and as entertainment. There's nothing to do in the *quartiers*—there are few bars, cafés, or movie theaters—and the welfare money their parents receive goes to feed the family. However, crime has dropped recently, Hafid says, as a result of the heavy policing begun by the current mayor.[2] "The prisons are full, and the meanest characters of the *quartier* are dead."

But relations remain tense between the French and Africans, or, as Hafid puts it, whites and blacks. "I prefer not to use the word 'French,'" he says. "Most 'French' Marseillais are just Italians or Portuguese who've assimilated, but they're the biggest racists of all. It's better to say 'whites'—the problems here are between whites and Arabs, whites and blacks. As for Arabs and blacks, we're brothers here, we're all from the *quartiers*."

Back on Rue Félix Pyat we meet Yusuf, a member of Fresh, who is of Comorian origin. Yusuf at first looks at me with startled hostility, but when Hafid tells him I'm American, his face lights up and he asks me who my favorite rap artists are—a question I can't answer, knowing nothing at all about the genre. Frowning, he steps back and says we will have to talk another day. He turns and walks off.

Although his father made the pilgrimage to Mecca, Hafid doesn't pray or concern himself with Islam, and neither, he says, do his friends of Muslim background; money, cars, the latest rap CDs, and cell phones mean more to them than religion. Young women from the *quartier* follow Islamic custom and tend to stay off the street, but those who venture out rarely wear head scarves, which, in Marseilles, are—like skullcaps, djellabahs, and three-day beards—

[2]In 1995 conservative candidate Jean-Claude Gaudin won the mayoral election—which put the Left out of power for the first time in Marseilles since 1953—and, hoping to attract investment and tourism, he launched a cleanup program designed to improve the city's image.

telltale signs of recent arrival. But among immigrants Islam survives as a unifier, bonding those from the *quartiers* and distinguishing them from the white French. Muftis in Marseilles, who draw together the parents of Hafid and his friends at Friday prayers, still retain authority, and I've arranged to speak with Sheikh Abdel Hadi, the mufti of the Great Mosque of the Sunna on Boulevard National.

The Great Mosque occupies the first floor of what might once have been a hardware store or restaurant. It lacks the soaring grandeur of such buildings in Muslim countries; there is no minaret; the sign, in Arabic and French, is small and unobtrusive; and one-way mirrored windows prevent those on the street from looking inside. I arrive as noon prayers are ending. As I enter, bearded men are streaming out, adjusting their skullcaps, slipping on their loafers, straightening their jackets. Wearing gray robes and a black-and-white kaffiyeh, Sheikh Abdel Hadi appears. He is muscular and intense, abrupt, and possessed of arresting dark eyes; his diction, the balanced and sonorous Classical Arabic of the Koran, bespeaks erudition, a lifetime of hard study in religious schools, and is devoid of traces of his native Algerian dialect or French.

The sheikh asks me to sit down on the floor in the corner, where he joins me after seeing off the remaining worshippers. We talk, or, rather, I ask questions and he orates, his voice ringing throughout the empty hall, his eyes flinty with something akin to disdain. The North Africans who've immigrated to France came in waves. The first wave were those who helped the French in the colonies; they were *jahil* (ignorant of Islam). They did not know Classical Arabic, only their dialects, so how could they possibly have taught their children the Koran, which must be studied only in Classical Arabic? There are no Muslims in the municipal government, and this indicates racism. The French government insists that religion and state be separate and forbids the wearing of head scarves; it does little to help the Islamic community, though Muslims have spent years working to build France. The sheikh is not complaining: his voice resounds with a sort of irritated defiance, as though the problems he describes are the inevitable lot of Muslims gone astray in a land of heathens.

In the 1970s, Islam began reviving, he tells me, and this has changed the world. When I counter that this may be the case across the Mediterranean but that here in France I've seen little sign of interest in Islam among the young and more evidence of French cultural influence, he cuts me off. "Our young have been influenced by the *zina'* [fornication] and *khamr* [alcohol] and drugs of France. This is natural. We're working to re-educate them. But they see that there's no answer to their suffering save Islam."

Won't a resurgence in faith hinder integration? I ask.

"*Integration?*" he responds. "We're not for integration. Islam tells us to cooperate with other *ahl al-kitab* ["People of the Book," or Jews and Christians] but not to integrate with them. We're for separation. Islam is in revival the world over, including here. It's the French who are going to be coming to us." He tells me my time is up, rises abruptly, shakes my hand, and goes upstairs, leaving me alone in the empty mosque.

I ponder the incongruity here in France of *zina', khamr, ahl al-kitab*, Koranic words bearing the stony resonance of the Sunna and the commandments, of implacable struggle and sin. The sheikh's rejection of integration runs counter to the basic precept of France's nationality policy—that immigrants accept French values and assimilate. Yet his position derives from irrefutable logic: if his followers integrate, they are no longer his flock, they have been conquered and converted. France's present-day policy of assimilation is, at root, a continuation of the *mission civilisatrice* of colonial days.

If the sheikh rejects integration, it hardly matters: the waning of religion (be it Islam or Christianity) in France portends a future in which race will mean more for North Africans than creed. In fact, it already does.

By reason of geography, restrictive visa regulations, and a policy of selective recruitment that favored the import of Arab labor, immigration from France's former colonies in sub-Saharan Africa has never matched that from North Africa. Black African immigrants account for only around 5 percent of France's foreign population. The Senegalese are the most numerous, followed by an expanding community of Comorians.

I'm having coffee with Nabou Diop, who was born in Senegal but just got her French passport, and her friend Agnes Yameogo, a French citizen with Burkina Fasan parents. Both are in their twenties and have worked as cooks in a Mexican restaurant near the Old Port. We're at Nabou's apartment, which is painted sunny yellow and looks out on a quiet side street splitting off from the hectic Cours Lieutaud. Haunting Senegalese music echoes from her CD player; children shout on the sidewalk below; the curtains are stirring with a breeze bringing in the warmth of the sun and the salty sea air.

Nabou is still relieved by her recent naturalization, which took six years. She has spent most of her life in France and speaks French without an accent, as does Agnes. Yet both are combative and have been stung by racism. Nabou had a hard time finding this apartment. Landlord after landlord, on hearing her French over the phone, mistook her for a white woman; when they met her, *hélas,* their apartments had "just been rented." She tells me old women sometimes grab their purses when they see her, as if she were a thief; her teachers in school tried to discourage her from pursuing a higher education, despite her good grades. She gives other examples. "When I visit Senegal," she says, clenching her small fists, "I feel European. But when I'm here, I feel black. I can't feel at home, even in Marseilles, the capital of Africa!"

Agnes pushes here glasses up the bridge of her nose and seconds Nabou, adding that Africans want to come to France because they will either "die of hunger or emigrate— it's not a question of choice. They're not going on vacation when they come here." The world belongs to the whites, she says. Whites are kings when they visit Africa, but they grudge blacks the chance to feed their families by working a few years in France. Although Agnes and Nabou have white friends, most of the people with whom they feel at ease are other Africans or Arabs from the *quartiers,* who share their sense of exclusion. On the television in the corner we see the faces of news-casters, all white; the blue screen seems to portray an artificial world from which blacks have been banished, Agnes says, and that must be by design.

The breeze stirs the curtain again, bringing in more warmth. *Le capital de l'Afrique.* The climate of Marseilles does call to mind northern Africa. Nabou and Agnes tell me that is why they chose to live here over Paris or Lyon, but wherever they go they are not at home.

The French Ministry of Justice, within whose purview fall mat-ters of naturalization, has stated, rather loftily, that nationality means "belonging. Belonging to a single history, belonging to a sin-gle destiny . . . France has never refused those who want to join its community." "Never" is not exactly the word. The decree of November 2, 1945, governing the status of foreigners on French soil has been amended some thirty times, with each instance making it harder to acquire citizenship or become regularized. In 1999 alone, French maritime authorities captured and deported some 10,000 illegals landing in skiffs or stowing away in ferries. Others who manage to sneak in do so stashed in the backs of trucks, or by hiding in the restrooms on trains, or by walking over the borders from Spain or Italy.[3] In all, some 100,000 illegals make it to France each year. Still others just overstay their visas. Foreigners caught in Marseilles *sans papiers* risk being arrested, locked up for several months in Baumettes Prison, then forcibly expelled by boat through the conveniently located detention center of the port of Arenc. Between 1991 and 1999 the percentage of those banished through Arenc's gates has almost doubled.

There is no way of knowing for sure, of course, but locals in Marseilles put the number of *sans papiers* at 20,000, though it could easily be much higher. The *sans papiers* form an easily exploitable labor pool of docile folk who staff kitchens, bus tables, drive trucks, sweep shops, scrub floors—who do, in short, all the work the French no longer want to do, often for as little as half the legal minimum monthly wage (now set at 5,600 francs, or about $740). The *sans papiers* help proprietors by saving them the social security tax that accounts for half the cost of labor; at the same time, by providing employers with an inexpensive alternative to lawful hires, they foster unemployment. However strict the laws and however rapidly deportation rates are rising, the police expel just enough illegals to appear to be enforcing the law but never so many as to interfere with the cleaning of streets or the busing of tables. This provokes suspicion of collusion—that politicians in power talk loudly but do little about *immigrés* in order to avoid alienating affluent voters (the kind who own restaurants, hotels, and trucking companies, for

[3]In the last five years, at least 3,000 people are known to have drowned making the trip from North Africa, a number that is increasing, but not as dramatically as it would be were not people using cell phones to call rescuers. In June, fifty-eight Chinese suffocated inside a produce truck bound for Britain. Other refugees have died in the cargo containers and holds of ships and planes; some have even fallen from the sky while trying to hide in the wheel wells of planes.

example), or to keep from offending the media (which has always been staunchly left wing) and the liberal sensibilities of the part of the electorate that sympathizes with the plight of the *immigrés*.

The most vulnerable *sans papiers* are the minors, mostly boys, who stow away aboard boats setting sail from Algiers, Oran, and Casablanca. Numbering around 300 at any given time in Marseilles, they gather in public parks and open squares, where their visibility protects them from police beatings and robbery. Some hitchhike out, either to farther points in France or to other EU countries. Many work in the jobs described above, but quite a few deal drugs, sell their bodies, or steal to survive.

At the Marseilles Palace of Justice courthouse I meet Amed Charaabi, a social worker of Tunisian origin employed by an association called Jeunes Errants. Jeunes Errants was founded in 1995 to aid runaway minors, most of whom were escaping the massacres in Algeria but who now tend to come from Sidi Bernoussi, Mouley Sheriff, and Ain Chauk—the spreading bidonvilles of Casablanca. Amed tells minors to return home (Jeunes Errants will pay for their tickets), where they at least have families; he gives them vouchers for meals and puts them up in hotels to get them off the streets.

An Algerian teenager is waiting outside Amed's office at the courthouse. His eyes are red and bleary, his hands chapped and trembling. Walking in on unsteady feet, he greets both of us with a courteous *La bes* ("Hello"), shakes our hands and taps his heart, and sits down in front of Amed's desk. The boy, whom I'll call Hussein here (Amed has agreed to allow me to sit in on the condition that I not reveal names), tells us his story in Algerian Arabic: He watched guerrillas of the Islamic Salvation Front (FIS) slit the throats of two of his neighbors. Then the FIS came after his brother, a policeman, and tried to coerce him into providing them with arms. To escape the pressure, his brother quit the police force, but then he lost his mind. Suddenly, Hussein found himself the sole family breadwinner, so he paid 500 French francs (about $70) to stow away in a container aboard a cargo ship bound for Marseilles. Since landing he has slept behind the railway station. Now, cold and hungry and having failed to find work, he has given up and come to Jeunes Errants for help.

Amed hands him meal tickets, calls around to find him a hotel room, and then explains his only option: application for territorial asylum. The process, during which applicants must prove they've been persecuted by their government, will take months and probably result in a refusal (France rarely grants asylum to Algerians, who flee, as a rule, poverty or the FIS, not the state), but this will give Hussein a chance to collect his wits and decide to head home.

Hussein rises and shakes Amed's hand, tapping his heart, and walks, still on unsteady feet, to the hallway and heads out, this time for a hotel.

In the days of empire, France's *mission civilisatrice* purported to "civilize" the *indigènes* (natives) and gradually turn them into *petits français*—junior French who would labor with alacrity to bring in the colonial harvest. The highest-ranking juniors were the *évolués,* or the evolved ones, colonial subjects trained to work in administrative positions. *Évolués* served two purposes: they cut down on costs by replacing French manpower, and they created the illusion that colonials were profiting from their subservient status, becoming "civilized," as it were. Both *petits français* and *évolués* were to serve the grandeur of France, and one day, or so the ideology posited, in the far, far (and ever receding) future, they would become "civilized" enough to be considered fully French. When independence came, well-positioned *évolués* often ended up running their countries.

Although the colonial era had come to a close long before I

arrived in Marrakesh, I found something like *évolué* culture still thriving there in places. Far from the manure-leavened dust, braying donkeys, and prayer calls of the Casbah, in the clean, once-French quarter of Gueliz, I would meet affluent young Moroccans who would gather in discotheques to speak French, show off their latest haute couture acquisitions, and argue over which Parisian arrondissements were chic, which passé. Many were going to France to study or live. As an Arabist, I found this Francophilia unsettling, even repugnant, in view of Morocco's history as a French protectorate,[4] but the Moroccans did not see it this way: among the elite, French and Moroccan culture had merged, they said, and given them a new identity, one superior to that of the Casbah dwellers. And besides, Morocco was poor, France rich. Was their desire to head north and be French really so tough to understand?

I'm drinking a cocktail with Nadia Borde and her sister Anissa, nées Benhalilou, at their loft-style home on Rue Berceau. Both were born in Algeria and are now in their forties; their father was killed fighting for France in the Algerian War of Independence. After his death, their family moved to Ardèche, near Marseilles, where their status as children of a veteran who had given his life for France facilitated their entry into a society still unused to North Africans. Nadia married a Frenchman and was the first Muslim to be wed in a Catholic church in Ardèche; her grandfather, although a devout Muslim, believed in assimilation and gave her away.

---

[4]France may have greater historical ties to Morocco, but this summer it was Spain that felt the brunt of its refugees. Having shut down its enclaves of Ceuta and Melilla along the Moroccan coast, Spain practically invited Moroccans (fleeing drought, child slavery, and prostitution) and economic and war refugees from sub-Saharan countries (which often have no extradition treaties with EU nations) to sail across the Strait of Gibraltar. "Spain is a doorway into Europe and we are just the doorman," said a Red Cross spokesperson. In August alone, police in one town in Spain intercepted some 600 refugees and some 70 Moroccan extras hired to act in a film about illegal immigration were inspired to sail the Strait themselves.

A librarian, Nadia has eyes that express a passion for learning, as do her flamboyant turns of phrase; her curves hint at a voluptuous attachment to good food and drink. Anissa, a speech therapist, is slender and patrician, frail from a recent struggle with cancer. Both are fair-complexioned enough to pass for French, which has helped them assimilate, but still they have felt alienated, especially when French have told them they "don't even look Arab."

Carrying our own wine, we pile into Nadia's car and drive down to Sur le Pouce, a Tunisian restaurant in Belsunce that serves no alcohol. "The owners have found a balance," Nadia says. "They observe Islam but don't bother others who have different customs. I like that." Sur le Pouce is filled with Arab and French young people downing harissa-flavored couscous, chicken and fries, red wine and pastis. We take a seat and order. I broach the subject of immigration, but we soon drop it: Nadia and Anissa no longer speak much Arabic and are not even accepted as Arab during visits to North Africa; Islam means nothing to them (Nadia is interested in Buddhism), and both talk about their distaste for extremists of any faith. Their hobbies are literature, travel, films (Nadia likes Oliver Stone), good wine and good food; the *quartiers Nord* are as foreign to them as they are to me.

The evening passes with couscous and wine, wine and baklava; our talk ranges over Putin and Russia, Nadia's readings, Nepal and India. They have assimilated and succeeded in their professions; they have moved beyond issues of ethnicity. Were they not now and then reminded of their Arab blood by strangers I sense they might rarely remember it.

Nadia and Anissa chose to adopt French and drop their native language. I think back to Gueliz and my antipathy to Morocco's hybrid culture; I now see that I was wrong. One's valor and value derive from subtler things than choice of language, and that choice is, in any case, largely predetermined by circumstance: by the prosperity associated with a language, by the access that language offers to a secure life, or, as with Nadia and Anissa, by the choice of a father to fight in one army versus another. The wealth and security of France inspire assimilation. The poverty of the Casbah can incite only flight.

Hafid and I have returned to Rue Félix Pyat in the *quartiers Nord* to meet Fresh, but the group has stood us up, and we get out of his car and walk around. He shows me what used to be the police station ("The kids burned it down") on the first floor of the high-rise where he used to live; we walk past it to the back lot. There is a crash and an explosion of glass: someone has thrown a sack of garbage out of a tenth-floor window, and it has landed twenty feet from us. We wander back toward the car, passing through the high-rise's first-floor hallway—a moldering green gallery of piss-splattered walls and fecal stench, rats and rubbish, shuffled through by an old Berber man in a white skullcap. As he passes us I say, "*Salam alaykum,*" but he gives me a dull stare and moves on, shuffling through more trash.

I watch him mount the stairs. Is this what this Berber, who would be so dignified in his village, has left his homeland for—to stomp through garbage in a reeking tenement? Hafid shrugs. "Well, the people here are hoping to move elsewhere. They think this is temporary. *I* moved out, after all." But the man is old, he may not have time. A decision to live in this filth screams desperation—what despair at home impelled this old man to come here?

We drive off to see Mokhtar, another of Hafid's friends, in the *HLMs* of Campagne-L'Evêque. At the entrance to one building we find him, a short and jumpy Comorian with manic eyes. We also meet Halim, of Moroccan origin; Berbali, another Comorian; and James, a Gypsy. Others come up to us, greeting us with *Wesh?*—slang for "What's up?" Hafid talks privately with Mokhtar, and I stand with the youths. James tells me they "steal a little, smoke a little *shit,* hang out, and have a good time . . . that's all." They're all second generation; they know little of their parents' homelands and care less; what counts is that they are from the *quartiers,* of immigrant origin. They owe France nothing ("We didn't ask to be born here"); they no longer go to school ("Why should we? For the French we're just Arabs, we're vandals and no one will give us work"). When a patrol of policemen roars by on motorcycles, the kids shout, *"Les condés!"* and jump inside to hide. But the police roar by, leaving a wake of exhaust drifting our way, and eventually the kids come back out.

Later we return to the center to spend the evening at Le Balthazar listening to rap. At Le Balthazar, teens—Arabs, Africans, and a few French—drink cheap beer in blue-lit murk and dance to the rumble-and-slash beat of NTM (*Nique Ta Mère*—"Fuck Your Mother") played by the DJ, Cash, a young Fenchman dressed in gangsta getup.

The kids in the *quartiers* have embraced black American culture and American rappers are idolized; their thumping verse of protest suits the anger of the second generation. Generational problems are growing: defiance and anger conflict with the bread-and-faith ideals of the first generation, but gangsta rap is winning out, eroding the old ways. One can imagine a time when the second generation will resent the illegals sneaking off boats and bringing with them the Third World, "immigrant" ways of the casbahs and villages.

If the *quartiers Nord* little resemble the working-class or affluent central and southern districts of Marseilles, life there is better than it is in the slums of New York City or Washington, D.C., and this has much to do with the largesse of the French welfare state. It also stems, paradoxically, from the prosperity induced by Euro-oriented policies of fiscal rigor—policies that one day could prompt the dismantling of the welfare state—and from measures introduced by Marseilles's Mayor Gaudin. Gaudin has spent money on the city's infrastructure to attract investment and promote tourism of the cruise-ship and conference-center variety, hitherto almost unknown in Marseilles; he has begun a policy of matching private investment with state funds. This has brought about some modest successes, or so the numbers (and many white French) say, reducing unemployment by 3 percent, reversing Marseilles's twenty-five-year-long drop in population, and increasing tax revenues. Gaudin's first deputy, Renaud Muselier, after explaining to me his government's chief accomplishment—"halting the spiral of decline"—launches into a prolix explanation of what clearly matters the most to him: his city's growing attractiveness to multinationals, its expanding music industry, and its readiness for the "New Economy." When I ask what he's doing for the *quartiers Nord,* he says the city is funding a program to encourage small *quartier* entrepreneurs to remain there. That's all.

The proprietors and shop owners catering to tourists are benefiting from the new prosperity, but it's hard to see who else is. Even this minimal prosperity, however, is already exercising its pull: more and more *sans papiers* are showing up on Cours Belsunce hoping to better their lives. Yet the cuts in public spending that may be necessary if France and Europe are to succeed in creating an economic union that can compete with the United States could, at least in the short run, worsen the plight of the *quartiers* by cutting welfare funds and bringing about American-style disparities of income.

May 1 is Labor Day in Europe. The local Committee for the Unemployed has told me that the *sans papiers* of Marseilles will be marching down La Canebière in the May Day parade to demand regularization. It is the Left, including the Committee, that has taken up the cause of the *sans papiers,* organizing them in marches and protests, agitating for their regularization, and opposing their deportation.

A warm, shifting breeze is blowing off the Mediterranean, soughing through the plane trees on La Canebière. The turnout for the parade is small—only 2,000 or so. Led by a bored-looking marching band playing what sound like Salvation Army tunes, the crowd carries banners bearing the slogans of yesteryear ("LONG LIVE THE PEOPLE'S WAR!" "WE DEMAND FULL EMPLOY- MENT!" "THE WORKING CLASS IS INTERNATIONAL!") mixed in with those of today ("STRUGGLE! SOLIDARITY! LEISURE ACTIVITIES!" "COMBAT GLOBALIZATION!"). One group of students bears a limp Soviet flag; a red-kerchiefed contin- gent marches, fists raised, under Che Guevara posters. Kurds hold- ing portraits of Abdullah Ocalan, leader of the Kurdish Workers Party, provide the only diversion: their loudspeakers blare the sav- age mountain bagpipe-and-drums music of Kurdistan into the soft clear air.

It turns out that no *sans papiers* are marching—perhaps they've been kept away by fear of the police, who are out in force. After the Kurds come the only marchers campaigning for immigrant rights, or one right, according to their banner: the right of noncitizens to vote in local elections. Where La Canebière cuts through Cours Belsunce they pass cliques of Moroccans and Algerians, who ignore them.

Disappointed by the absence of *sans papiers* (not to mention the anachronistic character of the march), I break away and head down to the quays of the Old Port, where crowds of young North Africans are out and about enjoying the sun. They are safe in their numbers; there are too many of them for the police to bother checking papers.

In the faces of these North Africans is the change coming to Europe. They have arrived as part of a migration that, like exoduses of ancient days, is taking place outside the control of men or the pale of law; it is a migration prompted by imbalances and inequalities grown too widespread, deep, and complex to rectify, at least anytime soon. Colonizer and colonized are reversing roles, but it is France that is benefiting the most, drawing its former subjects out of their failed homelands and profiting from their energy, youth, and low-cost labor, growing richer from their vibrant cultures. France is becoming, for the first time in its history, and against its will, a true *terre d'immigration* for peoples of all races. However distressing many French find this transformation, and whatever problems and discomfort all parties are suffering along the way, a confluence of demographic and economic factors on both sides of the Mediterranean ensures that it will continue, as certainly as the disparities between the First and Third Worlds will increase and multiply.

I reach the end of the quays and halt. The disparities between the two camps on either shore of the Mediterranean may eventually bring about a new dynamic, a dynamic of rage and destitution on one side and sated arrogance and barricades on the other. If this happens, egalitarian ideals may be a luxury even France will not be able to afford.

But that is conjecture; for now, there is sun, there is wind. From its perch high above the city, the gilded statue of the Virgin Mary atop Notre-Dame-de-La-Garde is splintering shards of sunlight into the azure. I draw in deep breaths of air blowing fresh from the Mediterranean, then head back to the parade to catch the last of the Kurdish songs.

Bibliothèque

The First Eden: The Mediterranean World and Man, Sir David Attenborough, William Collins Sons & Co. Ltd./BBC Books, London, 1987. The four parts of this book deal with natural history, archaeology, history, and ecology, and there is very good coverage of Mediterranean plants and animals.

The Inner Sea: The Mediterranean and Its People, Robert Fox, Alfred A. Knopf, 1993. *De rigueur.*

Mediterranean: A Cultural Landscape, Predrag Matvejevic, translated by Michael Henry Heim, University of California Press, Berkeley, 1999; previously published as *Mediteranski brevijar,* Zagreb, 1987; *Bréviaire méditerranéen,* Paris, 1992; and *Mediterraneo: Un nuovo breviario,* Milan, 1993. A beautiful, unusual book combining personal observations with history, maps, maritime details, people, and language.

The Mediterranean, Fernand Braudel, first published in France, 1949; English translation of second revised edition, HarperCollinsPublishers, 1972; abridged edition, HarperCollins, 1992. Still the definitive classic. *De rigueur.*

On the Shores of the Mediterranean, Eric Newby, first published by The Harvill Press, London, 1984; Picador, 1985. You have to travel with Eric and Wanda Newby to Italy, the former Yugoslavia, Greece, Turkey, Israel, North Africa, and Spain before arriving on the Côte d'Azur (the next to last chapter is entitled "Dinner at the Negresco"), but it's a pleasure every word of the way.

The Pillars of Hercules: A Grand Tour of the Mediterranean, Paul Theroux, G. P. Putnam's Sons, 1995.

The Spirit of Mediterranean Places, Michel Butor, The Marlboro Press, 1986.

World War II in the Mediterranean: 1942–1945, Carlo d'Este, with an introduction by John S. D. Eisenhower, Major Battles, and Campaigns Series, Algonquin Books of Chapel Hill, 1990. Laurence Wylie, author of *Village in the Vaucluse,* an excellent account of the year he spent in Roussillon in the 1950s, was told repeatedly by the people he met that he had come to their village too late, that he should have come before the war, when life was different. Yet Roussillon (he gave the village the fictional name of Peyrane in the book) escaped nearly all the tragic effects of the war (unlike neighboring Gordes). No Germans or Americans came to the village, there was no bomb damage, there were no reprisals or fighting in the commune itself. When he asked exactly how life was different, the replies were, "We were better off then. Life wasn't so hard. We got along better. There was a dance every Saturday night, and we were always visiting back and forth with each other over a cup of coffee. Now everyone stays at home. The war changed life." Although few French towns, if any, could have been less untouched physically, Wylie noted that "from all the stories one hears, and from all the nasty incidents that people today allude to but prefer not to recount, the effect of the war situation on life in the village was devastating, especially insofar as the ability of people to live comfortably together is concerned." Wylie learned that at the time of Liberation in 1945, a local *maquis* (Résistance) chief took over the governing of the commune. The chief received a telegram from a departmental committee office notifying him to arrest twelve supposed collaborators from Roussillon. He reportedly ripped the telegram up and remarked that the village's affairs would be dealt with as they always had been: as a family, with no interference from outside. Ian Norrie, author of *Next Time Round in Provence*, adds his own footnote to this account: "The Rousillonnais were not to be allowed to settle old scores or perpetuate feuds on a wave of fervent nationalism. They were one village; they were rebuilding their lives." Though Operation Anvil—the invasion of the French Riviera—is greatly overshadowded by the D-day landings, the Mediterranean theater of war was hardly insignificant, both psychologically and socially as Wylie has noted above, and strategically, as military historian d'Este outlines in this book. Eisenhower, in his introduction, reminds us that during just one Mediterranean campaign, battle deaths among Americans, British, and French totaled 32,000 men. "That staggering figure almost equals that of the 33,000 American troops killed during the entire Korean War (1950–1953). It even compares to the number (47,300) killed in the ten-year Vietnam conflict (1963–72) . . . By no means do these figures denigrate the traumas undergone by our soldiers in other conflicts; they merely explain our wonder at how such a large campaign as the Mediterranean could be treated as 'secondary.'" This is one of the few single volumes devoted to this arena of WWII, and though a bit dry at times, it's an interesting read with good maps and some black-and-white photos. ~A related companion to this book is Michelin map #103, Bataille de Provence: Août 1944, a reprint of the historical map originally published in 1947. It's printed in both French and English and should be available wherever Michelin maps are sold. If you can't find it, contact Librairie de France in New York (see Bookstores for information).

Mediterranean Architecture and Style

Mediterranean Color: Italy, France, Spain, Portugal, Morocco, Greece, photographs and text by Jeffrey Becom, foreword by Paul Goldberger, Abbeville Press, 1990.

Mediterranean Living, Lisa Lovatt-Smith, Whitney Library of Design, Watson-Guptill Publications, 1998.

Mediterranean Style, Catherine Haig, Abbeville Press, 1998; first published in Great Britain in 1997 by Conran Octopus Ltd., London.

Mediterranean Vernacular, V. I. Atroshenko, Milton Grundy, Rizzoli, 1991.

Villages in the Sun: Mediterranean Community Architecture, Myron Goldfinger, Rizzoli, 1993.

France

The Collapse of the Third Republic: An Inquiry into the Fall of France in 1940, William Shirer, Simon & Schuster, 1969. I wasn't surprised to find that Shirer (*The Rise and Fall of the Third Reich*) had written this book, only that I didn't know he had until recently. It is, as you might expect, as thoroughly researched and revealing as *Rise and Fall,* and he carefully illustrates, point by point, how the fall of France was an absolute debacle. Until reading this I hadn't realized the extent of the utter chaos—the complete lack of communication between high government officials themselves as well as with the public—that followed the news that the Germans were en route to Paris. As professor and French historian Marc Bloch recounts in the book, "It was the most terrible collapse in all the long story of our national life." Over a thousand pages, no photos, but with good maps. *De rigueur.*

Creating French Culture: Treasures from the Bibliothèque Nationale de France, introduction by Emmanuel Le Roy Ladurie, edited by Marie-Hélène Tesnière and Prosser Gifford, Yale University Press in association with The Library of Congress, Washington, and the Bibliothèque Nationale de France, Paris, 1995. The creators of the exhibit developed a theme for this project, which is to explore the relationship between culture and power in France, but I see this as nothing less than a history of France as told through its documents, manuscripts, books, orchestra scores, photographs, prints, drawings, maps, medals, and coins. Covering twelve centuries—from the time of Charlemagne to the present—you can imagine how extensive this collection is (the book runs to 478 pages). Some highlights include the "Letter of Suleyman the Magnificent to Francis I, King of France"; first edition of *The New Justine, or The Misfortunes of Virtue* by the Marquis de Sade; map of the battle of Austerlitz; and the handwritten *"J'accuse"* letter by Émile Zola in defense of Captain Alfred Dreyfus, which was then printed on the front page of *L'Aurore* on 13 January, 1898. I *love* this book. It's a masterpiece. Also included are a chronology of the history of France and good color maps.

Fragile Glory, Richard Bernstein, Alfred A. Knopf, 1990. To my mind, this is the best overall book about France since Fernand Braudel's classic mentioned below. It, too, is out of print, but I still see copies of it in used bookstores. Bernstein was the Paris correspondent for *The New York Times* from 1984 to

1987, and his book explores a variety of topics, including a chapter on *la France profonde,* which is in fact the best I've ever read on the true definition of "deep France," naming French children, the myth of the anti-American, immigrants, French aristocrats, politics and parties, Jean-Marie Le Pen, *les affaires,* the French struggle with its past. By the final chapter, Bernstein has laid the foundation for two major but sometimes contradictory conclusions: that France is still a nation greater than the sum of its parts, but that the French people are becoming more like everyone else, losing many qualities that once made them *différent. De rigueur.*

France on the Brink: A Great Civilization Faces the New Century, Jonathan Fenby, Arcade Publishing, 1999. As excellent as the older books recommended here are, an updated book on France was in order, and we now have Fenby's volume to provide us with thoughtful fodder for the early twenty-first century. Journalist Fenby—who has written for *The Economist, The Christian Science Monitor, The Times* of London, and has been editor of the *South China Morning Post*—is married to a Frenchwoman and was named a chevalier of the French Order of Merit in 1990. He's been reporting on France for over thirty years, and in this work he presents a full array of the country's ills and contradictions, some of which are familiar (the Résistance was smaller than we like to think; high unemployment; immigration; government corruption) but nonetheless remain for the French to reconcile. Readers who haven't kept up with the France of today may be alarmed to discover that some classic French icons—berets, baguettes, accordions, cafés, foie gras—are fading. In his review of the book for *The New York Times,* European cultural correspondent Alan Riding wrote that "the entire book serves as a valuable introduction to contemporary France." I would add that is also *de rigueur* reading.

France: The Outsider, Granta No. 59, published by Granta Publications, United Kingdom, distributed in the U.S. by Penguin Books USA, autumn 1997. This edition of the hip British literary magazine features modern France and *le malaise français* with essays by Patrick Chamoiseau, Luc Sante, Caroline LaMarche, David Macey, Assia Djebar, and others; a selection of contemporary French slang from *Le Dico de l'Argot fin de siècle* by Pierre Merle; and a photo essay, "The Farm at Le Garet," by Magnum photographer Raymond Depardon. As always, an insightful collection, and worth the effort to special order. (All *Granta* back issues are in print and can be ordered by sending $5 and the issue date to Granta USA, 1755 Broadway, 5th floor, New York, New York 10019; subscribers may order back issues—at up to 50 percent off—through the Web site www.granta.com.)

France Under the Germans: Collaboration and Compromise, Philippe Burrin, The New Press, 1996, translated from the French by Janet Lloyd. Robert Paxton referred to this book as "unsurpassed," and it is most definitely thorough and exhaustively researched. It's different from Paxton's own book in that Burrin, a Swiss historian, focuses on three sections of French society, each of which accommodated the Germans: French government, civil society, and a small but significant circle of journalists, politicians, and "ordinary" French people who voiced collaborationist opinions. Burrin seeks to dissect the meaning of the word *collaboration* itself, as it was first used by Pétain in October 1940 and which then passed into German as *Kollaboration*. It is important, as Burrin notes in his introduction, to understand how being occupied looked to the French then, and how they did not—perhaps could not—know what road they were going down and were not able to see the enemy for what he was. It may be too soon to refer to this work as a classic, but it already is to my mind. No photos, but a useful, long list of appropriate abbreviations and—best of all—a map clearly showing where the free and occupied zones began and ended.

The Identity of France, Fernand Braudel, in two volumes both translated by Sian Reynolds; *Volume I: History and Environment,* William Collins Sons and Co., Ltd., London, 1988; *Volume II: People and Production,* HarperCollins, 1988; first published in France under the title *L'Identité de la France,* 1986. This monumental work is phenomenal in its scope and originality. Braudel, who passed away in 1985, has been referred to as the "greatest of Europe's historians" and believed strongly in the necessity of world history. His genius was in his ability to link people and events across all time periods—in a single sentence. "Economic geography" was one phrase he came up with just before his death to describe his approach to history; yet he acknowledged that even this was not quite right. This is an unprecedented work, inexplicably out of print, but worth all efforts to track it down.

Mission to Civilize: The French Way, Mort Rosenblum, Doubleday, 1988. When Rosenblum wrote this, he was senior foreign correspondent for the Associated Press in Paris (he is now a special correspondent to the AP and is also the author of *Olives,* North Point Press/Farrar, Straus & Giroux, 1996). His career as a journalist took him to North and West Africa, the South Pacific, Asia, the southeastern U.S., the Caribbean, the Middle East, Canada, and all the former and present DOM-TOMS (*départements d'outre-mer* and *territoires d'outre-mer*) of France. Yes, this book is about France, but more specifically it is about the importance of *la mission civilisatrice* (read: colonization) to the French. Rosenblum recalls de Gaulle's famous remark: *"La France est la lumière du monde"* ("France is the light of the world"). He explains the seemingly contradictory French foreign policy; the difference between a *mauvaise foi* and *mauvais caractère;* the Rainbow Warrior *bavure* (*bavure* being a hitch or foul-up, notably by officials or police, which is so common that a smooth operation is referred to as *sans bavure*); *beurs* and *beaufs;* the struggles in Algeria and Vietnam and the atrocities committed in both; and the introduction of *"Faites mon jour"* ("Make my day"), *hypermarché* (supermarket), and *le fast food* into the language. *De rigueur.*

Portraits of France, Robert Daley, Little, Brown and Company, 1991. Daley has put together a miniature tour of French history and culture in this collection of twenty essays. He's combined a thousand years of French history in the book, with each portrait representing France as a whole. The portraits take readers to all corners of *l'hexagone,* including a number featuring southern French locales: Nice, Monte Carlo, Grasse, Avignon, and Les Baux. The Les Baux piece (subtitled "Drinking an 1806 Château Lafite") relates the time he and his wife drank an 1806 Lafite at Oustaù de Baumanière. It remains one of the very best essays about a wine experience I've ever read.

Realms of Memory: The Construction of the French Past, Pierre Nora, English-language edition edited and with a foreword by Lawrence Kritzman, translated by Arthur Goldhammer, Columbia University Press; *Volume I: Conflicts and Divisions* (1996); *Volume II: Traditions* (1997); *Volume III: Symbols* (1998). Originally published in France in seven volumes as *Les Lieux de Mémoire* (memory places), this astounding collection is at the top of my *de rigueur* reading list. I will go so far as to say that if you fancy yourself a knowledgeable Francophile and *haven't* read these, you are perhaps a *poseur.* This series is nothing short of a singular publishing event, hailed by *The Times Literary Supplement* in London as "a magisterial attempt to define what it is to be French."

The Road from the Past: Traveling Through History in France, Ina Caro, Nan A. Talese (an imprint of Doubleday), 1994. What a grand and sensible plan Ina Caro presents in her marvelous book: travel through France in a "time machine" (a car), from Provence to Paris, and experience numerous centuries of French history chronologically in one trip. I envy her and her husband, Robert Caro (the award-winning biographer of Robert Moses and Lyndon Johnson), for making such an unforgettable journey. I always plan my visits chronologically no matter *where* I'm going, so I am especially partial to Caro's method. Her route in this book takes travelers through Provence, Languedoc, the Dordogne, the Loire Valley, and ends in the Île-de-France. We not only progress chronologically, but the sites she has selected are the most beautiful examples representing each historical period. The journey begins in Provence in the first chapter, covering Orange, the Pont du Gard, Nîmes, and Les Alpilles. As the journey continues, you begin to see how every region and every period is related. Caro's approach presents a unique way of looking at France, at history, and at travel. This is a very special *de rigueur* companion.

Vichy France: Old Guard and New Order, 1940–1944, Robert O. Paxton, Alfred A. Knopf, 1972. It doesn't take long to discover that, among the number of books about Vichy, the definitive volume is Paxton's. If you're only going to read one, read this. An internationally recognized authority on this subject, Paxton was an expert witness at the trial of Maurice Papon in 1997 (see his editorial "Vichy on Trial," *The New York Times*, October 16, 1997). Understanding France during World War II is complicated at best, but is essential for understanding France at all today. Paxton documents the inner workings of the Vichy government, the politics between Philippe Pétain, Pierre Laval, and François Darlan, and the surprisingly slow growth of the Résistance. The revelation that the Vichy government enjoyed such mass support came as somewhat of a shock when this book was published in 1972. It is accepted knowledge that the French wanted to avoid the destruction of France at all costs, and Paris remains a beautiful city in part because of accommodation and collaboration. But the history of this period is certainly not as simple as that. As Paxton writes, "It is tempting to identify with Résistance and to say, 'That is what I would have done.' Alas, we are far more likely to act, in parallel situations, like the Vichy majority . . . The deeds of occupier and occupied alike suggest that there come cruel times when to save a nation's deepest values, one must disobey the state. France after 1940 was one of those times."

When Courage Was Stronger Than Fear: Remarkable Stories of Christians Who Saved Jews from the Holocaust, Peter Hellman, Marlowe & Company (Balliett & Fitzgerald Inc.), distributed by Publishers Group West, 1999; originally published as *Avenue of the Righteous,* Atheneum, 1980. In 1968, Peter Hellman visited Yad Vashem, the National Holocaust Memorial in Jerusalem, and was especially struck by the simplicity of the Avenue des Justes, better known in English as Avenue of the Righteous. The avenue is really a path lined with carob—and more recently, olive—trees, and under each tree is a small plaque displaying the name of a Christian (and in some cases a Moslem) who saved one or more Jews from Nazi persecution. Hellman recognized that this simplicity was deceiving, that there was a dramatic story behind each and every one of these plaques. He decided that very day that he wanted to learn more about these remarkable people. In this book he profiles five documented cases of the Righteous, each representing a different country (France, Italy, Belgium, Holland, and Poland). His only criterion was that the Righteous person still be living and accessible, which obviously narrowed the field a bit. I include Hellman's work here both because it is inspiring and significant, and because the chapter on Raoul Laporterie gives a very good account of life on both sides of the demarcation line (Raoul owned a clothing business on the occupied side but lived on the Vichy side, making it possible to offer his services as a *passeur,* someone who could slip Jews and others across the border). I consider this wonderful book *de rigueur,* but it comes with a warning: avoid reading it on public transportation unless you don't mind others seeing your tears.

Your Name Is Renee: Ruth's Story as a Hidden Child, Stacy Cretzmeyer, Biddle Publishing Company, Brunswick, Maine, 1994. While Raoul Laporterie's story in Peter Hellman's book above is of a *passeur*, Ruth Kapp Hartz's story is of a refugee, written by a college classmate of mine. It is, obviously, a bit more dramatic: Ruth, only four years old in 1941, and her family were foreign Jews (originally from Germany), and as such were targeted to be expelled from the Unoccupied Zone. They had left Paris soon after the Nazis arrived in 1940, and their lives since that time was one forced departure after another, moving from place to place in southern France, much of the time in hiding and several times nearly discovered. Without giving away the details, Ruth (alias Renee Caper) survived the war, and it wasn't until it ended that she realized she was wrong about how the French population had acted during the Occupation. Because she was sheltered in the south, where she was treated kindly and protected by a number of citizens, she truly believed that 90 percent of the population had been involved in the Résistance. Upon her return to Paris in 1946, she was shocked and confused to confront anti-Semitism. In the Afterword, she offers some thoughts on how to account for this difference. Two appendices cover the Nazi occupation of France and the French Résistance, and there are a few black-and-white photographs throughout the book. *De rigueur.*

The French

Culture Shock! France: A Guide to Customs and Etiquette, Sally Adamson Taylor, Graphic Arts Publishing Company, Portland, Oregon, 1990. Each Culture Shock! edition is authored by a different writer, and each is eminently enlightening. The France edition covers such topics as speaking and thinking in French, French film, the French attitude toward pets, why things close for lunch, do's and don't's in a restaurant, visas and work permits, queuing, being a guest in a French home, and office and business relationships. The Culture Quiz at the end of the book is particularly helpful. A really useful, basic guide that I consider *de rigueur* reading.

French or Foe?: Getting the Most out of Visiting, Living and Working in France, Polly Platt, Culture Crossings Ltd./Distribooks, Inc., Skokie, Illinois, 1996. Platt's on-the-mark book is without doubt the best one of its kind, and I consider it *de rigueur* for anyone planning to live, work, or study in France and anyone who really, really, really wants to understand France and the ways of the French. Platt's own company, Culture Crossings, which she incorporated in 1986, provides training seminars and workshops for corporate managers and executives and their spouses transferred to foreign countries. There is no other book as comprehensive as hers, covering such topics as perfecting the *mine d'enterrement* (funereal expression); French time; what *non* really means; what to expect at a dinner party; *se débrouiller* and *le système D;* the logic of French management, and more. In addition to explanations, Platt offers her own personal tips, such as the Ten Magic Words: *Excusez-moi de vous déranger, Monsieur, mais j'ai un problème.* You'll find this irresistibly indispensable.

The French, Theodore Zeldin, Vintage, 1984; originally published in Great Britain by William Collins' Sons & Co. Ltd., London, and in the U.S. by Pantheon Books, 1983. Zeldin's book is referenced entirely too often not to be considered the reigning classic. Zeldin is perhaps better known for his *France, 1848–1945* (Oxford), a monumental social history published in both a single-volume hardcover and a five-volume paperback series. Nearly all the works listed in his bibliography in *The French* are in French, so his perspective is not exclusively British/American. I feel the book is so good because, as Zeldin explains on the first page, he puts a lot of stock in humor. As we know, comedians are often the only people willing to blurt out the truth, and Zeldin believes "nothing separates people more than their sense of humor." He finds it interesting that the world knows so much about French cooking, wine, and the fine arts but little to nothing about French humor. Thus this book is filled with dozens of caricatures and cartoons, which help illustrate various points. In addition to six chapters, there are interviews with various French notables, including Brigitte Bardot, Yves Montand, and Paul Bocuse, and the concluding chapter, "What It Means to Be French," is alone a candidate for *de rigueur* reading.

The French: Portrait of a People, Sanche de Gramont, G. P. Putnam's Sons, 1969. Although published over thirty years ago, this book is still meaningful and truthful. Gramont is an astute bi-national observer (French-born, American-educated—at Yale and Columbia—and married to an American), and his book takes a different approach from Zeldin's above. It's divided into two parts, "Data" and "Forms of Exchange," and Gramont manages to be both critical and fond of the French, going to great lengths to explain why they are simultaneously so imitated and so misunderstood. It's a shame this is out of print, but I see it often in used bookstores.

The French Way: Aspects of Behavior, Attitude, and Customs of the French, Ross Steele, Passport Books, Lincolnwood, Illinois, 1995. One of my favorite books, this is a slim, handy A–Z guide to eighty-five traits of the French. Steele has compiled an interesting and useful list, including abbreviations and acronyms tourists will need to recognize; the significance of the *bleu-blanc-rouge;* how *cartes de visite* (business cards) are used; *cocorico!* (not cock-a-doodle-doo); the French meaning of the word *extra* and other false friends of English; *gendarmes, agents de police,* and *les manifestations;* the deeper meanings of the word *grandeur; l'Hexagone;* high tech; holidays; immigration; "La Marseillaise"; names and name days; numbers; *la France métropolitaine;* politeness and directness; *le système D;* sports; time; xenophobia; and *yéyé. Absolument de rigueur.*

NYONS
NYONS
CŒUR DE LA DRÔME PROVENÇALE

Château des Baux
MONUMENT D'EXCEPTION

villard de lans
VERCORS DAUPHINE
TOUT VERT OU TOUT BLANC

21-7-00

Provence

"*Provence is a country to which I am always returning, next week, next year, any day now, as soon as I can get on to a train.*"
—Elizabeth David, FRENCH PROVINCIAL COOKING

～

"*As one enters Provence from the north, there is a place that never fails to have a magical effect on my spirits. After Montélimar, the road passes through a gorge that pinches right up to the shoulder of the autoroute, then opens out upon a vast, vine-covered plain. The effect is emotionally exhilarating, like the untying of a mental knot, a release and a shock of open space within that mirrors the widening landscape without. Shortly afterward, a large road sign announces:* VOUS ÊTES EN PROVENCE. *Provence is good for the psyche. By the time I approach Cassis and that first breathtaking view of the glistening Mediterranean, I am singing, I am happy, I am chez moi.*"
—Kermit Lynch, ADVENTURES ON THE WINE ROUTE

Rome's Resort

BY ALEXANDRA FOGES

⌇

editor's note

....

One can go from town to town in Provence and witness the Roman conquest of the region. Here is an excellent piece focusing on eight glorious towns and monuments.

ALEXANDRA FOGES is a frequent contributor to *Condé Nast Traveler*, where this piece appeared in April 2000.

The Grand Hotel Nord-Pinus stands on the south side of the Place du Forum, in the middle of Arles. It isn't especially grand, despite its name, but it has the solid, reassuringly bourgeois air of many provincial buildings that were built halfway through the last century. The windows have green louvered shutters, the balcony is black wrought iron, and the plane trees dapple the summer sun in a way that positively *forces* you to sit down at one of the tables outside and order a glass of pastis. And since it was about two o'clock on a late August afternoon when I did just that, and since I was in France, my aperitif led inexorably to a dish of tiny, almost pitch-black olives that led, in turn, to a basket of bread, which was followed by some ratatouille and *loup de mer* suffused with the scent of fennel, lemon, and the Mediterranean.

It seemed, at the time, like a perfectly natural progression.

Earlier that day, I had been in Aix-en-Provence and had bought a book called *La Provence Romaine* in a secondhand bookstore lost somewhere in the maze of medieval streets behind the old town hall. It must have been published in the fifties; the photographs were black-and-white and slightly hazy, and even though I had to stop every few minutes to consult my Larousse, the story it told was thrilling.

I balanced the enormous book beside my plate and read about the Arena in Arles, built by the Romans in the first century A.D. to hold 26,000 spectators, baying for the blood of gladiators who fought to the death, either against each other or against exotic wild animals imported from Africa. An amphitheater that not only still stands but is regularly used by modern-day Arlesians, whose blood-lust has been redirected toward the only marginally more acceptable sport of bullfighting.

The book described the theater, where classical dramas were (and still are) performed, and Constantine's Baths, where the Romans indulged in their passion for spas, massage, and gossip. The Alyscamps, a long, mournful allée of marble sarcophagi and cypress trees, was where rich Romans went when they died, with much pomp and at considerable expense. And then there were the mysterious Cryptoportiques, buried deep beneath a Jesuit church, which were part of a Roman granary or sewer—depending on which source you believed.

It was clear that Arles had been, in some ways, a much grander and more magnificent town two thousand years ago. First of all, Roman towns were laid out on what any self-respecting Manhattan dweller will tell you is the New York City grid system. Those winding little side streets that we find so charming now are the work of the barbarian hordes who swept through Provence after the fall of the empire. Roman architects had a Cartesian passion for strict symmetry and proportion, and their town planning always followed the same pattern: the north-south main drag was called the Cardo, the east-west one the Decumanus. All the other, smaller streets ran parallel to them.

The Romans also built for the long haul—witness the vast Arena. And they built on a monumental scale—witness the great

Pont du Gard aqueduct, part of a waterworks that fed their baths at Nîmes. Or the Arles circus, now destroyed, which must have been at least three times the size of the Arena and was used for chariot races. Or the original forum, which was more than twice as big as the Place du Forum where I was sitting, about to take the next, inexorable step toward a large platter of cheese.

I put the book aside, looked up at the facade of the Nord-Pinus, and was amazed to see something that I had completely failed to notice before. Embedded in the corner of this otherwise quite ordinary nineteenth-century building were two colossal Corinthian pillars supporting the broken corner of an equally enormous pediment, grotesquely out of scale. There was something strange and almost frightening about these vestiges of Rome that had attached themselves, like some alien growth from the past, to my cozy little hotel. And yet there was also something deeply exciting about them.

I walked over to read a plaque on the wall of the hotel. The gigantic pillars and pediment, which reached all the way to the roof of the four-story building, had been part of a huge temple. They were all that remained of the ancient forum, which had once been the noisy, crowded, bustling epicenter of Roman Arles.

Later that night, I stepped out onto the balcony of my room and looked down at the sparkling lights in the Place du Forum. A bronze statue of Frédéric Mistral, with his flowing coat and poet's hat, dominated the square, and to his right a skinny young man—his emaciated arms covered in wild tattoos—took a gulp of gasoline and then . . . whoosh . . . used a lighter to set fire to his own breath. For a split second the square was lit by flames, but the people having dinner outdoors were too engrossed in each other, or in their food, to notice the poet, the fire-eater, or the Corinthian columns.

It must have been around midnight, but I was still haunted by the memory of the forum, and so just before I went back inside to go to sleep, I stepped to the edge of the balcony and reached out, across two thousand years, to touch . . . Rome.

Provence, whose name comes from the Latin word for this former Roman territory, Provincia, was part of the Roman Empire for more than five hundred years, from 118 B.C. to the fall of Rome in A.D. 476—years that left an indelible mark upon French art, culture, law, language, and life. Look at the Arc de Triomphe and you see a pompous copy of the triumphal arch just outside the Roman town of Glanum, near St.-Rémy. Walk around the Madeleine in Paris, on your guilty way to pick out some secret gastronomical indulgence at Fauchon, and you are looking at a bigger, cruder version of the mesmerizingly beautiful Maison Carrée in Nîmes. One of the handful of real superstars in the Louvre is a Roman statue, the still seductive, perfectly proportioned *Venus d'Arles,* whose breasts have defied age and gravity for two millennia. And in Provence, if you listen carefully you will notice that there seem to be a surprising number of men named Marius. And why? In honor of the great Roman general Marius, who defeated the barbarians near Aix in 102 B.C. and saved the empire.

After this decisive battle, the Romans expanded and consolidated their grip on Provincia, which now stretched north as far as Lyon and west to Narbonne. They built three massive roads: the Via Aurelia, the seventeen-hundred-mile road connecting Rome to Cadiz; the Via Domitian, which started near the Alps in Briançon and descended south from there to join up with the Aurelia; and the Via Agrippa, which followed the course of the Rhône, heading due north from the Mediterranean (which the Romans modestly called Mare Nostrum, or Our Sea).

If these roads were the arteries of Provincia, the flesh, bones, and brains were the spectacular new towns clustered along them.

Each was built as a mini-clone of Rome, with a forum, an arena, baths, a theater, temples, and a circus. So skillful were the architects, and so sophisticated the citizens, that Livy reported that these provincial towns were in fact "more like Italy than Italy." If you look at some of the intricate mosaic floors in the ruins at Vaison-la-Romaine, or at the chic, minimalist black-and-white floor in the Villa Maritima at St.-Cyr, or at any one of the elaborately carved marble sarcophagi in the museum at Arles, you see immediately just how luxurious life—at least for the upper classes—must have been.

Most of these towns were founded as retirement communities for the victorious Roman legionnaires, the Palm Beaches or Fort Lauderdales of the empire. A soldier would generally serve in the army for twenty years, and was ready, by the age of about forty, for his well-earned material reward in the sun. Nîmes, for example, was founded by the legions that defeated Antony and Cleopatra at the Battle of Actium; Arles was given to the Sixth Legion, which had fought against Pompey at Marseille; Orange was founded by the Second Legion.

As a strategy, it was brilliant: The soldiers got the land they craved, and Rome got the towns it needed to rule Provincia. It must be one of the great win-win stories of history. There are Roman ruins scattered all over southern France (with just a few farther north), but the most impressive ones, Nîmes, Arles, Orange, Glanum, and Vaison-la-Romaine, and the Pont du Gard, are concentrated around a fairly small area on both sides of the Rhône—all within a few days' march of each other. Or, in my case, a very lazy day's drive.

I came to Nîmes for the Maison Carrée and the equally famous Arena, but I somehow found myself swept into that essential and totally irresistible element of French life: the market. One end was dedicated to the nourishment of the body, with every conceivable fruit and vegetable grown in this fertile soil. (According to

Lawrence Durrell, Arles was called The Breasts by the Romans, so fruitful was she. Which may be one of Durrell's many lubricious fantasies, since I never found a reference to this in any of my other books.) The other end offered a deliciously anarchic jumble of objects for sale, ranging from some "Tee-Sheurts," a steal at ten francs apiece, to heavy, white linen sheets embroidered with the initials of long-dead brides, to some ragged red-and-gold Chinese puppets that looked as though they'd taken part in one too many performances. There were boxes and boxes of old books, with separate piles marked ALGÉRIE and INDOCHINE, telltale clues to France's ongoing obsession with her two most profound colonial traumas. Hard to resist a book called *J'étais Médecin à Dien-Bien-Phu,* especially since it had a full-color cover showing mangled corpses strewn across the mud, or *Attaché Navale à Moscou,* which somehow didn't promise quite the same degree of life-and-death drama. The stall holders were a laidback group—literally—lounging around on dusty old sofas behind their stands, far too busy chatting to their dogs, smoking furiously, or tending to the urgent chirp of their cell phones to be bothered with trying to sell anybody anything.

If the monumental arenas, the colossal circuses, and the grandeur of their aqueducts all evoke the alpha-male aura of Roman power and military might, then the mind-altering beauty of the Maison Carrée has always seemed to me to represent the feminine side of the Roman aesthetic. And, as if to prove my theory, many men have, over the centuries, fallen passionately in love with this sublime building. Colbert was so infatuated with it that he threatened to move the whole thing to the grounds of Louis XIV's newly constructed palace at Versailles, while Thomas Jefferson, when he was U.S. Minister in Paris, made a special journey south in order to see it. Even the bloodless Henry James fell for her charms, and Stendhal, who knew a thing or two about romance, wrote in 1837, "I have seen nothing as pretty as this pretty antique. It's the smile of someone who is habitually serious."

Walk slowly, very slowly, around the building and you will see just how it seduces your eye. Its design, like all Roman architecture, is not original: It is Greek in concept—Corinthian pillars support the pediment—but an enclosed central "room" (where the Roman religious services took place) has been added. The temple is not too big. The architect could easily have gone the grand route (it was a memorial to the Emperor Augustus's two sons), but he chose restraint instead and kept it small. And the Maison Carrée, like all great beauties, relies on its bones—in other words, its proportions—rather than its makeup (or its decoration) to deliver its irresistible impact.

A few years ago the mayor of Nîmes, Jean Bousquet, decided that the way to put his city on the European cultural map was to inject some late-twentieth-century architecture into the mix. Jean Nouvel designed some low-cost apartments, which have been endlessly featured in high-cost magazines, and Norman Foster was commissioned to design an art center, called the Carrée d'Art. After I'd made my pilgrimage to the Maison Carrée, I sat down on its front steps and looked left at the Foster building, which takes up one side of what was once the Roman forum. There's an element of chutzpah in the whole exercise: Its name clearly echoes that of the older building, its position demands comparison, and the fact that Foster has used the same number of ultraslim pillars on its facade drives the point home. But the truth is that if the Maison Carrée is Garbo, then the Carrée d'Art is an anorexic model turned starlet whose name you have already forgotten. There's nothing really *wrong* with Foster's building, except that it has a curiously unsubstantial air, and you can't help doubting that it will still be standing in two hundred years—let alone two thousand.

From beauty to the beast. Or at least that is how I felt as I walked from the Maison Carrée toward the Arena. The sheer size of the building (it seats 21,000) delivers its own crude punch; you don't *argue* with a structure this big. Rome rules, okay? Okay. But as I climbed up the scorching-hot stone steps toward the top row of seats and looked down, way down, at the sand-covered floor, I couldn't help remembering the bestiality of the "games" that were played here two thousand years ago. Half-naked gladiators hacked each other to death (there is a bronze statue in the Arles museum of a gladiator who looks like a wrestler dressed in a loincloth and armed with a sword, a helmet, and a riot cop's shield), tigers devoured antelopes, and on very special occasions, the blood-soaked amphitheater was flooded for a reenactment of the Battle of Actium, where the legionnaires who founded Nîmes had fought and defeated Antony and Cleopatra. (The symbol of the city, a crocodile chained to a palm tree, also originated with this battle.)

The water would be stained red with blood, and hundreds of slaves and prisoners would die each time this drama was performed. The funny thing about the Romans was that however horrific the show they were watching, the audience insisted on seeing it in style and comfort. They had to be shaded from the sun, the air inside the Arena was scented with perfumed water, and there had to be plenty of snacks and drinks for sale.

From the top of the terraces, you'll see some square holes carved into the stone at the edge of the Arena. These were anchors for the wooden masts that held up the velum, or canvas awning, which rolled out to cover the entire stadium. Two kids from Texas who couldn't have been more than twenty were sitting a few feet away from me, engrossed in their guidebook's description of this engineering feat. "Kinda like the Astrodome" was their verdict, and of course they were right. Except that the Romans did it without electricity, gas, steel, or a single crane, bulldozer, or computer.

A little while later, when I ran into the Texans again, I overheard one saying to the other, "She said I wouldn't respect her or treat her like a lady, but then she told me, 'But that's okay, because I'm not a lady.' And you know what? She wasn't." And then they both practically fell down the steps in a fit of filthy, uncontrollable, testosterone-fueled laughter.

Rousseau famously asked, when he first saw the Pont du Gard, "Why was I not born a Roman?" And, as I approached the monumental three-tiered aqueduct at dusk that day, I felt the same way. Who wouldn't want to be part of the most powerful empire on earth? Who can resist the almost pornographic attraction of military might and conquest? The Romans were just about as politically incorrect as you can get (not so thrilling, *pace* Rousseau, to have been born a Roman slave or woman), but two thousand years later, it is still impossible not to admire them.

The Pont du Gard is best seen from a distance, so your eyes can adjust to its size and take in the entire structure. After that, your legs can take on the challenge of climbing up and walking across it. To get this perspective, you can stumble around the banks of the Gard River; or you can paddle your way up to the *pont* in a kayak; or—and here's the best idea of all—you can sit on the shady terrace of Le Vieux Moulin, a restaurant that faces the aqueduct, order a *citron pressé,* and read about Marcus Agrippa, governor of Gaul, victor over Antony and Cleopatra, and architect of both the

Pantheon in Rome and this extraordinary feat of aesthetics and engineering that spans the river right in front of you.

The aqueduct, with its thirty miles of connecting covered canals, was built by Agrippa between 19 and 20 B.C. Nîmes already had plenty of drinking water for its fifty thousand people, but Agrippa thought nothing was too good for his veterans and felt that their new home in the provinces should have as many fountains as Rome. I stared hard at the monumental arches and the huge blocks of stone, some weighing more than six tons, and thought: All this for some *fountains*? But so accurate were Agrippa's calculations, and so well constructed was the aqueduct, that for nine hundred years it continued to carry water to Nîmes—and today, cars drive across its lower span. (The canals were originally sealed and water-proofed with a mixture of lime, pork fat, and unripe figs, which apparently did the job.)

The Romans, like the Egyptians, had the hubris to build for the future. They assumed—and, as it turned out, rightfully so—that structures like the Pont du Gard would be around for a very long time. Thus, they thoughtfully provided stone steps, which protrude from the walls to support scaffolding, so future generations of laborers could make sure Agrippa's aqueduct would stand for centuries to come.

After several days of absorbing the imperial glory that was Rome, I'd had enough. I wanted to see the other, private and familial aspects of their lives. What kind of houses did the Romans live in, where did they shop, what kind of pots did they cook in, what shape were the glasses they drank their wine from? How did the women pin up their hair, what was their jewelry like, and where did the men go when they wanted to get away from their wives?

To find out, I returned to the terrace of Le Vieux Moulin and consulted *La Provence Romaine*. Not far from ultrachic St.-Rémy, only an hour or so from Nîmes, were the remains of the Roman town of Glanum. I had a hazy memory of going there as a child, with my parents, sometime in the early sixties. My interest in the Romans was minimal, and all I recalled was being dragged around some sun-scorched rubble when I'd much rather have been lounging around on a sun-scorched beach. But in my address book, I still had the number of a couple, old friends of my mother's, who lived just outside St.-Rémy in the kind of "farmhouse" that no real Provençal farmer would be caught dead in. A quick call confirmed that, yes, they were both still alive and still together, and would be happy to have me join them for lunch, followed by a guided tour of Glanum.

The next day, just before noon, Michel (who, when I was ten, I had planned to marry—until my mother told me that he was already married to André) opened the door, and as I kissed him on both cheeks, I couldn't help thinking that the man I remembered as looking like a Greek god had, in the thirty-five years since I'd last seen him, turned into a . . . Roman emperor. But then again, the shy, mousy-haired ten-year-old had become a bossy, blond *femme d'un certain âge*. So I guess we were even.

We sat out on the terrace in the shade of an old fig tree, sipping Bellinis (one part fresh peach from the tree by the kitchen door, two parts Veuve Cliquot), and talked about—what else?—the Romans. André, an artist and fanatical Romanophile, told me with a smile that he had just finished painting on the dining room walls a series of murals copied from designs he had seen in Pompeii. An image from one of the famous hard-core murals, usually shown only to scholars—especially the kind of "scholars" who slip the guide a few thousand lira—flashed before my eyes. No, he couldn't have, could he?

Slightly nervously, I followed my hosts inside the house for lunch. And no, of course, he hadn't. One wall was a bucolic scene of trees, grape-heavy vines, and birds, and the others were a series of interior views. In one of them, a Roman lady in a delicately draped toga sat at a dining table not unlike the one we were sitting at, covered in a linen cloth and set with glass goblets and a plate piled high with a pyramid of green and purple figs. Even though these were not Roman paintings, they were close enough to the real thing to convince me, after I took my first bite of ripe fig, that some things hadn't changed at all in the last two thousand years.

After lunch we drove into St.-Rémy, or at least tried to. It was impossible to find a parking place. Finally, Michel just dropped André and me off, and we agreed to meet him at the Bar des Arts in an hour. If you look really hard in St.-Rémy, you can just about see the vestiges of a real town with a real life, hidden among all the chic little stores selling insanely overpriced baskets, handmade pottery, and antique linen sheets identical to those in the market in Nîmes— but with a zero added to the price.

I did discover a butcher shop with a beautiful prancing wooden horse in its window, which proudly advertised *taureau de camargue* and *cheval,* and struck up a conversation with the man behind the counter. We discussed the relative merits of beef and *taureau*— "Once you have tasted bull, beef will be so boring that you will never eat it again," he told me with classic masculine dogmatism. I said I'd have to take his word for it but promised to raise the issue with my butcher in New York as soon as I returned home.

Even the vegetable stores had been tricked up: One had Provençal-patterned fabric skirts covering the unsightly legs of its produce stands, and there was a charming old wheelbarrow parked outside, piled high with charming old bunches of basil, wilting in the noonday sun. André and I wandered back toward our meeting place, met Michel still cruising around looking for parking, and headed out to Glanum.

Unlike the Pont du Gard or the Maison Carrée, the town of Glanum forces you to work harder and use your imagination, combined with a guidebook, if you want to see how it must have looked when the Romans lived there. But André's enthusiasm was irresistible, and as he bounded ahead like an elderly mountain goat, I did my best to keep up. He showed me the foundations of a typical Greco-Roman house, with a series of surprisingly small rooms surrounding the atrium, and the family's private quarters farther back, around the open, columned peristyle.

A shallow stone basin with a drain in the middle stood in what must have been the kitchen. I tried hard to picture a Roman maid standing there, washing a pile of greasy dishes, feeling just as tired and frustrated as we all had before some American invented the miracle machine that would do it for us. We walked out of the ruins of the house toward the baths, or at least toward some bits of brick and stone that André assured me had once been a magnificent spa with a swimming pool and separate chambers—one hot, one warm, and one cold—where men went to relax, gossip, and doubtless escape, for a few hours, from their demanding wives.

My imagination was working overtime at this point, and I thought, churlishly (and sweatily), how accurate my childhood memory of sun-scorched rubble had been. After another hour of clambering around, trying to conjure up a whole temple from one broken column or a fountain from a fragment of carved stone, I was overcome with a guilty desire for a sun-scorched beach. Which was when my mind-reading hosts suggested we drive back to their house for a swim.

The sun had heated the water in the pool to the perfect temperature. As I swam lazily across it, I imagined that I was lolling about in the swimming pool of the Glanum spa, and I felt for the second time that day that in the end, not so very much separated us from our Roman ancestors.

I arrived back in Arles later that night. The fire-eater with the snake tattoos was still there, lighting up the Place du Forum with his gasoline breath, as I supposed he had been every night since I'd left. Although it must have been nearly midnight, I didn't feel like going to sleep. I wandered into the bar at the Nord-Pinus and felt as though I'd crossed the Pyrenees. There was a chandelier of multicolored glass, and I could just about make out a series of black-and-white photographs of bullfighters lining the walls, some famous (El Cordobés looking like the rock star he could have been) and some less instantly recognizable but no less handsome. In a cabinet I saw the suit of lights that the legendary Spanish bullfighter Dominguín wore when he fought in the Arles Arena in the 1950s, his pale-green silk jacket and waistcoat encrusted with rubies, sequins, and pearls, and so tightly fitted that it must have been as hot and constricting as a corset. And there in the corner was a small altar dedicated to the Virgin, where bullfighters pray before they enter the Arena, the sand-covered circle of death that links them irrevocably to the Roman gladiators.

Before going to bed, I went out on the balcony, reached across, and felt the rough surface of the column that had once stood on the forum, remembering the sublime beauty of the Maison Carrée, the grandeur of the Pont du Gard, and the bloodstained glory of the amphitheaters. The thought crossed my mind that despite the fall of the empire, Rome was ultimately the victor because so much of what it created—intellectually as well as physically—has endured. Julius Caesar, Marius, Emperor Augustus, Marcus Agrippa, and all the others must be smiling—triumphantly—in their respective graves.

Empire of Pleasures

The Romans, as we all know, were no fools. And so when they decided to expand their empire into the *provincia* of what is now France, the part they took over was the area that many people still consider the most seductive—Provence. The Romans controlled the whole of the southern portion of France stretching from the present-day Italian border, west to Narbonne, and then northward up the Rhône Valley as far as Lyon. Although there are Roman ruins scattered all over this part of the country, the most impressive ones—in Nîmes, Arles, Orange, Glanum, and Vaison-la-Romaine, and the Pont du Gard itself—are concentrated in a quite small area on both sides of the Rhône River. The sites are within a few hours' drive of one another, and all, happily, are conveniently located near some of the prettiest and best hotels and restaurants in France. The sybaritic Romans would have approved.

Arles

The Museum of Antiquity has one of the best collections of Roman art anywhere in France (4.90.18.88.88). About a 15-minute walk away is the Grand Hôtel Nord-Pinus. Not only the most charming hotel in Arles, it even has bits of a Roman temple embedded in its southwest corner—what more could the dedicated Romanophile ask for? Cocteau and Picasso used to stay here when they indulged in their passion for bullfights, which were (and still are) held in the old Roman Arena. The bar is an homage to the art of bullfighting, and in summer, lunch and dinner are served outdoors on the Place du Forum—the best place to eat in

Arles (4.90.93.44.44; info@nord-pinus.com; doubles, about $116–$195; *plats,* about $20–$30). The Hôtel d'Arlatan is also beautiful, occupying an old Renaissance palace near the Rhône River (4.90.93.56.66; hotel-arlatan@provnet.fr; doubles, about $90–$128). The Hôtel de L'Amphithéatre is more modest, but charming, right in the middle of Arles (4.90.96.10.30; contact@hotelamphitheatre.fr; doubles, about $42–$54).

Jardin de Manon is a simple, reasonably priced restaurant near the Roman burial ground Les Alyscamps. Good Provençal food, and often not a tourist in sight (4.90.93.38.68; plats, about $8–$24).

Fontvieille

The ruins of Barbegal are near this cheerful village, with its views over wheat fields and olive groves toward the bleached, jagged peaks of Les Alpilles. Fontvieille lies at a point almost equidistant from Provence's three most important Roman roads, in what is often thought to be the region's historical and spiritual heartland.

The Roman aqueduct, half hidden among the bushes and olive groves as in some idyllic Arcadian scene, was built in the 2nd century A.D. to carry water from Les Alpilles to a sophisticated mill complex that continued functioning right up to the fifth century. The eloquent ruins of this complex—the sole building of its kind to have survived since Roman times—can be seen by walking south down the quiet footpath that runs alongside the aqueduct's broken arches. After a few minutes, you emerge on a rocky slope in which a deep channel has been cut. Water once ran through here before descending the slope in two streams that activated eight pairs of connected mills which provided all the flour for Arles.

Fontvieille has a number of good places to stay and eat, chief among them being the family-run La Régalido. The hotel, exemplifying rustic chic at its most extravagant, is light and airy, and upper rooms have views over rooftops toward Les Alpilles. The dining room occupies the barrel-vaulted cellar of an early-seventeenth-century olive mill mentioned by Daudet. The food, of Provençal inspiration, is expensive but exquisite and is also served for much of the year in a large shaded garden ablaze with flowers (4.90.54.60.22; fax: .64.29; doubles, about $116–$253; *plats,* about $13–$25).

Fréjus

A large modern sculpture of an ancient galley stands at the motorway exit, a reminder that this now inland town was a major Roman port and naval base which reached the height of its fame after the defeat of Cleopatra's fleet at the Battle of Actium in 31 B.C. Today, after centuries of devastation and the silting up of the bay, Roman Fréjus has been reduced to fragments. Although it was never as lavishly endowed as Arles, Nîmes, or Orange, the scattered monuments here give altogether a fascinating idea of what the Roman township was like, and also have a considerable romantic appeal. The ruins include an amphitheater, a theater, and a twenty-five-mile aqueduct whose isolated redbrick piers rise above the fields like giant candles.

On the town's southern outskirts, a sufficient amount of archaeological evidence has been unearthed to have enabled historians to form a vivid and unique picture of a Roman port. An enjoyable walk skirts a long stretch of picturesquely overgrown Roman walls, leading to a charming country lane known as the Chemin de la Lanterne d'Auguste, which marks the line of the Roman quay and culminates in a well-preserved hexagonal structure thought by some to have been a Roman lighthouse.

In the center of Fréjus, the small Archaeological Museum (4.94.52.15.98) is attached to the Quartier Épiscopal, a fortified complex of Romanesque buildings that includes a circular baptistry revealing the influence of the Romans on Provence's early medieval architecture.

The excellent Hôtel L'Aréna, in the heart of the old town, is cheerfully decorated in a riot of Provençal tiles and pastel colors. An element of Roman hedonism characterizes its exotic garden, which has a swimming pool surrounded by potted palms, geraniums, and oleanders (4.94.17.09.40; info@arena-hotel.com; doubles, about $67–$87).

In a narrow old street around the corner from L'Aréna, the bistro-style Les Potiers serves a small selection of beautifully prepared light dishes in a simple, intimate setting (4.94.51.33.74; *plats,* about $9–$14).

La Turbie

The entrance to Provence from Italy is marked by the giant Trophée d'Auguste, which rises high above the coast at Monaco like some abandoned creation of Cecil B. DeMille's. Built between 13 and 5 B.C. to commemorate the Emperor Augustus's conquest of the Alps, it was originally crowned by a stepped dome supporting—nearly 165 feet above the ground—a statue of the emperor. Even today, reduced to a stump of colonnade resting on a massive plinth, it testifies with extraordinary eloquence to the military prowess of the Romans and to the imperial cult that took root so spectacularly under Augustus.

It may overlook the Côte d'Azur, but La Turbie is a village with remarkably simple hotels. Good food and reasonable comfort are to be found in the modern Le Napoléon (4.93.41.00.54; fax: .28.93; doubles, about $60–$67), while basic accommodation in a quiet and unrivaled location characterizes the late-nineteenth-century Le Césarée (4.93.41.16.08; fax: .1949; doubles, about $54–$76). The latter's country-style restaurant, Carpe Diem, makes the most of its panoramic views of the sea, and also claims to be the first wholly organic restaurant in France (*plats,* about $7–$12).

The town lacks the charm of Arles, so your best bet is to stay in the countryside and drive in to see the Roman sites. Le Vieux Castillon, in the village of Castillon-du-Gard, is about twenty minutes from town, very near the Pont du Gard. The hotel has been carved out of a series of ancient medieval houses, with authentically tiny medieval windows, and what your room may lack in size it more than makes up for in charm. The swimming pool is spectacular, overlooking the valley far below, and the restaurant is superb (4.66.37.61.61; fax: .28.17; doubles, about $146–$286; *plats,* $30–$60).

Le Castellas is also about thirty minutes from Nîmes, situated in an old house in the middle of the village of Collias. Less breathtaking than Le Vieux Castillon, it has a romantic outdoor terrace, and the restaurant is highly recommended (4.66.22.88.88; fax: .84.28; doubles, about $102–$104; *plats,* about $25–$54).

Au Flan Coco, in downtown Nîmes, is tiny, good, and inexpensive; in summer, be sure to pick a table on the sidewalk (4.66.21.84.81; *plats,* about $8–$14). When the renovation's complete, the Hôtel du Vieux Moulin will no doubt again be a great place to have lunch while you visit the Pont du Gard. You can, of course, also stay there, but the Vieux Moulin's real appeal is the view of the Gard River and the great Roman Aqueduct that spans it (4.66.37.14.35; fax: .26.48).

Orange

One of the most important centers of Roman Provence, this now-sleepy town has two of the grandest surviving monuments of the Roman world. Marking the approach to Orange for those who traveled south from Lyon on the Via Agrippa, the triumphal arch, circa 20 B.C., is the third-largest extant, as well as the prototype for such later arched gateways as Paris's Arc de Triomphe.

Walk in a straight line from the triumphal arch into the old center of Orange and you will eventually reach a square completely overshadowed by the sublimely proportioned Roman theater. Few other theaters of the world, and certainly no Roman one, can match the impact of this building, which is unique among ancient structures of this kind in having preserved its stage wall. To appreciate the full grandeur of the whole, you should make the steep climb to the top of the semicircular auditorium, which has a capacity for 9,000 spectators. Better still, try to attend one of the operas that have been regularly performed here in the summer months since the late nineteenth century (4.90.34.24.24; www.choregies.asso.fr/).

The friendly, old-fashioned Hôtel Arène overlooks a small square shaded by plane trees in the middle of a quiet pedestrian district a few minutes' walk from the Roman theater (4.90.11.40.40; fax: .45; doubles, about $66–$90).

A delightfully homey restaurant adjacent to the theater, Le Yaca is run by the energetic Faustino Perez, who serves simple but excellent local dishes such as fish soup and rabbit with garlic, all very modestly priced (4.90.34.70.03; *plats,* about $11–$14). For a more refined and inventive cuisine, Le Parvis occupies a traditionally elegant interior with rococo flourishes (4.90.34.82.00; *plats,* about $10–$19).

St.-Rémy-de-Provence

It has become the new(ish) St.-Tropez, albeit minus Bardot and the Mediterranean. Consequently, St.-Rémy is overrun with tourists in the summer—try to go in the spring or fall.

The early-nineteenth-century Château des Alpilles sits in a suitably grand park that you approach through a long allée of lime trees. It is elegant and supercomfortable and has tennis courts, saunas, a pool, and particularly pretty gardens (4.90.92.03.33; fax: .45.17; doubles, about $142–$170). Almost next door is the charming, less luxe, and less pricey Château de Roussan (4.90.92.11.63; fax: .50.59; doubles, about $68–$112).

The best place to eat is not in St.-Rémy but about twenty minutes away, in the delightful village of Eygalières. Le Bistro d'Eygalières is just one year old, and it has already earned its first Michelin star. The food is sensational, the decor is perfect, and there are even four rooms upstairs in case you can't bear to leave (4.90.90.60.34; *plats,* about $30–$50).

Vaison-la-Romaine

Until the beginning of the twentieth century, Vaison had few visible traces of its important Roman past. It had been one of the wealthiest towns in Provence, and excavations undertaken in the town center after 1907 soon resulted in what is by far the largest archaeological site in France. Divided essentially into two adjoining districts known as La Villasse and Puymin, the site, under the shadow of Mont Ventoux, has earned Vaison a reputation as the Pompeii of France. The remains are certainly extensive enough to allow you to imagine yourself back in Roman times, particularly the exceptionally well-preserved shopping street in the La Villasse district, and the many luxurious villas that once belonged to the rich merchants and retired legionnaires who were attracted to Vaison. Finds from the site, including a very realistic silver bust and an outstanding mosaic decorated with peacocks, are excitingly displayed in the modern Archaeological Museum. A Roman bridge, one of the largest in Provence, connects the former Roman town with the now quiet and remarkably attractive hill district, where the inhabitants took refuge during the Middle Ages.

Having taken over two adjoining sixteenth- and seventeenth-century buildings in the Renaissance showpiece of the upper town, Le Beffroi is a rambling hotel of great character, with spiral stone staircases, quaintly uneven tile floors, old Provençal furnishings, and outstanding views down to the Ouvèze River (4.90.36.04.71; fax: .24.78; doubles, about $70–$98). In the lower town the Hôtel Burrhus, which stands on the lively, café-lined Place de Montfort, is the best choice (4.90.36.00.11; fax: .35.39.05; doubles, about $36–$46).

Vaison's restaurants were unexceptional until the arrival of Robert Bardot from Lyon, whose Le Moulin à Huile was justifiably awarded a Michelin star in 1999. In a beautiful, isolated position on the south bank of the Ouvèze, Le Moulin has a terraced riverside garden that is an enchanting place to dine in summer. Its dining room is a vaulted, high-ceilinged cellar (4.90.36.20.67; *plats,* about $20–$24).

Reading

Modesty does not prevent us from recommending *A Guide to Provence,* by Michael Jacobs, as an introduction to this part of France (out of print). The *Michelin Green Guide* to Provence is a classic and, as such, will never go out of style ($20). The *Eyewitness Guide* to Provence and the Côte d'Azur is beautifully illustrated and had good recommendations for hotels and restaurants ($23). *La Provence Antique* is a fine, short, full-color guide to all of the Roman ruins (Éditions Ouest-France, available in France). *The Road from the Past,* by Ina Caro, is a wonderfully personal walk through France's history (Harvest, $16). *Caesar's Vast Ghost,* by Lawrence Durrell, is fascinating, crazy, and indulgent, but essential reading (out of print).

Marseille

BY ALEXANDER LOBRANO

∾

editor's note

Marseille, France's second largest city, has an undeservedly bad reputation which predates the release of *The French Connection*. I very much like
Marseille, and encourage you not to pass it by: behind some of its rather
ramshackle facades, the city is vibrant, energetic, and diverse; there is a
handful of superb architectural monuments; its Vieux Port is one of the most
picturesque in the Mediterranean; and its seafood restaurants are among the
best in the world. In its August 2000 issue, *Travel & Leisure* reported that
in a recent poll of French men and women twenty-five and under, Marseille
was voted as the top city to live in, followed by Montpellier, with Paris and
Bordeaux tied for third place. I believe that Marseille is a model of what
many cities in France will look like in the future.

ALEXANDER LOBRANO is European editor for *Gourmet* and contributes frequently to a number of magazines, including *Departures, France
Discovery Guide,* and *FRANCE Magazine,* where this article originally
appeared.

Nearly 150 years after Napoleon III's visit to Marseille, it's easy
to see why the majestic view from the Pharo gardens not only
seduced the emperor but inflamed his imperial ambitions as well. In
the distance, low bone-white mountains form a natural amphitheater that opens onto an expanse of red tile roofs and an endless
stage of azure sea. The emperor was so taken with the place that
the Palais de Pharo was built for him there. Although he never
stayed in the ornate mansion (Empress Eugénie preferred Biarritz),
his brief visit completely changed the destiny of the oldest city in
France.

The history of Marseille is irrevocably linked to its port, as the

Roman historian Justin relates in a 600 B.C. account of its founding: "In the days of King Tarquin, having dared to venture to the furthermost shore of the ocean, the Phocaeans [Greeks] reach the gulf of Gaul . . . charmed by this pleasant place, they asked for the friendship of King Nann of the Segobriges, on his territory, where they wished to found a city." Known as Massalia, it became one of the great ports of the ancient world.

The millennium brought Roman domination, followed by invasions that continued throughout the Middle Ages. The Marseillais experienced prosperity and ruin, plagues and crusades, independence and, in 1481, adherence to the French crown. Throughout it all, maritime trade remained the city's lifeblood.

Louis XIV was the first to undertake a major renovation of the port, developing the area along the Rive Neuve and ordering Marshal Vauban to construct the Fort St.-Nicolas and Fort St.-Jean on either side of the entrance. By the 1830s, however, the harbor had become a chaotic forest of masts, due to the huge increases in trade brought on by the conquest of Algeria. When Napoleon III visited in 1852, a new harbor, La Joliette, was being constructed to accommodate this growing traffic as well as the modern steamships that were replacing schooners.

With Marseille so vital to his far-flung empire, the Emperor gave his blessing to a series of projects that ushered in a period of unprecedented growth and prosperity. He personally laid the cornerstones for the grandiose Palais de la Bourse and the Cathédrale de la Major and approved further expansion of the new port. To service the growing harbor, he granted rail baron Paulin Talabot permission to build enormous warehouses some 1,300 feet long. Called Les Docks, this imposing structure of stone, brick and iron borrowed its name and concept from St. Katherine's docks in London. Baron Haussmann, meanwhile, was dispatched to reshape the city, tearing down old neighborhoods and installing wide boulevards similar to those he built in Paris. Most impressive was the rue Impériale (now the rue de la République), with its grand homes occupied by the city's wealthy shipowners and merchants.

When the Suez Canal opened in 1869, Marseille exploded, becoming the greatest boom town in nineteenth-century Europe and sharing with Chicago the title of "fastest growing city in the world."

The most eloquent expression of the ebullience of the era is undoubtedly the Palais Longchamp, a magnificent monument built to celebrate the arrival of a fifty-two-mile aqueduct transporting water from the Durance river to the frequently drought-stricken port. The massive neoclassical horseshoe-shaped colonnade with a triumphal arch at its center and museums (the Musée d'Histoire Naturelle and the first-rate Musée des Beaux-Arts) at each end crowns a hill landscaped with a massive series of fountains. This extravagant structure is awash in winsome allegory, the Durance itself being represented as sheaves of wheat, grapevines and bulls, symbolizing the power and fecundity of its waters.

Though it's difficult to fathom in view of its nineteenth-century wealth and power, Marseille's reputation declined rapidly after World War I, and for decades it has been ignored by French and foreigners alike. Its troubles began with the Depression and continued through World War II, when the city was badly damaged. Then came the advent of ships too large to use the Suez Canal and the loss of French territories in North Africa and Indochina, both of which dealt devastating blows to the port and related industries. At the same time, the city was called upon to deal with the repatriation of thousands of French colonists, most of them from Algeria. Gradually, Marseille acquired the image of being a rough, corrupt, economically troubled place.

Today, however, France's second-largest city appears to be summoning its strength to launch its next incarnation. As connoisseurs of urban life know, one of the most fascinating times to visit a city is on the eve of its rebirth. In the 1970s, New York and Barcelona both had a special atmosphere of faded grandeur that created a sort of broken charm that's now been lost to their revivals. In Marseille, the city's pulse is quickening, and you sense that this ancient place with a brawny, briny character is poised to sprint again.

Sit over coffee some sunny morning at La Samaritaine, a popular café on the edge of the Vieux Port, and you'll immediately notice the remarkable variety in the city's population. "Marseille has always been a city of immigration, with an extraordinary knack for producing talented French citizens," says Dominique Bluzet, the film producer known for *Uranus* and director of the city's thriving Théâtre du Gymnase. Indeed, all of the different flat breads in the world from crêpes to pitas to pizzas can be found here, and at the Pizzeria des Catalans, a great place to escape from the busy city center for a seaside lunch, they offer both Armenian and Merguez pizza. The city "smells of the different foods eaten by the Blacks, the Turks, the Greeks, the Italians, the Maltese, the Spanish, the Corsicans, the English and the Marseillais themselves," wrote Guy de Maupassant in 1884. A hundred years later he'd be obliged to add the North Africans and Vietnamese too.

Despite the looming presence of Jean-Marie Le Pen's National Front party and its "France for the French" sloganeering, Marseille practices a blasé cosmopolitanism that places it in the forefront of twenty-first-century cities. Two recent films—*Marius et Janette,* a love story set in L'Estaque, a Marseille district, and *Mémoires d'Immigrés,* a fascinating and deeply moving documentary by Yasmina Benguigui about the history of North African immigration to France—depict the city's ethnic insouciance in a way that might inspire other French cities to take a lesson. *Mémoires d'Immigrés* interviews French-born North Africans who say that only in Marseille have they been integrated into the life of the city, while *Marius et Janette* depicts the warm, communal life of a bunch of Marseillais of broadly diverse origins.

"Marseille resembles New York. It's ironic that both cities are much safer than their reputations would have you believe. Marseille has a lower felony rate than Paris, Nice and several other French cities," says Gérard Chenoz, director of Projet Centre-Ville, a municipal project to revive the city's old residential neighborhoods. "This is a city that brings together different people. It's always been a transit point between North and South, but it's also been an important intellectual and artistic crossroads. Like New York, the city has received successive waves of immigrants that have been initially snubbed but eventually accepted and integrated. After World War II, we slipped into a period of political inertia and the creative potential of this mix of people was ignored. But since the election of the new mayor, Jean-Claude Gaudin, the city has begun flexing its muscles."

Everywhere, you hear talk of its being an awakening Gulliver. Perhaps the most convincing evidence is Euroméditerranée, one of the most comprehensive urban and industrial renewal projects under way anywhere in the world. Launched in 1996, the entire project will take about twenty years to complete, with the most dramatic changes in place by 2001. Some $500 million in state and local funds have been earmarked for this initial stage, which involves rebuilding the Gare St.-Charles (in anticipation of the TGV line opening in 2000), renovating areas around La Joliette and rehabilitating neighborhoods in between.

Already, Les Docks has been transformed from an old warehouse into the region's most prestigious office space, thanks to the imaginative designs of local architect Eric Castaldi. And nearby,

European developers are investing in commercial and residential real estate, with the understanding that the city will upgrade lighting, sidewalks, schools and other municipal services. In addition to the Euroméditerranée projects, the city also plans to build a new tram system, expand the Marseille-Provence airport and revitalize urban areas in other parts of the city. In short, the entire downtown area is slated to be upgraded within the next two decades.

"What's driving this wholesale renovation is the emergence of a fifteen-nation free-trade zone around the Mediterranean basin," explains Thierry Martin, director of marketing and economic development for Euroméditerranée. "Marseille is in a position to become the capital of this zone." Investors are betting that major corporations, many of which have headquarters in northern Europe, will select Marseille as a hub for doing business with southern Europe and the Mediterranean countries. So far, their bet seems to be paying off: Les Docks is already 90 percent full. Among the new occupants are a number of U.S. firms, including Price Waterhouse, Deloitte & Touche, RSL Com and GE Capital Services.

Marseille's port, of course, is also an integral part of the city's comeback scenario. "It's the third-largest port in Europe, after Antwerp and Rotterdam," says Henri Roux-Alezais, president of the Port Authority of Marseille. "Importing and processing food is still a major activity, but oil, gas and mineral trade now make up the bulk of our business." Ferry traffic is also increasingly important, with boats shuttling more than a million passengers between Marseille, Corsica and North Africa each year. Last fall, one of the old cargo docks at La Joliette was leveled to make room for a new passenger terminal that will serve both ferries and cruise ships. "Five years ago, some 10,000 cruise-ship passengers came through Marseille," says Roux-Alezais. "Last year, that number was 80,000, and by 2000, we expect to reach at least 200,000. Our objective is to become the leading port of call for cruise ships in the Mediterranean."

Beyond its determination to remain a working port, Marseille is starting to realize the enormous value of its natural setting. "For centuries the Marseillais have considered the sea more as an economic asset than a scenic one," says Euroméditerranée director Martin. Today, however, the formerly bawdy port is bashfully starting to acknowledge its own beauty.

Hail a taxi at the port end of la Canebière, the famous Haussmannian boulevard that runs through the heart of the city, and tell the driver to take you to "Le Lunch, Sormiou." Twenty minutes later, you'll be coasting down vertical hairpin curves that lead through a forest of parasol pines to a tiny beach framed by ivory-colored cliffs and a turquoise sea. This magnificent spot is the first of Les Calanques, a series of inlets at the base of steep cliffs fronting the Mediterranean that are now protected as a national park. Now settled on the terrace of Le Lunch, sip a pastis, the only possible drink for this occasion since it's made in Marseille, and while you wait for a bowl of wonderfully ruddy bouillabaisse, contemplate the improbable fact that you're still within the city limits.

If its port hadn't been so good, Marseille might have bettered Nice as a resort, since its natural setting is even more spectacular than that of its much more assiduously courted sister city on the Côte d'Azur. Head east from the Vieux Port on the majestic Corniche Kennedy and you will pass Belle Epoque villas and the enormous manmade Prado beaches before arriving at the quaint little fishing village of Les Goudes. Head out of town in the other direction and, just beyond the port, you will discover the rough-

and-tumble charm of L'Estaque. Its beauty has been captured by so many avant-garde painters that you may have a strange sense of déjà-vu.

When Paul Cézanne first visited L'Estaque in 1870, it was a fishing village that was evolving into a working-class suburb with tile factories and cement works. In fact, in his most famous painting of the town, *Le Golfe de Marseille vu de l'Estaque* (1885), which hangs in the Art Institute of Chicago, there's a factory chimney smoking in the lower right-hand corner of the canvas. What attracted Cézanne, however, was the remarkable light and profusion of shapes composing the landscape. It was here that Cubism was born, thanks to the works not only of Cézanne, but the artists who followed him, including André Derain, Georges Braque and Raoul Dufy.

Marseille continues to attract artists and has an extraordinarily rich and varied cultural life that surprises visitors expecting a gruff, down-at-the-heels port. "Marseille residents love the theater," says director Bluzet. "It's a very extroverted city—it's the city of Yves Montand, Fernandel, Pagnol." During Bluzet's twelve-year tenure, the Théâtre du Gymnase has seen its subscription base grow from 2,000 to 16,000. "Plays have become a major form of entertainment in Marseille again. This city supports seven different theaters, remarkable given that its population is only around 850,000. The Marseillais are a very faithful and passionate public—their tastes are more Kevin Costner than Woody Allen. They like the color of life and want a strong story," says Bluzet.

Marseille has also made three dramatic additions to its extraordinary collection of museums: The new Musée de la Faïence, housed in the Château Pastré, a Provençal-style "country home" built in 1862 for a rich shipowner; the Musée de la Mode, devoted to costume history; and the Musée d'Art Contemporain, with works from the 1960s to the present. Together they are an excellent complement to Marseille's eleven other museums, several of which focus on the city's rich history. Visitors can discover the Musée des Docks Romains, with its *in situ* remains of a Roman warehouse next to the Vieux Port; the Musée du Vieux Marseille, housed in the sixteenth-century Maison Diamantée; and the Musée Grobet-Labadié, an intimate nineteenth-century mansion whose period rooms offer an intriguing glimpse into the cultivated tastes of the time.

Perhaps most impressive to outsiders, however, is Marseille's growing stature on the international contemporary art scene. The city is home to an impressive number of artists, both French and foreign, and the Musée d'Art Contemporain regularly devotes shows to iconoclastic creators whose works have received little attention in other major European cities. With its constantly changing mix of people, cultures and ideas, Marseille is proving to be the perfect venue for such exhibits.

"Culture can bridge all of the North-South schisms—in France, in Europe and around the Mediterranean basin," says Eric Michel, director of the Cité de la Musique. "In Marseille, it's already happening." Ruminating on the city's cultural life over coffee at the well-equipped Cité, a city-sponsored music center hosting music lessons and concerts for residents, Michel is characteristic of the dynamic, clear-minded public servants now steering the city forward. "Marseille isn't encumbered by a dominant bourgeoisie. Culture is therefore free both to mirror and to appeal to the splendid mosaic of the city," he says. A poster for upcoming musical events reflects this: Corsican, Spanish, Asian, Armenian, Provençal and Italian music concerts were slated. "We're one of seven municipal conservatories around the city—that is unique in France. But although the city has limited resources, we understand the need for neighborhood music centers—music has a special ability to bring together people who otherwise don't usually mix."

Marseille's neighborhoods are as heterogeneous as its population, and unlike many French cities, it has a fascinating architectural diversity. While la Canebière is lined with nineteenth-century wedding-cake facades, Le Panier, the oldest part of the city, is a classic Mediterranean warren of narrow streets and old houses surrounding La Vieille Charité, a seventeenth-century hospice housing a museum devoted to Mediterranean civilizations and another covering African, Amerindian and Oceanic arts. Near the Vieux Port you can see the monumentally dignified Palais de la Bourse, the vestiges of the walls of the original Greek city and, a few steps on, Belsunce, a neighborhood known for its splendid eighteenth-century *maisons particulières*. "The entire history of Marseille is displayed in its architecture," says architect Castaldi. "Rather than tearing down buildings, the city tended to expand. This process of accretion gave it a wonderful texture."

Thanks to people like Jeanne Laffitte, who publishes books specifically about Marseille, Provence, southern French lifestyles and gastronomy, the Marseillais have become more sensitive to their architectural heritage. Laffitte, whose offices are in a handsome eighteenth-century building that was formerly an arsenal (hence the name of her bookshop, gallery and restaurant, Les Arcenaulx), almost single-handedly led a fight to restore the dense neighborhood around the Place Thiars. "It was falling into ruin and city hall was completely indifferent. We had to fight," says the warm, cultivated woman at a desk piled high with books. "And in the end, we won." Through her efforts, a parking garage in the square was torn down, and the Fondation de France contributed funds to help launch the renovation of the neighborhood. The area is now crowded with restaurants and cafés and is one of the most animated parts of the city.

The lessons of this success are very much a part of the Projet Centre Ville. "For ten years, people had been moving out of the city, public spaces had been falling into disrepair, and the shops necessary to sustain a neighborhood were closing," explains project director Chenoz. To encourage the renovation of center-city housing, the city of Marseille has agreed to repurchase houses, paying 11 percent interest on the original investment, if buyers wish to sell after five years. Today, half of all housing renovation is being carried out by the private sector. School enrollments are rising, and the rental market is newly active.

"I have eternal confidence in this city," says Laffitte. An early-morning visit to the open-air fish market at the Vieux Port offers a colorful elaboration of her judgment. *"Du vivant aux prix du mort!"* cry the vendors, touting the quality of their live *poissons de roche, rascasse* and other small bony fish that are themselves almost inedible but become the heart of a good bouillabaisse when cooked into a thick paste. "Fish has been sold here for twenty-six centuries," says Pierre Minguella, proprietor of the Miramar, a Michelin-starred restaurant that serves the city's legendary dish. "In Marseille we've always had a talent for turning the difficult and undesirable into something delicious."

"Marseille" by Alexander Lobrano, *FRANCE Magazine*, Summer 1998. Reprinted with permission.

La Route Cézanne

BY LORRAINE ALEXANDER

editor's note

Here is a good piece outlining a suggested itinerary allowing visitors to explore in Cézanne's footsteps. It was originally part of a longer article on Aix-en-Provence, featured in the May 1993 issue of *Gourmet*.

LORRAINE ALEXANDER lives in Italy and has been a longtime contributor to *Gourmet*, writing often about France.

In 1899, when Cézanne was sixty, a critic wrote, "Can he really paint landscapes? He grasps their character . . . but runs aground in the art of separating his planes. . . . His meager knowledge betrays him." This is a judgment of consummate irony when one considers that Cézanne's landscapes of the countryside near Aix— and over a hundred of Mont Sainte-Victoire alone—are today among the works most associated with his great gifts.

Aix and Mont Sainte-Victoire are inextricably linked, precisely because of Cézanne's legacy, and to spend any time in Aix without venturing the six kilometers to the village of Le Tholonet and the mountain just beyond would be like visiting Granada without seeing the Alhambra. The best place to begin is the atelier, across the peripheral road north of the cathedral, on Avenue Paul Cézanne, that Cézanne acquired in 1901 (and which was saved from ruin as late as the 1950s, largely due to the efforts of John Rewald). It is a small house set in a garden of fig and acacia trees, begonias, and wild thyme; inside are the apples and bottles and busts that fill Cézanne's still lifes, as well as the spindly ladder he climbed to study their angles. There are even artificial flowers, which the painter preferred because they would not wilt before his work was done.

An excursion to La Sainte-Victoire itself starts where the D17 branches off Aix's peripheral road through a long *allée* of plane trees. Barely 3.5 kilometers farther along, past the banks of the Torse where Cézanne and Zola often walked, is Château Noir. Difficult to see from the road, this is where Cézanne rented two rooms to store his painting gear, and the house itself—neither a castle nor black, as it turns out—was the subject of seventeen canvases. Only a short walk down the road (to the left in a clearing of pine trees) was one of the artist's favorite spots for setting up his easel in view of his mountain, and along a nearby track are the caves that inspired some late, cubistic works.

Le Tholonet is a lively crossroads at which to stop for a cold beer or ice cream or simply to watch a game of *boules,* and behind the playing ground is another procession of plane trees, this one surely rivaling the beauty of the grand *allée* just outside Saint-Rémy-de-Provence. Beyond the village every turn reveals a new Cézanne landscape, with the mountain gaining ground until its 1,100 vertical meters become a looming, majestic presence. Lanes dwindling off the main road lead to fields perfect for picnicking; or, for those preferring a restaurant meal, there is the village of Beaurecueil's Mas de la Bertrande, where Sunday lunch is a popular family ritual, and the Relais Sainte-Victoire, well known for chef René Bergès's sophisticated, beautifully presented cuisine. One summer lunch here began with *rougets* in lavender butter, followed by roasted lamb with honey glaze, and finished with a gratin of red fruits in pinenut sabayon. The wine list is excellent, and there is no need to travel far for your choices. This is Palette country—one of France's smallest AOCs—with only two domains, Château Simone and Château Crémade, both of which produce marvelous wines. The he died at his home at 23, rue Boulegon, near Aix's Hôtel de Ville. The previous month he had written his son, also named Paul: "I go into the countryside daily . . . and spend my time there more agreeably than anywhere else I know."

Glimpses of the Real Provence

BY CATHERINE TEXIER

&

editor's note

It is very rare to run across articles about the lesser-known villages of Provence. Here is one I particularly like highlighting some authentic *villages perchés* off the well-trodden route. It originally appeared in the travel section of *The New York Times* on February 14, 1993.

CATHERINE TEXIER is a French novelist who lives in New York. She is the author of *Breakup: The End of a Love Story* (Doubleday, 1998, hardcover; Anchor, 1999, paperback), *Love Is Strange: Stories of Postmodern Romance* (W. W. Norton, 1993), and translator of *The Rap Factor* by Delacorta (Atlantic Monthly Press, 1993, hardcover; 1996, paperback).

Between the towns of Draguignan and Grasse in the Haut-Var, the upper region of the Var Department, runs a string of small fortified villages perched like fortresses atop the first folds of the lower Alps, across from the Esterel Mountains. They are the counterparts of their better known and more touristic cousins in the heights above Nice: St.-Paul de Vence, Vence, Tourrettes-sur-Loup. Built in the latter, all of five minutes from either restaurant, is lesser known and well worth a brief visit while you are in the neighborhood.

La Sainte-Victoire has assumed mythic proportions in these parts. Purportedly the site of the camp from which Marius defeated the Teutons in 100 B.C., it has gradually evolved into a place of pil grimage. (The cross at its summit replaces the old wooden Croix d Provence, erected by a Marseillais sailor in gratitude for surviving storm, that was eventually cut to bits by relic-seeking hikers.) Or one reaches the top by car or bus, masses of yellow *genét* (go spread over the "belt" plateau, or Cengle, that wraps around mountain's girth and still provides pasture for sheep. From height, as one turns south along the D56 past expanses of sunf ers, the Arc River's progress is signaled by the deep green veget that lines its course.

It is the Arc (and the parallel RN7) that leads to the fina along Cézanne's Road: the Pont des Trois Sautets, the tiny d backed bridge under which Cézanne painted the celebrated s *baigneuses* (bathers) that would soon inspire both Matis Picasso. Over the bridge and several kilometers back to th the second domain in Palette's exclusive AOC, Château and pausing here for a visit with Monsieur and Madame R whose family this most respected of Aix's vineyards has for two hundred years, is a fitting way to wind up a d country.

For many years Cézanne took a mule-drawn wagon Sainte-Victoire. Then one afternoon in October, 1906, working on *Le Cabanon Jourdan* (now at the Galleria d'Arte Moderna in Rome), rain began pouring do slipped and fell in a field at the foot of the mountain. Co never abide company while he painted, and so it was before he was found by a villager from Le Tholonet. T

Middle Ages, with a history dating back before Jesus, they have names like Seillans, Bargemon, Fayence, Callian, Figanières. Some of their sinuous lanes, most of them closed to cars, are barely wide enough for two people to walk side by side. Still paved with their original cobblestones with a middle gutter for the rainwater, they twist and sharply climb the slopes of the rock on which they cling. Hiding behind their ramparts, the villages, built to fend off the attacks of the dreaded Moors, strangely evoke the medinas of Morocco. Most have kept their tenth- or eleventh-century castles intact, with a chemin de ronde still circling under the ramparts.

Of course, this region has been discovered, mostly by English lovers of Haute-Provence, and Scandinavians and Belgians keeping their secret quiet. They have bought the medieval village houses and castles and renovated them into three- or four-story vacation homes full of character, with breathtaking views over the surrounding mountains. Fayence, Seillans and Bargemon have been partly gentrified, yet they are still deeply Provençal, involved in the production of olive oil (cold-pressed, the best you'll find in the south of France), essential oils from jasmine and lavender, and the famous Rosé de Provence, which you can taste and buy at the vineyards in the surrounding valleys. If you time your visit in late winter or early spring, when the mimosa blossoms burst into a vibrant yellow along the quiet roads, you will catch a glimpse of an authentic Provence the summer tourist can barely see.

A long weekend, or four days, will allow you to visit this area, which spans less than thirty miles east to west, about twenty-five miles north of the Mediterranean. If you take Autoroute A8 (also called Autoroute du Soleil), you can get off either at Le Muy (and take the D25 toward Callas) or at Fréjus (and take the D4 toward Fayence). The Draguignan-Grasse road (D562) is convenient for getting close to each of the villages, but I prefer the old, narrow mountain roads with the occasional hairpin turn (still very manageable with a good car), that take you to wild and very much untouched mountain vistas. You will rarely meet a soul, even in high season.

Fayence, 3,500 inhabitants, is the main village, although not, in my opinion, the most interesting. It is touristic and lively; up and down the steps of the old rue du Château are workshops and boutiques selling leather, Provençal fabrics, paintings on silk, olive wood sculptures and artifacts, lavender and essential oils (nearby Grasse is the center of the perfume production of Provence). The rue du Château leads up to the Tour de l'Horloge, with a beautiful panorama, north to the Plans de Provence and the Préalpes, and south to the Maures and the Esterel. The church has a sixteenth-century retable in gilded wood. The medieval village lies mostly south of Place de la République. The quaint little streets twist between the old houses with lavender or faded blue shutters.

One of the most interesting events in Fayence is the antique fair that takes place four times a year in Le Grand Jardin, a romantic] the old town. The next fair is scheduled to be held from April 17 to 25. Dealers exhibit antique Provençal furniture and objects, including the prized boutis (intricately quilted cotton bedspreads), along the pebbled alleys, while a makeshift café serves drinks and a light lunch on a shaded terrace.

From Fayence, and on the way to Mons, you can visit Notre-Dame des Cyprès, a twelfth-century Roman chapel, with a remarkable sixteenth-century retable, surrounded by cypresses. Take the D19 west of Fayence and follow the signs. Go back into Fayence and take the D563 through a wild and thick scrubland to Mons, perched on a rock at 2,950 feet with a spectacular view to the Italian Alps and Corsica. Originally a Celtic-Ligurian oppidum (a Latin word meaning fortress) settled before the Romans conquered Provence, Mons is now a quiet mountain village, whose cobblestoned streets vividly evoke its geography and its old social structure with their colorful names (all in Provençal), such as Caladoun Deboussadou (Breakneck Alley), Squeeze-Elbow Lane, Whistlers' Lane, Door-to-Door Ironsmith's Passage, Stone-Cutter's Street and so on. The wooden shutters of the old shops still hang, washed in faded blue. There are some beautiful vistas framed by the fortified doors. Take the vaulted staircase up to the Roman church (eleventh century), with its square steeple, its small side door in heavy wood studded with the traditional metal nails. It boasts five beautiful retables from the Baroque period.

From Mons, a very small and picturesque road goes along the Gorges de la Siagne all the way to Callian, one of the prettiest villages in the area. Like Montauroux, a couple of miles down the road, Callian has been restored by arts and crafts people. Its narrow, winding lanes, closed to cars, linked by steep stone steps, are shaded by the tall facades of the old houses, and everyone tends to their geraniums and bougainvillea. The eighteenth-century castle, recently rebuilt, dominates the village, next to the Chapelle des Pénitents, now converted into an art gallery.

From Callian and Montauroux it is a short drive to St.-Cassien, a man-made lake that dams the waters of the Siagne. Fishing, swimming and all manner of water sports are practiced in season.

Seillans, about ten miles west of Fayence on the D19, is a beautifully restored medieval village. A village favored by artists (Max Ernst made his home there for the last years of his life), it offers charming and comfortable hotels and restaurants. Its narrow streets en calades (paving stones edged with pebblestones of round silex, laid to provide traction for horses) climb between the ocher- and buff-colored walls. The old medieval facades, detailed with arches, corbelings and lintels, curve into vaults covering secret passages. The tourist office, near the Porte Sarrasine and the castle, publishes a brochure called "Balade Dans Seillans," unfortunately printed only in French, that gives a fascinating historical tour of the village. The castle, privately owned, cannot be visited. It was originally a Ligurian fortress, and the oldest section of the present castle was erected in the tenth century, probably against the Saracen invasions. It included a donjon, and the ramparts and houses that you still see below and against the castle. The Town Hall, at the rue de Clastres, which served as a prison in the Middle Ages, the rue du Four, the St.-Léger church, the chemin de ronde, built into the rock immediately below the castle, the rue de la Boucherie, the rue du Haut-Four and the Porte Sarrasine, with its charming fountain and lavoir, are all part of the original fortress.

The newer town, from the fourteenth century, lies below the rue de l'Église. Look for the rue du Mitan-Four, Passage de la Crotette and the little neighborhood around the rue de la Vanade that housed the tanners, the weavers and the granaries.

A number of small restaurants serve typical Provençal fare. One of the most charming is the Clariond, the restaurant of the Hôtel de France, on the Place du Thouron, near one of the old lavoirs, where you can have a festive meal or a simple pastis.

Notre-Dame de l'Ormeau, three-quarters of a mile outside Seillans on the D19 to Fayence, is worth a visit. The altar is surmounted by a beautiful sculpted and painted sixteenth-century retable.

A day's excursion from Seillans are the villages of Bargemon, Callas and Claviers, three sisters forever quarreling and competing with each other from their perches high on the hills near Draguignan. On the way, take a detour up the Col du Bel-Homme, a pass at 3,300 feet north of Bargemon, with a view of the Plateau de Canjeurs, a moonlike landscape of dry moorland where the French Army has a large base.

The D19 continues to Bargemon, built in the twelfth century and discovered in the twentieth by the English, who have renovated a number of the old houses and the medieval castle, recently parceled into exquisite privately owned apartments that share a garden, a swimming pool and a tennis court set among the olive groves. The other castle, below the village, has been owned for centuries (as it still is) by the old Provençal family of De Villeneuve-Bargemon. Like Seillans, the fortified part of Bargemon powerfully evokes a bygone era, and a walk on the rue Sous-Barry, with its splendid view, takes you very far from the bustle of the Côte d'Azur.

Here, too, the tourist office publishes a small booklet (in French) that takes you on a tour of the old village. Bargemon was also a Celtic-Ligurian oppidum, later developed as a fortress. The earliest ramparts date to the tenth and eleventh centuries. The castle was built around 920 to 950. Walk into the fortified village through the door flanking the church (which is part of the ramparts), or by the town hall, down the street, in front of a fountain complete with its trough, where the cattle used to drink and the tanners used to wash their pelts. On the door by the fountain you can still see the opening between the stones left for the portcullis to come down and close the fort. Make a right at the next fountain, and you can catch a glimpse of the castle from the Place du Château with its lovely double-curved stone staircase. You can also walk under its perfectly preserved dry-stone ramparts, organically built right into the rock. On the other side of the castle is the charming Place du Tertre.

From Bargemon it's less than four miles to Callas, clinging on the slope of a hill covered with olive trees and oaks. A couple of miles down the D25 toward Le Muy is the Gorges de Pennafort; park opposite the Gorges de Pennafort hotel and walk down the path following the stream. Waterfalls cascade from stone to stone between the cliffs of the canyon. One of the large flat stones at the edge of the gorge is called Samson's foot. According to the legend, the biblical Samson, fleeing his creditors, leaped across the canyon and his pursuers found only the print of his foot. A little path to the right of the canyon goes to the Notre-Dame de Pennafort chapel, isolated on a rock among the pine trees. Its nineteenth-century dome is erected atop an eleventh-century tower. Some of the best olive oil of the area is pressed at the Callas mill (a quarter-mile from the village), where it can be bought by the liter or the five-liter can and the installation visited. A little shop sells Provençal products (olive oil and honey soaps, Souleiado fabrics, olive wood objects and perfumes).

You can go back to Seillans through Claviers (the road branches out from the Bargemon road about a half-mile from Callas—drive through Claviers and about four miles out of the village make a left on the old railroad track, paved over as a road). Claviers is a small perched village, ignored by tourists, but with an eerie charm and gorgeous wild vistas. Park the car across from the *boules* or *pétanque* court, where the players throw day and night. Also stop at the Cercle de la Fraternité, on the edge of the cliff, for a pastis. The afternoon or the evening will fly by, and you will feel, for a few fleeting moments, truly Provençal.

Places to Stay, Places to Eat

Of the hotels and restaurants mentioned in this article, the only establishments I found in the current Michelin Red Guide and the Guide Gautié were Les Gorges de Pennafort, Moulin de la Camendoule, and Le Castellaras. However, this does not mean the other places do not exist, merely that they are not included in Michelin. I have retained their names, addresses, and telephone numbers as the author originally compiled, as there is a good chance that each of them is still in operation. Note that low season is roughly October through March.

Hotels

Les Gorges de Pennafort, Route du Muy, Callas (on the D25 toward Le Muy); 94.76.66.51. An old inn luxuriously renovated last year, overlooking the canyon of Pennafort and its waterfalls. Swimming pool.

Moulin de la Camendoule, Chemin Notre-Dame des Cyprès, Fayence; 94.76.00.84. An old olive oil mill set in a park with a large swimming pool.

Hôtel des Deux Rocs, Place Font d'Amont, Seillans; 94.76.87.32. This eighteenth-century manor house is charmingly renovated.

Hôtel de France Clariond, Place du Thouron, Seillans; 94.76.96.10. In the middle of the old town.

Auberge des Arcades, 12 Avenue Pasteur, Bargemon; 94.76.60.36.

Hôtel Lasousto, Place du Paty, Fayence; 94.76.02.16. Spectacular mountain views, but the bedrooms have primitive amenities.

Bargemon Restaurants

Le Bistrot du Vintage, Rue Jean-Jaurès (Route de Fayence); 94.76.71.08. Sophisticated new restaurant for the fashionable set. Provençal specialties with a nouvelle cuisine twist.

Auberge Pierrot, Place Philippe Chauvier; 94.76.62.19. Honest, family cuisine, right on the main plaza. Specialties: Claviers rabbit

with basil cream, Provençal tripes, John Dory with red pepper
sauce.

Les Arcades, 12 Avenue Pasteur; 94.76.60.36. Dining in the garden
under the fig trees and palm trees. Specialties: salmon in lemon
sauce, daube Provençale, salmon stuffed with John Dory mousse.

Seillans Restaurants

Le Clariond, in Hôtel de France Clariond; 94.76.99.28. Specialties:
farcis Provençaux, salmon with sorrel.

Le Pressoir, 5 Grande Rue; 94.76.85.85. Small quaint restaurant in
an old village house. Simple cuisine. Specialties: farcis, zucchini
fritters, rabbit with thyme and chanterelles.

Fayence Restaurants

Le Castellaras, Route de Seillans; 94.76.13.80. On the heights
above the village, in a beautiful garden. Refined and classy.
Specialties include lobster raviolis with sautéed artichokes, grilled
loup (Mediterranean fish) with mixed vegetables.

Le Poelon, 1 Rue Font de Vin; 94.76.21.64. In the heart of the old
village. Provençal specialties.

Callian Restaurants

La Taupinière, 6 Rue de la Calade; 94.76.59.17. Simple little
restaurant on a tiny, picturesque lane.

Callas Restaurants

Gorges de Pennafort, Route du Muy (D250); 94.76.66.51. Upscale
fare in the hotel's comfortable dining room.

The Camargue

BY CATHARINE REYNOLDS

~

editor's note

"When you feel surfeited with views," writes Ian Norrie in his wonderful book *Next Time Round in Provence,* "start on a tour of the Camargue where there aren't any; there is only horizon. Many parts of Provence are different but this one is more different than others. It excites not so much affection as a devotion which can verge on the mystical. Voices quaver, eyes mist over, cheeks glow when people tell you how they feel about the Camargue. It is the light, they say, the strangeness, the solitude, the space. Then come ecstatic references to the wild white horses, to egrets and flamingoes, and some go so far as to name it the most beautiful region in all France, let alone Provence."

The bird life in the Camargue is truly extraordinary, and the Parc Ornithologique maintains a variety of trails which offer visitors a good, overall introduction to the wetlands. Note that in addition to jeep and horse-riding tours, visitors can explore the delta by boat, canoe, and bike. Perhaps the most unique feature of the Camargue is that it is a true sanctuary from the bustling outside world.

CATHARINE REYNOLDS is a contributing editor of *Gourmet,* where this piece appeared in April 1998. Her "Paris Journal" column, which she wrote for the magazine for over twenty years, won a James Beard Foundation Award in 1998.

The opening footage of the wild white horses of the Camargue careering along the beach in Albert Lamorisse's short film *Wild Stallion* captured my childish imagination. Ever since, I've longed to visit the region, and I jumped when a week's break there was mooted.

A long northern-European winter had invaded our marrow, so the two of us were thrilled by the insolent Provençal sunshine that greeted us as we stepped off the train at Avignon after the three-and-a-half-hour trip from Paris. Little did I appreciate that this light—bright, hazy, glimmering, pearlescent—was to prove for me the hallmark of the trip.

We had reserved at Le Mas de Peint, located thirteen miles south of Arles. Crossing the Rhône, we perceived that we had entered a new, amphibious world: the Camargue, an island caught in the fork of the Grand Rhône and the Petit Rhône. The landscape is not gentle. Barely above sea level, the Camargue spreads flat over nearly three hundred square miles. Its marshy character, combined with the consistent sunshine, make it quite "other"—a world apprehended somewhere between earth, sea, and sky.

Since Roman times the region's inhabitants have had to struggle to wrest a living from this soil. Not for them the architectural pretensions of Loire Valley châteaux or even the *bastides* of their Provençal neighbors. They knew to build sturdy, ground-hugging *mas* (farmhouses) to resist that enervating prevailing wind, the mistral. The Mas de Peint, situated on its own 1,200 acres, is just such a fine seventeenth-century building.

Owner Jacques Bon's attachment to the place is innate; he was born there. His wife, Lucille, brought a designer's flair, which added discreet but efficient twentieth-century comforts and style to what remains essentially a working ranch. Four years ago they converted the barn adjacent to their house into an air-conditioned hotel, creating eight bedrooms and two suites as well as two welcoming reception rooms and a pair of side-by-side kitchens, one of which serves as the hotel's dining room.

With the help of Estelle Reale-Garcin they decorated in sympathy with the building's original vocation, counterpointing the region's brilliant sunshine with understated shades of terra-cotta, chamois, and teal. Our bedroom boasted bold beams, a handsome antique provincial chest, and pretty views. A claw-footed bath dominated our bathroom, shrouded in acres of ecru linen shower curtain. Everywhere fat white towels stood piled, embroidered with the Bon stock brand, which also marks the white bed linens. Quiet maids aproned in Provençal prints tend the bedrooms. This soft-spoken luxury characterizes the *mas* and in turn defines much of its clientele.

Coming down for pre-dinner drinks, we were treated to another aspect of this blend of simplicity and luxury. Checked curtains and dove-colored linen upholstery make the sitting room, with its broad fireplace, appealing. Wisteria winds round the pergola of the adjacent terrace, which was flooded with evening sunlight.

The dining room-*cum*-kitchen basked in the same radiance as we sat down at one of the small tables. An enormous nineteenth-century marble-topped kitchen sideboard commands the right side of the room, its splash back hung with copper utensils and plaited garlic. After selecting from the short list of regional wines, we tucked into four courses, all based on the region's local produce. Our fellow guests were mostly French, with a sprinkling of Britons, Italians, and Germans, and seemed to enjoy the delectable tomato tarts, the rich beef stew studded with olives, and the unctuous chocolate tart as much as we did.

Meals are table d'hôte, but who couldn't find things to please among dishes prepared from the Provençal larder of tomatoes, peppers, onions, and garlic? The Camargue adds its own specialties: red rice, beef from its jet-black cattle, and *tellines*. The first is a natural mutation of the rice that since the late 1940s—when France was losing Indochina—has been a mainstay of local agriculture. Red rice's nutty flavor and *al dente* texture make it an ideal accompaniment to the tender, flavorful local beef, which two years ago was granted full French gastronomic credentials, an Appellation d'Origine Contrôlée. *Tellines,* or wedge shells, are tiny, smooth-shelled bivalves that look like flattened pinky-beige olives. Panfried with garlic for nanoseconds, they set off the anisey tang of pastis, the Provençal apéritif par excellence.

At the Mas de Peint, most of these products are homegrown. The asparagus come straight from the kitchen garden, as do cabbages, fennel, leeks, artichokes, eggplants, and salad makings. The chicken and, of course, the beef also are produced on the property.

The enormous comfort of the Mas de Peint (and its pool) can too easily distract from the fact that it is the perfect base for a very active—albeit relaxing—holiday, full of riding, bird-watching, beach-walking, bicycling, and sight-seeing, including exploring nearby Arles, Nîmes, and the Romanesque treasures of Saint-Gilles.

Dapper Jacques Bon delights in touring the tables during meals to make sure each of his guests is finding what he or she seeks. With the slightest encouragement, he will schedule to take them around the ranch either on horseback or in his sport utility vehicle. And, though he doesn't speak English, his enthusiasm translates well, especially with a little help from Lucille, who spent time in South Africa.

We quickly planned a horseback tour. Both horses and cattle are the charges of *gardians,* a sturdy race of Mediterranean cowboys who speak with tangled Provençal vowels, typically wear shirts in the Provençal prints made familiar to us by Souleïado, and wield traditional *ferrés,* cast-iron tridents on chestnut poles, designed to keep their animals in line.

Jacques Bon's Camargue horses proved well-schooled but sufficiently spirited that I could still credit poet Frédéric Mistral's description of them as a "savage race unbent" for which "the ocean is the element." The Camarguais saddle, designed with pommel and cantle snugger than its Western counterpart and with "cage" stirrups in order to give the rider a very secure seat when wrestling with a reluctant beast, took some getting used to. Like all "white" horses, the Camargue foals are gray and grow paler over the first five years of their lives. They are small, never measuring more than 14¼ hands, but are not to be underestimated.

The black Camargue bulls can be distinguished from the Iberian fighting bulls that are often raised alongside them by their heaven-bent, lyre-shaped horns and relatively small size. The Camarguais herds are raised for the *course à la cocarde,* a variation on bull-fighting in which the white-clad *razeteur,* in a series of balletic if dangerous maneuvers, attempts to hook *cocardes,* or small ribbons or tassels, tied between the bulls' horns. Here bravery wins airs from *Carmen* and the bulls invariably live to fight another day.

In summer, both cattle and horses graze the flat, cracked-mud land that floods in winter. The terrain is covered with *sansouire,* sparse vegetation consisting primarily of clumps of glassworts— nearly the only plants that can survive the hypersaline water table. And mosquitoes thrive, making insect repellent essential from April through October.

The *gardian* who accompanied our rides was an endless source of information about the wildlife and what must be one of the world's most fascinating and fragile managed ecosystems. There is little that is natural about this environment, which from the mid-nineteenth century onward has been altered with dikes and, more recently, pumps to enable farmers to cultivate first vineyards and then rice. The latter crop also desalinates the land. During our two-hour ride, evidence of thriving populations of beaver, nutria, and boar was pointed out to us.

But it was the bulls and horses that absorbed us, and we vowed to plan another visit to coincide with the spring *ferrade* (branding roundup) or a local *course à la cocarde* or *jeux de gardians,* not unlike our rodeos. Both gather aficionados around steaming kettles of *boeuf des gardians,* the local stew made with bull meat.

Even nonbirders find themselves mesmerized by the Camargue's abundant birdlife. Early risers are rewarded with the best of nature's spectacle: great white egrets, ducks, eagles, black-necked grebes, passerines, and penduline and bearded tits. The showiest are France's only colony of flamingos, which inhabit an island in the Vaccarès Lagoon. Many species winter there, while others pause en route to Africa. Nearly eighty square miles of wetlands are protected as a European Heritage Site, and much of the rest of the area benefits from the protection of a bewildering variety of organizations. The Centre d'Information du Parc Naturel Régional at Ginès provides superb documentation about the area's feathered denizens, as does the Société Nationale de Protection de la Nature at La Capelière.

Even the chronically unfit can consider bicycling, thanks to the flat terrain. The Mas provides sturdy mountain bikes, suited to the gritty roads and paths. More than twelve miles of bicycle paths wind their way along the Digue à la Mer, which separates the Vaccarès Lagoon from the Mediterranean.

The Mas de Peint is within the commune of Arles, France's largest. The city itself could easily hold my attention for a week or more, but I found it equally fun to nip in for half-day visits. The church of Saint-Trophime, dedicated to the market town's proselytizer, dates from the eleventh and twelfth centuries. Its entrance features a tympanum of the Last Judgment, with the crowned Christ surrounded by the four Evangelists, including the angel-winged Matthew, and the three angels of judgment at the top. Saint-Trophime's cloister is still more impressive, with glorious sculptures on the capitals of the columns, especially those on the north side.

Opened several years ago, the city's triangular, cobalt-blue Musée de l'Arles Antique, with its artfully displayed paleo-Christian sarcophagi, rich mosaics, and Augustinian sculpture, occupies the same alluvial plain where, during the early Christian era, chariots once raced around the Roman circus, which accommodated twenty thousand.

We stocked up on *saucisson d'Arles*—a blend of beef, pork, and lardons marinated in red wine and Provençal herbs and aged several months or more. The original recipe dates from the seventeenth century. Authorities argue about whether the sausage must include donkey meat in order to be worthy of the name. Today much *saucisson d'Arles* is industrial-ordinary but not, we discovered, that at the Charcuterie Milhau, on the rue Réattu.

Our stay at the Mas coincided with Arles's Easter *féria*. A good dose of Ernest Hemingway's *Death in the Afternoon* and a childhood that included long stays in Mexico City and Madrid has left me with a passing understanding of bullfighting, so I was pleased when Jacques Bon assured me he could get tickets for the *corrida de rejón,* scheduled in the first-century Arènes de Arles.

The *rejón,* a sophisticated and challenging form of bullfighting undertaken by a man mounted on a highly trained horse, usually of Andalusian pedigree, showcases the complete complicity between man and beast and produces movements that evoke ballet in their complexity. The risk implicit rendered the experience at once dramatic and beautiful. One need not condone bullfighting to appreciate that it has been part of the fabric of life in this corner of the world probably since shortly after the Greeks founded a trading outpost there.

Afterward we retired to Arles's classic hotel, the Jules César, occupying a former convent, for lunch at its Restaurant Lou Marquès. Minutes after being seated, we found the dashing *rejóneadors,* with a cuadrilla of silky-haired groupies in their wake, placed at the table next to ours. They shared our enthusiasm for chef Pascal Renaud's Provençal cooking, including his John Dory with potatoes and tiny violet artichokes as well as his vegetable-filled ravioli, the flavors of which were bright as the old-fashioned dining room was somber.

The leading town of the Camargue itself, Saintes-Maries-de-la-Mer, is situated on the western side of the delta, beyond the Vaccarès Lagoon. Its honey-colored fortress-church is dedicated to both Mary Salomé, mother of the apostles James and John, and Mary Jacobé, the Virgin's sister, who in about A.D. 40 are said to have tossed up on the shore on a raft in company with their servant, the future Saint Sarah, patroness of Gypsies. Their relics have long made the port a place of pilgrimage. Unfortunately, folklore fosters commercialism. On the great annual feast days in late May and on the Sunday closest to October 22 there is singing and dancing in the streets and on the beach, but too often Gypsies badger visitors, assuring them long life in return for a "tribute," and the crowds can be oppressive.

Yet the town has enormous charm. Its radiant sunlight, which once captivated Vincent van Gogh, contrasts with shadowy interiors. The church, in particular, seems peculiarly mystical. A well on the right of the Romanesque nave attests to its role as a refuge for the inhabitants when marauding pirates and Barbarians plagued Saintes-Maries-de-la-Mer seven centuries ago. The saints' raft occupies pride of place above the altar. In the crypt around the brilliantly arrayed statue of Saint Sarah, seas of ex-votos reflect flickering candles—and the faith she inspires among Gypsies.

Farther afield, we visited Saint-Gilles, which knew its greatest prosperity in the twelfth century, when it was a staging point for Crusaders. (It also gained fame as a place of pilgrimage, located as it was on one of the four major routes to Santiago de Compostela.) Little remains of the period monastic buildings except the abbey church's splendid Romanesque facade—a Bible carved in stone—and the spiral staircase that once served the north bell tower. Both attest to the impressive skills of the twelfth-century masons, who are thought to have hailed from Toulouse. I found myself carefully unraveling the Easter Week story spread across the frieze.

Another day we drove to Nîmes, where the spectacular Arènes amphitheater rivals that of Arles. The classical symmetries of the

Maison Carrée, said to be the best-preserved Roman temple that has come down to us, left us spellbound. We were also delighted by architect Sir Norman Foster's extremely successful new Carré d'Art contemporary art museum, which occupies the western side of the square. Foster rose to the challenge of creating a well-mannered but fine building that succeeds in enhancing rather than diminishing the first century B.C. temple.

We returned to the Mas de Peint via Aigues-Mortes, located in the inhospitable marshes of the western Camargue. The city was built to order in the thirteenth century by Saint Louis to provision knights departing on the Seventh Crusade. We watched the sun set rosy from the ramparts and found ourselves better able to appreciate the poetry of Chateaubriand's description of Aigues-Mortes as "a tall ship aground on the sands, left there by Saint Louis, time, and the sea."

Nor did we limit ourselves to dinners at the Mas, but, following advice from the Bons, ventured into another nacreous pink sunset along the (very dubious) road west of the curious nineteenth-century company town of Salin-de-Giraud—and the salt pans whose production was essential to Marseilles soap—until we reached Chez Marc et Mireille at Beauduc. In the most rudimentary of beachfront settings we selected from sparkling, locally landed *loup* (bass), sole, *daurade* (sea bream), and turbot. While our choices were being grilled, we nibbled *tellines* and observed diners relaxed at wooden tables around us—local families, many of them with canine companions cached among the table legs. Flavorful dry Lubéron goat cheeses followed the firm-fleshed fish, capping an exceptionally satisfying supper. As we walked to the car, we circled to watch the waders and slender-billed gulls, marveling at this land caught between sea and sky, its horizontal panoramas, and its pearly light—a never-never land just an hour from Marseilles airport.

Hotels

Le Mas de Peint, Manade Jacques Bon, Le Sambuc, 13200 Arles; 04.90.97.20.62; fax: 04.90.97.22.20. (Doubles from about $178).

Restaurants and Shops

Charcuterie Milhau, 11 rue Réattu; 13200 Arles; 04.90.96.16.05.

Chez Marc et Mireille, Beauduc, 13129 Salin-de-Giraud; 04.42.48.80.08.

Restaurant Lou Marquès, Hôtel Jules César, Boulevard des Lices, 13631 Arles; 04.90.93.43.20.

This article originally appeared in *Gourmet*. Copyright © 1998 by Catharine Reynolds. Reprinted with permission of the author.

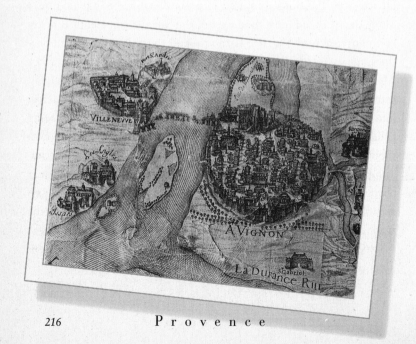

One from the Heart

BY WALTER WELLS

~∽

editor's note
....

Visitors to Avignon should not overlook Villeneuve-lès-Avignon (new town by Avignon), on the other side of the Rhône (in the Middle Ages Villeneuve was technically in Languedoc and thus in French territory, as the Rhône was the boundary between Papal territory and France). The fourteenth-century tower of Philippe le Bel houses a museum that holds two worth-a-detour paintings of the Avignon School by Enguerrand Quarton. One, *Coronation of the Virgin,* features famous monuments of Rome in the background but also Provence's Mont Ventoux. The other is actually a copy of the *Avignon Pietà,* considered one of the finest European paintings of its time, which was acquired for the Louvre by Charles Sterling (see "The Louvre Honors a Patron Saint of French Painting," by John Russell, in *Les Personalités* of my Paris edition). Additionally, the view of Avignon from Villeneuve is superb.

WALTER WELLS is managing editor of *The International Herald Tribune.* He lives in Paris and Provence with his wife, Patricia Wells.

Sky too blue, sun too bright, wind too strong, square too crowded, architecture too imposing, ramparts too formidable, history too ecclesiastical: Avignon is a city of excesses. Often skirted even on tours of Provence, with perhaps at best a nod toward the oft-sung bridge, the walls, and the wide, café-lined Place de l'Horloge, Avignon merits closer attention. Far livelier than other major stops in the Provençal interior, this sun-washed city of medieval and Renaissance facades can be sight-seen in a day, but known well in three. And it's right there at the heart of the region, the place to start from and to come back to for Provençal tours, particularly since its bustling streets and sophisticated shops can give big-city addicts a little respite from cypress-studded rustication.

After the sales pitch, a confession: It took me a very long time to like Avignon. Sure, there was wonderful architecture, and, yes, the shopping was the best in the region. But there was also something sinister about it, I thought, beginning with the dirty, crowded train station and extending to the Place de l'Horloge, where evidence of drugs and a certain low-grade hustle made me wonder if the city walls had been built to keep brigands in and the righteous out, rather than the other way around. Over years of living in the region my wife and I dreaded our forced trips there and avoided them. We chose longer drives to other train stations to meet visiting friends, and we transferred most of our *démarches administratives*—registering the car or settling tax questions—to regional offices in smaller towns in the Vaucluse *département*.

Then love happened. It was no stroke of mad passion that reversed those categorical first impressions, but rather a slow kindling of physical affection—for the brilliance of the light and the shade of the plane trees, each leaf a shimmering prism of green. Affection for the textures of stone and the noise of the student cafés in the rue Joseph-Vernet. Affection even for the unwashed flakiness of the performers in the *place*—for as much as anything they reflect Avignon's verve and energy.

At its best, travel is a series of intense experiences. And my experience in the two other principal cities in Provence's interior is not so intense. The charm of Aix-en-Provence is too official, too dressed up. And Arles is awash in a time warp, not Roman or Romanesque like the architecture, but a postwar haze, where everything is numb.

Not Avignon. Within its walls there's enormous energy. Forget as a tourist the industrial and commercial sprawl outside the ramparts, because it's nothing different or special. But Avignon *intra-muros* is a city of crisp corners and hard edges, of late-twentieth-century bustle played out against a stage set from antiquity under the klieglike illumination of the meridional sunshine.

The first impression Avignon leaves—the ramparts, the broken-off bridge, the Palace of the Popes—it owes largely to the medieval church. It's not necessary to dredge up the details (from tenth-grade world history or wherever) of the wrangles of the "Babylonian captivity"—a Holy See partly driven out of Rome by warfare and corruption, partly hijacked by an ambitious French king—or of the subsequent struggle between pope and antipope. All that is there for the reading in your favorite encyclopedia before leaving home or in the Michelin guide once you're here.

If you find the history imposing, wait until you see the papal palace. There's no spot to stand and take in its enormousness without craning your neck and swiveling your head. The full tilt from top to bottom is impressive, but the scan to get from end to end is incredible. What must the peasants have thought when they saw it in its fourteenth-century newness? What greater proof was there of the church's might, of their own minimal place in the order of things?

Inside, the hugeness is downright funny to modern sensibilities. Space has rarely been wasted so grandly. (Save the palace tour, by the way, for a rainy day or a windy one, when the mistral is whipping down the Rhône and the parasols on the Place de l'Horloge are furled and tied tight. Might as well put those cavernous rooms to practical use. And, frankly, except for the unforgettable dimensions, there's not much to remember about the interior.)

Besides the palace, there are the ramparts, built by popes to keep the city safe from the bands of thugs that roamed the medieval countryside. There is the museum of the Petit Palais (next to the big one) and its exceptional collection of thirteenth- to sixteenth-century Italian paintings as well as notable works from the Avignon School. And there are all the other cardinals' palaces, called *livrées* because the land to accommodate them was "liberated" from the less deserving.

But before getting down to serious touring, here's the second most important thing about this theatrical city: Today's Avignon is best known as the site of France's most prestigious theater festival, which fills the city every scorching summer, usually from mid-July to mid-August, with plays and players and crowds in clots too dense to pass through. So if you come then, come prepared. Wiser still, come another time, for English is *lingua non grata* for this event.

When you arrive, assuming the weather is warm, I say head for the Place de l'Horloge and take a seat at a café. (I usually choose a spot toward the upper end, close to the ancient carousel, both to admire the gilt decoration and to watch the children play.) It doesn't particularly matter *which* café—they're all pretty much alike, with service no slower and prices no higher at one than at another; just be sure you choose a comfortable chair and clear sight lines for observing the richly varied life of the square.

From the calm of early morning to the carnival midway of late evening, this *place* distinguishes Avignon for me. It's not typically Provençal, because it's bigger and noisier than the others. And if Avignon's modern-day influence is the summer theater festival, the Place de l'Horloge is theater in the round-and-round, a participatory stage set where performers and audience trade lines and roles constantly. If it's early morning when you install yourself, the parade will be calm and purposeful: businessmen and shopgirls on their way to work, children heading for school, housewives or maids heading for the market. And, of course, groups of tourists.

At lunchtime, you can observe the midday reunions—kisses on the cheek (usually three here in Provence, alternating from side to side) indicate good friends, whereas a single kiss on the lips, however fleeting, indicates greater intimacy.

As the day winds down, the *place* warms up, and it's then that one or two knots of street people—mostly young, many speaking German or Dutch or English and all wearing road grime—begin to give the *place* an unpleasant mood. It's then also that the performers begin limbering up, the quick-sketch portraitists solicit subjects, and the fortune teller reads upturned palms before upturning her own.

Late night is a time not to be in the *place*. Not because it's dangerous—it's constantly patrolled, and any sign of real trouble draws a clattering of police—but because in the late hours *les marginaux* are in charge. And as always on the midway at midnight, there's been too much to drink, too many shouts of rage. In mood, in tone, this *place* bears no resemblance to the morning's calm or the afternoon's softness. And the brightness of the street lamps is no substitute for brilliant sunshine and blue skies.

"What is it you like best about Avignon?" I asked a Provençal friend. *"La pierre,"* she said—the stone. Since in French *la pierre* is usually shorthand for real estate holdings, I hoped to pick up an investment tip. But no: *"La pierre et la lumière,"* she amended her reply—stone and light. Stones do dominate Avignon's texture, always have. The biggest one is the oldest one, the Rocher des Doms, a giant boulder between the Rhône and the papal palace that was the site of the first settlement, on high ground to escape the periodic ravages of the Rhône. Today the cathedral is there, Notre-Dame-des-Doms, built in the twelfth century but modified, pillaged, and rebuilt a number of times since. On the *rocher* also, peering out over the Rhône, is a quiet and underused park, a Provençal arrangement of natural elements rather than the sophisticated torturing—Île-de-France fashion—of those elements into what nature should have been. The wooden crutches propping up two winded parasol pines are charming evidence of kinder, gentler gardening.

Aside from the most visible stones, the papal palace itself, as imposing a medieval rock pile as ever existed, there's the protective stone of the ramparts and the crafted stone of the Pont St.-Bénézet, the bridge we've all sung about: *On y danse, tous en rond.* You can dance out onto it if you wish, or just admire its ruined grace from the vantage point of the park above. The bridge bridges nothing now except perhaps the centuries, four graceful arches stretching out into the Rhône toward the island in the middle of the river where the dancing really took place.

Rhapsodizing about *la pierre,* my friend would list hundreds of other sites and facades. Austere ones, like the tower and the fortress at Villeneuve-lès-Avignon. Others distant, like the rocky cliffs of the Gard, on the Rhône's western bank. I would certainly include one golden and luxurious facade, the Italianate Hôtel des Monnaies (once the papal mint), across from the papal palace. Now a music conservatory, this palace offers its front step as a frequent, unlikely perch for two middle-aged musicians, playing Les Paul and Mary Ford ditties on their electric guitars. Against other facades, it is the Mediterranean light that plays constantly and sometimes wildly, as when blue skies give way to tempestuousness.

There are dozens of stony spots that merit checking out, but here is my own short list, a highly personal selection of several intriguing examples of Avignon's special texture.

Start by looking down, at the pavement preserved in many city streets as well as the expansive parvis in front of the papal palace. Smooth oval stones, in tones of ocher and umber, were dredged up from the riverbed of the Rhône or the nearby Durance, then crowded edge to edge to make the surface. The effect, rugged and durable, speaks to the make-do practicality of the *provençaux.*

More conventional guidance to seeing a city says you must look not at the pavement, but up. Lift your gaze in Avignon, and chances are it will fall on one of the statues of the Virgin Mary adorning these stone walls. From niches over doorways, from perches high over street corners, and placidly surveying the irregular little *places* that dot the city's neighborhoods, these icons smile down benignly, some hundred and a half of them, grace notes for a graceful town.

For architectural grace, you could do far worse than to head for the rue du Roi-René. There, three mansions of contrasting styles are reckoned among the finest in town. At #17, the Hôtel Berton de Crillon is a restored Italianate marvel. Designed by a Bolognese architect, Domenico Borboni, and built in 1648–9, it now houses apartments. Across the street at #8–10, the Hôtel de Fortia de Montréal, also built in the 1600s, reflects a more sober Gallic style, built as it was for a military man. A few steps up the street at #12, the eighteenth-century Hôtel d'Honorati de Jonquerettes completes this monument to concentrated wealth. Here you might want to step into the adjoining courtyard (a relatively public space—parking for the offices the building now houses) where along the wall on the right you'll see *les satyrs à têtes coupées*. They aren't guillotine victims, but passageway props that lost their heads during a subsequent remodeling.

All three of these houses are from Avignon's second prosperous period, the prerevolutionary years when the region, still ruled from Rome and still not part of France, developed as a sort of free-trade zone. Art and culture flourished, and commerce, too. Avignon was known for its *indiennes,* those Provençal prints made famous in our time by Pierre Deux. Which brings us appropriately to the rue des Teinturiers, street of the dyers. A stream running alongside brought water and power to the old dye works, serving as one long millrace.

Although two waterwheels remain, locked motionless as memorials to a more active past, many have been taken out. But their power trains still run under the streets, and if an open doorway allows you a peek, you might see the racks of gears and drive shafts inside.

This entire street, quiet and cool, is a *site classé*, protected for its historical importance. I think of it as a tone poem, a reflective interlude to the bustle. (It's too far from the commercial center for business to thrive now.) The Caves Breyesse, at #41, is a veritable relic of old France. Customers still tote in cans and jars for refills from the *cave*'s metal vats, whether olive oil or *vin de table*. If so inclined, they can top themselves off, as well—at the *buvette*, 4.50 francs (about $1) a glass for bar-quality Côtes-du-Rhône.

Enough about tone poems—what is there to buy? Two areas of Avignon can satisfy that need, one chic and the other more democratic. For luxury shops, look to the neighborhood between the rue de la République/Place de l'Horloge and the rue Joseph-Vernet's quarter circle. Principally in the rue St.-Agricol, the rue Petite-Fusterie, and the rue Joseph-Vernet, you'll find sophisticated boutiques with clothing for women and men, china and glassware, rare books and antiques, pens and stationery, leather goods—this could be Madison Avenue in the 60s or the Avenue Montaigne, only in miniature. For a more youthful commercial experience, there's the tangle of pedestrian streets on the other side of the Place de l'Horloge, principally the rue des Marchands and the rue des Fourbisseurs. Here the boutiques are more *branchés,* cool, with-it. And practical, too, for in this sector you'll see the *quincailleries* for hardware, the *drogueries* for housewares, and the ever-present pharmacies. For the most practical of items, the covered food market is not far away, at the Place Pie. What charm is there is all inside this neo-nothing structure.

৵

Back to antiquity, back to one last favorite vantage point: the ruins of the popes' summer residence at Châteauneuf-du-Pape, an area known now for its full-throated wines, but remarkable also for the beauty of its panoramas. To get there, drive north on Route 7. A little beyond Sorgues, take the left that's clearly marked and pass through the famous stony slopes of this wine country.

From the village of Châteauneuf-du-Pape the road to the castle ruins isn't marked all that clearly, but no matter: From here you can see your vaulted and crenellated destination. And once there, it's not necessary to lift your eyes, for you're already lifted up. The silvery Rhône runs below, and its fertile valley stretches all around. In the distance there's drama—to the east, the Lubéron glitters; to the northeast, the vineyards of the Plan de Dieu ("God's Plain") run up against the snaggle-tooth Dentelles de Montmirail and the sandy white cap on Mont Ventoux. To the west and north is other mountainous relief. And to the south is Avignon's unmistakable profile. In the old days, when the pope was staying here, important news was flashed back and forth between this palace and the big one back in town.

You'll pass as you climb through the village a winery called the Domaine Hurlevent—"domain of the screaming wind." A truer name was never emblazoned, for here the mistral is no *bise,* as the *provençaux* call it, no gentle kiss, but thrusting and battering. Raw energy, natural and right for Avignon.

Bibliothèque

Aspects of Provence, James Pope-Hennessy, with photographs by Basil Collier, Little, Brown and Company, 1952, 1967. This exquisite book can be used as a guidebook but I tend to think of it as a guidebook companion that is also a great work of literature. In attempting to describe it, I can do no better than writer Rose Macaulay, who reviewed the book in its first edition for the London *Observer:* "His own impressions are vivid, sensuous and informed . . . it is one of the merits of this book that among its bright strange landscapes and towns, human beings and history also live." Here is one passage in which Pope-Hennessy reminds us of humans and history: "Like the history of every other country the early history of Provence is one of invasions and of war. Vineyards which now lie calm beneath the evening sky have been the scenes of vast and bloody contests, and half the fields we see are battlefields." *De rigueur.*

Caesar's Vast Ghost: Aspects of Provence, Lawrence Durrell, Arcade Publishing, Little, Brown and Co., 1990. Durrell was an adopted son of Provence, where he lived for over thirty years (he passed away in 1990). As he so thoroughly outlines, the Greeks settled in Provence long before the Romans discovered it. But the Greeks stuck to the coast, and it was the Romans who left an indelible mark inland. Julius Caesar's vast ghost is inescapably evident in the arenas, arches, bridges, aqueducts, and road systems that remain—in overall good condition—today. One of my favorite passages appears early in the book: "But nothing can do fair justice to the light—neither camera nor brush. It has a felicity and eloquence beyond all praise. These skies—the special wounded blue one finds sometimes in Mantegna's skies—are unique to Provence, for they are neither Greek nor Roman. They seem so freshly minted that the peasant faces you encounter in the Saturday market-place have all the poise and gravity of Roman medallions." To enhance his own observations, Durrell has added the comments and views of his two old friends, Jerome and Aldo. The opinions differ occasionally, but serve to enrich "our knowledge of the history and essence of the Midi and its people." With a number of beautiful color photographs, this is a *de rigueur* rumination.

Cahier de Provence, Arielle Picaud, Michel Le Louarn, Editions du Garde-Temps, 1996. In French and available in many of Provence's bookstores, this attractive paperback comes with a recommendation by my favorite magazine, *Maisons Côté Sud.* Similar to *Sara Midda's South of France,* it's a whimsical notebook *(cahier)* of the souvenirs of Provence, with some lined and blank pages for writing or affixing your own photos. The text is not lengthy or taxing for those who know a little French—I had to consult my Larousse a few times but otherwise it was fairly elementary. The cover features a small "window" filled with lavender, which makes your luggage smell great, as well as providing you with a whiff of Provence when you get home.

Colors of Provence, Michel Biehn, original photographs by Heinz Angermayr, translated by Rosanna M. Giammanco Frongia, Stewart, Tabori & Chang, 1997; © 1996 by Flammarion, Paris. I was initially inclined to dismiss this as just another pretty coffee-table book without much to say. In other words, a book I really didn't need. I could not have been more wrong. This is a stunning and wonderful achievement. Author Biehn, whose beautiful store in Île-sur-la-Sorgue is one of the most appealing on earth, introduces Provence by way of the colors that define it: red, orange, yellow, green, blue, white, gray, and black. This way of introducing Provence is shared by James Pope-Hennessy, who writes in *Aspects of Provence* that "I have already suggested that one's chief memories of a journey through Provence are colour-memories: and I realized this once more as I stood looking down at the Durance and at Sisteron, for the elms, poplars and even the fresh oak-trees along the river's banks showed dark against the startling apple-green of the water-meadows, and the faultless blue of the sky. Standing there I thought, as I had thought when seeing Provence for the first time through a grimy railway-carriage window, that it is a country that needs to be interpreted by painting rather than by writing." The text is personal and engaging, and the gorgeous photos are, to borrow a phrase from the publisher, "a visual banquet, a feast for the eyes." Best of all, Biehn shares addresses for stores where he likes to spend time, restaurants where he feels at home, and hotels where he would send his friends. *De rigueur.*

French Dirt: The Story of a Garden in the South of France, Richard Goodman, Algonquin Books, Chapel Hill, 1991. This is a memoir of the year Goodman spent in a small village near Avignon. He didn't just show up and move in; he started a garden, which, he writes, "connected me to France in a way more profound and more lasting than any other way I can possibly think of. Part of me is still there. And always will be . . . the garden is in my heart. Having a garden gave me a *place* to go in my village every day, a task to perform and a responsibility. You cannot ask more of a land in which you are a stranger. To feel the French earth, clear it, plant seeds in it, despair over it and, ultimately, to take from it, that was a precious gift." Goodman's adopted village he describes as "so small it doesn't even have a café. Or a bakery. Or a butcher shop. The number of Catholics is too small for the village to support its own priest; every six weeks a traveling priest who journeys from village to village comes to say mass at the tiny church here. It has no post office. No doctor. No gas station. No shop of *any* kind." The thing is, this description of the village Goodman lived in fits more villages all over France than the famous villages we visit as tourists. Beautifully written, and hard to put down.

In the South of France, photographs and text by Don Krohn, David R. Godine,

Boston, 1999. Of my favorite books on Provence, this one might be the best. Actually, Krohn has not limited himself to Provence, crossing over into neighboring Languedoc from time to time. Simply put, the text of this beautiful book is sensitive and informative, and the stunning color photos are of uncommon images. In the Afterword, Krohn reflects upon his life in the Herault region, where he lived with his family for a while. Although his observations are personal to his experience of *living* in Provence, I feel the final paragraph could be my own words as they so aptly describe how I feel after *visiting* Provence: "And at the end of each day, after the sun's intense heat and brightness had faded, there was always the serenity of the familiar view from my window. In the fading light and disappearing colors, in the cooling and fragrant evening air, the deep romanticism of the region was distilled into an image of the simple forms and soft shades of fields and hillsides. As I now remember that view out on the South of France, I recall the time spent there as if it were a long and richly colored dream."

A Guide to Provence, Michael Jacobs, Penguin, 1988. I kept reading of this book so often that I couldn't fathom why I had never seen it anywhere. Only recently did I learn it was, inexplicably, out of print, and after the last recommendation I came across I began a serious search to find a copy. Without too much effort I located one at a used bookstore, and now I know why it was recommended so highly: it is, quite simply, the best contemporary book I've ever read on Provence. The author holds a doctorate in art history and taught at an American art school in Provence. In addition to books he's published on art and artists, he has written another excellent guide to Andalucia. This is positively a book worth your most diligent efforts to find. (Note that it's paperback, not hardcover.)

The Magic of Provence: Pleasures of Southern France, Yvone Lenard, Elysian Editions, an imprint of Princeton Book Company, Publishers, Hightstown, New Jersey, 2000. I learned of this book through an advertisement in *France Today,* and I silently groaned, assuming it would be an imitation Peter Mayle. Do we need, after all, another Provençal memoir? Regardless, I did feel I had to investigate, and it was my good fortune to discover that this is not a Mayle wanna-be; it's an entirely enjoyable, well-written read. Lenard is French, and she and her American husband, Wayne, bought a second home (they also reside in Los Angeles) in the Lubéron some years ago. Their adventures are less house-related (they moved into the house after all the renovations were complete) and more about the history and customs of their village, food and wine, neighbors and guests. Recipes appear at the end of chapters, and relate in some way to the subject of each. This has become a formula I'm tiring of, especially since none of the recipes are unique, and all (except the Duchess's *Blanquette de Veau à l'Ancienne* and Madame Fabre's secret recipe) can be found in any of the Provençal cookbooks recommended in the *Saveurs Provençaux bibliothèque*. I would have preferred some dishes from her neighbors' tables. As it is, the only one I think is special is the *Apéritif Dinatoire* ("drinks-into-dinner party"), which has no exact translation, but to the residents of Lenard's village it means a cocktail party that either intentionally or unintentionally turns into an informal, simple dinner. But this small quibble aside, I could not get enough of Lenard's stories and truly did not want the book to end. "The Chicken Rustlers" might be my favorite chapter, but each one is a delight, and Lenard doesn't hesitate to also reveal the names of some favorite food purveyors and places to eat in the vicinity. And speaking of places to eat, I was so happy to learn that Lenard and I admire the best feature of the red Michelin guide: the red "R" (*repas*, or meal) listings for restaurants offering the best *qualité-prix* (good value places with a good quality-to-price ratio). As *de rigueur* as Mayle. (I couldn't resist opening her magicofprovence.com Web site, which revealed that the village is Ansouis. The site also offers some before and after pictures of the house and some photos of the castle, as well as "Yvone's Favorites," five miscellaneous recommendations for a hotel in Aix, a wine estate near Pertuis, an antiques dealer in L'Île-sur-la-Sorgue, a candied fruit *confiserie* in Apt, and a ceramics shop in Marseille.)

Mes Origines, Frédéric Mistral. I have not read this book, so you may find it strange that I am recommending it, but James Pope-Hennessy wrote of this that it "provides the best preparation for Provence I know. It is unsurpassed for this purpose by any set guide or travel-book yet written on Provence." So you see I felt I had to include it, and while I do not know if it's available in an English edition, I don't think you'll be disappointed, no matter what language you read it in.

Old Provence, Theodore Andrea Cook, originally published 1905; reprinted by Interlink Publishing Group, 2000. I first read of *Old Provence* in James Pope-Hennessy's *Aspects of Provence,* in which he refers to it repeatedly and admirably. I knew I had to find a copy, no matter how long or difficult the search, so I was so pleased that the folks at Interlink obviously felt the same passion for Cook's great work. This new paperback edition is one volume in Interlink's "Lost and Found Classic Travel Writing" series, and it's been referred to as the best book ever written about Provence. I would have to agree. Cook imparts every historical fact, myth, and legend (and his own opinions) about Provence, leaving no stone unturned. Do not be concerned if you initially find his writing quaint; it is, but it's also beautiful, erudite, and full of depth. To quote from the foreword, "what is perhaps most compelling about his observations of Provence is his insatiable human curiosity. He was not just another Edwardian traveller, scrambling over the ruins of some distant civilization. For what appealed to him was precisely the links, the historical continuity that bound together Roman Provence, medieval Provence and the Provence of 1900." In addition to the many quotes in Provençal, Cook provides translations for a list of Latin and Greek inscriptions, which is most helpful. *De rigueur.*

Provence, Ford Madox Ford, Ecco Travels, The Ecco Press, 1970; original ©
1935; illustrations by Biala. One of the classics, with charming black-and-white
line drawings. This paperback edition is a great bring-along, but is perhaps
even better if you read it *before* you leave, and is also great to *reread*—it's classic for a reason. It was Ford's description of nightingales that made me
obsessed to hear one sing, but in all my visits to Provence I have never heard
one (making my obsession now the Mother of obsessions). I remain optimistic
that on a trip in the not-too-distant future I will finally hear a nightingale, but
in the meantime, I have this book, which is swell consolation.

Provence, Peter Mayle, aerial photographs by Jason Hawkes, Random House,
1994. There are picture books galore with pretty images of Provence, but none
except this one show you what the region looks like from above. I love the vantage point of looking at Provence and the Côte d'Azur from the window of a
car or train, but looking at it from the air is something else entirely. These photos are incredibly fascinating, revealing the shapes of hilltop villages, hidden
Calanques, the seamless line of plane trees and rooftops lining the Cours
Mirabeau, the top of Mont Ventoux, salt pan configurations in the Camargue,
and stretches of uninhabited, pristine coastline. And of course Mayle's accompanying notes make this great to look at before you go (and great to have on
your shelf when you return).

Provence: Art, Architecture, Landscape, edited by Rolf Toman, text by Christian
Freigang, photographs by Achim Bednorz, Konemann, Cologne, 2000. I've
been very impressed with this new "Art, Architecture, Landscape" series. The
text is very thorough (the author of this Provence edition is an art historian
who has lived in the south of France for many years), the color photos are
great, and the price is significantly less than many other comparable illustrated
books. I'm particularly fond of the short biographies of significant personages
in the history of Provence found at the back of the book. Definitely the best
book of its kind I've yet encountered. *De rigueur.*

Running in Place: Scenes from the South of France, Nicholas Delbanco, The
Atlantic Monthly Press, 1989. In alternating chapters, Delbanco relates the
story of his life, his blissful honeymoon trip to Grasse with his wife, Dianne,
previous travels, and the 1987 experience of his return to France with his family of four, when they are fortunate to rent a house in Lourmarin, which
belongs to author Laurence Wylie *(Village in the Vaucluse).* It is a wonderful,
warm account, and multilayered, like his family history: The Delbancos were
originally Venetian-Jewish bankers who, in 1630, moved to Germany, remaining there for three hundred years. Nicholas's parents were both born in
Germany, but fled, separately, to London, where they were married in 1938.
He writes that "often, in my childhood, I had the sense of diminution: of pictures in museums that had once been in the family, of chauffeurs and upstairs

maids and cooks who fled at Hitler's advent, leaving the cupboard bone-bare."
France, and specifically the south of France, was a favorite vacation spot and
always held promise for him ("Those of my mother's family who did escape
the Nazis had done so by fleeing to Paris, then, slowly, south and west. France,
she used to tell us, was a civilized nation, a place to retreat to: heart's home"),
so much so that he occasionally referred to it as home when asked. A reviewer
for *The Boston Globe* wrote of this book that "the author's profound affection
for Provence earns this highly civilized memoir its place on the shelf beside
Ford Madox Ford," acclaim which I enthusiastically echo. *De rigueur.*

Sara Midda's South of France: A Sketchbook, Sara Midda, Workman, 1990. It is of
course no great secret that writers, photographers, and artists are the best at capturing the essence of the world around them. I believe this is because they have
a discerning eye and take the time to *really look* around them and see what's
what. This is often accomplished by remaining in one spot long enough to absorb
everything, which is why the prime seats at cafés, bars, and restaurants are often
occupé by these talented people. A quote I've long adored is one by Robert
Thomas Allen: "Most of my treasured memories of travel are recollections of sitting." Sara Midda must have done a lot of sitting to create these lovely, whimsical watercolor illustrations of daily life through the seasons in the south of
France. It's a most unique little book, with Midda's own handwritten notes and
assortment of quotes. It will perhaps most inspire those who've ever considered
keeping a journal—seeing this will make them bound right out and get one.

Spirit of Place, Lawrence Durrell, edited by Alan G. Thomas, Marlowe &
Company, 1969. Thomas, an old friend and bibliographer of Durrell, presents a
collection of Durrell's letters spanning thirty years together with excerpts from
Durrell's first two novels, short fiction, and travel essays. Durrell was well traveled, so this collection includes much more than the south of France. But as
Thomas notes, "Never really content when living away from 'the wine-drinking
countries which surround the Mediterranean basin,' Durrell and Claude [his
wife] set out to look for a home in the Midi." They found several homes in the
vicinity of Nîmes, and therefore many of the selected pieces are about the south,
from Gascogne to Grenoble and everywhere in between. I have read and loved
many of Durrell's books, and I think I am so fond of them because, as he notes,
"My books are always about living in places, not just rushing through them."

Thomas Jefferson's Journey to the South of France, Roy and Alma Moore,
Stewart, introduction by Lucia C. Stanton, Shannon Senior Research Historian
at Monticello, Stewart, Tabori & Chang, 1999. A creative idea for a book,
which pairs text from Jefferson's daily missives that he wrote during his three-
month trip throughout the south of France in 1787 with color photos, period
maps, portraits, engravings, and paintings. This journey did nothing less than
change Jefferson's life. He wrote, "If I should happen to die at Paris I will beg

of you to send me here, and have me exposed to the sun. I am sure it will bring me to life again." He developed a passion for architecture and architectural detail, and the Maison Carrée in Nîmes was his chief inspiration for the Virginia State Capitol in Richmond. I would have enjoyed more text and more descriptive information about the recipients of his letters, but for fans of Jefferson and Americana this is required reading. As one of the recipients, Madame de Tesse, penned, "I have been projected into future ages, and have seen the youth of America reading with enthusiasm and admiration all that has been collected about your travels."

Two Towns in Provence, M. F. K. Fisher, Vintage, 1983; *Map of Another Town* originally published by Little, Brown and Company, 1964; *A Considerable Town* originally published by Alfred A. Knopf, 1978; map and drawings by Barbara Westman. Some years ago, food writer Raymond Sokolov wrote for *The New York Times* that "In a properly run culture, Mary Frances Kennedy Fisher would be recognized as one of the great writers this country has produced in this century" (referring to the twentieth, of course). Sadly, M. F. K. Fisher passed away in 1992. Though she lived a rich and full life, I believe she still had much to share with us. To many people she may have been perceived solely as a food writer, and though I think her interest in food was sincere, I believe her true concern was for the basic needs of humanity. Many people may not realize she taught at an all-black college in Mississippi at a time when genteel white women didn't do such a thing; her generosity and kindness are legendary. I recommend bringing this paperback along not only because it is written wonderfully, passionately, and perceptively, but also because Aix-en-Provence (profiled in *Map of Another Town*) and Marseille (the subject of *A Considerable Town*), which occupy chapters in many books, are rarely, if ever, the *subject* of a single book. Also, I like Marseille, and so does Fisher, and I like her portrait of it. This is *de rigueur,* and I hope readers of this book will go on to read some of Fisher's other books, many of which have to do with France, including *As They Were* (Knopf, 1982; Vintage, 1983); *The Boss Dog: A Story of Provence* (Yolla Bolly Press, 1990); *Long Ago in France: The Years in Dijon* (Prentice Hall, 1991); *Serve It Forth* (North Point Press, 1989) and *Consider the Oyster* (North Point Press, 1988).

Views from a French Farmhouse, Julian More, photographs by Carey More, first published in Great Britain in 1985 by Pavilion Books Limited; first published in paperback in the U.S. by Trafalgar Square Publishing, North Pomfret, Vermont, 1992. This little book has been a favorite of mine ever since my friend Kathleen showed it to me in the days when we worked for the travel book division of the original Banana Republic. I love the text, the photos, and the warmth that emanates from its pages. One of my favorite passages reads: "In the roundness of these days we moved through the changing light, taking in the luminosity which, for centuries, has drawn artists and writers here like a magnet. It illumines the essential quality which makes Provence special. The Romans called it 'Genius Loci,' spirit of place: Lawrence Durrell has used it as a title; we celebrate it in poetry and pastis."

Village in the Vaucluse, Laurence Wylie, Harvard University Press, 1957. I was late in reading this, and after running across repeated mentions in books and articles, I finally found a copy at The Complete Traveller in New York (see Bookstores) about two years ago. It's a classic for a reason: An account of every aspect of daily life in one Provençal village, Peyrane (Wylie's fictional name for the beautiful village of Roussillon), it is unlike any other book on Provence. Wylie lived there for a year in the late fifties and though great changes have occurred in Roussillon since then, the fundamental characteristics of village life remain very much the same. Wylie covers geography, infancy, school, adolescence, marriage, politics, earning a living, health, being *brouillé* or *bien* with one's neighbors, the café, the outside world—in short, a thorough and vastly interesting picture of the Provençal village and its inhabitants. He concludes by writing that if Adam and Eve were to return to life, they might well choose Peyrane as their Paradise Regained. "Compared to most communities in the world today, Peyrane is well off. Its pattern of life seems balanced and sane. There is a bit of madness in the relationship of the Peyranais with the rest of the world. But when we look at life there and life elsewhere, it is not always clear on which side the madness lies." Puzzlingly out of print but *de rigueur.*

A Year in Provence (1990), *Toujours Provence* (1991), and *Encore Provence* (1999), all by Peter Mayle, all published by Alfred A. Knopf in hardcover, all by Vintage in paperback. What is there left to say about these three extraordinarily popular books? Plenty, actually. Remember that although *you* may be familiar with Peter Mayle, new readers are discovering his books all the time, and with good reason: they are wonderful, witty, and wise, as well as fun and interesting to read. I have known people to say things like, *"I lived in Provence for a while . . . I could have written those books!"* but of course, they didn't, and he did, and I seriously doubt anyone could pen them better than Mayle. As I mentioned in the introduction, Provence is still a special place, a corner of the world that has captured many visitors' hearts. It isn't perfect (what place is?), but as Mayle notes at the end of *Toujours Provence,* "It is of course true that there are crooks and bigots in Provence, just as there are crooks and bigots everywhere. But we've been lucky, and Provence has been good to us. We will never be more than permanent visitors in someone else's country, but we have been made welcome and happy. There are no regrets, few complaints, many pleasures." Now that these books are all in paperback, I encourage you to pack them in your bag—and reread them if it's been awhile or eagerly begin them if you're just starting out on your Mayle journey. *De rigueur.*

La Boutique
des Loisirs

Ets JoB ADAM et Cie - S.N.C. au Capital de 150.000 fm
R.C.S. B MENTON 330 915 265

La Côte d'Azur
(The Côte d'Azur—
French Riviera)

"Imposture, when recognized, is rather frowned on these days and the flight into pleasure occurs on leaden wings if at all. But the Côte d'Azur has always been a place to have your cake and eat it. Such has been its aim, not necessarily a trivial one."
—Mary Blume, CÔTE D'AZUR: INVENTING THE FRENCH RIVIERA

Riviera Revue

BY T. D. ALLMAN

~⁓~

editor's note

....

Though this piece appeared in the April 1988 issue of *Condé Nast
Traveler*, it remains mostly true, and is a good summation of selected spots
along the Côte d'Azur. I have retained the original prices, as they emphasize
how (stupendously) expensive the expensive places—such as the Hôtel du
Cap and the Louis XV—really were and still are. At press time, I was unable
to learn the status of Les Colombières, the wonderful hotel the author stayed
at in Menton.

The Riviera isn't what it used to be. What is? Not even nostalgia, as Simone Signoret reminded us. All the same, in my high-
season exploration of that long, languid strip of Mediterranean
shore that the French evocatively call the Côte d'Azur, I found idyllic places and caught, here and there, echoes of the laughter of the
Lost Generation.

On back roads, up in the hills, I picked wild bay, thyme, and rosemary so pungent the whole world seemed perfumed by *herbes de
Provence*. At Cap Ferrat, I wandered the gardens of the Rothschild
estate, and in Beaulieu I lounged on flowered terraces, perched on
craggy promontories, surveying views of the Mediterranean to make
your heart soar. At the Hôtel de Paris in Monte Carlo, I stared,
enraptured and appalled, at socialites whose necks were choked, and
fingers pinched and shoulders stooped, by jewels costing millions of
dollars. The emeralds and diamonds and rubies weren't what made
me gape. It was the faces. They were masks, gorgeous and grotesque
as those of New Guinea tribesmen.

Finally, in the hills above Menton, hard by the Italian border, I found a marvelously eccentric little hotel that made the disappointments worthwhile.

The difficulty for the eighties traveler is finding ways around the fact that the Riviera, once the haunt of the titled and celebrated, has been swept by a new kind of French revolution. In the last twenty years, hundreds of thousands have moved south into new, hastily built villas, apartments, and *multipropriétés* (time-sharing condos). Each summer, millions more French surge down the country's new freeways for *les campings* (trailer parks).

St.-Tropez, immensely popular with French tourists, provides the perfect introduction to the consequences of this Gallic version of Sunbelt shift. With its picture-perfect port, gorgeous sunsets, narrow winding streets, and pastel houses, the place must have been paradise back in 1956 when Bardot made *And God Created Woman* there. But there's no way eighty thousand people a day in summer can converge on a tiny village without changing its character. The change may not be to your taste, but that's precisely why some people like "St.-Trop." Nowhere else in these parts do chic and tacky run quite so cheek by jowl. At four in the afternoon, at La Gorille (The Gorilla), one of the most popular waterfront cafés, *French* tourists start lunching on frozen minute steaks washed down with Coke Classic. Meanwhile, ten feet away, people are drinking champagne on the afterdecks of million-dollar yachts.

As you stroll out along the breakwater in St.-Tropez, the yachts start out the size of apartments and grow to the size of apartment houses. Just opposite a café, a yacht registered in Kinshasa is tethered next to a floating palace registered in the Gulf emirate of Bahrain, and on another yacht the size of the Paris Ritz a mustachioed Arab surrounded by red gladiolus can be seen expostulating into a ship-to-shore telephone—trading arms, perhaps, or ordering his correspondence with Colonel North shredded. Like the quaint pastel buildings of the "old" town, mostly built since World War II, these yachtsmen are not quite what they seem. "The people on the yachts change every week or so," explained Philippe Cazilhac, a local boutique owner. "Only the yachts remain the same. Most of their real owners flee St.-Tropez each summer." The yachts, on the other hand, almost never leave the dock.

St.-Tropez is best at breakfast, when all but the German tourists are still asleep. By ten in high season, traffic jams of buses and boats are heading toward Pampelonne Beach; by noon the soft white sand of the best beach on the Côte d'Azur has turned the color of wall-to-wall sunburned flesh. The crowd here is French and Italian, with a leavening of Swiss, Dutch, Germans, and British—many of them cavorting in topless, and sometimes bottomless, abandon. You find shapes and sizes to suit every taste from Humbert Humbert to the American Dairy Association.

At sunset in midsummer the twisting, cobblestoned streets become a French anthropology lesson as the whole town turns into a vast outdoor restaurant and tens of thousands of people order the prix fixe dinners.

On the Place des Lices, the locals still play *pétanque,* the regional version of *boules,* but for every player there are ten tourists watching. At the nearby Café des Arts, the Provençal food is copious, delicious, and reasonably priced. The aisles are so thick with people you are lucky to be served by 11 P.M. By then the discos are filling up; many of them stay full until dawn. "America!" exclaims a young French woman for whom I bought a drink. "If I were rich, that's where I'd go for my vacation."

One evening, Larry Collins—genial author of *Is Paris Burning?* and other books—took me down to the Place des Lices to meet some friends. Eddie Barclay, the French impresario known as the king of St.-Tropez, was there. So were enough starlets, French pop singers, and other show-biz types to fill up an autograph book. As we sipped champagne, that's in fact what happened: Tourists pressed around, asking for autographs. Everyone was delighted to comply, and this vignette seemed, more than anything else, to reveal what's become of St.-Tropez in the last decade.

What if exhibitionism is not what you want? Even on the most crowded days, the view from the Citadelle is lovely. In the paintings—by Signac, Matisse, Bonnard, Dufy, Vlaminck, and Braque— inside the Annonciade Museum you can see, devoid of crowds, the light, the water, the mountains, the sky, the flesh tones that made St.-Tropez unique. Gassin, a nearby mountain village, is irre- deemably touristy-cutesy, but Ramatuelle, less than a twenty- minute drive from the topless throngs at Pampelonne, is still the real thing, in spite of the encroaching condos and building cranes.

Even in the heart of St.-Tropez, repose is intermittently sustain- able if you choose your lodgings well. My room in the annex of the Hôtel La Ponche—with gilded antiques, modern paintings, and French windows overlooking a little harbor that seemed to belong to me alone—was so alluring that I canceled plans to go out to dinner and laid out a little supper of wine, cheese, and charcuterie. A friend dropped by. We watched the sky and the sea at sunset turning pastel, just like the town. For a moment this perfect little world seemed glowing and tranquil as an old gouache. Then, just opposite, they began setting up the sound system. They turned on the klieg lights. They set up the ski jump. Only it was a bike jump. French kids on bikes were at the top of a little hill. One by one, they raced down the hill, pumping the pedals madly. The rider and his bike flew up into the pastel air, and then down, with a splash, into the pastel water— while the crowds of tourists applauded and danced to the music.

The music was "Do You Know the Way to San Jose?" My guest laughed at my chagrin and we sang another question to each other: "Do You Know the Way to St.-Tropez?"

Close your eyes as you head east through the overbuilt Ste.-Maxime and St.-Raphaël and along the Corniche de l'Esterel; things get much worse before they get better. Relief comes in Cannes in the form of interesting restaurants and cafés, and in some glorious old hotels and the well-tended gardens along the Croisette, the seafront boulevard. The public beach is a mere scrap of sand, raked clean every night, but the "private" beaches are open to all willing to rent an umbrella. The downtown area, around the Croisette, is touristy in an inoffensive, slightly naughty way. The usual merchants—Chanel, Cartier, Fred Joaillier—sell the usual trinkets. At night tall blond prostitutes prowl the streets, beckoning to vacationing Saudis, and the Bar Basque on the rue Mace is, as one guide puts it, *"un classique du circuit gay."*

Beginning in the sixties, Cannes made an effort to shed its dowdy image as a place where old ladies went to drink tea. A new American-style convention center was built, and freeways have ravaged sections of the upper city. Yet most of the old town, with the air of a Mediterranean village, has been preserved. The old Forville market is vivid with color, and along the beachfront enough of Belle Epoque Cannes survives to satisfy anyone's taste for nostalgia. The facade of the Carlton Hotel, with its twin cupolas said to be modeled on the breasts of the mistress of a Romanov prince, is as imposing as ever. Only a tad less genteel is the other grande dame of Cannes hotels, the Majestic, though one bright morning I witnessed a sight that restored my faith in French savoir faire. A man in late middle age, wearing the kind of pearl gray suit I might choose for a New York society wedding and clearly one of the hotel's managers, strode purposefully out of the hotel, across the garden toward the Croisette, where, three yards from the sidewalk, his progress was halted by the presence of a candy wrapper.

Motionless, he surveyed it with astonishment and contempt.

Would he stoop to pick it up? Of course not! Would he leave it lying there to sully the approach to the Hôtel Majestic? Unthinkable.

So, executing the kind of footwork star soccer players use when they're dribbling the ball downfield, with a series of discreet kicks he sent the offending crumpled piece of paper flying, first out of the garden onto the sidewalk, then off the sidewalk into the street, and finally into the gutter and down a drain.

The snazziest new hotel in Cannes, the Gray d'Albion, which gets rave reviews from French travel writers, has shiny escalators and a digital display board flashing the events of the day. It also has as its chef Jacques Chibois, the newest, brightest superstar in the firmament of nouvelle cuisine.

Dinner for two at his restaurant, Le Royal Gray, was more than $200. It included the chef's special canapés (soggy), ravioli stuffed with caviar, lobster salad with asparagus, veal cooked with truffles, roast lamb (all fine), and *"Le Léger Gâteau chaud de noix à la crème pailletée,"* which was a brownie.

The night our party was there, rock-and-roll played at top volume, for which the maitre d' apologized, but it accompanied our meal throughout. The restaurant's terrace surveyed a concrete wall. The dining room was a jungle of plastic flowers—this in the one part of France where flowers bloom all year, in a city that prides itself on the glories of its flower market.

Le Royal Gray, it should be emphasized, is no tourist trap. It has two Michelin stars. Gault-Millau recently awarded Chibois a coveted third *toque* (chef's hat), and a neighboring table of French tax accountants seemed pleased as punch with their *menus gastronomiques,* perhaps justifiably. Certainly Chibois is several cuts above the Riviera's most relentlessly publicized three-star chef, Roger Vergé. Vergé's art gallery, at Mougins, sells kitsch, and at Vergé's glorified cafeteria in Monte Carlo I encountered some of the worst food I've ever seen purveyed by a French chef of repute.

Just beyond Cannes is Antibes, where you can catch a glimpse of the Mediterranean idyll: not, alas, in the little fishing port Picasso loved so well but in the 150 or so paintings, ceramics, drawings, lithographs, tapestries, and sculptures he wrought in six months in 1946 in the mysterious fortress-palace of Château Grimaldi. He willed that the works should never leave the site of their creation: "If you want to see the Picasso of Antibes, you must come to Antibes." If you want to avoid Aquasplash and French Marineland, you must stay away.

Nearby Cagnes has a little museum full of memorabilia from the last years of Renoir's life. Pass as quickly as you can through Golfe-Juan and Juan-les-Pins, where buildings obstruct the vistas that inspired the postimpressionists. Head straight for Cap d'Antibes.

Cap d'Antibes, adorned with intact grand Belle Epoque villas, shrouding what's left of the Old Rich on the coast, is also the sight of the stunningly gorgeous, stupendously expensive Hôtel du Cap–Eden Roc.

Imagine your own private palace, touched by soft breezes and filled with Louis Seize antiques, overlooking your own private park of pine trees and white gravel walks leading to a cliff suspended over a Mediterranean so blue, suspended beneath a sky so blue, that you finally understand why they call it the Côte d'Azur. Better yet, reread the opening chapter of *Tender Is the Night*. This is the exact same spot where the Lost Generation found the Riviera. Scott Fitzgerald slept here. And so did Zelda.

If you're going to stay at the Hôtel du Cap, pack an extra suitcase and fill it with money. No credit cards, even though the meanest of rooms (a tiny single, with no view, on the ground floor) starts at about $260. If what you have in mind is a nice, big double with a glorious view and a terrace, count on spending more like $960 a night (15 percent service charge included, food not). Should you wish to partake of nourishment whilst in these celestial surroundings, budget about $1,300 a couple a day. If you don't run wild with the wine list, you might just make it. There's no beach at the Cap, but there is a beautiful, fairly crowded swimming pool hewn into the cliff side, and if you wish to swim in the sea, you can clamber down onto the rocks and use the diving board there.

Like most major Riviera hotels, the Hôtel du Cap has "modernized" itself, in this case by adding a restaurant complex called the Eden Roc. The food at the Eden Roc—caviar-truffle-type hors d'oeuvres, flambéed main courses, histrionic desserts—lacks a certain subtlety, but the view from your table to the Îles de Lérins is lovely. Not far away, however, is the Restaurant de Bacon, where, for somewhat less, you can enjoy what many agree is the best bouillabaisse on the coast.

In addition to your mere superrich, this Hollywood stage set of a hotel attracts Hollywood. Johnny Carson stays here; Bill Cosby keeps returning. Marlene Dietrich, Edward G. Robinson, and Erich Maria Remarque met in the bar. One Riviera memoir describes how George Raft walked to the pool with Norma Shearer, passing Charles Boyer. When I was there, Madonna was hidden away on the top floor and the lobby was full of expostulating Rodeo Drive–type folk, all demanding to change their $500-a-night rooms for, as the man ahead of me in line emphasized in the slow, loud English such people use with foreigners, "something better." Still, if your purpose is to find the "real" Riviera that exists only in twenties novels and fifties films, and damn the expense, put down this magazine right now and phone your travel agent. The Hôtel du Cap is it.

Whatever may be said about Nice, the next stop eastward, it's no stage set—and about the only place on the Riviera where you can take a vacation from taking a vacation.

The Promenade des Anglais, it is true, recalls Miami Beach, and the Casino Ruhl is just like those places in Atlantic City where people with plastic cups play the slot machines, only the gamblers here are from Maastricht and Düsseldorf, not Camden and Scranton. But in Nice, especially the old town, you find the exhilaration of both discovery and escape. What you've escaped is a world whose raison d'être is making money off tourists.

What you've discovered is a complicated Mediterranean, as opposed to French, city that existed long before either winter or summer sun became a commercial commodity.

Head away from the shoreline and suddenly you're in the Place Masséna—beautiful, powerful early-nineteenth-century buildings, all in the deep maroon rococo red that characterizes Niçoise architecture at its best. Well worth exploring is the Cimiez district in the hills behind the center city. The marvelous old Hôtel Regina there was turned into apartments decades ago, but you still can almost sense the spirit of Queen Victoria, who vacationed there, sunning herself. Nearby is a Roman amphitheater where a summer jazz festival is held. Not far away are the Matisse Museum and the Museum of Archaeology. Nice is rich in such cultural amenities—everything from the Chagall Museum to the icons in the Russian Orthodox cathedral. If you're a glutton for luxury, you'll love the Negresco, the big-deal hotel on the Promenade des Anglais that also houses the big-deal restaurant Chantecler.

The Hôtel Negresco, an official French historic monument "restored" with more hysteria than tact, glitters like a stupendous piece of costume jewelry. Not all that glitters, however, is paste. That immense chandelier in the Salon Royal is real Baccarat crystal, one of only two of its kind in the world. (The other was commissioned for the czar of Russia.) The wallpaper is so loud and the carpeting is so busy that you may assume that *couldn't* be real Gobelin tapestry on the wall, but it is.

Even in high season you can find places to stay in old Nice in all price ranges, so it makes a sensible base for exploring the region. In recent years the old town has undergone a SoHo-style revival, attracting artists and young people and becoming an engaging mélange of small galleries, restaurants, and *boîtes de nuit*. Cars are banned from the narrow cobbled streets. You can sit quietly at an outdoor café on the Cours Saleya and catch the scent of blossoms from the flower market.

When you leave Nice and head toward Monte Carlo on the Bas Corniche, something remarkable happens. You drive through Villefranche, St.-Jean-Cap-Ferrat, and Beaulieu, and for almost fifteen miles you find the Riviera more or less as it's supposed to be.

Here the hills plunging into the Mediterranean become mountains plunging into the Mediterranean—nearly vertical cliffs not even the most avaricious speculators could easily cover with condos. The rich and famous—the stupendously rich, the fabulously famous—got here first and so completely covered this section of the coast with palaces and villas that there's simply not enough room for the purveyors of ticky-tack to ruin everything.

Villefranche has the Riviera's loveliest harbor and the famous Cocteau Chapel, best seen at sunset. And across from St.-Jean-Cap-Ferrat is tranquil Beaulieu, a perfect little jewel box of a town with a perfect little jewel box of a casino. It does not have a sandy beach, but the two best hotels have delightful pools on rocky ledges and steps leading to the water. La Réserve and La Métropole are beautiful and refined. Though no one's giving anything away, they are also cheaper than places like La Voile d'Or in Cap Ferrat, where a double, with obligatory demi-pension, could cost about $900 a night. At La Métropole, where two acres of gardens lead to the sea, a double room facing the sea, with a terrace, is about $550 during high season. But that includes breakfast, and lunch or dinner, for two; the food is appealing.

Being less than five miles from Monte Carlo, Beaulieu is also an excellent base for taking in the sights of Monaco—and quite extraordinary sights they are.

I wish I'd been the first to say that Monaco is a sunny place for shady people, because that certainly captures the soul of the place.

It's no longer entirely accurate, however. Rainier III is the Donald Trump of princes. And thanks to his thirty-year campaign to turn Monaco into a Lefrak City for the flight-capital rich, his tiny domain today is so crammed full of skyscrapers that it's possible to walk all over the place without seeing the sun.

Americans may remember Grace Kelly as a fairy-tale princess, but people who know the Riviera see her marriage to Prince Rainier in a different light. "The Grimaldis were still dime-store princelings when Rainier married his Hollywood star," a well-connected lady informed me in Monte Carlo. "She was the one who opened the doors to the big money—Hollywood–Las Vegas money, New York and Philadelphia money, all sorts of money—and made this a place for the rich."

Hidden cameras are everywhere in Monaco. At every gala, plainclothesmen mingle with the social climbers. You may not notice it, but each time you enter the *salons privés* at the casino you will be photographed. Camping vehicles are absolutely prohibited in the principality. All these measures explain why some love Monaco more than anyplace else on earth. "It's the only place where I can wear my emeralds on the street," a woman I met in Palm Beach explained.

Even in broad daylight certain categories of persons will be either stopped at the border or, once spotted, hustled back into France.

I asked an acquaintance knowledgeable in such matters to item- ize some of the kinds of "undesirables" the Monégasque police might deport. "Oh," he answered, "young Arabs in dented cars; American and Scandinavian teenagers with backpacks who might sleep on park benches overnight; anyone without at least a few hun- dred dollars or a major credit card. Not everyone in those categories would be turned away," he emphasized, "at least during daytime. Only those who aroused suspicion. Anyone with a criminal record would be ejected." He added: "I mean the wrong kind of criminal record. Someone who'd embezzled more than a million dollars would not be inconvenienced."

Not that Monaco spurns those with rather less money to spend. At the fabled casino each night, a touristic *lumpenproletariat* stares into the slot machines, oblivious to the Belle Epoque splendors that surround it. The public rooms of the Hôtel de Paris and the nearby Hôtel Hermitage are also among the most sumptuous public spaces ever created.

Traditionalists and arrivistes alike adore the Paris, while the "fun" rich swear by the Hermitage, where even the toilets are superb artifacts of the Belle Epoque. The best suites (more than $1,000 a night) command views across the harbor of the Grimaldi palace and, when I was there, an immense CUTEX sign.

The Hôtel de Paris contains my favorite expensive restaurant on the Riviera. This is the Louis XV, and aptly named it is. Mme. de Pompadour would have gasped at the opulence.

At the Louis XV, chef Alain Ducasse, considered by many the up-and-coming chef of Europe, takes dishes normally found in peasant hovels or Chinese take-outs and turns them into marks of culinary genius. Specialties include pigs' feet, sweet-and-sour veal, and wonton soup—it's called "ravioli stuffed with foie gras with truffles in chicken bouillon," but that's what it is, a gilded version of wonton soup. The most memorable course is the vermeil finger

bowls. Service at the Louis XV is unhurried to the point of inter-
minableness. A dinner for two that began punctually at 9 P.M. ended
at 12:20 A.M. That didn't keep me from loving the whole two hundred minutes, because, just as you don't go to Monte Carlo for the
sunshine, you don't come to the Louis XV just to eat.

You're there for the theater. The gold plate and mahogany humi-
dors and crystal goblets—that synthesis of order and excess only
the French can really pull off—would have been sufficient unto
themselves. But then there were all these fashion tycoons from
Milan, and petrosheikhs from the Gulf, and men who looked like
Adolphe Menjou and women who looked like Bette Davis buying
dinner for girls who looked like Gidget and young men who looked
like the young Alain Delon. Best of all, there was the WASPy, yup-
pie American couple who were absolutely top drawer and also
spoke quite good French.

You had to have spent at least one summer in Maine to appreciate that, twenty feet away, this lockjaw couple was fighting a raging
battle. It went on until dessert arrived. At which point she stood up
and, without casting a glance in his direction, walked out of the
room. By then I was beyond shame about staring, and so, at another
table, was an Arab with a platinum Rolex and hair like Valentino's.
What riveted us was the double drama of this moment.

This woman's intensely beautiful face, when she rose, proved to
be attached to a body the shape and texture of an immense, unripe
pear. And this did not prevent—no, it deepened immeasurably—
the drama of the look of wounded adoration in her abandoned
companion's eyes.

Would some anguished scream fill the grand salon of the Louis
XV? Or would he mutter, "Frankly, my dear, I don't give a damn"?
A uniformed majordomo, hastening without seeming to hasten,
arrived at that moment, proffering cigars. He selected a Monte
Cristo; he ordered an Armagnac, which he sipped. When the bill

arrived, he scrutinized it and paid. Then he walked away—too slowly, too calmly; you could tell he was faking—to the door.

I didn't know whether to laugh or cry for the poor devil. But I do know I wanted to jump to my feet, applaud, and shout, "Author! Author!"

Menton, last place on the Riviera before you get to Italy, has a crowded beachfront. There are some fine old buildings downtown. Old Menton is worth a stroll, and the Menton market is a wonderful fake-exotic edifice—half Arab mosque, half Indochinese pagoda—a superb architectural folly born of the French colonial *mission civilisatrice.*

I wouldn't say more, except it was there that I found Les Colombières, the hotel I mentioned at the beginning of this article.

Les Colombières has only six rooms—each named, not numbered. It is set in ten acres of gardens just about to go to seed. The phones in the rooms don't work; there's no concierge. You're just given two keys—one to your room, one to the front door. My room was called Espagnol. Over the fireplace were etched in marble the words CAMERA AEDIFICATA ET DECORATA MDCCCCXXIII—F.B.

The man who embellished this extraordinary place in 1923 was Ferdinand Bac—aesthete, bon vivant, and bastard grandson of King Jérôme Bonaparte of Westphalia. Today Les Colombières is owned and run by the indomitable Mme. Bokairy. Staying there is like having an eccentric great-aunt who is sharing with you this old palace full of splendid books, paintings, and memories.

My room, actually my private apartment, was a treasure trove of Greco-Roman and Art Deco artifacts. The private balcony commanded a perfect view of the coast all the way from Italy to Monaco. The bed-sitting-room had a marble fireplace and hand-painted frescoes; the bathroom was out of the *Arabian Nights.* One noon, as I ate a pungent Italian cheese (purchased just across the border) and drank a mellow French wine (from Bandol, on the coast between Marseille and Toulon), a thunderstorm roared in from the Mediterranean, clawing the rocky shoreline, scratching its way toward the Alps.

The lightning bolts smote the trailer parks and condos like old gods of vengeance. Then the sky relented; the old town of Menton glowed like amber, making me want to stay there forever.

When I left the next morning I embraced Mme. Bokairy. I promised to return. "There is no other place like this left on this coast," she said. "I am eighty. I pray Les Colombières will be here when you come back."

Her words measured the fragility of this slender littoral where the Alps reach out to touch the Mediterranean, where people have always reached out, seeking year-round summertime of the soul.

St.-Tropez

BY HERBERT GOLD

editor's note

St.-Tropez is probably the quintessential French Riviera town, and although stretches of the Côte d'Azur today look more like Honolulu or Hong Kong, St.-Tropez still looks like the pleasant and pretty village it has always been, thanks to a building code that has prevented the proliferation of skyscrapers.

HERBERT GOLD has written about travel frequently for *Travel &*

Leisure (where this piece appeared in June 1988), the *San Francisco Examiner,* and other publications. He is also the author of over twenty books, including *Daughter Mine* (St. Martin's Press, 2000), *Best Nightmare on Earth: A Life in Haiti* (Prentice Hall Press, 1991), *She Took My Arm as If She Loved Me* (St. Martin's Press, 1997), and *Bohemia: Where Art, Angst, Love, and Strong Coffee Meet* (Simon & Schuster, 1993).

There was this girl on a bicycle with her skirts hiked up on the beach where we landed. We were surprised to see her in Downtown World War II, and she was surprised to see a hundred American Rangers."

My friend in the steam room at the San Francisco Press Club would find St.-Tropez somewhat changed. (For one thing, that girl is probably a grandmother.) But sensual surprise is still part of the deal in this French Riviera village, where *le high-life,* Brigitte Bardot and movie madness took over from the sleepytime centuries. Something in the sun, sea, cobblestones and faces still keeps faith with a history of Roman settlement and Gallic culture.

The port of St.-Tropez spreads out around a sparkling cove sheltered by a breakwater—restaurants, yacht harbor, cafés, hotels, pedestrian promenades and the Annonciade Museum. If you wind your way through a medieval tangle of streets—a ten-minute stroll, five if you're in an American hurry—you emerge onto the wide expanse of the Place des Lices: more cafés, music, an open-air market, smiling shops. And then, two minutes by foot up a slightly steep slope, there is the stillness of the Hotel Byblos compound; to the east, the Citadelle overlooks the sea.

That's the map of St.-Tropez. The town is like a cozy island with about 6,000 permanent residents; a visitor can learn it in a single day's strolling. The Plage des Graniers is just a few minutes' walk away. The other beaches require transportation, but the drive is only ten to twenty minutes, depending on which beach is your pleasure for the day.

A palimpsest, a tablet on which one thing is written over another, suggests the evolution of St.-Tropez. A joyous vacation-hangout culture was printed by history on top of an ancient port. For me, this linkage was oddly symbolized by Le Manège Enchanté in the Place des Lices. While their parents patiently waited for them to grow up, a covey of excited kids turned and turned on a carousel, riding a horse-drawn carriage, a desert jeep and a sleek spaceship, accompanied by Motown disco music from an ancient American tradition of about fifteen years ago.

But the flashing colored lights, the mothers and dads—that is pure Mediterranean village. And the luxurious, careless tourists—well, that's also French village, with Sweden, Spain, Italy and Beverly Hills well represented on the overlay. Yet the Café des Arts, with its players of *boules* in front, depicted fifty years ago in a painting that hangs in the nearby Annonciade Museum, looks much the same today.

We might want to correct certain daguerreotype images, however: seventeen-year-old Brigitte Bardot, shapely top and bottom, nuzzling various costars, directors, international playboys and husbands; monokinied starlets aiming their assets at the camera lads on the beach; a world hungry for scandal among cute little Côte d'Azur hotels and villas.

Today La Bardot, fifty-some and still shapely, does her nuzzling with small animals, having given up men and movies for pet husbandry and animal rights. The former starlets, replaced by new ones, have disappeared into starlet limbo. Many of the movie producers are now lean and limber, running barefoot on the beach in pursuit of cardiac fitness. But the essence of the handsome fishing village survives. There was a *reason* that St.-Tropez became a world center for funners and big spenders. The reason hangs on: sea, sand, air, café-sitting, an ability to perform wine-and-food rituals in what the French sometimes call *le relax.*

In the fifteenth century the little harbor received immigrants from Genoa. Some of their descendants must still be there; an Italian ebullience leavens the ironic French style. Besides studying the ruins of my Italian-Spanish-French bouillabaisse, fishbones and shells, I looked around for signs of ancientry. Ten kilometers west of St.-Tropez is Grimaud, a Provençal village with a ruined castle, a medieval Templars edifice and a low, thick-walled Romanesque church. A few kilometers south is the Chartreuse de la Verne, built in the twelfth century; to the southwest is Collobrières, with the remains of a Romanesque chapel.

The Maritime Museum in St.-Tropez is installed in the Citadelle, a sixteenth-century building; its souvenirs of ships and landings and Mediterranean wars give some perspective on the present comings and goings of yachts and sailing vessels. And the Annonciade, in a sixteenth-century chapel, has a splendid collection of modern French masters, including Matisse, Bonnard, Signac, Vuillard and Seurat.

My personal sense of St.-Tropez, however, has come not from the famous beaches and museums but from sudden discoveries: Italianate gates and sea-eaten painted doorways, a church and an elm tree at the Place de l'Ormeau, occasional marble street monuments and salt-sprayed paths. In the Rue Allard I found a chapel decorated with a Moor's head, no doubt celebrating some never-to-be-forgotten victory, now forgotten. The market at the Place aux Herbes—fruit, fish, those sun-fresh vegetables, flowers—provided daily entertainment.

Everywhere I found fountains, gardens, fig trees and un-Parisian smiles. My rule was always to turn in to the narrower street, and I followed ways too narrow even for motor scooters—but ample for the Tropézien peacocks to take their rump-proud promenade alongside me. On these quiet paths between garden walls, everyone is a celebrity, ruler of the stroll. One can imagine Greek and Roman visitors, Arab invaders, pirates and generals, revolutionaries—and, yes, my San Francisco Press Club friend, veteran of World War II, and Brigitte Bardot, veteran of the postwar cinema—hurrying down these walkways, pausing to pick a ripe fig.

For sightseers and celebrity-watchers, art lovers and health-seekers, St.-Tropez offers enticement aplenty. One early autumn Saturday I felt the stones of the Place des Lices beneath my feet, and the shouts and smells of a Provençal market filled the air. I achieved that marvelous peace of doing nothing amid the intensity of village business. Matisse entitled a painting of St.-Tropez *Luxe, Calme et Volupté,* and many other painters have celebrated this place that Guy de Maupassant called a "simple daughter of the sea . . . grown in the water like a shellfish." Colette found a nest here, and in her writings contrasted the laborious, sun-drenched local life with that of high-living visitors come to bask, flirt, loaf, compare yachts and couturiers. Anaïs Nin discovered another Tahiti in St.-Tropez; Errol Flynn found teenage companions; Françoise Sagan, subject for novels.

The smell of jazz mixes with the sounds of garlic (confusion is part of the charm). Even in winter, a white sunlight keeps visitors coming, uncovering more easily the natural glitter beneath the glitz. Outside the Annonciade, a peacock perched and seemed to blink at me—not a sculpture but a living bird, wearing its best feathers in honor of what would be Indian summer in my native Midwest.

A hundred years ago, geraniums were planted inside the walls of the city as a mosquito repellent. It seemed to work. Today the generously imported palms, cacti, aloes, agaves, yuccas and eucalyptus that once delighted Colette now delight me. Mimosa is a beautiful word and a beautiful smell.

On these autumnal strolls I rested from sniffing the fragrances by visiting the carvings of Tropézien legends, boats and martyrs in the little church. I studied guidebooks at a seaside café, dreaming of Romans and Saracens, knaves and saints, the great medieval wars that swept through the village. Then I'd have another *grand crème*—espresso and hot milk. Becoming an expert requires toil.

I discovered Château Suffren, with its stone tower that has survived the depredations of pirates and weather for 1,000 years. The Grimaldi Castle, the Jarlier Tower and its hanging garden have also endured through the visits of Arabs, Spaniards, Italians and miscellaneous brigands. What was left behind is an eclectic Mediterranean grace and peace for the ghosts who have struggled over this place.

At present, the chief local struggle is to bring in the nets filled with tunny. But besides its riches in the sea and on the vine, St.-Tropez has built ships, erected statues cast in tons of bronze melted from enemy guns, constructed castles and towers for those who profited from war, fishing or wine, or from having cleverly chosen noble parents. The castles are worth visiting: Saint Amé and La Messardière, the stately ruins of Borély, the intact gems of Pampelonne and La Moutte. (My favorite comment on château-visiting was pronounced by a stylish columnist for a San Francisco newspaper: "Today we visited a beige castle." Evidently it matched her suit.)

Unlike other places on the Riviera, St.-Tropez is not served by rail or major highway. The little extra effort needed to reach it has helped the traditional fishing-village ambience endure—although the T-shirt trucks still seem to get through. Especially after the hectic summer beach season, the village retains a modest stateliness.

Neither inflation, the fluctuations of the franc, nor the generations of tourists can alter the unique glow of sky and sea. The red tile roofs, the heartbreaking blue of water, the sun across mountains, the changes into evening twilight still attract artists. Holding a glass at a café terrace and meditating upon light can still turn a banker into a painter. I know a chemical engineer from Cincinnati who visited the Côte d'Azur and took early retirement from a soap company, finding he had a date with his palette.

The light is partly sky, sea, tile, sunsets, vineyards and pine forests, and partly in the mind—a quality of refraction off style, history and the skin of visitors nourished by the latest permutations of their investments. St.-Tropez is also a haven for a transient population of neckerchief-clad sports on their way elsewhere, shopping for souvenirs in the form of T-shirts or cocaine. Studying one's fellow tourists is part of tourism, and I received my postgraduate degree in Conspicuous Tasteless Extravagance in this lovely harbor.

I didn't meet Brigitte Bardot or Yves Montand, but here's the name-dropping part of my trip to the Côte d'Azur. I was sitting one evening with Bryan Southcombe, ex-husband of Charlotte Rampling . . . *that's the name I just dropped, folks* . . . when he said, "Well, I've never seen that before." "What?" I asked. A girl on a motorbike, wearing a miniskirt and nothing underneath, had just driven by, rising up off the seat so her skirt lifted. "Darn!" I said (not my exact words). "My mistake was paying such close attention to your description of Riviera art treasures, sir, that I missed this bit of local color."

"She noticed," he said; "she'll be back in a sec."

She didn't want me to feel left out. It was only a minute before she buzzed by again, wearing an ambitious smile.

The season was balmy, but lower in key than the celebrity-crazed days of summer. At Tahiti Beach a few starlets remained, and men who were a feast for connoisseurs of gold chains and neckerchiefs. (I imagined a sign at the entrance to Tahiti Beach like those on the roads to ski resorts: CHAINS REQUIRED.)

I enjoyed the lisping name of a unisex shop on the Place des Lices: "Clothing & Closed." I appreciated the literary T-shirt on a frisky child: "Rimbaud—No Man, No Law, No War Can Stop

Him." I found the disco in the Hotel Byblos, which promises nights that never finish: disco, at last, has found the disease for which it is the cure—jet lag. "Live on New York time," the bartender advised.

I admired the chutzpah of the owners of boats anchored in the yacht basin, enjoying feasts on deck, flowers and Champagne, while visitors stared and commented in many envious languages. Portside, Sénéquier seemed to be the most happening café, but in this democracy of hanging out, wherever you are is where it's happening. At Sénéquier I particularly enjoyed the group of what looked like kempt grandfathers fondly watching their team of Olympic Bee-Stung Lips champion granddaughters.

I also discovered the living museums of hair and nails. At Joffo Coiffure, for example, a window exhibit of wigs, falls and classic ponytails invites passersby to look inside. There a crew of white-shorted stylists is joyously at work, performing prodigies of marvelous complication and simplicity, preparing their clients for an evening of dancing, strolling and being watched.

While the visiting Dufy exhibit at the Annonciade deserved my attention, too, the best *outdoor* museum is that Mediterranean parade. Folks hold hands, giggle sweet nothings, sit over beers or mineral water at the waterfront terraces, the beaches and the Place des Lices. Things tend toward the youthy, beachy, yachty—not bad things to be.

I took a cooling brew at the Café de Paris, near a sashed, ribboned and stalwartly booted statue of a St.-Tropez mayor, erected during the reign of Napoleon III. Before me, painters were selling views of what I was seeing—sun, sea, sailboats, motor yachts. Behind, someone was singing a popular song with a refrain that translates as "I love you, me neither." When I strolled off into the maze of pedestrian streets, I found the Karmic Astrology Shop, offering both Traditional and Tropical star-reading, plus Biorhythms, Numerology and Tarot. Vacationers need philosophy, too.

A little farther on I stopped at Chez Mme. Marcel, a vitamin shop, for a high-potency carrot juice squeezed by a practitioner who was also selling sausage sandwiches.

In true artistic tradition, St.-Tropez has galleries and open studios everywhere. The Galerie de la Colombe in the Passage du Port specializes in Dalí, but also exhibits a newspaper article about the importation of counterfeit masterpieces from Taiwan. "They are pirates," the son of the owner reported indignantly. "But our Dalís all have certificates of guarantee. We sign them ourselves."

Dramatist Edouard Bourdet once advised the actors of the Comédie Française: "Only peasants lunch. A sandwich and a quart of Vittel will sustain you till dinner." In St.-Tropez I tried to vary this puritan rule at the Brasserie des Arts in the Place des Lices. A beer and a *salade niçoise,* plus all the people I could watch, would sustain me nicely till dinner—at least until my ice cream at the nearby *glacerie.* Hearing flute music in a hall across the square, I followed it like a child following the Pied Piper and found folk dancers practicing while painters worked on the backdrops for a village show. Next door at a bar called Le Sporting—Glacier, a band, competed on the terrace, playing an amplified rock version of "Les Feuilles Mortes." Groupies grouped nearby. Evening was falling—so soon?—and the strings of colored bulbs at Le Sporting performed their magic. The waiter informed me, with immense pleasure at my trust in his judgment, that he would help me choose the five best flavors of ice cream—but they were no longer serving ice cream.

"Guest workers" from elsewhere, perhaps Turkey or Greece, were cleaning the streets in red *Ville Propre* T-shirts. Laundry hung like banners from windows that overlooked winding medieval cobblestone paths. Bicycles clattered out of doorways, ridden by chic mothers with chic kids on baby seats. I once jumped out of the way as a mother gunned a motorbike down a hallway and onto the cobblestones. *"Bonsoir, monsieur,"* she said cheerily, with a little shrug because we had failed to collide.

The battered elm tree in the Place de l'Ormeau is said to have been planted by Henry IV—or so said the kindly gallery-keeper opposite, Jean-Marie Cupillard. The bell of the nearby church tolled loud and unelectronic. Monsieur Cupillard advised me to sit near the tree and meditate, then buy a work of art. I followed half his suggestions.

Winding my way back up toward the Citadelle, I was obliged to stop for another of my frequent ace-reporter meals—this is a land of good food, after all. The restaurant had a sign reading Le Clip; I sought to discover if it was indeed a clip joint. Alas for truth in publicity, it was not.

Except for the occasional startling sports car, the roads to the various beaches make St.-Tropez a mini-Moke, jeep, motorbike world. At Tahiti Beach I enjoyed the several species of starlet escorts: the wizened, wrinkled, pared-down jogger type; the traditional cigar-and-belly producer or agent type. There is also, of course, the revered international-playboy species, like the owner of the German-licensed red Ferrari parked in front of a sign promising an immediate tow. The beaches are said to be less polluted now (they are always less polluted than previously); Tahiti Beach had plenty of swimmers.

France, Provence, and the Riviera remain stubbornly themselves, no matter how many T-shirt shops drape their slogans over the grand history of this traditional best garden of the world. In St.-Tropez I found cobblestone alleys and fishing boats along with the carnival of beaches and cafés. But a person can't just visit museums and ancient churches *all* day. He's got to cast his veteran journalist's eye on a topless starlet now and then.

The Bare Facts

Where to Eat

My own theory, stubbornly tested and sometimes disproven, is that it's very difficult to find untasty food in France. So I tend to eat where and when I feel like sitting down—in St.-Tropez, on brasserie terraces, at cafés, in restaurants with views of water or the street, perhaps in a garden offering candlelit romance. The French like to eat out, and Mediterranean folks like to share the pleasure of eating out with casual company. In St.-Tropez, this adds up to a lot of restaurants.

When I tested the *salade niçoise* in cafés and brasseries on the beaches and in town, it never failed to both nourish my liver and entertain my palate. In early autumn I was able to find good eating without making reservations; I just followed my impulse, going by a local philosopher who says, "St.-Tropez is a paradise for chance meetings, a hell for appointments."

The Beaches

While the town of St.-Tropez has Provençal village charms, with its museums, cafés and waterfront, the beaches *(les plages)* are where the famous Tropézien action can be found. Tahiti Beach is probably the essence of the matter: a complex sand-and-sea amusement space, with boat docking, pools for those who tire of salt water, sauna, exercise studios, massage and Jacuzzi culture, shops, gardens, rooms for repose or sleep, and of course the endless parade of sunners on the sand and bathers in the still more endless soft Mediterranean.

Each beach has a slightly different ambience. Tahiti's is the most festive (read: "wild"). Tropezina also attracts movie stars and jet setters, but its scene, as one guidebook puts it, is more "sober." A restaurant there, Lou Pinet, at the hotel of the same name, is known for salads, grilled meats and fish during the day; gourmet cuisine at night.

Tabou Beach offers a more casual style, with lots of sport and physical exercise. (None of the beaches is exactly formal, of course.) Le Tabou is a friendly restaurant there.

All the beaches are only a few minutes' drive from the center of St.-Tropez, and visitors might want to test the various distinctions among them. I liked leaving my automobile at the Hotel Byblos and simply walking along the charming seaside path to a restaurant and beach called Plage des Graniers. In some sense, water is water, sun is sun, bikini is bikini.

Visiting the Area

Ramatuelle (from the Arabic meaning "God's gift") is a hilltop village with a seventeenth-century church. An artist's retreat, it provides an escape from beachy tourism and has superb views of the plain and the sea.

Another nearby village, Gassin, has a church dating from the thirteenth-century Knights Templar period. From here you'll get a view of the Alps and Italy, as well as a glimpse of the St.-Tropez bay far below. Grimaud is a wine and agricultural hub, with a spectacular ruined castle for historians and dreamers.

From St.-Tropez, you can take a boat ride to the Islands of Hyères. Their hidden attractions range from a nudist colony (although designating a special place for nudism on this coast seems a bit like carrying coals to Newcastle) and bird sanctuaries to the sea-weathered ancient fortress and peaceful little village on Porquerolles.

The Riviera in Winter:
Menton Then and Now

BY JOHN LUKACS

∾

editor's note

Many travelers don't venture far enough east to Menton, the last French
town on the Côte d'Azur before the Italian border, which is a shame because
it's a mellow and beautiful village. Menton's two-week Fête du Citron, held
every February coinciding with Carnival celebrations in Nice, is legendary
and worthy of a detour (it now rivals Monaco's Grand Prix and Cannes' film
festival in attendance).

Lemons are indeed one of the first things visitors encounter in Menton.
Whether it was a quince, an apple, or a lemon that Eve plucked from the
Garden of Eden, residents of Menton have never doubted it was a lemon,
and Adam and Eve surely ended their wandering here in this idyllic (and very
fertile) spot. This makes a handy explanation for the fact that Menton is the
only place on the Riviera where lemon trees bear fruit year-round. As the
trees can die if the temperature falls below 26 degrees (and it does drop
below 26 occasionally on the Côte), subtropical Menton does seem to be
blessed with its own microclimate.

JOHN LUKACS is the author of numerous books, including
Destinations Past: Traveling Through History with John Lukacs (University
of Missouri Press, 1994), *Confessions of an Original Sinner* (St. Augustine
Press, 2000), and *Five Days in London: May 1940* (Yale University Press,
1999). He wrote this essay for *Gourmet* in January 1988.

It is January, and the Train Bleu still runs from Paris to the French
Riviera, but it is not quite what it used to be: There is no dining
car, and the *wagons-lits* sleepers are not blue. Still, it is pleasant to
snuggle into one's compartment in the viscous darkness of the Gare
de Lyon, closing out the rest of the world (a sleeping car is now the
only thing that comes close to the yesteryear experience of sailing

away on a great ship, out of the reach of telephones) and waking up in the Mediterranean sunshine. Cannes and Nice and Monte Carlo flash by, and the train is nearly empty. Like the Train Bleu, the Riviera is not what it once was in winter. Then comes the last stop in France, Menton, at the easternmost bend of the French coast, two miles from the Italian border, unexpected. Unexpected because it is reminiscent of what the Riviera used to be.

It was in the 1830s that Lord Henry Brougham, English radical and Francophile, chose the Riviera for a winter sojourn because of its agreeable climate. This was a curious luxury at the time: Few people took winter vacations during the first half of the nineteenth century. But, then, the Riviera has a curious history. "Riviera" is an Italian word, and most of the area it denotes, including Nice, belonged to the kingdom of Savoy until 1860, when Napoleon III received it from Sardinia-Piedmont in payment for the help his armies had provided the year before in the liberation of northern Italy from Austrian rule. (Menton itself was purchased by France from the Grimaldi family, lords of Monaco, also in 1860.) Oddly the name "Riviera" stuck in every European language, English included. It was not until the 1880s that a second-rate French poet, Stéphen Liégeard, launched the phrase Côte d'Azur, the azure coast, with his book of the same name, for which he received a prize from the Académie Française. But the French still were not a traveling people, and they left the Riviera—a dormant backwater occasionally raided by pirates as late as the 1780s—to be discovered by the English aristocracy, following Lord Henry's lead.

As the English ventured southward, things began to change. The P-L-M line (Paris-Lyon-Méditerranée, the name suffused even now with romantic associations) had reached the coast, and it soon became fashionable—not only for the English—to visit the Riviera in winter. The king of Belgium pronounced it the most wondrous place on the globe and installed his mistress there for the winter months. The Russian aristocracy too discovered the charms of the Riviera. (There is a Russian Orthodox cathedral in Nice; if you lift your camera high enough, directing it above the fronds of the palm trees toward the bulbous domes, you may prove to friends that you've been to Moscow.)

Around the turn of the century the St. Petersburg–Nizza Express, then perhaps the most luxurious train in the world, ran from the icy fogs of the Neva to the orange-scented breezes of the Riviera three times a week. The Russians outdid the English lords in creature comforts: Their maids made up their beds in the *wagons-lits* with their own ducal linens. Soon enough less regal sorts traveled down to the Riviera not merely to escape the cold but to refresh their ailing lungs in the mild Mediterranean air. Not everyone found the cure a complete success, however, and so the Riviera became for some—Alexis de Tocqueville, Guy de Maupassant, and Marie Baskirtcheff among them—a fashionable place to die. By 1890 "the Riviera in winter" had become a magical phrase, full of aspirations of elegance, excitement, romance. Monte Carlo and Nice were crowded from Christmas to Easter, flowing with the fevered current of adventure and with the no less fevered undercurrent of social strivings. About 1905 the automobile began to arrive, bringing Grand Prix racing to Monaco and *concours d' élégance* everywhere else.

Following World War I came more change. For several decades it had been *de rigueur* to come only after Christmas and leave no later than April. Now people discovered the beauties of the Riviera's summer. *"Le soleil porte au lyrisme"* (the sun suggests the poetry of the region), the guidebooks said. Perhaps this had something to do with the changing, postwar ideals of human beauty: Women lifted the veils of their *chapeaux* from their faces and donned suntans, no longer marks of low breeding; skirt hems rose; and bathing suits shrank. After 1920 the P-L-M and *wagons-lits* posters were light blue and orange, the latter advertising summer scenes, fast trains on high viaducts, glistening beaches, white clothes, blazing light over the shining sea. The Riviera had found its place in the summer sun, and such notables as Somerset Maugham and F. Scott Fitzgerald, the Prince of Wales and Winston Churchill, would motor from their enclave at Villefranche as far east as Monte Carlo for an evening. But seldom to Menton.

Menton was sedate and "bourgeois," a word with a reputation that, in the 1920s, was not particularly attractive. The town had its quota of annual visitors, mostly of the English upper-middle class, and some settled in Menton for good. Its climate was (and still is) warmer than the rest of the Riviera, with an average temperature of seventy degrees in the winter, experiencing a night of frost only once every ten years; its hotels and *pensions* were comfortable and a whit less expensive than those in Cannes and Nice; but it was not ultra-chic. Unlike the rest of the Riviera, Menton was famous for its flora rather than for its human fauna. Its celebrated lemon trees produced forty million lemons each year. It was a garden lover's paradise. Sir Thomas Hanbury, an English merchant more Italophile than Francophile who had made his fortune in the China trade, built for himself a great castle at La Mortola, east of Menton, a magnificent 250-acre garden, and a museum, which he gave to the city.

With the flood of mass tourism that followed World War II, the reign of cement and concrete began to wield its disfiguring influence; the French themselves started to travel in droves; and the Riviera became a great summer receptacle, emptying out in winter. Why escape the cold to go to the Riviera when it was possible to fly to warmer climates within a few hours, and for not much money? In the 1950s the Costa del Sol edged out the Côte d'Azur, and the

Canaries, Morocco, Tunisia, even the Antilles, were coming on fast.

Menton looked on from the periphery, eluding some of this fate. Of all the spots along the Riviera, it has changed the least—and survived much: pirate raids during the eighteenth century; the quarrel between France and Italy during the nineteenth; a fair-sized earthquake in 1887; a cannonade in 1940, when Mussolini declared war on France (a brave handful of French troops held off the Italian army for more than a week around the customs posts on the seaside highway); wartime occupation; and a good deal (but, of course, not all) of the postwar destructions perpetrated by the construction industry.

Lying in a well-protected cove, a half-moon of a bay divided by a jetty, Menton lives a double life: Above the hotels that line the seaside promenade is the agreeable maze of streets in the old town. Automobiles wend their way with difficulty through some of these streets, not so much because they are narrow but because of their many turns. Still, the scents of lavender and thyme beckon, and the aroma of garlic that is ubiquitous in the old quarters of Marseille and Nice is less pervasive here. The occasional sign for a tearoom, in English, is reminiscent of Menton's Anglophile past; but more numerous are the small café-bars crowded with handsome young people, Italianate in their looks and temperament. Nonetheless the English presence lingers: The main quay is named after King George V, and a few English still take their tea in the short winter twilight under the awnings of the hotel terraces.

The warmth of the sun prevails in Menton. At noon, in January, the air is soft rather than semitropical, and the whiteness of the light fills it without dazzling the eye. The clientele is no longer overwhelmingly English but composed of people from the great cities of Western Europe: middle-aged men in their somewhat stiff but well-cut dark double-breasted suits and their well-preserved, long-necked wives. Or mistresses? Unlikely. The age of the *grandes horizontales* on the Riviera is long past; and Menton is not Cannes with its hordes of half-naked amateurs.

Menton does not blaze, but it shines. It is not a diamond but a pearl. It is, at its best, an outpost representing solidity, good value for good money, the security of comfort and good food. The cuisine of Menton is appreciated *because* it is provincial rather than cosmopolitan, international rather than supranational, a mixture of Provençal and Ligurian and Piedmontese. In contrast to many other places, Menton offers no definite distinction between those restaurants favored by the local citizenry and those catering to visitors. Northern Italian establishments are faring well just now. During the last ten years it has become fashionable for Milanese and Turinese to spend winter weeks in Menton, a few hours south of the chilly yellow fogs of their cities in the Po valley, while their children whoop it up on the ski slopes of Courmayeur and Sestrières.

Fifty years ago "smart" meant "new." Now it often means "old-fashioned," and in some respects Menton is an old-fashioned place. Not entirely, of course. To the west its growing suburbs—modern, indistinguishable from the rest of the Riviera—march along the coast to the pine-covered promontory of Cap Martin, where not so long ago only a few, nearly solitary villas stood. On the eastern side of Menton the bay of Garavan bends toward the Italian border. This stretch, where the

pleasant sight of red-tiled roofs provides ample antidote to the few high buildings, is blissfully less traveled. The reduced traffic is an improvement not only over the neighboring present but also over the remote past: An extension of the Via Aurelia of the Roman Empire had run through what is now called Menton, along its stone path from Genoa to Marseille, but today the three great *corniches* of the Riviera end before Menton, on the other side of Cap Martin.

Whether one arrives in Menton via Italy or France, the best way to arrive is arguably still by train. Motor traffic on the Riviera is horrendous at almost any time of the year. And, though there is Pan American service from New York to Nice, the first glorious waft of Mediterranean air that touches the face as one steps from the terminal building quickly vanishes. Buses make the run from the airport along the coast, dropping travelers on their way, with Menton the last stop, but much is lost in transit, and one grows sleepy and satiated by the Riviera scenery as the bus lurches forward through Monte Carlo. How much better it is to step out of a sleeping car at Menton's station on a winter morning. The station may be an indifferent building, but by the time one reaches the taxi stand the world has become a magical springtime of oleanders, hibiscus, and lemon trees. The drive through an alley of pollard trees, which create violaceous shadows under a benevolent sun, brings the visitor to any of a number of small hotels where the smell of freshly aired carpets mixes pleasurably with the faint whiff of machine oil and furniture polish in the elevator. And across one's room, beyond the balcony doors, the sea glistens. A room with a balcony is indispensable, of course. This is, after all, the Riviera.

Cap Ferrat: A Place in the Sun

BY LORRAINE ALEXANDER

~

editor's note

One of the prettiest walks I've ever taken in my life is the one which hugs the coast of the Cap Ferrat peninsula, described in this piece. The tourist office (at 59 avenue Denis-Semeria) in Saint-Jean-Cap-Ferrat, the peninsula's only town, publishes a good map of this eleven-kilometer picturesque pathway, which winds past Plage Paloma to Pointe Hospice on the thumb of the peninsula, then on to a lighthouse, the top of which rewards climbers with scenery to die for (which is good because most of what you'll see is off-limits, unless you have a prior invitation). One doesn't need an invitation to visit the Villa Ephrussi-Rothschild, however, and while I find the interior to be somewhat forgettable, the magnificent gardens are anything but: they include themes such as Spanish, Provençal, Asian, exotic, etc., complete with ponds, waterfalls, benches, and, of course, stunning views all around.

LORRAINE ALEXANDER, introduced earlier, has contributed many pieces about France over the years to *Gourmet,* where this piece originally appeared in February 1995.

In one of M. M. Kaye's popular romantic novels of exotic foreign intrigue, a wizened eccentric throws a treasure into the sea, allowing the narrator to expound on the evils of money "because all it led to was progress; and he was against progress because it seldom led to happiness, and more often only meant hideous buildings, ugly factories, dirty railway yards, and noisy motor cars . . . and exploitation. He preferred coconuts, cloves, and charm."

Kaye's characters never lived out their dramas in places as accessible as the French Riviera, but her fiscal philosopher might well have got the idea to jettison his gold in favor of the three Cs after a tour of the rampant development that has overtaken parts of that coast. On the other hand, it is a virtual certainty he never set foot on Cap Ferrat, the ultimate place in the sun.

Barely five miles from the Nice airport and several worlds from anything approaching touristic meltdown, Cap Ferrat has long been synonymous with luxury, the kind money can indeed buy, whether purchased a day at a time in its hotels and restaurants or, more permanently, in villas bearing such names as Beautiful Horizon and, yes, Happiness. It is a jut of land extending two miles into the Mediterranean, in the spur-shaped crook of which the charming port of Saint-Jean-Cap-Ferrat nestles. At the neck of the cape, Villefranche to the west and Beaulieu on the Italian side stand like sentinels, framing one's entry into what instantly seems a hushed, tranquil glade, as far from the hustle and hairpins of the corniche road as any secret garden.

Gardens are, in fact, what cover many of Cap Ferrat's mere 580 acres. Its climate is considered among the mildest along the entire Côte d'Azur, a direct benefit of the mountains (the Maritime Alps, lending their name to the Riviera's *département*) that fringe the water here: Facing south and devoid of any but scrub vegetation, they store the sun's heat and dispense it back along the shore, while blocking clouds from scuttling seaward. It is true that on my several trips I have never known a wet, gray day on Cap Ferrat—though rain comes often enough to keep the gardens growing and the mistral can blow with typical fury even under a clear sky.

If a balmy climate has long made the coast of southern France hospitable to botanical species, many of them foreign—neither the olive nor fig, lemon, cypress, not even the plane tree is indigenous— it has had a similar effect on people. Much of the Riviera's history has been written without a trace of Gallic accent by people seeking glamour, health, escape, and, in the early years of the century, the patina only the gilded Old World could bestow on social ambition. As demand must always exceed supply on such a slim slice of exotica as Cap Ferrat, its precincts were soon pulsing with what Noël Coward called, sizing up his own and future eras, "the rich riff-raff of the international set." Isadora Duncan had a studio in Saint-Jean. The Duke of Connaught, the youngest of Queen Victoria's children, opened the gardens of his villa there to all ranks whenever the Royal Navy docked in Villefranche. Closer to home and our own day, Daisy Fellowes, of the Singer sewing machine family and reputed to be "one of the first women in the fashionable world to have her nose changed," spent summers cruising on her yacht but dropped anchor when invited to the cape for lunch.

W. Somerset Maugham, who came to Cap Ferrat in 1928 and lived there year-round (except during wartime) until his death in 1965, surely qualifies as this sequestered promontory's most famously talented resident. Having already written *Of Human Bondage* and seeking a life free of the strictures imposed by English society, he bought twelve acres of prime Cap Ferrat property. The parcel included Villa Mauresque, named by its former inhabitant, a Monsignor Charmeton, who had resided in Morocco before becoming father confessor to Leopold II, King of the Belgians. The monarch was in fact Cap Ferrat's chief landholder at the time and, from all accounts, a down-to-the-bones despot, who lived long and licentiously off a fortune accumulated in what was then the Congo.

Maugham had the minarets removed from the roof of Villa Mauresque—and the window across from his desk sealed up to keep the view's beauty from distracting him as he wrote. He also planted what he claimed were Europe's first avocados. And, like many Cap Ferrat residents then and now, he was an esteemed host: Wallis Simpson had her Christmas dinner at Villa Mauresque immediately following the Duke of Windsor's abdication, and Winston Churchill was a welcome guest.

Fashions and the fashionable, by their very nature, come and go. But the buildings the fashionable erect as their way stations frequently survive (barring war, abuse, or natural disasters), their foundations set deep in the terrain of history. The elegant Hotel Bedford, a Belle Epoque bellwether whose name alone reflected the heavily English leisured class that checked in, lasted long enough to be renovated in 1985–88 and reborn as the luxurious Royal Riviera Hotel. Its spacious rooms are oases of hushed comfort, and its small sand beach, a flight of steps down from the formal-feeling grounds and pool, lies sheltered along Beaulieu's pretty bay.

Dinner indoors, at Le Panorama, is a grand affair: The elaborate dishes on chef Yves Merville's lengthy menu include *tatin* of *foie gras,* butterflied red mullet, and luscious red fruits set on shortbread in a caramelized citrus sauce. By day, with sun and a soft breeze beckoning, however, a casual lunch at a La Pergola table poised between pool and bay can have equal appeal—even greater, if your kicked-down espadrilles are starting to seem like the only shoes worth owning. Shrimp with guacamole *mousseline* and squid salad with basil were as inviting one afternoon as the scene itself, and dessert was a lovely medley of fruit *sorbets* artistically arranged like spherical dollops of paint on a "palette" plate. A children's menu, rare in this realm of grown-up pleasures, offers fish fingers and cheeseburgers, both served with . . . *crème de ketchup.*

Buildings are not alone in their ability to cling to life. Gardens too, well-tended ones, can set down roots that span centuries. The bulk of what was once King Leopold's botanical garden estate (the still privately owned Villa Les Cèdres) has long outlived his dubious reign; its thirty-five acres—minus a few that have become a public zoo—support what Roderick Cameron, in his book *The Golden*

Riviera, calls "whole forests of bamboo" and "an assembly of cacti . . . without peer in Europe."

Cap Ferrat's grandest horticultural garden is part of the Villa Rothschild, a near neighbor of both the present Royal Riviera and the former royal reprobate. The villa and gardens, bequeathed to the Institut de France in 1933 by Baroness Béatrice Ephrussi de Rothschild, are spread over the cape's narrow isthmus and open every day from mid-March till mid-November, weekends and most holidays the rest of the year. The baroness called the enormous pink—her favorite color—and white Renaissance-style villa that dominates the gardens a *palazzino* and named it the Île-de-France after the luxury liner; people say she would survey the work of her thirty gardeners, all wearing sailors' berets with pompoms, from the second-story loggia, as if standing on the bridge of that great ship. (People also say that, no Bo Peep, she would prod the gardeners with her pink umbrella or whack them with her pink purse when displeased!)

The villa was built between 1905 and 1912—the imperious daughter of the Bank of France's governor going through eleven architects in the process—and is now a museum of fine porcelains and furnishings, but the seven theme gardens that fan out from it are a museum in their own right. Occasionally, when the present staff of four gardeners is unable to keep up with their colossal task, some of the gardens must be closed. On my last walk through them—and with a mistral blowing so loudly that the very amiable curator James de Lestang and I, leaning into the gusts, could barely hear one another—the Provençal section was looking ragged enough to be essentially off-limits.

The lapidary garden is, naturally, immune to such ravages. Created by Marchand des Raux, head gardener as of 1935—and an acquaintance of Matisse, who sometimes came here to draw—this romantic nook was fashioned in part from the stones left over from the villa's construction. It is a garden of fountains, arches, and gargoyles; a shady, peaceful place where hydrangeas bloom under a large camphor tree. Farther along, past the so-called Japanese garden (its ceramic pagoda is actually Chinese) and through the cypress-lined Florentine allée, is the rose garden, a splendor during the baroness's time but destroyed by frost in 1956 and replanted with four hundred new bushes only in 1991. Down its trellised slope toward the Rade (inlet) de Villefranche stands a stone baldachin, carved with the initials of Béatrice Ephrussi and prompting me to wonder who, beyond her name, this woman was. A pillager of Italian churches, some have said, though this would scarcely distinguish her from other aggressive collectors. Elisabeth de Clermont-Tonnere, who painted her portrait and was thus in a unique position to study her subject, said in tones verging on the biblical, "She has houses built and razed . . . orders groves to be displaced, and commands flowers to grow during the mistral."

Once you turn and climb up through beds of succulents to the gardens' highest point, Beaulieu's Baie des Fourmis, symmetrically balancing the Villefranche inlet, and the coast of Italy come suddenly, spectacularly into view. It is also from this vantage that the formal, central garden—*à la française,* despite such Italian elements as its water steps—descends back toward the villa, which in sunshine looks like a fabulously frosted cake. But the Temple of Love, where "Amour" used to stand, is now empty, the statue having been toppled during a storm. (Romantics saddened by the demise of "Amour" can take comfort in the view to the west: The turquoise tiled roof, until recently the residence of an Egyptian noble, is the same one Cary Grant, the Cat, scampered over in Hitchcock's Riviera classic *To Catch a Thief.*) Visitors are still able, of course, to pause here and gaze over giant palms into the flanking bays, dotted with sailboats in fine weather, or down to the carp-filled pools and seventeenth-century Tuscan urns that lead back to the villa.

It would be a shame to leave the Rothschild gardens without stopping at the villa's pretty tearoom, where a selection of savory and sweet tarts as well as salads and hot or iced teas provide a soothing break. While inside, you may also want to see some of the richly furnished rooms. The paintings scattered about (Bouchers and Fragonards, a Monet of the Seine and a Renoir of his olive trees in Cagnes), the Flemish tapestries, and the coromandel screens are beautiful, but some of the salons, undoubtedly reflecting the baroness's abbreviated stays, seem as austere as an unfeeling heart.

Her dressing room is more personable. Its eighteenth-century pea-green panels are decorated with carousels and crowns, fancy hats and flowers, and in one corner is her manicure "kit," which would comprise a modern traveler's entire allotment of carry-on luggage. In the adjoining bedroom is one of the antique silk gowns she collected and, beside the bed, a Sèvres breakfast tray. The villa's porcelains are, in fact, its pride, and in glass cases set in a wide bay window are several entire Sèvres services, circa 1756. The oldest piece, dated 1740, is from the Vincennes workshops created by Louis XV. Elsewhere in the house is perhaps the most endearing of the porcelains on display: a Meissen (also circa 1740) orchestra of musical monkeys.

At the farthest possible geographic remove—a very relative notion on Cap Ferrat—from the baroness's estate is another monument to the Belle Epoque with its own glorious garden: the Grand-Hôtel du Cap-Ferrat. Apart from the hotel's sumptuous décor, seamless service, and stunning swimming pool, dramatically designed into the rocks at the cape's tip, it is the garden, created by Zhor Maissen, a dedicated horticulturist (and wife of the general manager when the Grand-Hôtel was still the Bel-Air), that delights today's guests. Among the flowering specimens are eight types of hibiscus; fourteen kinds of mimosa, which burst forth in tones of yellow in winter; blue, white, and (very rare) pink echiums; and masses of brilliantly hued daisies and oleander. Because Cap Ferrat's soil has a high iron content, blue flowers, such as plumbago and solanum, thrive here. And then there are the trees: parasol pine, cypress, eucalyptus, olive, kumquat, and fig, as well as orange, lemon, and grapefruit.

The feast does not end in the garden. For twenty-six years Jean-Claude Guillon has been chef here, and Le Cap's food—lobster and sole *gâteau, blanquette* of shrimp in vermouth sauce with black truffles, and (leaving the deep, fish end of the menu) duckling with rosemary honey—is splendid. And wine steward Daniel Delcassé is as conversant on the subject of ancient vines as he is with such note-worthy local vineyards as Clos Saint Joseph, which makes a won-derful, well-structured, never-exported white. Among the excellent desserts when I dined here were *crème brûlée* with lavender from the garden and a daring, delicious fennel tart with star-anise ice cream. (On the down side, if you are tempted to have a snack in the comfy piano bar—named for Maugham, whose villa was nearby—be pre-pared: A heavy-on-the-mayo club sandwich costs a sobering 180 francs, or just over $30.)

The mistral that had blown so mightily at the Villa Ephrussi continued through the night but subsided by midmorning of the next day, washing the sky clean. Not the best of swimmers, I cele-brated the return of calm by taking the hotel funicular down to the pool, to learn to "sing" with my head in a water-filled clear plastic salad bowl—the first step in swimming instructor Pierre Gruneberg's program for all of us "who are not happy in the water." His method is confidence-inspiring and as famous on the Riviera as those who have signed his scrapbook of celebrity students during his forty years' tenure. My reward for graduating from bowl to laps was the poolside Club Dauphin's *sandwich gourmand:* three toast rounds, one with smoked salmon; one with *langoustine,* lobster tail, and caviar; and the third with shrimp salad. I was beginning to contemplate a career as a concessionaire for Pierre's plastic bowls when I knew it was time to leave.

Saint-Jean, once a humble fishing village, provides a gentle change from the occasional overdose of pampering, and the footpath that takes you there can be picked up just beneath the Grand-Hôtel's pool and cabanas. It's an easy half hour's walk, past unlovely wire fences on the land side but with a seaward sweep that includes Cap d'Ail and Monaco. On the sunny morning I set out for the Les Fosses inlet and Saint-Jean, fishermen cast their lines at intervals along the rocks and an Italian runner greeted me and the day with a lilting *"che bella giornata!"*

Once past a car-block gate, you can bear right and rejoin the footpath proper, which continues to Sainte-Hospice Chapel and Paloma Beach. Or you can stroll, as I did, directly to the port via Avenue de la Libération. I arrived early, just as the village was coming to life: shops and cafés opening up, the clatter of dishes, the smell of bread, the music of halyards jostling against masts. From the steps of Saint-Jean-Baptiste you can see over berthed yachts, lying about like passive, pale sirens, to the deceptively plain Voile d'Or, where chenille bedspreads, gilded consoles, and vases of long-stemmed roses epitomize old-style, unblushing *bien-être.* Lunch there, on the garden terrace, brought chef Jean Crépin's *langoustines de chalut,* surely the best on earth—crisp outside, melting inside, with a subtle Chinese-inspired sauce.

Across the harbor is chef-owner Jean-Jacques Jouteux's intimate, highly regarded Le Provençal, another mecca of fine dining, and especially fine fish. *Daurade royale* (sea bream) was presented whole on twigs of fennel in a copper pan, boned tableside, and served with crushed black olive sauce and lightly cooked spinach. Roasted Saint-Pierre (John Dory), one of Jouteux's signature dishes, came wrapped in crisped fig leaves and decorated with a wide strip of dried orange peel, the contours of which complemented the leaf shapes. Both fish were moist and delicate and well paired with a white wine from near Saint-Tropez, Château Minuty's Cuvée de l'Oratoire. My dinner companion and I decided to order the cheese course as soon as we learned that the menu's fresh goat cheese, from the Massoins Arlequine farm, is purchased raw and then cured at the restaurant. For dessert we shared "five little tastes" that included chocolate torte and fig *clafouti*—which allowed us a satisfying sampling while keeping quantity and cost under a semblance of control.

Cap Ferrat does not always require such deep pockets as Le Provençal does. A five-minute walk away, down to a row of pretty portside restaurants and cafés, is Le Sloop, where a very well prepared five-course prix-fixe midday meal of fresh and smoked salmon, zucchini blossoms stuffed with herbs and ricotta in basil cream, roasted *daurade royale* with potato coins, cheeses, and wild strawberries with almond *tuile* and ice cream cost less (155 francs) than Le Provençal's main course alone. And the view, from a vantage close upon the slips of Saint-Jean's sleek seagoing clientele, could only be improved upon if all traffic were eliminated so near the terrace tables. At night, a dockside stroll and dinner here—or just coffee and Cognac—bring the present and all its possible pleasures into focus.

Up near the Voile d'Or, the Capitaine Cook offers a full range of fish and crustaceans in pleasant surroundings; and farther along Avenue Jean Mermoz a nineteenth-century villa with balustraded terraces, French doors, and a lovely Mediterranean garden has been converted into the Hôtel Brise Marine. The furnishings are modest and the rooms small, but these details cannot diminish the beauty of the ample sea and garden panoramas from this quiet, residential corner of Saint-Jean.

Inland, on Cap Ferrat's high saddle, is the Clair Logis, another former private house, this one built in the 1920s and purchased in 1949 by the grandmother of the present owner, Pierre Melon. The main dwelling's nine guest rooms, named for flowers—Tuberose, Lavande, Myrtille, and so forth—are simply but sweetly decorated (those in the annex are less appealing), many have small balconies with stone balustrades (mine was threaded with magenta bougainvillea), and all the bathrooms have been recently modernized. Breakfast is served at umbrellaed tables along the path leading to the front entry, and beginning the day here, looking out over the broad, beautifully landscaped grounds, can be bliss. You may have to ring the desk bell twice or carry your own bags up the stairs if Monsieur Melon has gone into Saint-Jean on an errand, but the Clair Logis's advantages are a gracious parkland setting and a homey environment at exceptionally reasonable rates.

As the song says, though, the best things in life really *are* free, even on Cap Ferrat, where a turnoff to the tiny Plage de Passable leads to an easy footpath that meanders along the undulating cliff face. (The path looks at first glance private but is eventually signposted, joining the circuit that had taken me from the Grand-Hôtel into Saint-Jean and continuing to the Royal Riviera's beach.) You'll find shade under canopies of pine boughs where stone benches have been thoughtfully positioned, and sun on the rocky points that afford views back to Villefranche and around Mont Boron to Nice. Residents may pass by on their dog-walking duties, but otherwise you are likely to have the path down to the lighthouse to yourself. Any stop along the way will seem the perfect place to read or chat or merely listen to the waves and the echoing church bells of

Villefranche, ringing over the water as they have for all others who have lingered, as if under the spell of the same gentle Lotus-Eaters Ulysses met, along this languorous shore.

Hotels

Hôtel Brise Marine, 58 avenue Jean Mermoz, 06230 Saint-Jean-Cap-Ferrat; 04.93.76.04.36; fax: 04.93.76.11.49.

Hôtel Clair Logis, 12 avenue Centrale, 06230 Saint-Jean-Cap-Ferrat; 04.93.76.04.57; fax: 04.93.76.11.85.

Grand-Hôtel du Cap-Ferrat, 06230 Saint-Jean-Cap-Ferrat; 04.93.76.50.50; fax: 04.93.76.04.52.

Royal Riviera Hotel, 3 avenue Jean Monnet, 06230 Saint-Jean-Cap-Ferrat; 04.93.01.20.20; fax: 04.93.01.23.07.

La Voile d'Or, 06230 Saint-Jean-Cap-Ferrat; 04.93.01.13.13; fax: 04.93.76.11.17.

Restaurants

Le Cap (see Grand-Hôtel du Cap-Ferrat).

Capitaine Cook, 11 avenue Jean Mermoz, 06230 Saint-Jean-Cap-Ferrat; 04.93.76.02.66.

Club Dauphin (see Grand-Hôtel du Cap-Ferrat).

Le Panorama (see Royal Riviera Hotel).

La Pergola (see Royal Riviera Hotel).

Le Provençal, 2 avenue Denis Séméria, 06230 Saint-Jean-Cap-Ferrat; 04.93.76.03.97.

Le Sloop, 06290 Port-Saint-Jean-Cap-Ferrat; 04.93.01.48.63.

La Voile d'Or (see Hotels).

This article originally appeared in *Gourmet*. Copyright © 1995 by Lorraine Alexander. Reprinted with permission of the author.

La Vie en Èze

BY GULLY WELLS

❧

editor's note

. . . .

Its other attributes aside, the elevation of Èze—about 1,300 feet—is really its ultimate asset. When you're standing in the Jardin Exotique looking down at the sea and the *bas corniche,* the din of the Riviera is nothing more than a faint murmur.

GULLY WELLS is literary editor of *Condé Nast Traveler,* where this piece originally appeared. She writes often of France and the French.

If you pretend to have any originality as a traveler, you should probably keep pretty quiet about your secret dream of visiting the Côte d'Azur. Everybody knows that this great classic is on its last— but still elegant and, in the right dusky light, still sexy—legs. Like that Grandest Horizontale of them all, Venice, this famous sliver of coastline undoubtedly looked even more exquisite fifty years ago. Where didn't? And, even if true, who cares? A great beauty is always a great beauty, even when she is a great *older* beauty.

The romantic in me wants to believe that true travel legends never die, they are just waiting for a new generation to discover them. And so, with this in mind, I called a friend in Paris and told him I was thinking of visiting an embarrassingly well-known medieval village above Monaco. His—utterly predictable—response was to tell me, with the world-weariness of a true Parisian, that this particular village had probably been "over" before I was born. He suggested that, instead, I go to a hamlet high in the Vaucluse, at least four hours from the coast, where a brilliant young chef was serving organic food, and the place had yet to "take off," so I'd be way ahead of the crowd.

But what if I didn't want to be original or avant-garde? What if I wanted to wallow in nostalgia and pretend I was Zelda, or Coco, or Brigitte? What if I craved a view out over the heartbreaking blue of the Mediterranean, with the shadow of Corsica just visible on the horizon and the lights of St.-Jean-Cap-Ferrat twinkling like rhinestones far below?

What if I wanted to experience, just this once, a real travel legend? What then? Not much point in climbing up into some scrubby hills for some free-range *lapin* and a bowl of field greens *sauvage*, was there? I could hear the sigh on the other end of the telephone, and my friend was forced to admit that there probably wasn't.

The place I chose instead is called Èze. Many years ago, someone had sent me a postcard of a fortified medieval village clinging to a vertiginous rock that overlooked the Mediterranean. At the summit were the ruins of an ancient castle, a lemon-yellow church, and serpentine streets lined with old houses that coiled around the hill like a snail's shell. But it was the pure cobalt blue of the sea, a thousand feet below, that stuck in my memory. This part of southern France is full of hilltop villages. Èze is the only one in the whole of Provence that has this sublime view. It sits high above the Côte d'Azur, about halfway between Nice and Monaco, serenely overlooking the Baie des Anges and St.-Jean-Cap-Ferrat. The surrounding cliffs, known as *falaises* in French, are so wild and steep that even now, when this must be some of the most valuable land in the world, the developers have admitted defeat, and the mountains tumble down to the sea covered only in wild thyme and clumps of crooked pine trees.

Èze is one of the oldest settlements along the coast. As the author of a local guidebook put it, *"Èze prend ses racines dans la nuit protohistorique."* But once dawn broke on that protohistoric night, a bewildering succession of people moved through the area. Ligurians were followed by the wild and woolly Celts and then the Greeks. The Liguro-Celts, in turn, were defeated by the Roman legions from the south. Invaders approached from the sea, which meant that every house in the village was built facing the sublime view—convenient for the well-heeled Parisians who began to buy property here after the war. The castle was destroyed so many times that all that remains is a battered shell surrounded by a *jardin exotique* consisting of some truly hideous cacti.

I arrived in Nice at just about the worst possible time of the year; it was high, hot summer, toward the end of August. There was tourist gridlock along the whole of the coast, and I felt more like Roseanne than like Zelda, or Coco, or Brigitte. Maybe the cool mountain air of the Vaucluse was not such a silly idea after all. But this moment of doubt began to fade as soon as we started climbing up the Moyenne Corniche, became even fainter as we approached Èze, and vanished the instant I walked through the gates of the Château de la Chèvre d'Or.

The streets of Èze are far too narrow for cars, so the taxi left me at the entrance to the Château. My bags disappeared, and I was left to wander along the path that meanders through the hotel's gardens. In some moods, I am convinced that the only hotels in the world I ever want to stay in are those that were once somebody's house. This mood took over in Èze. The Château had belonged to an American violinist named Zlato Balakovick, who was born in the Balkans and ended up in New York. He fell in love with Èze in the early 1920s, long after Nietzsche—who was an infatuated and constant visitor in the 1880s—but long before the postwar invasion.

Balakovick arrived at a time when the village was virtually abandoned. He figured out where the best view was, bought the ruined house on that site, and went about transforming not just his own home but the fortunes of the whole village, inspiring a renaissance of Èze in the years between the two World Wars. The Château became a hotel in 1960, but if you choose your room carefully, you can still pretend that you are the spoiled guest of an indulgent host who has invited you to loll about in his stunningly beautiful house.

There is no unplanned noise in the garden of the Château. All I could hear was the cool gurgle of water being directed toward the swimming pools and fountains, the swishing of the sprinkler system, and, up above, in the clear blue sky, the distant sound of money being burned at a very high speed—the *thwacka, thwacka, thwacka* of rotating helicopter blades. The path led me to a terrace with a shallow pool at its center and some tables with white umbrellas set up along the edge of a stone wall. Below was the view I had seen on the postcard; the camera had not lied. The sea was cobalt, but with patches of emerald green and sapphire and so translucent that you could, even from this amazing height, see clear to the bottom. There were elegant yachts hovering in the middle of the bay, too bored to move, and smaller boats that eagerly wriggled their way across the water, with undulating white tails of wake that made them look like slow-moving sperm intent upon capturing the ovum of St.-Jean-Cap-Ferrat. I sat down beside one of the tables, ordered a bottle of Domaine Ott rosé (in honor of Zelda) and a salad of field greens *sauvage* (in honor of the pioneering chef in the Vaucluse), turned my body toward the heat of the sun (in honor of Coco and Brigitte), and drank my own private toast to the Côte d'Azur.

When I was a little boy, I used to know an old lady who had met the great Nietzsche," Xavier Cottier told me with great pride as he handed me a glass of Champagne and an *oeuf farci,* while the mayor of Èze looked on approvingly. The Cottier family has lived in the village for about nine hundred years, and Xavier, who is its unofficial historian, continued: "Nietzsche used to stay at a small hotel in Nice in the rue de la Paix, but he loved to walk around Èze and always said, '*C'est quand l'inspiration créatrice coule en moi le plus richement que mes muscles foncionnent le mieux*' ['It is when the creative impulse is strongest in me that my muscles work at their best']. Which is why he wrote *Thus Spake Zarathustra* here and why we have named the Chemin Nietzsche for him."

We were sitting on the terrace of the Château Eza, a medieval house (now a hotel) that in the 1920s had been bought by the Prince of Sweden, who somehow succeeded in creating, on this coast of light and sun, a gloomy, dark castle that must, I suppose, have reminded him of home. But, no matter, it still had the magical view and now, even more important, a brilliant chef.

Provençale *pistou,* which can be a kind of rough-and-ready soup (and can be called Piss Stew when it is really bad), was here transformed by using the freshest ingredients—baby clams, miniature *haricots verts,* and, most crucial of all, the best olive oil—to create a perfect first course. Next arrived a pigeon that had been roasted in honey and spices and was surrounded by a necklace of tiny sweet turnips. Then salad and some bell-shaped chèvre that came from Corsica, whose outline the mayor had claimed to see from the terrace before dinner: "*Vous voyez, là-bas,*" he'd said, directing my gaze toward the unblemished horizon. "*Ah, oui,*" I'd replied, lying. "*Oui, je la vois.*"

A little sorbet, a short respite, and then the dessert of roasted fresh figs and vanilla ice cream *faite maison,* but I had already admitted defeat with the Corsican goat cheese and so said good night to the mayor and M. Cottier and walked back to the Chèvre d'Or through a labyrinth of cobbled alleyways. The evening ended with instant sleep, but I awoke just before the pink light of dawn to find one of the village cats purring happily in his sleep at the foot of my bed. A sleeping cat—every hotel should have at least one.

⌒

Èze is so small and, it has to be admitted, so overtouristed in the summer that after a day or so you are in the mood for a side trip, either down to the coast or up, farther into the hills. Or both. I chose to mix the Romans with the Rothschilds.

The Romans had, of course, taken the high ground and constructed at La Turbie, six years before the birth of Christ, a huge stone monument marking their victory over the forty-five Ligurian tribes that had been unwise enough to resist their rule. The Rothschilds, just as naturally, had taken the low ground and had built, on Cap-Ferrat in 1906, their own enormous monument to the fruits of capitalism, the Villa Ephrussi. Both are perfect reflections of the values, martial and monetary, of their creators.

I asked one of the cabdrivers in Èze if he thought I should go to La Turbie, and although he was just about willing to take me there, he shrugged his shoulders, lit a cigarette, and said of the Roman monument, *"C'est pas grand' chose."* He could not have been more wrong. It is a very big thing indeed. And magnificent. And still, even in its ruined state after two thousand years, manages to concentrate your mind on the power and the glory that was Rome. Which must have been just what its architects wanted.

I read the names of all those long-forgotten and defeated tribes who had been destroyed by the legions. The Senate constructed Le Trophée des Alpes in honor of the Emperor Augustus, and it originally had a circular colonnade that included niches for statues of each of Augustus' campaign generals, as well as a twenty-foot statue of the emperor at the top of its cone-shaped roof. Although most of the stone had been cannibalized over the centuries, you still have a sense of its gargantuan size from the proportions of the podium. When Jean-Jacques Rousseau first saw that other monument in France to the supreme power of Rome, the Pont du Gard, he described the sensation of "vanishing like an insect in this boundless edifice," and you know precisely what he meant. But there is another—faintly shameful, in our very un-Roman and oh-so-politically-correct days—feeling that overwhelming military power can arouse, and that is a desire to identify with the victors. A feeling that Rousseau also clearly had when he went on to say, "As I humbled myself, I could vaguely feel something which raised my soul, and I said to myself: 'I wish I were a Roman.'"

The cabdriver from Èze who had been so reluctant to take me to La Turbie was elated at the thought of the sybaritic, fin de siècle, and totally over-the-top beauty of what he called the Palais Rothschild on Cap-Ferrat. *"C'est ravissant,"* he promised. In a way, he was right. The "Palais Rothschild" epitomizes the glory days of the Côte d'Azur. It is a monument to the extravagance of one woman, Béatrice Ephrussi, who was born a Rothschild, the daughter of a director of the Bank of France, and who decided in 1906 to build her dream house along this stretch of unspoiled coastline. Her dreams ranged far and wide, at least in terms of their "artistic" influences, and were interpreted by between twenty and forty different architects.

On the outside, the villa seems to be Northern Italian and Renaissance in inspiration. Except that it is painted lipstick pink, not a shade that you see very much of around Florence or the Veneto. Inside, her dreams float off in a number of other directions: The central patio is Italian downstairs and Spanish with Moorish touches upstairs, hung with a number of medieval and Renaissance works of art. From the patio I wandered through a series of stifling formal salons, dining rooms, and boudoirs, so stuffed full of Louis XVI furniture and Gobelins tapestries that even Marie-Antoinette would have said "Enough!" The same formality was repeated out-doors, where there was not just one garden but seven. I was almost asphyxiated by the perfume of thousands of pink roses, until I decided that this was it—I'd had it. I'd seen how the other 0.0001 percent used to live, and I wanted to be back up in the hills looking at the gilded excesses of the Côte d'Azur from a safe distance.

By the time I got back, it was dusk, and the only sound I could hear in the garden came from the fountains, which were gurgling like contented babies. I took off my shoes and climbed down the cool stone steps toward the pool and sat with my feet dangling over the edge of the wall, looking down at Cap-Ferrat. The lights were just beginning to glitter as the Grande Dame got herself ready for another night out. She was still lovely, and the shimmering lights made me think of a beautiful woman of "a certain age" in a silver-sequined dress: A little optimistic, perhaps, but what the hell—after dark she can still get away with it. I also thought of Scott and Zelda and the summers they spent nearby at the Villa America on Cap d'Antibes, with its huge garden full of lemon trees. I remembered Fitzgerald's description of this part of the coast—"the diffused magic of the hot sweet South . . . the soft-pawed night and the ghostly wash of the Mediterranean far below"—and imagined that he could have been looking through my own eyes. The legend hadn't changed so much after all, but then again, real legends never do.

Èze is an easy—and spectacular—fifteen-minute drive from the Nice airport. Choose your hotel carefully, and you will be insulated from the crowds that besiege the coast. Avoid the height of the summer: Aim for May or June or late September or October.

Lodging

The summit of the summit is the Château de la Chèvre d'Or. Its meandering garden has lots of hidden corners and a stunning pool that overlooks the Mediterranean. The best room is No. 20, tucked away by itself below the pool, with its own private balcony. In the evening, the food in the slightly stuffy (in both senses) dining room leans toward the fussy and pretentious, but the simple grilled fish and salads served at lunch, under white canvas umbrellas by the pool, are delicious (04.92.10.66.66).

Dining

The most interesting food in Èze is at the Château Eza. The chef produces traditional Provençale food of the most imaginative kind. In the summer you eat outdoors on the terrace, where the view lives up to the extraordinary cuisine. The Château Eza is also a hotel, but the rooms are dark and charmless and there is no garden or pool (04.93.41.12.24).

Riviera Retro

BY LINDA DANNENBERG

∽

editor's note

Les Îles d'Or (Porquerolles, Port-Cros, and Le Levant, also known as the Îles d'Hyères after the town of Hyères where the ferry disembarks) seem about a hundred years behind the times. In many ways they remain an antidote to civilization, and their natural features are a strong reminder of the paradise the Mediterranean once was.

Nature—and a few creature comforts only the French provide so well—is the main reason to visit the islands, only a short ferry ride away from *le continent* (the mainland). The islands haven't received a great deal of publicity in the States, but readers can find more information in some of the guidebooks recommended in *Renseignement Pratiques* and at the French tourist offices in the U.S. and in France. Note that there are no cars on the islands—Port-Cros and Porquerolles are national parks, after all—and only island merchants and those providing services (like hotels and restaurants) are allowed to have cars and drive, so visitors must leave their cars on the mainland. Bikes are available for rent on Porquerolles, but otherwise count on your own two feet. I rarely meet anyone who's been to the Îles, which I suppose is both fortunate and not; but I urge you to go, even as a day-tripper.

LINDA DANNENBERG is the author of *Pierre Deux's French Country* (1984), *Brittany: A French Country Style & Source Book* (1989), *Pierre Deux's Normandy: A French Country Style & Source Book* (1988), *Paris Bistro Cooking* (1991), and *Paris Boulangerie-Patisserie* (1994), all published by Clarkson Potter; *Perfect Vinaigrettes* (Stewart, Tabori & Chang, 1999); *French Tarts: 50 Sweet and Savory Recipes* (Artisan, 1997); and coauthor of *Ducasse: Flavors of France* (Artisan, 1998). She also writes frequently on French lifestyle and design for *Town & Country, Wine Spectator,* and *Victoria.*

Windsurfing in the mistral is but one of the physical pleasures fueled by the exaggerated forces of nature on the Îles d'Hyères, the French Riviera's Golden Isles. Passionate love is another. Porquerolles and Port-Cros are astonishingly unspoiled beauties just a few miles off the Côte d'Azur, where breezes fragrant with eucalyptus and heather blow across empty beaches and *sauvage* landscape. Sparsely populated and imbued with a sense of privacy and discretion, the islands have been the locus for more than a score of published French love stories. How many unpublished love stories have been played out here is anyone's guess.

Pinewoods, palm trees, fields of lavender, and banks of mimosa—here is the Riviera before the onslaught of condominiums, campgrounds, and gridlocked caravans. On the Golden Isles (named for the sunlight that is reflected off the mica cliffs) there is more luxuriant vegetation now than there was a century ago. Today, Porquerolles and Port-Cros offer the best of the Riviera: the sun, the sweet, clean air, a gentle climate, and of course, the sea, all without crowds, without cars, and without the manic chic. (The third Hyères island, Levant, is divided into a naval installation and a world-famous nudist colony.)

Porquerolles, the largest of the three, is a tight little island a few miles off the Côte d'Azur that refuses to reveal its charms to the day-tripper. Oh, one can pass a few happy hours on the Plage d'Argent, the silvery, pine-shaded beach near the village, and have an enjoyable meal and a stroll around the town square before the ferryboat leaves for the mainland. There might even be time for a short bike ride. But the respite and the romance that the island offers come only after an investment of days. It is worth taking the time to get to know Porquerolles and its secrets.

Some of this arc-shaped island's most beautiful spots are accessible only by boat. In a streamlined yacht or in one of the sturdy old *pointus* (small wooden launches with pointed bows and sterns) for rent at the port, one can explore hidden creeks and coves like the sublime Calanque de L'Oustau de Dieu, sheltered by soaring cliffs on the island's southern coast. Tiny sand beaches, shady copses carpeted with pine needles, and intimate shelters under rock formations make memorable settings for picnics and long, private afternoons.

The 3,000-acre island's densely wooded interior is marked with twisting paths and shaded lanes that cut narrow swaths through olive groves, vineyards, and deep, silent forests. On one of the yellow mountain bikes for rent from Bob Ghiglion at the Relais de la Poste, and then eventually on foot, one can reach the most primeval regions, visit elusive *châteaux-ruines,* and climb to dramatic vantage points accessible only to the intrepid.

Much of the island has remained as it was during the days of the Romans more than two thousand years ago. Subsequent invasions by the monks of Lérins, by Turks, and assorted pirate bands, left few traces other than scattered stony ruins. A village was built in the mid-nineteenth century as a military garrison; the central parade field still bears its original name, the Place d'Armes.

After the turn of the century, Porquerolles became the private domain of François-Joseph Fournier, a French engineer and adventurer who had made a great fortune in Mexican silver mines in the late 1890s. In mid-life Fournier returned to France and fell in love with a younger woman. As an engagement present, he offered to buy her the island of Porquerolles, and she accepted. The Fourniers developed the land and planted orchards, vineyards, and olive groves.

When Fournier died in 1935, his land went to his seven children. Five of them sold their land to the state (which still holds eighty percent of the island) to inhibit real estate development. The twenty percent not protected by the state is vulnerable to a group of off-island developers and speculators who want to build housing developments around the tiny village square. This is the basis for an island controversy that has divided the *porquerollais,* not equally, into anti- and pro-development factions. Most residents and seasonal regulars are afraid of seeing their little Eden become a paradise lost.

The island has a legion of faithful full- and part-time residents, many of whose families have been coming to Porquerolles for generations. The calm, unpretentious atmosphere here is not without sophistication. Many of the *porquerollais,* at ease in their faded Lacoste shirts and baggy cotton slacks, in fact hail from Paris. *Le tout Porquerolles* often gather at day's end for a drink and gossip on the terrace of Rémy Dufour's L'Escale, a café just up from the port.

Among the most visible of the island's rather casual social nucleus are actress Mylène Demongeot and her husband, film producer Marc Simenon, whose father, Georges, first came to Porquerolles in the twenties; painter Martin Dieterle and writer Caroline Lebeau; Eli and Jacqueline Jacobson, who produce the trendy ready-to-wear line Dorothée Bis; Sébastien Le Ber, a Fournier grandson and the *vigneron* who produces the island's Domaine de L'Ile wines, and his wife, Barbara; and Le Ber's sister, Caline, who with her husband, Georges Richard, operates the island's finest hotel, Le Mas du Langoustier.

Set off by itself on seventy-five acres at the southwestern tip of the island, Le Mas du Langoustier is a rambling Provençal inn full of charm and offering plenty of privacy. Many of the sixty-five rooms and apartments are decorated with opulent Provençal cotton prints and furnished with sculpted antique armoires, commodes, and chairs from the Midi. At night, cicadas add their music to the warm air scented with herbs and jasmine. The hotel itself is supremely tranquil and discreet. Even when all the rooms are occupied, one rarely crosses paths with another guest (this may explain why it is popular with politicians). Only at dinnertime are guests within earshot of one another, gathered either in the dining room or out on the terrace overlooking the hills that slope down to the sea.

Meals at Le Mas du Langoustier are justly celebrated, prepared with imagination and a light touch by chef Jean-Louis Vosgien. At a recent dinner, appetizers included a warm quail and almond salad garnished with wild mushrooms; sliced marinated salmon with fresh basil, served with lemon chutney; and shellfish-stuffed ravioli flavored with fresh tarragon. Among the tantalizing main course possibilities were slices of baked lobster in a sweet-and-sour sauce accompanied by a warm artichoke salad; fillet of *loup* (monkfish) braised in a delicate sea urchin sauce and served with an assortment of stuffed vegetables; and a succulent fillet of beef garnished with truffles.

Porquerolles' other restaurants and hotels are almost all clustered around the Place d'Armes. Agreeable dinners, with an emphasis on seafood, are served in the garden of Les Glycines or at the Arche de Noé. A few steps off the Place is L'Orée du Bois, a cheerful garden restaurant with a striped yellow awning and rose-bordered terrace, where one can order a lively, refreshing *blanc de blancs* from Cassis to accompany the appealing Provençal menu. A pizzeria, a simple beach restaurant at the Plage d'Argent, and some cafés serving sandwiches and salads complete the island's culinary spectrum.

The tiny, steep island of Port-Cros, only three miles long and one mile wide, is rich in the literature of love. The most famous story, told by Eugène Melchior de Vogüé in his fervent, moving novel, *Jean d'Agrève,* concerns the nineteenth-century lovers Hélène and Jean, who meet aboard a ship and eventually find love and overwhelming passion on Port-Cros. But she is married, and he is a naval officer who must return to sea. Their story is said to be true. During the inevitable separation that follows their affair, their letters cross, there is a misunderstanding, there is torment. By the time Hélène breaks with her past and returns to Port-Cros, Jean has left for Indochina. After nursing the sick and wounded repatriated from the Tonkin, Hélène dies on the island from yellow fever. Jean and Hélène are reunited only in death in the small cemetery high on a hill in Port-Cros. Other literary lovers—Jetta and Hubert, Hervé and Flora, Agnès and the Gypsy—fare better, but the island remains a setting for bittersweet love.

At first glance Port-Cros appears to be anything but strikingly romantic. Upon arrival one sees simply the diminutive port with its semicircle of cafés, shops, and restaurants, and a few small homes set above the village in the hills. Most of the day-visitors who take the one-hour boat trip from the mainland towns of Le Lavandou or Hyères spend their time right here at port. But stretching off from the port are the narrow *sentiers,* pathways that wind through luxuriant greenery around and across the island. One will lead you through the Solitude Valley and pass by Le Manoir d'Hélène, a nineteenth-century manor house built by a nobleman and named for the lover Hélène. Another will take you to Port-Man and a startling green amphitheater surrounding a bay.

Take any one of these walks and the entrancing spell of Port-Cros will begin to take hold. It beguiles all the senses, a combination of delicately perfumed air, the feeling of a light steady breeze on the skin, the bedazzlement of the Provençal sun reflected up from the sea, and the heady, heavy silence broken only by one's own footfalls or words.

"At five o'clock the boats pulled out, charged with a humanity eager to return to their domestic preoccupations. The island was left alone with its lovers," wrote Gérard Prévot in his 1957 novel, *Les Chemins de Port-Cros*. It would be a shame to visit Port-Cros for just a few hours, especially since one can overnight in Le Manoir, a nostalgic and secluded hotel that resembles a colonial mansion from a lost empire, the Congo in the 1920s, perhaps. The graceful Lloyd Loom wicker furniture set around the gardens is of the period, while the house itself was built in the early 1900s.

Run by Pierre Buffet, whose family owns much of the island, Le Manoir is full of personal touches, from gorgeous bouquets of flowers on windowsills and landings to intriguing artwork in the salon and the cozy writing room. The twenty-six rooms are spacious and comfortable without being particularly stylish. Three of the best, facing the front gardens, are numbers 22, 25, and 26, each with its own terrace that catches the morning sun.

In addition to the beautiful promenades, you can also windsurf and swim at the Plage du Sud de la Palud. And then there is the Aquascope. This strange-looking, waterborne tank, originally developed for underwater reconnaissance, is used by Jean-Jacques Marabel to give half-hour tours of the shimmering marine world surrounding Port-Cros, the only domain in Europe to be classified as an underwater national park. After overcoming the initial discomforts of settling into a round shell six feet underwater, you begin to enjoy the eerie marine landscape.

Relatively unknown outside of France, the Îles d'Hyères would like to stay that way. "The islands are not big enough for everybody," says Le Ber, "so their appeal must continue to be very limited." Or deliberately unsung. Within sight of the Côte d'Azur, this tiny, remarkable archipelago is a hundred years away in spirit and ambience.

Looking Down on the Riviera

BY JOEL STRATTE-MCCLURE

∽

editor's note

Revered sons of Provence, Frédéric Mistral and Jean Giono, each defined the boundaries of Provence differently. They both, however, were equally dismissive of the coast, which they considered to have nothing whatever to do with the "real" Provence. Mistral and Giono would perhaps have considered the *villages perchés*—fortified villages clinging to summits just a few miles inland from the Côte—worthy of inclusion in their geographic realm.

While I admit to enjoying the Riviera coastline as much as anyone else, if not more so, it is the *villages perchés* that are more indelibly etched in my mind. A few miles really does make a difference.

Freelance writer JOEL STRATTE-MCCLURE was born in North Dakota and now lives in Valbonne with his family. He has written guidebooks to Paris and other European cities, and was formerly bureau chief for Fairchild Publications in Paris, and Monaco correspondent for *People*. His work has appeared in a wide variety of periodicals, including *ARTnews*,

Boston, France Discovery Guide, Time, and *The International Herald Tribune.* He is currently keeping a record of his 16,000-kilometer trek around the Mediterranean Sea, which began on January 1, 1998.

Real Riviera residents, in contrast to casual visitors, often bemoan the incessant growth that continues to clutter the Mediterranean coast between Italy and Cannes. The resulting problems of security, pollution, congestion, and environmental decay have prompted many to consider leaving the south of France.

The it's-time-to-return-to-North-Dakota sensation hits me 3.5 times a year (the average for foreign residents is 4.3 times annually), and I have found only one way to deal with this paroxysmal state of fear and trembling.

I head, occasionally on foot with my dog Bogart, to my favorite perched village, Gourdon, and sit on the terrace of the Taverne Provençale or Le Nid d'Aigle. There I order a simple lunch—a *salade niçoise,* a melon, and a peach sherbet with fresh mint—and look down reflectively (and superiorly, I might add) on a coastal population that has increased from 887,120 people in 1982 to 980,703 at the end of 1990.

Gourdon's lofty altitude—1,650 feet above the Loup River and 2,510 feet above sea level—puts civilization in perspective with a panoramic view that on a clear day takes in the whole Riviera shooting match—from beyond Nice to Italy, out into the sea to Corsica and west to the Esterel Massif.

From up here, as I usually conclude after an hour of relative solitude, the Riviera might beat North Dakota.

Gourdon is only a fifteen-minute drive from my home in the hillside town of Valbonne. But like many of the seventy-five (or so) other perched villages in the Alpes-Maritimes, the French *département* containing the congested French Riviera, it seems a world away.

I often arrive in Gourdon in a warlike and stressed frame of mind, which recently has been compounded by the construction of a perfume factory halfway up the mountain. Fortunately, the town's thirteenth-century château, itself built on the foundation of a ninth-century Saracen fortress, has comforting vaulted rooms and a small chapel (still used for services on special Sundays) that simultaneously calm me down and make me feel adequately protected.

The château-cum-museum—flanked by three levels of terraced gardens designed by André Lenôtre—contains not only a self-portrait of Rembrandt, an Aubusson tapestry, and a writing table that once belonged to Marie-Antoinette, but also enough ancient armor to combat a contemporary invasion. I envy the French industrialist owner, although he did have to pay for its restoration in 1972, because he can permanently look down on the coastal havoc and hordes from his aerie.

Gourdon, populated by 231 hearty souls, does not have any of the fancy hotels (there are in fact *no* hotels) or too-touristy shops that typify many perched villages on the coast, like Èze. Nor is it quite as pristine as some of my other favorites, like Peillon (where I go when I am having the Riviera equivalent of a nervous breakdown), which has had the good sense to ban boutiques.

Gourdon is in between the two. There are some thirty artisan workshops, craftsmen's cubbyholes, and operative showrooms that sell glassware, pottery, perfume, soaps, and a plethora of local produce and products. But unless a busload of tourists has arrived or it is the middle of summer (when real Riviera residents do go back to North Dakota or wherever they come from), Gourdon is not overwhelmingly crowded.

In fact, I have never even seen both of the two tennis courts (a recent addition and seeming incongruity) in the local perched playground in use at the same time. And the shops in Gourdon are informal enough to keep me coming back not just to browse but also to buy soaps, herbs, and oils. Everything for sale, for example, in the Fabrique de Savons de Toilette—including the *eau de parfum,* lavender-scented herbal sachets, and bath oils—is homemade from natural products. I also like to drop in on Charles Balembois, the glassmaker at the Verrerie d'Art de Gourdon, who actually sings (or screams, some say) while he creates intricate crystal figurines and tries to convince me to join the Fondation de la Préservation de la Pensée Humaine au Bonheur d'Exister (rough translation: Foundation for the Preservation of Human Thinking on the Good Fortune of Existing), which he created here in 1964.

Gourdon is particularly refreshing because some perched villages, like Èze or St.-Paul-de-Vence, have become inexorably absorbed into the coastal suburbia. These now resemble Disney World, though Èze, perched some 1,400 feet above the Mediterranean and frequently called the "crown of the Riviera," has banned cars from its old village and is worth a visit for the panoramic view, exotic garden built in the ruins of the town's crumbling château, and fourteenth-century chapel. Indeed, some romantic real Riviera residents still go to Èze, situated between Nice and Monaco, because it's a favorite spot for lovers.

But St.-Paul-de-Vence so resembles a film set that—once they find a parking place—visitors can be excused for thinking they are in a movie when they arrive to find Yves Montand playing *boules* in front of the Café de la Place. It perhaps takes a visit to the local history museum, where different costumes represent bygone days and depict the town's "evolution," to remember that it wasn't always this way.

Fortunately there are dozens of perched, fortified hillside villages—constructed on mounts, peaks, mesas, domes, buttes, hills, pinnacles, crowns, and summits—to give a frenzied existentialist like me a much better vantage point of our lives and times.

The less wrecked are located not on the coast but in the *arrière pays,* which, though properly translated as "back country" or "hinterland," I tend to consider a combination of Adventureland, the Middle Ages, and nirvana. Much of it seems straight out of *The Hobbit,* for lack of a more classical literary allusion.

Physically, of course, the *arrière pays* is the pre-Alps and Maritime Alps, which rise from the Mediterranean to nearly 16,500 feet above sea level. But the terrain, vegetation, cooler climate, ecosystem, and almost everything else are a world apart from the coast. Rivers—the Esteron, Loup, Var, and Vésubie—crisscross a country of steep slopes, terraced agricultural plots, flourishing forests (of beeches, firs, and pines), and a breed of people not preoccupied with tourism trends or the rate of the dollar.

The definition of what is perched and what is merely hillside is, in the end, subjective. Initially, the perched villages were surrounded with ramparts and, distant from both farming land and water supplies, built this way for protection. This precaution was anything but stupid during the era of Germanic invasions, Muslim pirates, and Middle Ages mercenaries.

Today some are deserted, some are casually maintained, some strictly promote a Provençal way of life and language (street signs are often in both French and Provençal), and some purport to be the next Èze or St.-Paul.

My own definition of a perched village (partially plagiarized from the photographer who accompanied me in the hills for this story) is multiple. First of all, an authentic perched village looks as if it will fall down if one rock or boulder is removed. Although it sometimes depends on the vantage point, the villages mentioned here, mostly built with stones from the surrounding hillsides, could all fall down. (In fact, some are in such need of repair that they may do so before you get a chance to check them out.)

They are usually built around a church or château, have houses buttressing one another, are difficult to access, and are impossible to attack by car. Their inhabitants do not hang clothes out the window or breed cats just for the effect. And they are not overtly commercial (Gourdon shopkeepers are still civil, creative, and friendly, but I actually prefer perched villages where there are no shops at all and inhabitants buy their bread and meat from mobile *boulangeries* and *boucheries* that pass each morning).

More important, the local *boules* players in a perched village *must* be able to beat me. (When I played in St.-Paul with Nall, an American artist from Alabama, the tourists took pictures of us, which was so ridiculous that we now play in the privacy of our own yards.) Finally, the food in restaurants should be symbolically less expensive than "down below."

Despite my rigid definition and high standards, I do like some villages simply for the relief I experience when I see them. Just knowing I'm leaving the coast and industrial zones in the dust, or sand, gets me excited.

Gattières, Carros, and Le Broc, for example, are just minutes away from the Nice–Côte d'Azur International Airport on the road that runs toward Isola 2000 and other near-Riviera ski resorts. These three towns have been Èze-ed (they have modern versions of the perched apartment complex right next to the perched cemetery and the perched supermarket), and often look better from afar than up close.

But they each contain some scenic features, especially small chapels or panoramic views, which give me an initial breath of fresh air.

The D1 road from Bouyon (eighteen miles from St.-Laurent-du-Var with a nice café in the central *place*) to relatively untouched Bonson marks the real transition to wilderness west of the Var. (Incidentally, most of the roads to perched villages are narrow and require skillful driving. However, many real Riviera residents—who usually take pride in tailgating and regard it as a personal insult if they are confronted with a red light, which they usually run—sometimes drive sensibly in the back country. Take heed: Do not, no matter how small your car, try to drive within the villages—just park below and walk around.)

Other perched villages, closer to Nice and the coast as the sea gull flies, are more pristine and austere. Not only are they relatively untouched, but some are fortunately fighting to stay that way.

In Peillon, after spending five minutes negotiating an illegal parking place one Sunday in June and battling for an unreserved table at the Millo family's Auberge de la Madone (it looks away from perhaps the south's largest gravel quarry, which scars the valley), I saw a poster proclaiming THE BACK COUNTRY MUST NOT BE A VICTIM OF THE COAST'S FRENETIC DEVELOPMENT.

"We have been fighting to prevent any and all boutiques in the village but do allow music and concerts in the square from time to time," says the Auberge's spunky Marie-Josée Millo Clavel, whose current home lies between the house in which she was born and "my final resting place in the cemetery." She vows that "we will do everything we can to avoid making Peillon turn into an Èze, because our clients want to experience the real thing—not find shops that sell department store trinkets at twice the price. And that's the way we want to keep living."

Unfortunately, the food at the Auberge, cooked by Marie-Josée's brother, is so delectable that coastal residents beat a path (the road to Peillon is not much bigger than a path) to her door to sample offerings like the *tourton des pénitents au coulis de tomates douces*—a dish that uses twelve to fifteen herbs, depending on the season, and resembles, she says, "an omelet without the eggs."

Peillon is located on a rocky spur in the Paillon Valley, some ten miles from Nice. The first houses, built within the walls of a castle dating from the twelfth century, were constructed in the 1400s. The Baroque-style parish church, with a storybook tower and superb working clock, was restored in 1982. The Chapelle des Pénitents Blancs (White Penitents' Chapel) includes frescoes by Giovanni Canavesio representing the Passion of Christ.

Like all these villages, the walkways are cobblestone, and you can meander in a labyrinth of streets that has not changed much in configuration through the centuries. I have yet to hear anyone complain about the almost complete lack of commerce (there is a local sculptor who sells his works).

Many perched villagers are proud of their heritage. Frequently on Sunday the village of Peille, a two-hour walk (uphill) from Peillon and built near the ruins of a castle, hosts a local fête in the main square. The restored city hall has an exhibition of photographs and maps displaying the evolution of the town, and young schoolchildren take great pride in giving visitors a heartwarming guided tour of their past.

The city hall has also published guides (in French) to well-restored Peille that indicate lintels, inhabitants, the date of construction, and other details, including the various building stages of the Ste.-Marie church from the eleventh through the sixteenth centuries.

Most villages provide at least rudimentary comforts for travelers. The Hôtel Belvedere in Peille has five rooms, while the Auberge de la Madone in Peillon is very well renovated—though not quite at the level of the Colombe d'Or in St.-Paul or the Château Eza and Château de la Chèvre d'Or in Èze (all excellent hotels in these crassly commercial perched villages).

Each village has its claim to fame. Farther east, Castillon proclaims itself an "artists' village" while Ste.-Agnès touts itself as the highest perched village on the coast.

Ste.-Agnès is only two and a half miles from Menton and less from the *autoroute* that parallels the sea between Genoa and Marseille. But at a 2,178-foot elevation and with a population of just under one hundred, it seems much more distant. This is perhaps because it takes at least forty-five minutes to get to Ste.-Agnès on a windy road that heads from Menton up the Gorbio Valley.

Yet though Ste.-Agnès has traditionally turned its back on Menton and the coast, it could be the next Èze. In fact, it wants to be.

"We need to keep the village alive, and the best way to do that is to generate income through tourism and shopping," explains Roger Tibert, who owns the Logis Sarrasin restaurant. "I like what they have done to Èze!"

There are already some boutiques with smart names in Ste.-Agnès, like Lampe d'Aladin and Frédéric Pelissier's A Touch of Glass. Pelissier, who helped renovate a Victorian house in Berkeley, California, speaks English and sells an exciting array of glass lamp shades for about 450 to 20,000 francs.

Eerily and Èze-ily, the Michelin green guide to the French Riviera seems to recognize the future already. It gives Ste.-Agnès itself only one star but awards two stars to what it calls "a splendid view of the Provençal motorway" from the top of the town.

This oversight aside, Ste.-Agnès is a superb village that merits a day's visit before it really becomes Èze-in-the-Hills. Its ninth-century streets are made of sharp stones, which actually massage the feet (as you climb to admire the view of the motorway), and one of France's national walking paths passes right through the village. There are two hotels (Le Saint-Yves and La Vieille Auberge), but many visitors prefer to stay in the three *gîtes* in the village (there are another five within three miles of town), which rent for approximately 3,000–4,500 francs a month in the summer.

And I like Ste.-Agnès because I can get an omelet at Roger Tibert's for about 20 francs and a rabbit *plat du jour* for about 45 francs.

If Ste.-Agnès already seems too Èze-y, head farther back toward the Alps. There, more rugged, austere mountain villages are even more removed from the climate and clamor of the sea.

Lantosque, about 1,650 feet above sea level and a forty-five-minute drive from Nice (on a quite good road), is renowned for the kayaking on the Vésubie River in the gorge below it. But I particularly like its simple cemetery, topped with a high cypress, because the family tombs with many Italian and Provençal names remind me that this region (which belonged to Italy until 1860, when the county of Nice was returned to France) does have a past.

In addition, the buildings in Lantosque afford a spectacular spectrum of colors and construction in various stages of freshness, brilliance, or decay. The best aspect of the simple but comfortable Danish-run Hostellerie de l'Ancienne Gendarmerie is the dining room that looks up at the hovering village.

No perched village is an island, of course, and each is surrounded by an array of flora, fauna, views, and walks. And there are some worthwhile side trips, like the Church of the Madonna in Utelle, which attracted about thirty thousand pilgrims in 1938 and even has crutches left in the entrance to illustrate that some were healed.

A few real Riviera residents, troubled slightly more than I by all the growth and development, are beginning to head even farther into the back country. They go beyond Lantosque and St.-Martin-Vésubie to the spectacular Mercantour National Park.

But I'm not yet at that stage. Visits to the nearby perched villages 3.5 times a year are enough to keep me sane until I decide for myself—rather than let 980,702 other people influence me—to head back to North Dakota. Though each time I return home from Gourdon, I wonder whether I am heading down the right side of the mountain.

Bibliothèque

Côte d'Azur: Inventing the French Riviera, Mary Blume, Thames and Hudson, 1992; first published in paperback in the U.S. in 1994. A delicious and fascinating read from the first word to the last, and best of all, it's a paperback, making it a candidate for the bring-along pile. With dozens of black-and-white photos, you never want this to end. *De rigueur.*

DuMont Guide: French Riviera—Art, Architecture, History, Rolf Legler, translated by Russell Stockman, Stewart, Tabori & Chang, 1986; originally published 1982 by DuMont Buchverlag GmbH & Co. The practical travel suggestions on the blue pages at the back of this book might lead one to classify it as a guidebook, but I view it as more of a history book with a special focus on art and architecture. It's the best book of its kind in paperback, with 53 color photographs and 105 drawings, engravings, floor plans, and maps, and I have yet to find another book published in the U.S. quite like it. It is very much worth the effort to obtain this undoubtedly hard-to-find title.

French Riviera: The '20s and '30s, Charles Bilas, Lucien Rosso, and Thomas Bilanges, Vilo International, 1999. The authors take a unique look at the Riviera, focusing on the years when it blossomed into the *luxe* place it became, paralleling the blossoming of the Hollywood movie business. Hotels, private villas and palaces, and casinos are featured with accompanying illustrations (over 160), most in color. Many of these architectural gems and follies—in the art deco and art moderne styles of the times—are not showcased in other books.

Great Villas of the Riviera, text by Shirley Johnston, photographs by Roberto Schezen, Rizzoli, 1998. This lavish book features twenty sumptuous villas on the Côte d'Azur, including some you can visit (Villa Île-de-France, Villa Kerylos, and Château de la Napoule) and most you can't (La Mauresque, L'Ermitage, etc.). Without this book, you'll never know of the splendor behind the facades, and in fact, you won't even know the facades because you'd never be able to find most of these private palaces. A feature nearly every villa in this book shares is a view of the Mediterranean to die for, reason enough to page through this book.

Monaco
(Principality of Monaco)

"To better understand the Principality of Monaco one should remember the answer that Doge Marco Foscarini gave to an ambassador who made light of the modest size of Venice: 'You err, Excellency. Nations are not to be measured, but weighed.'"

—René Novella, MONACO 360°

A Promenade in Monte Carlo

BY RACHEL BILLINGTON

～

editor's note

As I noted in *Renseignements Pratiques*, Monaco is best explored simply by walking around, and there is perhaps no grander capital to stroll in than Monte Carlo.

Though this piece, which appeared in "The Sophisticated Traveler" section of *The New York Times Magazine* on March 13, 1988, is thirteen years old, nearly everything about Monte Carlo remains the same: you need only substitute a few names of the rich and famous. The personal lives of the Rainier royal family have changed, and, of course, the Louis XV Restaurant is no longer "the newest Monte Carlo wonder" and "the young chef Alain Ducasse" is now a Michelin eight-starred celebrity.

RACHEL BILLINGTON is the author of *Loving Attitudes* (William Morrow, 1988, hardcover; Penguin, 1989, paperback), *Theo and Matilda* (HarperCollins, 1990), *Occasion of Sin* (Summit, 1982), *A Woman's Age* (Summit, 1979), and *All Things Nice* (Black Swan, 1969), among others.

In Monte Carlo, there's the old, the new and the newly old. The newly old buildings are the newest, as seen in the still-unfinished Metropole Hotel, which is being rebuilt in the style of the Belle Epoque, with pillars, marble floors and "riotous overdecoration," as one Monacan lovingly described it. The truly old, which is Monte Carlo's claim to a place in architectural history, is exactly the same—except it is genuine. The Casino was built in 1878, as was the Opera House, known as the Salle Garnier after Charles Garnier, who designed it as a smaller version of his Paris Opera House.

The Salle Garnier was opened in 1879 by Sarah Bernhardt, who was always welcome in Monte Carlo because she was a spectacular loser at the gaming tables. The Ballet Russe de Monte Carlo, under the direction of Diaghilev and with Nijinsky as star, performed there. (The only reason one American dancer-turned-actress named Grace Kelly had ever heard of Monte Carlo was because of the Ballet Russe.) John Mordler, the director of the Opera House, says he had never believed the story of Nijinsky's jump from one side of the stage to the other until he saw the Salle Garnier. "So famous and yet so small," as one auditioning singer commented.

Then there's the Hôtel de Paris, which looks like a film set and was actually being used as one by Dino de Laurentiis when I was staying there, and the Hôtel Hermitage, whose Salle d'Hiver has the prettiest glass dome outside of a Tiffany lamp shop but whose pillars resemble steel girders, a curiosity explained when one learns that the designer's best-known work was the Eiffel Tower. Nor must one forget the Café de Paris, which

is both old and newly old, since the facade is being retained while the rest is being reconstructed. The sounds of building in the winter are as loud as the sounds of fireworks in the summer and Grand Prix racing cars in the spring. Monte Carlo is never a quiet place.

Which brings us to the new, constructed over the last twenty years and giving a fair imitation of Manhattan *sur mer*—except that the entire Principality of Monaco is only a little more than half the size of Central Park. From a distance, it seems to be composed entirely of skyscrapers, jostling each other for space between the mountain of La Tête du Chien at their backs, the sea in front and the borders of France to the west and (after a little more French soil) Italy to the east. These tall apartment buildings are called by romantic names—Park Place or Columbia Place or even Buckingham Palace—that fail to disguise their essentially selfish nature: each hides the view of the one behind. Pity the Persian prince's villa now up for sale and hidden behind twenty floors of concrete, or indeed any pink-washed remnant of a more graceful age. Prince Rainier was once asked why he had not stopped the building of skyscrapers. His reply: "I am not a dictator."

Prince Rainier lives on Le Rocher, the Rock, where the royal palace of the Grimaldis sits in its own charming toytown square with its own toytown soldiers and band—two trumpets and two drums. On the Rock are the grand Oceanographic Museum, directed by Jacques Cousteau, the houses belonging to Princess Caroline and Princess Stephanie, the mayor's house, the Palais de Justice and the Conseil National. You have to own a Monacan license plate to drive on the Rock and have a great deal of money to live there. At the highest point, the Cathedral stares impassively seaward.

Which brings us to Princess Grace. For she is buried inside, under a flat stone inscribed in the same way as for all the other deceased royal princesses ("Gratia Patricia Principis Rainier III uxor") but utterly different because her grave is always cluttered with flowers—roses, poinsettias, carnations, humble daisies. "People come from all over the world with their posies," says

Virginia Gallico, who was principal lady-in-waiting to Princess Grace. "We haven't the heart to tidy them away."

When Princess Grace died in 1982, 30,000 people wrote in sorrow. Her face still adorns a butcher's shop in the market in the Place d'Armes, a flower shop in the fashionable Avenue des Beaux-Arts. In the newly reclaimed area of Fontvieille there are a lake and a park and, in the center of the park, a rose garden dedicated to the Princess, with a statue of her rising out of the rocks and a quotation from a poem she wrote: "What is so special about a rose that it always seems more than a flower? Perhaps it is a mystery it has gathered through the ages. . . ."

The roses in Monaco seem to flower all year round. The seasons are signaled instead by the changing promenade along the seafront. In the winter, the crowds of tourists disappear, leaving the older residents to take their poodles for a peaceful breath of air. Monte Carlo as much belongs to poodles in the winter as it does to tourists in the summer. In the winter, elegant, no-longer-young women wearing hat and pearls sip a 3 P.M. brandy in the Hôtel de Paris bar or play bridge in a smoke-filled upper room of the Country Club. The Country Club has an official waiting list of four years, although a friend of mine, a new resident, got in immediately. "I knew the right people," she admitted cheerfully.

In the summer, the young rich show off to each other at the Beach Hotel, whose row of striped beach tents gives it the air of a medieval pageant. (Placement is everything, to be at either end a disaster.) In summer, 8 P.M. is the time to visit the bar at the Hôtel de Paris, have a word with Louis and check out the latest in Dallas-style glamour. After dark the place to be seen is the Sporting Club, where the famous Salle des Etoiles seats 500 for dinner and, in case it gets a little stuffy, the whole roof slides back to reveal the great glittering firmament above.

Tourists are informed that Monte Carlo is *"un rêve"*—"a dream." This seems most true in the evening, when one is leaning on a parapet in front of the palace courtyard and staring across the harbor, where lights twinkle from little white yachts and blaze from Niarchos's gigantic yacht. It is true at lunchtime on the terrace of the Saint-Benoît restaurant, where the view of the sea is endless and a poodle laps from a bowl under a chair. It is especially true in the Louis XV Restaurant, the newest Monte Carlo wonder, where the young chef Alain Ducasse presides over a salon boasting more gold per square yard than Fort Knox. The effect of all that gold is lightened by white walls and medallion portraits of charmingly painted ladies, and by white tablecloths and riotous flowers. There are seven courses on the set menu, heralded by the *"Pâté chaud de Colvert de Sologne et foie gras en Pithiviers, sauce rouennaise des chicons poêlés."*

The South of France had always been the winter quarters for the leisured upper classes. The English, in particular, liked to leave their climate for several months of the warm south. Even now the really chic, particularly the Monacans, avoid July and August.

In the 1860s, the previously impoverished Principality of Monaco was transformed into a fashionable destination when François Blanc, founder of La Société des Bains de Mer, lured the rich and titled to something unique, his newly built Monte Carlo Casino, a precursor of the present Casino.

Trying to compete with the man who broke the bank at Monte Carlo was never the only reason to come to "good old Monte." Nowadays gambling receipts account for only 4 percent of the country's income, despite the huge success of a new American-style casino at Loews Monte Carlo. It seems soulless, vulgar and dull—if you're not a gambler. But in his most recent book, *Easy Money,* David Spanier, an expert on gambling, claims that the new casino has its own "easy, open and classless Western style." The Société des Bains de Mer owns 50 percent of Loews Monte Carlo; thus 50 percent of the profits from the new casino goes to support the old-fashioned Monte Carlo Casino down the hill.

Walking through the stately and ornate rooms of the Monte Carlo Casino is like going back a hundred years. "It's our Versailles," comments my escort, Pierre Cattelano, a veteran of casinos throughout Europe, now returned to his home country to work once more in the rooms where he began as a croupier in 1935. Then, he says, people stayed on for months, not days. From the Salle Américaine to the Salle Européenne to the Salon Privé and the Salon Super Privé (entirely lined in leather) the Casino unfolds, becoming with every room and every bar quieter and more secret. Until, that is, one gets to the innermost sanctum, the Salle Blanche, again white and gold, dazzling, out of this world, reserved for high rollers and presided over by a painting by Gervais, *Les Grâces des Trois Florentines.*

Monte Carlo is filled with surprises, most of them the result of the confrontation of the old with the new. Mr. Cattelano, the elegant representative of *nostalgie,* has an apartment at the top of the tallest skyscraper—from which he can tell the time by the Casino clock. The outer rooms of the Casino shudder with the noise of slot machines. A seascape, painted 100 years ago and showing Monte Carlo as a beautiful and deserted picnic spot, looks down unbelievingly. The slot machines will go into the Café de Paris when it's finished being re-created, taking with them, presumably, the players with their plastic pots filled with change and their extremely un–Belle Epoque sneakers and sweaters and jeans.

A British writer, Grant Richards, noted in 1927: "I like Monte Carlo. I do not like it as much as I did in 1899. . . . It has become democratic for one thing, and it has become much more moral." Living off the wicked flavor of the past is obviously not something that appealed to the Rainiers even before the war. The present

Prince is likened by financial journalists to the head of a flourishing business, Monaco Inc., that has very wide and sometimes conflicting interests. The big money in Monte Carlo now comes from corporate taxes levied on overseas companies that do at least 25 percent of their business outside Monaco.

The resident (unless he is French) can avoid personal taxation but that does not mean he is living in fairyland. Leave the seafront and you might be in any busy French provincial town—except that the apartment blocks are higher and the traffic heavier. An inspired innovation, Héli Air Monaco, whisks you across the rippling blue sea from Côte d'Azur Airport in Nice to Monte Carlo for less than the cost of a taxi. It is a pleasure—until you reach the heliport at Fontvieille, the home of light industry, and must make your way by taxi through tunnels and exhaust fumes to the Place du Casino. If you are staying at a hotel in that vicinity, however, you can then walk to most of your destinations.

Walking is the way to enjoy Monte Carlo. If you get tired of pâté and truffles at the Hermitage or another grand hotel, you can walk to Rampoldi and eat Italian. Since so much of the country is halfway up a mountain, there are public lifts in appropriate places. And walking in Monte Carlo, unlike most places in the world, is absolutely safe at any time of the day or night. Monte Carlo has no unemployment and no muggers. This contributes to its popularity with those who number diamonds among their best friends. Police in Monte Carlo arrest first and ask questions later. That's the price you pay for security and for an enthusiastic police force with limited experience.

Monte Carlo is closely guarded and its cultural life is closely controlled. John Mordler points out that, of all countries in the world, Monaco devotes the biggest percentage of its budget to the arts—

7 percent or, in 1987, $32 million. All cultural events are under the patronage of Princess Caroline, but Prince Rainier is also involved.

Many of the most interesting of Monte Carlo's cultural organizations were set up by Princess Grace or founded in her memory. One of the last things she did before her death was to choose a dishwasher and table for a canteen in the Académie de Danse Classique Princesse Grace. This is according to the ebullient Mme. Marika Besobrasova, who came to Monaco from Russia and, with the help of Princess Grace, founded her international school for pupils from thirteen to eighteen years of age. The Académie de Danse Classique is a direct link to the Ballet Russe and a nice antidote to Loews Monte Carlo.

The exotic gardens, with thousands of succulents growing out of the rocky mountainside, is hard to miss (and involves a heavy price in tourist crowds and traffic). Another Garnier creation, a pink-washed villa that houses the Doll Museum, is hard to find because it has been masked by a concrete chunk of an apartment building. Inside is a parade of dolls collected by Madeleine de Galea in Paris during the late nineteenth century. Many of the biggest and most elaborate are mechanical dolls that dance, eat, smoke, breathe, blink, write and, in fact, do almost everything but speak— which is rather a relief.

A collection of even more special interest lies in the city, at 9 rue Princesse Marie de Lorraine, where Prince Rainier used Princess Grace's books on Ireland, collected by her in the sixties, as the basis of an Irish Library. The Princess's books are recognizable by their bright green, shamrock-shaped bookplates; they include plays by her Pulitzer Prize–winning uncle, George Edward Kelly.

Prince Rainier's ambition for his country is well known. As one Monacan commented sagely, "We couldn't have a principality without a prince"; another added that Rainier had brought the country from the nineteenth to the twentieth century. Young Prince Albert is now beginning to take his mother's place in royal photographs. He can be seen working in his palace office late in the evening—that is, when he's not in training for bobsled competitions or driving his Porsche down the narrow streets of the old city. Princess Stephanie is described by palace representatives as a "businesswoman" operating mostly in America, who has not much to do with Monaco at the moment. Which leaves Princess Caroline—now seriously married and the mother of three children—as front person for the royal team. Gossip has it that she may be the barrier to Prince Rainier's remarriage. Two royal ladies would, apparently, be one too many.

To an outsider, the change in Monte Carlo that Grant Richards noted between 1899 and 1927 feels curiously true fifty years later: "The pace is set by the rich and respectable bourgeois rather than by the butterfly and the spendthrift." Monte Carlo does have its glamorous residents, its Helmut Newtons, Boris Beckers, Placido Domingos, Karl Lagerfelds, but essentially it is a place for the rich and respectable. After all, it is nearly as difficult to become a resident as to go through the proverbial needle's eye.

Somerset Maugham called Monte Carlo "a sunny place for shady people." With the advent of tall buildings and conventional commercial prosperity, it is tempting to reverse it to "a shady place for sunny people."

Bibliothèque

To say there are not many single volumes available on Monaco is an understatement. Many of the guidebooks recommended in *Renseignements Pratiques* include good historical and descriptive information, but for a wonderful look at the Principality—both visually and verbally—see *Monaco 360°* (text by René Novella, photographs by David Maria Galardi, Priuli & Verlucca, Editori, 1999). The text—surprisingly informative and interesting for a coffee-table book—is in Italian and English, and the photographs panoramic (it's not named *360°* for nothing) and gorgeous.

Saveurs Provençaux
(Provençal Flavors)

"Provence begins with a France that tastes of Italy and ends where it tastes of Switzerland."
—Leslie Forbes, A TASTE OF PROVENCE

Tasting Inventory

BY RANDALL ROTHENBERG

❧

editor's note

Philip and Mary Hyman, the American subjects of this piece (which appeared in May 1996) have an encyclopedic knowledge to match the extraordinary encyclopedia they're working on: *L'Inventaire du Patrimoine Culinaire de la France*. Although the Hymans track down food products from all over France, *miel de Narbonne* can be considered unique to "greater" Provence. As Ford Madox Ford reminds us, "Provence on the East of the Rhône became *Provincia Romana* and the Roman Province, joined to what was Roman on the right bank, towards Spain, became the home-territory of the whole region that the Romans called *Gallia Narbonensis*. If you wrote a capital V upside down and divided the space between its arms by a descending straight line which would be the Rhône, the triangle on the right of the dividing line would be the true Provence with which we are concerned. That on the left of the line would be the sort of quasi-Provence that contains Montpellier, Béziers, Carcassonne, and Perpignan and that finally merges into a sort of Catalan-Spanish territory. The whole would be Gallia Narbonensis called after Narbonne of the honey."

RANDALL ROTHENBERG is an author, editor, magazinista, and one-time newspaperman who specializes in communications and culture—which includes writing about food, naturally.

With the type of scrutiny that hunters reserve for underbrush, Philip Hyman pauses outside the window of Fauchon, the lavish food emporium on Paris's elegant place de la Madeleine, and peers at a display of honey. Not sighting his quarry, he enters. Passing displays of *myrtilles* from the Loire and *moutarde* from Bordeaux, he stops before a wall filled row upon row with jars of honey. "Do you have *miel de Narbonne?*" he asks a young shopgirl.

"In the nineteenth century, it was one of the two most famous

honeys in France," Philip explains after she retreats. "It's a rosemary honey. Through the late nineteenth century, you mentioned
Narbonne"—a dusty wine town five miles from the Mediterranean
in southern France—"and the immediate association was rosemary
honey. There's a thirteenth-century reference. We have a dictionary
for eighteenth-century merchants; it talks about Narbonne honey.
I've seen a 1908 document that discusses the difficulty of finding
it—the expansion of the vineyards was destroying the rosemary. We
want to see if it still exists, if Narbonne still produces a honey that
carries its name."

Mary Hyman, pug-nosed, scholarly, more excitable than her
droll husband, peers up from a counter she's been surveying. "The
only honey with rosemary here comes from Spain," she says.

Philip's eyebrows ascend. "Spain!"

The shopgirl returns with a fair rendition of a Gallic shrug.
"They have no honey that claims to be from Narbonne," Philip
sighs after she concludes her whispered counsel.

Although the Hymans' interest is strictly academic, the reason
for it is anything but. They are among the lead players in France's
latest grand project, an Eiffel Tower of scholarly research: to catalog every extant traditional food product in each of the nation's
twenty-six internal and external administrative regions.

When the decade-long endeavor is completed near the end of this
century, France will finally know how many cheeses it produces—
allaying Charles de Gaulle's apprehension about the governability of
a place so fragmented that the number remained obscure. Not only
cheeses, but pâtés, sausages, pastries, candies, liqueurs, jams, hams,
lambs, and melons—any and every regional food specialty (save
wine) that history shows to have a place in the nation's conscious-
ness. The very name of the encyclopedic enterprise—*L'Inventaire du
Patrimoine Culinaire de la France*—just begins to hint at the seri-
ousness with which the French treat their food heritage.

Which makes the Hymans' role in assembling it that much more delicate. The only two historians the French government deemed worthy and capable enough to discriminate among culinary fact, fable, fancy, and fad, they happen to be Americans: she a preppy from Ossining, New York, and he a Jewish doctor's son from Mobile, Alabama.

The Hymans make a beeline for the nearby Maison du Miel.

"I'm looking for a Narbonne honey," Mary tells the woman behind the counter in fluid French, which, unlike her husband's, bears no American taint. "It's from rosemary flowers."

The shopkeeper nods animatedly. She's heard of it. A very strong taste. Not like *miel du Gâtinais* or other, more popular brands. But no, she hasn't had it for a very long time.

Miel de Narbonne isn't even on the Hymans' must-find roster. They are merely trying to get a head start in scouting southern France. They've actually been far more concerned of late about Alsace and the mystery of *langue fourrée*, a smoked beef tongue wildly popular in the nineteenth century around Strasbourg but which seems to have disappeared.

Thus far, they and their collaborators—two French ethnologists, an agronomist, and a handful of part-time field researchers they supervise—have found enough to publish inventories for Île-de-France, Bourgogne, Nord-Pas-de-Calais, Bretagne, Pays-de-la-Loire, Poitou/Charentes, Rhône/Alpes, Franche-Comté, and Provence/Alpes/Côte d'Azur. The volumes contain detailed histories and descriptions of each product selected, as well as explanations of their uses, composition, and variations. At the end of the books are recipes featuring the products and addresses of suppliers; among the ground rules for inclusion is that a product must be "living"—in other words, still available for sale somewhere in France.

Sadly, the books contain no photographs or illustrations to guide inveterate market browsers who, having read about *boudin noir de Paris* (a Parisian blood sausage made with onions that dates to 1393), are eager to find it in the stalls at the foot of the rue Mouffetard. This is, after all, a government, not a Gallimard, project.

The books, though, are merely one component of an ambitious effort by the Conseil National des Arts Culinaires (CNAC) to sustain the glories of French cuisine. The government agency, founded in 1989 by Socialist culture minister (and foe of American cultural imperialism) Jack Lang, is planning a program that will bring tourists to farms, working with retailers to sell regional products, and sponsoring a program in which children in some five hundred schools are taught how to taste.

"Do you know any other country that would arrange for the education of taste? Any other country? Taste is very important to us," Alexandre Lazareff, the urbane thirty-nine-year-old director-general of CNAC, said to me over dinner recently at Lucas Carton, one of Paris's best restaurants.

Lazareff is a living model of his own maxim. A scion of the family that created both the afternoon tabloid *France-Soir* and the weekly women's magazine *Elle*, he readily admits to experiencing "pornographic pleasure" the first time he sneaked a peek at his parents' Gault-Millau guide. After graduating from the prestigious Sciences-Po and the École Nationale d'Administration and joining the ranks of France's senior bureaucrats, he continued for years to write saucy nightlife guidebooks and restaurant reviews for *Le Figaro*.

"We have our memories, our roots. 'Casey at the Bat' evokes something for Americans. Here, *pain d'épice* evokes my youth. And food gives the French something to talk about. Americans," Lazareff said, his matter-of-factness underscoring his disdain, "have nothing to talk about."

It was Lazareff who, at a desperate moment, found the Hymans. Encomiums of taste aside, CNAC's role is intensely political. Like the more restricted *appellation contrôlée* designation for wine, cheese, and a few other products, the agency's *L'Inventaire* provides a basis, should one ever be needed, for furnishing legislative protection to French food products—safeguarding them, in this era of GATT and European unification, from the ravages of free trade.

Recognition of the value and importance of these products—what the French call *valorisation*—would also help preserve them at home, in the process protecting the small farmers and bourgeois merchants who constitute a potent political force in France. Indeed, in each region to be inventoried, a committee of local experts (the head of the bakers' union, perhaps the director of a cheese cooperative) is convened to assemble a list of products it deems culturally important. That list is then compared with the one drawn by the Hymans from historical references, such as ancient cookbooks, menus, government surveys, and travelers' diaries. Field research—including visits to *charcuteries* and *pâtisseries*—further refines the catalog.

Yet shortly into its first year, *L'Inventaire* was fumbling along, heightening the political sensitivities and threatening the project with collapse. To organize the enterprise, CNAC needed historians whose methods were unimpeachable and whose conclusions would be firm.

"You're walking on thin ice sometimes. You can't just tell people that something they've believed since the seventeenth century is not true," says Philip Hyman, a bearded forty-eight-year-old. Poitou/Charentes, France's second-largest producer of rabbits, wanted its lapin listed. The Hymans said no—the industry had only existed for twenty years. He continues: "What we're doing is very fact-based, an extremely well documented approach, which is at the opposite extreme of the folklore"—trafficked by chefs, published by the likes of Waverly Root, and tenaciously memorable—"that says, 'Louis Quatorze liked this.'"

The Hymans are unlikely historians. They met in 1969, when living across the hall from each other in a sixth-floor walk-up on the rue Gay-Lussac in the 5th Arrondissement. Philip was an escapee from graduate school in the Midwest who had been so overwhelmed by Paris on his first trip to Europe that he decided to stay. Mary, three years his senior, was honing her French in preparation for a career as a language teacher back in the States. At first they ignored each other. Rebuffs became repasts when they discovered their mutual passion for food; marriage followed a year later.

To finance their stay, Mary took a job as a translator and Philip rewrote badly composed English texts. They decided to combine forces by translating an old cookbook, and then another, for the American market. To augment their income, Mary became a specialist at devising two-hundred-character recipes to accompany the stock photographs that French food magazines bought by the bushel. Eventually they built comfortable careers translating the works of Paul Bocuse and other doyens of nouvelle cuisine.

It was, literally, a hand-to-mouth existence. "We had to test all the recipes," Philip recalls, "which meant we ate for free."

Their work with antique recipes eventually led them to write articles for obscure food journals about such subjects as plagiarism in eighteenth-century French cookbooks. Their work came to the attention of Jean-Louis Flandrin, a leading cultural historian, who urged them to become his students at L'École des Hautes-Études, one of the nation's leading graduate schools. It cost nothing, so they went, in a few years earning advanced degrees that established them among the few historians in all of France with expertise in both food and books—exactly the background the CNAC needed to rescue its floundering culinary inventory.

"I have a confession to make: We weren't very excited about choosing Americans to do our *Inventaire,* but we had no choice," Lazareff told me. "And we're open-minded enough to accept anyone who shares our values. Philip and Mary are more French than the French. They chose France. That's why they know so much about products and geography, and why nobody has criticized them for being American."

Continuing their quest for honey, the Hymans stroll over to Galeries Lafayette, which has recently added a food hall on its second floor. There they find *miel de Provence, miel du Canada, miel du Gâtinais,* and *miel de Lavande.*

"Can I help you?" an aproned clerk asks.

"*Miel de Narbonne?*" Philip inquires.

"Ah, no."

Political shoals may have been circumvented, but scholarly reefs underlie *L'Inventaire.* Indeed, the entire project is an Aristotelian conundrum, forcing its authors to question continually whether the essence of a product lies in its name, its ingredients, or its history. The Hymans' answers—the closest France comes to an official designation of culinary truth—put the lie to the untutored assumption of American foodies that classic French cuisine is eternal and unchanging.

"People go to the southwest and they say, 'Oh, the Périgord, foie gras, this has been going on a long time,'" Philip tells me over a lunch of saddle of rabbit in a mustard glaze, a new variety of wild-tasting strawberries called *mara des bois,* and *croquants de Cordes* biscuits. "What's really interesting is that today it's almost entirely duck liver, whereas as recently as fifty years ago it was almost entirely goose liver."

"You'll see this with cheeses a lot," Mary adds. "A famous cow cheese—for example, Saint-Marcellin from the Rhône/Alpes—you find out was equally famous two centuries ago, but it was a goat cheese."

A pair of field-workers, Muriel Menguy and Laurent Terrasson, drop into the Hymans' comfortable, book-filled apartment in the workaday 18th Arrondissement, on the far side of Butte Montmartre. Muriel has just been to the Academy of Medicine, where she photocopied a 1797–98 study of the substances used to make bread. Philip flips through it.

"Bread made with white beans. Bread made with millet. Here, in Carpentras, a bread made with buckwheat. Normandy has a pure buckwheat bread—we knew about that. But Carpentras, no." He taps at his Macintosh PowerBook. "This is all database material."

Sometimes, such evolutionary enigmas create problems for the Hymans. There was, for example, the case of *dragées de Verdun,* tiny sugarcoated confections traditionally served at baptisms. History records that in Verdun, site of the famous World War I Allied victory, *dragées* were traditionally made with aniseed. At some point, almonds were substituted.

"This creates a problem for us," Mary says. "What do we do about a product that has the historical name but is different? Should we include it and just say that the center is different? Or is it a different product masquerading under a traditional name?" To find out, they turned to Laurent, a wiry pastry chef, to glean from the one manufacturer still making the candies the reasons for the shift.

To date, repeated calls have not been returned, but Laurent

(who, after all, did manage to locate the lone *pâtissier* in all of the Midi-Pyrénées who still makes the spit-roasted cone-shaped cake called *gâteau à la broche*) intends to keep after him. "It's Inspector Clouseau, you know," he says.

A bit of melancholy underlies the detective work, however. Whenever they travel in France, the Hymans say they are struck by the proliferation of hypermarkets, the vast superstores selling everything from *mousse de canard* to *mouche-trappes* that are taking the place of the specialty markets which keep the small producers in business. More than once, between research and publication, they have seen the very last manufacturer of a centuries-old food item go out of business, taking a piece of La France Profonde with him.

Not to worry, says Alain Senderens. History lives, he says, in novelty.

Senderens is the president of CNAC, a largely honorary but nonetheless unusual position for him. For if anyone would appear to represent apostasy in French cooking, it is the chef-proprietor of Lucas Carton, one of the nation's three-star temples of nouvelle cuisine. Senderens is the man who dared marry the noble foie gras with that peasant fare, cabbage . . . and steam them! Even today he continues to shock traditionalists; among the entrées on his current menu is *ris de veau croustillant aux écrevisses et sa garniture de maïs éclaté*—sweetbreads and crayfish garnished with popcorn.

Yet this heretic considers himself a historian and believes *L'Inventaire* can provide the foundation upon which new dishes will be built. "Nobody really invents in a void," Senderens told me over a glass of champagne in the private upstairs dining room of his restaurant. "There's always something that precedes it."

By way of example, he pointed to his signature dish, *canard api-*

cius, a two-thousand-year-old recipe he found in an ancient Roman cookbook. The sweet, crisp duck (which Senderens insists on serving with a 1976 Banyuls, a rich, portlike, fortified wine from Languedoc-Roussillon) is made with apricot and quince and roasted in honey.

"*Miel de Narbonne?*" I wondered.

"Never heard of it," the chef replied. "Honey from the Pyrénées I know. But I've never heard of *miel de Narbonne.*"

Provence Olives and the "Liquid Gold" Oil

BY CARY MARRIOTT

~

editor's note

Even if its olives were not famous, Nyons is worthy of a detour even for those who may not have planned to include northern Provence in their itineraries. Nyons (one of the few French words where the final "s" is pronounced) is my favorite town in all of Provence, notably for its pretty setting along the banks of the Eygues River, its weekly market on Thursdays, its proximity to the lavender fields of Vinsobres and the pottery ateliers of Souspierre and Dieulefit, the absence of many Americans, and because it's the home of Lydie Marshall and her À La Bonne Cocotte cooking school (see "Cooking Schools" in *Renseignements Pratiques* for specifics).

Writer and traveler CARY MARRIOTT has lived in Nyons and has contributed frequently to *Gourmet, The New York Times,* and a number of other publications.

NYONS . . . SON SOLEIL ET SES OLIVES proclaims the sign on the road into town. Any Provençal town can boast of the sun, but Nyons's olives—that is different. These are no ordinary black olives. Plump and unctuous, they are the peerless tanche variety, unique to the two river valleys that define the Nyonsais region. The olives and their extra virgin oil claim their own appellation *d'origine*. This guarantees the variety of olive—where it was grown, how it was cultivated; it also guarantees that the olives were cured only in sea salt and water and that the oil was extracted from the first cold pressing.

In this French town of 6,000 in the department of the Drôme, at the northern reach of Provence, olive oil is taken as seriously as wine. The Confrérie des Chevaliers de l'Olivier (loosely translated as the Brotherhood of the Knights of the Olive Tree) was founded in Nyons in 1963 to defend the olive tree and its culture, threatened by a devasting freeze that killed half the 500,000 trees in one night in 1956. Every year on the Sunday before July 14 the group sponsors an olive festival called Les Olivades. In this small-town spectacle the chevaliers, dressed in their Christmas-green capes and olive-branch-festooned hats, parade though the streets along with other *confréries* in assorted colors (including golden honey, wine, truffle brown). This is followed by a procession of flags from all the olive-producing countries. They end up at a tree-shaded, open-air theater on the banks of the Eygues River for the induction of new members.

Les Olivades takes place expressly in July to spread the word to the many summer visitors in the region of Nyons's "liquid gold," as Homer described the oil, but the olive is actually a winter fruit. In December and January, six mills in the region cold-press the fruit using virtually the same process the Romans brought to this part of Provence along with the olive some 2,000 years ago. Outside the Moulin Autrand down by the Pont Roman (one of two distinguishing landmarks in Nyons), I watched two elderly women nimbly sort out unripe olives amid a waist-high bunker of cartons, crates and sacks of the fruit. Destined for eating, the largest olives would first be cured for about six months until they turned tender and savory, their skin the deep-brown color of a monk's robe (as one Frenchman described it).

Inside the mill, with oil production at full tilt, everything seemed slippery, including the air, as three men pushed, pulled and dumped the olives and their crushed pâté from one step to the next. Once sorted, rinsed and the leaves removed, the smallest olives, pits and all, 440 pounds at a time, went into a slowly spinning, metal basin where two churning granite wheels crushed them. From this basin a blackish-brown paste oozed out onto two-foot-round mats, called scourtins, once made in the exact form of a giant straw beret, but now flat without the beret's lip and made of more durable nylon. One man stacked the scourtins, heavy with olive paste, about a hundred high onto a dolly, then rolled them onto the press. As the press came bearing down, a thick black liquid—a mixture of the fruit's oil and water—cascaded over the sides of the scourtins. A centrifuge then separated out an opaque green oil, later made clear when filtered through cotton. In the end, into each bottle went the juice of eight to eleven pounds of fruit and nothing else, according to Josy Autrand-Dozol, a fourth-generation olive oil maker who runs the mill with her husband, Jacques Dozol. "No chemical treatment," she said. "Nothing artificial." I was to hear this "all natural" refrain in Nyons as often as the litany of olive oil's health benefits—in particular its role in reducing the risk of heart disease.

Is the celebrated olive oil of Nyons the best? Is a Burgundy better than a Bordeaux? In terms of quality the oil is certainly first-rate; in terms of flavor it is a matter of taste. Made solely from the very ripe tanche olive, its mild flavor makes the oil of Nyons particularly good for cooking since it imparts some but not too much flavor to a dish. Oils from farther south tend to be fruitier and made from a mixture of olives, including green ones—olives picked before they are ripe. Riper olives, such as the tanche, produce a milder oil.

"A good Nyons 'cru' should taste like winter fruits—apples and pears," says Christian Teulade, director for the last twelve years of the Nyons Cooperative, which handles the olives of about 400 growers and churns out thousands of liters of olive oil a day during the peak of the harvest season, producing a third of all the oil. "If you are not used to olive oil, Nyons oil is a good place to start," Mr. Teulade added. "It's like someone just beginning to appreciate wine might drink white wine rather than red." He says he has five different olive oils in his kitchen—two from Italy and three from France: one from the Gard, one from the Bouches du Rhône and, of course, one from Nyons. "You wouldn't drink the same wine with every dish and you wouldn't use the same vinegar for everything either—it's the same for olive oil."

A friendly rivalry exists among the local producers as to whose oil is best. "Nyons's is the champagne of olive oils and the cooperative's is the Dom Pérignon," says Mr. Teulade with a smile. As with wine, everything—from soil, to sun, to pruning, to irrigation—affects the flavor, as well as how long the olives sit before pressing. At the cooperative, where modern equipment has replaced traditional mill methods and science comes before art, the oil ends up the mildest. For that reason Christian Cormont, the chef at Le Petit Caveau, a Nyons restaurant, uses the cooperative's oil for cooking and the Autrands' crisp, fruitier oil for salads.

Purists will choose the oil from either the Vieux Moulin in Mirabel-aux-Baronnies or the Moulin du Puits Communal in Buis-les-Baronnies. Neither filters its oil. Instead, these most traditional of mills decant it—any sediment falls to the bottom and the maître de moulin taps the oil from above, leaving a cloudy, thick-looking liquid and a stronger aroma. "If a little bit of pulp gets in the bottle, it doesn't matter," says André Michel of the Puits Communal mill in Buis. "With that comes a bit more flavor." Alain Farnoux, at the Vieux Moulin in Mirabel, whose great-grandfather was the first in his family to make olive oil, told me that the fancy word of the moment to describe olive oil is "ardent." When asked about the flavor of his own earthy oil he was more straightforward, *"Elle est bonne!"*

The American shopper might expect to find Nyons olive oil on the shelf at the local gourmet food store, but except for a small percentage that escapes as export to neighboring European countries and to other parts of France, locals and tourists buy it all on the spot. The olives themselves only pop up in the States once in a while, which is even more regrettable, considering their rich, full flavor. The tapenade of Nyons olives puréed with herbs and capers, readily available here, merits the "Provençal caviar" name.

Travelers who make their way to Nyons will find a town most remarkable for its setting—on the banks of the Eygues River in a fold of the Baronnies Mountains. The area defined by the appellation stretches south and east of Nyons between the Eygues and Ouvèze Rivers and takes in more than sixty communities, including such charming villages as Vinsobres, Puymeras and Brantes. A fifty-mile drive that the Nyons tourist office calls the *route d'olivier* circles this rugged, hilly enclave. This is not the Provence of Souleiado shops (the chic Provençal fabric maker) and swimming pools but rather an agricultural back country of cherry, apricot, almond and olive orchards. Along the route you see no great sea of olive trees, just small swells lapping along the hillsides and the banks of the winding rivers, predominantly around the oil mill towns of Nyons, Mirabel-aux-Baronnies and Buis-les-Baronnies. Forever green, the olive tree's leaves are pale on their underside and a deeper shade of green on top. When the wind blows and the sun is at the right angle, a plantation of olive trees looks like a wave of silver. The trunks vary in size and shape, depending on their age, and the older ones are twisted and knotted—each one as individual as the wrinkles on an old person's face. There are trees said to be a thousand years old in the area.

North as Nyons is, it barely seems to belong in Provence in a geographic sense. But the olive tree firmly roots it there. "The whole area of Provence is made homogeneous by the universal culture of the olive and vine," wrote James Pope-Hennessy in *Aspects of Provence,* "and the unmistakable stamp of a great civilization which Rome has left upon this country like the deeply cut impression of an imperial seal." Once in the region there is no shortage of ways to sample the oil and the olive. In Nyons you can elbow up to the tasting bar at the cooperative to swirl, sniff and sip this year's olive oil cru, or try the tapenade omelet at the Brasserie Belle Époque; or buy the delicious olive bread at La Halle aux Fromages (both on the main Place de la Libération). At Le Petit Caveau the chef serves picodon (local goat cheese) with tapenade in puff pastry, and six miles outside Nyons on the olive route, La Charette Bleue, a favorite local restaurant, serves faux filet with tapenade and salmon cured in lemon and Nyons olive oil.

If the oil and olives of Nyons taste good, it may also have something to do with the faith and determination of the people who grow the olives and produce the oil. The olive tree has needed nurturing in France and nowhere has it received more attention than in Nyons. The appellation is one indication of that. It took close to ten bureaucratic years to achieve and came in the wake of the February 1956 freeze. They still talk about the freeze here in hushed terms as "the night one heard the trees cry out." With a mistral blowing ninety miles per hour, the temperature plunged from around fifty degrees to zero in a matter of hours. The trunks and branches of the trees, which were full of sap after a mild December and January,

splintered with a sinister cracking noise—like a glass of ice cubes being filled with hot water. The "indomitable and eternal" olive tree, as Sophocles called it, will perpetually regenerate itself. But a farmer requires a certain amount of patience and imagination to tend the tree. There had been many freezes before, but this time man had the bulldozer, so many farmers tore out the trees—which can take ten years to bear fruit and twenty before they give a regular harvest—and replaced them with faster producing grape vines and other fruit trees.

To save the industry, a group of concerned local people organized the Syndicat de la Tanche and pursued the appellation. They aimed to save not just a tree, but rather the fruit of a civilization that dates back thousands of years, the very symbol of their heritage and of Provence. The passion became manifest with the founding of the Confrérie des Chevaliers.

Besides Les Olivades, the Confrérie sponsors the Alicoque festival on the first Sunday in February, when the neighborhood gets together to celebrate the new oil. The oil is blessed in the town church the night before. At the main event the next morning in the medieval Place des Arcades, long tables covered with white paper cloths and laden with bowls of the new oil and garlic cloves await the arrival of toasted baguette rounds. By eleven many hundreds stand poised for the tasting. When at long last the small mountains of bread appear, a frenzy ensues. The crowd snatches up the pieces, rubs them with garlic, dips them in the faintly fruity olive oil and eats them with a glass of local Côte du Rhône wine. Just as at Les Olivades, at the Alicoque the Confrérie inducts new chevaliers who pledge "to defend the olive tree and all the riches, both material and spiritual, that it brings." As this vow suggests, the olive tree yields more than delicious fruit and oil for the Nyonsais table. "The olive trees," Freddy Tondeur, president of the Confrérie, says in a deep, resonating voice, "they are our Chartres."

Along the Provençal Olive Route: Mills and Restaurants

Getting There

A map showing a drive through the olive-growing areas and other regional information can be obtained at the tourism office, Syndicat d'Initiative de Nyons, Place de la République, 26110 Nyons; 04.75.26.10.35.

The Mills

All the mills operate in December and January, sometimes into February, depending on the harvest. In addition to oil, olives, and tapenade, they sell a variety of regional products.

Coopérative du Nyonsais, 9 place Olivier de Serres (on the route to Orange), Nyons; 04.75.26.03.44. Best place to buy olives for its variety of sealed packages and sizes and consistently good product.

Moulin Autrand-Dozol, 8 promenade de la Digue (next to the Pont Roman), Nyons; 04.75.26.02.52.

Les Vieux Moulins à Huile, 4 promenade de la Digue, Nyons; 04.75.26.11.00. Two beautifully restored eighteenth- and nineteenth-century mills giving a sense of the history of the industry. Now the backdrop for a boutique selling regional crafts and books as well as olive oil from the trees of the owner Jean-Pierre Autrand.

Moulin à Huile du Puits Communal, rue du Puits Communal, Buis-les-Baronnies; 04.75.28.03.30.

Le Vieux Moulin, rue de la République, Mirabel-aux-Baronnies; 04.75.27.12.02.

The following are a few places for sampling the olive and oil of the Nyons region:

Le Petit Caveau, 9 Rue Victor Hugo, Nyons; 04.75.26.20.21. Small, pretty restaurant with blue-and-white Provençal tablecloths. Four-course menu; extensive but expensive regional wine list.

La Charette Bleue (five miles from Nyons on the D94 to Buis-les-Baronnies); 04.75.27.72.33. Always busy (consider reserving). Good value. Regional menu.

Auberge de la Clu, Plaisians (outside Buis on the way to Brantes); 04.75.28.01.17. Hearty Provençal country cooking. Four-course menu.

Olive Bread

La Halle aux Fromages, 17 Place de la Libération, Nyons; 04.75.26.38.20. Superb olive bread baked in a brick, wood-burning oven from a regional boulangerie called **Pain d'Épi** (04.75.27.41.72). If you are driving the olive route and reach the village of Curnier about 1:30 or 2 take a short detour to Montaulieu (Mount of the Olives in Provençal)—the bakery is outside the village on the right-hand side. Bread straight from the oven is sold at this time Monday through Friday.

Shopping

La Scourtinerie, 36 rue de la Maladrerie, Nyons; 04.75.26.33.52. Provence's one remaining scourtin maker; now produced in assorted shapes, colors and sizes as placemats, doormats and rugs. Also sells oil from the Vieux Moulin in Mirabel and other regional food products and crafts.

Lydie Marshall, cookbook author and owner of the cooking school
À la Bonne Cocotte, gives weeklong cooking classes at her medieval
château in Nyons. (See page 50 for information.)

This piece originally appeared in the travel section of *The New York Times*
on July 5, 1992. Copyright © 1992 by Cary Marriott. Reprinted with
permission of the author.

Bouillabaisse

BY JEFFREY ROBINSON

editor's note

I've sampled fish soups and stews in various Mediterranean ports of call
and have prepared a few at home. There aren't many dishes I like better than
fish soup, but there is no fish soup that is better than bouillabaisse. Period.
There may be disagreement over *la vraie bouillabaisse*, but as far as I'm concerned, if there's no richly flavored *soupe de poisson* with bread and rouille
served with a separate platter of fish, it's just, well, fish soup, and you don't
know what you're missing.

Due to the contradictory nature of bouillabaisse, I've included two
pieces on this Provençal specialty. Visitors may frequently see restaurants
that offer bouillabaisse once a week and require advance orders (signs will
say SUR COMMANDE). One of the most memorable side trips I ever made was
to Marseille from the tiny town of Le Trayas, along the Corniche de l'Esterel
near Cannes. My husband and I set out in the morning in order to make our
twelve-thirty reservation at Chez Fonfon: first we took the little coastal train
to St.-Raphael, where we transferred to a bigger train for the hour-and-
forty-five-minute ride to Marseille. Once in Marseille, we then caught a bus
to a stretch of the city's coastal road, where we had to negotiate a flight of
stairs down to the quiet Anse des Auffes . . . *et voilà,* Chez Fonfon, and its

justifiably famous bouillabaisse. My husband was of course aghast that the cost to get there was more than the meal, but I say it was worth every franc.

JEFFREY ROBINSON lived for twelve years in the south of France. He is the author of eighteen books, including biographies of Princess Grace of Monaco and Brigitte Bardot. His investigative nonfiction credits include *The Laundrymen, The Merger, The Manipulators,* and *The Hotel: Backstairs at the World's Most Exclusive Hotel,* which is about Claridge's in London. Robinson wrote this piece for the October 1975 issue of *Gourmet* and now lives in Great Britain.

People take their bouillabaisse very seriously in Marseille. That city is to that soup what New York is to . . . well, ball-park hot dogs, water bagels, and, maybe, pastrami sandwiches. Marseille, however, is a city largely lacking in charm. There are wide avenues, but the streets are dirty. Some sections are bleak and tough, and there are often rude nuances cutting through the French. There are sandwich kiosks on every corner, sometimes two per corner, and the mistral whips down the Rhône, banging shutters and getting on everyone's nerves. When the wind blows you hear a lot of people mumbling, "*Quel sale vent,*" which it is.

Yet at the bottom of the main street, La Canebière, is the Vieux Port—and here's where you make your bouillabaisse connection. The fishermen and their women who jam the morning market sell from stalls in front of their boats. They have lived with bouil-labaisse all their lives; the fish they catch end up in it, they claim their predecessors created it, they speak of it as their birthright. They tell you flatly that no matter where else it's served, *la bouillabaisse marseillaise* is the one by which the others must be judged.

The only problem is that this most famous local son seems to be something of a gastronomic Abominable Snowman. Risking the chauvinistic *bouches-de-Rhône* wrath, I must confess that everyone

I spoke with gave me a different description—and everywhere I ate I was given a different soup.

In the simplest of terms bouillabaisse is nothing more than a pot-au-feu gone maritime. The definition is something like "a soup from the region around Marseille, made of fish cooked in white wine or water, or both, and seasoned with garlic, saffron, pepper, orange rind, oil, tomatoes, bay leaves, parsley, and various other herbs of Provence."

Erudition, however, is given short shrift.

"*Monsieur,* I can assure you that this is the real bouillabaisse."

"*Mon vieux,* here you have found *la vraie bouillabaisse marseillaise.*"

"*Écoutez,* bouillabaisse has been in my family for generations. This is the real one."

Now it's tough enough finding two Frenchmen to agree on anything, but finding two from Marseille to agree on bouillabaisse? *Bonne chance.* Okay, the fishermen did say yes to bouillabaisse being a slew of fresh fish boiled together. No one contested that part of the cast should be made up of *congre* (conger eel), *crabe* (crab), *moules* (mussels), and *crevettes* (shrimp). *Langouste* was the turning point. (This is not lobster; it is spiny lobster, the sea crayfish that has no claws.) Regarding its inclusion, some of the fishermen said yes, if you like. Others insisted never.

The discussion then took on a typical local flavor. With plenty of arm waving and shouting and the French equivalent of "What makes you such an expert, Pierre?" the "*d'accords*" were hushed. They couldn't even decide on the best fish for the soup. It seems that in Marseille you get to choose any five or six of the following: *rouget, grondin, vive, baudroie, rascasse, rouquier, loup, saint-pierre, merlan,* and *lotte.* But don't bother dusting off your French dictionary unless you plan on shopping in Marseille. In the United States the selections can be made from: halibut, bass, hake, haddock, red snapper, perch, cod, whitefish, rockfish, and pollack. Mathematically, if you prepare bouillabaisse once a week with any five or six of the ten possibilities, there are enough combinations to last the better part of a decade, without repeating the same recipe. You can see then that this is no ordinary operation.

This fish soup even has a past. Some foreign aficionados swear that history is filled with references to bouillabaisse in ancient Greece, Spain, and Morocco. (They don't swear it too loudly in Marseille, however.) What's more, in Italy there's *zuppa di pesce;* in Belgium there's *waterzooi à la flamande;* and there are even French variations on the theme: *chaudrée* on the coast of Charente, *cotriade* in Brittany, *bourride* in some areas of the Mediterranean, and *bouillabaisse marseillaise* in Paris, where they cough and stammer a lot when you ask them what fish they've included.

Beyond the flattery of imitation, one well-known French cookbook has elevated the origin of bouillabaisse, suggesting that Venus concocted it to put her husband to sleep so that she could enjoy a peccadillo on the sly. (The French are very fond of that version.) The poet Méry was so taken with bouillabaisse that he fashioned verses for it—and this was long before grown men on Madison Avenue were doing the same thing for American soup companies. (Here the French merely shrug, not too impressed, because they know that nothing rhymes with "bouillabaisse.")

In truth, the soup's beginning is likely an unromantic tale: One day a fisherman's wife gathered the remains of the morning's catch and boiled it all together. The soup couldn't always be the same because the leftovers varied, and it was probably named when the woman explained to her neighbor, "*Quand ça commence à bouillir, baissez.*" (When it starts to boil, lower the flame.)

For the film, enter now some princess, countess, or otherwise prominent lady from Paris who one day gets lost and stumbles into the little fishing village. She finds it quaint and stays, eventually being served the local lunch. When she returns home, guess what becomes the "in" thing? As travelers begin coming to the southern coast of France, and, in particular, to the area between Marseille and Toulon, restaurants open to cater to them, and, thanks to the lady from Paris, the visitors ask for bouillabaisse. Before they can tote up *l'addition,* what was once a simple seafaring-man's lunch has become a dinner gone to finishing school.

These days along the Vieux Port of Marseille it's not hard to see that visitors are willing to pay for a pedigree. The fanciest restaurant there sells bouillabaisse for about ten dollars, because someone has to support the six waiters who serve it, whereas the average price should be somewhere in the four- to six-dollar range. Anything less isn't bouillabaisse, and anything more is for snobs. The real bouillabaisse is a poor man's meal, a *plat de pêcheur* made with inexpensive fish. Whatever else it may or may not be, it is always made with *poissons bon marché.*

The economy factor is another strike against *langouste,* which doesn't add any distinctive taste to the soup anyway. And the taste of each ingredient is important. Everything must boil together to create a synergistic blend, and each ingredient must make a contribution. *Langouste* adds not so much to the flavor as to the price, because it is anything but cheap.

Down the *quai* there's a fellow in a tuxedo standing in front of a restaurant grabbing elbows with a "Psst, want to buy a great bouillabaisse?" Another place has a kettle of bouillabaisse painted on the front window; yet another has an old man in hip boots on the sidewalk who, while continually reopening the same oyster, suggests that you try his restaurant for "the real thing."

Taking an "ask-the-truck-drivers" approach, I stayed with the fishermen. And one of the first things they said was that bouillabaisse is not a soup to be had before a main course. It *is* the main course. They also said, and I guess this holds true for all seafood dishes prepared in coastal areas, that there are good times and not-such-good times for making bouillabaisse. Because the fish must be fresh it seems you should check the weather early in the morning—like before dawn—and never bother with bouillabaisse unless the weather is perfect. If it isn't, then the catch will probably be light and you can expect that the bouillabaisse won't be made with fresh fish.

The word "fresh" is so important that there are some in Marseille who would have you believe you can't possibly eat bouillabaisse in the evening because the fish will have lost their freshness. Lunch, they say, is the last chance.

Also, one should not expect a bouillabaisse to be ready in ten minutes. If it is, something's wrong. It should take twenty to thirty minutes to prepare. Again, the name explains the reason why. *Boui,* from *bouie,* which means boil; and *abaisso,* from *abeissa,* which means lower. You boil, and then you lower the heat. Actually, you end up doing it twice, and, therefore, the soup should be called bouillabaisse-bouillabaisse, but it's easy to see why it's not.

What you do once you've assembled your cast of minor sea monsters is not difficult. Leave the smaller fish whole and slice the larger ones after removing the heads and tails. For every six pounds of fish and crustaceans you'll need two cups of thinly sliced onions, one cup of thinly sliced leeks, three pounds of coarsely chopped tomatoes, a half cup of fennel or a half teaspoon of dried and crushed fennel seeds, a teaspoon of dried thyme, two bay leaves, two parsley sprigs, a quarter teaspoon of crushed saffron threads, plus salt and freshly ground black pepper.

All the vegetables and seasonings should be put in a large pot;

then you add either eight cups of water or six cups of water and two cups of white wine, plus three-quarters cup of olive oil. The crustaceans are put in, and the firm-fleshed fish go on top of the crustaceans. Make sure there's enough stock to cover the seafood, put on the lid, and boil the soup briskly. (The heat must be extremely high to properly combine the water, wine, and oil.) After eight or nine minutes turn off the heat and add the tender-fleshed fish. Turn on the heat again and boil the soup for another seven or eight minutes, being careful to thoroughly cook the firm-fleshed fish without overcooking the more tender ones.

After boiling the soup the second time, strain the stock into a serving bowl and spread the seafood on a platter. In Marseille the stew is served with a bread called *marette*. If you can find or make large croutons, so much the better; otherwise any bread will do. The idea is to put a *marette* in the middle of everyone's bowl and cover it with *rouille*, which is basically nothing more than a paste of pimiento, peppers, garlic, and, occasionally, mayonnaise. Several different pieces of fish should be arranged around the crouton; then the stock is poured over it all. As the crouton absorbs the broth the *rouille* mixes with it, combining the diverse flavors. And that is *one* of the ways that the real bouillabaisse appears.

One day after my visit to Marseille Herself insisted that I join her for her bouillabaisse, "*la vraie bouillabaisse.*" An ingredient she used that I hadn't seen in Marseille was *girelle,* a small fish found mainly in the waters around Cannes, which gives the saffron color of the soup a deeper hue. Instead of *rouille* she included several sauces: *verte,* ravigote, *rémoulade,* curry sauce, tartar sauce, and a *sauce piquante*. Each gave a new flavor to the bouillabaisse, and I was fascinated.

The following noon I invited the lady to accompany me on an

exploratory expedition, and we were off to the port at Villefranche, where we found *langouste* in the bouillabaisse and a waiter who promised us that this was the way it was always served in Marseille. That evening in Golfe-Juan we both took notice of the boiled potato sitting in the middle of the soup. We did not press the issue by mentioning that the restaurant owner claimed to have been raised in Marseille and assured us, "*Toujours les pommes de terre.*" The following afternoon in Cannes the bouillabaisse was without potatoes and without *langouste*. It was also without wine and without mussels, which the waiter said should never be included in a real bouillabaisse. What this bouillabaisse had going for it was a *rouille* made without mayonnaise. There was also a small bowl of grated cheese, to be sprinkled into the soup and onto the *rouille*.

That was when I decided to quit. I had "*bouillabaissed*" three times alone in Marseille and four times in the company of Herself, totaling seven soups in six days. I may not have the soup again for quite a while, thank you, but I now suggest a loosely drawn conclusion, deduced somewhere along the way: There are no right ways to make the real bouillabaisse, only a lot of wrong ways. And what it all seems to boil down to is, I guess, *chacun à sa vraie bouillabaisse*. But don't say that too loudly in Marseille.

This article originally appeared in *Gourmet*. Copyright © 1975 by Jeffrey Robinson. Reprinted with permission of the author.

Bouillabaisse:
Tempest in a Fishpot

BY GULLY WELLS

෴

editor's note
....

GULLY WELLS is literary editor for *Condé Nast Traveler* and writes
often about French people and places. She contributed this piece to the May
1994 issue.

When I was younger and even more foolish than I am now, I
spent a winter in a small house in the depths of Provence. For
some reason I became obsessed with the idea of cooking a bouillabaisse. And who better to advise me in this tricky enterprise, I
thought, than the two ladies who were my closest neighbors?

Not only was I foolish but I was also stupid and naive. Mme. X
and Mme. Y, who both fancied themselves the Julia Child of the
Midi, arrived in my kitchen "cruising for a bruising," and did
almost come to blows as they argued over what constituted a bouillabaisse *véritable*. Mme. X came from Toulon and was therefore
determined to add potatoes. "*Absolument dégueulasse*," spat Mme.
Y, who was born in Marseille but had acquired the Parisian habit of
including lobster, and even mussels, thus provoking the vitriolic
response from Mme. X: "*Complètement stupide*."

Whether this referred to the ingredients or to Mme. Y, I never
discovered. But what made the whole scene even more alarming was
the fact that both ladies were armed with large carving knives (to
attack the fish I'd got up at dawn to buy in the market, I hoped). In
the end, I silenced them both with generous portions of evenly distributed flattery and a couple of bottles of very expensive Domaine

Tempier rosé de Bandol. I can't even recall how the bouillabaisse turned out, but I do remember thinking I would *never, ever* get involved with cooking it again. Which I didn't for a good fifteen years, until last summer.

If there is any agreement at all on the subject of bouillabaisse, which I sometimes doubt, then maybe it begins and ends with the premise that it is a fish stew from the Mediterranean that can only—and should only—be cooked and eaten within spitting distance of that legendary inland sea. Not even my quarrelsome neighbors would argue with that. Some purists (usually people who come from Toulon or Marseille) will tell you that *la vraie bouillabaisse* is found only in their hometown and in a few places along the coast between these two culinary lodestars. Others will allow that the permissible area extends as far as Menton to the east. Still more fanatical aficionados, when you innocently ask which restaurant serves the best bouillabaisse, will look at you with a mixture of pity and contempt and tell you, quite categorically, that "*on ne mange pas de la* vraie *bouillabaisse dans un restaurant.*" The only possible place to eat this stew is in the house of somebody who knows how to cook it. And where might that be? Every time I asked that question—whether in New York, London, or the village where I happened to be staying, not far from Bandol—I received the same answer: "*Mais, chez Lulu Peyraud, bien sûr.*" But of course.

The Domaine Tempier, which has been in Mme. Peyraud's family since 1834, produces some of the best wine in this part of Provence, including the rosé that stopped Mme. X from killing Mme. Y in my kitchen all those years ago. The vineyard is small, seventy acres, and sits in a gentle valley between Toulon and Marseille, with the family's old *mas* (farmhouse) at its center, surrounded by vines and cypress trees, its terrace shaded by yet more vines trained over an ancient pergola. An outside staircase, smothered in ivy, climbs up one side of the house, and around the back there is a clump of southern France's ubiquitous plane trees, their mottled bark made of what looks like Stormin' Norman's cast-off battle fatigues. There are various salons and a formal dining room—kept cool and dark in the summer months, with the shutters closed—but the heart of this house is its kitchen. A huge fireplace dominates the room. Raised off the ground, it was built as much for cooking as for *chauffage.* A copper cauldron sits like a throne at the center of the hearth and is the only pot that Lulu would ever *dream* of cooking bouillabaisse in. The rest of the kitchen is firmly located in the last century; no (visible) refrigerator, stove, or dishwasher. These regrettable modern intrusions are carefully hidden away in cupboards behind antique wooden doors. For Lulu Peyraud is a perfectionist, and her aesthetic code extends from her house to the wine her family produces, to the food she is famous for cooking . . . and, most especially, to her bouillabaisse.

A bouillabaisse day begins at dawn, when Mme. Peyraud sets off for the market in Bandol. Although certain fish are considered essential—*rascasses* (scorpion fish), *baudroie* (anglerfish), *rouquiers* (wrasses), *vives* (weevers), and *serrans* (combers)—any number and variety of others may be added *selon l'arrivage,* or "depending on what the fishermen bring in that morning." (Incidentally, if you ever see this phrase, or just the initials SA, on a menu, you are already in the right kind of restaurant.) *Murène* (moray eel), *mérou* (grouper), and *Saint-Pierre* (John Dory) are all especially prized, but the list could also easily include *loup de mer, chapon, rouget grondin,* as well as octopus, crab, and the controversial mussels.

A different variety of small rockfish is used to make the broth, or "*soupe,*" that is the basis for bouillabaisse. These tiny fish, some as small as an inch long, include spiky red and black *rascasses;* miniature green crabs known as *favouilles,* which add a peppery flavor; and *cigales de mer,* which are considered the sweetest of all the crustaceans.

Assembling this encyclopedia of fish is only the beginning. Or, as Etienne Fauche, the onetime mayor of Cassis, put it, "The secret of a successful bouillabaisse may be summed up as follows: live fish in large variety, good olive oil, and top-quality saffron. The only difficulty in executing this dish consists in bringing it to a boil rapidly and fiercely."

Which is where Lulu's copper cauldron enters the picture. The name should give us a clue: *Bouillir* means to boil and *baisser* means to lower. And so the cooking principle is established. First you boil like crazy (to prevent the oil and water from separating), and then you quickly lower the heat so that the entire cooking process never takes more than twenty minutes.

If a blood feud can start over the ingredients that belong in a true bouillabaisse, then whole wars must have been fought over how, when, and where the dish was conceived. It's possible that the idea came with the Greeks when they established a settlement in what was to become Marseille around 600 B.C. Although they did introduce the olive (one essential part of bouillabaisse) to Provence, they can't have been the first people on earth to think of putting some fish in a pot and cooking them over a fire. Fish stews existed wherever there were fish. Along the Mediterranean coast of Tuscany, in Leghorn, you find *cacciucco livornese,* which, like bouillabaisse, is made from many different kinds of fish; in France there is the *cotriade* in Brittany; in the Basque country, *tioro;* in Spain, the Catalan dish *suquet;* and in New England, clam chowder. Essentially, bouillabaisse was a stew that fishermen made on the beach (over a driftwood fire, which lent it a slightly smoky flavor) in a large pot with the small leftover fish that they couldn't sell. They added a few stalks of wild fennel, olive oil, and seawater in lieu of salt. *Et voilà!* Not food that any remotely well-off person would have eaten until this century, when everything was turned upside down and bouillabaisse became one of the most expensive and desirable dishes at any restaurant along the Côte d'Azur.

Lulu's recipe is not so very different from the fisherman's special. One of her sons builds a fruitwood fire outdoors, and the long table is set up on the terrace. While Lulu starts cooking, glasses of chilled rosé or a young red Domaine Tempier are passed around, with platters of toasted bread spread with *tapénade* and a puree of anchovies. (Note: The "toast" is even better if the slices of bread are simply left to dry in the hot sun.) The *soupe* is prepared in advance—the small rockfish, olive oil, tomatoes, garlic, onion, and fennel are boiled together and strained. The saffron, serious fish, and potatoes are added to the cauldron after the fire has subsided a bit. And the *rouille* (a deep orange, garlicky mayonnaise that contains cayenne peppers, bread crumbs, saffron, and the liver of the *baudroie* fish) is put on the table.

Twenty minutes later we sit down. First the *soupe* is served over toast that has been rubbed with garlic and covered with *rouille;* then, on separate plates, as a second course, comes the fish, accompanied by yet more *rouille* and just enough *soupe* to keep the fish moist. And what wine to serve with bouillabaisse? "*Un vin nerveux,*" Lulu said, which I took to mean something as young and naive and nervous as I'd been when I first tried to cook this inimitable Provençal dish. I later discovered that what she meant was indeed a young wine, one that was a little "jumpy," in which you can still taste the tannin, giving it a certain sharpness and clarity. A bottle of Domaine Tempier (*rouge*) de Bandol 1990 would be perfect.

Unlike her fanatical fans, Mme. Peyraud did not claim that the only place one could possibly imagine eating bouillabaisse was *chez elle* or *chez* anyone in particular. Both she and her close friend and neighbor Richard Olney were only too happy to point me in the direction of the best local restaurants that serve bouillabaisse . . . "*mais toujours selon l'arrivage.*"

If you believe the Greeks and Waverley Root, and *one* of my argumentative neighbors, then Marseille is where you begin. And if you believe Mme. Peyraud, as I'm more inclined to do, then the place to head for is Chez Fonfon. Almost impossible to find, this restaurant is hidden in one of the only *calanques* left in the heart of Marseille. These inlets, which are really miniature fjords, existed all along the coast, but those within the city have been built over, with the exception of the Vallon des Auffes. The only way to reach it is by walking along the seafront and then, when you come to the Monument aux Morts d'Orient, taking the first, *extremely* steep staircase down to your right. At the very bottom you will find a tiny inlet, an oasis in the middle of the city. Little fishing boats slurp about on the water, cafés and restaurants crowd the quay, and the feeling, with no cars to intrude, is of *le vieux Marseille*.

Chez Fonfon looks as though it has always been here. The owner, M. Mounier, an old friend of Mme. Peyraud's, has been cooking bouillabaisse since the 1950s. This is about as far away from the *menu touristique* as you can get. The restaurant is small—if you discount the second floor (which you should), there are only about fifteen tables—and the food is presented without fuss, frills, or pretensions. You sit looking out the window at the boats that have brought in your fish, and if you are interested (as I was), your waiter will tell you the name of each fish as he presents it, carefully arranged on a platter, before it is cooked.

Although fish is obviously the thing to order here, should somebody—God forbid—request *steak frites* (as my brother did), there will be no raised eyebrows, just the best grilled steak and the crispest *frites,* produced at the same time as the aquarium full of petit *chapon, galinette, rouquier, congre,* and *rouget grondin.* Afterward, there are *îles flottantes,* but all I could cope with after this surfeit of sea creatures was a *digestif* of marc and espresso.

At the other geographical extreme of bouillabaisse country (assuming you are of the ultraorthodox persuasion) lies Toulon, and a few miles east of Toulon, in Le Pradet, on a rocky promontory surrounded by olive trees, sits L'Oursinado. If Chez Fonfon is Marcel Pagnol country, then L'Oursinado is where Alain Delon and Romy Schneider would have gone for (an adulterous) bouillabaisse in the sixties. It has an air of slightly passé, but still sexy, chic. L'Oursinado is hidden away on its own spit of land. The outdoor tables are shaded, the air is scented by umbrella pines, and far, far below, the blue Mediterranean sparkles as the waves crash against the rocks. Here, you are asked to order your bouillabaisse when you book your table, and when the fish are presented (cooked) on their cork platter (to retain the heat), they look like a still life painted by an early Dutch master. The hideous spiky *rascasse,* whose mysterious role in the bouillabaisse is to bring out the flavor of the other fish, since it has no discernible taste of its own, stares at you with unblinking eyes, its mouth agape; little red crabs and mussels are scattered around the edge of the platter, and in the middle are thick slices of conger eel, pink *rouget,* and firm, white *loup de mer.* The only way to eat the smaller fish is with your hands, so after the feast is over, finger bowls and clean napkins are produced along with madame's *spécialité de la maison:* crème caramel. The trees shine with garlands of tiny lights as the ritual bottle of locally produced marc appears on the table, to settle all those fishy creatures that I imagined were still swimming around inside me.

Richard Olney, an American who lives near Mme. Peyraud and an acknowledged master when it comes to the art of bouillabaisse, once wrote: "Bouillabaisse is never far from my mind—the concept representing a sort of absolute value, a yardstick by which other fish stews may be measured."

It is both subtle and complex, its provenance stretching backward into the murky depths of time and sea. Bouillabaisse has always been the reigning monarch of the fish-stew kingdom.

Infused with love (one legend has it that the *soupe* was invented by Venus to put her husband, Vulcan, to sleep when she had a rendezvous with Mars) and hate (how could I forget Mme. X and Mme. Y and their knives), in this part of Provence, at least, it is an elemental part of life. The olive oil, the fennel, the saffron, the garlic, the fish—they are all of a seamless piece, something that nobody would dream of questioning, except, of course, when it comes to what constitutes *"une vraie bouillabaisse."*

Sound Bites

Brasserie New York, Quai des Belges, Marseille; 04.91.33.60.98.

Chez Aldo, La Madrague-de-Montredon; 04.91.73.31.55.

Chez Fonfon, Vallon des Auffes, Marseille; 04.91.52.14.38.

L'Oursinado, Le Pradet, Toulon; 04.94.21.77.06.

Tétou, Le Golfe-Juan; 04.93.63.71.16.

The Chickpea's Shining Moment

BY CARA DE SILVA

editor's note

I have not conducted an extensive survey of *socca*. In fact, the only *socca* I've ever had is Thérésa's, and while that hardly allows me to qualify it as the best, I, too, hope that *socca* will still be scraped and served off the top of a big steel drum at the edge of Nice's daily *marché*, for another twenty years and more.

CARA DE SILVA is a former food editor of *Newsday* and the author of *In Memory's Kitchen: A Legacy from the Women of Terezin* (Jason Aronson, 1996).

Positioned in front of a long line of customers at Nice's Marché aux Fleurs, Thérésa Ashor stands scraping *socca* into small paper cones. "My doll" . . . "My sweet" . . . "My cousin," she says, as each buyer approaches the pan that holds the huge chickpea flour crepe. "Here, let me give you a little extra because you are so kind" . . . "so dear" . . . "so beautiful."

I watch this Niçois soft sell appreciatively until finally it is my turn.

Thérésa, an earthy woman in heavy makeup and dangling earrings, smoothes her apron, readjusts her black cap, and cocks her head. "How would you like it?" she asks, smiling at me. "Soft?" "Well done?" "Crispy?" I lick my lips. My mouth waters. But I don't know the answer. It has been more than twenty years since I had my first—and only—taste of *socca* at a New York street fair. Remarkably, I have never forgotten it.

True, my devotion to chickpeas is fierce. Ask others about their favorite foods and they invoke chocolate, or maybe caviar, ice cream or pizza.

Personally I think this humble legume can hold its own with any of them.

Give me *socca*, spicy Indian channa dal, creamy hummus, or even chickpeas straight out of a can, and I am contented.

But it wasn't only love of *pois chiches* that made this rustic preparation linger in my memory. Somehow, to me, the venerable *socca* symbolized an older, perhaps less dazzling, but more romantic Nice—that of Queen Victoria, Matisse, the czars, the early days of the Promenade des Anglais, summering English aristocrats, the Belle Époque and the distinctive Niçois when they were still Italian speakers. All were people, places and times that I found captivating.

Certainly, other traditional dishes were evocative and delicious, too. Who could resist *pan bagnat, pissaladière, salade niçoise* or the remarkable *tourte de blettes* (a sweet or savory "pie" made from Swiss chard)? Yet it was only *socca* that held my imagination completely in thrall.

Of course, the black pepper-dusted pancake that lay like curls of scrambled egg in my paper cone that day in the Marché aux Fleurs was far better than the one whose memory I had cherished for so long. Both here, at Chez Thérésa on the Cours Saleya, as well as in the Brooklyn version, the dish was a simple baked mixture of chickpea flour, water and a little olive oil, which together produced a taste more seductive than that simple combination of ingredients would suggest. But there was more still to this one. Smoky from the wood-fired oven in which it had cooked, its texture at once soft and crisp, the spicy flavor of the pepper complementing the nutty flavor of the chickpeas, it exceeded even my well-honed expectations.

And it also made a perfect beginning to an informal round of *socca* eating—and research. My stay in Nice was to be a brief one, but while there I wanted to do more than get my fill of *socca*. I wanted to find out as much as I could about it.

Advised by the tourist office to restrict my explorations to the port, the Cours Saleya and Vieux Nice, the oldest part of the city and the area where *socca* was most widely available, I ambled curiously through streets lined with the graceful buildings of other eras and pictured them filled with the *socca* eaters of their time. And I wandered, too, past restaurant signs painted with folk figures in traditional Niçois dress. *"Aqui sí manja una bouona socca"* ("Here we eat a good socca"), said one in dialect.

"For Nice people, *socca* is a habit, a very old habit, not something folkloric," Yvette Blacas of the Lou Pilha Leva Restaurant told me in a gently chastising tone when I asked for information about this native dish. "They eat it as you would eat croissant or pain au chocolat in Paris. Any time. Elsewhere in France, people eat sandwiches, but here *socca*. On Sunday afternoons, people walk in the Promenade des Anglais eating *socca* from paper cones, or they come here for *socca* afterward. People from Nice eat *socca* all the time."

The more I explored, the more my eyes told me she was right. But why? I knew a comparable pancake existed in Toulon. Another, called *cecina,* came from Tuscany. And from Fred Plotkin's *Recipes from Paradise: Life and Food on the Italian Riviera,* I learned that there was a chickpea crepe called *farinata* in Liguria. Was one of these the source for all the others? And what was it that had brought the omnipresent *socca* to this sensuous city on the Bay of Angels?

Local legends about its origins were intriguing. The most common credited the dish to a group of workmen from the Italian village of Cuneo who centuries ago emigrated to Vallouise, a town in southeastern France famous for its pottery. Out of the chickpea flour the workers carried with them, they made pancakes in the same kilns in which they baked pots and bricks.

Then, years later, too old to continue their hard work, they moved to Nice, bringing the city the beginnings of *socca*. (Although it is in the Piedmont, the province of Cuneo abuts Liguria, so the crepe may well have started out as Liguria's *farinata,* crossed the border into Cuneo, and then continued on into France.)

The story is charming. But I prefer a different one. Recounted by Jacky Bonnet of the restaurant René Socca—who also informed me that in Niçois dialect "*socca*" means a "spanking"—it goes something like this: Centuries ago, when the Turks attacked Nice, they camped next to its walls and did their cooking there. To rout the invading army, the people of Nice threw hot olive oil down on its soldiers. When they fled, the chickpea flour pancakes they had been making were left behind. (In an amusing variant, the hot oil lands on small mounds of raw chickpea flour, cooking it, and thus producing the first *socca*.)

Unfortunately, there was no time to try to determine which of these stories was fiction and which, if any, was fact (the Turks did invade Nice in 1543 under Barbarossa, the Turkish admiral, but did they leave *socca* behind?). Yet each added flavor to the different versions I tasted as I made my way around Vieux Nice. Though I couldn't discriminate among the crepes like a native, the subtle differences in style between makers, and the effect of wood, gas, and electric ovens on *socca*, began to reveal themselves to me as I sampled.

At René Socca, where tables spill onto the street, the pancake, cooked in a wood-fired oven, was thicker and chewier than the one at the Marché aux Fleurs, but still delicious. At Lou Pilha Leva it was tasty, but cooked by electricity (a measure to some of the loss of tradition), it lacked the ancient flavor added by fire. At Les Caves Ricord, the cooking medium was gas and the preparation definitely less compelling. And at Nissa Socca, the addition of a pinch of cumin to the batter gave a lively and unexpected accent to the dish.

But in the end—perhaps because hers was the first I had had after all those years of waiting—Thérésa's *socca* seemed to me to be the best.

Before leaving to catch my train for Paris, I returned to her stand at the Marché aux Fleurs for a last taste and a last look. As I watched, fragrant pans of *socca* arrived on a bicycle, brought from the glowing oven where the dish is made by her husband; savvy market pigeons pounced on crusty crumbs of *socca* as soon as they fell to the ground, and Thérésa, serving a nattily dressed customer, coyly addressed him as "my handsome one."

Already nostalgic, I reached into my handbag for a postcard I had bought during my stay. Though the antique photograph it reproduced was taken a century ago, it showed a *socca* seller vending her wares almost exactly where Thérésa stood now. The comparison was comforting. It made me feel that even if I don't get back to Nice for another twenty years, *socca* will still be there.

A Stirring Treatise on Ratatouille

BY JEFFREY ROBINSON

editor's note

The reason ratatouille in both the U.S. and France is often a tired cliché, and bad, is because its simplicity is deceiving. Ratatouille, much like the Spanish soup gazpacho, is much more complex than putting all the ingredients together in a pot and cooking until tender (or, in the case of gazpacho, blending the ingredients until pureed). In fact, for ratatouille to achieve its depth of flavor, most or all of the vegetables must be cooked separately before they meet in one pot. This is more time-consuming than it is difficult, but the reward is worth the effort.

You may want to prepare the authentic ratatouille recipes featured in this piece before a trip to Provence in order to recognize a true version of it during your stay. Note that a handsome edition of Jacques Médecin's cookbook is available in many shops in Nice. (Note too that Médecin is no longer mayor; an anti-Semitic supporter of the National Front, he fled the country in the early 1990s when it was reported he had diverted money for the Nice Opera into his bank account. He stayed in Uruguay until 1995, when he was extradited to France, and died in 1998.)

JEFFREY ROBINSON, whose work is featured elsewhere in this book, wrote over six hundred published articles and short stories during his twelve years in the south of France, including this one, which appeared in the June 1979 issue of *Gourmet*. He moved to Great Britain in 1982 to concentrate on writing books.

G ood ratatouille (pronounced something like rat-ta-two-ya) is very good and bad ratatouille (pronounced exactly the same way) is very bad, and, according to the little old ladies in Nice who have been making this vegetable stew for fifty or sixty years, it's all in the stirring.

You find these little old ladies wearing black dresses and black scarves, carrying netted shopping sacks through the morning market at the Cours Saleya in the heart of Old Nice. They're there every day, early, before the tourists arrive, and they bargain with other little old ladies who wear black dresses and black scarves and who sell the fresh produce. Buyer and seller say, "*Bonjour, Madame*," to each other. Then the woman buying inspects the tomatoes. She shakes her head no, and the woman selling says that they are very good for cooking. The woman buying says no again but continues to look until she spots two or three that will pass. The woman selling takes them and then reaches down to find three or four or five others before she puts them all together on the scale. "*Voilà*," she says. "These are the best tomatoes in the market today."

But the woman buying mumbles, "They are overripe and too expensive for this time of the season."

The woman selling, after checking to see that no one is within earshot, replies, "You can have these for twenty *centimes* less per kilo."

The woman buying shrugs that she would only take them for thirty *centimes* less per kilo.

The woman selling nods, "*D'accord,* just don't tell my husband."

Chances are good that even with the thirty-*centimes*-less-per-kilo bargain the woman selling has recouped her losses by her reading of the scale and that the woman buying knows it, but that neither cares because this is all part of a game they've been playing for heaven knows how many years. Anyway, the woman buying now has her tomatoes and is free to move on to the next stall where she can play the same game for her zucchini.

Once upon a time one of the women buying was Tante Mietta, the cook in the home of the grandmother of the present Mayor of Nice. And when it comes to ratatouille, which in Niçois is la rata-touïa nissarda, the local favorite son, Jacques Médecin, says he's willing to put his reputation on the line, even in off-election years.

"I grew up," he relates, "in a house where good food was a family tradition, and I feel strongly about the local cuisine." The mayor is also, by the way, author of a guide to Niçois cooking. "Among other things, the region around Nice offers arid mountainous countryside, extraordinary climate, pretty girls, flowers, fruits, vegetables, tough and lusty youth, art, and a very special way of cooking. Dishes like ratatouille are typical. And it seems to me that my generation is the final depository of these ancestral traditions."

The mayor's grandmother, under the sharp eye of Tante Mietta, inscribed the recipes of her generation in a notebook. "Here's where you find the ratatouille that Nice is famous for," the mayor told me. "One of the problems with this dish, in particular, is that all too often it turns out wrong; the ingredients aren't right, it's overcooked or badly cooked or undercooked; it's not sufficiently mixed, it's hard, it's muddy. Contrary to popular belief, good ratatouille is a time-consuming and difficult dish to prepare. It demands your patience and attention. But once you've tasted what it is all about, once you've tasted the ratatouille of my grandmother and Tante Mietta, you'll see why it enjoys the reputation it does."

In their recipe Grandmother and Tante Mietta claimed that there is no exact proportion of ingredients for a precise number of servings. Besides, ratatouille is such a versatile dish that they always made much more than they could possibly use at any one meal. It would keep for days, and there were literally dozens of ways it could be served.

Based on this, the mayor suggests two pounds of eggplant, two pounds of green peppers, two pounds of zucchini, two and a half pounds of tomatoes, two pounds of onions, five pinches of crumbled thyme, ten small cloves of garlic, one bunch of parsley, twenty basil leaves, then flour, oil, salt, and pepper.

Slice the eggplant and zucchini into half rounds and very lightly flour them. Put them into different saucepans. Rid the peppers of their seeds and stems and cut them into long thin slices. Put them into a third saucepan. Finely chop the onions and put them into yet another saucepan.

Add a little olive oil to each pan, about three tablespoons' worth, and very lightly simmer the vegetables. You must allow each to cook at its own speed, and you'll know it is done when the skin is soft enough to be easily pierced by a fork.

As the vegetables are ready, combine them in a large pot, still over a low flame, and add salt and pepper to taste. What you're doing here is trying to bring the four vegetables together at the time when each has lost its toughness yet guarded its own distinct flavor.

Now, while this is going on, in a large pot with a heavy bottom, you should be simmering in olive oil the garlic, which you've chopped, the basil leaves, the herbs, and the tomatoes, which you've crushed. This is to form a thick sauce, and it will require frequent stirring.

When the sauce is ready and the vegetables are ready—and be careful with the timing because it's easy to miss and must be right—pour the sauce over the vegetables and continue to stir. In the Niçois dialect *rata* means dish or meal and *touïa* means stirred, and, if you haven't stirred enough, don't be too shocked to find dinner closely resembling a colorful rubber cement.

Once the vegetables have been well mixed into the tomatoes and herbs, pour off any excess oil and serve.

Slightly different is a variation on the theme by sculptor James Ritchie. He's been living in the hills of Vence, just behind Nice, since coming from Montreal seventeen years ago. He says he never had a Tante Mietta, so he had to learn the hard way—by trial and error. Some seventeen ratatouille years later, at least according to a local American writer who shall remain nameless (the very same who during the hungriest days of his période de vache maigre found out, also by trial and error, which of his friends knew how to cook), Ritchie is as creative when it comes to ratatouille as he is with large blocks of pure white Carrara marble.

To serve six to eight (freeloaders know talent when they see it), he starts with six medium-size onions, a dozen good-size tomatoes, two medium-size eggplants, six medium-size zucchini, one green pepper, one red pepper, five garlic cloves, three bay leaves, plus olive oil, salt, freshly ground black pepper, thyme, rosemary, and basil.

Peel and chop the onions and put them in a large saucepan with warm water and salt. You'll need enough water so that the onions won't burn. Put them over a low flame and cover.

Then peel the tomatoes and set them aside.

Cut the zucchini and the eggplant into small pieces. Chop the garlic and the herbs and mix them in a casserole with salt. Once that's done, mix in the zucchini and the eggplant.

Chop the peppers into one-half-inch squares.

By now the onions should be transparent, which means they are tender, and that's when you mix them with the zucchini and eggplant and herbs and one half cup of olive oil. Stir and cover the casserole, putting it back on the low flame for fifteen to twenty minutes. But keep an eye on it and don't forget to stir.

When the vegetables are partially cooked, say at about the fifteen-minute mark, add the green and red peppers.

Like the old "pinch of this and pinch of that" business, you'll have to judge the timing for yourself, although the vegetables should simmer twenty to thirty minutes. And that's when you add a good-sized bunch of finely chopped basil, then the tomatoes, and another one half cup of olive oil. Cover the ratatouille and cook—but stir frequently—for about thirty minutes more.

Ritchie insists that the dish must simmer and *never* boil and should be served over large elbow pasta or brown rice, with a covering of freshly grated Parmesan cheese.

Although I'm relatively certain that Jacques Médecin and James Ritchie have never personally discussed each other's ratatouille— "You're a great sculptor"; "You're a great mayor . . ." is perhaps the closest they've ever come to exchanging recipes—it wouldn't be surprising to find them agreeing that ratatouille is one of the world's most versatile dishes. In fact, its multitude of uses is one of the most interesting things about it. Be it *à la Médecin* or *à la Ritchie*, ratatouille is the mainstay of the simple Niçois family's summer meal. The dish is delicious, economical, and can easily be disguised in an infinite number of ways.

You can wrap an omelette around it for a fascinating vegetable breakfast. Or, mix large chunks of tuna with it and bake it as a casserole for *ratatouille à la basquaise*.

It mixes with ravioli (*à la provençale*) or works on crêpes with finely chopped parsley (*crêpes fourrées*). You can stuff tomatoes with it or serve it as a bed for cannelloni (also *à la provençale*).

Put the ratatouille in a pie plate with a thin pie crust and bake it. Or, if you like, add some poached eggs to the top. That's called *tartelette à la grecque.*

If you're into making your own pizza, try it with ratatouille instead of ordinary tomato sauce and then get really creative by adding slices of ham, green olives, chunks of tuna, ground beef, mussels, mushrooms, anchovies, whatever.

Along the south coast of France, *daurade* is frequently baked on a bed of ratatouille, but certainly any fish can be prepared that way. Try it with sea bass, adding olive oil, thyme, marjoram, salt, and pepper. Under a medium flame it should take twenty-five to thirty minutes.

Stop a dozen Niçois and you're likely to get a dozen different ways of reusing ratatouille, but the favorite of that previously referred to American writer is *ratatouille pipérade,* which as a July or August meal dazzles even the most finicky politicians and sculptors.

Take your ratatouille and put it in a casserole and break a few eggs over it. Then add salt, cayenne, and various herbs (here the general heading *herbes de Provence* covers a multitude of sins). Broil the dish under a low flame and serve it with smoked ham or spicy sausage. On the side should be some heavy dark bread and the local red *vino.*

Yes, the timing of the ratatouille—that is, getting all the vegetables to wind up cooked at the same time without having any overcooked or undercooked—isn't the easiest thing to manage. But once you've got that down pat, the combinations are endless. In all honesty, though, I must admit that I've never really put my ratatouille to the ultimate test: I've never invited any of those little old ladies from the morning market home to try to out-ratatouille them. That brave I'm not. There are some little old ladies in Nice who would have you believe that to serve the dish in any way, shape, or form other than as plain and simple ratatouille is a sacrilege. (In some cases, however, their granddaughters are suitably impressed, which quite frankly is what the *pipérade* is all about.)

Yet, when it comes to ratatouille, those little old ladies are full of advice, and listening to them is worth getting out of bed at some awful hour, like dawn. One tells you that you must never skimp on the olive oil. She says that you cannot use too much, but that if you use too little your ratatouille will not be edible.

Another reminds you to always, *toujours,* always add the tomatoes after the rest of the vegetables are cooked. If you don't, she promises, the results will be disastrous.

Yet another says you must simmer the vegetables. Don't boil them. And be sure to use freshly ground black pepper and sea salt and very fresh vegetables.

And then every one of them, a clear one hundred percent of those little old ladies, says stir . . . and stir . . . and stir.

Occasionally, one of their husbands comes along and says, "No one can make ratatouille like my wife."

And that means *no one*—except the next guy's wife when the next guy is about to tell the same story.

"Nope," he goes on. "My wife makes the finest ratatouille you ever ate. You can tell how superior it is once you've tasted how bad a bad ratatouille can be."

At first he uses the word *mauvaise* to mean bad, and after a moment he decides that what he meant to say was *dégoûtante,* which is considerably worse than the usual bad.

"I guess the most abominable concoction I ever tasted was the ratatouille they served us during the war."

It seems that ratatouille, at least for some companies, found its way into mess halls as the French equivalent of the "beloved" American creamed chipped beef on toast.

"They served us ratatouille for breakfast, lunch, and dinner, and I can still remember the song we made up about it."

At this point the little old ladies walk away, and someone says, "Oh, Georges, not again." But Georges takes a deep breath and sings, "*C'est pas de la soupe, c'est du rata. . . .*"

Army songs being what they are the world over, Georges' song freely translated means that Jacques Médecin and James Ritchie and all the little old ladies at the morning market in Old Nice know a hell of a lot more about ratatouille than the French Army.

For those who might find the "pinch of this and pinch of that" method a little too vague, we append specific amounts and measurements.

Ratatouille Jacques Médecin

Cut 2 pounds green peppers lengthwise into ¼-inch strips and put them in a heavy saucepan with 3 tablespoons olive oil. Chop 2 pounds onions and put them in another heavy saucepan with 3 tablespoons olive oil. Halve lengthwise 2 pounds small eggplant, cut it crosswise into ¼-inch slices, and in a colander toss it with ¼ cup flour. Put the eggplant in a large heavy saucepan with 3 tablespoons olive oil. Halve lengthwise 2 pounds zucchini, scrubbed and trimmed, cut it into ¼-inch slices, and toss it in a colander with ¼ cup flour. Put the zucchini in another large heavy saucepan with 3 tablespoons olive oil. Cook each vegetable over low heat, stirring, for 10 minutes for the onion, 12 minutes for the eggplant, and 15 minutes for the pepper and the zucchini, or until each is tender. Transfer the vegetables to a large flameproof casserole, add salt and pepper to taste, and simmer the vegetables over low heat, stirring, for 30 minutes, or until the mixture is a very coarse purée.

In another large flameproof casserole combine 2½ pounds tomatoes, cored and quartered, 10 small garlic cloves, chopped, 2 cups parsley sprigs, minced, 20 fresh basil leaves, or 6 teaspoons dried, and ¾ teaspoon thyme and simmer the mixture in ¼ cup olive oil, breaking up the tomatoes and stirring, for 30 minutes, or until the sauce is thickened. Stir the sauce into the eggplant mixture and simmer the mixture, stirring, for 10 minutes, or until it is a coarse purée. Skim off any excess oil. Makes about 4 quarts.

Ratatouille James Ritchie

In a saucepan barely cover 6 onions, chopped, with salted water, bring the water to a boil, and simmer the mixture, covered, for 20 minutes. In a saucepan of boiling water blanch 12 large tomatoes for 30 seconds and peel and core them. Cut 6 zucchini, scrubbed and trimmed, and 2 eggplants into ½-inch dice. Mince 5 garlic cloves with 3 bay leaves and fresh basil (or dried, if necessary) to taste, in a large flameproof casserole combine the mixture, and add thyme and rosemary to taste. Stir in the eggplant and the zucchini. Cut 1 green pepper and 1 red pepper into ½-inch pieces. Drain the onion and add it to the eggplant mixture with ½ cup olive oil. Simmer the mixture, covered, stirring, for 15 minutes, add the peppers, and simmer the mixture, covered, stirring, for 15 minutes. Stir in the tomatoes, a handful of fresh basil leaves, chopped, or 3 tablespoons dried, ½ cup olive oil, and salt and pepper to taste and simmer the mixture, covered, breaking up the tomatoes and stirring, for 30 minutes, or until the vegetables are tender but not soft. Simmer the ratatouille, uncovered, for 15 minutes, or until it is thickened. Makes about 4 quarts.

Provence's Almond Calissons

BY KATHLEEN BECKETT

~

editor's note

    Calissons d'Aix can now be found in specialty food shops in the U.S., but nothing beats buying them in one of the beautiful shops on Aix's Cours Mirabeau. And although perhaps less traditional, I swoon over the *calissons* dipped in chocolate.

Aix-en-Provence is known for many things—the shielding plane trees lining its broad Cours Mirabeau, the healing waters sprinkling in its fountains, the elegance of its centuries-old buildings and the excellence of its ancient university. One of the city's biggest attractions, however, is a little iced diamond of marzipan, the celebrated *calisson d'Aix*.

The almond candies appear in the windows of the town's plentiful pastry and candy shops, sitting prettily on paper doilies, wrapped in ribboned cellophane sacks, or packaged in white boxes that echo the *calisson*'s distinctive shape. Redolent of the sweet almonds and mellow Cavaillon melons that flourish in this part of France, the *calisson d'Aix* has been compared, with typical French eloquence, to the paintings of Cézanne and the music of Mozart, often part of the repertory of the city's renowned music festival.

Some of the most delectable almonds come from the South of France (though these days Provence no longer grows them abundantly, so almonds are imported from the Mediterranean basin). With the assistance of the Industrial Revolution, Aix became a candy center in the 1800s, and its numerous confiseries produced almond nougats, almond pralines and almonds dipped in white icing, called *dragées*. (A traditional gift for baptisms, *dragées* are often displayed in candy shops next to pairs of white baby booties.) But any candy maker can produce almond bars and marzipan. A *marc deposée*—a designation similar to an *appellation controllée*—assures that only those in Aix can make a true *calisson*. And every year, the city's dozen or so *calissoniers* do just that, producing more than 500 tons of the singular sweet to sell from their family-run shops or to ship overseas.

One of the oldest *calissoniers* is the exquisite A La Reine Jeanne, a white-and-gold jewelbox of a candy shop with marble floors and etched glass vitrines on the Cours Mirabeau. The store is named after the wife of King Réné, who, history records, served the first *calisson* back in 1454. It is run today by Joseph Brissac and his sisters, great-great-grandchildren of the firm's founders.

A La Reine Jeanne sells *calissons* under a crystal chandelier and makes them in its dark, cramped basement. The method has remained unchanged for five generations. A half-dozen rather rudimentary machines and three young apprentices do the work. A young man in rubber boots runs the almonds between two metal rollers that look like the ringers of an old washing machine to rid them of their brown husks, then shovels them into another machine to crush them. He next mixes the almonds with fruit confits of glazed Cavaillon melon and oranges in a huge metal pot with rotating blades. Then he scoops the mix into a deep metal pan. The golden paste gets another crushing and the addition of enough sugar to make the health-minded blanch as pale as the sweet almond paste.

Two young women in pink dresses and white caps and aprons then take over; their duty is to fashion the fruit-and-nut mixture into *calissons*. They push the paste with the palms of their hands into a form like a stencil with thirty-six tear-shaped holes backed with white rice paper. The candies used to be cut by hand, in crisscrosses, which resulted in their diamond shape. Age has softened the angles and the *calisson* is now rounded, more like a pointed oval a couple of inches long. After slathering the paste with royal icing, a mix of egg whites and sugar, the women lift trays of the boat-shaped sweetmeats into a huge oven, and bake for twenty minutes.

Calissons taste smoother and more cakelike than traditional marzipan. One variety is dipped in chocolate. Their flavor varies from house to house, as each *calissonier* carefully guards his own secret recipe. One will use a touch more melon, another a twist more orange. "But I never use California almonds. They have no taste," said Jean-Pierre Borrelly, *calissonier* at the Confiserie Brémond Fils, a fixture on the Cours Mirabeau since 1830.

The right ingredients are essential. To make the true *calisson d'Aix,* Mr. Borrelly quotes Marçel Pagnol: "You need one-third almonds, one-third fruit confits, one-third sugar, and a quarter savoir faire."

Aix residents point out that the number three is part of local lore. The *calisson* not only has three ingredients, but three layers—icing, paste and rice paper. The city was founded in the year 123 by Caius Sextius Calvimus (three names) and originally called Aquae Sextiae Saluvium (three names). The designation was later changed to Aix-en-Provence (again, three names) or, simply, Aix (three letters). *Calissons* are served three times a year—on Sept. 1, Christmas and Easter—at Notre Dame de la Seds to commemorate the end of the great plague of 1630. With its bottom layer of rice, or azym, paper, the *calisson* replaces the host and is believed to guard against sudden death and contagion. The priest offers the sweetmeats from his chalice, repeating three times *"venite ad calicem"* (come to the chalice). The congregation replies, thrice, with the Provençal *"venes toui i calissoun"* (we are coming).

It's generally believed the religious rite gave the candy its name, but, as with most things, there are two sides to the story. The eminent Provençal literary figure, Frédéric Mistral, insisted the *calisson*

was named after the *canissoun*, a reeded platter on which *confiseries* display their confections. The almond treat has been muse to others in the arts over the years. The troubadour Claude Bruyes sang its praises back in the sixteenth century, and Madame de Sévigné devoted one of her letters to the *calisson*, thanking her daughter for sending a shipment to her in Paris.

Aix's *calisson* makers made present-day history last year by baking the world's largest *calisson*, a feat documented by the *Guinness Book of World Records*. Almost 500 pounds heavy, 12 feet long and 5 feet tall, the mammoth *calisson* was wheeled past a proud citizenry down the Cours Mirabeau, under its plane trees and past its three fountains, then devoured by all those desiring a taste of Provence in a bite.

Satisfying a Sweet Tooth

Calissons d'Aix are sold in pastry and candy shops throughout Aix-en-Provence. Prices are the same: about $2.50 a 100 grams (less than a quarter-pound, or about four *calissons*), $3.50 for the chocolate variety. The candies will keep, refrigerated, for three months.

Three of the best-known establishments are located on the Central Cours Mirabeau:

A La Reine Jeanne (32 cours Mirabeau, 13606 Aix-en-Provence; 04.26.02.33).

Confiserie Brémond Fils (36 cours Mirabeau, 13606 Aix-en-Provence; 04.27.36.25).

Confiserie Béchard (12 cours Mirabeau, 13100 Aix-en-Provence; 04.26.06.78).

The Wines of the Sun

BY ANTHONY DIAS BLUE

~

editor's note

As I've noted in my previous books, I believe that crops that grow together, go together. It is no accident that the wines, apéritifs, and digestifs of Provence pair so remarkably well with the local ingredients and dishes.

Here are two pieces that present an overview of the Provençal *appellations* (note that the Côtes du Lubéron is not mentioned; it has only been an *appellation contrôlée* since 1988, and has more often been included in the Côtes du Rhône a.c.) and some typical drinks to enjoy before or after a meal.

ANTHONY DIAS BLUE is wine and spirits editor of *Bon Appétit* and the author of numerous books, including the *Zagat Survey 2000: San Francisco Bay Area Restaurants* (1999), and *The Complete Book of Mixed Drinks* (HarperPerennial, 1993).

Both the making and the drinking of wine are integral, immutable parts of life in Provence. And they have been from what seems like time immemorial—well, at least from time beginning twenty-six centuries ago. That's because Provence was the first area of France to be planted with grape vines. When Greek traders from Asia Minor arrived in the Phoenician city of Massila (modern Marseille) around 600 B.C., they established vineyards.

The Romans, in typical Roman fashion, expanded on what the Greeks started. From their beloved *Provincia* the Romans carried vines north up the Rhône Valley and into the rest of France. From the Mediterranean port city *Forum Julii* (today called Fréjus) they shipped large quantities of wine to Italy. In the Middle Ages, Provençal wine was exported to England after King Henry II married Eleanor of Aquitaine; in the seventeenth and eighteenth centuries Provence was second only to Bordeaux in wine production. The demand for Provençal wine continued to rise in the nineteenth century, resulting in a massive expansion of vineyard area.

However, in the middle of the nineteenth century, that demand began to decrease. The wines of the neighboring region of Languedoc were on the rise, and the newly efficient railroads transported large amounts of them to Paris. Provence was in trouble. As if competition weren't enough, there was disease, too: in short order, wilt disease, mildew and phylloxera. To recover from the last, winemakers in the region had to economize by adopting more efficient planting techniques and growing more prolific grape varieties. Mere survival became paramount; quantity was more important than quality, and that's how things remained for a long time. Red, white or rosé, wine was an everyday thing, an innocuous quaff that locals consumed with food; rosé was the top choice of the tourists who packed the Riviera.

Today, fortunately, things are changing. Serious winemakers are experimenting with dozens of varietals—some native, some from other parts of France and some from Italy—and new techniques in order to make better wines. In general, wines from Provence still are neither the subtlest nor the most elegant in the world, but they are intensely flavored, kissed by the sun and sea, and are natural companions for the distinctive regional cuisine. There are even some outstanding new bottlings.

Provence Proper

Provence has a climate that is ideal for growing grapes: mild winters and long, hot, dry summers, with fresh winds from the Mediterranean keeping those summer temperatures from climbing too high. The north wind known as the mistral is problematic, but luckily, the Lubéron mountains protect the region from the most damaging effects of the gusts. Because of the mistral, young vines in parts of Provence are traditionally planted at an angle so that the wind will cause them to grow straight over time.

There are eight Appellations Contrôlées (ACs) in Provence: Bandol, Bellet, Cassis, Coteaux d'Aix-en-Provence, Coteaux Varois, Côtes de Provence, Les Baux-de-Provence and Palette. Let's talk about them.

Some of the best-known wines of Provence come from Bandol, a resort town located on the coast between Toulon and Marseille. Bandol red is an intense, spicy, age-worthy wine made from a minimum of 50 percent Mourvèdre—a dark, luscious, plummy varietal. Mourvèdre is also the lead grape in Bandol rosé, the area's most famous and expensive wine. Bandol white is fresh and fruity, and has a distinctive aniseed aroma. Domaine Tempier, Château Pradeaux, Château de Pibarnon and Château Ste.-Anne are leading Bandol producers.

Bellet is a tiny AC located north of Nice, the city in which most of the wine seems to be consumed. There is Bellet red, rosé and white; the last is the best. Prices for Bellet are inflated, as production is extremely limited and demand is high.

Cassis is a beautiful village overlooking a Mediterranean harbor between Marseille and Bandol. Vines are cultivated on the walled, terraced slopes to the south of the town. The red made here is nothing special, and the rosé is agreeable, but the white has a fine reputation. Floral and herbal with a slightly salty tang, it has good body and goes well with the local seafood. Producers to look for include La Ferme Blanche and Clos Ste.-Madeleine.

Coteaux d'Aix-en-Provence, located primarily north and west of the town of Aix-en-Provence, offers some of the best wine values in Provence. Half of the wine produced here is rosé, 40 percent is red, and the remainder is white. The red resembles Bordeaux or Côtes du Rhône rather than other area wines. Top producers of this AC include Domaine de Trévallon and Château Barbelle.

Coteaux Varois is a large area of vines around the town of Brignoles. Grapes from here are transformed into over 30 million bottles a year of red, rosé and white. The quality has tended to be mediocre, but it is improving.

Côtes de Provence is the largest appellation in Provence, with three main areas of production: the coastal vineyards running from St.-Tropez to Toulon; the valley north of the Massif des Maures around Les Arcs; and the vineyards farther northeast and west of Draguignan. Rosé is the staple wine here. The old style was heavy and quite alcoholic; the new style is lighter and lower in alcohol. Red is the next most important color in this AC, and today it sports a modern style as well. Producers to look for include Commanderie de Peyrassol, Domaine Richeaume, Domaine de la Malherbe and Château Barbeyrolles.

The appellation Les Baux-de-Provence lies in a circle of mountains near the historic hill town of the same name. Most of the production here is red, and the quality tends to be high because the estates are small and private. Labels to check out include Mas de Gourgonnier (which makes a lovely rosé, too) and Mas de la Dame.

Palette, a tiny appellation just east of Aix-en-Provence, consists of two properties: Château Simone and Château Crémale. Each produces red, white and rosé of a fairly high standard.

Vin De Pays Pioneers

Aside from the strictly defined appellations, there is much room in Provence for expansion in the appellation of *vins de pays,* or country wines, and several winemakers have set up shop to explore the possibilities. Two Burgundians—Aubert de Villaine, the outspoken owner of Domaine de la Romanée-Conti, and Jacques Seysses of Domaine Dujac—have created Domaine de Triennes in Nans-les-Pins, forty-five minutes north of Toulon. The two appreciate the freedom of Provence, where, as de Villaine put it, "the benchmark has yet to be set."

The Triennes house style is structured and balanced, with a minimum of intervention during fermentation and aging. The wines are simply labeled by varietal, an American concept that is catching on here and elsewhere in France. Unlike the owners' regal Burgundies, these vins de pays are zesty and ready to drink now. A fresh and snappy Merlot with herbs and plummy fruit and a brisk and lively Cabernet Sauvignon with tangy acidity and lots of raspberry fruit head the list. The Triennes Reserve is a lush Cabernet-Syrah blend with good balance and lively fruit.

Near the tiny hamlet of Châteauvert, about an hour east of Aix-en-Provence, proprietor Philippe Bieler and his American winemaker, Bob Lindquist, are making news at Château Routas with a series of wines named after historic French figures. "The vineyards here are old and interesting," said the affable Lindquist, who is also the proprietor of Qupé Winery in Santa Barbara, California, "but they haven't been taken seriously for centuries. For years there has been very little attention paid to the quality of wines here."

Bieler, a passionate cook, bought the château for its "proximity to epicurean raw materials"—like the truffles he often adds to his guests' scrambled eggs—but the business of wine is foremost at this property. The Routas Cyrano (named for the big-nosed poet and swashbuckler Cyrano de Bergerac) is a fleshy, ripe Syrah, while Pyramus (named for a botanist ancestor of Bieler's) is a white blend with deeply extracted flavors and a lush finish. The official Coteaux Varois appellation, which includes most of the Routas wines, was created only in 1993—a sign that greater things are to come from this area. "I think that Grenache and Syrah have enormous commercial potential with American consumers," said Lindquist.

The Southern Rhône

When talking about Provence in a discussion of wine, we are talking about a truncated region. That is because French wine law separates the southern Rhône (which is geographically part of Provence) and its wines from Provence and its wines. But, for the purposes of our discussion, we will include them here. They are, in fact, more closely related geographically and stylistically to their Provençal siblings than to the wines of the northern Rhône, with which they are normally grouped under the traditional heading "Rhône Wines."

A number of well-known appellations constitute the southern Rhône, including Côtes du Rhône, Châteauneuf-du-Pape, Gigondas and Tavel. Widely varying recipes for *encépagement* (how much of which grape is used in a blend) mean that wines of this area tend to differ more from one another and from producer to producer than do the wines that are farther up the river. One example is red Châteauneuf-du-Pape, which can legally be made from up to thirteen grape varieties but, depending on the producer, can also be made from as few as two or three.

Many American wine drinkers get their first taste of this part of France from bottles marked *Côtes du Rhône,* an appellation that has become practically synonymous with French red wine. A whopping 90 percent of Côtes du Rhône comes from the area that centers on the historic town of Orange, known for its first-century Roman amphitheater.

While wines of the Côtes du Rhône are often undistinguished, there are an increasing number of producers offering more interesting bottlings. Meffre, Guigal, Jaboulet Aîné, Vidal-Fleury, Delas and Tardieu-Laurent are doing estimable work here. The renowned Perrin family has played a vital role in the current revival of this AC, as well as of the whole southern Rhône region. Its white and red Perrin Reserves are a good value for everyday drinking, and Perrin's Cru de Coudoulet de Beaucastel releases—a fresh, peachy white and a tangy, bright red—are wines to be taken seriously.

One cannot discuss the Perrin family without mentioning its estate, Château de Beaucastel, considered the leading producer of Châteauneuf-du-Pape, which is perhaps the southern Rhône's greatest appellation. The Château de Beaucastel red and white fetch some of the highest prices for wines from this region and are thrilling, idiosyncratic bottlings. "We have an identity," the personable François Perrin explained, "and we must keep it. There is no point competing with or copying an Australian or Californian, just because that style is in fashion." (That point of view has not prevented this talented family from establishing an estate in central California, soon to produce eagerly awaited Rhône-style wines.)

Respect for personal style—this singular identity—is widespread among the best producers of this appellation, and that gives the wines from the area their character. Other deft Châteauneuf-du-Pape producers to look for include Clos du Mont-Olivet, Domaine de Montpertuis, Domaine de Mont-Redon, Domaine de la Mordorée, Château de la Nerthe, Château Rayas, Domaine du

Vieux Télégraphe and Tardieu-Laurent, the last a relatively young, high-quality *négociant* with one foot in Burgundy and the other in the Rhône.

A similar dedication to excellence and individual expression can be found in the sixteen communes entitled by French law to append their individual names to the larger Côtes du Rhône appellation. These fall under the Côtes du Rhône-Villages rubric. I am very impressed with the quality of the wines from the village of Cairanne, including the exciting, muscular offerings of Domaine du Trapadis made by the intensely serious Michel Charavin. When I found a pair of ladies' nylon stockings near a vat of Syrah in his small winery, I asked him why they were there. He replied unsmilingly, "I use them to add yeast during fermentation."

I also like the Cairanne wines from Domaine Richaud, where Marcel Richaud, a charming vintner with blue eyes and movie-star good looks, makes robust, fruity reds and endearing whites. And I like the top-quality releases from the local cooperative Cave de Cairanne, which blends the wines of 260 growers into appealing, well-balanced bottlings.

Considering that Côtes du Rhône-Villages wines generally sell for well under $20, they offer excellent value for the money. Other Côtes du Rhône-Villages bottlings to look for come from the towns of Séguret and Sablet. And if your taste runs to sweet whites, check out the offerings by Domaine de la Soumade and Château du Trignon from the town of Rasteau, and Jaboulet Ainé and Chapoutier from the town of Beaumes-de-Venise.

The lovely village of Vacqueyras was elevated to its own appellation in 1990 because of the richly fruity reds it produces. These wines are often blends of Grenache with Syrah and Mourvèdre. Look for wines from Tardieu-Laurent, Domaine de Boissan, Jaboulet Ainé, Vidal-Fleury and Château des Tours.

Gigondas earned its appellation status in 1971. The incredible bottlings of Domaine Raspail-Ay are certainly among the best made here. The reds are keepers that will repay cellaring; the rosés are available for more immediate enjoyment. The dedicated proprietor of this forty-five-acre estate, Dominique Ay, has as rustic a look as his region. His shiny stainless-steel winery may be one of the most modern in the area, but "we are totally traditional here and do everything *en famille*," he asserted. Other producers of note in Gigondas include Domaine du Pourra, Domaine Santa-Duc, Château du Trignon, Tardieu-Laurent and Domaine de Boissan.

Tavel and Lirac, just north of Avignon, are historically known for rosé. Tavel is still in the rosé business and is the only French appellation to make just rosés, but Lirac has taken credit for some exceptional reds lately. The imposing but welcoming facade of Château d'Aqueria can be seen from the highway. This estate offers wines from both appellations—a superbly fruity Tavel rosé with bright, tangy grapefruit and a long, clean finish; a lovely white Lirac; and a rich, complex red Lirac with gobs of black fruit.

Domaine de la Mordorée, where chemical-free organic agriculture is strictly practiced, makes an elegant Tavel with plump berry fruit, and an excellent Lirac in both red and white. "The vineyards and the wines here are benefiting from a return to traditional methods," noted owner Christophe Delorme.

The extremely productive appellation Côtes du Ventoux sits where the Rhône Valley merges with Provence to the east. *The* outstanding red produced here is La Vieille Ferme, made by Jean-Pierre Perrin, co-owner of Château de Beaucastel. He also makes a lovely rosé.

The Côtes du Lubéron, a relatively new but promising appellation in the hills along the north of the Durance Valley, is putting out some attractive reds and rosés. The ambitious wines of Jean-Louis Chancel's Château Val-Joanis are drawing serious attention to this southernmost Rhône region. Other producers of note include Clos

Mirabeau and Château de l'Isolette. The white La Vieille Ferme belongs to this AC.

Considering that the south of France is particularly blessed by the sun and the sea, the steady improvement of the wines of Provence and, to a lesser degree, of the southern Rhône (which had a much easier row to hoe) should come as no surprise. As Philippe Bieler of Château Routas put it, "I live in the most beautiful place in the world, and I am surrounded by terrific wine."

More and more producers seem to be equally confident and are developing their own strong, individualistic styles. The future of Provençal wines—not to mention the present—is very bright indeed.

Before and After

It is customary throughout Provence to have an aperitif before a meal to whet the appetite, and a liqueur, spirit or sweet wine afterward to bring things to a spectacular finish. Here are some recommendations for what to drink when you're visiting the area, and what to look for when you're here—but long to be there.

Aperitifs

More than any other beverage, pastis is the drink most closely associated with the south of France. Pastis is an aperitif made by steeping various herbs and spices in alcohol. Star anise is the predominant flavor and gives this potion its distinct licorice taste.

Pastis is a common refresher on hot afternoons. A small portion is served in a tall glass, and water (usually dispensed from a ceramic or glass pitcher—and sometimes poured over a sugar cube placed on a small slotted spoon) is added, which instantly turns the drink a milky white (hence its nickname "the milk of Provence"). Then the mixture is stirred, with ice cubes being the final flourish.

Thanks to its taste, pastis was a popular successor to absinthe, the notorious anise-infused spirit that was especially fashionable in the nineteenth century among writers and artists like Oscar Wilde and Vincent van Gogh. Absinthe was banned in France in 1915 (as it had already been in most other countries) because it was made with wormwood, a hallucinogenic and very toxic plant. (The famous Pernod, which is served throughout France in the same manner as pastis, is actually a tamer, legal version of absinthe.)

Today, the pastis of the south of France still bears a close resemblance to its infamous forebear but contains no wormwood. Major pastis brands produced in Provence and available in this country include Ricard, Prado, Granier and the elegant Henri Bardouin.

An herb-based aperitif to enjoy when in Provence is Suze, flavored with the earthy gentian root. One of Suze's biggest fans was Pablo Picasso, who in 1912 created a well-known cubist collage of a Suze bottle and glass.

Homemade and artisanal aperitifs and liqueurs are also common, but unfortunately they are rarely found commercially in the United States. Vin de noix (red or rosé wine flavored with walnuts) and vin d'orange (white wine flavored with orange) are two favorites to look for in restaurants or cafés. A Provençal adaptation of the classic aperitif known as kir is kir Provençal (red wine laced with *crème de mure,* a delicious blackberry liqueur). Herb-based liqueurs include farigoule (from thyme) and génepi (from yarrow).

After-Dinner Drinks

When you visit Provence, there are several popular after-dinner drinks to try. Local vintners often use the pomace (grape pulp) left over from winemaking to distill marc de Provence, a potent brandy served at the end of a meal as an aid to digestion. The herbal elixir called Aiguebelle, a liqueur that resembles the better-known Chartreuse, is still made by Trappist monks at the abbey of Notre Dame, founded in 1137 near Montjoyer. Either version of Aiguebelle, green or yellow, can be served as a *digestif.*

Although the notable sweet wine Muscat de Beaumes-de-Venise is commonly enjoyed as an aperitif, it is also wonderful sipped after dinner, either with dessert or on its own. Made from the ancient Muscat grape, this light, fortified wine originates in the town of Beaumes-de-Venise on the slopes of Mont Ventoux. Labels available in America include Chapoutier, Jaboulet Ainé and Meffre. Serve this refreshing wine chilled.

Wine Talk

BY FRANK J. PRIAL

∿

editor's note

This piece brought a big smile to my face, and I believe it may contain the only reference to a "vinously minded historian."

FRANK PRIAL is the wine columnist for *The New York Times* and writes about wine for a variety of other publications. He is also the author of *Wine Talk* (Times Books, 1978) and coauthor, with Rosemary George and Michael Edwards, of *The Companion to Wine* (Prentice-Hall, 1992).

On August 15, 1944, ten weeks after D day, another Allied force disembarked on the beaches of France. On that day, some one thousand vessels stood off the Mediterranean coast and put several hundred thousand American and French troops ashore at St.-Raphaël, St.-Tropez and Marseille.

Their mission: to race north through the Rhône Valley to join the Allied forces fighting their way eastward from the Normandy beaches toward Paris and the Rhine. The landings and the campaign that followed were known as Operation Anvil.

Anvil never captured the public's imagination as did Operation Overlord, the D day cross-Channel invasion. With good reason: the landings were virtually unopposed and the Germans offered only token resistance as they fled north to join the final battle for their homeland.

But for one participant, at least, Anvil had special significance: it was to him a campaign to save the great vineyards of France from the beer-drinking Huns.

Wynford Vaughan Thomas was a British war correspondent attached first to the American troops under General Alexander Patch, the overall commander of Anvil, and later to General Jean de Lattre de Tassigny, who led the French part of the operation.

I am indebted to the historian and writer Robert E. Quirk for a copy of Mr. Thomas's reminiscences about the campaign, first published in an essay collection called *The Compleat Imbiber* in London in 1963.

Mr. Thomas got his first inkling of what Anvil would be like when he stormed ashore with the Americans at St.-Raphaël. When the ramp on their landing craft dropped down, they rushed into the warm surf and up the beach through a smoke screen. Coming out of the murk, they spied a Riviera villa that had escaped the prelanding shelling.

"The door opened," Mr. Thomas wrote, "and an immaculately dressed Frenchman appeared. He carried a tray on which were ten glasses and a bottle of Veuve Clicquot '34.

" 'Welcome, gentlemen,' he said in French and added in English, 'even if you are a bit late.' "

Writing ten years after the landing, Mr. Thomas said "time softens controversy and the history of distant wars grows mellow like '49 Burgundy."

One look at the map and the route taken by the invading armies, Mr. Thomas said, made the raison d'être of the campaign clear: "Ahead of the advancing troops was grouped such a collection of noble names that the mouth waters as the hand types them: Châteauneuf-du-Pape, Tavel, Tain-l'Hermitage, Château Grillet, the Côte Rôtie, and, beyond, the greatest objective of them all— Burgundy and the Côte d'Or!"

Among those who planned Anvil was a French general and wine lover, Lucien de Montsabert. Mr. Thomas said that he had no documentary proof but that he felt certain it was General de Montsabert who sent the American troops through the Basses-Alpes.

"Their job was vital, but the vinously minded historian will note that it did not take them near a single vineyard of quality," he said. "Now follow the advance of the French Army. Swiftly they possessed themselves of Tavel, and after making sure that all was well with one of the finest *vin roses* in France, struck fiercely for Châteauneuf-du-Pape. The Côte Rôtie fell to a well-planned flanking attack."

Meanwhile, the Americans were working their way up the eastern, mostly vineyard-free side of the Rhône River. Visiting the American headquarters, Mr. Thomas found the commanders a bit disturbed. They thought the French were dragging their feet. "They're staying too long at some place called Chalons something or other," an officer said.

Indeed they were. Chalon-sur-Saône is the southern gateway to the great Burgundy vineyards, which the French above all wanted to avoid turning into battlegrounds.

"We must not forget 1870," a French officer told Mr. Thomas later that day. The officer said that one of the last battles of the Franco-Prussian War had been fought around Nuits-St.-Georges, an important Burgundy wine town, and that Prussian reserves, rushing to the front, had marched through and destroyed the legendary vineyards of La Tache, Romanée-Conti and Richebourg.

At that point, Mr. Thomas wrote, a young officer rushed in to announce that weak points in the German defense had been found. "And, Colonel," the officer said, "every one is on a vineyard of inferior quality."

The Germans were quickly put to flight, and within a day or two, the correspondent and General de Montsabert were racing up the highway through Burgundy.

"A blown bridge here, a demolished house there—what could these matter beside the great, overriding fact of the undamaged vineyards stretching mile after mile before us?" Mr. Thomas wrote.

Soon the French troops—or at least the officers and correspondents—were savoring the best from the cellars of Aloxe-Corton and Vosne-Romanée. The wines, Mr. Thomas said, had been hidden behind false cellar walls. To allay the suspicions of the Nazis, labels of great wines had been repasted on cheap ones, which the conquerors drank with relish.

"I have drunk great wines in many parts of France," Mr. Thomas said, "but never have I tasted such nectar as was offered to me during the early days of the liberation of Burgundy. That whole enchanted period of my life is a symphony of popping corks."

Bibliothèque

Cookbooks

It seems to me that one cannot separate Provençal food from Provençal history. Really good cookbooks—ones that offer tried-and-true, authentic recipes, as well as detailed commentary on the food traditions of the country or region and the history behind the recipes and the ingredients unique to the cuisine, are just as essential to travel as guidebooks. I read these cookbooks the way other people read novels; therefore, the authors have to be more than just good cooks, and the books have to be more than cookbooks. All of the authors and books listed below fit the bill, and because they are *all* my favorites, I feature them alphabetically. I use each of them at different times throughout the year and couldn't envision my kitchen without a single one. I also do not provide lengthy descriptions of these titles as I think it is sufficient to state that they are definitive, and stand quite apart from the multitude of Mediterranean and Provençal cookbooks crowding bookstore shelves. I have also included a few articles and titles that aren't strictly cookbooks, but are interesting and relevant nonetheless.

Mediterranean (Provence is well represented in each of these titles)

A Book of Mediterranean Food, Elizabeth David, Penguin, 1988.

Cod: A Biography of the Fish That Changed the World, Mark Kurlansky, Walker and Company, 1999. I include this wonderful book here because, as Kurlansky notes, "From the Middle Ages to the present, the most demanding cod market has always been the Mediterranean." Fresh or dried salt cod is a ubiquitous Mediterranean staple (except in the Muslim countries), making an appearance in such dishes as *sonhos de bacalhau* in Portugal, *brandade de morue* in France, *baccala in umido* in Tuscany, and *filetti di baccala all'arancia* in Sicily. The fascinating story of cod crisscrosses the globe from Newfoundland, New England, the Basque coast of Spain, Brazil, West Africa, Scandinavia, and other locations, but the Mediterranean is never very far from the thread.

The Feast of the Olive, Maggie Blyth Klein, Aris Books (Addison-Wesley), 1983; Chronicle Books, revised and updated edition, 1994.

From Tapas to Meze, Joanna Weir, Crown, 1994.

Mediterranean: The Beautiful Cookbook, Joyce Goldstein, Collins (produced by Welden Owen), 1994.

Mediterranean Cookery, Claudia Roden, Knopf, 1987.

Mediterranean Cooking, Paula Wolfert, HarperCollins, 1994.

The Mediterranean Diet Cookbook, Nancy Harmon Jenkins, Bantam Books, 1994.

A Mediterranean Feast: The Story of the Birth of the Celebrated Cuisines of the Mediterranean, from the Merchants of Venice to the Barbary Corsairs, Clifford A. Wright, William Morrow and Company, 1999.

Mediterranean Light, Martha Rose Shulman, Bantam, 1989.

The Mediterranean Kitchen, Joyce Goldstein, Morrow, 1989.

The Mediterranean Pantry: Creating and Using Condiments and Seasonings, Aglaia Kremezi, photographs by Martin Brigdale, Artisan, 1994.

Mostly Mediterranean, Paula Wolfert, Penguin, 1988.

Articles

"The Mediterranean: A Delicious Voyage of Discovery," *Bon Appétit,* May 1995. A special collector's edition featuring twenty-seven Mediterranean ports of call, including Nice and Porquerolles. To order this back issue, contact Condé Nast Publications, P.O. Box 57781, Boulder, Colorado 80322; 800-765-9419. Back issues are $5.50 for second-class mail and $7.50 for first-class delivery.

Provençal

Chez Nous: Home Cooking from the South of France, Lydie Marshall, HarperCollins, 1995, hardcover; *A Passion for My Provence,* HarperPerennial, 1999, paperback.

The Cuisine of the Sun: Classical French Cooking from Nice and Provence, Mireille Johnston, Random House, 1976.

Flavors of the Riviera: Discovering Real Mediterranean Cooking, Colman Andrews, Bantam, 1996.

The Food and Flavors of Haute Provence, Georgeanne Brennan, foreword by Patricia Wells, Chronicle Books, 1997. One of the few books dedicated to little-visited Haute Provence, I like this not so much for the recipes but for the background information Brennan provides about living and eating by the seasons and the typical ingredients grown and cultivated here. In fact, the book is organized by these key ingredients: wild herbs and lavender, olives and olive oil, wild mushrooms and truffles, cheese, the *potager,* sheep, goats and pigs, game and fish, nuts, honey and fruits.

The Food Lover's Guide to France, Patricia Wells, Workman, 1987. Though this is mostly a guide to restaurants and food specialty shops throughout France, the essays Wells provides on food items unique to Provence and the Côte d'Azur—including *le melon de Cavaillon,* honey, *fruits confits,* wines and cheeses of Provence, and *mesclum* (the real thing, not the mixture often found in U.S. supermarkets with Asian greens added)—are great and informative reading.

French Country Kitchen: An Evocation of the Food, People, and Countryside of Southern France, Geraldene Holt, preface by M. F. K. Fisher, Fireside (Simon & Schuster), 1987; originally published in Great Britain by Penguin.

French Provincial Cooking, Elizabeth David, Penguin, 1970, originally published in Great Britain by Michael Joseph, 1960; first published in the U.S. by Harper & Row, 1962.

Provençal Light: Traditional Recipes from Provence for Today's Healthy Lifestyles, Martha Rose Schulman, Bantam, 1994.

Provence: The Beautiful Cookbook, Richard Olney, Collins Publishers, San Francisco, 1993. Olney's introduction contains one of the most perceptive passages ever written about Provence and food: "Those who look at Provence in a distant and detached way no doubt find it a single region with no precise definition. Yet this is a profoundly false impression. Provence is not one but many regions, and those who care to explore its depths and discover its secrets, who seek to understand its culinary truths, will speak of 'the Provences,' in the same way as the historian or the geographer approaches this amazing southeastern corner of France. The plural, in fact, appropriately defines these lands of the sun, which do not allow themselves to be tamed easily. Nor is it a simple matter to know their flavors. This is a region whose personality is revealed only to those who take the time to pursue it: to those prepared to take their taste as a leisurely stroll, who know that the garden's treasures are not to be devoured but rather looked at, conversed with, gathered with love and then eaten in relaxed enjoyment."

Provence Gastronomique, Erica Brown, photographs by Debbie Patterson, Abbeville Press, 1995. In addition to recipes, there is a visitor's guide to restaurants, places of interest, specialties of the region, markets, and fêtes at the back of the book.

Recipes from a Provençal Kitchen, Michel Biehn, Flammarion, 1999. I have to admit that the recipes in this beautiful book aren't particularly unique or as thorough as in other Provençal cookbooks, but just glimpsing the gorgeous cover and the interior photographs *inspires* me to cook, and that, sometimes, is enough.

A Taste of Provence: Classic Recipes from the South of France, collected and illustrated by Leslie Forbes, Little, Brown, 1987, hardcover; Chronicle Books, 1991, paperback. Try to find the hardcover edition, if you can, as the handwritten text was abandoned for typeset words in the paperback, which I think completely robs the work of its spirit. More than a cookbook, as Forbes provides an abundance of folklore, historical background, lovely illustrations, and restaurant notes.

A Taste of Provence: The Food and People of Southern France with 40 Delicious Recipes, photographed by Carey More, written by Julian More, Henry Holt, 1988. More a beautiful photography book than a cookbook, although the recipes I've tried (especially the one for *tapenade,* which I think is the best version I've encountered) are authentic and good.

Not a Cookbook, but a Culinary Classic

The Physiology of Taste or Meditations on Transcendental Gastronomy, Jean Anthelme Brillat-Savarin, translated by M. F. K. Fisher and with illustrations by Wayne Thiebaud, Counterpoint (by arrangement with The Arion Press), 1994, distributed by Publishers Group West; original translation copyright 1949, The George Macy Companies, Inc.

Articles

"Delicious Provence: Splendid Food in a Magical Setting," *Bon Appétit,* May 1999. A special collector's edition featuring some great articles by food writers such as Mort Rosenblum, Georgeanne Brennan, Susan Hermann Loomis, and Martha Rose Schulman. A piece I particularly like is "The Flavors of Provence," which highlights twenty essential dishes made with twenty essential ingredients: lemons, lamb, zucchini, artichokes, goat cheese, asparagus, almonds, beef ("beef is not really a Provençal staple, except maybe in the Camargue, where French cowboys still ride a marshy range. But *daube* [which in Provence is made with beef] is as ubiquitous and as appreciated as Marcel Pagnol paperbacks"), anchovies, garlic, honey, *herbes de Provence,* tomatoes, wild mushrooms, Swiss chard, fennel, eggplant, basil, olives, and bell peppers. To order this back issue, contact Condé Nast Publications, P.O. Box 57781, Boulder, Colorado 80322; 800-765-9419. Back issues are $5.50 for second-class mail and $7.50 for first-class delivery.

"The Goat Is the Cow of the Poor: Some Provençal Cheeses," Edward Behr, *The Art of Eating* No. 27, Summer 1993. Some readers may already know of this absolutely excellent, critical, and superbly written quarterly newsletter. Although not exclusively about Provence or France, Behr has devoted several issues to various aspects of French food and restaurants over the years, and each of them is worth the effort to special order. Of this Provençal cheeses issue, I would say: don't go without it. Behr and his wife spent two weeks in Provence in pursuit of traditional cheeses, and this issue contains some of the most comprehensive writing on goat and sheep's milk cheeses—including Banon, brousse, Picodon, and Pelardon—anywhere. Due to the number of Provençal cheeses that visitors will encounter at *marchés* and restaurants, I consider this *de rigueur* reading. Further, if you really want to learn about the food traditions of France and other countries, and care about the food you eat and its future, you'll definitely want to subscribe to this stellar periodical, which has been described as "One of the most respected publications in the food world" by *Chef's Edition* on National Public Radio. "Provence" (No. 55, Fall 2000) is a more recent issue, and the three topics Edward Behr delves into are "The Cooking of Poor People" (in which he interviews Guy Gedda, a retired Provençal chef), "Wine from a Southern Climate" (referring to Domaine Tempier and Château Simone), and "Olive Oil from the Valley of Les Baux" (referring to a new olive oil, Castelas, which Behr says is "the first Provençal olive oil I've liked"). Some of the finer cookbook and cookware stores sell individual issues of *The Art of Eating* (Kitchen Arts & Letters in New York stocks it regularly), but to receive it in your mailbox you should subscribe: Box 242, Peacham, Vermont 05862; 800-495-3944; www.artofeating.com; back issues are $9 each, $7.50 each if you order four or more).

"Hidden Provence," Mireille Johnston, *Saveur* No. 1. It's hard to find much material on the Département des Alpes-de-Haute-Provence, so this article is especially welcome. As Johnston writes, "In Haute Provence, you will look in vain for hillsides covered with vacation villas, for pretentious shops and galleries, for Souleidao-wrapped resort hotels. Real people live in Haute Provence, in real towns and real countryside." In addition to traditional recipes of this pocket of Provence, there are recommendations for places to stay and eat, as well as family-run sources for candy, honey, olive oil, cheese, *santons,* and ceramics. Contact *Saveur* at 800-429-0106. Back issues are $5.95 each (three or more issues are $3 each), shipping and handling is $2 per issue (or $1 per issue for three copies or more), and credit-card orders are accepted by phone. To send a check, write to DC Reader Services, Back Issues Department, P.O. Box 2898, Lakeland, Florida 33806, and include a note indicating the issue date.

"Secrets of Vieux Nice," Colman Andrews, photographs by Antoine Bootz, *Saveur* No. 8. The delicious specialties of the Côte d'Azur's capital—*tripes à la niçoise,* socca, *salade Niçoise, farcis a la Niçoise, estocaficada,* ravioli, zucchini blossom beignets, and more—are presented in great detail with accompanying recipes. As Andrews notes, "Nice is one of the few cities in France—Lyon is another—that can be said to have its own cuisine." Very much worth ordering this back issue if your library doesn't have it. See contact information above for *Saveur.*

About French Wine

Adventures on the Wine Route: A Wine Buyer's Tour of France, Kermit Lynch, Farrar, Straus & Giroux, 1988, hardcover; North Point Press, 1995, paperback; preface by Richard Olney. Kermit Lynch, a Berkeley, California, wine merchant, is a wonderful storyteller, especially when he's talking about wine, which he is, of course, in this book. Besides being entertaining, readers will learn a lot about French wine—and the men and women who make it—while reading of Lynch's journeys. This is a unique book, and individual chapters cover some wines of Provence, Northern Rhône, Southern Rhône, and neighboring Languedoc. Every chapter is great, but the one I appreciate the most is "Southern Rhône," in which the author goes to a renowned restaurant on two different occasions and causes an (unintended) scene each time, the first over credit cards (they weren't accepted, and he didn't have enough cash) and the second over a wine that was "off" and—*quelle surprise*—expensive. M.F.K. Fisher called this "one of the pleasantest and truest books about wine I've ever read." I call it a candidate for the *de rigueur* list.

Alexis Lichine's Guide to the Wines and Vineyards of France, Alexis Lichine, Alfred A. Knopf, 1989, 4th edition. Lichine—former wine exporter, grower and wine-maker (Chateau Prieuré-Lichine), author, and all-around wine authority—really knew how to bring wine to life. Even though this wonderful book is out of print (Lichine passed away in 1989, and Prieuré-Lichine was sold in 1999), it can still be found at some wine shops and bookstores. This is a book for both travelers—with chapters on suggested tours as well as hotel and restaurant recommendations (though these can't be relied upon because the book is a bit out of date, I have found that some of this information is still accurate)—and for wine buyers, with lengthy profiles of each wine-growing area (twenty-one in all, including a chapter on cognac, Armagnac, and calvados) and chapters on storing and serving wine, tasting wine, wine and health, and buying wine (which includes a vintage chart).

Larousse Wines and Vineyards of France, Arcade Publishing, Little, Brown and Company, 1991. Both a dictionary and an encyclopedia, this tome (639 pages) is, in my opinion, the best single volume on French wine-growing areas. This comprehensive work covers every topic relevant to French wine and was written by sixty-eight authors, each one an expert in his or her chosen field. You will find it a trusty authority whenever you refer to it. Maps, over 500 color photographs, charts, in-depth entries on vinification, glasses, soil, tasting, champagne secrets, etc., and two glossaries—one of French tasting terms and the other of technical terms—complete the package.

Touring in Wine Country: Provence, Hubrecht Duijker, series editor Hugh Johnson, Mitchell Beazley, 1998. The "Touring in Wine Country" series is designed for traveling wine lovers interested in including vineyard visits to their itineraries. This Provence edition features suggested routes, color photos, maps, wine and food notes, and practical information for the nine appellations of Provence. Lightweight and good to bring along.

Wines and Vineyards of Character and Charm in France, Fodor's Rivages (Fodor's Travel Publications, division of Random House, Inc.), 1998. *Finalement,* an English translation of this Rivages guide, popular for years among Europeans. French-wine enthusiasts will find this an indispensable guide, and very much worth perusing. There are individual sections on the wines of Provence and Northern and Southern Rhône, including detailed road maps, color photos, and all the practical information for visitors. Also indicated are other languages spoken by the vintner (this is worth noting; unlike at wineries in the States—especially in California—you will almost always meet the vintner/owner or a family member, not a representative).

Wines of the Rhône Valley, Robert M. Parker Jr., Simon & Schuster, 1997. To quote Parker, "When I drink a great Rhône, it is as if my heart and palate have traded places." Forget about ordering Burgundy and Bordeaux when you're in Provence: you'll find a great number of wonderfully rich, delicious Provençal wines (mostly red but a few notable whites) that pair remarkably well with the local cuisine. In this book, Parker covers wines of the Northern and Southern Rhône, including some esoteric Rhône wines such as Costières de Nîmes, Côtes du Vivarais, and Côtes du Ventoux. At the back of the book is a visitor's guide, glossary, and an alphabetical list of food specialties of the Rhône Valley.

And Good Books About Wine in General

Jancis Robinson's Wine Course, BBC Books, London, 1995.

Making Sense of Wine, Matt Kramer, Quill (an imprint of William Morrow & Co.), 1989.

The Oxford Companion to Wine, edited by Jancis Robinson, Oxford University Press, 1994.

Pairing Wine and Food: A Handbook for All Cuisines, Linda Johnson-Bell, Burford Books, 1999.

Tasting Pleasure: Confessions of a Wine Lover, Jancis Robinson, Viking, 1997. French wines are mentioned or featured throughout the twenty-four essays.

Vineyard Tales: Reflections on Wine, Gerald Asher, Chronicle Books, 1996. Six of the twenty-nine essays are about a variety of French wines, including the Rhône wines Hermitage and Crozes-Hermitage.

À Table!
(To the Table!—
Dinner Is Served)

"The high-spirited, playful Provençal cuisine (the Provençaux like to describe it as spirituelle—*"witty"*)*, with its staples of tomatoes, garlic, saffron, sweet and hot peppers, salt anchovies, olives, olive oil, and the native wild herbs, although certainly unique, is much closer to that of other Mediterranean countries than to any other regional French cuisine. It is family cooking, not restaurant cuisine; the professional cook who can bring the right homey touch to it is very rare indeed. It is the only part of France that has always approached vegetables with respect and imagination, reserving a place apart on the menu for the vegetable entrée (between the fish and the roast for a festive meal or between the hors d'oeuvre and the main course for a simple lunch)."*
—Richard Olney, *The Taste of France*

Coastal Cuisine

BY ALEXANDRE LAZAREFF

∿

editor's note

Here is a little tour of Marseille's best eateries.

ALEXANDRE LAZAREFF is a regular contributor to *FRANCE Magazine* and is director of the Conseil National des Arts Culinaires, the organization overseeing the publication of the multivolume encyclopedia *L'Inventaire du Patrimoine Culinaire de la France*.

A culinary portrait of Marseille can only begin with the Vieux Port—an authentic, working fishing port, not some glitzy marina packed with pricey yachts. If you need convincing, just take a stroll through the daily morning market on the quai des Belges. While fishermen sit on their barges mending their nets, their wives hawk a bountiful catch of wriggling eels, scorpion fish, gurnard and other fish typically found in bouillabaisse. Cheeky remarks fly between the venders, who remain superbly indifferent to the traffic of urban passersby.

This old port—so much more welcoming than its Saint-Tropez counterpart—offers some pleasant gastronomic surprises. The city has recently done away with the old covered terraces and cleared out the streetwalkers, with the surprising result that you can still find some serious eateries. Miramar, for example, serves such wonderful fish that you quickly forget the funky decor. The seafood here is about as fresh as it gets—try the marinated *coquilles Saint Jacques* or the wonderfully daring combination of sea urchins with ginger.

Then there's Maurice Brun, where the proprietor carries his role of Provençal purist to the extreme, chewing out the occasional customer who salts the fish. And New York is the local equivalent of Paris's Brasserie Lipp, a see-and-be-seen kind of place where celebrities frequently stop by to schmooze with the proprietor. Chances are the local press will be on hand—conveniently enough, they also frequent this Vieux Port fixture. After all, it is here, over a bowl of *soupe au pistou* or the catch of the day, that local gossip is exchanged and election campaigns are plotted.

Another perennial favorite is Chez Fonfon. Tucked in a setting reminiscent of a Pagnol film, Fonfon sits on a creek below the corniche, with picture-perfect views of little fishing boats and drying nets. Fonfon's bouillabaisse is, simply, the best in Provence.

Not far away, Les Arsenaux stands on what was once the site of the royal arsenal—and what was, until recently, an urban wasteland dominated by a parking garage that had choked the life out of one of the area's few plazas. The tireless Jeanne Laffitte (who subsequently became deputy mayor) campaigned for years to have this eyesore removed so that an Italian-style pedestrian square could be created and the neighborhood renovated. Work finally got under way in the late 1980s, and the results are exemplary. Now a book-store-gallery-tearoom-restaurant, Les Arsenaux is a first-rate cultural center as well as a fine place to eat. Habitués can pick up a book—some are published by the proprietor herself—and then enjoy a hot or cold *soupe au pistou* and redfish fillets with eggplant and fennel seed. But remember, you absolutely must order your *bourride* or bouillabaisse in advance.

Another shining star among Marseille's hotels and restaurants is Le Petit Nice, a wonderfully serene Relais & Châteaux inn owned by the father-son team of Jean-Pierre and Gérald Passédat. Perched on the edge of a rocky promontory below the Corniche Kennedy, the villa is surrounded by the Mediterranean, its poolside terrace shaded by the knotty branches of a hundred-year-old spindle tree. At his father's urging, Gérald Passédat completely refurbished the bedrooms, turning them into jewels of contemporary design. And Gérald's kitchen—for years, a domain lovingly tended by his father—is the best around. Passédat is the only restaurant in Marseille that can truthfully claim to serve haute cuisine. Indeed, only the Passédats can get away with bringing the broth *after* the fish when they serve bouillabaisse or garnishing lobster with *violets de la Méditerrannée,* soft oysters with a bizarre color and consistency. Even the olive bread is a miniature masterpiece.

The city also boasts a great patisserie: Villedieu (16 la Canebière; 04.91.33.63.11). Three generations of Villedieux have now received the much-envied title of *Meilleur ouvrier de France*— truly a unique case. There's also Maurice Mistre (L'Atelier du Chocolat, 18 place aux Huiles; 04.91.33.55.00), who specializes in chocolate leaf, creating delectable pages that can be read, turned and devoured. Unfortunately, it has become impossible to find *panisses,* made from chickpea flour, or *chichis frégis,* twisted beignets flavored with orange-blossom water. The tradition of *navettes,* however, remains alive and well. Marseille families still line up on February 2, *le jour de la Chandeleur,* to buy these pastries shaped like Mary Magdalene's boat. But if you want to avoid the crowds, you can purchase them at Le Four des Navettes (136 rue Sainte; 04.91.33.32.12) and save them for the big day.

You might top off your visit with an excursion to *les calanques,* the rocky inlets along Marseille's coast. How has this sprawling city managed to preserve such wild spaces? It seems incredible that one can still find cabins without water or electricity so close to the city center and seemingly suspended between sea and sky. In this edge-of-the-world landscape, a few shacks that can barely be characterized as restaurants serve simple yet tasty grilled fish. Le Lunch (Calanque de Sormiou; 04.91.33.60.98) enjoys the best word-of-mouth reputation. But look around. There are others.

Miramar, 12 Quai du Port; 04.91.91.10.40.

Maurice Brun, 18 Quai Rive-Neuve; 04.91.33.35.38.

New York, 7 Quai des Belges; 04.91.33.60.98.

Chez Fonfon, 140 Vallon des Auffes; 04.91.52.14.38.

Les Arsenaux, 25 Cours Estienne d'Orves; 04.91.54.77.06.

Passédat, Hôtel Le Petit Nice, Corniche Kennedy, Anse de Maldormé; 04.91.59.25.92.

This article originally appeared in the Spring 1995 issue of *FRANCE Magazine.* Reprinted with permission.

Dining in the French Countryside

BY CATHARINE REYNOLDS

~

editor's note

The original of this piece was actually much longer and highlighted special places to eat in six regions of France. For this book I have only included the one restaurant chosen for Provence, Le Vieux Castillon.

CATHARINE REYNOLDS, introduced in the "Provence" section, is a contributing editor of *Gourmet,* where this piece appeared in October 1998.

T*erroir*—the very word sounds earthy. But what precisely does this noun bandied about by French gastrophiles mean? I gesticulate expansively as I struggle to explain: *Terroir* is a Frenchman's native soil. Even the most urbane boulevardier can become near-maudlin about his *terroir,* acknowledging roots reaching back to a province, a village, a family vegetable patch. Though his regional accent has long since vanished, his allegiance to the land of his fathers remains intact.

Applied to food, *terroir* encompasses regional cooking—dishes that spring from their native loam and showcase the best of local products and traditions. A few years ago *cuisine du terroir* became the mantra of eaters casting aside the affectations of *nouvelle cuisine* in favor of the hearty, homey creations that, enthusiasts would suggest, have nourished Frenchmen since the days of Vercingetorix.

The typical dishes of any region are a direct by-product of availability. And, in spite of today's broader range of possibilities, we all find a consoling harmony—not to mention a flavor bonus—in eating just-plucked produce.

With wines, the link between place and product is blazoned across the labels. This is equally true of many of France's most savory commodities, even those we have come to accept as generic. Thus, as a child, I was enchanted to learn that the Camembert I adored was named for a village buried in the Norman hedgerows. Only later would I analyze how almost all my favorite fare advertised its origins: *boeuf bourguignon, volaille de Bresse, sauce béarnaise, salade niçoise.*

Autoroutes catapult visitors in a trice from Burgundy's rolling hills to the east's granitic Alps, from the Loire's alluvial limestone to the sandy pine barrens of the Landes, from Normandy's salt meadows to Picardy's sugar-beet fields, spinning a kaleidoscope. And each change in landscape brings with it differing crops and livestock—all of which are fundamental to the lusty flavors of French regional cooking.

In the rush to check out temples of *Michelin* three-star excellence, too many foreigners sail past less glossy restaurants run by chefs who have opted to stay down on the farm, electing a life close to nature and the local purveyors. Yes, the best of these products are available nationwide (indeed, worldwide), but they taste infinitely better on their home territory, or so we confirmed in sampling the earthly delights of French *cuisine du terroir.*

Provence—Le Vieux Castillon

Our taste buds changed gears as we motored into Provence along roads marked by gray-green olive trees. The mere sight of the groves whetted our appetites for sunny fare—which is just what we found at Le Vieux Castillon, a thirty-three-room inn occupying a series of converted village houses linked by flowered galleries and shady gardens in the hill village of Castillon-du-Gard, fifteen miles northeast of Nîmes.

Seated in the airy dining room overlooking the pool, we found the scents of the *garrigue,* or herb-entangled underbrush, transposed to the table: rabbit sausages flavored with truffles and Cabécou goat cheese stuffed with olives. The *grissini* tipped with black olives that we nibbled while choosing pumpkin soup with snails and garlic croutons only confirmed our sense of place. A fennel "marmalade" sparked the roasted John Dory that followed, and the lamb was perfumed with thyme and rosemary. For dessert, a lemon-thyme-pear essence was counterpointed by suave brioche French toast, the whole enhanced with honey ice cream and chocolate.

For the last fifteen years chef Gilles Dauteuil has masterminded such cooking at Le Vieux Castillon, marshaling the best of the region's larder. The polished presentations reveal his early training as a pastry chef, but they never betray his ingredients, from the zucchini and garlic blossoms to the *chapon de mer* (red scorpion fish) hauled from the Mediterranean only hours before. He enjoys taking inquisitive travelers to see a nearby shepherd who makes Le Vieux Castillon's gently ripened Pélardon goat cheeses, clearly taking inspiration from the Provençal countryside—a landscape very different from the northern flatlands where he was born. He waxed lyrical describing Provençal fare and enthused over the wealth of local cookbooks that are an ongoing source of renewal and discovery for him and, in turn, for the diners who come to bask in the Midi.

Le Vieux Castillon, rue Turion-Sabatier, 30210 Castillon-du-Gard; 04.66.37.61.61; fax: 04.66.37.28.17; closed from early January to late February.

France's Rolling Pizza Parlors

BY PATRICIA WELLS

editor's note

Patricia Wells has written often of the cuisine of Provence, but she is the only food writer I know to have written of the ubiquitous pizza trucks of the region, offering delicious and quick fare for natives and visitors alike. She provides a list of markets at the end, and though this article was written in 1988, the market days remain the same.

PATRICIA WELLS is the restaurant critic for *The International Herald Tribune* and is the only foreigner, and the only woman, to have held the post of food critic for the French newsweekly *L'Express*. Wells is also the author of a number of books, including *Patricia Wells at Home in Provence* (Scribner, 1996), *The Food Lover's Guide to Paris* (fourth edition, Workman, 1999), *The Food Lover's Guide to France* (Workman, 1987), *Bistro Cooking* (Workman, 1989), and *Simply French: Patricia Wells Presents the Cuisine of Joel Robuchon* (Hearst Books, 1995). Eighteen years ago, Wells and her husband, Walter, bought an eighteenth-century *mas* named *Chanteduc* ("song of the owl") in Provence, where lucky apprentices can attend her cooking school (see *Renseignements Pratiques* for details).

M y fascination with pizza trucks began several years ago at Christmas time, when near our home in Provence I spotted a small gray Citroën van for sale at a local gas station. For reasons even I don't understand, I began to dream of owning that truck—a battered, twenty-five-year-old vehicle that had been customized into a mobile pizza stand, complete with wood-burning oven—and making the tour of markets up and down the Rhône valley.

My dream has not come true, but I've satisfied myself by collecting photographs and lore on the pizza trucks of Provence, chatting with the bakers and sampling the varied pizzas and snacks sold from the vans throughout the year in markets and in village squares all over the region.

Traveling from market to market, following my nose as the fragrance of freshly baked pizzas wafted through the air, I have kept mental notes on styles and makes of trucks and on the assorted pizza toppings that seem most popular.

What, one might ask, is pizza doing in Provence? Some believe that flat bread dough topped with local flavorings and baked in stone bread ovens have been popular in the region since the days of the Romans.

Others say pizza came along later, seeping over the border from Italy and up from the region of Nice, which, until the middle of the last century, was part of Italy. In either case, it all makes sense, as the traditional toppings, from cheese to anchovies, black olives to ripe red tomatoes, are native to the region.

The pizza truck's presence at the market also makes sense historically. For centuries, itinerant merchants sold ready-to-eat snacks, such as homemade *pissaladière* (flat rectangular bread tarts topped with onions, black olives and anchovies), *fougasse* (ladder-shaped bread sprinkled with anchovies or pork cracklings), as well as dried figs wrapped in fig leaves, for local people to eat out of hand as they conducted their weekly marketing.

Pizza truck fare serves as modern-day fast food, snacks for eating during the morning while shoppers wander through the market stalls. Modern-day housewives who are too busy to cook on shopping day place an order for a pizza to go when they arrive at the market, then pick up the pie just before closing time, to take home for the noon meal.

The contemporary itinerant pizza truck merchants travel hundreds of kilometers each week, stationing themselves at markets and in village squares on a more or less regular scheduled route.

The creativity of pizza truck decors, as well as the menus, are limited only by the merchant's imagination. In Carpentras on Friday market days one finds no fewer than eleven trucks, including an immense green and white Peugeot van—Pizza Chez Bernard—advertising pizza au feu du bois, or specialties baked in a wood-fired oven.

I spotted one of my all-time favorite pizza trucks in the lively village of Forcalquier one Monday in July, when the weekly market was in full swing. There, right in front of the Post Office, stood Pizza Chez Michel, a bright blue and white van with advertising for snacks painted on it with Kodachrome clarity. Pizza Chez Michel offered a superb pizza sprinkled with wild cèpe mushrooms, another with goat cheese and anchovies, and yet another layered with paper-thin slices of home-cured country ham. The woman behind the counter also dispensed thin buckwheat crepes sprinkled with Grand Marnier, a pizza *armènienne* (sprinkled with ground meat, olives, tomatoes and garlic) and baguette sandwiches of sliced pâté or sausage.

The biggest truck I ever spotted was in the tiny village of Banon, population 950. About half of the space at the Tuesday morning market held on the *boules* court was taken up by a truck the size of a double-wide house trailer. The truck was outfitted with a wood-burning oven for baking crisp pizzas and for roasting farm-fresh chickens.

The most unusual offshoot of the pizza truck I ever saw was parked in the center of the market in the village of Digne, where an iridescent blue panel truck offered marketgoers a taste of America. The Rockburger, painted with a giant cartoon of a multidecker hamburger and a crushed can of Coca-Cola, offered rockburgers, rockmonsieurs (grilled ham sandwich topped with grated cheese) and rockdogs, with frites, "Coca," and all the Heinz ketchup your heart desires.

No one I have spoken to seemed to have any idea of exactly when the pizza truck became such a fixture in the villages of Provence. However, one recent Sunday in the village of L'Îsle-sur-la-Sorgue, a merchant assured me that his 1960s Citroën was custom-outfitted with a small gas oven more than twenty-five years ago. "Today," remarked the current owner, Remy Plauche, "you can buy factory-made models, but they just don't have the charm."

Monsieur Plauche—whose spiffy orange and white van still bears the name of the original owner, Monsieur Meyssard—travels from village to village offering his specialties by the portion or *entier*. At about $1 for a slice of cheese-and-anchovy pizza and $5 for a ten-inch pie, Monsieur Plauche's prices are typical of all the mobile pizza sellers.

On a good day, a pizza baker might sell up to one hundred

pizzas, with toppings ranging from the ordinary (tomatoes and anchovies) to the unusual (mussels and shrimp).

Although most of the pizza bakers of Provence may never rate Michelin stars for their culinary excellence, there are tips to searching out the best pies. First, look for those baked in wood-fired ovens: the wood flame imparts a richness and subtlety you don't get with gas or electric ovens. Second, keep the topping as simple as possible (my favorite is sprinkled with shavings of the local goat cheese, known as *picodon*). And finally, ask the baker to make yours "*bien cuit,*" or well done, in hopes that the crust will be properly crispy and crunchy.

Pizza to Roll

Following is a selected list of markets, and market days, on which pizzas from Provence and the Alps/Côte d'Azur can be sampled. Markets are held in the mornings only, usually starting at around 9 A.M. and closing at noon.

Monday: Aix-en-Provence, Bollène, Cavaillon, Forcalquier.

Tuesday: Aix-en-Provence, Banon, Vaison-la-Romaine.

Wednesday: Arles, Cassis, St.-Rémy-de-Provence, Sisteron.

Thursday: Aix-en-Provence, L'Isle-sur-la-Sorgue, Maussane-les-Alpilles, Nyons, Orange.

Friday: Aix-en-Provence, Carpentras, Cassis.

Saturday: Arles, Saint-Rémy-de Provence, Saint-Tropez.

Sunday: L'Isle-sur-la-Sorgue, Sarrians.

This piece originally appeared in the travel section of *The New York Times* on June 5, 1988. Copyright © 1988 by Patricia Wells. Reprinted with permission of the author.

A Memorable Meal:
In M.F.K. Fisher's Footsteps

BY MARY CANTWELL

∽

editor's note

I was prepared to like this piece before I read it because I had so enjoyed Mary Cantwell's book *Manhattan, When I Was Young. Sans doute,* not only did I like it, I *loved* it, most of all because I so identified with her desire not to trust the small details of a journey to memory. I always scribble in my journal when I'm traveling, prompting my husband to cringe and some staff to assume (mistakenly) I'm an important reviewer!

MARY CANTWELL was the author of several memoirs, including *Speaking with Strangers* (Houghton Mifflin, 1998, hardcover; Penguin, 1999, paperback) and *Manhattan, When I Was Young* (Houghton Mifflin, 1995, hardcover; Penguin, 1996, paperback). She wrote this piece for the July 1999 issue of *Gourmet.*

My husband and I were crammed into a small Fiat, equipped with a *Guide Michelin,* a list of places we wanted to see, and M.F.K. Fisher's *Map of Another Town,* which we had nicknamed the "*Guide* Fisher." In Aix-en-Provence it was Fisher's restaurants and lodgings we looked for, her perceptions we were trying to share. I have seldom been happier than during our lazy walks along the Cours Mirabeau.

Never before or since has a journey, like that one through the south of France, lived up to my every illusion. One day we even experienced a mistral, whose gusts, true to promise, made leaving our cozy, map-strewn car as much an emotional as it was a physical assault. The Riviera, we said sagely (as if we knew), was spoiled, but did it matter when driving a few miles inland was all it took to

À Table!

be transported to Roman France? And medieval France? And the France of Marcel Pagnol?

One drowsy afternoon we drove across a great plain, through air that seemed the color of honey. We had been lured in that direction by the label on a wine bottle—a picture of a ruined tower—and my husband wanted to see the place where the wine came from. Perhaps if I hadn't had my nose stuck in *Michelin,* the landscape that passed us by might have struck me as beautiful. Instead, I was saddened to learn (as I read aloud) that two millennia ago that peaceful plain had been literally bloody. In 102 B.C. the Roman general Marius fought a battle there, saving Provence from the barbarians. For decades thereafter, the warriors' bones were used to make fences.

I wanted to turn back, to Aix, maybe, or to the Palace of the Popes in Avignon, but by then that ruined tower had turned into the Grail. So on we drove, while I, who soaks up atmosphere the way wool picks up lint, slowly drowned in misery. Then we saw a small town that looked as if it had grown out of the hillside in which it was niched.

It was named La Tour d'Aigues. To the left of the town *place* was the roofless ruin of a sixteenth-century château that had been torched during the French Revolution. In one room an enormous shiny-leafed bush with white flowers reached toward the sky. Looking out from an arched entrance, we could see the *place* and, beyond that, the plain. From that height it looked like a Brueghel landscape. By then it was sundown, and in the shadow cast by a wall of the château, old men were playing *pétanque.* Young men were playing pinball in a café, the second floor of which was a restaurant. When we climbed the stairs and saw it, I reached for the little travel diary my mother had given me. For once I didn't want to trust my memory.

I scribbled: *Roses on every table, matching curtains and table-cloths that might have been run up by a grand-mère. Dresser with baskets of fruit, big bunch of pussy willows. The waitresses—an old woman and a young girl. They gave us a pissaladière niçoise fresh from the oven. Then we had beautiful white asparagus in a vinaigrette. B. had marvelous frogs' legs, and I a trout spitted on fennel. Local white wine, local chèvre. Crème caramel and tarte aux pommes.*

I had never had white asparagus before, and I loved it immediately. My quite-ordinary supermarket stocks it now, and I am forever working on the quintessential vinaigrette. But I know no American restaurant, however fond it may be of proclaiming itself an honest-to-God bistro, that measures up to that one in La Tour d'Aigues. That small second-story room is the reason I gave up haute cuisine on the spot (up to then we'd stopped at every three-star on our route).

Until that evening, I had never realized how a few elements—a little kindness, roses picked from somebody's garden, and food that had been transported no more than a mile from where it was nurtured—could constitute a kind of "yes" to life. That great plain ceased to bother me, and its grim battle receded to what it should have been all along: a mere mention in my *Michelin*. All that was bad was erased by everything that was good in that little town.

Because perfection never comes twice, I haven't returned to Provence, and my only souvenirs are photographs of triumphal arches and columns, cloisters and churches, and one of myself in a purple shirt and orange corduroy trousers. (I must have been visible for miles.)

Ironically, we never found the ruined tower from the wine label. But do I regret not finding it? I don't think so. My memory sees it even if my eyes did not, and, like all unrealized desires, it still lures.

"A Memorable Meal: In M.F.K. Fisher's Footsteps" by Mary Cantwell. Copyright © 1999 by Mary Cantwell. Originally published in *Gourmet*. Reprinted by permission of the Estate of Mary Cantwell.

À Table!   411

Bibliothèque

Eating & Drinking in France, Andy Herbach and Michael Dillon, Capra Press, Santa Barbara, 2000. This is one book in the "What Kind of Food Am I?" series (others are on Spain and Italy), and I *love* it. First of all, it's a small paperback that fits easily in a pocket, so you won't look like a nerd in a restaurant as you look up a word. More important, it's *really* thorough: seventy-eight pages of French menu words and methods and styles of cooking (which, as we all know, is what trips people up the most), such as *canard à la presse* (roast duck with red wine and cognac), *hongroise* (served with paprika and cream, means "Hungarian"), *pommes à l'anglaise* (boiled potatoes), and *oeuf à l'Huguenote* (poached egg with meat sauce). Plus, these guys are funny: in the margins, they note, "You won't want to confuse *ris* (sweetbreads) and *riz* (rice)," "*jambon persillé* (parsleyed ham) is generally shredded and served in jelly and frankly it's not up our alley," "*tripoux* . . . sounds fancy, still tripe," and next to the entry for ketchup, "if you're looking this up you've had too much to drink." There is also a list of their favorite restaurants around France (over twenty in Provence and along the coast), and an English-to-French pronunciation guide including useful phrases such as: What is this?; I did not order this; I am a vegetarian; overcooked; and rare. There are a few misspellings in the book, and I disagree with the authors about *marrons glacés* (perhaps they never had them?), but I wouldn't go to France without this in my bag.

Guide Gantié, Jacques Gantié, 2000. I read of this book in Peter Mayle's *Encore Provence.* Mayle writes that the guide describes "750 *bonnes tables* from one end of Provence to the other." He adds, "Read it and eat." The *Guide* is theoretically available in both French and English editions, but the French version is more widely available, even at English-language bookstores (my copy is from The Cat's Whiskers in Nice—see "Bookstores" in *Renseignements Pratiques* for address and telephone). But even if you don't read French, you can't go wrong, as the majority of entries are marked with one, two, three, or four olive branches, one being a *"coup de coeur"* (a menu that stands apart though sometimes the establishment is modest or not widely known) and four being a *"table d'exception"* (approaching perfection). The 2000 edition lists 800 *bonnes tables* as well as 500 *produits gourmands* (which appear on the green *"Paniers du Sud"* pages) for Provence, Côte d'Azur, and Liguria and Piedmont just over the border in Italy. (Additionally, there are some *tables du Sud* listings for Paris.) *De rigueur.*

The Food Lover's Guide to France, Patricia Wells, Workman, 1987. Although this book is over a dozen years old, I still highly recommend it. Many of the restaurants, *fromageries, charcuteries, boulangeries,* and shops selling *spécialités régionales* of Provence and the Côte d'Azur are not only still in business but thriving. *De rigueur.*

Michelin France: Hotels & Restaurants, better known as the Red Guide. The Michelin Red Guide was first published in 1900, and it's easy to see how it has maintained its excellent reputation for just over a century. I think of the Red Guide as being a nearly perfect book: it offers good accompanying maps, alphabetical entries by city or town, wine suggestions, twenty pages of maps indicating the location of three-star establishments, and "Bib Gourmand"— my favorite—places, school holidays calendar, license plate codes, international dialing codes, and a Euro conversion chart. Though the hotel and restaurant descriptions are in French, they are accompanied by many easy-to-decipher symbols, which are explained in English in the introductory section of the book. I'm an especially big fan of the *Repas* "Bib Gourmand" listings. These are good-value places defined as offering good food at moderate prices, and I think these are more often "worth a detour" than the three-star palaces. Just as I've written about Michelin's The Green Guide, travelers will always be in capable hands with a Michelin Red Guide—it's like the Steady Eddie of guidebooks. However, Michelin does not provide the sort of review commentary I find useful, which is why I also enthusiastically recommend consulting Patricia Wells's book and the *Guide Gantié* above. Each guide has its strengths, and using them both will cover all the bases.

Articles

"Provençal Contemporary," Colman Andrews, *Saveur* No. 20, July/August 1997. Some of Provence's—and France's—best new cooking from Auberge de Noves outside Avignon, Le Cagnard in Haut-de-Cagnes, and Le Mas du Langoustier on the Île de Porquerolles. To order a back issue, contact *Saveur* at 800-462-0209.

~Perhaps better than an entire book on restaurants and cafés is simply a handful of carefully chosen addresses. These I have found at the back of some good cookbooks, notably *Flavors of the Riviera: Discovering Real Mediterranean Cooking,* by Colman Andrews (five restaurants are recommended in Nice), and *Provence Gastronomique* by Erica Brown (a few restaurants are recommended for a number of towns in Provence). Both of these titles are detailed in the *Saveurs Provençaux bibliothèque.*

Les Personalités
(Natives and Passionate Visitors)

" 'Naturally you love Provence,' says a character in Colette's novel La Treille de muscat, 'but which Provence? There are several.' It is vital to remember this when discussing any aspect of the region, beginning with the Provençals themselves. Any generalization about a people is suspect, but those made about the Provençals seem to be particularly so. The region's southern climate has led travellers to describe its people in the same hackneyed terms that are commonly applied to all those living in a Mediterranean climate . . . 'There is no single Provençal person,' suggested the chronicler of the Félibres, 'there are just Provençal people.' "

—Michael Jacobs, *A Guide to Provence*

Matisse on the Riviera

BY LORRAINE ALEXANDER

❧

editor's note

Although Matisse didn't arrive on the Côte d'Azur until the middle age of his long life, his name has become synonymous with the Mediterranean. The real treat, for me, at the Musée Matisse, is the casual appearance of his red-and-ivory-striped chair, familiar to us all from a number of his paintings. What I would give to take that chair home!

The Chapelle du Rosaire in Vence is a completely different—and in some ways more rewarding—visual treat. On my visits to the *chapelle* there have never been more than a handful of tourists inside, leaving one to contemplate Matisse's creation in relative silence. My suggestion for a perfect day on the coast might begin by first selecting a pair of comfortable walking shoes. Depending on where you're staying, plan to walk either up or down the footpath that connects Old Nice with Vence. As I prefer walking down the hill, I would visit the *chapelle* first, and then make my way down the footpath, pausing at the Fondation Maeght. (The path is not strenuous and it follows a stream for part of the way; inquire at the tourist office about the exact location of the footpath—it's not difficult to find, but you do have to know where to look.) After lunch or an early aperitif in Nice, end your day at the Musée Matisse, where you can reflect upon your rewarding journey. To return to your original starting point, visitors may want to take the bus (there is hourly service between Nice and Vence) as the route provides some of the most spectacular scenery in the world.

LORRAINE ALEXANDER lives in Italy and has been a longtime contributor to *Gourmet*, where this piece appeared in September 1994.

The year was 1917. George M. Cohan wrote "Over There," and Freud published *Introduction to Psychoanalysis*. Dixieland jazz was in, and the Romanovs were out. And, the week before Christmas, forty-eight-year-old Henri Matisse arrived at Nice's Hôtel Beau Rivage, moving into a narrow room with a large window opening onto the Mediterranean. He was suffering from bronchitis and needed, quite literally, breathing space "far from Paris and my cares." But it rained for a month. "Finally," he wrote, "I decided to leave. The next day the mistral chased the clouds away, and it was beautiful. I decided not to leave Nice and have stayed practically the rest of my life."

Matisse had grown up in the north of France, where sun and color were as rare as kumquats. His grain-merchant father wanted him to study law, which he dutifully did. But in 1890, during a long convalescence from appendicitis, his mother gave him a box of watercolors. And the rest, as they say, is art history.

The "great colored reflections of January" had cast their seductive spell, and for the next thirty-seven years Matisse would produce, mainly in Nice and nearby Vence, a prodigious body of work—paintings and line drawings, sculptures and tapestry cartoons, book designs and ceramics, the "Dance" murals of the Barnes Foundation, the cutouts of *Jazz,* the stained glass of the Rosary Chapel. And now, forty years after his death, there is a growing conviction—aided by the 1992–93 New York and Paris retrospective exhibitions and the world tour of the Barnes collection—that Matisse will be considered the greatest painter of the modern age.

Matisse's art, deliberately devoid of troubling subject matter, lightens the world's load rather than adding to it. His aim was never consciously to shock or confound. What we respond to in his canvases and cutouts is harmony and the purity of saturated color, set before us as celebrations of beautiful women, decorated rooms, flowers and fruits, sea and sky, and finally that dazzling Mediterranean light—more often than not filtered through a window that remains an invitation to lush, limitless possibility and the horizon's serenity.

Matisse painted four canvases in his cramped Beau Rivage room above what became, with the Armistice, the Quai des Etats-Unis. He was already famous: He had met Gertrude Stein and her art-collecting family a dozen years earlier; his works figured importantly in the fabulous collection of modern art acquired by the pioneering John Quinn. *Blue Nude* (1907) had been featured in New York's groundbreaking Armory Exhibition in 1913—and been burned in effigy by art students in Chicago. He was, too, a dedicated paterfamilias, long settled with his wife, Amélie, and three children on the outskirts of Paris. But it was the Riviera that seized him and would condition the creative vision of the second, hugely productive, half of his life.

The stretch of Mediterranean coastline that claimed Matisse was a simpler place in 1917 than it is today, though it had already reinvented itself several times over. Tobias Smollett, who lived for two years, from 1763, in what is now Nice's *vieille ville,* was the first writer of note in English to describe the area. What he had to say about Nice made good reading but very bad cross-cultural blood. The typical *niçois* was a "dirty knave," the women were "not particularly well favored except for their teeth," and the food was mainly sour bread, salt fish, and bad butter. About the only thing Smollett could like were the gardens, by which "I can scarcely help thinking myself enchanted."

Smollett's *Travels Through France and Italy* delivered far from a crushing blow to Nice, of course; the redoubtable doctor himself even put in for a posting as the city's next consul. (Request denied.) Either he was a glutton for punishment or the Riviera had managed to cast the net of its spell over even this very feisty fish.

Part of the Riviera's lure, then as now, was its climate. Smollett had tuberculosis, and for the next century and a half many of the rich and famous who rushed to the coast did so, like him, as much in pursuit of life itself as of the good life. The railroad—"a cannon-ball style of travelling" in the view of one observer—reached Nice in 1864, and, from that moment on, the Riviera grew with the speed of a headlong express. By century's end Queen Victoria was wintering at the Excelsior-Régina, built in her honor in Cimiez, Nice's residential hill where the Roman town of Cemenelum had thrived in the second century B.C. But

Queen Victoria was not to be the Régina's only illustrious tenant; from 1938 until he died, in 1954, Matisse lived and worked in his Régina apartment across the street from the Romans' ruined arena—and from the grove of olive trees that would one day front Nice's Musée Matisse.

For the two decades preceding that move, however, Matisse remained mainly in or near Nice's old quarter, creating a body of work that would later be assigned to his "Nice period." When the Beau Rivage was requisitioned to house demobilized American soldiers in 1918, Matisse first moved next door, to number 105, Quai des Etats-Unis, where he painted his daughter, Marguerite, in her plaid coat and his son Pierre practicing the violin; then, for an even briefer stay, to a nearby villa, which produced several landscapes. Soon, however, he was back in a suite of hotel rooms, this time at the Hôtel de la Méditerranée, which stood a few blocks from the landmark Negresco, on the Promenade des Anglais, until it was demolished in the 1930s. Here, in Italianate rooms rented over a period of four years, he posed his gauze-draped models on antimacassared armchairs or on the balustraded balcony that would give them, and us, sweeping views of the Baie des Anges and Carnival-time's Fête des Fleurs.

Finally, in September 1921, Matisse found the premises that would suit his needs for the next seventeen years. At 1, Place Charles-Félix, the neoclassical structure that illumines the Cours Saleya when its golden stone is infused with late-day sun, there was space enough, and most of all there was light enough. (The enormous window of the fourth-floor atelier remains easily visible from the east end of the Promenade's beach.) Here Matisse occasionally left his painter's easel to work on book illustrations, pen-and-ink drawings, tapestry designs for Beauvais, and sets and costumes for Diaghilev's Ballets Russes. But during most of the 1920s and 1930s he was still painting his odalisques, Moorish screens, and the anemones and dahlias, magnolias and ranunculi, lemons and pineapples that fill many of his best-loved canvases.

There can be little doubt where all those fruits and flowers came from. The Cours Saleya's daily market must have been as much an organic art-supply store for Matisse as it is a part of present residents' food-shopping rounds. Its stands of Cavaillon melons, snowy-headed cauliflower, bright bell peppers, and herbs and olives galore are legend on the Riviera, as are the cafés whose tables edge up to them.

Le Safari is my favorite. This is where the neighborhood comes for lunch, and so it was here that I sat down with sculptors Sacha Sosno and Arman to talk about Matisse, whom Sosno had visited at the Régina and been encouraged by as a boy; drink the house red; welcome serendipitous arrivals; and order. What came first was platters piled high with steamed mussels and then, handed overhead as if borne on waves, mounds of sliced raw artichokes dressed only

in olive oil and lemon. But one of the party had ordered the house ravioli with *boeuf en daube* filling to begin, and once these had been sampled more of the rich little squares came as main courses—and real, humming contentment set in. My own main course, a specialty promoted by Sosno, who is an eager cook when he's not in his marble-filled workshop just off the Place de l'Ancien Sénat, was nothing more or less than delicious golden chanterelles sautéed with garlic and parsley.

The following Monday I came back for the Cours Saleya's weekly antiques and flea market and, after rummaging through vintage lace and old silver, settled in with a friend for another Safari lunch. What we wanted by then was a dose of mercy—food that was typical but light—and we got exactly that: *salade niçoise* and a perfect *bagna cauda,* the Provençal fast-day (that is, meatless) plate of boiled vegetables with pungent anchovy sauce. It was a glorious, sunny day, and hot enough, even under our umbrella, that we decided on *panachés* (half beer, half fizzy lemonade) instead of wine, and ended with bolts of espresso to propel us into the afternoon.

At the Safari, I chose lunch and the animated market crowd over dinner; dinner, on the other hand, is the only meal served at La Merenda, a few blocks away. Some people complain that the service at this minuscule mecca of Nice cooking is less than friendly. The night I went, however, someone let slip an audible sigh when told that the zucchini blossom *beignets* were *finis,* and when her second choice arrived—excellent stuffed and panfried sardines—so did the kitchen's single remaining *beignet* and an indulgent smile from Madame. Pasta *au pistou* was luscious, even if its buttery flavor seemed odd, with Alziari, the most famous olive-oil merchant in the city, just steps away on rue St.-François-de-Paule. La Merenda serves regional classics—ratatouille, lentils with sausage, tripe in white-wine sauce—and plenty of bustle, but you have to be brave to secure one of its seven tables: In an age when people without

answering machines are considered cranky if not actually perverse, La Merenda's lack of a telephone has an almost antediluvian charm. Still, reservations are taken, and if you stop by to make them several days before you want to dine you will have cracked the code.

Back on the extension of the Cours that leads to the Beau Rivage is one more outpost of genuine Nice food: La Petite Maison. The paneling and house poodle, posters and pink gladioli, ceiling fans and gilt mirrors are reliable clues that this is an old-style place likely to give value for the franc. Two fish dishes were excellent: grilled salmon encrusted with peppercorns and served with anise cream; and grilled *loup de mer* (sea bass), which came with violet artichokes, chanterelles, and a healthy splash of olive oil.

And now to bed. Matisse's old room at the Hôtel Beau Rivage vanished when the section he occupied was turned into apartments; but the part facing the rue St.-François-de-Paule offers reliable comfort, businesslike efficiency—messages delivered on your television screen—and of course great location. In summer La Plage Beau Rivage is an attractive spot for a beach lunch as well as a romantic setting for drinks.

A simpler but more personable hotel is La Pérouse, beyond the Galerie des Ponchettes (where works by Dufy are on permanent display) on the curve of road that leads to Nice's port. La Pérouse is, like the Beau Rivage, mere steps from the Cours Saleya but also affords unobstructed views of the Promenade and bay as well as the surprise of a pool and patio set in the cliff behind it and shaded by lemon trees. The small grill room operates only in high summer.

To reach the Cimiez district and Musée Matisse from Nice's old quarter requires a good town map if you have chosen to drive yourself rather than go by taxi or bus; in any case you will head north and west, paralleling for a time the Paillon riverbed. To one side of

the museum's grounds is the Franciscan monastery where Matisse is buried, and to the other, across the rue de Matisse, is the Régina, the artist's principal residence for the last decade and a half of his life. (The Régina's former splendor is now dulled and peeling, more evocative of Miss Havisham than of Queen Victoria, and the former Matisse apartment has been divided in two and stripped of anything recalling its famous resident. The curious may nonetheless find, as I did, an obliging tenant to lead them along the side terrace for a glimpse of Matisse's third-floor bay windows.)

When the "new" Matisse museum opened last June, many art lovers could hardly believe all the waiting was finally at an end. The original museum had opened in 1963, sharing space with Nice's archaeology museum in a red and ochre villa built in the seventeenth century. Though it had been altered (its façade is largely trompe-l'oeil), the villa was classified as a landmark, making the addition of a modern structure aboveground impossible. A competition was held, a design settled upon, and in 1987 digging was undertaken to the north of the villa—until more Roman ruins were uncovered. Work was eventually relocated to the west, where construction proceeded unhindered by history, thanks to the Roman Empire's environmental protection policy: This area had been traversed by an aqueduct, and in order to keep the water supply unpolluted no dwellings had been erected. All this, along with scandals in city hall and the election of a new mayor, makes it easy to compute the delays.

A curving sweep of white stairs leads down to the reception hall, where Matisse's enormous *Oceania, the Sky* and *Oceania, the Sea* (1946–47) and *Flowers and Fruits* (1952–53) are allowed their full dramatic impact. The neutral tones of the *Oceania* pair can be a shock, coming from this supreme colorist. The motifs were inspired by Matisse's 1931 trip to Tahiti, but because he found the light there disappointing (he was enchanted, on the other hand, by New York

City's winter light) he put color aside in favor of creamy stencil and silk-screen flora and fauna on fields of natural linen.

The result is as subdued and elegant as the impeccably tailored linen suits Matisse typically wore. He looked, in fact, more like a fastidious psychoanalyst than an innovative artist, as can be seen in the many photos of him at the museum. And form did follow function: His life was orderly, dominated by work; he spoke the beautiful, concise French of cultivated men of past eras; and he could, in person and in such works as the *Oceania* pair, transmit a powerful calm. The calm was not seamless: Matisse was sensitive to the most casual remark, an insomniac, a perfectionist; his painter friend Edmond Cross characterized him as "anxious, madly anxious." Still, or perhaps because of his personal torments, Matisse's goal was always balance, and here it is, at the outset, in the serene palette and weightless equilibrium of his sea and sky worlds, and even— though this time admitting color—in the rhythmic, repetitive design of *Flowers and Fruits*.

Matisse's cutouts, of which *Flowers and Fruits*—actually a study for a ceramic mural—is the largest and last completed, were made according to a very particular technique. Poor health at the end of his life made standing for long hours at an easel insupportable, and so he instructed assistants in the coloring of specially made squares of paper. Mixing his own paints, he had them cover the squares in quick, overlapping strokes to create smoothly monochromatic swatches. Matisse himself did the cutting, but only after repeatedly drawing his shapes, then smudging the outlines to help him see them as volumetric. When he was satisfied with a design and ready to cut, he put the final drawing out of sight, chose music to complement the feelings he wanted to express, and then cut, in precise strokes and often in rhythm with the music, the form he had memorized. "To cut out color quickly," he said, "reminds me of chiseling sculptures."

Sculpture was the medium Matisse turned to in order to resolve problems of depicting mass in his paintings, and the four "Back" bronzes that completed the entry display when I visited illustrate this principle. "I sculpted," he said, "to impose order on my mind. . . . I painted like a painter; I did not sculpt like a sculptor." The "Backs," two of which still belong to Matisse's inheritors, are bas-relief figures still clinging to the painter's two dimensions, not yet liberated in space. They were finished in numbered succession from 1909 to 1931, and their progression toward abstraction mirrors the artist's own course.

Upstairs are more sculptures: first, the series of "Jeannette" heads, looking like bulbous, rather eerie flowers; and then, as we proceed to the central room of the villa, numerous small standing and reclining nudes, all from the 1920s, that in fact are contemporary with the odalisques Matisse was then painting in his Place Charles-Félix studio. These "miniatures," attitudes relaxed, arms often draped about their heads, are a lesser-known part of Matisse's body of work (he did about seventy sculptures in all, however, a number that indicates their importance to their creator) and another revelation of his graceful hand.

A room documenting the education of that supple hand is close-by, but on our way are some of the drawings that show it off best. In the 1936 *Portrait of a Woman* (Mrs. Dorothy Paley) shading still played its role in realistic rendering, but in the 1951 *Portrait of Claude* (the artist's grandson, now the head of the family firm of inheritors) we see the ultimate distillation of drawing for Matisse: a few deft lines, squiggles for eyes, and yet the regard so expressive and specific. Matisse never stopped being a student; his son Jean took a revealing photo of him in 1946, when he was seventy-five, drawing at the Louvre. The purpose of so much practice was to make the stroke of his hand a taking of flight, a movement free of thought by the time it marked the surface he would sign. Christian

Arthaud, assistant curator of the museum, told me that Matisse actually closed his eyes to do some of his drawings, including one here of Rabelais; this was his ultimate test of himself, not a game, and his signatures are the stamps of his own approval.

The room of Matisse's earliest paintings will surprise many visitors. They are mostly academic copies—exercises that provided income when bought by the state—and dark little still lifes and landscapes: *Still Life with Books* (1890), which Matisse considered his first real painting; a vase of three timid daisies peering out from murky depths; and a Breton village, its palette wholly of the north. The only glimpse of light and things to come is a small canvas painted in Corsica, soon after his marriage, when he first found the Mediterranean.

Also on this floor, you will discover another aspect of Matisse's diversity: his book designs. For Matisse the open book was equivalent to a canvas, and his concern was to create, as always, balance and harmony, playing dark against light, white space against decoration. Matisse knew many of the writers whose works he illustrated—Apollinaire, Aragon, de Montherlant—and admired the others, among them James Joyce, medieval poet Charles d'Orléans, and symbolist poet Stéphane Mallarmé. (Every phase of the Mallarmé project, his first endeavor in book design, was bought by the Cone sisters of Baltimore, whom Matisse considered his ideal patrons, and now belongs to the Baltimore Museum of Art.)

Upstairs you will pass through several rooms with a mix of such instantly recognizable paintings as *Still Life with Pomegranates* (1947); unfinished ones, such as *Nymph in the Forest/Verdure,* complete with erasures, which was a study for a tapestry design; objects the artist collected as well as painted, including a Moroccan samovar and a rococo chair; many more marvelous drawings and cutouts, among them *The Wave,* which the museum has adopted as its logo; forty-odd preliminary works for the Barnes *Dance* murals;

and finally a multitude of early versions of the decorations for the Rosary Chapel in Vence.

What you will not find is a mine of Matisse's greatest masterpieces, one reason being that the visionary collectors of his work were not primarily French; instead they were Russian (until the Revolution, when private collections were confiscated), to a limited extent German (until Nazism pronounced modern art "degenerate"), and, especially, American. By the end of the 1920s Dr. Barnes's holdings alone, amassed in Merion, Pennsylvania, included sixty Matisses. In France, on the other hand, the first critical study of Matisse did not appear until he was fifty, and his "Nice period" canvases, so full of beautiful images, were dismissed for years as merely decorative. In spite of this, Xavier Girard, the Matisse museum's curator, has pursued a mission of honoring the artist on his home ground, and the resulting gift to us all is 68 paintings and cutouts, 236 drawings, 57 sculptures, and more—all on view in the environment Matisse chose above all others.

In January 1941, Matisse was operated on for cancer. War was raging, too, of course, and the precarious location of Cimiez, unprotected above Nice, added to his worries. In March, 1943, an arsenal on the Cimiez hillside was in fact bombed, and in July Matisse left the Régina for the relative refuge of Vence. He went with Lydia Delectorskaya, who had been his wife's nurse and then his model in the 1930s—she is the cool, lovely blonde of *The Blue Eyes* and *Woman in Blue*—and who by this time had supplanted Amélie (the couple separated legally in 1940) to become his companion and devoted gatekeeper. The house they rented for nearly six years was called Le Rêve (the dream), and it was here that Matisse embarked in earnest on his cutouts and the chapel decorations that would turn Vence into a place of artistic pilgrimage.

My advice is to come to Vence—only five miles inland and one stop (exit Cagnes) from Nice on the *autoroute*—for more than a hasty visit to the chapel; the surrounding hills provide a greener scene as well as several fine museums that will complement your Matisse itinerary. (The *autoroute* is the best way to come if you do not wish to risk motorized mayhem on the smaller roads, which would seem to promise a gentle approach but are so poorly sign-posted you may find yourself, as I did, being asked directions on a ribbon of asphalt by the equally lost driver of a fork-lift crane.) Vence's medieval gates and fountains are animated by the commerce of its shops and market stalls, and the Auberge des Seigneurs, near the Peyra Gate, is a good choice for dinner, especially on a chilly night when its fire is blazing and the typically lively crowd that gathers for grilled meats and the house *marc* turns the rustic room into a Gallic mead hall.

For comfortable accommodations—and fresh house-baked croissants at breakfast—you need only follow the signs for the Col de Vence, crossing avenue Henri Matisse, to fall into the friendly lap of the Hôtel La Roseraie, a blush-pink house with sage shutters that was recently restored by owners Maurice and Monica Ganier. Many of the dozen modestly priced rooms, decorated with generous splashes of Souleïado fabrics, have southern exposures over the pool and garden and beyond to Vence's Romanesque church tower.

Farther up the hill and just beneath the *baous,* or stone bluffs, that dominate the landscape above Vence is the Château du Domaine Saint-Martin, which combines beautiful lodgings with the fine cooking of chef Dominique Ferrière and the wine connoisseurship of sommelier René Leroux. (A Clos Saint-Joseph, white and of the region, was a delicious discovery one evening.) Meals are taken in the glassed-in dining room, on the adjoining terrace, or poolside amid flowering oleander, and guests can stay in the main house, separate pine-shaded villas, or one of the spacious bastides nestled into the eave of the *baous*. Waking up to sunshine and breakfast on a bastide terrace pitched over olive and cypress groves with views down to Cap d'Antibes comes at a price, but this is the best excuse in these hills to cut loose and fly high if your purse permits.

Such stratospheric spaces can be a barrier to a genuine experience of place, but the area's many fine-art collections soon comprise a *table d'orientation:* Galerie Beaubourg, opened only last summer (the sculpture garden is a field day of Armans, Sosnos, and Césars, among others); Les Collettes, Renoir's house-museum in Cagnes-sur-Mer, where two Matisse watercolors mark his visit to the Impressionist master only weeks after his arrival in Nice; and the Fondation Maeght. I went to the Maeght in a rainstorm, hoping to find Matisses among the abundant Mirós and glorious, gaunt Giacomettis, but there are none here, though the gift shop does a brisk business in posters of his work.

Not that those poignant Giacomettis in the Maeght's central courtyard aren't worth jumping puddles to see. Still, the gray, Matisse-less morning had put a literal damper on my vision of lunch on a sundappled terrace. Until, that is, I sat down to the Auberge du Clos du Loup's *marmite de poissons* with a friend, a bottle of Château Maravenne rosé (a Côtes de Provence from near La Londe), and—would I make this up?—a house tape of "Singin' in the Rain." Our moods soared from soggy to sublime once the tureen of red mullet, weever, scorpion fish, and cod—no interloping lobster here—in a broth perfumed with coriander and saffron was set before us. This, desserts of poached pears with chocolate sauce, Gene Kelly, and the grape vine framing our window made the wet world outside slip swiftly away.

Visitors to the Maeght who had reserved a table at the famous Colombe d'Or, in nearby Saint-Paul-de-Vence, were probably not as lucky. Though the very pretty guest rooms and terrace and especially the art (Picassos and Calders and a Matisse drawing included) have made its name, the Colombe d'Or has fallen victim to its own celebrity. On three different occasions the food was only average, the service indifferent, even harried, and the art poorly lit and labeled. In summer, tour buses clog the access road, and Saint-Paul itself, delightful off-season, feels like a theme park. The best time to go is early morning, before the likes of you and me have arrived in force, or at night, when you can sense the romance of this village and hear your own footsteps on the cobblestones. The real beauty here, for both its restaurant—indoors or terrace—and rooms, is Le Saint-Paul, tucked into the village center but with splendid views out over the crumbling ramparts. The Café de la Place is a good spot to enjoy a ham sandwich, the hot plat du jour, or just a cold beer and to watch a game of *boules*—Montand played here!—or the local poodles on parade.

One thing you will discover in this fascinating region is that environments change abruptly within only a few kilometers. The Hôtel Le Hameau, just outside Saint-Paul, is a charming family-run cluster of converted farm buildings interspersed with grapefruit and mandarine groves. Trellised grapes and passion flowers shade the path to the parking area, and many of the rooms have semiprivate balconies or patios. There is a pool, too, on a slight rise from which magenta bougainvillea, looking like patches of Matisse gouaches, can be seen draped over the white-stucco walls and archways.

The peaceful simplicity of Le Hameau would have appealed to Matisse, had it been rentable fifty years ago, but instead he settled into the second floor of Villa Le Rêve on what is now Vence's Avenue Henri Matisse. The modest house still stands, well back from the road, but the inside was unfortunately hacked into cubby-holes when the villa was converted to a guest hostel. The outside has barely changed, however. The olive trees Matisse called *pieds de mammouth,* or elephant feet, remain near the entry, and the French doors and balcony—Matisse's window onto Vence—still look out over the weedy front yard seen in old photographs, ringed with clementine, cherry, and Chinese persimmon trees as well as palms. These are the exuberant palms we glimpse in *Red Interior* (1947) and *Interior with Egyptian Curtain* (1948), and the olive trees appear through the window in *The Silence Living in Houses* (1947), an unusually somber title for an unusually joyless painting.

But even Matisse, celebrator of color and life, had been subdued by events: He was increasingly confined to the wheelchair his son Pierre had sent him from New York; in 1944, Amélie, then seventy-three, had been briefly jailed by the Gestapo for typing Résistance newsletters; Marguerite, fifty, working in Brittany to help prepare for the Allied landing, had been denounced and put on a train to Ravensbruck (she escaped when the train was derailed by an Allied air raid); and Jean, who had become a sculptor, was also in danger, smuggling explosives for the Résistance.

If the suspense and worry emerged on a few of Matisse's canvases, he still shared the soaring aspirations of his mythic *Icarus* with its passionate red heart, and in 1947 Tériade published this and a host of other cutouts in *Jazz,* which writer and lecturer Rosamond Bernier calls "one of the most beautiful of all twentieth-century books." It was beginning to seem that the more Matisse's health and the world at large unraveled, the more his creative will gained strength.

Matisse's Rosary Chapel—and that is how we think of it, though he was not its architect—has become the sacred heart, in a way, of the entire Riviera's rich artistic life. Matisse's intention was merely "to balance a surface of light and color against a solid white wall covered with black drawings." But, as one enters the chapel, the shock hidden within those unassuming words takes hold, for the juxtaposition of the bright green, blue, and yellow stained glass against the stark black and white of the rest of the interior challenges every preconceived notion of church decoration.

Matisse was never conventionally religious. Sister Jacques-Marie, who first asked his advice about a single window for the proposed new chapel in 1947, instructed him in matters of church symbolism and dogma once he had taken on the project. She admired him, and he in turn trusted her, for she had, when only sixteen, nursed him after his surgery and later, when she was still Monique B., even posed for him. Their friendship was the catalyst for what Matisse eventually called the summation of his life's work.

The white chapel, only about fifty by thirty feet, sits amid cacti and palms on a hilltop shared with the Foyer Lacordaire, a Dominican rest home for about forty women. (Public entry is restricted to mid-mornings and afternoons on Tuesdays and Thursdays most of the year, to guarantee the residents' privacy, but in summer open hours expand to include afternoons every day except Sunday and Monday.) Matisse gave himself completely to the chapel's colossal challenge. He sold some of his own lithographs and drawings to help with the financing, and in the end took on every inch of the decoration, from the stained glass and ceramic murals to the sculpted crucifix and candlesticks and the confessional door, a tracery of carved wood that looks like an all-white Moorish screen. But Matisse's primary interest—apart from the harmony of the whole—was the stained glass.

Six windows along the nave and nine behind the nuns' transept pierce the south wall in slender vertical strips of blue and yellow leaves against green fields. On either side of each strip are wall embrasures that serve as solid stalks schematically but, in practical terms, act as louvers to lessen the heat entering the building. The effect is of the garden's actually coming indoors, its reflections transferred to the white "canvas" of the tiles. Matisse's colors, recalling the sun, the sky and its reflection in the sea, and vegetation, were consistent with his belief in the stability (and harmony) to be gained in using two colors—here, blue and yellow—in combination with a third that would "bring them into agreement," in this case green. He also believed that certain colors carried with them specific emotional charges—a blue, for example, might "penetrate the soul"—and so color was more than a structural building block; it was an expression of feeling.

The Tree of Life pair of windows in the chapel's shallow apse repeats the colors of the south wall's glass, though here the yellow leaves resemble a philodendron's and the blue ones are cactuslike ovates, all rising to a half-sun disk. The artist, as always, took much of his inspiration directly from nature: A former neighbor of his in Vence told me their first encounter occurred when Matisse knocked on his door, introduced himself timidly, and asked if he might photograph a particular tree, a *figuier de barbarie,* on the neighbor's property; permission was of course granted, the tree's broad cactus pads almost certainly serving as models for this part of the chapel.

The Tree of Life windows light the chapel's altar, chiseled from the same stone as the Pont du Gard's. Its mass is nonetheless dwarfed by the thick black lines of Matisse's fifteen-foot-high drawing of Saint Dominic, which covers the north transept wall. Matisse left Le Rêve in January, 1951, returning to the Régina, where the dimensions of his apartment were almost exactly those of the chapel, and so some of his late sketches for Saint Dominic he actually did to scale on his own walls, standing on a ladder and drawing with a piece of charcoal tied to the end of a seven-foot bamboo pole—a strenuous feat, even for a well man.

There were numerous preliminary versions of the Virgin and Child mural, too, on the north nave wall, and each was simpler than the former. The point, as usual, was to refine the image to its essence, and above the sacristy door you will see an ultimate distillation: The outstretched arm and the poignant tilt of the Child's head convey the tenderest intimacy in only a half dozen lines.

The torturous progress to Calvary recounted in the Stations of the Cross mural, spread over the chapel's back wall, is almost painful to look at by comparison. The lines are abrupt, the rhythms disjointed, shattering the chapel's peace at least momentarily. Matisse is telling a violent story, and the viewer's discomfort is perhaps a measure of the affective immediacy of his accomplishment.

Matisse's chapel was consecrated in June, 1951, but because he was too ill to attend he sent a short letter to the presiding bishop, as unhesitating and direct as a final stroke of ink: "I present to you in all humility the Chapel of the Rosary. . . . I consider it, in spite of its imperfections, my masterpiece. May the future justify this judgment. . . ."

Hotels

Château du Domaine St.-Martin, avenue des Templiers, 06140 Vence; 04.93.58.02.02; fax: 04.93.24.08.91.

Hôtel Beau Rivage, 24 rue St.-François-de-Paule, 06300 Nice; 04.93.80.80.70; fax: 04.93.80.55.77.

Hôtel Le Hameau, 528 route de La Colle, 06570 St.-Paul-de-Vence; 04.93.32.80.24; fax: 04.93.32.55.75.

Hôtel La Pérouse, 11 Quai Rauba-Capeu, 06300 Nice; 04.93.62.34.63; fax: 04.93.62.59.41.

Hôtel La Roseraie, avenue Henri Giraud, 06140 Vence; 04.93.58.02.20; fax: 04.93.58.99.31.

Le Saint-Paul, 86 rue Grande, 06570 St.-Paul-de-Vence; 04.93.32.65.25; fax: 04.93.32.52.94.

Auberge du Clos du Loup, route de Grasse (D6), 06480 La Colle sur Loup; 04.93.32.88.76.

Auberge des Seigneurs, place du Frêne, 06140 Vence, 04.93.58.04.24.

Château du Domaine St.-Martin (see Hotels).

La Merenda, 4 rue de la Terrasse, 06300 Nice (no phone).

La Petite Maison, 11 rue St.-François-de-Paule, 06000 Nice; 04.93.92.59.59.

Le Safari, 1 Cours Saleya, 06300 Nice; 04.93.80.18.44.

Le Saint-Paul (see Hotels).

Colette's Riviera

BY JUDITH THURMAN

～

editor's note

Sidonie-Gabrielle Colette is not a name we immediately associate with the Mediterranean, yet she was as thoroughly seduced by the region as Henri Matisse.

JUDITH THURMAN is the author of *Secrets of the Flesh: A Life of Colette* (Alfred A. Knopf, 1999) and *Isak Dinesen: The Life of a Storyteller* (St. Martin's Press, 1982, hardcover; Picador, 1995, paperback), for which she won the National Book Award.

In 1991 I spent a vibrant year in Paris researching a book on Colette's life, then eight somber years in my New York study writing it. While I was in France, I visited her native Burgundy, her apartment at the Palais-Royal, and two of her country houses. But I didn't have the leisure or the means to explore her haunts on the Riviera.

By last summer my first draft was done, and no commission has ever been more timely or welcome than this one: to compare the sensuous images in Colette's letters and books with the living landscapes and sensations that inspired them. The Riviera, of course, has been developed, even pillaged, in the course of a century, not least by writers. So one must search for poetic affinities rather than for literal matches between Colette's Riviera and its contemporary counterpart. Some things, however, have endured: the austere beauty of the hills; the unbridled hedonism of the coast; the intensity of the light; the temper of climate and people; the potent erotic savor of the whole southern experience.

For half a lifetime, Colette had scorned what she liked to call *le bas de la France,* "the bottom of France." She had always, she says, "childishly" imagined the road from Paris to the Mediterranean as "a downward slope, easy and fatal." Then suddenly one summer—in 1925—she took the fall and tumbled into love with the Midi.

It was one of those affairs for which one impetuously forsakes old ties, in this case a "dream house" on the Breton coast where she had vacationed for thirteen years, first with her lesbian lover, the Marquise de Morny, then with her second husband, Henry de Jouvenel, their daughter, his two sons (the elder of whom, sixteen-year-old Bertrand, became her lover there), and a large circle of friends.

Colette's infatuation with the Riviera was to last longer than either of her first two marriages: fourteen years. It was a "family romance" in many senses. Through her father, the improvident

Captain Colette, who called her Bel-Gazou—a Provençal expression that means "lovely babble"—Colette had *le bas de la France* in her blood. He came from the great shipbuilding port of Toulon, where his own father had been a naval officer, and the Colette family owned a very pretty piece of real estate on the cliffs outside town, at Le Mourillon.

In the youth of her first marriage, Colette often stayed with friends in Nice—the poet Renée Vivien owned the delightful Villa Cessole in the hills above the city—or in Monte Carlo, where her husband, Willy, gambled away the fortune that, in part, she'd earned for him by writing the *Claudine* books. Having signed his wife's novels, which invented the modern teenage girl and became the biggest best-sellers of the *fin de siècle,* Willy kept the royalties and cobbled the series into a play, also wildly successful. In the spring of 1903, she and Willy took Claudine on tour to the casino towns of the Côte d'Azur.

A few years later, Colette had divorced Willy and gone onstage herself. She was soon, in her own right, one of the most scandalous and popular French music-hall artistes—famous for appearing without a leotard, or much else, in pantomimes with titles such as *The Flesh, The Cat, Egyptian Dream,* or *The Gypsy Girl.* The reliable money was in the provinces, so under the aegis of her impresario, Baret, she became a virtuoso of the one-night stand, playing thirty-two cities in as many days. On the downhill train from Paris to Nice, and uphill from Monte Carlo to Paris, she wrote *The Vagabond,* using her makeup case as a desk. In Marseilles, she stayed in the same modest hotel (today called the Mercure Beauvau) that once received Chopin and George Sand. The view from its front windows has barely changed: the masts of pleasure boats and fishing launches; the glittering, tacky, and vital old port shaped like a horseshoe and hedged with sprawling cafés and bars, some of ill repute. When her show was over she would wolf down a velvety bouillabaisse like the one still proudly served at the Restaurant Michel on the rue des Catalans. Yes, she loved the garlicky breath and the lilting accents—her father's accent—in which an irrepressible public shouted out its admiration for her charms. But a season in the "pretty, false Midi" wasn't—"and I'll say it again," she wrote—worth a chill November day with the mists rising from the bogs of her native Burgundy.

Yet it was to the Côte d'Azur that she returned when de Jouvenel discovered her five-year liaison with his son, and asked for a divorce. Bertrand had been pried from her embrace by his parents, and engaged to a young woman he was shortly to marry. The fifty-two-year-old Colette was at the height of her powers; as usual, she found solace in her Olympian productivity. She was working simultaneously on two novels, a screenplay, and a hefty weekly quota of reportage and criticism, as well as acting the part of Léa in a revival of the drama she had adapted from *Chéri,* her own great novel about the romance of an aging courtesan and a young gigolo. Her sensual appetites were undiminished, including her appetite for adventure. But she had come to regard love as a fatal trap.

That didn't mean, however, that she wasn't willing to walk into it again with her beautiful, sea-colored cat's eyes wide open. Earlier that winter, her friend Marguerite Moreno, who was playing Chéri's mother, introduced her to Maurice Goudeket—thirty-five, an intense, courtly, raven-haired dealer in pearls and an obliging "extra man" at society dinner parties, who had adored Colette's work since adolescence. The meeting was inconclusive, so Colette and Moreno cooked up a second "chance" encounter—at Easter, on the Riviera. Maurice, Moreno, and some mutual friends were staying at the Eden Palace, on Cap d'Ail, a delicious Belle Époque hotel, expensive and discreet, with balconies and a manicured parterre overlooking the sea. It is still as charming to look at, and no doubt as romantic to inhabit, as it was then, though when I rang the bell the concierge informed me that it had become a private apartment complex. But perhaps because Colette's name also rang a bell, he opened the wrought-iron grille and invited me in to inhale the perfumes of a secret garden.

Colette arranged to join Moreno and her party—and to make the ploy seem spontaneous. "I was quick," she admitted. By July, the great writer and her "exquisite boy" were inseparable and would remain so. Their vacation on Cap d'Ail had not yet changed her opinion of the south, but Maurice had taken a two-week lease on a pink villa in the Var, with the Mediterranean at the foot of the garden. Game for every new pleasure that her "Satan" had to offer, Colette accompanied him.

By day, the heat was torrid, bleaching the sea and sky and melting the resin of the pine trees. The two lovers gaily braved sunstroke to go touring in Maurice's open car, stopping to bathe on deserted beaches with sand "as white as flour and finer than pollen." The nights were so mild they dragged their mattresses onto the terrace, and awoke to the setting moon and the "dark orange dawn." She had discovered her native element, Colette gushed to Moreno, which was this landscape, and "love, too."

In the neighboring village of Ste.-Maxime, recently colonized by the Parisian theater and fashion worlds, Colette had friends—actors, models, directors. The lovers could have dined in chic, familiar company every evening, but preferring nightlife of a rougher, more local color, they often drove to St.-Tropez, just across the gulf.

St.-Tropez's old port is now jammed with charter yachts out of the Cayman Islands and beefy tourists in knockoff Versace T-shirts. But the peeling stucco houses—pink, yellow, and terra-cotta, with worn green and turquoise shutters—haven't changed. Nor has the stately, low-slung Place des Lices, at the heart of the village, where there is a thriving open market on Saturdays.

While the narrow side streets are solidly stocked with branches of nearly every major luxury store found in Paris, Milan, and New York, Colette's sandal-maker, Rondini, is still in business at 16 rue Georges-Clemenceau, and he still makes Colette's "Spartacus" sandals. After she broke a leg in 1931, she took to wearing them, even in winter, and they became her trademark.

In the summer of 1925, however, St.-Trop was still a somnolent place with no traffic and a rustic piano bar frequented by fishermen and a few adventurous artists. Here they drank rosé and ate grilled fish caught that morning. Colette consumed "enormous" quantities of garlic and raw onions, and exulted to her aristocratic friend, Anna de Noailles, about the charms of the "beautiful sailor-boys" who danced together under a bare lightbulb. A week into her honeymoon with the man and the place, Colette surprised another old friend, Francis Carco, with the announcement of her conversion: "What country! No kidding, Francis, I don't want any other." Her father would have been pleased to hear it.

This idyll in the Var so utterly seduced Colette that before she left she decided to sell her house in Brittany and buy a property near St.-Tropez. Her friends turned up a peasant farmhouse with four small rooms, off the route des Salins. It had no plumbing or electricity, but the well was deep and full, and there was a wisteria-draped terrace that faced north. The house stood on slightly more than 2½ acres of land, planted with vines and fig trees. Beyond the garden was a *pinède*—a stand of old pines—and a path that led through the vineyards, past a rotting gate "which a child could break through," to a deserted beach. "Without having to negotiate a single step," wrote Colette, she was in the sea.

Colette christened the house La Treille Muscate—the muscat vine. She immediately began to settle down in her imagination: the big, luminous room for her lazy hours and the small, dark one for writing; a kitchen garden scented with tarragon and sage; an abundance of tomato and pepper plants, of wild mushrooms and untamed roses. There were no mosquitoes, so she would sleep on the terrace with the mistral ruffling her hair, and wake to see the first rays of a copper sun tincturing the milky water.

To the fastidious Maurice, La Treille Muscate, as he wrote in his memoir, would never be "really beautiful or really comfortable," although Colette would give it—magically, as she had given all her Edens—the illusion of being so. She would also do some of her greatest writing here: *The Pure and the Impure,* which she called her "personal contribution to the sum total of our knowledge of the senses," and which is something deeper, too—a meditation on the way human beings eroticize their first bonds. And she would make the house, St.-Tropez, and its landscape the setting for her master-piece, *Break of Day:* "The finest Côte d'Azur book," writes the coast's most astute recent chronicler, Mary Blume, "in which a middle-aged writer named Colette renounces the pleasures of the flesh, and in particular the sunburned, salt-flecked flesh of a hand-some young man, for the sterner demands of art. [*Break of Day*] is a book of considerable nobility whose composition was undoubt-edly eased by the presence of the sunburned, salt-flecked young man whom Colette married in 1935. Like so much of the Côte d'Azur, it is all a cheerful imposture."

The destiny of ravishingly scenic coastal real estate with a caressing climate seems to be ruled by a set of laws as inexorable as natural selection. First come the artists, then the rich, then the aspiring rich, and finally the masses. It wasn't long before Pastecchi's, the St.-Tropez piano bar, was charging Deauville prices and crowded with celebrities and moguls in couture beach pajamas air-kissing over their champagne buckets. Soon there were traffic jams of Hispano-Suizas and Bugattis triple-parked in front of the little shop where Colette bought her stationery and toilet paper. (They have since been replaced by Jaguars and Ferraris.) In 1932, having quixotically entered the beauty business, she opened her own boutique on the port, selling cosmetics with the Colette logo and—in a white lab coat—doing makeovers of the famous actresses who, it was noted, came out looking ten years older than when they went in.

While the glamour of St.-Tropez has never quite palled, it was even then being diluted by the campers, the tents on "her" pristine beach, the proliferation of nasty little snack bars with American names—"Hollywood-Beach," "Seawood Lodge"—and the souvenir stands selling postcards of "Collette's villa [*sic*]," which she bought up wholesale and sent, half-furious, half-amused, to her friends. She deplored the cars full of foreign "sheep" (including those from Paris) that created gridlock on the corniche. By the mid-1930s, it was only at dawn that she could swim in the Baie des Canoubiers without being pestered for an autograph or offended by German nudists showing too much chalky flesh, or by amorous couples pushing the envelope of flamboyance. Colette admired discretion. She also liked having things to herself.

As the years passed, her haunts on the Riviera became the naturally inaccessible rather than the socially exclusive ones. She was invited to dine on the burnished yachts moored in the new marinas, and in the flashy villas going up in the hills, where white-gloved servants waited on languid convives who later retired to swap wives, daughters, or occasionally sons. But she much preferred the family suppers of ratatouille and fish soup at the farmhouse of her closest neighbors, Vera the ballerina and Julio the dentist; or a prebreakfast walk with her bulldog through the *pinède,* where she soaked her espadrilles in the dew and feasted on stolen figs; or an expedition with her friend Moune to the hill towns—Grimaud, Bormes-les-Mimosas, Èze, Haut-de-Cagnes—to explore the ruins and to buy old pottery for a song. If the heat abated or a novel was stuck, she might set out for a daylong hike, with a picnic, through the Dom Forest.

Today there is little tourism and almost no commerce on the shadowy N98 out of Bormes-les-Mimosas, which runs through the Dom. Twelve miles west of St.-Tropez one passes a small vineyard—Domaine des Campaux—which produces one of the delicately spiced and delicious local Côtes de Provences. The old stone *maison de maître,* surrounded by a flagstone terrace, has been converted recently to a bed-and-breakfast, with rustic rooms and a wholesome table d'hôte. It looks much as La Treille Muscate must have when Colette discovered it.

You may decide, with her, to bypass the coastal resort towns east of St.-Tropez and spend half a day finding the twelfth-century Chartreuse de la Verne, set in a grove of ancient chestnuts. Drink from the sacred stream and count your blessings. You might also, in her honor, stop at the Restaurant du Café de France, in Grimaud, for a plate of roasted yellow peppers, meltingly sweet and smothered in raw garlic.

If you do nothing else in St.-Tropez (besides sun, gorge, ogle, and shop), you must bike or drive down La Route des Salins, which runs past Colette's farmhouse, to the Plage des Salins, where the *sentier littoral* begins. This footpath of ocher sand winds for miles along the coast, through fragrant scrub, with unspoiled views of the sea. You can clamber down the rocks for a swim, your communion with the elements uninterrupted by greasy toddlers carrying Barney floats, brokers with laptops, or topless models flaunting perfect bodies.

After her morning swims, Colette loved working among the lizards and the stray cats in her own garden. She dug an irrigation ditch for her tangerine trees and mulched them with heaps of seaweed, which she carried from the beach and rinsed in well water. In September, she helped her farmhands bring in the grape harvest. And only when the new wine was in its casks did she close up La Treille Muscate and return to the gray light of Paris.

In 1939, when Hitler signed his "pact of steel" with Mussolini, Colette and Maurice sold their house in St.-Tropez and bought a country place closer to the capital. She was beginning to suffer from the excruciating arthritis of the hip that eventually crippled her. During the exceptionally frigid and damp first winter of the war, Colette's doctors advised her to go south for some relief, so she and Maurice booked rooms at the Hôtel Ruhl, in Nice. She told friends that the garlic, the oranges, and the flower market had restored her, at least a little.

Old cities, like old trees, have deep taproots that can't be shaken as easily as resorts are by the storms of change, and Nice, like Marseille, is an inexhaustibly real place. Visit "her" flower market in the Cours Saleya, with its ancient pastel houses, two stories high, and lunch on *salade niçoise* at the Riviera's most charming hole-in-the-wall, Chez Palmyre. There were two Chez Palmyres in Colette's life, one a famous lesbian bistro in Belle Époque Paris, the other a

tiny restaurant in St.-Tropez, where an aged "Ma Palmyre" did all the cooking, and this is the latter reincarnate. It is even possible that Colette ate here—Mme. Palmyre of Nice, now eighty-four, has been in business since the 1930s and still does all her authentic Provençal home cooking for a devoted, native clientele.

In winter I might have chosen, as Colette sometimes did, to stop at the Negresco. But since it was July I avoided the heat and congestion of downtown Nice by staying at Le Cagnard, in Haut-de-Cagnes. This handsome hotel has been artfully assembled from several ancient village houses and decorated in a medieval style. A few doors away, on Place Docteur-Maurel, I found the only shop on the Riviera that tempted me to spend some of the mad money I had been saving for the Casino de Monte Carlo. Terraïo sells classic pottery with pure shapes, the color of the dusky sea.

Chronic pain dimmed but never entirely extinguished Colette's wanderlust, and at the end of her life she was still writing prodigiously. Her confinement focused her powers, and in the course of the four war years in France, this invalid entering her seventies produced eight books, including her last and most famous novella, *Gigi*. When peace returned, Maurice took her south as often as he could, hoping to revive her spirits in the southern climate that had nurtured their early love. They stayed with Simone Berriau, the actress and producer, who had a house overlooking the salt marshes near Hyères, and with the count and countess—Charles and Pata—de Polignac, who rented a luxurious villa in the hills south of Grasse. Practically next door, you will find one of the most refined hotels in the region, Le Moulin des Mougins, run by Roger Vergé. It is just off a main road, but like a Frenchwoman with a flaw to her beauty, it goes to heroic lengths to be alluring, and succeeds admirably.

The Polignacs introduced Colette and Maurice to their cousin, Prince Pierre of Monaco, and in May of 1950, encouraged by her fan the prince, Colette made the first of what was to become a series of annual trips to Monte Carlo, living in a ground-floor suite of the Hôtel de Paris, which had a wheelchair entrance and a private garden. She regaled Pata with descriptions of the appallingly inelegant foreign tourists and the crowds of assorted millionaires and minor royalty—the characters, she said, from a somewhat tedious operetta. The following winter, as Colette was being wheeled into the operatically opulent Salle Empire, with its frescoes of peacocks, tigers, and naked women, she stopped to watch a film being shot in the lobby. The leading actress was an enchanting young beauty switching fluently from English to French. Without hesitation, Colette announced to Maurice that she had found "our Gigi for America": Audrey Hepburn.

Having ventured and lost 200 francs in my first ten minutes at the roulette table, I, unlike Colette, decided that I would never voluntarily return to Monte Carlo. But it was great pure impure fun for a while. The Hôtel de Paris still caters to millionaires, minor royalty, and appallingly inelegant foreign tourists, many of them our compatriots, and the ambiance today is more *Dynasty* than *Merry Widow*. But Colette would have enjoyed the sybaritic new spa, the three-star cuisine, and even, I suspect, the hotel beach, where surgically enhanced beauties in four-inch mules, dripping with diamonds and Tahitian pearls, are kept busy on their cell phones. To what purpose? Reread *Chéri*.

The Facts

The "downhill" TGV (France's super-express train) gets you to Marseille from Paris in four hours, just enough time to read Colette's *Break of Day,* and perhaps Mary Blume's absorbing and sharply observed *Côte d'Azur.* Rent a car in Marseille and head for St.-Tropez, stopping in Toulon for a coffee in one of the shaded squares around the opera house. You might find some fine old editions of Colette's work in the charming book kiosks, or you can search the musty philately shops for the rare stamps once cherished by Colette's fey, musical brother, Léo.

Hotels

Hôtel Mercure-Beauvau Vieux-Port, 4 rue Beauvau, Marseille;

04.91.54.91.00; fax: 04.91.54.15.76; doubles from about $110. Still a haunt of French writers and literary romantics.

Le Yaca, 1 blvd. d'Aumale, St.-Tropez; 04.94.55.81.00; fax: 04.94.97.58.50; doubles from $250. Colette wintered here in 1927, when La Treille Muscate was undergoing one of its periodic renovations.

La Réserve de Beaulieu, 5 blvd. Général Leclerc, Beaulieu; 04.93.01.00.01; fax: 04.93.01.28.99; doubles from about $330. La Réserve opened in 1890. It has since been renovated, but the shell-pink rooms, dazzling views, and antique *politesse* of the service give an exquisitely creamy taste of the old Côte d'Azur.

Hôtel Belle-Vue, 14 place Gambetta, Bormes-les-Mimosas; 04.94.71.15.15; fax: 04.94.05.96.04; doubles from about $30. A modest, somewhat funky establishment with a charming terrace.

La Grande Maison, Domaine des Campaux, Bormes-les-Mimosas; 04.94.49.55.40; fax: 04.94.49.55.23; doubles from about $85. Mother-and-daughter proprietors Laurence Lapinet and Joyce Naveau rent out rooms.

Le Cagnard, rue Sous-Barre, Haut-de-Cagnes; 04.93.20.73.21; fax: 04.93.22.06.39; doubles from about $150. Several refurbished village houses.

Hôtel de Paris, place du Casino, Monte Carlo; 37.7/92.16.30.00; fax: 37.7/92.16.38.49; doubles from about $350. Colette wintered in this Monaco classic.

Restaurants

Restaurant Michel, 6 rue des Catalans, Marseille; 04.91.52.30.63; dinner for two about $88. For bouillabaisse.

L'Olivier, Hôtel La Bastide de St.-Tropez, rue des Carles, St.-Tropez; 04.94.97.58.16; *dinner for two about $150.* Set among old olive trees, this restaurant offers excellent cuisine—rabbit cooked in olives, scallops roasted in garlic.

Restaurant du Café de France, 5 Place Neuve, Grimaud; 04.94.43.20.05; dinner for two about $67. Local melon with ham, roasted yellow peppers smothered in raw garlic, fresh cold tomato bisque.

Le Moulin des Mougins, Quartier Notre-Dame-de-Vie, Mougins; 04.93.75.78.24; dinner for two about $200. Owned and run by one of the great chefs of France, Roger Vergé.

La Pinède, 10 blvd. de la Mer, Cap d'Ail; 04.93.78.37.10; dinner for two about $83. An unpretentious grilled-fish kind of place right on the beach.

Chez Palmyre, 5 rue Droite, Nice; 04.93.85.72.32; dinner for two about $23. The menu is drawn from family recipes.

Castelroc, Place du Palais, Monaco; 37.7/93.30.36.68; lunch for two about $65; closed for the season until May 13. Delicious fettuccine with white truffles.

Shopping

Rondini, 16 rue Georges-Clemenceau, St.-Tropez; 04.94.97.19.55. Where Colette had her sandals made.

Poterie Augier, 40 rue Clemenceau, St.-Tropez. Modern versions of the milky-green Provençal pottery that Colette liked.

Market, Place des Lices, St.-Tropez. At the heart of the village; Saturdays until 1 P.M.

Gérard Panay, 22 rue Jean-Alard, Bormes-les-Mimosas;

04.94.71.31.90. The old Provençal pottery and local landscape art collected by Colette.

Diagram, 11 Cours Saleya, Nice; 04.93.80.33.71. A picturesque array of antiques, pottery, and fabrics.

Terraïo, 12 place Docteur-Maurel, Haut-de-Cagnes; 04.93.20.86.83. Classic pottery with pure shapes; milky turquoise platters and bowls.

Villa America

BY JEFFREY ROBINSON

∽

editor's note

Gerald and Sara Murphy, American expatriates for a time, remain the most celebrated couple ever to spend time on the Côte d'Azur, and surely their Villa America remains the symbol of sought-after invitations. It never occurred to me to see if the villa was still around, but it obviously did to Jeffrey Robinson, as he relates in this piece.

Writer Julia Markus wrote a piece for *The New York Times Magazine* some years ago about Antibes during the time the Murphys entertained their famous friends at Villa America. The final paragraph of the piece is a beautiful summation of those days then, but ours now, too:

"What does the Riviera have to give us today? Scents of perfumed trees and aromatic herbs and the sea. No amount of traffic cuts through it. The smell of things as precious as when the world—and expatriate wealth—was young. It gives us the Mediterranean, seemingly wide as an ocean, with the sailboats and the audacious yachts gliding by. The covered market, the twisting streets, a bride coming out of the Hôtel de Ville, the absolute sense of life. If Picasso in his black hat and black shorts no longer points to Olga in her tutu at La Garoupe—if that moment is lost forever except in Sara Murphy's photograph—there is still the Picasso Museum displaying his Antibes work in an atmosphere of an eternally tropical day. But it's not the life of the few anymore. "Many Fêtes," Fitzgerald wished Gerald and Sara in his dedication to *Tender Is the Night.* Antibes is still to be enjoyed. But now it's the life of the many, and we all want to have a good time."

JEFFREY ROBINSON, whose work appears elsewhere in this book, lived in the south of France before moving to England. He has contributed a number of food and travel articles to *Gourmet,* where this piece appeared in 1989, and is the author of many nonfiction books, including biographies of Princess Grace of Monaco and Brigitte Bardot.

No one at Cap d'Antibes remembers Villa America now. Even when you ask some of the old-timers where it is—or, rather, where it used to be—you merely receive a long, blank stare and then a shrug. Too much time has passed. But that doesn't change the fact that Villa America was a very special place.

It was Gerald and Sara Murphy's summer home during the 1920s.

It was, with modifications, Villa Diana in *Tender Is the Night.*

It was a place to hang out with Scott and Zelda, Hemingway, Picasso, Léger, Cole Porter, Dorothy Parker, Robert Benchley, Monty Woolley, Archibald MacLeish, John Dos Passos, and Ford Madox Ford. It was a place where the Lost Generation played. And it was a swell place.

There will always be something terribly romantic about France in the 1920s. The "war to end all wars" was over; the good guys had won, the shattered glass had been swept away, and the next war was still a long way off.

These were "*les années folles,*" the crazy years, of flappers and the Charleston, of Stravinsky and Diaghilev and Les Ballets Russes. It was an era of well-lit cafés and absinthe, of women in meshed hose and cellar *boîtes* (nightclubs) where black musicians just over from the Deep South were playing something new called jazz.

People were in the mood to party, and Paris was the place to do it.

And the Murphys were the hosts par excellence.

Sara Wiborg was born in Cincinnati in 1883, the oldest child of a local ink magnate. She was a beautifully delicate girl, graced with poise, every cultural advantage, and a rich father.

Gerald Murphy was as handsome as Sara was stunning. He was born in Boston in 1888, an heir to the Mark Cross fortune. He attended Hotchkiss, Andover, and then Yale, where he was Skull and Bones (he would later harbor a deeply felt resentment toward the secret society, the origin of which he never revealed) and voted Best Dressed in the class of 1912.

Sara and Gerald married in 1915. Daughter Honoria was born in 1917. Their first son, Baoth, came along in 1919, and their second, Patrick, was born the following year.

By that time Gerald was bored with business and wanted greener pastures. As he was later quoted, "There was something depressing to young married people about a country that could pass the Eighteenth Amendment."

With Sara's annual income of close to seven thousand dollars, then a tidy sum, and Gerald's own fortune, the Murphys had the freedom to do what they wanted, go where they pleased. So they packed up, grabbed the children, and headed for France, arriving in Paris in 1921 and bumping headfirst into cubism. Gerald was so smitten with it that he told Sara, "If that's painting, it's what I want to do." And just like that, Gerald became a painter.

He was considerably more, however, than a wealthy dilettante amusing himself. In fact, he and Sara, as was generally conceded, pretty much defied categorization altogether.

Once Scott Fitzgerald got to know them, he tried to convince Hemingway that "the rich are different from you and me."

"Yeah," came the response, "they've got more money."

Gerald and Sara did have more money, and yet they stopped short of rushing to join the expatriate millionaires on the fashionable Right Bank avenues that fan out from the Arc de Triomphe. (Ironically Scott and Zelda, hardly well off, rented a large, well-furnished flat facing the Arc at 14, rue de Tilsitt.) Instead, once the Murphys had moved into town from Saint-Cloud, they took a top-floor apartment on the Left Bank at 23, quai des Grands-Augustins, in the Sixth Arrondissement, looking out over the Seine and Île de la Cité. Gerald also rented a studio, in Montparnasse, at 69, rue Froidevaux.

Paris was a good place for an aspiring artist to be. Gerald met and got to know Picasso, Miró, and Gris; saw their work in the local galleries; and quickly found acceptance for his own paintings as part of the "American Precisionist" school.

Paris was also a good place to meet those Americans who were about to claim the decade as their own. Sylvia Beach's Shakespeare and Company bookshop-*cum*-lending library was nearby at 12, rue de l'Odéon. Gertrude Stein and Alice B. Toklas lived off the Luxembourg Gardens at 27, rue de Fleurus. And that's where the Murphys met Hemingway.

Ernest Hemingway had come to Paris in 1921 with his first wife, Hadley, on the advice of Sherwood Anderson. Home became a fourth-floor walkup at 74, rue du Cardinal-Lemoine, in the heart of the Latin Quarter and just off the Place de la Contrescarpe. (The Hemingways didn't know it at the time, but James Joyce had begun writing *Ulysses* a few doors down, at number 71.) Two years later, after their son John (Bumby) was born, they moved to an apartment over a sawmill at 113, avenue Notre-Dame-des-Champs, down the block from Ezra Pound's place. Later, when the Hemingway marriage broke up, Gerald Murphy helped Ernest bridge the troubled waters with a four-hundred-dollar loan and lodging in his painter's studio.

In turn Hemingway became the Murphys' guide to a side of life they might not otherwise have discovered. He introduced them to Scott and Zelda Fitzgerald, instructed them in the subtleties of all-day bicycle races, explained in detail how to become a regular at the right Left Bank cafés, took them skiing at Schruns in the Austrian Tyrol, and personally presented them to the world's best bullfighters at Pamplona. Together they sat on wicker chairs at Le Sélect and Le Dôme, La Coupole and La Rotonde, all in Montparnasse. Together they drank and sometimes ate at Les Deux Magots and Le Flore and the Brasserie Lipp along Boulevard Saint-Germain. Together they observed and discussed and judged and mixed with White Russian exiles, Spanish painters, and French poets—the "inmates," as Hemingway called the café dwellers. (When Hemingway wanted a place to drink alone and write, he kept to himself at the Closerie des Lilas. It was warm inside in winter and a fine place to sit outside in spring and summer.) Unlike Villa America, these old Paris haunts remain, their wicker chairs out front, filling up early with tourists and writers, shop clerks and poets.

The Murphys were more than a decade older than the Hemingways and the Fitzgeralds, and more family-oriented, building their lives around their three children. They may well have thought of themselves as expatriates, but in truth they never turned their backs on things American, as did so many others in France during those years. They imported the latest records, knew the latest dance steps, and supposedly had shipped from the States the very first waffle iron ever seen in Paris.

What really made the Murphys special, however, was their sense of adventure. In the early 1920s only laborers got suntans, and not by choice; they got that way by working in the fields. Anyone with money *wintered* on the Côte d'Azur but was never seen there in July or August. Anyone except the Murphys. They single-handedly started the trend that changed the Riviera into a summer resort.

Arriving in the South of France for the summer of 1923, they discovered Antibes, out of season and shut tight. Undaunted, Gerald bribed the manager of the Hôtel du Cap to remain open on a partial basis with a skeleton staff of three. Picasso and his family came to visit. Before summer's end the Murphys had fallen in love with the place and decided to buy a home in the area. In 1924 they found a property, purchased it, and renamed it Villa America.

Back in the mid-1970s, while I was living not far from Nice and just after I had read Calvin Tomkins's book about Gerald and Sara, *Living Well Is the Best Revenge,* I got it into my head that I wanted to see Villa America. But I quickly discovered that, if it was still there at all, it was no longer called Villa America.

The logical place to begin my search was the Antibes city hall, just off the morning marketplace. In those days the municipal archives were crammed into a maze of low-ceilinged rooms on one side of the building's attic. The sign on the door read OPEN 10–12, 3:30–5:30, CLOSED WEDNESDAYS, WEEKENDS, AUGUST, AND AFTER-NOONS IN JULY. And even when I managed to thread the needle, showing up on the right days at the right times, the man in charge— a stereotype complete with pencil-thin mustache, blue functionary's smock, and a Gitane dangling perilously from his bottom lip— either wasn't there or wasn't interested in unlocking the door. "Bureaucracy" is, after all, a French word.

Waters do sometimes part, however, and access was occasion-ally mine. What records remained from before the war were filed in huge green books, each entry carefully recorded by hand. The ledgers referred to papers that had long since been stuffed into car-tons, now covered in dust, and piled one on top of the other, six high and four deep.

"May I see the one on the bottom, please?"

"*Alors . . .*" (arms waved in great agitation) came the response.

It took several visits, but eventually I found the villa's original deeds. They showed that the fourteen-room Chalet des Nielles had been built in 1904 and that Gerald Murphy (whose listed profession was "*artiste peintre*") was its third owner. He bought the house and 7,600 square meters of land for 350,000 francs in September, 1924. The following July he added 771 square meters to his holding, at a cost of 18,500 francs. And in 1926 he bought the missing triangle of 347 square meters, which completed the property and for which he paid 14,000 francs.

Gerald and Sara now owned the second largest estate (8,718 square meters) on Cap d'Antibes, surpassed only by the Aga Khan's property near the lighthouse. Having spent 382,500 francs (about $530,000 in 1988 terms) to buy the land—Sara's annual income from her trust fund had been increased to $40,000 in 1922, or just under $300,000 in 1988 dollars—they brought American architects to France to remodel the main house; build a guesthouse (to be called La Bastide); construct an oddly shaped, two-story studio at the bottom of the garden, sort of a Provençal watchtower with green-shuttered windows; and add two cabanas and a garage with living quarters. While this was going on, Gerald supervised the clearing of La Garoupe beach: He persuaded all his friends to help pluck the cane and seaweed from the beach, then built cabanas on it and claimed it as his own. In 1932 the Murphys also bought a tiny farm across from Gerald's studio on the Chemin des Nielles. Called La Ferme des Orangers, it was dubbed "the cow shed" and reserved for overflow guests when the main house and La Bastide were full.

Villa America sat surrounded by eucalyptus trees on the crest of a hill in the middle of the cape, with sweeping views of the sea, a half mile or so inland from La Garoupe. You can find the shell of it today by driving fifty yards down the narrow Chemin des Mougins, off the Boulevard du Cap, and keeping all eyes peeled to the right.

When I finally located the house the name on the gate was Villa Fiamma, and it was owned by Edmund Uher, a German industrialist who'd bought the house from the Murphys in 1950 for 5.2 million francs. Utterly unaware of Villa America's history, he found the literary connection only "vaguely amusing." He did mention, however, that the Murphys' former housekeeper and gardener were living in Gerald's old studio, which Uher had sold to them and which the occupants now called L'Atelier.

Baptistine-Marie and Joseph Revello, both pushing eighty when we met in 1974, lit up when I asked if they remembered the Murphys. "The family was only here about two months a year," Marie said, "yet they maintained the house and the staff all year long. There were seven gardeners and five or six staff in the house. Monsieur and Madame were both very pleasant, very nice to us, and everyone liked them. They had lots of friends and were always planning parties." (Having modeled the characters Dick and Nicole Diver in *Tender Is the Night* partially on Gerald and Sara, Fitzgerald dedicated the novel to the couple with the line "Many Fêtes.")

"They loved their children and did everything for them," Marie went on. "There were picnics and treasure hunts, and the family filled the property with animals. I remember there were two cows, one called Violette. Birds were in cages everywhere, and they even had a pet monkey."

Hemingway hadn't yet become famous, and neither Marie nor Joseph could recall which of the Murphys' guests he was. Scott Fitzgerald was just a blur in their combined memories. But Zelda was not.

"I remember that woman very well," Marie insisted. "I could never forget her. She drank a great deal. A pitcher of Martinis at a time. She laughed and danced and must have said many unusual things, because people were always looking at her strangely. She was, as we say, *fada* [a bit crazy]. But she was the most beautiful woman here. Everyone on the staff called her *La Jaconde* [the Mona Lisa]."

With each party, Villa America slipped more deeply into the French experience that became an indelible part of the twentieth-century American-expatriate literary soul.

"There was no one at Antibes this summer," Scott Fitzgerald wrote—tongue in cheek?—to a friend in 1926, "except me, Zelda, the Valentinos, the Murphys, Mistinguett, Rex Ingram, Dos Passos, Alice Terry, the MacLeishes, Charlie Brackett, Maude Kahn, Esther Murphy, Marguerite Namara, E. Phillips Oppenheim, Mannes the violinist, Floyd Dell, Max and Crystal Eastman, former Premier Orlando, Etienne de Beaumont—[it was] just the right place to rough it, an escape from the world."

But with the 1930s everything changed.

Patrick Murphy was diagnosed as having tuberculosis in October 1929, and Gerald and Sara moved the family to Switzerland, where they lived for a year and a half in hopes that the better air would help the child recover. A seeming cure was effected, and the family returned to Antibes for two years. In July 1932, they returned to the United States. Then suddenly in 1935, Baoth, away at boarding school, died of spinal meningitis. A year and a half later Patrick died too, finally beaten by the disease he'd fought for almost half his young life. Gerald had ceased painting when Patrick's illness had first been diagnosed, and now he told Sara he never wanted to return to Villa America. In a letter to Fitzgerald, a desolate Gerald Murphy wrote, "In my heart I dreaded the moment when our youth and invention would be attacked in our only vulnerable spot, the children."

The party was over.

∽

At first, the house was rented. Among the people who lived there for a time were the Dolly sisters, who supposedly painted every room black and hung mirrors on the ceilings.

Then came the war, and the house was shut, left empty.

In 1949 Uher heard the villa was for sale. "I'd been renting next door and didn't know anything about the Murphys except that they wanted to sell. Many people feared just after the war that the Russians were going to attack Europe, and the main condition Murphy set down was that the sale had to be handled in American dollars. No one knew exactly how much he wanted, so I made an offer and two days later he cabled saying okay."

At the time there were six houses on the property. Uher sold what he didn't want, including La Bastide and L'Atelier, reducing the size of the estate by about half.

"I changed many things," he continued. "There was, for instance, a large stairway at the entrance, which I took down. I converted the two bedrooms on the main floor into one large living room. I'm afraid my taste and the Murphys' taste were not quite compatible. The architect they'd hired didn't know the Mediterranean, and the villa didn't fit here. Maybe it would have worked in Beverly Hills, but Villa America wasn't right for the Riviera."

The only thing left from the Murphy days, he claimed, was the wrought-iron garden furniture. (A bedroom suite had remained for a time, but when Sara asked to have it Uher returned it to her.) Still, I wondered if perhaps there might be anything else, such as the Villa America sign I knew had existed. He thought about this for a moment, started to suggest that a painting might once have been stored in the basement, then quickly changed his mind and said no, there was nothing else.

Intrigued that a painting might indeed exist, I wrote to Archibald MacLeish, the last survivor of the band of friends from those days. I told him I'd found the villa and thought he'd be amused to know the Dolly sisters had lived there at one time. He answered that he remembered Villa America very well, but that his wife assured him he didn't remember the Dolly sisters.

In response to my mention of Uher's hint about a possible painting, MacLeish noted the Museum of Modern Art's then recent (1974) one-man show of Murphy's work and his belief that all the canvases had been accounted for at that time. Accounted for or deemed missing, as it turned out. According to the New York museum's catalogue for that exhibit, of the ten works Gerald was known to have completed during his remarkably short but fine seven-year painting career (1922–29), four were missing. Confusion continues to plague the question of the artist's total production. Still, today, thanks to a gift made by MacLeish just before Gerald Murphy's death from cancer in 1964, *Wasp and Pear* is part of MOMA's permanent collection. Two other Murphy paintings belong to the Dallas Museum of Fine Arts; in 1960 Douglas McAgy had been the first American museum director (of the then Dallas Museum of Contemporary Arts) to admire his work and exhibit it in his "American Genius in Review" show.

In 1983, after attending a party given by the owner of the Ferme des Orangers (who for some years had been laboring under the mistaken impression that the Ferme was the actual Murphy family villa), my wife and I set out to drive by Villa America for another nostalgic look. We found it reduced to a construction site. All that was left of the house was the original four walls. I subsequently learned that Uher had sold the place in 1976 to a young Swiss watch tycoon for just over a half million dollars, and as soon as the latter had taken possession he'd begun ripping it to pieces. I have since returned to find a house with Greek Revival columns, a huge marble veranda, and a swimming pool. If it was Beverly Hills for the Murphys, it's Riyadh now.

Only one relic of those "feted" summers remains, a wooden sign that reads VILLA AMERICA À 50 MÈTRES. Painted by Gerald in his atelier with the help of his children, perhaps as a summer-morning project before their ritual trek to the beach, it now decorates the wall just over my word processor as a reminder of the debt so many American writers have owed to France. That's what lives. That and the image of hallowed ground fifty meters down the road . . . a sign pointing in the right direction for would-be Fitzgeralds and would-be Hemingways who couldn't be at Cap d'Antibes sixty-five years ago, when everybody who was anybody partied at the Murphys'.

Picasso at the Beach

BY LORRAINE ALEXANDER

∽

editor's note

Years before there was a Musée Picasso in Paris, and before I had visited the Museu Picasso in Barcelona, I went to the Musée Picasso in Antibes during a three-week spring vacation on the Côte d'Azur. I spent hours and hours inside the Château Grimaldi, marveling over the great space it afforded an artist; but when I finally walked outside on the back patio, which overlooks the Mediterranean, I had to catch my breath: this, I decided, was not only a *great* place for an artist to work but a *perfect* one. I remained on the patio for the rest of the day, feeling I was the luckiest person alive to be there in that beautiful spot (and not at all sure when I might be fortunate enough to sit on a patio overlooking the Mediterranean again). On repeated visits, I still find the museum, and that patio, to be inspiring.

LORRAINE ALEXANDER, who also wrote the piece on Matisse in this section, contributed this article to *Gourmet,* where it appeared in August 1998.

B uilt on the site of Antipolis, a Greek trading post established several centuries B.C., present-day Antibes is a cheerful maze of prosperity and palm trees set down between (bigger) Nice and (brighter) Cannes. The old center of town is a hive of history and the particular beauty that a castle and a Provençal market bestow, while Cap d'Antibes, a residential enclave to the west, is all location-location-location, as cool and cosseted as a goddess reclining on rose petals. In 1946, when Pablo Picasso arrived in neighboring Golfe-Juan with Françoise Gilot—an aspiring artist a third his age and his latest love—to spend the summer in cramped rooms near the beach, the coastal roads were rutted tracks, wartime shortages persisted, and rooms of any sort were hard to find. An acquaintance tried persuading Picasso to decamp to her estate in Cap d'Antibes, but he replied that his apartment had "vitamins."

Picasso, a vigorous sixty-five, had long been famous: Decades earlier, before World War I, he and Georges Braque had pioneered cubism, chiseling reality into planes, and *Guernica* had been painted in 1937, adding social conscience to the perceived attributes of his growing mystique. In the weeks after the Liberation of Paris, GIs waited in the courtyard beneath Picasso's rue des Grands-Augustins studio for an autograph.

In postwar Antibes, everyone knew *le maître* was among them. Imagine the scene that August, then, when Picasso, brown as a beetle in shorts and striped T-shirt—the fisherman's attire that had become his uniform—was approached on the beach by an elegant, linen-suited man laboriously pushing a bicycle. He turned out to be the curator of Antibes's Château Grimaldi museum, modest by any standard and not yet reopened after the war. When they parted, Picasso had a set of keys to the twelfth-century castle and free use of its top floor as his studio. For the next four months he hewed to a fierce work routine, standing in silence for hours at a time, from after lunch till late at night, when spotlights were directed on the paintings, throwing the rest of the vast room into darkness. In this way, Picasso explained, he could become almost hypnotized, as if in a trance. He told Françoise that while he worked he left his body outside the door, "the way Moslems take off their shoes before entering a mosque."

The newly improvised discipline suited Picasso: mornings to read his mail and swim; lunch at Chez Marcel (now the Bistrot du Port) in Golfe-Juan or near the museum; then to work in the Romanesque castle, with views across the water to Antibes's old fort, which he admired for its "austere and intelligent geometry." By the time Picasso left in late November, he had completed forty-four drawings on paper and twenty-five paintings on whatever he could find, mostly laminated plywood and fibro-cement, using marine paint and carbon recycled from arc lamps on loan from a film stu-

dio in Nice. The following summer he returned to paint *Ulysses and the Sirens,* and in 1948 the entire body of work completed on the premises became the core collection of Antibes's Musée Picasso, the first museum ever dedicated to a living artist.

Among the many appeals of visiting *this* museum in *this* place is the symbiosis between the two: painting after painting of sea urchins and soles, eels and octopuses, a wedge of watermelon, a fisherman leaning on a bar table; and minutes away one of the prettiest covered markets of the Riviera, lined with bar-cafés and displaying its own still lifes of fish and melons. The market is, of course, appealing for its own sake, too. Last spring melons from Carpentras and Martinique sat alongside violet artichokes, white asparagus, and tiny blue-red radishes peering out from their foliage. One table was spread with spices and herbs—powdered bay leaf the color of old jade, an olive-wood bowl of mustard grains—and next to it were urns of fragrant white acacias. When I asked the vendor what he does with this flower other than inhale, he launched into recipes for acacia *beignets,* acacia jelly. . . . Reminders of a previous year's market purchases were heavy, incised blocks of Marseilles soap—eucalyptus and honey—that remain as sculptures by my washbasin at home.

Within the museum's light-soaked rooms, the complement of environment and art shifts. Picasso's braying geometries and black gashes seem at first to rail against and then find a kind of cure in the calm of the castle's smooth, balanced mass. The nudes—flat and cold, on a green background, a white bed; Ingres's odalisques translated into triangular faces and bowling-pin legs—seem flung, unsuspecting, against the rough-cast walls. The ageless, figurative fauns are the most naturally at home, in one room serenading a third-century stela from the museum's archaeological archive. The effect is ultimately as harmonious as the fauns' imagined music, the whole structure transformed into a monumental stone pedestal for Picasso's abstractions.

The first large painting one sees, *Ulysses and the Sirens,* was the last executed, entering the collection when the early idyll of the beach holiday was over. A citrus-slice mouth mimes a scream—but there is still a sea-dream quality in the blue-and-green palette. And it is this dream that inhabits these rooms: at the center a pregnant Françoise, Picasso's "woman/flower"; all around her the frolicking goats, nymphs, centaurs, and smiling, flute-playing fauns of mythology. These are the images that dance across *Joy of Life,* the artist's beachparty bacchanal and the heart of the collection, and gaze sweetly at us from triptych and table case. "I never see fauns and centaurs in Paris," Picasso said. "They all seem to live here."

Picasso's Antibes period blends fantasies of antiquity with mundane water pitchers and coffeepots, culled from flea markets and trash heaps and domestic incidentals. He came upon Chez Marcel's owner, a big, rude woman, selling sea urchins on the sidewalk . . . and began that very day *The Sea Urchin Gobbler.* When photographer Michel Sima brought a wounded owl into the studio, Picasso made a splint for its leg and began creating tender portraits of this bird-companion on his makeshift "canvases" and eventually on his ceramic plates and sculpted pitchers. Perhaps he recognized his own notoriously intense stare, the Andalusian *mirada fuerte,* in the animal's eyes. Compassion is not a trait much associated with Picasso, but throughout his life, dogs, cats, birds, and even goats filled his homes and studios, and here, in Antibes, even the terracotta *Standing Bull* smiles.

Picasso's outpouring in Antibes is a celebration of the Mediterranean, of his submersion in its ancient myths and present

pleasures. As a thoughtful viewing requires time, it's a happy circumstance that some of the nearby restaurants are as good as they
are; minutes away by foot, they all stand ready to fuel a visit or subsequent discussion. La Jarre is the prettiest (beamed and vaulted
ceiling, lush bouquets, damask linens on well-spaced tables) and
with the most polished and personable service. Shrimp roasted with
gingerroot and salmon on sorrel sauce were beautifully cooked, and
as both were pink we drank what always seems best in warm
weather here anyway, a rosé, this one from Bandol.

L'Armoise, popular for rich meat dishes exuding the woodsy flavors of southwestern France, is intimate by way of being both
minuscule and utterly romantic. Le Brulot, on the other hand, is a
caldera of boisterous energy as high-borne platters of grilled steak
and fennel-scented fish levitate to packed tables. *Socca,* a chick-pea
pancake, is a regional specialty and a fine starter as you adjust to
the dark and din of this Midi mead hall.

Sea urchins are legally fished off Antibes, Cap d'Antibes, and
Golfe-Juan all year except summer. Anyone strolling the market-
place will pass the Café des Chineurs, where the sign DÉGUSTATION
D'OURSINS would surely have tempted Picasso. Another marketplace
meal might be picked up at the Maison du Poulet. I was lured by the
bin of homemade potato chips out front and the friendly banter of
the aproned owner, who explained that the shop spit-roasts not only
farm-raised chickens but also pork, rabbit, and leg of lamb. You can
order the meat whole or by the slice, stash it in your tote along with
a bag of those terrific chips and some market fruit, and proceed to
La Garoupe, on the way to Cap d'Antibes (see below), for a picnic
on the beach where summer tourism began on the Riviera.

In May 1948 Picasso and Françoise moved to a tiny house called
La Galloise in Vallauris, known for its red earth and potteries, in the
hills behind Golfe-Juan and Antibes. Their arrival grew out of an
encounter as serendipitous as the one that had led Picasso to the

Château Grimaldi: Suzanne and Georges Ramié, owners of the respected Madoura pottery, had ventured to the beach at Golfe-Juan—Picasso's office—and offered to put a section of their workshop at his disposal. It was the beginning of a new passion for the artist, bringing together both painter and sculptor by way of a medium as ancient as the colony of fauns and satyrs he'd excavated in Antibes.

With Suzanne as his teacher, Picasso began by applying paint to standard forms but was soon manipulating the wet clay to startling effect. Over the ensuing years he single-handedly revived Vallauris's flagging industry, creating among much else the seventy-five playful, daring ceramics that would complete Antibes's collection. His production was rapid and often repetitive, but the best pieces are powerful and for many come as a delightful surprise. Picasso wanted us to redefine what we see—from cubism forward—and so a vase becomes a bird, a plate a bullring, its sloping rim lined with spectators. Janine Vincent, Madoura's manager, is lavish with praise. "He did things no one else could do, applying lithographic techniques to clay, for example. His hands were divining rods. *Il savait tout!*"

Madoura, which has the exclusive right to Picasso's limited editions, has many of his ceramics on display and for sale, beginning at about $600 for a small engraved tile. In 1977 Vallauris's sixteenth-century château became a museum where more of his work can be viewed, including numerous photographs, a fine bullfight series of plates, and a striking head of Jacqueline Huot, whom he met in 1954, when she was a shop assistant at Madoura, and married in 1961. Adjacent to this collection is the deconsecrated chapel where Picasso's *War and Peace* mural reveals itself as a kind of twentieth-century cave painting. Still, the images of violence and peace are standard ones; more affecting, to me, is his *Man with Sheep* sculpture, in the market square across the street.

For visitors to Vallauris, a restaurant with exuberant style and reasonable prices is Le Manuscrit, a former perfume factory on the nondescript road that leads, farther on, to La Galloise (still in family hands). Diners gather outdoors or on a glassed-in terrace, a human-scale terrarium filled when I was there with enormous yellow lilies and masses of billowy hydrangeas. A flavorful fish terrine coated in vodka *crème fraîche,* "country" salad, and white- and dark-chocolate *croustillant* stood up to the splash of the surroundings. Most fun of all are the big, jauntily fringed umbrellas scattered among the tables—all that's needed to recall Robert Capa's 1948 photograph of Picasso holding a similar one high over the laughing, prancing Françoise, which endures as a frame snatched from his singular, long career and their moment at the beach.

Cap d'Antibes

In 1923 Gerald and Sara Murphy, a stylish American couple credited with making the French Riviera fashionable in summer (before them, tans were what happened to farm laborers and anyone else who couldn't get out of the sun) checked into the barely-up-and-running Hôtel du Cap with their children and their friend Picasso, who came with his mother, first wife Olga, and son Paolo. The only other guests were a Chinese family who'd been wintering there. Today the hotel, splendid on its green carpet unrolling toward the sea and waterside Eden Roc, is an icon to the understated yet quite fabulous luxury only cash can contemplate (credit cards are not, in fact, accepted). Pink geraniums line steps down to pine grove and pool; rose gardens spill out toward a small spa facility; and tentlike cabanas, for guests only, cost approximately an extra $270 a day. Picasso returned on occasion, as has roughly half the high society of this century. The hotel's setting and pervasive pampering—the gift of awaking to a fleetingly white-capped sea and the salt air's clarity after a night rain, then curling up on toile de Jouy as breakfast is rolled in—redefines *luxe, calme,* and *volupté*. Paradise paled somewhat when a trio of expressionless, business-suited body-guards settled in like a shipwreck on the Eden Roc's terrace, but lunch indoors—the best scallops, with "melted" leeks, ever designed onto a plate, garlicky cod-flecked potato *gnocchi,* and a 1990 Château de Bellet—restored the spell.

If the Hôtel du Cap caters to an international clientele, the smaller, simpler Hôtel Beau-Site, its near neighbor, feels entirely European, the sort of place where a retired schoolteacher, sleekly stylish newlyweds, and a family of four from Neuilly or Nuremberg might spend a week or two of nodding acquaintance at the poolside snack bar. Accommodations are pretty and light-filled, with pastel-painted furniture and shiny new bathrooms; downstairs a large-screen television and leather sofa anchor one end of a spacious room otherwise given over to breakfast tables and a square bay of windows overlooking the patio. A double in summer runs a mere 600 francs, approximately.

Another modestly priced place tucked amid the high walls and elec-tronically monitored gates of Cap d'Antibes is La Bastide du Bosquet, its green-shuttered, petal-pink façade a Pagnol fantasy. Straggly flowers mill over the front gar-dens, lending a sweetly unkempt air, while inside the eighteenth-century house sunflower-yellow

and sky-blue walls set off antique chests and wardrobes. (The family business has been, for generations, furniture restoration.) In sum, Arts & Crafts meets Pierre Deux—the prototype, that is. Anyone prizing beautifully hand-glazed tiles and the sibilant music of cicadas above room service and puffed pillows will find the unselfconscious ambiance—a reason some film people hide out here at festival time in Cannes—a very special luxury.

Finally, where well-being along this coast is concerned, there is always the exemplary bouillabaisse served at coolly classic Restaurant de Bacon to consider. Accompanied by a stunningly framed view, over teal water, of Vieil Antibes, it is as good as lunch gets. Had Picasso been time-traveling the day I dined here, my bowl would surely have inspired another still life for his museum across the bay.

Hotels

La Bastide du Bosquet, 14 chemin des Sables, 06600 Antibes; tel./fax: 04.93.67.32.29.

Hôtel Beau-Site, 141 boulevard Kennedy, 06160 Cap d'Antibes; 04.93.61.53.43; fax: 04.93.67.78.16.

Hôtel du Cap–Eden Roc, boulevard Kennedy, 06602 Antibes; 04.93.61.39.01; fax: 04.93.67.76.04.

Restaurants

L'Armoise, 2 rue de la Touraque, 06600 Antibes; 04.93.34.71.10.

Le Brulot, 3 rue Frédéric Isnard, 06600 Antibes; 04.93.34.17.76.

Eden Roc (see Hôtel du Cap, above).

La Jarre, 14 rue Saint-Esprit, 06600 Vieil Antibes; 04.93.34.50.12.

Le Manuscrit, 224 chemin Lintier, 06220 Vallauris; 04.93.64.56.56.

Restaurant de Bacon, boulevard de Bacon, 06600 Cap d'Antibes;
04.93.61.50.62.

An American in Provence

~~

editor's note

Food writer Richard Olney passed away at the age of seventy-one on
August 3, 1999. He was never as well known to Americans as Julia Child or
Elizabeth David, but his influence to those in the culinary profession—and
to American home cooks who *did* know of him—was profound.

In addition to his popular *Simple French Food* (IDG, 1992, paperback)
and *The French Menu Cookbook* (Simon & Schuster, 1970), his other excellent books include *Lulu's Provençal Table: The Exuberant Food and Wine
from the Domaine Tempier Vineyard* (HarperCollins, 1994), *Romanée-
Conti: The World's Most Fabled Wine* (Rizzoli, 1995), and *Richard Olney's
French Wine & Food: A Wine Lover's Cookbook* (Interlink Publishing
Group, 1997).

This tribute to Olney was compiled by *Gourmet* magazine, where it
originally appeared in the November 1999 issue.

When Richard Olney, a native Iowan, moved to Provence in
1961 to find a solitary place to paint, he was unwittingly
taking what has become a central step in the journey of many
famous food people. But unlike M.F.K. Fisher, Elizabeth David, or
Julia Child, Olney stayed.

Among the outsiders who discovered Provence, Olney may have
been the one who best appreciated the rhythm of the life of the

land. From his rustic perch on a hillside near Toulon he wrote and edited more than thirty-five books on food and wine (many were volumes in the Time Life *The Good Cook* series, which he developed). His most influential book, *Simple French Food,* was published in 1974 and caused an entire generation of American chefs to reconsider the way they cooked. His last, a memoir called *Reflexions,* is being published this month by Brick Tower Press.

Last year Marion Cunningham, a close friend of Olney's and a cooking legend in her own right, traveled to Solliès-Toucas with a writer and photographer for *Gourmet.* Her purpose: to remind a new generation of food and wine lovers about Olney and his gifts as a teacher. It turned out to be Cunningham's last trip to Olney's home. Olney unexpectedly passed away in July. He was seventy-two.

"We arrived at his property on top of a steep hill on a warm early-October afternoon," says writer Peggy Knickerbocker, who accompanied Cunningham. "We walked along his purslane lawn, past his handmade fountain and fish pond, under the grape arbor, and under a line of crisp, freshly laundered dish towels—the aviary and chicken coop in sight—then entered the kitchen through a veil of strung-together corks, a wine lover's curtain to keep the flies out. Looking impish with his short dark hair, a pink work shirt, and red suspenders, he could not have been more welcoming as he stood tending the crackling wood in his fireplace, the focal point of his house and, really, his life."

It was that fireplace and his skills as a cook that drew a fairly steady stream of chefs, cookbook writers, journalists, and wine pros, some more welcome than others, to his door—and eventually into his memoir, a funny, often catty document of his life in and out of favor with the food establishment. Some visitors came with preconceived ideas of the good life in Provence that only occasionally matched the reality of Olney's kind of simple living. "This is not a house," said one outraged French wine merchant to

Olney, as the story goes in *Reflexions*. "It's nothing but a shack!"

To many others, however, Olney's kitchen represented the ideal of French country cooking.

"Richard's house was the way all of us Americans would love to think all French homes look," Cunningham says. "It was very rustic. It was as if the house were part of the little hillside. Nothing was hidden. There weren't doors you went in and out of—everything ran together. And everything there told you who he was and what he did. The kitchen was in the center of the house, but he would usually eat outside."

"A simple wooden table abutted a broad square column that appeared to hold up the house," Knickerbocker says. "The work area was totally approachable, with no extraneous kitchen machines. At least two dozen knives, sharp and ready for work, were poked into the space between the cutting board and the wall. Simple track lights focused only on the work at hand. It was one of the simplest kitchens I've ever seen, and unquestionably the most efficient."

What follows are other memories of a few of the many people who traveled to Richard Olney's house in Provence.

Alice Waters, chef, Chez Panisse, Berkeley

I can remember every detail of my first visit to Solliès-Toucas: the climb up the steep hill to his little house set amid terraces of ancient olive trees, the clicking of the cicadas, the rustle of the leaves in the wind, the aroma of the wild herbs all around us, mixed with the smell of Richard's Gauloises.

He received us wearing nothing but an open shirt, his skimpy bathing suit, a kitchen towel at his waist, and a pair of worn espadrilles. He invited us into his house, which consisted basically of one room in which he worked, ate, and entertained when weather prohibited dining on his idyllic terrace. I can close my eyes and see the boulders with which Richard and his brothers had built the fire-place at the head of the house, the copper pots hanging above, the marble mortars on the mantelpiece, the column by the table papered with wine labels, the lovely platters and tureens displayed on hard-to-reach shelves, the windows out to the garden where the table under the grape arbor had been laid with beautiful linens.

He served us a spectacular salad, full of Provençal greens that were new to me—rocket, anise, hyssop—with perfectly tender green beans and bright nasturtium flowers tossed in and dressed with the vinegar he made himself from the ends of bottles of great wine. That salad was a revelation and inspired countless *salades composées* in the years to come. My first visit ended, many hours later, in the same way all my subsequent visits ended: in a kind of ecstatic paralysis brought on by extraordinary food, astonishing wines, and dancing until dawn to seventy-eights of Edith Piaf and *bal musette* music.

Marion Cunningham, cookbook author

The last time I saw Richard I asked him, "If you could eat at any restaurant in the world, where would you eat?" His reply: "At home." I visited Richard at least half a dozen times, and the food was always incredible. You could remember it for the longest time. Richard felt that you should know a few basics about how to cook, and from there you should be able to do whatever you wished. That was why he had wings in the kitchen: He could put things together.

When we were cooking, he seemed to hear bubbles I didn't hear and smell things I didn't smell. He was like a parent with a small child. He just heard new things that most people didn't. When I was there this last time, I was reminded of that while watching him brush olive oil on a leg of lamb. He'd made a brush of some herbs. His food was always stunningly good. Everything he said, he could make come true on the plate.

And when it was time for you to leave, he never wanted you to go. He would say, "Wait until I finish my drink, and then you can go."

Kermit Lynch, wine writer and merchant

Richard produced wonderful works about food. No one talks as much about his wine books, but I think they will certainly last longer than anybody else's from our era. The whole story of wine is in those books. And his writing is wonderful. Those books are so complete and elaborate.

Richard was completely honest to himself. The most horrible criticism he could make of somebody was to call them a whore, and what he meant was that they weren't true to themselves.

When we went to his place after he died, Richard's brother found his checkbook, and on it Richard had written "*artiste peintre.*" Not writer. Not cook. He would always say he was working on his last book. He would say, "Oh, I think now I'm gonna get back into painting."

Gerald Asher, wine writer

I first met Richard more than thirty years ago. In those days he was still painting a little while contributing the main monthly cooking feature to *Cuisine et Vins de France,* then the very bible of French gastronomy. It was quite a feat for an American with no professional food experience to be teaching France its own classic dishes.

"Turn left there," my friend said. "That's his driveway." Staring with disbelief at what appeared to be a sloping concrete retaining wall with a dirt track rising steeply above it into some dense, scrubby bushes, I put the car in lowest gear and made a run at it, not daring to hesitate—even in the track's hairpin turns—until I had made it all the way to the top. I pulled in under a tree at the side of a dirt yard.

Richard had not been expecting us, but out of nothing and a scrap of something else, he produced a salad and a neat stack of perfectly round omelets of varied hue and a medley of flavors. We sat very happily at a round table under a vine on the little terrace in front of the double-windowed room that was virtually his whole house. Only later did I discover all the little multicolored lights wound into that vine. They were turned on at dusk every evening, even when Richard dined there alone in a swimsuit.

To Richard, life was an occasion.

Judy Rodgers, chef, Zuni Café, San Francisco

Richard taught me how to teach myself. His books encouraged a high level of *intelligence* about cooking—as opposed to desperation. He said, sort of: "Cook smart. And have fun." He was the teacher who knew he was smarter than you, and yet you loved it. He was an intriguing combination of hilarious, warm, and intimidating.

One time we went back to his place from northern Italy with truffles that he'd picked out, and he made dinner. He had a beat-up Le Creuset pot, with some cracks in it, and some eggs. Our meal was just the eggs, the butter, the chopped white truffles, and the salt. The seasoning was garlic, but the only way it got in was by his rubbing it on the wooden spoon he used to stir the eggs. And it mattered exactly how this wooden spoon got rubbed with the cut clove of garlic before he stirred the scrambled eggs and white truffles. That definitely got my attention.

Bibliothèque

Marie Bashkirtseff

I Am the Most Interesting Book of All: The Diary of Marie Bashkirtseff (Volume I), Marie Bashkirtseff, Phyllis Howard Kernberger (translator), Katherine Kernberger (translator), Chronicle Books, 1997. I had never heard of Bashkirtseff until I stood in front of her portrait at the Musée des Beaux-Arts in Nice. Then I saw paintings *by* her, and I was intrigued. Until this book was published, however, all I knew of her was that she was a Russian aristocrat who led a daring life and became a painter. Her life was much, much more than that, and in the same way that the writings of Vladimir Nabokov and Nina Berberova are valuable records of the vibrant Russian community in Paris, Bashkirtseff's are representative of the Russian community on the Côte d'Azur.

Paul Cézanne

Cézanne and the Provençal Table, Jean-Bernard Naudin, text by Gilles Plazy, recipes by Jacqueline Saulnier, preface by Alain Ducasse, Clarkson Potter, 1995; originally published in French by Éditions du Chêne—Hachette Livre. This book—and the related Matisse and Renoir titles listed below—is one title in a series generally shelved in the cookbook section of bookstores. I've never used any of them for the recipes (which represent Provençal specialties of the time) because it is far too difficult to reach the back pages of the books, where the recipes can be found; but the photographs—color reproductions of the artist's paintings juxtaposed with the actual settings—are intoxicating. Someday I might actually try a recipe from one of these titles, but in the meantime I never tire of reading the text or looking at photos of the Jas de Bouffan outside Aix, Les Collettes, or the open windows to the Mediterranean.

Colette

Creating Colette, Volume 1: From Ingenue to Libertine, 1873–1913 and *Volume II: From Baroness to Woman of Letters, 1912–1954* (both by Claude Francis and Fernande Gontier, both Steerforth Press, both 1999) and *Secrets of the Flesh: A Life of Colette* (Judith Thurman, Alfred A. Knopf, 1999). I very much enjoy Colette's fiction, but I enjoy reading *about* her even more. These biographies are definitive and delicious in every respect. The selected bibliography in *Secrets of the Flesh* underscores the great number of Colette biographies that have been published. I was somewhat surprised when these three volumes all appeared in 1999. It does beg the question, why so very many biographies? I think a reviewer for *The New York Times Book Review* answered it well when she wrote, "Perhaps because with each new biography Colette becomes more representative as a woman who negotiated between the privileges and the punishments of a society that constrains women by idealizing them; in her concerns, contradictions, aspirations and ambivalences she remains a continuing gauge for the life of so many French women of the 20th century." Two other biographical Colette books of which I'm particularly fond are *Colette—Earthly Paradise: An Autobiography Drawn from her Lifetime Writings* (1966) and *Belles Saisons: A Colette Scrapbook* (1978), both by Robert Phelps, both published by Farrar, Straus & Giroux. Additionally, Maurice Goudeket, Colette's second husband, whom she unsuccessfully hid from the Nazis (but successfully managed to free from deportation to Auschwitz), wrote his own book about life with Colette: *The Delights of Growing Old* (A Common Reader edition; see Bookstores in *Renseignements Pratiques*).

M.F.K. Fisher

M.F.K. Fisher, Julia Child and Alice Waters: Celebrating the Pleasures of the Table, Joan Reardon, Harmony Books, 1994. Although this book is a tribute to three women who changed the way Americans think about food and cooking, it is also a book about the common thread which inspired and united them: France—particularly Provence—and *la cuisine Française*. I found it absolutely fascinating, and while I already greatly admired each of these writer-cooks, I was surprised to learn the degree to which they were pioneers in the food world and the degree to which they were devoted to each other. I do not think it's an exaggeration to state that due to Julia Child's PBS television series, the Food Network is able to exist and thrive today; that due to M.F.K. Fisher's passionate writing on gastronomy (which was ultimately about life and how one lived it), publishers and readers realized food was more than something to eat, and cookbooks and food publications are now more popular than ever; and due to Alice Waters's insistence upon fresh, seasonal food, we have more farmer's markets across the country (twenty-eight in New York City alone!). *De rigueur* reading for anyone interested in food, France, and America.

Marquis de Sade

At Home with the Marquis de Sade: A Life, Francine du Plessix Gray, Simon & Schuster, 1998 and *The Marquis de Sade: A Life,* Neil Schaeffer, Alfred A. Knopf, 1999. I was surprised that two biographies of Sade were published within a few months of each other (anniversary of his death, I wondered, or possibly the bicentennial of the date he was released from prison?); but the appearance of these seems to be coincidental. Both of these authors have tried, successfully I think, to present Sade in a broader and more sympathetic light than he's ever been portrayed before. Ultimately I was more interested in Gray's work because she focused on the the two women who were most important in Sade's life: his wife, Renée-Pélagie de Sade, and his mother-in-law, Madame de Montreuil. Much more complex to me than Sade was his wife, who remained unbelievably forgiving and consenting up to the day Sade was released from the Bastille, when she changed her tune.

Henri Matisse

Matisse: A Way of Life in the South of France, Jean-Bernard Naudin, text by Gilles Plazy, recipes by Coco Jobard, Rizzoli, 1998; originally published in French by Éditions du Chêne-Hachette Livre.

Gerald and Sara Murphy

Living Well Is the Best Revenge, Calvin Tomkins, Modern Library, 1998; originally published by Viking Press, 1971; *Everybody Was So Young,* Amanda Vaill, Houghton Mifflin, 1998, hardcover; Broadway Books, 1999, paperback. F. Scott Fitzgerald's *Tender Is the Night* is my favorite Fitzgerald book. When I first read it, I knew it was loosely based on the dazzling American expatriates Gerald and Sara Murphy, but I had no clue how much of it was fiction. With the appearance of these two books, the Murphy facts and fictions have been sorted out. The Modern Library edition, at 172 pages, is the smaller of the two, but is not a lesser book in any way. Tomkins, longtime art critic for *The New Yorker,* relates their story concisely and engagingly. Black-and-white reproductions of Gerald's paintings and sixty-nine photographs from the Murphys' family albums are included (the color painting featured on the jacket, *Cocktail,* is also Gerald's and is part of the collection at the Whitney Museum of American Art). Amanda Vaill's book runs to 361 pages and also includes two inserts of black-and-white photos. Her book is simply more—more detail, more background, more recent material (there are even a few photos from the '40s and '50s, whereas in the Tomkins book a notation appears after the last photo: "The Murphys' family albums do not go beyond 1933, the year they came to America"). Initially, I wasn't sure what Gerald meant by his remark, "Even though it happened in France, it was all somehow an American experience," but after reading these two books I saw that this is very much an

American tale, and a rather tragic one at that. If you're going to read one book you might as well read them both. The slim hardcover can easily be devoured on the flight over, and you'll finish the paperback in the wee hours of the first or second night because you won't be able to resist.

Pablo Picasso

Life with Picasso, Françoise Gilot and Carlton Lake, McGraw-Hill (hardcover), 1964; Anchor/Doubleday (paperback), 1989. In his introduction to this engaging book (once I began reading it I was incapable of putting it down), Carlton Lake says of Gilot: "I realized that she had an infinitely deeper and truer appreciation of Picasso's thought and work than anyone I had encountered." Lake certainly encountered enough people in Picasso's circle of friends and acquaintances to make such a statement. And judging from other works I've read about Picasso, I believe his observation is correct. Although Gilot and Picasso never married, they did have two children together, Paloma and Claude. Though they met in Paris, the greater part of their life together was spent in Provence and on the Côte d'Azur. I have great admiration for Gilot, who is an accomplished artist in her own right (for a complete look at her *oeuvre,* see *Françoise Gilot: Monograph, 1940–2000,* Acatos, Lucerne, Switzerland; text in English.). In 1970, Gilot married Dr. Jonas Salk, who passed away some years ago. And so she has spent much of her life with two of the most influential people of the twentieth century. She remains no less fascinating a figure.

The Sorcerer's Apprentice: Picasso, Provence, and Douglas Cooper, John Richardson, Alfred A. Knopf, 1999. Richardson, author of Volumes I and II of *A Life of Picasso* (both published by Random House), presents here a personal and entertaining slice of life in Provence from about 1949 to about 1970. It is, of course, a life completely absorbed by art and artists and all manner of eccentric personalities, and it is the story of Richardson's complicated relationship with modern art (especially cubist) collector Douglas Cooper. I couldn't stop reading it, and I can't imagine you will, either. With numerous black-and-white photos and reproductions.

Auguste Renoir

Renoir's Table: The Art of Living and Dining with One of the World's Great Impressionist Painters, Jean-Bernard Naudin, Jean-Michel Charbonnier, recipes by Jacqueline Saulnier, Simon & Schuster, 1994.

VILLE DE NIMES

TOUR MAGNE

N⁰ 22734

La Parfaite - Nîmes

Hubert ROBERT (1733-1808)

La Maison Carrée

LOUVRE INV. 7648

R. M. N.

VILLA EPHRUSSI DE ROTHSCHILD
Les plus beaux jardins de la Côte-d'Azur

Plein Tarif Adulte 49.00F
7.47 EUR

032448/1/1003 20/05/00 14:01/17402

Ce billet, valable pour une seule visite, n'est ni repris ni échangé.
Le Musée décline toute responsabilité en cas d'accident.

Le Jardin Espagnol

Jardins, Musées, et Monuments

(Gardens, Museums, and Monuments of Note)

"The South of France has been the playground for cultural and political figures for well over a century, but there is one art form in which it has excelled above all others. Almost every major French painter of the twentieth century has passed some time there and Provence can claim, with some justification, to be the heartland of modern French art. Artists, therefore, do figure prominently . . . in the museums and monuments that are such a highlight of the region as a whole."

—Paul Stirton, BLUE GUIDE: PROVENCE & THE CÔTE D'AZUR

Relish the Rhône

BY CLIVE IRVING

editor's note

The Rhône, one of two great rivers of Provence (the other is the Durance), is impressive. Lawrence Durrell, in *Caesar's Vast Ghost,* says that of the four major rivers of France, "the Rhône is the most various to study and perhaps the most delightful to explore, for in its relatively short course (it is the shortest of the four) it cuts across the two hemispheres which together make up the temperament of France itself: the cold dark north and the sun-dazzled Mediterranean. In a manner of speaking it *is* France and if you journey along it you can study it as a sort of summation of the French character and of French history."

CLIVE IRVING is a frequent contributor to *Condé Nast Traveler,* where this piece appeared in May 1995. In this piece he follows the Rhône from Switzerland to Saintes-Maries-de-la-Mer.

It began with a furtive rattling of the window shutters and a faint howling around the medieval casements. Night sounds where there had been many night sounds through the ages. By morning the howling was incessant. I pushed open the shutters against a forcefully resistant wind. Fifty feet away, in the ruins of an ancient chapel, its nave open to the sky, the trapped wind sucked up white powdered stone and took on the form of an incubus driven mad with the constraint.

This was a pervasive, inhabiting wind. It raged across the hill above, tearing into freshly bloomed cascades of yellow broom so that the color writhed. Cypresses, the most exposed of the trees, flexed acutely in the line of the wind. They signaled its direction—and identity. The intruder came from the north, sucked down the great valley of the Rhône and into Provence like a jet stream. This was the mistral.

The evening before had been different, a foretaste of summer in a backwater of southern France called Drôme-Provençal. I had followed a minor tributary of the Rhône, the Jabron, into a valley and to a medieval village called Le Poët-Laval. There, on a hillside, I found a commandery originally built by those ardent Christian hosts, the Knights of Malta, in the fourteenth century. The commandery is now a hotel, Les Hospitaliers. Dinner on the terrace overlooking the Jabron Valley had been serene. A light, warm breeze wafted up its scents: lavender, lime (the *tilleul,* whose fresh blossoms are locally dried for use in a soothing herb tea), broom, and even the ripe cherries that hung heavy in the orchards below.

Then came the mistral to remind us that Mother Nature can be a spoiler, too.

My memory of the mistral was of something warmer and more congenial. It had been many years earlier in the crucible of the southern Midi, at Carcassonne. Then the wind had been at my back, urging me on to Spain while it remained domiciled in France. With enduring luck, I had never felt it again.

Until now. The concierge at Les Hospitaliers admitted that it was unusually late in the spring for the mistral to strike, and offered with mathematical certainty that it would last for either three, six, or nine days.

I checked with a more scientific source. A mistral is generated when two vast rotations of pressure converge: high pressure over the mountains and plateaus west of the Rhône and, to the east, a low-pressure storm system over the Alps and northern Italy. The Rhône Valley acts as a funnel between these two systems, drawing down cold, desiccating air from the Alps. The wind can be miles high, and it gathers force as it roars toward its nemesis, the Mediterranean.

I could see one effect immediately. The sky was rinsed clean of haze. This produced a stark, intense light that seemed to curb or even eradicate shadows. Where there was shade it was suddenly chill. This polarization of light and temperature driven by violence was, I suddenly realized, very familiar—it invests the final landscapes of Vincent van Gogh.

A few days later, in the remnants of the Plaine de la Crau southeast of Arles, with the mistral tearing across the last fields before the sea and the cut grasses as yellow as corn, I was looking at van Gogh's palette, needing only art to intervene. Van Gogh's derangement, whatever its cause, must have embraced the whiplashed intensity of light as soul mate.

The blaze of colors he found when he arrived in Provence was not inert, and his olive trees have the gnarled ligaments that come from fighting the mistral year after year.

The mistral is a living force, blowing grit in your face and perspective into your vision. It shapes the lands of the Rhône as profoundly as history. Often, it drove people to extremes. On an exposed and isolated hunk of rock at Grignan, near Montélimar, is a castle made famous because it was a home to Marie de Rabutin-Chantal, who, as Mme. de Sévigné, bequeathed a classic of French literature, the acutely observed letters she wrote to her daughter Françoise-Marguerite recounting seventeenth-century court life. Snuckered into the bowels of the castle is a glorious church, the Eglise de St.-Sauveur—located there precisely to gain shelter from the mistral. I found Grignan a bleak and grim place, causing me to wonder whether Mme. de Sévigné wasn't really a closet masochist disguising her vice with ripe accounts of the local food. Pellets of gravel lashed at me as I composed this thought—hurled by the mistral, but also, possibly, by the lady's ghost.

I had been following the Rhône southward for a week. This river may lack the sweep of the Danube or the wayward twists of the Rhine, but without it Europe would be only half the fun. The Rhône Valley allowed the Romans to penetrate the heart of the Continent, and so permanently acquaint the dour north with licentious Mediterranean habits.

The Rhône is also the alimentary canal of France, figuratively and actually. More fine food is dispensed and gorged along its banks than anywhere else in Europe—or the world, for that matter. Hundreds of wines, a few exceptional, many others of strong identity, are made from vineyards within the river's reaches. I wanted to see what the Rhône's gifts to life could be like in total. But I made a sacrifice. I excluded Lyon.

I also chose not to track the Rhône to its source in Switzerland but, instead, picked it up just south of Lake Geneva, where it flows into Savoie. Then, with more instinct than method, I went on my riparian way. My final goal was the Provençal delta land known as Bouches-du-Rhône—mouths of many kinds were going to be active in the course of this journey, including my own.

At Bellegarde-sur-Valserine, thirty miles west of Geneva, the Rhône takes a sudden sweeping turn to the south. The river is not yet at full bore; it's overpowered by the titanic escarpments of the Jura on the west bank and the Haute-Savoie on the east. The Savoie Mountains have raw-rock teeth at their peaks, ribbons of dense woodland beneath, and then pastures and meadows tilting down to the narrow cut of the Rhône. Goats clamber the upper pastures; cows addled with the rich grasses slumber below.

Wherever in France the cuisine springs so evidently from the terrain, it's the directness of the translation that stuns you. Savoie is to dairy products what Texas is to beef: The place oozes cream, butter, and cheese. The infusion of mountain herbs and flowers in the raw milk is still palpable on the tongue, even when tasting an aged cheese, like the hard Beaufort of Savoie, which matures for up to two years.

The pastoral qualities of the Rhône are now, however, frequently sublimated to France's need for electricity. There are twenty-two hydroelectric plants between the Swiss border and southern Provence. Many are, in effect, dams, filling valleys upriver of them and controlling the flow downriver. Yet for vast stretches of the Rhône you are unaware of this engineering.

For example, a little downriver from the third dam at Génissiat, the small town of Seyssel, overlooked from the west by the Montagne du Grand Colombier, one of the Jura's most imposing ridges, gives no hint of creeping industrialization.

On the gentler slopes of the eastern bank a wine is made that rarely leaves France: Roussette de Seyssel. The white wine, like the cheese, picks up something of the herbal flavor of the earth and makes an agreeable aperitif or, as I found with a superb local salmon-trout, a good match for fish. Savoie isn't a place to find great wines, but great wines are often too big to fit into these minor miracles of France. This kind of serendipity, the matching of an obscure local wine with a local dish, is one of the things that make a journey along the Rhône worthwhile; you'll probably never taste the wine again, and if you did, out of context, it would not be the same.

Between Savoie and Lyon the Rhône meanders through tamer landscapes, and then, powered up by the Saône, it becomes the serious river where the Michelin men, having scattered their stars through Burgundy and Lyon, reach the final stretch known as the Côtes du Rhône. But there is more here for the senses than a gastronomic binge. The river, now wide and strong, pulls all the attention southward, where the sky, for the first time, intimates heat.

Traveling in the 1920s, Ford Madox Ford noted the same change: "Somewhere between Vienne and Valence, below Lyons on the

Rhône, the sun is shining, and south of Valence Provincia Romana, the Roman Province, lies beneath the sun. There is no more any evil, for there the apple will not flourish and the brussels sprout will not grow at all." (Palate bludgeoned by northern food, Ford had developed a particular aversion to the brussels sprout.)

He was right. Descending the Rhône Valley becomes incrementally more sensuous. You know the north is at your back and that Ford's Provincia Romana is waiting with its looser temperament. Twenty miles south of Lyon, Vienne shows little sign of its Roman past. Yet here was one of the largest theaters of Roman Gaul, as well as a temple specializing in orgiastic celebrations of the goddess Cybele. Traces of the theater remain, but Vienne is pervaded more by modern mercantile France than by hot-blooded paganism. I had a different object of desire in mind, a few miles farther south, where urbanization faded.

It concerned a grape, viognier. This is a tricky grape to cultivate, and until recently there were fewer than a hundred acres of it in the world. For some reason it has now become a voguish grape, with new plantings in California and Provence, but nothing will alter the fact that the peculiar qualities of the viognier flower to their optimum in only one place, the hills above Condrieu, south of Vienne. Condrieu is one of the Rhône's ancient ports, and a remarkably congenial town.

Remarkably, because at this point the Rhône Valley becomes the jugular of French infrastructure: As well as the river, three north-south roads—the N86, the N7, and the A7—bunch together here, as do two railroads, an old one that runs through Condrieu itself and the TGV that whips down the Rhône's east bank.

Nonetheless, it is the vineyards that catch the breath: In places on the precipitous west bank they are nearly vertical. The vines grip onto little poles. Of the Côte Rôtie, a little north of Condrieu, the ravenous gourmand A. J. Liebling wrote: "I fancied I could see that literally roasting but miraculously green hillside, popping with goodness like the skin of a roasting duck." At Condrieu the Rhône makes a sudden half-S turn, which means that for a short stretch the west bank actually faces south. This twist, with the combination of soil, microclimate, and steepness, gives the viognier the perverse setting it likes best, like a bat selecting a particularly vertiginous cave.

What is the outcome? A white wine with a short, fragile life in the bottle that delivers a balance of fruit and flowery scent unlike any other. A handful of producers craft this wine under the Condrieu appellation; a separate appellation of viognier, Château Grillet, has a longer life and a higher reputation but, to my taste, is overrated and certainly overpriced (about a hundred dollars for an undersize bottle, even on site).

I had little idea how the viognier would open up my palate. But the gods of taste were with me. There is a small hotel on the river at Condrieu, the Beau Rivage. Its restaurant has one Michelin star, and I ordered a specialty, *quenelle de brochet au salpiçon de homard*—rendered more prosaically, fish dumpling in lobster sauce. With it I chose a bottle of 1992 Condrieu, Les Chaillets, by a producer, Cuilleron, whose vineyard is only two and a half acres. The quenelle was creamy, and the lobster sauce lifted it to perfection—or so I thought.

Perfection, however, was yet to come. It is the custom at the Beau Rivage to serve a palate refresher called *granité;* in my experience this is usually a simple, icy sorbet. This time it was a composition of inspired eccentricity: a sorbet flavored with lemon and thyme. The cool, fresh herb subsumed the citron's tartness. When I sipped the Condrieu, the *granité* fused with the elusive fruits of the wine, and the whole was exquisite. Another small miracle of France.

Every time I relish France, I recall who it was who led me over the threshold of the experience, who taught the relevance of place to food. In 1960, Elizabeth David published what would become an enduring masterpiece, *French Provincial Cooking.* French provincial life, with all its exact rituals of intensely localized cooking, seeped from every page. One of the few dishes that I mastered from the book's recipes was a *terrine de campagne,* a coarse pork and veal terrine laced with garlic, juniper, and cognac (in the pre-Cuisinart age, these recipes were often arduous and exploratory—"better still, if your butcher will provide it, back fat, which is the pork fat often used for wrapping around birds for roasting").

The origin of this recipe, so redolent of the bourgeois cuisine I love, was the restaurant of a hotel remote in the Ardèche mountains. It happened that I was now only two hours away from the source, and I decided to find it.

There is a discernible wildness in the mountains that taper away on either side of the Rhône, especially to the west, where the Massif Central lurks, unseen but felt. Between this core of France and the Rhône is the Ardèche, a brooding presence beyond the river's west bank all the way from Vienne to Provence, a vast crunching of valley, mountain, plateau, and gorge. To reach my objective, the town of Lamastre, I had to follow the gorge of the Doux River from where it met the Rhône at Tournon. After crossing the Doux on a bridge with high, slender piers, the road became a dizzying corniche, climbing for more than twenty miles into cooler air, with paling blue skies and a sharp, cleansing wind.

Lamastre remains much as Elizabeth David found it: an agricultural center of stoic individuality. The Mairie was plastered with Communist party posters for the European elections. The source of my recipe, the Hôtel du Midi, was in a corner of the main square. It was smaller than I imagined, white with chocolate-colored window shutters. The name Barattero was above the door, over a yellow and white awning. In the 1950s, when Elizabeth David found the hotel, the then–Mme. Barattero had done her own cooking for thirty years. The hotel remains in the family, but today the kitchen is run by Bernard Perrier, acclaimed as one of the Jeunes Restaurateurs d'Europe.

Nothing has been lost. Elizabeth David noted the bond between the hotel's kitchen and the local charcuteries, and it remains the most distinctive influence: robust Ardèchois sausages, terrines, and pâtés that leave no part of pig, duck, or fowl to waste. The charcuterie plate, several kinds of sausage and hams, uncontaminated by preservatives, glistens with the moist freshness of the meat. Around the corner from the Midi, I found the Vallon charcuterie, a cool palace devoted to the arts of pork. The *rillettes de porc,* seasoned pork fat with a matted, stringy texture, long my chosen form of death-by-cholesterol, were masterly. Perrier's single Michelin star doesn't really describe his or the region's style, which needs no authentication from lofty levels. It's an antidote to refinement, immune to modishness. And, as Elizabeth David wrote, if you happen to be traveling south, make the detour.

In fact, after this detour I changed my tactics. I no longer clung to the river. Like any river, the Rhône is a sum of its tributaries, and each tributary brings its own experience. Along the southern Rhône, isolated dukedoms, baronies, and sects resisted incorporation into a larger state for centuries—the assertive statehood that seems so characteristic of France was late in subduing places as iconoclastic as these, each fortified by its own epics, each rooted in feudal allegiances (the last anarchy of France is that of the table—too many cheeses to pasteurize into a nation).

The wind that had chilled Lamastre, borne from the Massif Central, did not ruffle the Rhône. There was a nice, hazy torpor to the west bank, and the N86 was relatively lightly traveled. It is a little-used and rewarding wine route. From the Côte Rôtie south for a hundred miles or so, the vineyards of the foothills bore many minor names and a few great ones: St.-Joseph, Cornas, St.-Péray. Across the river from Tournon were the two Rhône monarchs on their hills: Hermitage and Crozes-Hermitage. Mixed among the west-bank vineyards were orchards, cherries being picked, and fields of poppies. You could reach out and touch summer. It was just a little farther south.

Midway between the two exits for Montélimar on the A7 there is a sign, not to a place but to an idea: LE PORT DU SOLEIL. Two years ago, when I was driving to Provence on a gray fall day, the sun had actually broken through at precisely this point. A lateral valley cuts its way to the Rhône from the east, and high wooded ridges tail back toward the Alps. Today, a corona of heat fringed the ridges, the blue of a flame. The flame of Provincia Romana.

It would be wrong to accept the Romans as the sole sensual zeitgeist of Provence, despite their many physical remnants. It's more a wider Mediterranean atmosphere, with its odd blend of lusts and enervation, that permeates the Rhône's southern flanks. The Greeks probably gave the river its root name, Rhodanos. Celts and tribes from northern Italy preceded them. The Roman machine, once it rolled in during the last century B.C., found much to its taste, access to plentiful wine being one. The legions were as susceptible to the natural assets as we are; Caesar sent his worn-out veterans, layered with scars from bleak and distant garrisons, to enjoy their twilight years in Provence. The Roman spine was, over the decades, helped on the way to its decay by the good life encountered in the Rhône delta.

Now the colonizing legions are Mayle-inspired house hunters. The Provençal fantasy has seeped from the coast northward to the Lubéron. I gave these pastures a wide berth, heading instead for Drôme-Provençal, a regional label that was new to me. The department of the Drôme, with its capital in Valence and named after a tributary of the Rhône, has been left untouched by fantasy marketing; it's just another place on the left as you zoom south. I had briefly touched its northern border, the sheer-walled valley of the Isère River leading to Grenoble and the Alpine ski resorts. This southern flank, with its commingling of Mediterranean and Alpine light, is a borderland, regardless of departmental maps—the deeper I went into it, the more independently physical its identity became.

The road following the Jabron River was suddenly squeezed into a defile. The Montagne du Poët, nearly three thousand feet high, descended in a series of densely wooded spines from the north, and from miles away, in the dark skirts of the mountain, I saw the limestone turrets of medieval Le Poët-Laval, the only reflectors of the southern sun. The Knights of Malta must have chosen this site with care, spiritually aligned with the light they emanated from.

Les Hospitaliers is still a sanctuary. A small pool has been built into the ramparts without softening the commandery's severe outer fabric: The comforts are all within, including a series of small dining rooms with bare stone walls.

On my first evening these were empty. Dinner was served on a terrace under almond trees. In the long June twilight the valley below slowly dissolved into a shroud of river mist.

The nearest town, Dieulefit, showed no sign of creeping Mayleism. In the main square a friendly, plain bar, the Brasserie du Levant, was clearly the close kin of its namesake in the 1914 Baedeker I use to check lineage, and it faced a wonderful relic of old France, a Grands Magasins spelled out in the original Deco type— a nickel-and-dime emporium layered in junk and bare essentials. In a classic avenue of plane trees, men played *boules* without the histrionics you see closer to the Mediterranean.

Was I hallucinating? I seemed to be in a lost France of those Clouzot movies with the young Signoret or Montand. What would the right date be? I settled for 1957; it felt right but needed authentication.

This came soon enough. I went south and farther into the

mountains, into an area known as Les Baronnies. The name lingered from three medieval baronies that ruled there and, more to the point of my mission, this was also a source of one of the Rhône's tributaries, the Ouvèze, noted for its trout. The river and the roads snake into valleys where all urgency dissipates. Slopes carpeted in broom, lavender, myrtle, and other colors I didn't recognize followed the river, but the higher reaches were wind-scoured bare with lime leeching like melting snowcaps. Mont Ventoux, a limestone massif more than six thousand feet high, blocked off the south.

The Ouvèze waters an enchanting town, Buis-les-Baronnies. A corridor of plane trees, planted in 1811 as a gift from Napoleon to celebrate the birth of his son, follows the river into the town square. It was market day. Lavender, scented soaps, honey, and lime flowers mingled with olives, pears, apricots, cherries, and sausages and charcuterie on the stalls alongside a cool fifteenth-century arcade. And it was here, in a restaurant called La Fourchette, that 1957 became edible.

Always eat where the market people eat is an infallible rule. In La Fourchette they were lapping up the three-course seventy-franc menu (that's about twelve bucks). I had a charcuterie plate, piquant hams and sausages; a grilled trout so fresh it must have leaped straight from the Ouvèze to the plate; a pear poached in red wine to the consistency of aromatic jelly; and a young, greenish chardonnay, a *vin du pays* Baronnies. A dozen or so tables were served, single-handedly and charmingly, by the patron's wife. The patron was, of course, cooking. Another of the minor miracles of France.

Later, tracking the Ouvèze upstream into the lengthening shadows of Mont Ventoux, the weather turned as Spielberg would have directed after such a time warp: weirdly oppressive. Les Baronnies are locked in their own densely bucolic theater with an occasional, really mad flourish like the church at Pierrelongue, which was built atop a sugar-loaf rock with no space to spare. The ripeness of the land fuses with stagnant, heavy air and erodes the will. Breaking free of it was a relief. But at Les Hospitaliers that evening the air had a new mischief. Diners retreated from the terrace. There was a sound in the trees like water on a reef.

The mistral, defying the triserial predictions, raged for four days. Then I began to understand better its imprint on the land, how cultivation had been defensive: cypresses used as screens for vulnerable crops, walled gardens for early-budding flowers, villages built into the wind's lee on southern slopes, with narrow streets walled off at the perimeter. Because this was a late mistral, it caught the fields of lavender and lavandin (a less fragrant hybrid) as they were coming into color and created effects of strange beauty, whole hillsides liquid in waves of color. Some lavender is grown on gravel in rows, like vines, and these fields danced like woven robes.

Leaving the valleys and heading farther south brought no relief. The Rhône Valley loses definition in the plains south of Orange, with the massifs folding back, leaving only a few saw-toothed spurs in the path of the wind. The mistral is released with renewed force. A vestigial limestone shard of the Lubéron range called Les Alpilles, which seems to have been detached bodily and blown toward the sea, lies immediately south of St.-Rémy. It's a beguiling optical illusion, since it seems more massive than it actually is—its highest peak is only 1,312 feet.

On a spur of Les Alpilles is Les Baux, a source of legends as romantic as those of the Arthurian court. For a while from the eleventh century, the lords of Baux dominated the Rhône delta, but the surviving shell of their fortress, the Eagle's Nest, doesn't seem martial; instead, you feel the aura of the medieval voluptuaries who turned it into a love nest. During a pacific interlude in the thirteenth century, troubadours courted a ménage of beauties culled from the noble families of the south. They lived a kind of pre-Pre-Raphaelite idyll paced by lutes and poems, broken eventually by civil wars and religious repression. On the heights the mistral was an abrasive reminder of Les Baux's fall. A contest of spirits arose in the wind: The lashing northern air, carbolic, like Switzerland, pitted against the whole amorous embrace of the south.

But the south held out. Below Les Baux lies the exquisite and perfectly formed St.-Rémy. The Provençal gift for distilling pleasurable oils, juices, and scents, as though making manifest a spirit in the earth itself, is here in concentration. The ancient inner town, well insulated from the mistral, is a warren of delectables. Cottage-size restaurants, patisseries, charcuteries, and herbalists retain an artisanal eye over quality and presentation. The one problem is intrusive cars, driven with Gallic temper through alleys seldom wider than the vehicle—if ever a whole town should be made into a pedestrian precinct, this is it.

On the western edge of the old town, on the site of the medieval ramparts, the Place de la République is even more exposed to traffic, but it also has the best bars. I began to devise a new category: bars out of reach of the mistral. The Brasserie du Commerce, on the northeast corner, qualified. Over an *assiette de jambon cru,* washed down with a plummy rosé from Les Baux, I finally came to terms with the damn wind: The sky was picking up that tinge that foretells the Mediterranean, even when you are a good way from it. Mistral or not, I was going to go where nothing could shield me, the Camargue, to the end of the river.

Unlike almost all other great rivers, the Rhône has no final sweeping estuary to the sea. At Arles, it divides into the Petit Rhône and the Grand Rhône. I already knew the squalor of the Grand

Rhône's last miles as it reaches Port-St.-Louis. It falls within an industrial sprawl of ports, refineries, and an aerospace plant. I chose to follow the Petit Rhône as it slithers through the western stretches of the Camargue wetlands and meets the Mediterranean placidly.

Thirty years ago, the Camargue (it probably got its name from Caïus Marius Ager, a Roman general) was a place people talked of confidentially, a secret, wild place with white horses and black bulls with large, sharply spiked horns (the bulls bred for the bullfights at Arles and Nîmes). The mosquito-plagued lagoons to the west had not yet been cleared and turned into a resort coast, and most of the summer crowds turned east at Avignon, heading for the Riviera, missing the Camargue with its large, unmolested wetlands and exotic bird population. An attempt was made to turn the delta into a rice granary, but that didn't seem to threaten the remoteness.

I had heard stories of cars being blown off the road by the mistral on the route into the Camargue from Arles. Mine wasn't, but the wind was merciless. A few bold cyclists trying to ride north into Arles were incapable of movement, and dismounted. There were virtually no windbreaks. Lagoon grasses, sea lavender, and glasswort patchily covered salt-streaked earth (the salt pans of the southern Camargue yield a major harvest of Mediterranean sea salt).

But the impression of bleakness conceals a vulnerable ecosystem. The Camargue is the only place in France where many bird species will breed, including herons, egrets, terns, and flamingos. An ornithological park at the Pont de Gau covers sixty hectares (about 150 acres) and, with a series of well-posted walks, gives access to a world that otherwise can easily be missed. But efforts like this to preserve the natural life compete with trashy distortions of the old Camargue—"ranches" promoting rides on the native horses, for example. In the mistral the horses were huddled around water troughs, rumps to the wind. They didn't resemble the white horses of legend; most were a sad, soiled gray.

The Petit Rhône meets the sea at the southern tip of the Camargue just west of Stes.-Maries-de-la-Mer. In the summer of 1888, while the yellow house at Arles was being repainted, van Gogh took a trip to Stes.-Maries-de-la-Mer, then a small fishing port. He made drawings that were to guide his painting, and one of these paintings, *Fishing Boats on the Beach,* explodes with a new energy of color. The beached boats have spiky masts piercing a yellowing sky that seems to boil with heat and wind. It's as though van Gogh trapped on canvas not just the equivocal light but the strange, gaseous forces energized by the Rhône as they hit the Mediterranean.

When I finally reached the Mediterranean, it was at Stes.-Maries-de-la-Mer, and there was the same combustible quality in the light. The mistral confused horizons, mixing driven yellow dust and water into a foaming mist. But no sailboats had left harbor, and the beach van Gogh painted was now bordered with a spreading ribbon of villas. Stes.-Maries has become a resort, like many on this coast, a place dedicated to summer without the culture to support any other life.

The last bridge on the Petit Rhône, the Pont de Sylvereal, reminded me of many in the Carolinas and Georgia, a single metal span without ceremony. In its final stretches, the Petit Rhône is an amiable, unhurried river devoid of the roiling currents I saw on the Rhône's upper reaches in Savoie. A lazy day of fishing can be had from its banks without even realizing that these are the dissipated waters of one of Europe's greatest rivers.

A little west of the Petit Rhône, farm stands sold sweet muscat wines and sacks of rice and olives. There were vineyards on a vast alluvial plain that don't appear on any appellation map, owned by the same company that harvests the Camargue salt.

It was an unprepossessing site, with wind whipping sand

through the vines, but, at 4,200 acres, it produces the largest wine crop in France. In his *World Atlas of Wine,* Hugh Johnson praises the vintners and says that under their brand name, Listel, the light and fruity table wines show promise. Much of this stuff, though, will end up as cheap supermarket wine in wine-glutted Europe.

The late above-mentioned A. J. Liebling, whose girth eventually cleared sidewalks, is a dangerous muse for a writer in France. He rightly instructed that "the eater's apprenticeship must be as earnest as the cook's." His appetite eventually killed him. I had been earnest all the way down the Rhône, but Liebling would have thought my intake risible. There was one last gesture to make to him, though. Of all the wines he imbibed, Liebling kept returning to Tavel.

Tavel's color, mingling burnt orange and cherry, is a root pigment of Provence, suspended in a bottle. At its best it hits the tongue with an instant recognition of the place: earth and sun consummated. I'm not a rosé fan, but Tavel stands alone and, in salute to Liebling, I wanted to drink it within reach of its source. Tavel is one of the most Romanesque vineyards in the southern Rhône. It's encircled by the Gard forest, and the village roofs have a roseate shimmer.

A few miles southwest of Tavel is Castillon-du-Gard, where the core of a medieval town has been converted to a hotel, Le Vieux Castillon. This has been done so discreetly that the hotel is virtually invisible. The rooms are spread out in a cluster of medieval shells linked by courtyards and alleys. The hotel's restaurant is at the highest level, giving views over many vineyards. It was here I had my Tavel moment: a bottle of 1992 Domaine de la Forcadière.

By pure luck I had found what the wine guru Robert Parker ranks as the finest Tavel, from an estate with 114 acres and a demand that often outstrips supply. It was a double hit, because with the wine I had a whole grilled *dorade*—the French name for Mediterranean bream, which, so legend has it, was sacred to Aphrodite. If she'd tasted it with Tavel, she would certainly have been even more wanton.

Taking a walk at dusk, I saw what at first seemed a Tavel-induced crepuscular phantom—three tiers of perfectly sculpted arches stretched, pale pink, across a valley against the darkening outline of a high plateau. But it was real enough: the most spectacular piece of Roman engineering I have ever seen, the Pont du Gard—the Golden Gate Bridge of 19 B.C.

The Roman obsession with pure water has left its traces all over Europe. As Augustus Romanized the cities of the southern Rhône, the demand for water outstripped supply. In Nîmes the Roman hedonists found their baths running dry. Nobody knows exactly who should be credited with the solution—Augustus allegedly put Agrippa on the case. In any event, the engineers fixed on a water source, the Fontaine d'Eure, thirty-five miles north of Nîmes, as their salvation. The terrain between the source and Nîmes is a folding of gorges and the high, rocky scrubland called *garrigues*. To span this distance with an aqueduct required a variety of works: troughs, very long tunnels, covered ducts, and, to leap the Gard at a narrow-necked gorge, an aqueduct carrying a canal 160 feet high and 900 feet across.

The engineers' solution was as elegant as it was breathtaking: three vaulted levels, the first with its piers implanted on the embankments and spanning the river; the second, on top of the first, straddling the gorge; and the third, the actual aqueduct—all of this built from quarried limestone, with some blocks weighing six tons, positioned without mortar. Over the course of the thirty-one miles, the gradient was precisely planned to achieve a flow of forty-four million gallons a day.

And here it was, two thousand years later, still intact. I've seen Roman waterworks from Budapest to Bath, but always remnants whose original scale was lost. The scale of the Pont du Gard is astonishing. In the morning, when I reached the gorge, some people immune to vertigo were cavorting across the highest span; I took the middle, which was converted to a road bridge in the thirteenth century. Kayakers were coming down the gorge beneath. Others were picnicking on the banks. The scents of sage and mint drifted from the *garrigues*. The mistral had died the night before. Provincia Romana was back in balance, ripe and content.

Tracking the Rhône

The French Rhône, 300 miles long, divides into two worlds: butter in the north, and olive oil in the south. In Savoie, on a terrace bordered by lupines, marigolds, and roses, I had a sole poached in cream. In Provence, next to a market where freshly bottled oils range in color from dark green to translucent honey, I had monkfish grilled in oil and garlic. Regional identities are fixed firmly by kitchen flavors—and wine.

The wine most literally claimed by the river, Côtes du Rhône, is in fact the least dependable. The appellation is vast and loosely prescribed. At its outer limits in the valleys of Provence, it loses any defining quality. In contrast, Côte Rôtie, restricted to about 320 acres on a spectacular right bank hillside, embodies the rich, toasted-earth quality that sets a red Rhône wine apart from any other.

On the River

More or less any Rhône wine of quality is reachable from the N86, the old road that tracks the river from Lyon to Provence (the N7, on the opposite bank, is a nightmare).

North of Lyon, as the Rhône snakes eastward toward the Alps, there is no parallel road of any note until Savoie. The Savoie Rhône can be admired with a one-day circuit: Take the N508 south from Bellegarde-sur-Valserine, and then the D992 to Seyssel, where it crosses to the west bank. A few miles below Culoz, the Rhône divides around a twin-peaked mountain. Follow the west bank to Belley, then the N504 to Yenne.

You're heading for a great coup de théâtre. The road tunnels under the massive Mont du Chat and emerges into a transformed world: facing Lac du Bourget, with monumental vistas to the Alps. Return north on the N201, skipping the bland spa of Aix-les-Bains, and pick up the D991, which follows the eastern Rhône bank to Seyssel. There, visit the caves of Varichon & Clerc, which bottles the best Savoie wines, including Roussette de Seyssel.

Off-River

South of Vienne, the tributary valleys lead to entrancing landscapes. For the northern Ardèche, take the D534 from Tournon (on the N86) to Lamastre. For the southern Ardèche, from St.-Just (on the N86) take the D201 to St.-Martin-d'Ardèche and the corniche that runs along the northern face of the Gorges de l'Ardèche, the D290. This is the French Grand Canyon, where last December stunning Stone Age cave paintings were discovered.

For a France lost in time, head east from Montélimar to Les Baronnies. Pause first at Grignan on the D541, where Mme. de Sévigné holed up from the mistral, then head on to Nyons, famous for its lavender, truffles, and light, golden olive oils. Go south on the D538 to an easily missed left turn onto the D46 to Mollans-sur-Ouvèze. You're now in the increasingly mountainous Baronnies. Take the D5 to Buis-les-Baronnies, where the restaurant and market prices are locked in 1957. Finish with a run up the D546 into the upper Ouvèze Valley, a tranquil trout-fishing Elysium.

West of Avignon, do what the Romans did: Take the N100 to

Remoulins, the D981 to a dead-end at Pont du Gard. Picnic under the stupendous aqueduct. Loop back to Remoulins and take the D19 and the D981 to Uzès, where the old medieval town flies banners in the local red and yellow colors. The *garrigues* around Uzès and, to the south, the gorge of the Gard River, as it runs to the Pont du Gard, are worth the detour.

In the Delta Lands

Skip the Grand Rhône south of Arles. The Camargue, even though given to rinky-dink ranches, is worth visiting for the Pont de Gau ornithological park on the D570, north of the soulless resort of Stes.-Maries-de-la-Mer. The park was founded in 1949 and now protects sixty hectares (about 150 acres) of vital habitat. The visitors center has a large-scale model for orientation and English-language guides to the walks. Take binoculars.

Just west of the Camargue is Aigues-Mortes, a walled medieval port left marooned when the coastline silted up. From the Tour de Constance, on the ramparts, where Protestants were once incarcerated, you can get an eyeful of the town and the salt flats that run out to the Mediterranean. And, to the east, you can pick out where the Petit Rhône dribbles into the sea, but a sliver of its former self.

Accommodations

The north: Near the river in a small, dead-end village called Eloise, near Bellegarde-sur-Valserine, Le Fartoret has modest, motel-style rooms but a fine restaurant with views over rich Savoie pastures (04.50.48.07.18; fax: 04.50.48.23.85; doubles from about $60). For luxury and style within easy reach of the Rhône, the Imperial Palace in Annecy is on the crystal-clear lake with views of the Alps (04.50.09.30.00; fax: 04.50.09.33.33; doubles from about $175).

Mid-Rhône: The Beau Rivage at Condrieu is the best-sited hotel on the river; handsome rooms, informal but classy restaurant, wine list definitive of the two superb local wines, Côte Rôtie and Condrieu. Ask for a river view (04.74.59.52.24; fax: 04.74.59.59.36; doubles from about $125).

Southern Rhône: Les Hospitaliers is in Le Poët-Laval, half an hour east from the Montélimar South exit of the A7. It has an excellent restaurant, good-value local wines. Be sure to ask about the location of rooms, and specify a view of the valley (04.75.46.22.32; fax: 04.75.46.49.99; doubles from about $100). Le Vieux Castillon, in Castillon-du-Gard, is the kind of place Caesar would have retreated to as he directed the Roman debauch: great pool, expensive restaurant, fine wine list. Also check carefully on room locations and sizes (04.66.37.00.77; fax: 04.66.37.28.17; doubles from about $150).

The Camargue: Only one place has real class. Outside Stes.-Maries-de-la-Mer, the long-established Mas de la Fouque, hidden at the end of a private road bordering a lake rich in wildlife, has loyal clients and a limited capacity, so book early. Access to riding, pool, tennis, good restaurant (04.90.97.81.02; fax: 04.90.97.96.84; doubles from about $390).

Definitive Restaurants

Bad meals are hard to find on the Rhône, but when in doubt, sniff out where the locals eat. Three restaurants in the southern Rhône have won international reputations, which means reservations are essential:

In the days when the N7 was the only summer route to the Riviera, nerve-shattered drivers found respite at the tables of La Pyramide in Vienne, where Fernand Point predated the stars of nouvelle with his butter-based artistry. Point has gone (but a street is named for him), and, after a relapse, his place has two Michelin stars again. The butter is less wanton, the wine list exceptional (04.74.53.01.96).

In Valence, another great city on the Rhône, the Pic has been fine-tuning for its three Michelin stars for three generations. Many rate it the best on the Rhône, eluding the stamp of either butter or oil, using both with finesse. It has the defining wine list of the Rhône Valley (04.75.44.15.32).

The small riverside town of Mondragon has a power plant named after it, but also has La Beaugravière, a restaurant that moved Robert Parker, premier wine nose, to berate the Michelin for passing it over. It now has a grudging two knives-and-forks. Parker was right: The wine list alone, without fancy prices, is up to his mark, and the food has a regional authenticity that's harder and harder to find (04.90.40.82.54).

Just Your Garden-Variety Riviera

BY KAREN BAAR

∽

editor's note

There are lovely gardens to be found all over the world, but those of Provence and the Riviera are surely among the most sensuous, fragrant, and breathtakingly beautiful.

This piece highlights three gardens on the coast, any one of which could be described as not-to-be-missed. But inland Provence shelters a number of other, equally spectacular, versions of earthly paradise.

KAREN BAAR is an avid gardener who lives and writes in Connecticut.

The steep, terraced hillsides that rise above the narrow, twisting Riviera roads are planted with silvery olive trees and tall, black cypresses that resemble exclamation points. The scent of rosemary and lavender fills the air, and pale-yellow snapdragons and lemon-colored broom dot the rocky terrain. Here and there grow huge agaves and aloes, exotic neighbors to roses and bougainvillea.

Conspicuous display has been a pastime here for quite a while, and if your taste runs to gardens, the Riviera's one step from paradise. First, there's the climate, with its mild, sunny winters. When wealthy consumptives and their families first began wintering here in the 1800s, they were surprised to find that many plants thrived year-round. Then there's the coastline's dramatic backdrop of steep limestone cliffs, blue water, and golden light—perfect settings for gardens that lead to a view of the sea. Writing from Nice in 1765, Tobias Smollett, a physician credited with popularizing the Riviera among the English, confided in a letter: "I can scarcely help thinking myself enchanted. The small extent of country which I see is all cultivated like a garden. Indeed, the plain presents nothing but gardens full of green trees, with oranges, lemons, citrons, and bergamots which make a delightful appearance . . . roses, carnations, ranunculuses, anemones, and daffodils, blowing in full glory with such beauty, vigor, and perfume, as no flower in England ever exhibited."

The Baroness's Green Thumb

Like many of the cosmopolitan elite who arrived during the Belle Epoque, Baroness Charlotte Beatrix Ephrussi de Rothschild, a daughter of the French branch of the banking dynasty, bought land on Saint-Jean-Cap-Ferrat, one of the quietest, wealthiest parts of the Riviera. Her first coup was snatching almost eighteen acres on the narrowest part of the isthmus from the hands of Belgium's King

Leopold II. The Baroness took the local penchant for display to a new level, making the grounds as much a part of her plans as her palatial villa.

The Baroness built her palace by the sea to house her art collection, which includes masterpieces from around the world; her gardens showcase an international collection of styles as well. To create the Ephrussi estate, the rocky outcrop had to be completely leveled, and enormous amounts of soil and water brought in. It was a colossal undertaking that took seven years, from 1905 to 1912, and twelve architects to complete. The results are still breathtaking. Villa Ephrussi de Rothschild is an Italian palazzo with rose-colored stucco walls and panoramic views of the sea. The house was built, sometimes literally, around the art that the Baroness collected; the stone entrance, for instance, once led to a fifteenth-century Catalan cloister.

The Baroness's museum of gardens sounds ambitious, but one flows effortlessly into the next, creating a wonderfully unified whole. Walking through a hedge of clipped yews, you arrive at a lovely pool and wide canal, the French garden. A water staircase descends a small hill topped by Temple d'Amour, which the Baroness, not to be outdone by the Sun King, ordered copied from the Trianon at Versailles. In classic French-garden style, the shrubs are tightly clipped, the lawns are immaculate, and there are neat beds of calendula. Below lies the Spanish Garden, with its charming fern-filled grotto and a fish-shaped fountain that spews water from its mouth. Nearby, the Exotic Garden, planted in steep terraces, offers expansive views of the turquoise sea. A huge agave, which blooms only once in fifty years, puts forth its tall, asparagus-like flower spike, preparing for its brief moment of glory. Here, too, are towering aloes: some eight feet tall, many in flower, and all standing starkly against the deep azure sky.

Prince Albert's Jardin

Exotics are the surprising grace notes in Riviera gardens. While the climate is cooler and wetter than, say, parts of Mexico or Madagascar, the Riviera's landscape provides a natural nursery for cacti and subtropical blooms. Rain runs quickly off the steep, terraced slopes, and the coast is sheltered from the chill of north winds by mountains and warmed by the sea.

Nothing surpasses Monaco's Jardin Exotique when it comes to showcasing the range of Riviera plant life. Overlooking the Mediterranean, 7,000 varieties of exotic plants grow from a precipice on the Moyenne Corniche. Hacked out of a steep cliff over the course of twenty years during the reign of Albert I, known as the Scientist-Prince, the Jardin Exotique, which opened in 1933, deserves a visit just to admire its extraordinary engineering. A labyrinthine network of well-paved paths leads gradually down the steep slope, making hairpin turns and crossing chasms on small bridges with hand-hewn wooden railings. Carved out of the cliff are pools filled with tiny fish. Huge, artificial rocks made of cement are scattered around the garden to add dimension and more diverse places to plant. Tree-sized cacti, some one hundred years old, are tethered to keep them from toppling over. Aloes and euphorbias grow in the sheer rock faces, in crevices, and along paths. The combined effect of the vertiginous views, plants that look like living sculptures, and flowers in magenta, orange, yellow, and purple, is mesmerizing.

A Noble Passion

Huge gardens are rarely privately owned these days. Simple economics prohibit the armies of gardeners and expensive outlays required for their upkeep. In the days of the Baroness Ephrussi, a staff of thirty gardeners, dressed in sailor costumes and berets with red pom-poms, carried out her every whim.

Now, Riviera gardens are designed on a more intimate scale. One of the loveliest is the Villa de Noailles in Grasse, an English garden made by a Frenchman. It's a garden of romance, an Eden created by the Vicomte Charles de Noailles not for show, but *"pour sa famille et ses amis."* For the last thirty years, it's been open to the public, an unusual gesture in a place where the wealthy traditionally hide behind high walls and locked gates.

A plant lover as well as a patron of avant-garde artists like Cocteau and Man Ray, de Noailles saw the garden as an art form. He attempted a cubist garden in Hyères but was frustrated by the dry, hot site which killed the plants he loved in English gardens: magnolias, camellias, and tree peonies. He moved to Grasse in 1947, where he gardened until his death at age ninety in 1981. There, he had abundant water, which he used in his design. Filling stone troughs, dripping down fountain walls—the sound of water is everywhere at Villa de Noailles.

The garden, like so many others on the Riviera, is built on a steep slope. The terraces have formal hedges, within which the shrubs and flowers grow seemingly wild. The grassy paths, filled with low wildflowers—buttercups, red clover, and hawkweed—are narrow, designed to accommodate only one person at a time.

Taking the long, broad staircase to the bottom of the garden, you walk through grassy terraces, past a huge stand of bamboo, and down a path past a beautiful small maple with brilliant red-orange leaves. You emerge in a lush glade of magnolias. Nearby flows a stream with a small cascade. Except for the sounds of birds and running water, you are enveloped in quiet, as the sun slowly descends toward the glowing gold of a Riviera sunset.

Riviera: Down the Garden Paths

Many Riviera hotels have lovely gardens. At Le Manoir de L'Etang in Mougins, a small, family-owned hotel that used to be a private mansion, you can stay in a room furnished with local antiques and eat breakfast on the terrace in the midst of a beautiful Mediterranean garden (66 Allée du Manoir; 04.93.90.01.07; from $95). Hostellerie du Château de la Chèvre d'Or is a luxurious hotel in the ancient hilltop village of Èze. The charming period rooms are each distinctively decorated (some in Provençal, some in Louis XV, some modern). The hotel has a pretty (if rather formal) garden, but the real attraction here is the view. I'll never forget watching a thunderstorm break over a hilltop across the valley from my room (rue du Barri; 04.92.10.66.66; doubles from about $250). In Monaco, the Hôtel Hermitage (square Beaumarchais; 377.92.16.40.00; doubles from about $330), built at the turn of the century, overlooks the Mediterranean and is only a short walk from the Monte Carlo Casino. After viewing gardens, you can indulge yourself at Les Thermes Marins, Monte Carlo's seawater baths (2 avenue de Monte-Carlo; 377.92.16.49.40; single seawater treatments run $50–$100; a day package consisting of four seawater treatments costs $135).

Restaurants range from outdoor cafés to five-star establishments. I enjoyed lunch at Restaurant Maximin (689 chemin de la Gaude, Vence; 04.93.58.90.75; prix-fixe lunch is about $33 per person). For a livelier scene, Le Safari (1 Cours Saleya, Nice; 04.93.80.18.44; lunch is about $50 for two), on the central market in Nice, serves wonderful fish dishes. And La Coupole (Hôtel Mirabeau, 1 avenue Princess Grace, Monte Carlo; 377.92.16.65.65; prix-fixe menus start at about $53 per person) offers creative dishes served in a luxurious setting.

With the exception of the Villa Noailles, the gardens are open to the public almost every day in high season. The Villa de Noailles allows visitors on Fridays from 2 p.m. to 4 p.m. from February 15 to May 15 (57 avenue Guy de Maupassant, Grasse; about $7). I'd recommend calling the Grasse Tourist Office to confirm

(04.93.36.66.66). Through November 1, the Ephrussi de Rothschild (Saint-Jean-Cap-Ferrat; 04.93.01.33.09; about $8) is open from 10 A.M. to 6 P.M. You can traipse through Monaco's Jardin Exotique (62 boulevard du Jardin Exotique; 377.93.15.29.80; about $7) from 9 A.M. until dusk.

Maeght Foundation, Where Art Is Fine and the Grass Green

BY ROBERT WERNICK

∾

editor's note

Wildly popular Saint-Paul-de-Vence (best visited in the early morning or at the end of the day) is one of the most beautiful villages in the world. The Fondation Maeght may be its biggest draw, and with good reason: it's a wonderful museum, described by the *Ulysses Travel Guide* as "a perfect union of nature, architecture and art." I am envious that writer Robert Wernick had the opportunity to meet Aimé Maeght while researching this article, which appeared in the June 1979 issue of *Smithsonian*. Maeght passed away soon after, but his spirit is evident in every corner of the foundation.

ROBERT WERNICK, who lives part of each year in Paris, travels around the world writing articles on an enormous variety of subjects that interest him, among them museums, food, artists, goats, the devil, the gin rummy championship of the world, and chimneys.

Discreetly grandiose, the "Fondation Marguerite et Aimé Maeght" sits perched among the pines on a foothill of the Maritime Alps near the medieval walled village of Saint-Paul-de-Vence, between the snow-capped peaks and the warm blue sea. Every day a long file of cars comes curling up the narrow road from the coast, bringing visitors to admire its superb display of modern art, half in–half out of the landscape.

A frequent question is "How do you pronounce the name?" The answer is unexpectedly simple: you pronounce it "Mahg."

Aimé Maeght was born in northern France, in Flanders, and did not have his first view of the Mediterranean until he was twelve years old. It was 1918, after four years of German occupation, and he was lying on a stretcher, almost dying of malnutrition. He was to live on this lush, warm coast for twenty-five years. After his sufferings in the north, this strip of coast has remained a vision of paradise for him.

One spot in particular appealed to him—a steep rugged bit of wilderness just below Saint-Paul-de-Vence, a few acres of pine and live oak rising out of the tangled underbrush known as the *maquis*. In time, Maeght was able to buy the land he had long coveted.

Soon bulldozers were moving in, water rights being acquired, brush being torn up, plants brought in. Maeght always liked to think in big terms. His house overlooking the property has grown over the years. The rooms are filled with masterpieces: Etruscan vases on the sideboard, a Giacometti chandelier in the living room. On the terrace overlooking the swimming pool, a couple of hundred guests can be served the dinners which Maeght orders from a three-star restaurant. An aviary houses hundreds of birds. There are orange trees, lemon trees, a vineyard which produces enough delicate red wine to serve guests all year long. Thirty-nine thousand plants were brought in to turn this parched hillside into an opulent garden. In dry summers (almost every one), while all the countryside turns brown, the sprinklers are continuously twirling and the Maeght gardens and lawns are always green.

But Maeght from the beginning had ambitions for something more than a luxurious private residence. He wanted a place where artists could meet, relax, work undisturbed if they chose. He built a guesthouse, a graphic arts shop completely equipped with presses, inks, paper, and so on, where artists could experiment at their ease. He built a ceramics workshop with a traditional wood-burning oven and a modern electric one.

Beyond all this, he wanted a showplace—not a museum in the traditional sense but a space, partly indoors and partly out, in which important works of art could be admired in a setting worthy of them.

He first began talking about the project in 1950, on a visit to Cambridge, Massachusetts, with master architect José Luis Sert of Harvard's Graduate School of Design. It was a project after Sert's own heart; it was the kind of thing he had often discussed and sketched out over café tabletops in Paris in the 1930s. He wanted to design a space for the display of art, in which the artists themselves could collaborate in the conception and the execution. The structure, or group of structures, would follow what Sert calls the "anonymous architecture of the Mediterranean peoples." It would rise as naturally and unobtrusively out of the landscape as any village of the region—Saint-Paul-de-Vence, for example, a cluster of squarish houses with terraces, gardens, patios. Like a village, it could be expanded in any direction by adding new buildings.

The actual work on the site began in 1960, and the first phase of construction took four years. In accordance with Sert's ideas, the artists themselves were called in constantly for observation and advice. The foundation was inaugurated formally in July 1964, with a speech by André Malraux.

It is easy to understand Malraux's enthusiasm. The foundation is surpassingly elegant, drenched in air and light, thoroughly Mediterranean. The works of the artists are well placed, well lighted; they invite an unhurried walk that takes you indoors and out, up steps and down.

The entrance gate opens onto a large sculpture garden, where amid tall slender pines the works of a score of modern sculptors rise like so many man-made trees, in raw granite, polished bronze or wood, or twirling strips of metal.

A Calder mobile is by the entrance, a happy choice, for there are always children coming with their parents.

The buildings are of standard modern concrete, its bare whiteness livened by bricks baked in the traditional Provençal way over wood fires. They are easy to get into and out of, there are glass doors everywhere, there is as much to see outside as in. Beside the exhibition halls and the administrative offices, there is a chapel in memory of the Maeghts' young son Bernard, who died of leukemia—a chapel with a medieval Christ and a stained-glass window by Braque. There is a library well stocked with reference books and documents on modern art, a cafeteria, an auditorium where lectures or concerts can be given—where exponents of the avant-garde like John Cage or Merce Cunningham can come to demonstrate their latest experiments. There are ceramic murals and mosaics; one, by Pierre Tal Coat, scrawls like a prehistoric graffito along a garden wall. All in all, it is a place of easy enchantment.

The exhibition halls are on different levels, owing to the slope on which they are built. But the roof is at the same height for all, and so they all have different proportions. The works in these rooms are constantly being changed out of the boundless reserves of the foundation. And two or three times a year there are major exhibitions covering some great name or some striking feature of contemporary art. A special show dedicated to Miró will open July 7. The eighty-six-year-old artist will attend and his new stained-glass windows done for the foundation will be unveiled.

There is always the pleasure of the unexpected to be found here, as when you turn a corner and come across a quiet pool full of fish—blue mosaic fish by Braque—or a perpetual-motion fountain by Pol Bury, a jumble of stainless-steel cylinders which scoop up water, rise to the horizontal, lose their balance, spill out the water, following a complicated rhythm. There is also considerable drama, notably in the placing side by side of two of the most spectacular displays of the foundation, Giacomettis and Mirós.

Giacometti has a hall to himself, and a terrace just outside. Through both of them loom or stalk the familiar Giacometti figures: men, women, dogs, thin-limbed, hieratic. The sun shines bright and pleasant, it might be any village square of the warm south, and all these creatures remain locked in their monomaniac solitude, staring out at a world in which they have no part.

Turn the corner from the terrace, and the world changes explosively. Here is a space baptized "the Labyrinth," which was turned over to Miró to people as he pleased with the products of his imagination. Everywhere you turn there is a Miró winking or leering or grinning at you. There is a monster cavorting on a roof, another planted with outstretched legs like a puppy dog on the terrace floor. There is an egg-shaped marble called *Woman with Her Hair Undone*. There is an *Arch of Triumph* which might be a prehistoric megalith sprouting horns. There is a ceramic egg, a ceramic goddess, ceramic waterspouts and gargoyles overlooking a pool. There is a giant bronze pitchfork, a bronze girl painted in all the brightest Miró colors.

The choice of all these particular artists who are represented in the Fondation Maeght is no accident. They are all artists represented by, and sold by, the Galerie Maeght on the rue de Téhéran in Paris, which for more than thirty years now has been a key presence in French and international cultural life. There are also Maeght galleries in Barcelona and Zurich, and an American office in New York City.

Maeght's career began with a lucky accident, purposefully exploited and followed till it led to his current eminence.

It was back in 1932. Maeght and his wife, Marguerite, owned and ran a small print shop in Cannes. He spent long, hard years studying the craft of lithography, and he specialized in turning out the gay, colorful posters which were in demand for shows at the casinos of the Riviera. One day a satisfied customer, Maurice Chevalier, sent around another customer—a shy, elderly man with a gray mustache who had a watercolor he wanted reproduced for use as a poster advertising a charity event. His name was Monsieur Bonnard. First name, Pierre. The Maeghts could not do enough for him. He in turn was delighted by the printing job. He told the Maeghts he wanted to put up the original watercolor for sale at an auction at the charity event. "I know those auctions," said Maeght. "You won't get 2,000 francs for it; leave it with me and I will get more than that." He put it in his window alongside some posters of his own, and within twenty-four hours had sold it for 5,000 francs. A new dealer had appeared in the art world.

Over the next decade, Maeght gradually built up his business, enlarged his circle of acquaintances. Artists were thronging through the south of France in those days; many of them were doing decors and costumes for the Ballet Russe de Monte Carlo. Picasso was there often, Matisse, Dufy, Chagall—a whole company of great names. The Maeghts got to know them all, and Marguerite especially developed a talent for helping them with little daily problems.

Relations grew especially warm with Bonnard and Matisse during the war years. Both painters lived near Vence and the Maeghts had a property there, including a cow whose milk helped them all survive the privations of the bad years. It was Matisse who urged

Maeght to go to Paris as soon as the road was clear. When the Germans were out of the way in the summer of 1944, he got into a car with his elder son and with Bonnard and headed for the capital to make his name and fortune.

It was a considerable gamble. The art world of Paris was in a shambles after four years of isolation under German occupation. Many of the big dealers had had to flee for their lives when the Nazis came. Others who stayed open were being accused of collaboration with the Germans. No one knew what it would be like.

Maeght had no doubts and was prepared to think big. He was one of those who realized, more or less dimly, that the whole world of art was about to undergo an immense change. The artists he had met in the thirties were well-known figures; their days of poverty and obscurity were long behind them. But their reputations were still limited; the man in the street would barely recognize their names. A new day was dawning in which they would become world figures, millionaires, superstars. GIs flooding through Europe had discovered at least two personalities to whom they were making massive pilgrimages. One was the Pope. The other was Picasso.

Maeght might have had Picasso, he says, when he opened his gallery in Paris and began to spread his wings, but that would have left little room for other commanding personalities. He preferred to sign up all the rest: Braque, Matisse, Chagall, Miró, Léger, Calder, Giacometti, the giants of the school of Paris, the revolutionaries who had blasted out new roads for the art of the twentieth century.

He worked in a grandiose style befitting names like these. His gallery was princely. His receptions on opening nights were imperial: he would take over a major restaurant and invite two or three hundred people. He published handsome books about his artists, he offered them unlimited hospitality. His principle of business has always been to offer to buy artists' works outright instead of selling them on consignment. This ensures them an income and ensures *him* a plentiful supply of works of art.

For the first two decades after the war all the years were good. Maeght became immensely rich, and his vaults were stuffed with the works of masters. He realized he had a unique opportunity to create a monument in his lifetime, and the monument now stands sparkling on the hillside by Saint-Paul-de-Vence.

It is one of two such monuments that have been recently created in France—both enormously popular, providing an instructive contrast in contemporary taste. The other is the Pompidou Center—Beaubourg—in Paris, for some a brilliant conception, for others an unholy mess.

The Fondation Maeght has its crowds, though they are counted in the thousands rather than the millions, unlike Beaubourg, which by last summer had clocked its ten millionth visitor. Everything at the foundation is uptown, first class. Even in the cafeteria, instead of the ordinary five-and-dime furniture, you sit on cast-iron chairs designed by Diego Giacometti, Alberto's brother. The visitors following their serpentine way through hall and terrace, chapel and garden, treat it all with proper respect.

Will it last? Maeght himself is now seventy-three, a vigorous erect widower, with the haughty well-pomaded look of the aging matinee idol. He is still very much in charge of his gallery, he still follows every detail of life at the foundation with his imperious perfectionist eye. He has not quite finished building there. Once he had a grandiose scheme for a 1,200-seat theater. But bureaucratic bickerings on the part of the local authorities—who were always a little suspicious of Maeght because he was promoting the works of foreigners, Parisians, and doing little for the village artisans who carved picturesque pepper mills out of olive branches—blocked the construction. He is happy today that they did; the big theater would have been a monster that would have devoured all the energies of the foundation, and he is thinking now of three small theaters for all kinds of work in any form—stage, film, dance, opera.

But there is a limit to the size of the foundation, and in general it has probably been reached. For one thing, it costs enormous amounts of money, and though Maeght's profits over the years have been huge, they are not limitless. The market has been slowly drying up, and his great names are leaving the scene one by one. The center of artistic gravity shifted noisily and decisively to New York during the 1950s. The great names on which he had built his fame and fortune belong to the past—or to the future. For the present, he has had to replace them with new ones—like Chillida, Rebeyrolle, Riopelle—familiar to collectors, but hardly as famous or as profitable as the older giants.

Those giants were once thought of as wild men—or even wild beasts, *fauves*—rampaging through the house of art and wrecking all its dainty furniture. Today they appear rather as the last representatives of the classic French traditions of order and harmony and good taste. The roar of the *fauves* today sounds like a shepherd's flute.

Maeght has provided an ideal home for their works. Sooner or later the property will revert to the French state, it will be run by the bureaucratic book instead of with loving zeal; banana peels may well pile up under the pines. But for the moment Aimé Maeght has every reason to be proud of what he sees when he looks down from his manor house at the visitors coming up the road from the coast. He has provided a fitting home and showcase for the things he loves.

Originally appeared in *Smithsonian*, June 1979. Copyright © 1979 by Robert Wernick. Reprinted with permission of the author.

The Boulevard: Live the Dream

BY GULLY WELLS

editor's note

....

The first time I went to Aix-en-Provence I was a student living in Paris. I had found a dirt-cheap fare for a bus en route for Nice—though the "bus" turned out to be a guy's private car. The three other passengers were also (duped) American students. We left Paris in the evening, where it had been raining for what seemed like forty days and forty nights, and at some early hour the next sun-filled morning we stopped for *café* at Les Deux Garçons on the Cours Mirabeau. Anyone who's been there will understand when I say I thought I'd died and landed in *le septième ciel* (seventh heaven). I would be hard-pressed to name a more beautiful thoroughfare, described so lovingly by M.F.K. Fisher in *Two Towns in Provence:* "It is probable that almost every traveler who has ever passed through Aix has been moved in some positive way by the view from one end of the Cours or the other, by the sounds of its fountains in the early hours, by the melodious play of the pure clear sunlight of Provence through its summer cave of leaves. Some of them have tried to tell of their bemused rapture, on canvas and sketch pads and on scratch-pads and even postcards, but they have never been satisfied. It is a man-made miracle, perhaps indescribable, compounded of stone and water and trees, and to the fortunate it is one of the world's chosen spots for their own sentient growth."

GULLY WELLS, whose work appears elsewhere in this book, is literary editor for *Condé Nast Traveler*, where this piece appeared in February 1998.

In a dusty side room at the top of a staircase in an old museum in the heart of Aix-en-Provence, there's a series of maps of the city. One of the earliest is dated 1468 and shows the familiar asymmetrical outlines of a medieval town: the tangle of crooked streets and alleys, a few disproportionately massive churches, all enclosed within the claustrophobic embrace of the surrounding walls. Walk slowly around the room and eventually you will come to another map that was made about two hundred years later, in 1680. The city looks, at first glance, pretty much the same, but if you study it more carefully, you will see that a huge chunk of the southern wall has disappeared and in its place is a wide boulevard lined with a double row of trees. To the south of this street, on land that had once been outside the city limits, a whole new *quartier* has been created, built on the then-revolutionary grid pattern. Designed with Cartesian severity, streets as straight as arrows bisect blocks of houses at precise right angles, with not a wiggly or meandering lane in sight: It could almost be New York. Look at the next few maps, which span the eighteenth and nineteenth centuries, and you'll see that the city has grown, the ramparts have come down, and it has gradually expanded, devouring the surrounding fields, woods, and villages. But at its center that one elegant boulevard remains. And today, if you flew over Aix in a small plane and asked the pilot to swoop down low over the center of town, you would still see, in the middle of the city, its aorta—the Cours Mirabeau.

As a piece of town planning, the Cours is wonderfully free of any practical purpose. Queen Marie de Médicis had brought with her from Italy the concept of a wide urban boulevard (the Cours-la-Reine in Paris was also inspired by the Italian model) which Italians used for their daily passaggio. The Cours was constructed in the mid-seventeenth century as a place where the aristocracy of Aix could parade around in their carriages and sedan chairs in order to see and be seen. This was not a road that actually led you anywhere, other than up or down the complicated, slippery snakes and ladders of the social ladder. The Cours quickly became the most fashionable address in town. *Hôtels particuliers,* built from the local honey-color stone, lined both sides of the street, and it was generally agreed that the grandest houses were those on the south side, which backed onto the new Quartier Mazarin, with their huge shady gardens and stables at the rear. One of the very oldest is the Hôtel de Maurel de Pontevès, which was built in 1647 and is directly opposite the famous Deux Garçons café, so that today you can sit and sip your *citron pressé* and gaze upon the Schwarzenegger-like torsos of the two Herculean Atlantes who support the balcony over the doorway. Their lapidary beards are as tightly curled as the hair under their muscular arms, and even though the hotel is now the Court of Appeals, splendor manages to shine through its prosaic modern-day function.

It was Leonardo da Vinci who said, "Let the street be as wide as the height of the houses"—an architectural axiom that has usually been ignored—but in Aix they remembered that perfect proportion, like great bone structure in a face, is the secret of lasting beauty. The Cours Mirabeau happens to be 440 meters long and 44 wide, while none of the houses are more than four stories high, and there is something mysterious about this geometry that makes the result of the equation eternally pleasing to the eye. Not only did the architects do their math right, but they also knew that nature had to be included in the construct—and they understood that there is something organically satisfying about the combination of stone, water, and trees.

The double rows of plane trees on each side are now about the same height as the town houses, and in the summer, their boughs brush up against the buildings and reach across to meet in the middle of the street, like the vaulted roof of some vast cathedral, so that the fountains and the people who still parade up and down the Cours, just as they did 350 years ago, are bathed in a soothing, dappled golden-green light.

Long before I arrived in Aix last summer, the mother of an old friend who has lived there all her life and who can remember a time when carriages still drove along the Cours sent me a clipping from a local newspaper, *La Provence*. I think she probably meant it as a warning. It was her way of telling me that things had changed, and of tempering with the present-day reality whatever rosy memories I had of the Cours Mirabeau from my last visit almost twenty years ago. It was clear from the article that the feeling in Aix was that the Cours needed help. About 50 of the 170 plane trees were so diseased that they would have to be replaced, the parking situation was described as "anarchic," the noise from the horns of "enraged drivers" was unbearable, and the sidewalks were being invaded by café tables and chairs, leaving little space for pedestrians.

The elegant lady with the perfect bone structure was, in the words of *La Provence,* in need of a good "lifting," if not a total transformation. My heart sank as I went on reading, and I began to worry that the aristocratic boulevard, which had charmed everyone from the eponymous Comte Mirabeau of Revolutionary fame (it was named in his honor in 1876; before that it had been simply known as Le Cours) to Marcel Pagnol, to Picasso, to the great American essayist M. F. K. Fisher, had fallen prey to the same disease that had destroyed so many other iconic places in the world and was being buried under a tide of traffic and late-twentieth-century trash.

Some instinct told me that I should see the Cours for the first time in the early morning, while it was still cool and relatively empty, before the traffic took over and the waiters' tempers became as frayed as the cuffs of their black jackets. I might even be able to hear the water splashing in my favorite fountain, the Neuf Canons, whose basin had been constructed in Louis XV's time, with especially low sides, for the thirsty sheep that were driven each year through the town on their spring migration to the hills. And so I got up soon after six and wandered down the hill from my hotel into the labyrinth of narrow streets that lead through the old town, out onto the broad green swath that unites the *vieille ville* with the Quartier Mazarin.

I arrived in the square behind the post office as the market was being set up: Wasps hovered over candles made from honey-scented wax, the seductive perfume of ripe peaches and melons mingled with the aroma of huge bunches of deep green basil, and little red tomatoes the size of pearls and feathery *girolles* mushrooms the color of Halloween pumpkins were piled up in baskets like so much costume jewelry. Even at this hour, the bourgeoise Aixoise, ladies who would rather die than go shopping without first doing their hair and makeup, and whose finely grained leather handbags and silk foulards betrayed their almost religious devotion to quality, were out patrolling the stalls, on the lookout for the very best delicacies to set before their demanding families that night. I crossed the square and kept on walking until finally I came to a narrow street and followed its every crooked turn until it ended in a thick forest. I had arrived on the Cours.

The great green cathedral nave seemed unchanged, the fountains in the middle still bubbled away, and the waiters at Les Deux Garçons actually had early-morning smiles on their faces. The traffic was a long way from "anarchic," and not a single driver sounded his horn as I crossed to the middle of the road and bathed my hands in the warm sulfuric water of my second-favorite fountain, "Old Mossback," whose spout emerges from a strange misshapen mountain of moss. The Romans were passionate about Aix's warm springs, and the town, which the Romans called Aquae Sextiae in honor of the Consul Caius Sextius, was founded in the second century B.C. as a kind of R and R outpost for exhausted legionnaires. Even today its inhabitants firmly cling to their belief in the medicinal properties of its water. I settled down in a chair on the terrace of Les Deux Garçons and ordered a café crème, *s'il vous plaît,* in my best French accent. If I just sat there long enough, I felt, the whole of Aix would eventually pass before my eyes, like some strip cartoon on an endless loop. It was the perfect vantage point.

The first drama of the morning happened just after eight, when a large woman carrying a bedraggled black poodle that was dripping water all over her high-heeled gold sandals marched by with a man who looked about as unhappy as the dog and who kept repeating plaintively, "*Non, j'ai pas poussé,*" as she crooned softly into the poodle's damp ear, "*Mon pauvre petit, mon pauvre petit.*" What crime was committed? Had the man pushed the dog into the fountain? And why? I ordered some more coffee and a croissant and resigned myself to never knowing the answers.

Soon after the Poodle Pusher disappeared into the Passage Agard, two young mothers strolled by and sat down at the table next to mine. They clearly had some serious gossip to attend to and ordered two double espressos before they each lit a cigarette and inhaled deeply. I strained to catch what I could of their conversation, but again the crucial elements of the plot eluded me and I had to make do with inadequate snippets ("I told her it was the last time, but then his mother offered me . . ." "Francette will kill him eventually, you know that . . ." "He begged and begged her, but she said she wasn't a pig . . .").

Even today the pace of life along the Cours seems palpably slower than in the "real" world. The young mothers were in no rush, and the rest of the breakfast crowd on the terrace of Les Deux Garçons had all settled down behind their newspapers for an unhurried and civilized start to the day.

Inside, in the olive green and gold Directoire salon on the left—the one that is decorated just as it was in 1792, when the café first opened its glass doors for business—a man sat alone at the table in the center of the room. This was clearly his office. His papers were scattered all around him, books were piled up on the tiled floor at his feet, and the waiters patiently filled his coffee cup at intervals as he sat scribbling away with a fountain pen that leaked blue-black ink onto his fingers. (When I happened to return to the café later that day for a predinner aperitif, he was packing his papers into an old leather briefcase, after a long and, I hoped, profitable working day.)

Toward lunchtime the pace began to quicken. Serious food was about to be eaten, which demanded white linen tablecloths and napkins, and a waiter added a list of the day's specials to the menu, which stood in a glass case on the sidewalk, like a siren, seducing people inside with its whispered promise of *oursins,* belon oysters, *cervelles aux beurre noir,* and crayfish Provençal. I watched as my neighbors sat down: a middle-aged couple, with wedding rings embedded in folds of flesh, who studied the menu with the pornographic intensity of true gourmands. A bottle of Sancerre and *fruits de mer* to start, then a Côte du Rhône with their meat, followed by some discreet hand-holding (perhaps they weren't married—at least to each other—after all?), and then they each had dessert (forget that "one order/two spoons" American nonsense), with coffee and cognac for monsieur. By the end I felt, just by osmosis, deliciously drunk and contented.

But as the day wore on and I walked slowly down the Cours, I began to see what the article in *La Provence* had been talking about. Although the south side of the street has mostly kept its aristocratic style, with banks and a few elegant patisseries occupying the ground floor of the former private town houses, things had gotten a little out of control on the other side.

Outside Monoprix, the T-shirts and bikinis and plastic sandals were dangling from clothes racks on the sidewalk. Next door, a fast-food joint called Quick had an enticing color picture of a hamburger the size of a football in its window, and farther along, a shoe store had set up some permanent glass vitrines on the street.

The café owners, not unreasonably, want to pack in as many customers as they can, and if that means putting more tables and chairs on the already congested sidewalk, why not? The other problem is, of course, the automobile. Some places—like Siena, for example—have solved the dilemma by simply making the city center a pedestrian zone, but the feeling in Aix is that this wouldn't work.

When I spoke to Alexandre Medvedowsky, who is in charge of urban planning for the mayor's office, he told me that they were seriously considering banning all parking. "Our problem is that we have some older and more conservative Aixois who would like to turn the Cours into a museum," he explained over breakfast at the Villa Gallici, "with no cars at all and much less commercial life. But we don't want the center of our city to be dead. We want to keep it alive so that people will continue to live and work there."

Medvedowsky has appointed three different companies to propose solutions to the question of how best to restore and preserve the Cours. The cost is estimated to be more than ten million dollars, and the entire project will be completed by the year 2000. [By the fall of 2000 work was still under way on the Cours, but officials were optimistic that the project would be complete by 2001.]

The truth is that even with the T-shirts and the traffic, the inherent beauty of the Cours Mirabeau still manages to shine through.

As I sat downstairs at Le Grillon, surrounded by portraits of that great promoter of *la vie provençale,* Frédéric Mistral, I looked at some old postcards that I had bought at an antiques store the day before. A sad-looking man stood beside his donkey, which was piled high with straw, in front of the same fountain I had bathed my hands in early that morning. There was a streetcar behind him (in those days, you could take the tram all the way from Aix to Marseilles), and on the other side of the street were parked some black cars, the kind you associate with gangsters in Chicago, with generous running boards and bug-eyed headlamps.

Apart from the donkey, it wasn't so very different from the scene before my eyes as I glanced up and saw a similarly sad-eyed young man playing *Boléro* on his flute, with a battered hat at his feet containing a few coins. I looked at another postcard; this one was of the then-new La Rotonde fountain, which stands guard over the entrance to the Cours. I could see it to my right, spouting water high up into the air from its triple tier of basins, completely at odds with the cozy familiarity of the Louis XV sheep's fountain and the warm, watery slopes of the Old Mossback.

My third postcard was of a shop front, with the name BECHARD just visible above its doorway. It was impossible to make out what the shop sold, but I remembered passing a patisserie of the same name earlier in the morning and decided to go back, postcard in hand. Tiny glacé fruits were arranged in multicolored pyramids behind glass, and a *tarte aux citrons,* whose lemon slices were so thin that you could see straight through them, sat in the middle of the window, just behind a silver basket of twisted twigs of candied orange skin covered in bittersweet chocolate.

The lady at the counter smiled when she saw the old photograph and confirmed that Béchard had been at this corner for *"presqu'une centaine d'années,"* and added that she hoped it would be there for another hundred. Then she turned away to serve a gentleman who looked as though he had just stepped out of one of my postcards. He must have been in his seventies, with a neatly trimmed white beard and birdlike face.

He was wearing a perfectly tailored black suit, sparkling jet-black buttons on the jacket's cuffs, and a stiffly starched white shirt with a high, Edwardian collar. Even though it must have been eighty degrees outside, he had on soft black kidskin gloves, black boots, and a black straw homburg and was carrying—what else?—a silver-topped ebony cane. Just looking at him as he chose his champagne chocolate truffles, and seeing them packed up in an elegant red and gold box and tied with ribbon, my faith in the unchanging and unchangeable nature of Aix-en-Provence was completely restored. If gentlemen like this still bought chocolates like these from a shop that had stood on the same corner for a hundred years, then all must be well in the world. And on the Cours Mirabeau.

Think of the Cours Mirabeau as the backbone of Aix. It cuts straight through the center of the old town, with the newer seventeenth- and eighteenth-century Quartier Mazarin to its south and the truly ancient winding streets and alleys of the *vieille ville* to its north. The Quartier Mazarin is more residential, with some magnificent private *hôtels particuliers* backing onto secret walled gardens. There are some very chic interior-decorating stores, antiques shops, and boutiques in this part of town, but it is quieter than the other side of the Cours, where you'll find lots more restaurants, cafés, markets, and street life.

In the heart of the Cours area, the Hôtel des Quatre Dauphins is, in my opinion, your best bet. A tiny old hotel on the historic Place des Quatre Dauphins, it has all the old-world allure that you could wish for, and none of the drawbacks (04.42.38.16.39; fax: 04.42.38.60.19; doubles, about $55–$70). The Hôtel Negre Coste is directly on the Cours Mirabeau, but it can be noisy and lacks charm. The Hôtel des Augustins, on a side street, was once an

Augustine abbey. Not much remains of that beyond a vaulted ceiling or two, but it is now a comfortable, if uninspired, hotel (04.42.27.28.59; fax: 04.42.26.74.87; doubles, about $100–$200).

But if you enjoy a fifteen-minute walk from the Cours and money is not a factor, the Villa Gallici is the place to choose. An old villa with its own beautiful garden, heavenly pool, and impeccable service and food, this is your best bet in Aix, without question. The terrace alone, with its fountain and plane trees, is worth the journey for breakfast, drinks, or a slow lunch—the ratatouille with poached eggs is recommended, with the local rosé (04.42.23.29.23; fax: 04.42.96.30.45; doubles, about $150–$310).

The north side of the Cours is lined with cafés and restaurants, but only a few are worth visiting. My favorite is still Les Deux Garçons, which has been there since 1792 and serves the most reassuring kind of simple brasserie food: oysters, steak frites, omelettes, gigot d'agneau (04.33.4.42.26.00.51; entrées, about $10–$32). Le Grillon is only fifty years old, but it looks as though it's been there forever. The food is not grand, but the people-watching is (04.42.27.58.81; entrées, about $7–$16). Antoine Côté Cour, in the flowering courtyard of an old mansion, serves simple grilled food (04.42.93.12.51; entrées, about $8–$24). At Le Clos de la Violette, next door to the Villa Gallici, you will be served some of the best cuisine in this part of Provence. Not cheap—and some would say a tad pretentious (who really needs chocolate-covered basil leaves?)— it's still worth a detour, as the Michelin says (04.42.23.30.71; entrées, about $28–$37).

The Cours Saleya of Nice

BY DOONE BEAL

~

editor's note

No trip to the South of France is complete without a visit to its outdoor *marchés*. In *Bon Appétit*'s special issue on Provence (May 1999), Susan Hermann Loomis wrote that "Each market underscores the Provençal emphasis on quality ingredients, fresh produce, artisanal production and seasonal culinary inspiration, and does so with its own style, personality— and personalities. And when it comes to friendliness, a trip to a Provençal market will fill the heart as much as the basket." I love every market I've been to in Provence and along the Côte d'Azur, but my favorite is the market on the Cours Saleya in Nice. Most markets in Provence happen only once or twice a week, but the gathering on the Cours Saleya is daily, except Monday, when the space is occupied by a flea market. Among the many memorable treats I have purchased here are *fraises des bois* (wild strawberries, available only in the spring, which taste like no strawberries you've ever had) and a variety of goat cheeses (I have yet to taste an American goat cheese as delicious as those in the south of France). Provisions procured here in the morning for a lunchtime picnic at Castel Plage or in the park atop La Colline du Chateau are all the ingredients one needs for a day *bien passé* (spent well).

DOONE BEAL lives in London but has spent so much time in France— much of it in the south—that she considers it a home away from home. Over the years she has contributed numerous pieces to *Gourmet,* where this piece appeared in May 1986.

Under the striped awnings glow tubs of poinsettias alongside stacked carnations ranging from shell pink through coral to scarlet and crimson. In one stall yellow lilies and miniature purple gladioli are being swiftly, deftly assembled into a bouquet, and from another the ravishing scents of jonquils, mimosa, and hyacinths mingle and waft over to our terrace table at La Madrague.

Signal among many definitions of bliss is, surely, to find oneself lunching outdoors under the high blue heaven of a perfect day. As with many other experiences, no French meal ever tastes quite so good as the first, but I don't entirely attribute the enjoyment of La Madrague to the euphoria of the occasion, nor even to that of its setting. Launched with a bottle of fine 1983 Sancerre, the dishes were all simple but perfect of their kind: the oysters, clams, and *étrilles* (baby crabs) arrayed on a bed of seaweed; the slippery white fillets of *turbotin* with *sauce mousseline* and a fluffy boiled potato; and the *coquilles Saint-Jacques maison* in a creamy wine-based sauce with rice. The variety is extensive in this, one of the choicest of the many seafood restaurants in the corner of old Nice known as the Cours Saleya. Just inside the door lie serried ranks of sole, red mullet, *loup de mer*, and shellfish of every sort from which to choose; and, proudly presented for the inspection of a neighboring table, were the glistening speckled gold and silver, sage and russet ingredients of a bouillabaisse prior to being plunged into the cooking pot. Casual as the restaurant may appear to be, there is nothing rough-and-ready about La Madrague.

Repaved over an underground car park and now one of Nice's newest pedestrian precincts, the Cours Saleya frames the daily domestic flower market (the famous wholesale one has been relocated near the airport) and the fruit and vegetable market. On the Cours' shadier, southern side are the fish stalls, several of which double as restaurants. Among these are Au Bistroquet, with its excellent fish soup, and Le Réveil—now rather smart with brown-and-white-checked cloths and well reputed for its seafood—the oldest fish stall/bar of them all, which at one time played host to the fish porters.

Lying just behind Quai des Etats-Unis, the Cours, with its triple-bracketed lamps, presents a beguiling prospect. The Baie des Anges glistens through white stone arches, and, ahead, looms the steep green bluff of the Château—the hill that was the site of Nice's fortress, destroyed in 1706. Beneath the hill a handsome yellow stucco building, the upper floors of which once housed Matisse's studio, is a survivor of the early nineteenth century, when the Cours was the elegant promenade of old Nice. It seems on the verge of a renaissance, for this cornucopia of scent and color, together with its baskets of oysters and *oursins* (sea urchins), crab, and crayfish, is one of the most attractive corners of the Vieille Ville (Old Town). It is also one of the most entertaining, especially for lunching—and, in summer, dining—outdoors, serenaded by Janni, a strolling guitarist, whose repertoire ranges from *Carmen* to *Zorba.*

According to a resident friend, café and restaurant tables on both sides of the Cours meet in an almost seamless center during the high-summer season, and even on a sunny winter day—the sort of day that won Nice its original reputation well over a century ago—business is brisk. Closer inspection, and some local chat, reveal a greater variety of establishments than is at first apparent, for no two are exactly alike, and there are subtle distinctions between those that are tourist-oriented and those that cater to local patronage. On Mondays, there being neither fish nor flowers, the *antiquaires* and *brocanteurs* set up their stalls for what has now become one of the most important markets of its kind along the whole of the Côte d'Azur. The dealers gather chiefly at the Civette du Cours, a *bar-tabac* the interior of which is unadorned but where one can lunch, surrounded by the colorful scene outdoors, from a choice chalked up on a blackboard. Both the grilled sardines and the *lapin au vin blanc* are very special. Almost next door, at 1 Cours Saleya, is Le Safari, abuzz in the evening and much more soigné, though still very typical of Nice, with a pleasant interior and a flaming spit for grilling *scampi* and *langoustes.* On another day we had a dozen oysters and *oursins* here, relaxing over a leisurely bottle of wine in the midday sun: at 160 francs, a cut-price treat indeed.

The food of Nice is scarcely *grande cuisine,* but at its best it is fresh, piquant, and zesty. Consider *socca,* a delicious chick-pea-flour pancake that seems to be the monopoly of the cafés of the Vieux Port. (A tiny restaurant at 5 rue Réparate, Nissa Socca, specializes, as the name would suggest, in this dish and offers a splendid version.) Also *pissaladière,* a crisp onion and anchovy tart with black olives; *pistou,* a garlic, basil, and Parmesan-based soup, or a sauce that goes particularly well with pasta and gnocchi; and *fleurs de courgettes farcies,* stuffed zucchini flowers, which are among the more subtle and delicate offerings—to name just a few traditional dishes. I was frustrated in my quest to visit La Méranda (4 rue de la Terrasse), one of the prime sources of local fare, just off the Cours, as the restaurant was closed when I arrived. But a peek through the window revealed a tiny, tightly packed bistro where—such is the reputation of Monsieur Giusti's cooking—people are happy to crowd in and take their chance. The objective is strictly to eat rather than to linger and relax, and for lunch one goes either very early or very late (dinner is served only until 9:30), for there is no telephone and thus no reservations can be made.

However, I was compensated by a restaurant of similar type and reputation, albeit slightly more spacious: La Taverne du Château, 42 rue Droite, also just inland from the Cours and, incidentally, the site of some interesting antiques and bric-a-brac shops. At La Taverne one can and should reserve or, better still, call in personally and stake claim to a particular table, the evening trade being slightly less hectic than at lunchtime. Casual local customers gather for their *anis* at the long zinc bar; gourds, ropes of garlic, and drying peppers hang in festoons from the ceiling; and, under the aegis of Madame Bonifassi, there is an air of hospitable bustle. Apart from bouillabaisse, which must be ordered ahead, the specialties include *beignets* of sardines, eggplant, zucchini, or whatever else might be in season. The dishes of the day, and I counted twenty, are chalked on a blackboard, and we chose *beignets d'aubergine, gnocchi au pistou,* feathery crisp *friture* of whitebait, and a luscious traditional *osso buco* before finishing our meal with a delightful *crème renversée*. This is the place to come when you are really hungry.

The tall, narrow streets of old Nice, through which daylight scarcely penetrates, feel much more Italian than French—and not surprisingly, for Nice was reunited with France only in 1860. Garibaldi was born here and baptized in the parish church of Saint Augustin (it still seems odd to me to see the square named for him labeled Place, rather than Piazza, Garibaldi). Farther along rue Droite, which is bannered aloft from side to side with lines of washing, the Palais Lascaris is a small gem of an Italian (in fact, Genoese-style) *palazzo* of the seventeenth century, discreetly restored and now classified as a *monument national*. Its balustraded, marble staircase leads to state apartments on the second floor. Here Flemish tapestries hang beneath trompe l'oeil ceilings frescoed with mythological romances and dramas. The rooms are tiny but sumptuous, as is the beautiful chapel with its unusual triple-mirrored altar and the bedchamber—separated from the anteroom by clouded glass and gilded panes—where cherubs cavort. It's possible to see the *palazzo* in just ten minutes or, on the other hand, to spend a couple of hours there, imbibing its ghostly, rather Guardiesque nostalgia.

Pursuing the Italian idiom, Chez Don Camillo, at number 5 rue des Ponchettes—another street of tall, elegant old buildings at the eastern end of the Cours Saleya—is quiet, gracious, and rather formal, like the lunchtime clientele, in furs and hats as opposed to the jeans and sweaters of the market. The pasta is, as one might well expect but does not always find, a star turn: steaming hot and cooked perfectly *al dente*. The *pâtes aux truffes noires* (noodles with black truffles) were memorable. *Saltimbocca, osso buco,* and all the usual *escalopes* were listed, but I never can resist *feuilletés* of any kind, and, because they were clearly a specialty of the chef (I always take my cue from the choices of neighboring tables), we decided on one of *rognons de veau au marsala* and another of *fruits de mer,* the latter proving to be a particular success. Discretion forbade, but among the desserts the *mille-feuilles* looked all but irresistible, and so did the *profiteroles glacées au chocolat.* Don Camillo's menu is somewhat limited, but each item is very well prepared. This is also a good restaurant for the evening meal should one prefer to escape the gregarious melee of the Cours Saleya itself.

Almost next door to the restaurant are two galleries of interest: Anne Marie Rey and Krivy, both of which house series of temporary exhibitions. Anne Marie Rey, who was born in this part of old Nice, has garnered among many other items a fascinating collection of posters and postcards of contemporary art from all over Europe. Spurred by the relatively new antiques market, such establishments seem likely to increase and revive the prestige of an area already graced by the Galerie Ponchettes and the Galerie des Arts Contemporains (at 77 and 59 quai des Etats-Unis respectively).

Nestled in the crosshatch of side streets immediately off the Cours Saleya, on rue Saint-Gaetan, is Aux Essences de Grasse, an apothecary's collection of some hundred different flower essences and *eaux de toilette.* These can be bought singly or combined in a brew of one's own personal devising that, according to Monsieur

Polipot, takes some eight hours to complete, depending on the fixative used. A scholar of his trade and a mine of fascinating information, M. Polipot also sells soaps, oils, and perfumed oils for burning in lamps.

One of us smelling of lavender and the other of jasmine oil, we made our way toward the opera house end of the Cours and the charming Salon du Thé La Petite Ferrier on the corner of rue Saint-François de Paule. This is the street where Napoleon resided briefly in 1796, shortly after his marriage to Josephine, and where he penned some of his most passionate letters to her, including such turns of phrase as ". . . my emotion thunders in my ears like a volcano. . . ." There are no traces of thundering passion visible in this tearoom, however: Civilized and soothing—a group of comfortable armchairs clustered beneath a potted palm and tables laid with pristine napery and silver—it is a popular luncheon rendezvous (you can also breakfast here) offering an ambiance and choice of food quite different from its neighbors. Some half dozen inventive and delicious salads are available, for example, and always a dish of the day, such as roast duck with turnips. Other items include *blini* and *brouillades* (scrambled eggs, with chives or black truffles) as well as plain grills. In fact plain in the best sense is part of the restaurant's appeal, for in this instance it implies top-quality ingredients. We had an irreproachable *sole meunière* accompanied by a fine white Côtes de Provence, recommended by the owner, Marc Fischler, who attends every table personally and takes a genuine interest in his clients' pleasure. As for the *pâtisserie* and other desserts, which are outstanding, you choose from as tempting an array as I have seen in some time. For the record, the *îles flottantes* with a *coulis de framboise* were really spectacular. All in all, La Petite Ferrier is one of the brightest blooms in a restaurant bouquet of as much variety, in this tiny area of old Nice, as those beneath the gaily striped awnings of the Marché aux Fleurs.

Socca Nissa Socca
(Crisp Chick-Pea-Flour Pancake)

1¼ cups chick-pea flour (available at Italian markets and some specialty foods shops)
1 teaspoon salt
¾ teaspoon ground cumin
¼ cup olive oil

Into a bowl containing 1⅓ cups cold water sift the chick-pea flour, a little at a time, whisking constantly, and skim the froth with a skimmer. Whisk in the salt and the cumin and let the batter stand at room temperature for 4 hours. Pour the oil into a well seasoned 12-inch pizza pan with a ¾-inch-high lip and tilt the pan to coat the bottom evenly with the oil. Stir the chick-pea batter, add about 1⅓ cups of it to the pan, or enough to measure a thickness of ¼ inch, and whisk the mixture gently to blend it with the oil. Bake the mixture in the upper third of a preheated 450°F. oven for 30 to 35 minutes, or until it is golden brown and crisp. The *socca* may be eaten directly from the pizza pan with a knife and fork or it may be cut into wedges and served warm with drinks. Serves 4 as an hors d'oeuvre or 2 as a main dish.

Bibliothèque

Jardins

Gardens in Provence, Louisa Jones, photography by Vincent Motte, Flammarion, 1992. Jones has lived in the south of France for over twenty years, and she is passionate about the gardens found there. The text in this survey is informative and engrossing, and the accompanying photos are incredibly beautiful. I especially like the visitor's guide, which includes private gardens open to the public, public parks and gardens, unusual plant sources, wine properties, hotels and restaurants, guided visits, garden décor, common plants found in Provençal gardens, and a bibliography.

Gardens of the French Riviera, Louisa Jones, photography by Vincent Motte, Flammarion, 1994. A companion guide to the Jones and Motte title above, this is another must-have for garden lovers. The photos are just as gorgeous as in the Provence book, and in addition to the descriptive features of Côte d'Azur gardens, Jones also includes gardens designed by landscape artists such as Harold Peto, Russell Page, and Jean Mus. Again, the visitor's guide is fabulous, providing information on private gardens open to the public, nurseries specializing in Mediterranean plants, garden associations, hotels and restaurants, guided visits to Riviera gardens, plants in Riviera gardens, and a bibliography.

Gardens of the Riviera, Vivian Russell, Rizzoli, 1994; first published in Great Britain in 1993 by Little, Brown and Company, Ltd. Another book on Riviera gardens but different from Louisa Jones's book above in that Russell also presents chapters on English gardens and gardeners, French purists, style barons, contemporary and botanical gardens, and a guide to gardens open to the public. It is worth remembering that though a number of plants we think of as being native to the Riviera (and to Provence) were "imported" from elsewhere, they nonetheless thrive as if they were born here. As Russell notes in her introduction, "It is the chronic lament of everyone who knew the Riviera as it once was that the best is gone, and this sense of a lost paradise is part of the poignancy of the story. Yet the vines and the cypresses, the fragrant mimosa and eucalyptus, the 'musical comedy palms' all settled in at last, have made the Riviera their home, and the air still retains that intoxicating luminosity, in the presence of which everything else can somehow be forgiven . . . Thus the story of gardeners and their gardens on the Riviera does not end—for those who persevere, and who adapt, the love affair remains fresh and exciting. And as Michael J. Arlen concluded comfortingly, 'the Mediterranean is still the Mediterranean.'"

Renoir's Garden: A Celebration of the Garden That Inspired One of the World's Greatest Impressionist Painters, Derek Fell, foreword by Jacques Renoir (great-grandson of Pierre-Auguste Renoir), Simon & Schuster, 1991. A companion book to Les Collettes, the nine-acre estate near Cagnes-sur-Mer, which Renoir purchased in 1907. Les Collettes was to Renoir what Giverny was to Monet. There are only a few original paintings inside the house, but I don't feel this detracts from what is a lovely place to visit. I enjoy visiting artists' homes because I like to see the rooms, the surroundings, and the grounds which inspired the artists; after all, if I wanted to see Renoir canvases, I would be infinitely more satisfied by visiting one of the museums holding strong collections of his work, such as the Barnes Foundation outside Philadelphia, the Phillips Collection in Washington, D.C., or the Musée d'Orsay in Paris. The images of Les Collettes were photographed in three seasons, so this book is an especially nice record for visitors who will only see it during one.

Marchés

Markets of Provence: A Culinary Tour of Southern France, foreword by Patricia Wells, text by Dixon Long, recipes by Ruthanne Long, photographs by David Wakely, CollinsPublishers, San Francisco, 1996. As stated in the introduction, "Anyone planning to visit Provence will find that focusing on the markets is a good way to experience the region." The inviting photographs aside, this is a most useful book with lots of practical French phrases, shopping tips, a conversion chart, seasonal specialties, typical Provençal foods to look for, a market glossary, and suggestions for restaurants, sites, and shops. The book is organized by days of the week, with one market and town highlighted for each day. At the end of each chapter is a list of each day's other markets in Provence, so visitors really can plan an entire itinerary around the *marchés.* Note that the Côte d'Azur markets are not included. *De rigueur.*

Musées

Artists and Their Museums on the Riviera, Barbara F. Freed with Alan Halpern, Harry Abrams, 1998. It's not remarkable that so many of the twentieth century's great artists worked on the Côte d'Azur simultaneously, but that so much of their artwork remains, often in their former studios and homes. These museums are typically small, personal, and of exceptional quality, and I like to think their presence saves the Côte d'Azur from being solely another Mediterranean playground. Like the author of this useful book, I have been repeatedly filled with joy and inspiration whenever I visit the museums along this coastline. Color and black-and-white photos, thorough descriptions, a good bibliography, and practical information make this guide *de rigueur.* (Note that, in general, most museums are closed on Tuesday.)

Fauve Painting: The Making of Cultural Politics, James D. Herbert, Yale University Press, 1992. This book goes beyond the usual comparisons of Fauve canvases to analyze them within the political and cultural trends of their time.

The Fauves: The Reign of Color, Jean-Louis Ferrier, Editions Pierre Terrail, 1992. Features the works of Matisse, Derain, Van Dongen, Braque, and Dufy.

Peintres de la Couleur en Provence, 1875–1920, Reunion des musées nationaux, Paris, 1995; published on the occasion of the exhibit of the same name shown at the Hôtel de la Region Provence-Alpes-Côte d'Azur, Marseille (January 28–April 28, 1995) and the Musée du Luxembourg, Paris (May 15–August 15, 1995). "Good landscape painting," to again quote James Pope-Hennessy, "makes public a personal interpretation of the place portrayed, and thus enhances the general appreciation of it, providing, as it were, a new lens through which others can look. Provence, which has been so much painted, provides numerous instances of this—what van Gogh did for Arles, what Cézanne did for the environs of Aix or Corot for Avignon and for Villeneuve." This comprehensive book—in French but still of interest even to those who don't read the language—amply illustrates Pope-Hennessy's observation with color reproductions of works by artists well known and less so, including van Gogh, Gauguin, Cézanne, Bonnard, Renoir, Signac, Adolphe Monticelli, Felix Ziem, Achille Emperaire, Louis Leydet, Joseph Garibaldi, Alphonse Moutte, Henri-Edmond Cross, André Derain, Henri Manguin, Albert Marquet, and Francis Picabia.

Single-Artist Books and Catalogs

The following are definitive volumes (some are comprehensive catalogs that accompanied museum exhibitions), and are worth an effort to find. However, most of these books are not *catalogues raisonnés*—I've only included titles that represent an artist's oeuvre in the south of France; for definitive books covering the full range of an artist's work, see the *Musées, Jardins, et Monuments bibliothèque* in my Paris edition.

Bonnard at Le Cannet, Michel Terrasse, preface by Jean Leymarie, fourteen black-and-white photographs by Henri Cartier-Bresson, Pantheon, 1988; English translation copyright 1988 by Thames and Hudson, London; originally published in France as *Bonnard et Le Cannet* by Editions Herscher, Paris, 1987. A *Washington Post* review of a 1984 Bonnard exhibit at the Phillips Collection opened as follows: "The food is French, the sun is hot. A young woman lithe and naked, escaping from the heat, floats calmly in cool water in a clean enameled bath. Bees buzz in the garden . . . the bedroom sheets are linen . . . the apricots are ripe . . ." I have always loved those lines, which seem to capture the work of someone born and bred of Provençal soil. Bonnard, however, was not from the south of France, yet his creative output there prompts us to assume he was. A great number of his canvases were created at Le Bosquet (The Grove), the house he bought at Le Cannet, near Cannes. Filled with color reproductions, this book doubles as an art history text, and many of his most familiar paintings feature nearly every corner of Le Bosquet—the garden, dining room, kitchen, staircases, sitting room, bathroom, Bonnard's bedroom, the spare bedroom, and his studio.

Bonnard: The Late Paintings, published to accompany the exhibition of the same name organized by the Musée National d'Art Moderne, Paris (February 23–May 21, 1984); the Phillips Collection, Washington, D.C. (June 9–August 25, 1984); and the Dallas Museum of Art, Texas (September 13–November 11, 1984).

Calder's Universe, Jean Lipman, Running Press, Philadelphia, in conjunction with the Whitney Museum of American Art, 1976, 1987. Originally a Philadelphian, Alexander Calder worked for many years in Aix-in-Provence, and I find him to be as talented as Picasso in many respects.

Cézanne, Harry N. Abrams, 1996. Published in conjunction with the Cézanne exhibition held at the Galeries Nationale du Grand Palais (September 25, 1995–January 7, 1996), the Tate Gallery in London (February 8–April 28, 1996), and the Philadelphia Museum of Art (May 30–August 18, 1996).

Cézanne: Landscape into Art, Pavel Machotka, Yale University Press, 1996. Machotka photographed the sites of Cézanne's landscape paintings—nearly all of which were painted in Provence—from the same spot and at the same time of day. A unique and beautiful book.

The Paintings of Paul Cézanne: A Catalogue Raisonné, John Rewald, Harry N. Abrams, 1996. Large, boxed hardcover set in two volumes, the texts (volume I) and the plates (volume II).

Paul Cézanne: Letters, edited by John Rewald, translated by Seymour Hacker, Hacker Art Books, 1984.

Chagall: A Retrospective, edited by Jacob Baal-Teshuva, Hugh Lauter Levin Associates, 1995.

Fragonard, Jean Montagne Massengale, Masters of Art Series, Abrams, 1993.

Fragonard in the Universe of Painting, Dore Ashton, Smithsonian Institution Press, 1988.

La Guerre et la Paix, Sylvie Forestier, Reunion des Musées nationaux, 1995. In French, with excellent photos of the difficult-to-photograph *La Guerre et la Paix* mural in Vallauris, which Picasso painted in 1952–53. This is the only book I've found devoted to this singular work.

Fernand Léger, Carolyn Lanchner, with essays by Carolyn Lanchner, Jodi Hauptman, and Matthew Affron, and contributions by Beth Handler and Kristen Erickson, The Museum of Modern Art (distributed by Harry Abrams);

published in conjunction with the exhibition "Fernand Léger" at The Museum of Modern Art, New York (February 15–May 12, 1998).

Fernand Léger: The Rhythm of Modern Life, Prestel, Munich, New York, 1994; published on the occasion of the exhibition "Fernand Léger, 1911–1924: Le rhythme de la vie moderne," Kunstmuseum Wolfsburg (May 29–August 14, 1994) and Kunstmuseum Basel (September 11–November 27, 1994).

Henri Matisse: A Retrospective, John Elderfield, The Museum of Modern Art, 1992.

Matisse and Picasso, Yve-Alain Bois, foreword by Joachim Pissarro, Flammarion, 1998; accompanied the exhibition "Matisse and Picasso: A Gentle Rivalry" at the Kimbell Art Museum, Fort Worth, Texas (January 31–May 2, 1999). The Matisse-Picasso relationship is well documented, but this beautiful book is the best of its kind in comparing and contrasting their artwork.

Monet and the Mediterranean, Joachim Pissarro, Rizzoli, 1997. Published in conjunction with the exhibition of the same name held at the Kimbell Art Museum, Fort Worth, Texas (June 8–September 7, 1997) and the Brooklyn Museum of Art, New York (October 10–January 4, 1998).

Francis Picabia: Accommodations of Desire—Transparencies 1924–1932, Kent Fine Art Inc., New York, 1989. A slim but beautifully printed book with the text on thick, ivory paper and the color plates on glossy stock. Picabia moved to Mougins in the early 1920s.

Francis Picabia: Anthology, Centro Cultural de Belem, Portugal; published to accompany the exhibit of the same name (June 6–August 31, 1997).

Picasso: La Provence & Jacqueline, Actes Sud, 1991; published to accompany the exhibit of the same name in Arles in the Espace Van Gogh. In French with good quality color and black-and-white reproductions.

Picasso's Ceramics, Georges Ramié, Chartwell Books Inc., 1974.

Seurat, Alain Madeleine-Pedrillat, Skira/Rizzoli, 1990.

Paul Signac: A Collection of Watercolors and Drawings, essays by Marina Ferretti Bocquillon and Charles Cachin, Harry N. Abrams, 2000. The only book still in print devoted to Signac's sketches and watercolors in their entirety. Charles Cachin is Signac's son-in-law.

Chaim Soutine: An Expressionist in Paris, Norman L. Kleeblatt and Kenneth Silver, 1998; published in conjunction with the exhibition of the same name at The Jewish Museum, New York (April 23–August 16, 1998); Los Angeles County Museum of Art (September 27, 1998–January 3, 1999); and the Cincinnati Art Museum (February 14–May 2, 1999). The title notwithstanding, this book does cover the life and work of Soutine during the time he was in the south of France, and is an excellent, thoughtfully produced volume.

The Complete Letters of Vincent van Gogh, in three hardcover volumes as a boxed set, Bulfinch Press, 2000; first published 1958. The ever-insightful James Pope-

Hennessy refers to van Gogh's letters as being "without any equal in the literature of the European painting of the nineteenth century," and notes that van Gogh's letters from the south "are of an interest and importance it is hard to over-state." It was van Gogh, after all, who wrote that "The future of modern art lies in the south of France." In the introduction to this beautiful set, V. W. van Gogh writes that "The letters of Vincent van Gogh make fine reading for everybody. For people who usually do not care about artistic matters, they form a splendid human document of great interest. For art lovers and art historians they are of great importance. Frequently one who starts reading by chance or merely out of curiosity goes on for quite a while. Of course one cannot be expected to read the whole at a stretch—there are too many pages for that. The letters at the end, however, hold the same interest as those at the beginning, and one does not get tired of them." These beautiful volumes do not make good traveling companions, but there are several good paperback editions available.

Van Gogh in Provence and Auvers, Bogomila Welsh-Ovcharov, Hugh Lauter Levin, 1999.

Van Gogh: Vertigo of Light, Jacqueline and Maurice Guillaud, Guillaud Editions, Paris, Clarkson Potter, 1991. A gorgeous, unique book pairing text from van Gogh's letters with stunning reproductions (nearly all of which were painted in Provence), some printed on thin tissue paper to allow light in.

Series

Discoveries (originally published in France by Gallimard, English translation copyright by Abrams and Thames & Hudson). These colorful paperback books are a terrific value: they're jammed with information; the quality of the reproductions is good; they're lightweight and easy to pack because of their size (approximately five by seven inches); and the price is right. Titles in the series that are appropriate for traveling in the south of France include *Cézanne: Father of 20th Century Art; Chagall: The Art of Dreams; Matisse: The Wonder of Color;* and *Van Gogh: The Passionate Eye.*

Pegasus Library (Prestel, Munich, London, New York). Pegasus is similar to Discoveries but is primarily a hardcover imprint (only a handful of editions are also published in paperback) and is a little more scholarly. The books are not pocket-sized but are still slender, lightweight, and packable. Appropriate titles include *Cézanne in Provence; Marc Chagall: Daphnis and Chloë;* and *Van Gogh in Arles.*

World of Art (Thames & Hudson). This good series is a paperback line and individual books can be hefty but are still lightweight enough to bring along. Appropriate choices for traveling in the South of France include books on Bonnard, Cézanne, Matisse, Picasso, and Fauvism.

RÉPUBLIQUE FRANÇAISE

4.20 LA POSTE

RÉPUBLIQUE FRANÇAISE

LA POSTE

Plaisir
d'Offrir

Des Belles Choses
(Good Things and Favorite Places)

"In the past ten years Provence has become the art de vivre *capital of France, giving even Paris a run for its lifestyle. Thirtysomething Parisians, Japanese hungry to comprehend the sun-soaked culture, Americans in search of The Next Big Thing— all are looking to the Midi for clues about how they should be eating, decorating, living."*
—Christopher Petkanas, TRAVEL & LEISURE, MAY 1998

Objects of Desire

BY KAREN TAYLOR

∿

editor's note

This piece, which appeared in a special regional issue on Provence in *FRANCE Magazine,* highlights some of the *objets* which so define Provence and its sunny *art de vivre.*

In her introduction, Karen Taylor noted that "In and of themselves, these objects are wonderfully seductive, but they become absolutely irresistible once you discover the stories behind them. . . . In this fast-moving, high-tech world, objects that have survived time and changing fashions are a reassuring, comforting presence."

KAREN TAYLOR is editor of *FRANCE Magazine.*

When it comes to setting a Provençal table, you can forget fragile, gold-rimmed porcelain—here tastes run toward the casual and rustic. Such pieces are easy to find: Every outdoor market has stands brimming with cerulean blue, emerald green and mimosa yellow ceramics, and handwritten signs indicating nearby "*potiers*" proliferate along roadsides. But for those in search of age-old tradition and quality, there are only a few addresses to consider.

La Faïence

One of these is Faïencerie Figuères, a small atelier where Marcel and Gilberte Figuères, along with their two sons, are singlehandedly reviving *faïence de Marseille,* a style that appeared and vanished within little more than a century.

Faïence, which refers to glazed ceramics that are finer than earthenware but not as fine as porcelain, was produced in Marseille as early as the late seventeenth century, although at the time few people could afford it. Then in the early 1700s, the same new affluence that fostered the development of other decorative arts created a demand for elegant tableware.

At first, the designs reflected influences from Rouen and Spain. By the 1750s, however, artisans at Marseille's fifteen factories had developed a style that was clearly their own, characterized by elegant shapes decorated with Chinese motifs, flowers, animals, landscapes and seascapes. Their popularity was as intense as it was brief, cut short by the Revolution, which sent many wealthy clients to the guillotine. By 1806, there was not a single *faïencier* left in the city.

Gilberte Figuères specializes in copying pieces from Marseille's Musée de la Faïence, located just a few minutes from her atelier. She typically spends ten hours patiently reproducing a single plate by La Veuve Perrin, famous for her exquisite floral patterns. Of course, all that work can be lost if there is a problem during firing. When this does happen, destroying as many as fifteen pieces at once, Gilberte remains philosophical and simply starts over. Currently, she is working on a large platter for a gentleman who donated his original to the museum.

Marcel, who looks like a kindly cobbler with wire-rimmed glasses and a snowy white mustache, specializes in trompe l'oeil, also popular in the eighteenth century. The most traditional pieces are the plates of lemons, olives, mushrooms, figs, mussels or other foods native to the region. In recent years, he has also begun crafting individual pieces of fruit, nuts and vegetables, many of them indistinguishable from the real thing. The secret, he says, is in his glazes, all of which are custom mixed. "Sometimes I put as many as ten layers on a single piece so that the brilliance comes from within, just like a real piece of fruit."

A very different type of faïence can be seen in Apt, where Jean

Faucon carries on the town's unique tradition of solid and *marbré* ceramics. The marbré, or marbleized, effect is achieved by mixing combinations of brown, red, yellow, green and cream-colored clays from the area. Holding up a broken plate, Faucon shows how the colors are the substance of the plate itself, not painted on the surface. "It's sort of like a marble cake," he says—but that's about all he will reveal about his secret technique.

Marbré first appeared in Apt in the 1770s, complementing what was already a style unlike any other. Here, artisans never painted faïence. Instead, they used transparent glazes to show off the rich earth tones of the local clay. All decorations—flowers, acanthus leaves, putti, animals—were sculpted or in relief. Faucon picks up a piece of clay, rolls it between thumb and forefinger and deftly shapes petals that slowly become a rose. "It can take all afternoon to sculpt the lid to a soup tureen," he sighs.

Compared with Marseille's sophisticated pieces, Apt's faïence is warm, unpretentious, even rustic—and didn't suffer from the Revolution. In fact, local production reached its apogee from 1815 to 1870, with faïenciers selling their wares at the famous *foire* in Beaucaire and exporting to Algeria, the Middle East, even South America. Had they banded together during the next decades, they might have been able to survive the new competition from porcelain and mass-produced faïence. Instead, most of them went out of business.

The style would likely have disappeared completely were it not for Faucon's grandfather, who revived the art in 1942. Today Faucon and his two employees turn out traditional as well as more innovative designs, including a fresh blue-and-cream marbré (made from colored, not natural, earth) with rims and sculpted ornaments in matching cream.

These pieces are coveted by collectors the world over, and Faucon now exports 50 percent of his production. Aptésiens also appreciate this art, buying pieces for weddings and other special occasions. "It's expensive," he acknowledges, "but people understand why when they see how it's made. That's the reason I sell it only here at the atelier, not in shops. I want customers to realize that when they buy one of these pieces, they are buying a bit of history."

Also helping to keep the Apt tradition alive is Faucon's friend, Antony Pitot. Unlike Faucon, Pitot came to faïence by accident—a car accident, to be precise. Due to extensive injuries, this former gym teacher was obliged to choose a new métier. "I hesitated between wrought iron and faïence," he laughs. "I guess I've always liked fire!"

Working alone in a small atelier, Pitot turns out pieces of such exceptional quality that they have been selected by no less discerning clients than furniture designer Jacques Grange. Although he dabbles a bit in marbré, most of Pitot's pieces have either deep-green or ocher-yellow glazes. Their scalloped and octagonal shapes, he explains, date back to the days of Louis XIV, who ordered that everything metal—including tableware—be melted down to finance his war effort. This created a great demand for ceramic tableware, and artisans simply used the same molds that had been used for silver and gold dishes.

Pitot too sells only out of his atelier, a marketing strategy that hasn't kept clients from finding him: On a wall, he has a map of the world studded with dozens of pins marking the hometowns of his far-flung customers.

Le Tissu

Jackie O and Japanese tourists. Picasso and Camargue cowboys. Napoleon and Josephine. The common denominator? All have succumbed to the seductive charm of *"tissus provençaux."*

More than any other object, these fabrics have come to symbolize Provence the world over. Perhaps because they sum up the essence of this region: The cotton fabric suggests the casual, comfortable lifestyle, while the intense, saturated colors echo the vibrant hues found in the Provençal landscape. As for the designs, even the most elegant patterns are disarmingly approachable, inviting you to adopt a mood to match their cheerful nonchalance.

Also known as *indiennes,* these delightful fabrics do in fact owe their origins to the East. The historical details vary somewhat from source to source, but it is generally believed that brightly printed cottons first made Europeans smile sometime during the early 1600s, when they were introduced by Portuguese and Dutch trading ships arriving in Marseille.

The aristocracy, accustomed to wearing heavy brocades, silks and damasks, immediately embraced these gaily painted fabrics, integrating them into their wardrobes and decors. They willingly paid a fortune for imports, inspiring entrepreneurs in Marseille to attempt to produce indiennes locally.

Annie Roux, author of *Le Textile en Provence,* writes that the industry got off the ground in 1648 when local playing-card makers applied their block-printing techniques to fabric. Initially, everything was done by hand: Pigments were made from plants, then workers carefully dipped handcarved blocks into the dye and pressed them onto the fabric, one color at a time. Sometimes, women would use paintbrushes made from their own hair to fill in printed black outlines.

Before long, domestic and imported indiennes were in such demand that silk and wool makers began to panic, and in 1686 they persuaded the government to outlaw printed cottons altogether. The decree had about the same effect as Prohibition: People wanted them more than ever. Clandestine mills churned out the coveted fabric, and smuggling proliferated. Meanwhile, members of Louis XIV's court openly flaunted the ban. But not everyone got away with such defiance: Michel Biehn, author of several books on regional textiles, writes that the gendarmes sometimes seized dresses right off women in broad daylight.

Thanks in part to Madame de Pompadour's influence, the interdiction was finally lifted in 1759. Almost overnight, factories began springing up throughout France. By the early 1770s, local producers were offering quality on a par with that of Indian imports and designs integrating French motifs. It was also during this period that the people of Provence adopted these fabrics for their regional dress.

Production of indiennes finally ebbed in the late nineteenth century, eclipsed by new fabrics from mechanized mills in the north. The few businesses that remained in Provence subsisted largely on local orders for scarves and material for costumes.

One of these was the Manufacture de Laurade in St.-Etienne-du-Grès, which limped along until Charles Deméry took over the helm, introducing modern printing techniques and embarking on an ambitious marketing campaign. By the 1950s, he had put Provençal fabrics back on the pages of international fashion magazines.

Then in 1976, the family business split, spawning what are now the two biggest names in Provençal fabrics: Souleiado and Les Olivades. Over the years, both have evolved into producers of high-end home furnishings and fashions, with boutiques around the world selling everything from table linens and porcelain to sheets, towels and jewelry. (In the United States, Les Olivades is sold exclusively at Pierre Deux stores; Souleiado has its own shops.) Like all prestigious fabric houses, both keep their look fresh, presenting new collections every year.

Imitations, of course, abound, with nearly every outdoor market and souvenir stand in the region hawking colorful printed cottons. But Jean-François Boudin, head of Les Olivades, isn't too worried. "We don't consider them competitors. We cater to a niche market—customers who expect faultless quality, not only in printing but also in the selection of raw materials, innovative design, marketing and customer service."

One newcomer, Créations Anny Verlene en Provence, is eyeing that very market. Open last year, the Aix-en-Provence company produces designs inspired by Mediterranean and Provençal themes. Sold in upscale home furnishings boutiques in France, the line is currently being introduced to the trade in the United States.

Those interested in the history of Provençal fabrics will want to visit Souleiado's museum in Tarascon, devoted to Provençal costumes as well as art, faïence and furniture. The visit, which requires an advance reservation, includes the old ateliers (virtually unchanged since the day the last artisan block-printed fabric there) and the cobwebbed attic, where Souleiado stores its prized collection of some 4,000 fruitwood printing blocks.

Les Olivades, meanwhile, invites visitors to tour the only textile mill still producing indiennes in Provence. Although modernized, the process continues to respect the roots of this ancient craft: Silkscreen printing is used to apply one color at a time, with some designs requiring sixteen separate applications. In all, the printing process involves eight steps, including the painstaking inspection of every centimeter.

Having developed a new respect for these fabrics, visitors are ready for the best part: a stop at Les Olivades's factory store, where they can scoop up exquisite tablecloths, clothes and home accessories at up to 50 percent off.

Le Mobilier

It's a husband's vacation nightmare: Traveling in Provence, his wife falls in love with a massive armoire or a towering *buffet à deux corps* and insists on shipping it stateside, cost (and time) be damned. The scenario, according to local antique dealers, is not all that uncommon.

What is it about Provençal pieces that makes them so irresistible? Perhaps it's their lilting lines, rounded corners and exuberant carvings. Or the warm walnut patina, the cheerful painted finishes and the simple rush seats. All of these elements, in any case, have typified Provençal furniture since the eighteenth century.

Prior to that period, most Provençal dwellings were quite modest and had little in the way of furniture; the few wealthy homes were furnished with pieces shipped from Paris. Then in the early 1700s an affluent bourgeoisie emerged in towns along the Rhône, building *bastides* and *hôtels particuliers.* To furnish them, they turned to artisans who had learned their craft building vessels in Marseille and Toulon. Before long they were producing the comfortable, rococo-inspired furniture of Louis XV's Paris—designs that would become the foundation for what is known today as Provençal style.

While retaining the fluid lines characteristic of these pieces, artisans adapted them to local tastes, eschewing gilt and bronze in favor of sculpted flowers, olive branches, shells and other regional motifs. This interpretation showed up in armoires and commodes but also in furniture peculiar to Provence, such as the *panetière,* a sort of wooden cage mounted on the wall for storing bread; the *garde-manger,* or pantry; and the *pétrin,* a table with a compartment used to prepare dough.

This golden age of furniture making continued well into the next century, taking new inspiration from changing tastes in Paris. Production waned in the late 1800s, however, when industrially produced furniture flooded the market. Today, the region's authentic *ébénistes,* or cabinetmakers, can be counted on one hand—and even then you'd probably have a finger or two left over.

One of these is Mélani et Fils, located near Arles. René Mélani started the company in 1958 and later apprenticed his two sons, Olivier and Frédéric. Olivier will take you through their spacious showroom, enthusiastically commenting on the exquisite panetiers and pétrins, buffets and commodes. He takes most pride, however, in showing visitors the one piece that is not for sale: a magnificent armoire nearly eight feet in height. Four years in the making, it is the sum of Mélani's rare savoir-faire.

Like most unpainted Provençal furniture, it is made from walnut. But not just any walnut. Mélani uses only 100-year-old trees, and for this piece dipped into its prized stock of 150-year-old walnut, selecting perfectly aged planks with just the right grain. Then the *ébéniste* designed the piece, giving it harmonious volume, graceful lines and perfect balance. Each panel and door was made by hand, then passed on to the sculptor. Using some 200 tools, he deftly chiseled the intricate basket of flowers and other decorative flourishes. Finally, after assemblage and finishing, a master *ferronier* supplied the handsome hinges and lace-like hardware that run the length of the doors.

Babsky, located near St.-Rémy, also makes walnut reproductions but increasingly caters to the growing demand for painted furniture. Made from linden, these pieces now account for 80 percent of its business. According to Serge Babsky, whose father founded the company in 1958, customers are increasingly looking for pieces that are unique. In this age of mass production, he says, that is the ultimate luxury.

In addition to crafting buffets, libraries and armoires to clients' specifications, Babsky will also custom-design interiors for every room of the house. His luminous finishes—the formula is a closely guarded family secret—now grace fine homes in the region as well as such prestigious establishments as the Oustau de Baumanière hotel in Les Baux.

Anyone doubting the superior quality of such hand-crafted pieces should visit Ateliers Laffanour, near Carpentras. Standing in his showroom, Georges Laffanour will not hesitate to lift up one of his lovely chairs and throw it down on the stone floor. "My father liked to do that," he chuckles, obviously pleased with himself. Picking up the undamaged chair, he explains, "An oak chair would have broken. But this chair has been handmade from properly aged wood from plane trees."

Georges and his brother Gérard offer a range of Provençal styles in both walnut and painted finishes. There's the *fauteuil bonne femme,* a wide, low piece perfect for pulling up to the fireplace; and the *marquise,* an adorable little chair with a double back, made for women wearing long, full skirts ("they didn't actually sit, they alighted," says Georges). Then there's the *chaise à nourrice* or *chauffeuse,* a very low chair made for nursing or warming yourself by the hearth; and the *radassier,* a three- or four-seat settee wide enough to accommodate the ample derrières of gossiping matrons.

In business since 1840, Ateliers Laffanour still makes these chairs the way it always has: by hand. "Of course, we now use machines to turn pieces before sculpting them," explains Georges. "That eliminates the most onerous part of the job." The patterns used in the machine, however, are hand-carved. For Georges, there is simply no other way to make a chair. "Oh, you can buy so-called Provençal chairs made in China, but personally I wouldn't even put one in my garage to hold an oil can." And please don't mention the word varnish to him. "Our chairs are waxed, *never* varnished. That would be like putting ketchup in bouillabaisse!"

Atelier Laffanour's craftsmanship has earned it the 1997 Prix Jacques Léon, awarded to outstanding Provençal artisans, as well as a long list of clients, including some of the area's best restaurants. But for Georges, the supreme compliment came from François Nourissier, a member of the Académie Française: "What I like about your chairs is that when I'm sitting at the dinner table, I forget all about them."

Les Carreaux

It's a delicious sensation: You come in from the hot Provençal sun, kick off your shoes and feel the cool, smooth tiles under your feet. Ahhhh. In these southern climes, terra cotta has long been the floor covering of choice. Prized for its rustic beauty, it becomes more lovely with time, taking on a rich, silky patina.

Introduced in Provence in the sixteenth century, hexagonal *tomettes* and square tiles were an instant hit, keeping homes cool in summer and requiring little maintenance. And thanks to the region's many clay deposits, tiles were soon being made locally, notably in Salernes and Apt.

In those days, the process took about two months, as everything had to be done by hand: Workers excavated, washed and mixed the clay before cutting it into tiles, which were then dried, fired and cooled. Getting them to market was equally slow and laborious, with horse-drawn carts carrying them to towns throughout the region. Many were destined for Marseille, where they were loaded onto wooden ships headed for North Africa. By the late 1800s, production and shipping had improved dramatically, thanks to the introduction of hydraulic mixing machines and the railroad. It was the heyday of Provençal tiles, which found their way to markets as distant as Tonkin.

Like a host of other industries, tile making suffered enormous setbacks during the two World Wars, and many factories simply never reopened. "By the 1950s, the industry was in a state of crisis," recalls Pierre Boutal, who took over the family business in Salernes in 1957. "Nothing here had changed since the nineteenth century; we just couldn't compete with mass-produced products."

Boutal was determined to turn things around. In the early 1960s, he teamed up with Jean Faux, a ceramist from Vallauris, and, after much trial and error, developed a process for adding colorful glazes to tiles. "My big break came in 1965, when the architect for a planned community near St.-Tropez decided to use my tiles, both terra cotta and glazed. Their colors and shapes were uneven, but he liked them that way! Suddenly, our rustic tiles became trendy, and Salernes got a new lease on life."

Carreaux Vernin, one of the only tilemakers remaining in Apt after the war, also owes its survival to Boutal. "We were really struggling back then," says Brigitte Benoit-Vernin, "but when we began producing glazed tiles, business picked up." Today, Vernin produces some of the region's most beautiful hand-cut terra cotta, glazed enamel and hand-painted tiles. Their irregular surface is considered part of their charm, but Vernin ruthlessly inspects each one for imperfections that are largely invisible to the untrained eye. This attention to detail has earned them clients ranging from the Aga Khan and Christian Dior to châteaux, museums and churches throughout France.

There are other tilemakers scattered throughout the region, but Salernes remains the undisputed center for this craft. A tour of the town's fifteen factories should begin at Sismondini, a small operation located on a wooded hillside outside of town. Still a family-run business, it has changed little since it was established in 1847. Here, the air is filled with the sweet smell of pine mingled with smoke from the original woodburning kilns. Some twenty-five tons of wood are needed for each firing, a technique that gives tiles a distinctive "*flamé*" look.

The only other factory to use woodburning ovens is Terres Cuites des Launes, known also for its practice of dusting each freshly cut tile with lavender ashes, imparting a finely textured finish. Like Sismondini, the factory produces only hand-cut terra cotta floor tiles, using either local red clay or a honey-colored clay from Apt. The result of these artisanal methods is a wonderfully rare combination of rustic charm and elegance.

Elsewhere in Salernes, products range from hand-crafted to semi-industrial. Several of the larger factories have in fact pretty much abandoned terra cotta floor tiles in favor of decorator tiles for kitchen and bath. Among them is Pierre Basset, whose family has been in the business for four generations. Known as the "*couturier du carrelage*," he has developed some 3,000 different patterns. "And if we don't have what you're looking for, we'll custom design whatever you want," he promises. "Just bring in a swatch of fabric or describe what you'd like, and we'll hand-paint tiles to match."

But when it comes to originality, no one can touch Alain Vagh. Just for fun, he covered a speedboat in tiny red tiles, a jeep in blue, a cement mixer in lime green and a grand piano in yellow. People have tried to buy these fantastical creations (some are displayed in his showroom), but they're not for sale. "I'm no artist," he laughs. "These are just a way for me to let off some creative steam." What he does sell is classic terra cotta, glazed and hand-painted tiles, considered to be among the best available.

Vagh, who took up his trade in the symbolic month of May '68, still has long hair and ideals dating from that era. "I decided that the only way to be free in a capitalistic society was to become the boss," he explains. He also believes that freedom carries certain responsibilities: "When you live well from what you do, you must protect your craft. In Salernes, quality has made us what we are, and we mustn't lose sight of that. Innovation is important, but you mustn't sell your soul in the process." A reference, no doubt, to competitors who import cheap tiles from Portugal or Morocco and simply glaze them on site.

For Vagh, innovation has taken the form of a wafer-thin ceramic veneer for piano keys, which may prove to be a better substitute for ivory than plastic. "It's a serious application for the thin tiles I developed for my 'sculptures.' Concert pianists are currently testing these new keys, and so far they like them—they say ceramic is less slippery than plastic. But it will take fifteen or twenty years to see how they hold up."

In the meantime, Vagh is contemplating becoming the Christo of tiles. "I'd really like to cover a WWII bunker with a mosaic of a giant pink starfish. It would be a great way to transform a symbol of horror into something joyful!"

Ocres

One of the most enchanting moments in Provence occurs in the late afternoon, when the sun's golden rays caress the textured façades of houses clustered along narrow village streets. Wedged between azure blue sky and velvet black shadows, these romantically weathered reds, yellows and greens positively glow.

Nowhere is this effect more dramatic than in Roussillon, a town drenched in blood-red ocher from surrounding quarries. Nearby, other deposits yield the infinite shades of yellow, green, red and brown that bathe interiors and exteriors throughout the region.

Archeologists have found evidence that ocher, a natural pigment, was used in prehistoric times, notably in the famous Lascaux cave paintings in Dordogne. The Egyptians, Greeks and Romans also relied on ocher paints for their frescoes, and medieval French artisans dabbed them on the walls of gothic cathedrals.

The ocher deposits in the Vaucluse, the largest in the

world, are believed to have been initially exploited by the Romans, who exported ocher via Marseille. After they left, the resource was seemingly forgotten until 1785, when Jean-Etienne Astier, a cooper from Roussillon, "rediscovered" its qualities.

Astier's timing was perfect: The dawning Industrial Revolution ushered in all sorts of new products that could be colored by ocher: rubber seals for jars, rubber boots, linoleum, cigarette filters. . . . The industry boomed throughout the nineteenth century, with exports streaming into Europe, the United States, Russia, Asia, South America and Africa. Then came World War I and the loss of the Russian market, the Depression and the weakening of U.S. sales, and most devastating of all, the development of cheaper synthetic pigments. After peaking at 40,000 tons annually in 1929, ocher production in the Vaucluse fell to the 1,000 tons now mined by the Société Française des Ocres, the area's only remaining ocher company.

Visitors to the Vaucluse can now wander through acres of fantastical landscapes formed by abandoned open-air quarries. In Roussillon, water has eroded the soft cliffs, sculpting them into stalagmite-like shapes forming the "Val des Fées." Near Rustrel, exposed layers of multicolored earth have been dubbed "*le Colorado Provençal.*" Old ocher mines, meanwhile, are now used for cultivating mushrooms.

In 1994, the Usine Mathieu, an ocher factory that shut down in 1960, was reopened as a space devoted to preserving ocher's historical legacy and to exploring new applications for pigments. Known as the Conservatoire des Ocres et Pigments Appliqués, it is a unique undertaking. "We didn't want this to be a museum," says Mathieu Barrois, who conceived the project with his wife, Barbara. "Our vision was to run this place like a business. Essentially, our objective is to educate the public, disseminate information and train professionals."

What they had in mind could be seen during a visit one afternoon last fall. In a grassy area surrounded by pine trees, a young man initiated children in the art of making pigments. After dispatching them across the lawn to scrape rust off an old truck, he demonstrated how to make ink from rust. Then he showed his wide-eyed audience how to make blue ink from a red flower.

Inside the old mill, a woman presented her new CD-ROM on color theory, and visitors admired displays of various wall treatments achieved with ochers and oxides. Nearby, Jean Petit, a chemist who has studied pigments for fifty years, talked about molecules as if he were telling a bedtime story: there were the good guys and the bad guys, the mischievous ones, the shy ones. Eyes twinkling, he held his audience in suspense, awaiting the inevitable chemical outcome of mixing these characters.

Back outside, Mathieu Barrois demonstrated how ocher was processed "in the olden days." People gathered around as he aimed a high-powered hose at a pile of yellow earth, watching the golden liquid zig-zag down the hill in narrow troughs. The extracted earth, they were told, is 90 percent sand and 10 percent ocher, so the idea is for the heavier sand to settle out during this process. At the bottom of the hill, the ocher and water mixture flowed into shallow basins; there, the water would slowly evaporate, leaving cakes of ocher that, in the past, were ground into powder at the mill. Mathieu's vintage mills are not yet back in service, but visitors were sent off to inspect the "yellow mill"—indeed, every crevice from floor to ceiling is still very yellow—and the "red mill," where yellow ocher made red by baking was processed.

Before leaving, they were invited to stop by the small corner selling books (ranging from basic how-to's to scientific treatises), beautifully packaged ochers and oxides for artists, and sacks of pigments for outdoor and indoor use.

Throughout the year, the Conservatoire holds conferences and workshops, many of them attended by international decorators, who claim that ochers have a unique luminosity that simply can't be matched by latex paints. In Provence, at least, there are many who share their enthusiasm; homeowners throughout the area have been dragging, ragging, sponging and stenciling their walls with these pigment, sometimes using the boldest of hues.

Not everyone is thrilled about this new trend. Michel Biehn, a Provence native and author of *Colors of Provence,* says, "There is a lot of color in this region, but except for Roussillon, color has traditionally been in nature, not in buildings. Provençal villages have always been harmonious masses of beige and gray—they are beautiful. Colorful façades are really more of an Italian idea."

So how did they become "typically Provençal"? The culprit, according to Biehn, is the enormously successful *Pierre Deux's French Country,* first published in 1984. "There's a photo everyone seems to remember of a red house in Nice with blue shutters. Now, people who want to be 'authentic' think they have to paint their house red!"

"Objects of Desire" by Karen Taylor, *FRANCE Magazine,* Summer 1998.

Des Belles Choses

G ranted, it's quite personal, but this is my list—in no particular order and subject to change on any day of the week—of
some favorite things to see, do, and buy. I am mindful of what James
Pope-Hennessy wrote in *Aspects of Provence* that "The task of sin-
gling out a landscape for description is even more invidious than
that of choosing monuments and towns. Each traveller in Provence
will make his own discoveries and stick to them, forming and carrying away from the countryside his own mental pictures, not those
of any guide." He went on to single out the view from Les Baux,
the Pont du Gard, the shore of Hyères, and Forcalquier as special
places for him. Some of these are my favorites, too, but I have others, and I am happy to share them with you here in the hope that
you will also enjoy them, and that you will reciprocate by sharing
your discoveries with me.

A word about shopping: I am not much into acquiring things so
as a general rule shopping is not one of my favorite pastimes; but I
enjoy buying gifts for other people, especially when I'm traveling.
To borrow a quote from a great little book called *The Fearless
Shopper: How to Get the Best Deals on the Planet* (Kathy Borrus,
Travelers' Tales, 2000), shopping is "about exploring culture and
preserving memory—the sights, sounds, smells, tastes, tempo, and
touch of a place." Most of what I purchase, therefore—even for
myself—falls into the food and wine category, because for me, food
and drink are inextricably linked to a place, especially if that place
is Provence. Every time I smell the cloth sack of *herbes de Provence*
when I open my pantry I am instantly transported back to the outdoor *marché* where I bought it, and I even remember talking to the
vendor about how hot it was that day and what I liked most about
Provence. A bottle of Domaine Tempier Bandol or Domaine Ott

Rosé aren't just types of local wine—they're Provence in a bottle, one deep, rich, and spicy and the other light, sparkling, and dry. Similarly, I also like to buy sensuous items that smell nice, like soaps, lotions, bath oils, and fragrances for the home. The assortment of soaps that are now in my bathroom aren't just useful cleansers—when their scents hit me I am instantly in a good mood, reminding me of the gardens and perfumes of the south of France. To quote again from Kathy Borrus, "I am surrounded—not by things but history and culture and memory." I have found that even the supermarkets of France sell beautifully packaged items of yummy stuff that in the U.S. are either hard to find or expensive, or both.

And a word about stores: I have a particular knack for "discovering" shops that a year or so later end up in books and articles; therefore, as it would be redundant to list some of my favorite retailers that are also featured in the books under "Shopping/*Les Souvenirs*" in the *Bibliothèque* that follows, I have only mentioned them if I had something extra to say about their wares. And you might want to adopt my motto of "when in doubt, buy it now." I learned years ago that the likelihood of being able to retrace my steps to a particular merchant *when it was open* was slim. If you spy a sweet *fougasse* in the window of a *boulangerie* or a piece of Provençal pottery that has your name all over it, *allez* (go) and get it, for Pierre's sake. One has regrets only for the roads not taken, or in this case the *objet* not purchased! Visitors should be aware that, in general, most shops are closed on Sunday (and some on Monday morning as well).

~Rows of plane trees, poplars, and parasol pines.

~Any outdoor *marché*, but especially those in Carpentras, Nice (Cours Saleya), and Nyons.

~The park atop the Colline du Chateau, Nice. I prefer to get there by climbing the stairs, which can be accessed from the rue du

Chateau in Vieux Nice. It's a long climb up, but sweeping views are your reward. It's also a great spot for a *pique-nique,* so time your visit to follow a morning spent gathering provisions at the Cours Saleya *marché.*

~Le Moulin des Caracoles (5 rue Saint-Francois-de-Paul, 04.93.62.65.30), Nice. An excellent shop just steps away from the Cours Saleya selling a wide range of beautiful and functional Provençal specialties, including glass items from Biot, tabletop linens and ceramics, books, and a variety of food products. It's not that you can't find some of these things elsewhere, but the quality here is particularly irresistible.

~The lobby and dome of the Hôtel Négresco, Nice.

~La Merenda restaurant (4 rue Terrasse; no telephone), Nice.

~Musée Dufy/Galerie des Ponchettes (77 quai des Etats Unis), Nice.

~Henri Auer (7 rue St.-Francois-de-Paul; 04.93.85.77.98), Nice. A family business for almost 200 years and the best place to find bursting-with-flavor *fruits confits* and *confitures,* all beautifully wrapped, of course.

~The trompe l'oeil facade of the Musée Matisse, Nice.

~The magnificent staircase and eighteenth-century pharmacy of the Palais Lascaris (15 rue Droite), Nice.

~Escale en Provence (7 rue du Marché; 04.93.85.23.90), Vieux Nice. This enticing shop sells the best assortment of Provençal gifts, specialty food products of the region, and floral decorations that I've seen anywhere, including those signature glass bottles of *bain moussant* in a variety of shapes, sizes, and scents (these are the real things, not knock-offs made in China with labels written in English).

~Radio Monte Carlo (98.3 FM). The disc jockeys pronounce this station's identification with great flair, sounding positively Italian.

~Oliviers & Co. (about a half dozen locations in Provence, and others throughout France). A chain of shops with a theme tailor-made for *The Collected Traveler:* olive oils and related products from around the Mediterranean. Founder Olivier (which appropriately means "olive tree" in French) Baussan created this wonderful concept in the early 1990s, with each store offering extra virgin, first cold-pressed oils from a variety of regions of Provence, North Africa, Spain, Italy, Israel, and Greece. In addition to straightforward olive oils, the stores sell herbal and citrus-infused oils, vinegars, olive oil soap, pottery, olive wood spoons, condiments, empty bottles and flasks, and *scourtins* (the round, woven disks used in olive harvesting, which also make great placemats!). Additionally, an excellent book is available at each store, *Olive Oil: A Gourmet Guide,* by Olivier Baussan, with recipes by Jacques Chibois (chef at La Bastide St.-Antoine in Grasse) and photography by Jean-Charles Vaillant (Flammarion, 2000; distributed in the U.S. by Abbeville Press). The lovely photos and recipes aside, the book is a mine of information about the different types of olives that grow around the Mediterranean. Baussan also reveals a surprising tip about the phrase "first cold press." Though a bottle of olive oil has little chance of selling without this label, Baussan notes that it "has been meaningless for many decades. It dates from the time when presses lacked the power to extract all the oil at a blow and it was necessary to do a second milling and pressing adding hot water, which naturally resulted in an inferior product. However, once powerful modern hydraulic presses were introduced, only a single pressing was necessary. We have made a pointless slogan of the problems of the old process." The book also was honored with "Best Book of the Year" by the World Cookbook Fair Awards. At the time of this writing, in the U.S. there are only Oliviers stores in New York; to learn of other possible future U.S. locations, or to place mail orders, call

877-828-6620. Baussan also founded—though no longer owns—the chain of l'Occitane stores (see below), and both companies are Provençal home-grown.

~L'Occitane (various locations in Provence, and throughout France). Stepping into a l'Occitane store is like walking into a sun-filled van Gogh painting, and the wares are equally as tempting: soaps, lotions, shampoos, cosmetics, and fragrances for men and women, all made with natural essences from plants and vegetables. Fortunately for some of us, there are now a number of l'Occitane shops in selected U.S. cities, which might make a gift from one of the stores seem common; but the range of products is so appealing, and the gift wrapping so nice, that a present—for yourself included—from l'Occitane is anything but ordinary. If you do live near a l'Occitane store, you might want to stop in before you leave to look at its sun-care line and some travel-size products, including a travel kit with shampoo, cold cream, hair care, and hand cream. I like the square, tin boxes for soap and the small rounds of solid perfume concentrate, especially great for hot days when my antiperspirant isn't working as well as it should. Tiny bottles of perfume extract are available in a range of scents, as well as small tins of shea butter for dry hands. All the shaving supplies for men are in plastic bottles.

~The crunch of aged ivory-colored gravel underfoot as one walks through gardens and along pathways.

~Le Trophée des Alpes, La Turbie.

~The Salle des Mariages in the Hôtel de Ville, Menton, decorated by Jean Cocteau.

~The tiles and wall paintings in the Palais des Papes, Avignon.

~Librairie Roumanille (19 rue Saint-Agricol; 04.90.86.01.24), Avignon. Founded by the *félibre* Joseph Roumanille, with an enticing selection of books (old and contemporary) and prints of Provence.

~Papiers-Plumes (45 rue Joseph Vernet; 04.90.82.68.77), Avignon. A shop with beautiful and unique photo albums, scrapbooks for all occasions, datebooks, pens, papers, and envelopes galore.

~Any brand of *pastis,* in the evening, at "my" café ("My" café is initially any café I choose, but in order to discover which café I want to frequent, I have to settle in at a few first. By trip's end, I will have identified one or two which are "mine").

~The Pol Bury fountain and Alberto Giacometti courtyard at the Fondation Maeght, St.-Paul-de-Vence.

~Musée National Picasso La Guerre et la Paix, Vallauris.

~The terrace of La Colombe d'Or, St.-Paul-de-Vence. If you show up in-between meals, and ask nicely, you can walk around and look at the fabulous artworks by the likes of Miró, Picasso, Modigliani, Matisse, Chagall, and—my favorite—*The Girl with the Parrot* mosaic, by Léger.

~Signs advertising *"Le Snack."*

~Gordes, but it must be visited before Roussillon. (Besides its singular position, the best feature of Gordes to me is the views it provides from its walls.)

~Roussillon, every inch of it. I suggest taking a short hike along the path in the surrounding ocher quarries first and then heading up the hill to the village. Be sure to bring along a pair of old walking shoes and old socks for the hike, as the ocher dust discolors everything. Resist the temptation to touch the powdery dust as it *will not come out* if it gets on your clothes.

~Sous L'Olivier (place du Chateau; 04.90.72.11.90), Gordes. This *épicerie de choix* also sells beautiful Provençal postcards and greeting cards.

~Abbaye de Sénanque, one of the finest examples of twelfth-century monastic architecture in Europe and one of three Cistercian abbeys in Provence. Also, its justifably famous and much-photographed lavender field, when in bloom, is worth a detour.

~Musée Municipal de l'Annonciade, St.-Tropez.

~The village of Grasse, the Musée Jean-Honoré Fragonard, and the Parfumeries Fragonard, which offers informative tours with no pesky touts making you feel guilty if you don't buy anything. The chapter "How to Be a Nose" in Peter Mayle's *Encore Provence* is a good preparatory read.

~Le Petit Caveau (9 rue Victor Hugo; 04.75.26.20.21; fax: 04.75.26.07.28), Nyons. An excellent restaurant not only for its food (do not miss the local *pelardon* cheese in olive oil and herbs at the end of your meal) but for its wine. Instead of choosing a bottle, diners can choose the "*Trois Verres*" option, selecting a different glass to accompany each course.

~An outside table at Le Salon du Thé Bouquinerie (Le Poët-Laval). You don't need reservations or directions to this wonderful little café—the village of Poët-Laval, near Nyons in northern Provence, is so small you'll discover it on your own.

~Poterie du Bouton d'Or at Les Ateliers de Souspierre (Le Bridon, 26160 La Begude de Mazenc, on the road to Le Poët-Laval and Dieulefit; 04.75.46.26.46). Workshop and store with a beautiful selection of Provençal pottery, including some discounted seconds (which, with such little blips and bubbles, hardly seem like seconds to me). Prices here, as well as at other area potteries, are not cheap, but are definitely less than what you would pay in the States.

~The SNCF local running along the Côte d'Azur.

~Château de Taulignan (a *chambre d'hôte* just outside Vaison-la-Romaine; 04.90.28.71.16; fax: 04.90.28.75.04). A gorgeous but moderately priced bed-and-breakfast in a château dating from 1549, with views all around of vineyards and gentle hills. Kind hosts, a delicious and wholesome breakfast prepared with care, swimming pool, and being just one kilometer from Vaison make this an exceptional lodging.

~Le Cigalou (45 cours Taulignan), Vaison-la-Romaine. A small, pretty restaurant with light, flavorful dishes of the south, like *salade du sud*, *pistouade* on toasts, and local fish with *aïoli*.

~The synagogue in Carpentras (tucked away in the corner of place de l'Hôtel de Ville), the oldest in France. Not hard to find, but it isn't well marked on the outside; once inside the entryway, you have to ascend the staircase to enter the light-filled, beautiful temple. When I visited, there was only one guide/attendant, who spoke no English, but her French was clear and enunciated and anyone who knows a little of the language should have no trouble understanding her speak of the architecture, history, and present-day Jewish community.

~The extremely pleasant town of l'Îsle-sur-la-Sorgue, and the extremely pleasant store La Maison Biehn (7 avenue des Quatre Otages). Even if you have no intention of buying anything, stop by to see the nineteenth-century mansion that houses the beautiful Provençal wares of the shop. Owners Michel Biehn—author of *Colors of Provence* and *Recipes from a Provençal Kitchen*—and his wife, Catherine, have put together a unique selection of antique quilts, clothing, furniture, linens, and irresistible *objets*.

~Notre-Dame de la Garde, Marseille, which surely occupies one of the most covetous sites in the Mediterranean world.

~The views from the Jardin Exotique in Èze.

~Swimming in the saltwater pool at the Monte-Carlo Beach Club (note that if you're thinking of bringing your Frisbee, it's *interdit*).

~The Jardin Exotique and Fontvieille Park in Monaco.

~The town of St.-Remy.

~Provençal olive oil, from Coopérative Oleicole de la Vallée des Baux (rue Charles-Rieu, Maussane-Les-Alpilles; 04.90.54.32.37;

this is the oil that everyone raves about, but typically sells out so fast you can't get any. Your best bet is to buy it from the Cooperative, but in the event it has sold out, some shops in Les Baux and St.-Remy stock it, or you can contact Zingerman's in Ann Arbor—422 Detroit Street, Ann Arbor, Michigan 48104; 888-636-8162; fax: 734-769-1260—which usually always has some on hand); Coopérative du Nyonsais

(place Olivier de Serres, Nyons; 04.75.26.03.44; the Cooperative sells the famous olive oil of Nyons in bottles and containers of varying sizes, as well as vacuum-packed Nyons olives, olive oil soap, and local wines, which can be tasted before purchasing); and Alziari (14 rue St.-Francois-de-Paule, Nice; 04.93.85.76.92; Alziari also sells other olive-oil-based products and Provençal honey, and will ship internationally. Thankfully, Kitchen Arts & Letters in New York also stocks a small quantity of Alziari olive oil—see Bookstores for contact information). And a word about the cost of quality olive oil: readers familiar with my *Central Italy: The Collected Traveler* know that producing olive oil is a labor of love; the retail price is often not high enough. Peter Mayle echoes this in his "Discovering Oil" chapter in *Encore Provence*, when he states, "Nobody gets rich from growing olives." High-quality olive oil is always, in every case, staggeringly expensive to make.

~Le Pont du Gard (Nîmes). Nîmes is technically in Languedoc, a province I will cover in a separate edition; but as the Pont du Gard is so close to the border of Provence (about 50 km from Avignon), I had to include it here. I'm not exaggerating when I describe the Pont du Gard as being awesome, magnificent, and sublime. And I love how Lawrence Durrell has written of it in *Caesar's Vast Ghost:* "It is the size, of course, as well as the realization that the whole construct is slotted together in pieces of honey-colored stone without the help of mortar. Each individual block is the size of a motorcar! How did the Roman engineers manage to raise these vast chunks so high into the air? But water was precious, water was life, and the Roman was uxorious to a fault about land and its fruits. Provence signified something like married plenty!"

~The city of Nîmes, which to me has a very Spanish feel to it. To quote Thomas Jefferson, Nîmes "possesses not only the most impressive Roman monuments in France but also life and vitality beyond tourism."

~*Les croquants aux amandes* from Maison Villaret (13 rue de la Madeleine; 04.66.67.41.79), Nîmes. These delicious, *really* crisp (you have to dunk them in coffee or you risk cracking your teeth) biscuits are a signature specialty of Nîmes, from a shop which has distinguished itself since 1775.

Bibliothèque

Classics

Italo Calvino, in his thoughtful book *Why Read the Classics?* (Pantheon, 1999), notes, "Classics are books which, the more we think we know them through hearsay, the more original, unexpected, and innovative we find them when we actually read them." Don't postpone joy, then! Here's a selection to choose from, to read or reread, poetry included. These are available in several different publishing series (Modern Library, Plume, Penguin Classics, etc.) in both hardcover and paperback—the choice is yours.

The Anchor Anthology of French Poetry: From Nerval to Valéry in English Translation, edited by Angel Flores; introduction by Patti Smith, Anchor, 1958, 2000.

The Count of Monte Cristo, Alexandre Dumas.

Bella-Vista, Colette, various published editions, but the Modern Library minipaperback is perfect for traveling.

Charles Baudelaire—poems.

Letters from My Windmill, Alphonse Daudet, originally appeared in 1866 in *Le Figaro.*

The Red and the Black, Stendhal.

A Sentimental Journey, Laurence Sterne.

The Stranger, Albert Camus.

The Three Musketeers, Alexandre Dumas.

Fiction, Short Stories, and Mysteries

The Avignon Quintet: Monsieur, or, The Prince of Darkness; Livia, or, Buried Alive; Constance, or, Solitary Practices; Sebastian, or, Ruling Passions; Quinx, or, The Ripper's Tale, Lawrence Durrell, Viking, 1975.

The Fly-Truffler, Gustaf Sobin, W. W. Norton, 1999; first American edition, 2000. I decided early on in the life of this series not to review works of fiction, not because I don't have favorites, but because I feel it's more important for readers to recognize the wealth and diversity of companion reading available. I am making an exception with this work, however, because it is such a masterpiece both in a literary sense and in the way it portrays the very essence of Provence: it is one of just a few books—fiction or nonfiction—which so accurately depicts the heart of the region and the *Provençaux.* Sobin has lived for over thirty-five years in Provence, and though I don't know exactly where, he obviously is familiar with *Haute Provence,* old Provençal dialects, and rapidly vanishing peasant customs. The cultivation of silkworms, for example, is one custom which has barely survived. He writes that when silkworms begin spinning their cocoons, the only thing that interrupts them is a tremendously loud noise, like a thunderclap: "When a thunderstorm was seen approaching, women—in preparation—would gather, begin ringing bells—goat bells, sheep bells—or beating, gently at first, against shovels, frying pans, cauldrons in an attempt to prepare their little nurslings for the far more invasive sounds of the thunderstorm itself. They'd increase the volume of those cacophonous medleys with each passing minute. In response, the silkworms wove all the faster, and their thread, as a result, went unbroken throughout the ensuing thunderstorm." The book is filled with little scenes and images like that one, which remain with the reader long after the final page has been turned. And interestingly, Sobin includes a passage which matches a reference made by Laurence Wylie in *Village in the Vaucluse*: "Next morning, Cabassac discovered his poor bereaved aunt had prepared the entire house for mourning, as well. She'd done so in the most traditional Provençal manner. She'd draped all the mirrors in the house with black crepe and detached the pendulum from the tall grandfather clock in the hallway. According to ancient custom, these measures allowed the spirits of those recently deceased to rise all the more readily, unhampered by either their own reflection or any gratuitous reminder of human time." (I found this interesting because it is an ancient Jewish custom to cover the mirrors in a home after someone has died, and I wonder if the custom originated elsewhere and made its way to Provence from Spain or Italy.) *The Fly-Truffler* is to be read slowly and savored.

French Folktales, Henri Pourrat, selected by C. G. Bjurstrom, translated and with an introduction by Royall Tyler, Pantheon Books, 1989. One can learn a great deal about people by reading their folklore. This collection, like all the editions in the Pantheon Fairy Tale and Folklore Library, is a delight. These 105 legends are, as Tyler writes in the introduction, "stories to eat with your pocket-knife, among friends. They are delicious, and the days they taste of will never come again."

The Garden of Eden, Ernest Hemingway, Scribner Paperback Fiction, 1986.

The Horseman on the Roof, Jean Giono, North Point Press, 1996.

J'Accuse: The Dark Side of Nice, Graham Greene, The Bodley Head, London, 1982.

Loser Takes All, Graham Greene, Viking Penguin, 1989.

The Man Who Planted Trees: A Story by Jean Giono, engravings by Michael McCurdy, Chelsea Green Publishing Company, Chelsea, Vermont, 1985.

My Father's Glory and My Mother's Castle, Marcel Pagnol, with a foreword and a recipe by Alice Waters, North Point Press, San Francisco, 1960; foreword/recipe copyright 1986.

Perfume: The Story of a Murderer, Patrick Suskind, John E. Woods, translator, Alfred A. Knopf, 1986 (hardcover); Washington Square Press, 1995 (paperback).

Perfume from Provence, Winifred Fortescue, preface by Patricia Wells, illustrations by E. H. Shepard, Hearst, 1993.

The Pleasing Hour, Lily King, Atlantic Monthly Press, hardcover, 1999; Scribner Paperback Fiction, 2000.

The Rock Pool, Cyril Connolly.

The Rover, Joseph Conrad, Owl Books, Heart of Oak Sea Classics Series, 1999; originally published in 1923.

Tender Is the Night, F. Scott Fitzgerald, Charles Scribner's Sons, 1933, 1934; © 1948, 1951 by Frances Scott Fitzgerald Lanahan.

The Three Fat Women of Antibes, W. Somerset Maugham, Mandarin, London, 1990.

The Unquiet Grave, Cyril Connolly, 1945.

Design, Decorating, and Entertaining

At Home in France: Eating and Entertaining with the French, Christopher Petkanas, foreword by Marie-Hélène de Rothschild, photographs by Jean-Bernard Naudin, Phoenix Illustrated, London; first published in 1990 by George Weidenfeld & Nicolson, London, distributed in the U.S. by Sterling Publishing Company. All about *l'art de recevoir,* the art of receiving or entertaining as practiced by the French. Though there are recipes included, this is a cookbook/lifestyle book unlike any other. Petkanas, who is also a regular contributor to *Travel & Leisure,* presents eighteen individuals or families who are famous for their *recevoir* hospitality, six of whom, including Simone Beck, coauthor with Julia Child of *Mastering the Art of French Cooking,* entertain in Provence.

Authentic French Provincial Furniture from Provence, Normandy and Brittany, H. Algoud, Leon Le Clerc, Paul Baneat, Dover Publications, 1993.

Country Houses of France, Barbara and Rene Stoeltie, Taschen, 1999.

French Provincial Furniture, Robin Ruddy, Schiffer Publishing, London, 1998.

Pierre Deux's French Country, Linda Dannenberg, Clarkson Potter, 1984. *Travel & Leisure* special correspondent Christopher Petkanas referred to this groundbreaking book as "the style book that gave the world Provence fever." Seventeen years later, it's still the style book by which all others are measured.

Provence: The Art of Living, photographs by Solvi Dos Santos, text by Sara Walden, foreword by Sir Terence Conran, Stewart, Tabori & Chang, 1996.

Provence Interiors, Lisa Lovatt-Smith, edited by Angelika Muthesius, Taschen, 1996.

Quilts of Provence: The Art and Craft of French Quiltmaking, Kathryn Berenson, Henry Holt & Company, 1996.

Really Rural: Authentic French Country Interiors, Marie-France Boyer, Thames & Hudson, 1997.

Rare and Out of Print

The French Riviera, Pierre Devoluy and Pierre Borel, The Medici Society, London, 1924.

The Riviera: Painted and Described, William Scott, A. & C. Black, London, 1907.

Shopping/Les Souvenirs

When I'm looking for singular gifts other than culinary items, I've enjoyed consulting *The Riches of France: A Shopping and Touring Guide to the French Provinces* (Maribeth Clemente, St. Martin's Press, 1997). The first section—"The Essentials"—includes real nuts-and-bolts information on exchange rates, VAT, customs and duties, shopping hours, returns, discount shopping, sizes, mailing purchases home, packing tips, and more. This is the most thorough book I've seen, and a separate chapter is devoted to Provence. Clemente's recommendations have proven exceptionally helpful in searching for unique gifts for business colleagues and friends. Another book I really like is *Provence: A Country Almanac* (Louisa Jones, Stewart, Tabori & Chang, 1999). This unique book is really an almanac (but with beautiful color photographs), divided into four chapters, one for each season of the year, and includes recipes, folklore, poems, and quotations. Each chapter highlights various gardens, museums, festivals, restaurants, crafts, and time-honored traditions for each season, and I have used Jones's recommendations to find my way to a number of addresses I had not run across in any other books. ~Some good shopping vocabulary words to know are *soldes* (sales); *dégriffés* (refers to clothing where the labels have been cut out); *moitié-prix* (half price); *coin des affaires* (refers to the bargain section of a large store); *deuxième choix* (seconds); *tout doit disparaître!* (everything must go!); and *je regarde* (I'm just looking, thank you; useful for any type of shopping or browsing).

Related Nonfiction

The Collected Stories of Katherine Mansfield.

Letters to Anaïs Nin, Henry Miller.

Fascinating France: A Cultural Quiz Deck on the Language, Arts, and History of France, text by Nancy Noblett, Knowledge Cards, Pomegranate. While in transit, test your knowledge with these forty-eight mini-lessons in the cuisine, history, language, architecture, and geography of France. The deck of cards packs easily, and some of the questions are: "Who was the composer of *Bolero?*" "Can you name five French writers and their corresponding literary movement?" and "Lavender, Roman ruins, the Riviera, bouillabaisse, and the mistral are associated with what well-known region of France?" (Okay, they're not all as easy as the last.)

France: Landscape, Architecture, Tradition (Manufacture Française des Pneumatiques Michelin/Bulfinch Press, 1995) and *To Live in France* (James Bentley, photographs by Michael Busselle, Thames & Hudson, 1997). Usually, coffee-table books on France don't interest me, but these two I like. They both feature sections on Provence and the text is interesting and worth reading. To quote from the Michelin/Bulfinch book: "In the Midi the visitor is struck by the immediate sense of having been transported somewhere totally different. The Mediterranean captivates the imagination. It heralds the tropics and the southern seas; it conjures up the images of caravanserai and the aromas of spice; it feeds the maddest of projects. It is this sense of the exotic that makes its appeal to hordes of holidaymakers who head towards its summer resorts, and to thousands of others who come here in retirement to seek the dream of eternal rejuvenation."

French Dreams, photographs by Steven Rothfeld, introduction by Richard Reeves, Workman Publishing Company, 1993. With writings by the likes of Edith Wharton, Balzac, Gérard de Nerval, Baudelaire, Henry James, Colette, and Gertrude Stein to accompany the dreamy photos by Rothfeld, this is a special treat to buy for yourself, and it also makes a nice gift for your favorite Francophile. The images—handmade Polaroid transfers—are not the predictable pictures one sees in so many other books on France (and many seem to have been taken in the Midi). It's a beautiful package for those who appreciate beautiful things.

Seaside Interiors, Diane Dorrans Saeks, edited by Angelika Taschen, Taschen, 2000. Only two of these to-die-for interiors are on the Côte d'Azur (one in Cannes, the other in Monte Carlo), but I love this *Interiors* series, and this particular edition is particularly irresistible.

The South of France: An Anthology, compiled by Laura Raison, Cadogan Publications, London, 1985. Profusely illustrated with black-and-white drawings by Cézanne, Cocteau, Matisse, Picasso, van Gogh, Aubrey Beardsley,

Braque, and others, this is a brilliant anthology composed of letters, poems, recipes, and excerpts from novels and short stories by those who have visited or lived in the Midi. Raison has arranged the material into ten themes: towns and ancient places; rural life; heroes and villains; arts and the artists; travelers; Riviera towns; Riviera lifestyles; love songs; food and wine; and endings. It's a superb collection (sporting a jacket with a favorite painting of mine, Bonnard's *Côte d'Azur*, from the Phillips Collection), crying out to be dipped in to, at any point, again and again.

Traveler's Journal (Peter Pauper Press), *Voyages* (Chronicle Books), and the *Lonely Planet Travel Journal* are my current favorite journals. The first two are spiral-bound, which I like because the pages lie flat. *Traveler's Journal* features five clear plastic sleeves at the back for ticket stubs, photos, receipts, etc. (brilliant). *Voyages*—a bigger journal measuring about 8½″ by 11″—features an elastic band that wraps around the book from top to bottom (not quite as good as plastic sleeves, but the band helps to keep loose stuff inside). The *Lonely Planet* journal is different from each of these by being rather sleek-looking, with a black, faux-leather cover measuring approximately 4″ by 4″. Pages are lined on one side and blank on the reverse, and at the back of the book is a ton of essentials: twelve pages of maps of the world, calendars for 1999–2002, address pages, useful Web sites, clothing and footwear sizes, international dialing codes, metric/imperial conversions, a time zone conversion wheel (very nifty), and a pocket inside the back cover for all the loose ephemera one accumulates.

Traveller's Literary Companion: France, John Edmondson, Passport Books, 1997. This is one book in a series that explores the relationship between writers and places, and it includes extracts from literary works; maps; biographies of the writers; a town-by-town guide to each *département* highlighting writers' houses and museums and anything of literary interest; and a list of recommended novels, plays, and poetry. Each chapter focuses on a particular region of France—there is one for Provence, Côte d'Azur, and Monaco—and readers are led all around *l'Hexagone* and introduced to French authors and others who wrote in France. With numerous black-and-white photos of writers, there is no other book like this for literary enthusiasts.

Travels with Alice, Calvin Trillin, Avon, 1989. Not all of the fifteen essays in this witty and entertaining book are about Provence or even France, but I couldn't resist including it here because Calvin Trillin is on my short list (as in top five) of favorite writers. "Hanging Around in Uzès," "Full Basket," and—my favorite—"Damp in the Afternoon" are the only three pieces with the south of France as backdrop, but it doesn't matter: Trillin is irresistible, and a traveling companion *par excellence*.